THE
NAVY LIST
2013

Compiled on the 27th January 2014

information & publishing solutions

Published by TSO (The Stationery Office) and available from:

Online
www.tsoshop.co.uk

Mail, Telephone, Fax & E-mail
TSO
PO Box 29, Norwich, NR3 1GN
Telephone orders/General enquiries: 0870 600 5522
Fax orders: 0870 600 5533
E-mail: customer.services@tso.co.uk
Textphone 0870 240 3701

First printed edition published 2014
ISBN 9780117731219

This edition is printed in the UK for The Stationery Office Limited
on paper containing 75% recycled fibre content minimum.

Printed in the United Kingdom for The Stationery Office
P002677176   C2   11/14

PREFACE

This edition of the Navy List has been produced largely from the information held within the Ministry of Defence's "Joint Personnel and Administration" system (JPA) as at 27th January 2014.

Officers who succeed to peerages, baronetcies or courtesy titles should notify their Career Manager.

Serving officers who notice errors relating to their data in the Navy List should ensure that the data held within JPA is accurate & up to date. If you are unable to make these corrections within your JPA account, you should seek assistance either from your JPA administrator or Career Manager. All other errors or omissions should be brought to the attention of the Editor of the Navy List. Readers who should wish to comment on this edition of the Navy List are invited to write to:

Mrs Cliona Willis
The Editor of the Navy List
Mail Point 2.2
West Battery
Whale Island
PORTSMOUTH
PO2 8DX

Due to the wide-availability of the Defence Intranet, free distribution of the Navy List in hard copy format has ceased. Anyone who is unable to access the Navy List via the Defence Intranet may request copies of a CD-ROM version from the Editor at the above address.

CONTENTS

Section 8

Section 9

vi

MEMBERS OF THE ROYAL FAMILY

HIS ROYAL HIGHNESS THE PRINCE PHILIP, DUKE OF EDINBURGH, KG, KT, OM, GBE, ONZ, AC, QSO, AC, GCL, CC, CMM

Lord High Admiral of The United Kingdom .... 10 Jun 11
Admiral of the Fleet .... 15 Jan 53
Captain General, Royal Marines .... 1 Jun 53
Admiral of the Fleet Royal Australian Navy .... 1 Apr 54
Admiral of the Fleet Royal New Zealand Navy .... 15 Jan 53
Admiral of the Royal Canadian Sea Cadets .... 15 Jan 53
Admiral of the Royal Canadian Navy .... Jun 11

HIS ROYAL HIGHNESS THE PRINCE OF WALES, KG, KT, GCB, OM, AK, QSO, PC, ADC

Admiral of the Fleet .... 16 Jun 12
Commodore-in-Chief, Her Majesty's Naval Base, Plymouth .... 8 Aug 06

HIS ROYAL HIGHNESS THE DUKE OF CAMBRIDGE. KG, KT

Lieutenant .... 1 Jan 09
Commodore-in-Chief Scotland .... Aug 06
Commodore-in-Chief Submarines .... Aug 06

HIS ROYAL HIGHNESS PRINCE HENRY OF WALES, ADC

Commodore-in-Chief Small Ships and Diving .... Aug 06

HIS ROYAL HIGHNESS THE DUKE OF YORK, KG, GCVO, ADC

Rear Admiral .... 19 Feb 10
Admiral of the Sea Cadet Corps .... 11 May 92
Commodore-in-Chief Fleet Air Arm .... Aug 06

HIS ROYAL HIGHNESS THE EARL OF WESSEX KG, GCVO, ADC

Commodore Royal Fleet Auxiliary .... 1 Jan 11
Commodore-in-Chief Royal Fleet Auxiliary .... Aug 06

HER ROYAL HIGHNESS THE PRINCESS ROYAL, KG, KT, GCVO, QSO

Admiral Chief Commandant for Women in the Royal Navy .... 15 Aug 12
Commodore-in-Chief, Her Majesty's Naval Base Portsmouth .... Aug 06

HER ROYAL HIGHNESS THE DUCHESS OF CORNWALL, GCVO

Commodore-in-Chief Naval Medical Services .... Aug 06
Commodore-in-Chief Naval Chaplaincy Services .... 2 Oct 08

HIS ROYAL HIGHNESS PRINCE MICHAEL OF KENT, GCVO

Honorary Rear Admiral Royal Naval Reserve .... 1 Jun 04
Commodore-in-Chief Maritime Reserves .... Aug 06

HER ROYAL HIGHNESS PRINCESS ALEXANDRA THE HON. LADY OGILVY, KG, GCVO

Patron, Queen Alexandra's Royal Naval Nursing Service .... 12 Nov 55

VICE ADMIRAL OF THE UNITED KINGDOM

Honorary Rear Admiral Sir Donald Gosling KCVO RNR .... 2 Apr 12

PERSONAL AIDES-DE-CAMP TO THE QUEEN

Admiral His Royal Highness The Prince of Wales, KG, KT, GCB, OM, AK, QSO, PC, ADC
Rear Admiral His Royal Highness The Duke of York, KG, GCVO, ADC
Commodore His Royal Highness The Earl of Wessex, KG, GCVO, ADC
Vice Admiral Sir Tim Laurence, KCVO, CB, ADC

PRINCIPAL NAVAL AIDE-DE-CAMP TO THE QUEEN

Admiral Sir George Zambellas KCB, DSC, ADC, DL... 9th April 13

NAVAL AND MARINE AIDES-DE-CAMP TO THE QUEEN

Commodore N L Brown ADC .... Appointed 30 Jul 11 Seniority 30 Jun 10
Commodore P A McAlpine OBE, ADC .... Appointed 19 Dec 11 Seniority 08 Feb 11
Brigadier MW Dunham OBE..Appointed 15 Jun 12 Seniority 09 Jun 09
Commodore SW Garrett OBE..Appointed 27 Mar 13 Seniority 21 Apr 08
Commodore GT Little OBE .... Appointed 26 Jul 12 Seniority 17 Jul 12
Captain R Fancy OBE.. Appointed 07 Jan 13 Seniority 1 Mar 10

EXTRA NAVAL AND MARINE EQUERRIES TO THE QUEEN

Vice Admiral Sir James Weatherall KCVO, KBE
Vice Admiral Sir Tom Blackburn KCVO, CB
Vice Admiral Tony Johnstone-Burt CB OBE
Rear Admiral Sir John Garnier KCVO, CBE
Rear Admiral Sir Robert Woodard KCVO
Commodore A J C Morrow CVO

NAVAL AND MARINE RESERVE AIDES-DE-CAMP TO THE QUEEN

Commodore AC Jameson ....Appointed 23 Apr 13 Seniority 01 Jul 11
Colonel R M Bruce ADC RMR..Appointed 20 Jun 03 Seniority 01 Jun 97

HONORARY APPOINTMENTS

HONORARY CHAPLAINS TO THE QUEEN

The Reverend S. J. Brown, QHC, BD
Father Andrew Mcfadden, QHC, VG, PhB, STL
The Venerable M.G Poll QHC, BA (Hons)
The Reverend B. R. Clarke, MBE, QHC, MA, FRGS

HONORARY PHYSICIANS TO THE QUEEN

Surgeon Rear Admiral C McArthur, QHP, BM, BCh, BAO, MRCGP, LRCP, DObst, RCOG Dip FFP
Surgeon Commodore A.S. Hughes, QHP, MBChB, MRCGP
Surgeon Captain The Honourable RMC McNeil Love QHP

HONORARY SURGEON TO THE QUEEN

Surgeon Commodore A Walker QHS, OBE, FRCS
Surgeon Captain M J Midwinter CBE QHS RN

HONORARY DENTAL SURGEON TO THE QUEEN

Surgeon Captain (D) R.E. Norris, QHDS, MA, FFGDP, MDGS, RCS(Eng), BDS(Lond)

HONORARY NURSE TO THE QUEEN

Captain I.J. Kennedy, QHNS, QARNNS

HONORARY OFFICERS IN HER MAJESTY'S FLEET

ADMIRAL

His Majesty King Carl XVI Gustaf of Sweden, KG ....25 Jun 75

His Majesty Sultan Haji Hussanal Bolkiah Mu'izzaddin Waddaulah Sultan and Yang Di-pertuan of Brunei Darussalam, GCB, GCMG .... 4 Aug 01

HONORARY OFFICERS IN HER MAJESTY'S ROYAL MARINES

COLONEL

His Majesty King Harald V of Norway, KG, GCVO ....18 Mar 81

DEFENCE COUNCIL 2013

The Rt Hon
Philip Hammond MP
Secretary of State for Defence

Dr Andrew Murrison MP
Parliamentary Under Secretary of State and Minister for International Security Strategy

Lord Astor of Hever DL
. Parliamentary Under Secretary of State and the Lords Spokesman on Defence
Unpaid

Philip Dunne MP
Parliamentary Under Secretary of State and. Minister for Defence Equipment, Support and
Technology (including Defence Exports)

The Rt Hon
Mark Francois MP
Minister of State for the Armed Forces

Anna Soubry MP
Parliamentary Under Secretary of State and Minister for Defence Personnel, Welfare and
Veterans

Jon Thompson
Permanent Under Secretary

Admiral Sir George Zambellas KCB DSC ADC
First Sea Lord and Chief of Naval Staff

General Sir Peter Wall GCB CBE ADC Gen
Chief of the General Staff

Air Chief Marshal Sir Andrew Pulford KCB CBE ADC RAF
Chief of the Air Staff

General Sir Nicholas Houghton GCB CBE ADC Gen
Chief of the Defence Staff

Air Chief Marshal Sir Stuart Peach KCB CBE ADC BA MPhil DTech DLitt FRAeS RAF
Vice Chief of the Defence Staff

General Sir David Richards GCB CBE DSO ADC Gen

Professor Vernon Gibson
MOD Chief Scientific Adviser

Bernard Gray
Chief of Defence Materiel

David Williams
Director General Finance

THE ADMIRALTY BOARD

Chairman
THE RIGHT HONOURABLE PHILIP HAMMOND MP
(Secretary of State for Defence)
(Chairman of the Defence Council and Chairman of the
Admiralty Board of the Defence Council)

THE RIGHT HONOURABLE MARK FRANCOIS MP
(Minister of State for the Armed Forces)

MR PHILIP DUNNE MP
(Minister for Defence Equipment, Support and Technology)

MR ANDREW MURRISON MP
(Minister for International Security Strategy)

MISS ANNA SOUBRY MP
(Minister for Defence Personnel, Welfare and Veterans)

LORD ASTOR of HEVER, DL
(Under-Secretary of State and the Lords Spokesman on Defence)

ADMIRAL SIR GEORGE ZAMBELLAS KCB, OBE, ADC, DL
(First Sea Lord and Chief of Naval Staff)

VICE ADMIRAL PHILIP JONES CB
(Fleet Commander)

VICE ADMIRAL DAVID STEEL CBE
(Second Sea Lord)

VICE ADMIRAL SIMON LISTER CB, OBE
(Chief of Fleet Support)

REAR ADMIRAL DUNCAN POTTS
(Controller of the Navy)

REAR ADMIRAL CLIVE JOHNSTONE CBE
(Assistant Chief of Naval Staff)

MISS LOUISE TULETT CBE
(Finance Director (Navy))

KEY PERSONNEL

4* NAVY COMMAND

Chief of Naval Staff/First Sea Lord
Admiral Sir George Zambellas KCB DSC ADC DL

3* NAVY COMMAND

Fleet Commander & Deputy Chief of Naval Staff
Vice Admiral Sir Philip Jones KCB

Chief of Naval Personnel & Training and Second Sea Lord and Chief Naval Logistics Officer
Vice Admiral David Steel CBE

Chief of Materiel (Fleet)
Vice Admiral Simon Lister CB OBE

CHIEF OF STAFF (INTEGRATED CHANGE PROGRAMME)

2* Chief of Staff (Integrated Change Programme) (COS(ICP))
Rear Admiral Malcolm Cree MA

1* Assistant Chief of Staff (Integrated Change Programme) (ACOS(ICP))
Brigadier Richard Spencer OBE

DIRECTOR CARRIER STRIKE

Director Carrier Strike
Rear Admiral Graeme Mackay

NAVAL STAFF - NAVY COMMAND

2* Assistant Chief of Naval Staff (Policy)
Rear Admiral Clive C C Johnstone CBE

1* Head of Naval Staff
Commodore Jim Lines RN

COMUKMARFOR

2* Commander UK Maritime Force (COMUKMARFOR)
Rear Admiral R K Tarrant

1* Deputy COMUKMARFOR (DCMF)
Commodore Jeremy Blunden LVO Royal Navy

1* Commander UK Task Group (COMUKTG)
Commodore Jerry P Kyd

COMUKAMPHIBFOR

2*Commander UK Amphibious Forces & CGRM (COMUKAMPHIBFOR & CGRM)
Major General   Martin Smith MBE

KEY PERSONNEL

COMOPS

2* Commander Maritime Operations (COMOPS)
Rear Admiral M J Parr

1* Commander 3 Commando Brigade RM (Comd 3CDO BDE RM)
Brigadier S M Birrell DSO

ASSISTANT CHIEF NAVAL STAFF (A&C)

2* Rear Admiral Fleet Air Arm and Assistant Chief of Naval Staff (Aviation & Carriers)
Rear Admiral Russ Harding OBE

1* Assistant Chief of Staff Carrier Strike & Aviation (ACOS CSAV)
Commodore Matt Briers

1* Commanding Officer RNAS Yeovilton (CO VL)
Commodore R Alexander OBE

ASSISTANT CHIEF OF NAVAL STAFF (CAPABILITY)

2* Assistant Chief of Naval Staff Capability (ACNS Cap)
Rear Admiral D L Potts

1* Assistant Chief of Staff Maritime Warfare (ACOS MW)
Commodore Guy A Robinson OBE

1* Assistant Chief of Staff Information Superiority (ACOS IS)
Brigadier David Evans

1* Assistant Chief of Staff Surface Ships & Submarines (ACOS SSM)
Commodore Ian Shipperley

1* Assistant Chief of Staff Land & Littoral Manoeuvre (ACOS LLM)
Brigadier Bill Dunham

1* Assistant Chief of Staff Maritime Capability (ACOS Mar Cap)
Commodore Alex Burton

ASSISTANT CHIEF OF NAVAL STAFF (SUPPORT)

2* Assistant Chief of Naval Staff (Support) (ACNS Spt)
Rear Admiral Ian Jess MA

1* Commodore Portsmouth Flotilla (COMPORFLOT)
Commodore Paddy A McAlpine OBE ADC

1* Commodore Devonport Flotilla (COMDEVFLOT)
Commodore Richard Farrington CBE

1* Commodore Faslane Flotilla (COMFASFLOT)
Commodore Mike Walliker OBE

KEY PERSONNEL

1* Assistant Chief of Staff Afloat Support (ACOS AFSUP)
Commodore Robert W Dorey MA RFA

1* Assistant Chief of Staff Logistics & Infrastructure (ACOS Logs & Infra)
Commodore A T Aplin MBE

Commanding Officer HMNB Clyde
Commodore Keith Beckett

Commanding Officer HMNB Devonport
Commodore Graeme Little OBE ADC

Commanding Officer HMNB Portsmouth
Commodore Jeremy Rigby MA

Naval Base Transfer
Mr David Diamond

Finance Director Navy

2* Finance Director (Navy)
Louise Tulett CBE

1* Assistant Chief of Staff Resources & Plans (ACOS RP)
Commodore David Dutton OBE

1* Command Secretary & Deputy Civilian Workforce Advisor
Giles Ahern

1* Head of RN Communications
Commodore Gary Sutton

FORF

2* Flag Officer Regional Forces (FORF)
Rear Admiral John Clink OBE

1* Naval Regional Commander Eastern England (NRC EE)
Commodore Martin Atherton

1* Naval Regional Commander Northern England (NRC NE)
Commodore S R Baum

1* Naval Regional Commander Scotland & Northern Ireland (NRC SNI)
Captain Chris Smith

1* Naval Regional Commander Wales & Western England (NRC WWE)
Commodore Jamie Miller CBE

KEY PERSONNEL

Assistant Chief of Naval Staff (Personnel) and Naval Secretary

2* Assistant Chief of Naval Staff (Personnel) and Naval Secretary
Rear Admiral S J Woodcock OBE

1* Commander Maritime Reserves (COMMARRES)
Commodore Andrew Jameson

1* Commodore Naval Personnel Strategy (CNPS)
Brigadier R A Magowan MBE

1* Commodore Naval Personnel (CNPers)
Commodore Mike Farrage CBE

1* Naval Assistant (NA)
Commodore Ross ALBON OBE

1* Assistant Chief of Staff Medical (ACOS MED)
Surgeon Commodore R M C McNeill Love

1* Commodore Naval Legal Services (CNLS)
Commodore Andrei Spence

FOST

2* Flag Officer Sea Training (FOST)
Rear Admiral B J Key

1* Deputy Flag Officer Sea Training (DFOST)
Commodore John Weale OBE

1* Commander Operational Training (COM OT)
Commodore TJL Williamson MVO

1* Commander Core Training (COMCORE)
Brigadier Ged Salzano MBE

Chaplain of the Fleet

2* Chaplain of the Fleet
The Reverend Scott J Brown CBE QHC BD

OFFICERS ON THE ACTIVE LIST
OF THE ROYAL NAVY, THE ROYAL MARINES,
THE QUEEN ALEXANDRA'S
ROYAL NAVAL NURSING SERVICE
AND RETIRED AND EMERGENCY OFFICERS SERVING

Person Name	Substantive Rank	Seniority	Branch	Specialisation	Organisation	Location
A						
Abbey Rachel Faye	Lt RN	07-Sep-10	ENG	ME	FOST DPORT SEA	HMNB DEVONPORT
Abbott, Duncan A J	Lt RN	01-Nov-07	WAR	GSX	HMS DIAMOND	
Abbott, Grant P	Maj	01-Oct-09	RM	GS	FLEET CAP	NCHQ
Abbott, Katherine Y L	Lt RN	01-Dec-03	WAR	PWO	HMS DAUNTLESS	
Abbott, Sir Peter (Charles), GBE, KCB, MA	Adm	03-Oct-95				
Abbotts, Michael C	Lt Cdr	01-Oct-11	ENG	AE	CHFHQ (SHORE)	RNAS YEOVILTON
Abel, James A	Lt RN	01-Nov-05	ENG	WESM(SWS)	DES/COMFLEET	USA
Abel, Nigel Philip	Lt Cdr	01-Oct-07	WAR	P CDO	CHF(MERLIN)	RAF BENSON
Abernethy, James R G	Cdr	30-Jun-04	WAR	PWO(N)	FLEET ACOS(RP)	NCHQ
Ablett, Daniel J	Surg Lt Cdr	01-Nov-09	MED	GS	INM ALVERSTOKE	GOSPORT
Ablett, Eleanor L	Cdr	30-Jun-11	LOGS	L	HMS BULWARK	
Abouzeid, Adam A	Capt	01-Sep-09	RM	GS	CTCRM - CW	EXMOUTH
Abraham, Paul CBE	Capt RN	30-Jun-08	WAR	SM(CQ)	DI - ICSP	MAIN BUILDING LONDON
Ackland, Heber K MVO	Capt RN	10-Dec-13	LOGS	L	FLEET COMNDER DCNS	NCHQ
Adam, Ian K	Cdr	30-Jun-09	WAR	PWO(A)	FMW CENTRE	HMS COLLINGWOOD
Adam, Murray W	Lt RN	01-Nov-06	WAR	PWO(SM)	HMS VIGILANT	
Adams, Alistair J	Cdre	05-Nov-12	WAR	PWO(C)	PJHQ (UK) J6	NORTHWOOD
Adams, Andrew M	Capt RN	18-Jan-10	ENG	MESM	SIT - ABBEYWOOD	MAIN BUILDING LONDON
Adams, Edwin S	Lt Cdr	01-Oct-09	WAR	P SK4	845 SQN	RNAS YEOVILTON
Adams, George	Lt Cdr	01-May-09	ENG	ME	FLEET CAP SSM DIVISION	NCHQ
Adams, Henry D	Lt RN	01-Sep-12	WAR	SM(X)	MCM1 CREW 6	FASLANE
Adams, Joanne F	Lt RN	01-Apr-08	WAR	O SKW	857 NAS	RNAS CULDROSE
Adams, Jonathan T	Lt	01-Sep-11	RM	GS	42 CDO RM - M COY	PLYMOUTH
Adams, Keith J	Lt RN	01-Sep-11	ENG	AE	FLEET HQ	NCHQ
Adams, Lee M	Capt	01-Apr-11	RM	GS	NCHQ	
Adams, Matthew	Capt	20-Jul-07	RM	SCC	ARMOURED SUPPORT GROUP	RNAS YEOVILTON
Adams, Megan A	SLt	30-Jun-07	MED	MEDICAL	BRNC DARTMOUTH	
Adams, Peter	Cdr	01-Sep-09	ENG	TM	FOSNNI - YOUTH C	ROSYTH
Adams, Victoria R	Lt RN	01-Sep-12	WAR	GSX	HMS DAUNTLESS	
Adams, William John MBE	Lt Cdr	01-Oct-08	WAR	GSX	OP ATALANTA	NORTHWOOD
Adcock, Edward G	Lt RN	01-Nov-12	WE		HMS SUTHERLAND	
Addison, Timothy M	Capt	01-Sep-10	RM	GS	40 CDO RM - COMD COY	TAUNTON
Adekoluejo, Gbadebowale A	SLt	01-Sep-11	ENG	AE	DCEME	HMS SULTAN
Adey, Joanna L	Lt Cdr	01-Oct-10	ENG	TM	RNSME HQ & ATG	HMS SULTAN
Adkins, Paul S	Lt RN	16-Dec-11	WAR	C	FLEET CAP IS DIVISION	NCHQ
Adlam, Charlotte	Lt RN	01-Jan-09	ENG	WE	DEFAC CMT	SHRIVENHAM
Adshead, Stephen P	Surg Lt RN	01-Mar-12	MED	GDMO	HMS VIGILANT	
A'Hern, Paul Vincent	Lt RN	01-Sep-09	WAR	GSX	RN EXCHANGE NORWAY	OSLO
Ahlgren, Edward G OBE	Cdr	30-Jun-09	WAR	SM(CQ)	UKRBATSTAFF	HMNB PORTSMOUTH
Ahuja, Vijay Yogesh	Surg Lt RN	05-Aug-09	MED	Anaes	INM ALVERSTOKE	GOSPORT
Aindow, Alice Lucy	Mid	01-Nov-13	WAR	GSX	BRNC DARTMOUTH	
Ainscow, Peter D	SLt	17-Nov-11	ENG	ME	DCEME SULTAN	HMS SULTAN

Person Name	Substantive Rank	Seniority	Branch	Specialisation	Organisation	Location
Ainsley, Alex S.	2Lt	01-Sep-11	RM	GS	CTCRM OFFICERS	EXMOUTH
Ainsley, Andrew M J	Lt Cdr	01-Oct-08	WAR	PWO	PJHQ (UK) J3	NORTHWOOD
Ainsworth, Alan	Lt RN	01-Jul-04	ENG	WE	DEFENCE ACADEMY	SHRIVENHAM
Aird, Pauline	Lt Cdr	01-Apr-05	ENG	ME	AIR 22GP - LYNEHAM	RAF LYNEHAM
Aitchison, Ian	Lt Cdr	31-Mar-03	WAR	MEDIA OPS	HQ ISAF	KABUL HQ ISAF
Aitken, Andrew J	Cdr	30-Jun-11	WAR	SM(CQ)	HMS TALENT	
Aitken, Neil D	Lt RN	01-May-07	WAR	ATC	ARCC KINLOSS	RAF KINLOSS
Aitken, Steven R	Lt RN	01-Jan-01	WAR	P LYNX	RN EXCHANGE FRANCE	PARIS
Ajala, Ahmed R A	Lt Cdr	01-Oct-04	ENG	WE	FLEET CAP RCAP	NCHQ
Akerman, Andrew E	Lt RN	01-Aug-08	LOGS	L	HMS OCEAN	
Alberts, Ian	Surg Lt RN	07-Aug-13	MED	MEDICAL	BRNC DARTMOUTH	
Albon, Joshua G	SLt	01-Apr-11	WAR	P UT	CHF (MERLIN) 1	OXFORD
Albon, Mark	Cdr	30-Jun-06	WAR	HM	FLEET HM UNIT	PLYMOUTH
Albon, Ross	Cdre	07-Jul-08	LOGS	L BAR	NAVSEC	PORTSMOUTH
Alcindor, David J	Lt Cdr	22-Apr-10	WAR	SM(AWC)	MOD SSPAG	MAIN BUILDING LONDON
Alcock, Christopher	Capt RN	30-Jun-07	WAR	O SK6	HMS NELSON	
Alder, Mark C	Lt Cdr	01-Oct-10	ENG	MESM	NCHQ CNPERS	PORTSMOUTH
Alderson, Richard J	Maj	01-Oct-04	RM	GS	CAREER TRAINING	AUSTRALIA
Alderson, Stuart J	Lt RN	01-Sep-13	ENG	MESM	DCEME SULTAN	HMS SULTAN
Alderton, Paul A	Lt Cdr	01-Oct-09	ENG	WE	NAVY MCTA	HMNB PORTSMOUTH
Aldous, Benjamin	Lt Cdr	01-Nov-07	WAR	PWO(A)	DEFAC JSCSC ACSC	SHRIVENHAM
Alessandro, Santino S	2Lt	01-Sep-13	RM	N/A	CTCRM OFFICERS	EXMOUTH
Alexander, Amy L	Lt Cdr	01-Oct-08	ENG	WE	HMS NELSON	
Alexander, Oliver D D	Lt Cdr	01-Oct-06	WAR	MCD	SDU 1	FDS PORTSMOUTH
Alexander, Phillip M D	Lt Cdr	01-Jan-09	ENG	MESM	NBC CLYDE BABCOCK	HELENSBURGH
Alexander, Robert S OBE	Cdre	04-Dec-12	WAR	P SK6	RNAS YEOVILTON	
Alexander, William A D	Lt RN	01-Jan-06	WAR	HM	RN EXCHANGE N ZLAND	NEW ZEALAND
Allan, Chris R	Lt Cdr	01-Dec-05	WAR	PWO(C)	FLEET COMOPS NWD	NORTHWOOD
Allan, Fraser Stuart	Maj	01-Oct-09	RM	GS	NCHQ	
Allan, John Martyn	Lt RN	08-Dec-09	WAR	O SKW	854 NAS	RNAS CULDROSE
Allan, Robert Campbell-Ross	Mid	01-Sep-13	ENG	AE	BRNC DARTMOUTH	
Allcock, Andrew J	RN Chpln	05-Jan-09	Ch S		DEFENCE ACADEMY HQ	SHRIVENHAM
Allcock, Edward C	Surg Lt Cdr	07-Aug-07	MED	Anaes	MDHU PORTSMOUTH	PORTSMOUTH
Alldridge, George M	SLt	01-Feb-11	WAR	HM	MWS COLLINGWOOD	
Allen, Alexander P.	Lt RN	01-Jan-07	ENG	ME	DES/COMFLEET	ABBEY WOOD
Allen, Benjamin J	Mid	01-Sep-13	WAR	GSX	BRNC DARTMOUTH	
Allen, Elinor Jane Rd	Cdr	30-Sep-05	WAR	OP INT	NPT RES MOBILISATION	HMNB PORTSMOUTH
Allen, Jason L	Lt Cdr	01-Oct-13	WAR	PWO	MWS COLLINGWOOD	
Allen, Lloyd N	Lt RN	11-Dec-09	LOGS	L	HMS OCEAN	
Allen, Nicholas C	Lt RN	08-Jul-12	WAR	P UT	RNAS YEOVILTON	
Allen, Patrick L	Cdr	30-Jun-08	WAR	O SKW	FOST DPORT SEA	HMNB DEVONPORT
Allen, Paul M	Lt Cdr	01-Oct-04	WAR	O LYNX	DES/COMJE/HELS	RNAS YEOVILTON
Allen, Richard	Cdr	30-Jun-06	WAR	SM(CQ)	DES/COMFLEET/SM	ABBEY WOOD
Allen, Richard M	Cdre	01-Jul-13	WAR	SM(CQ)	BDS WASHINGTON	WASHINGTON USA
Allen, Stephen M	Capt RN	08-Jan-13	WAR	O SK6	FLEET CSAV	NCHQ
Allen, Timothy W	Lt RN	01-Sep-08	WAR	GSX	MCM2 CREW 1	PORTSMOUTH
Allen-Scholey, Spencer G	Lt RN	09-Apr-10	ENG	MESM	HMS VIGILANT	
Allen-West, Bart J	Lt RN	05-Aug-11	LOGS	L	DES/COMLAND/LCS	RAF NORTHOLT
Allfree, Joseph	Lt Cdr	01-Jan-03	WAR	AAWO	HMS DRAGON	
Allibon, Mark C	Cdr	30-Jun-00	WAR	PWO(A)	DES/COMFLEET	ABBEY WOOD
Allison, Glenn	Lt Cdr	01-Oct-08	WAR	P SK4	651 SQN	RAF ALDERGROVE
Allsopp, Mark D	RN Chpln	02-Jun-08	Ch S	Chaplain	CTCRM	EXMOUTH
Almond, Nicholas	Lt Cdr	01-Oct-12	ENG	AE	DES/COMJE/HELS	RNAS YEOVILTON
Alston, Richard	Maj	01-Oct-08	RM	C	HQ 3 CDO BDE RM	PLYMOUTH
Althorpe, Damian S	Capt	01-Apr-11	RM	SCC	CHFHQ (SEA)	RNAS YEOVILTON
Alvey, Joshua T.	Mid	01-Nov-13	WAR	GSX	BRNC DARTMOUTH	DARTMOUTH
Amery, Miles T	SLt	01-Dec-13	WAR	GSX	MCM2 CREW	PORTSMOUTH
Amor, Matthew	Lt RN	01-Sep-10	ENG	WESM(TWS)	HMS AMBUSH	
Amorosi, Riccardo G	Lt Cdr	01-Oct-11	ENG	WE	HMS NELSON	HMS NELSON
Amphlett, Nigel G	Capt RN	07-Jun-10	WAR	O LYNX	ATTACHE/ADVISER HAGUE	BRUSSELS
Ancona, Simon J	R Adm	14-Oct-13	WAR	O SK6	ACDS MIL STRAT	MAIN BUILDING LONDON
Anderson, Andrew E	Lt Cdr	01-Oct-10	WAR	ATC	FOST DPORT SHORE	HMNB DEVONPORT

Person Name	Substantive Rank	Seniority	Branch	Specialisation	Organisation	Location
Anderson, Bruce W.	Maj	01-Oct-11	RM	GS	Op LANSBURY	AFGHANISTAN
Anderson, Bryan A.	Lt RN	12-Jul-13	WAR	INT	1 CAREER	SHEFFORD
Anderson, David E	Lt RN	06-Apr-07	WAR	O SK6	RNAS CULDROSE - AED HQ	RNAS CULDROSE
Anderson, Garry S.	Lt Cdr	01-Oct-07	WAR	INT	FLEET COMOPS NWD	NORTHWOOD
Anderson, Joseph	Mid	01-Feb-13	LOGS	L	HMS RALEIGH	
Anderson, Kevin	Lt RN	01-Jun-03	ENG	TM	DEFENCE ACADEMY	SHRIVENHAM
Anderson, Mark E	Lt Cdr	01-Oct-05	WAR	PWO	HQ ARRC COMND GROUP	GLOUCESTER
Anderson, Martin	Lt RN	31-Jul-09	WAR	SM(X)	FLEET COMOPS NWD	NORTHWOOD
Anderson, Michael I	Lt RN	01-May-07	WAR	O MER	750 SQN SEAHAWK	RNAS CULDROSE
Anderson, Neil	Lt Cdr	01-Oct-11	ENG	WE	DES/COMLAND/LCS	ABBEY WOOD BRISTOL
Anderson, Peter D.	Mid	01-Sep-13	WAR	GSX	BRNC DARTMOUTH	
Anderson, Robert G	Capt RN	01-Jul-08	ENG	WE	FLEET CMR	NCHQ
Anderson, Stephen R	Lt Cdr	01-Oct-08	WAR	O LYNX	FOST DPORT SEA	HMNB DEVONPORT
Anderson, Timothy J	Surg Lt RN	04-Aug-10	MED	GDMO	HMS DRAGON	
Andrew, Paul R	RN Chpln	04-Jan-10	Ch S	Chaplain	40 CDO RM	TAUNTON
Andrews, Alistair J	Lt RN	01-Apr-09	WAR	P SKW	849 SQN	RNAS CULDROSE
Andrews, Christopher	Lt Cdr	01-Oct-09	ENG	IS	OCLB BIRMINGHAM	BIRMINGHAM
Andrews, David	Mid	19-Apr-13	WAR	O UT	BRNC DARTMOUTH	DARTMOUTH
Andrews, Dominic M	Lt RN	01-Oct-13	ENG	WE	DES/COMFLEET	ABBEY WOOD BRISTOL
Andrews, Iain S	Lt RN	01-Sep-01	WAR	MW	MWS COLLINGWOOD	
Andrews, Justin P	Lt Cdr	01-Oct-11	ENG	WE	HMS IRON DUKE	
Andrews, Liam James R	Lt RN	01-Nov-13	WAR	SM(X)	HMS VIGILANT	
Andrews, Louisa J	Lt Cdr	01-Oct-10	WAR	HM(AM)	LOAN DSTL	FAREHAM
Andrews, Nicholas G.	Lt RN	01-Mar-11	WAR	GSX	HMS MERSEY	
Andrews, Paul	Lt Cdr	01-Jun-94	LOGS	L C	DES/COMFLEET	SOUTHAMPTON
Andrews, Rick	Lt RN	01-Sep-07	ENG	MESM	DES/COMFLEET	ABBEY WOOD BRISTOL
Andrews, Robert C	SLt	01-Sep-11	WAR	P UT	824 SQN	RNAS CULDROSE
Andrews, Steven J.	Lt RN	13-Oct-12	MED	MS(CDO)	MED SQN CDO LOG	BARNSTAPLE
Angliss, Roger J.	Lt RN	08-Apr-05	WAR	O MER	820 SQN	RNAS CULDROSE
Angus, Donald J C	Surg Lt RN	19-Aug-13	MED	GMP	INM ALVERSTOKE	GOSPORT
Aniyi, Christopher B.	Cdr	30-Jun-09	ENG	ME	DES/COMFLEET	ABBEY WOOD
Ankah, Gregory K	Lt Cdr	01-Dec-04	ENG	ME	DEFAC JSCSC ACSC	SHRIVENHAM
Annett, Ian G.	Capt RN	11-Mar-13	ENG	WE	FLEET CAP IS DIVISION	NCHQ
Anrude, Jack F MC.	Capt	01-Sep-10	RM	GS	ARMOURED SUPPORT GROUP	RNAS YEOVILTON
Ansell, Christopher	Lt Cdr	01-Oct-06	WAR	PWO(C)	HMS SUTHERLAND	
Anstey, Robert J	Cdr	30-Jun-05	WAR	SM(CQ)	NUCLEAR CAPABILITY	MAIN BUILDING LONDON
Aplin, Adrian T MBE	Capt RN	24-Nov-09	LOGS	L	DES/COMLAND	ABBEY WOOD
Apps, Julian C.	Capt	01-Sep-04	RM	GS	UKRBATSTAFF	HMNB PORTSMOUTH
Arend, Faye Marie.	Lt Cdr	01-Oct-06	LOGS	L	FLEET SPT LOGS	NCHQ
Arkell, Thomas C	Capt	01-Sep-13	RM	GS	40 CDO RM - DGHR(O)	TAUNTON
Armand-Smith, Penelope H	Lt RN	01-Jan-05	WAR	HM	FLEET COMNDER DCNS	NCHQ
Armitage, David G	SLt	01-Feb-11	WAR	P	HMS RICHMOND	
Armour, Angela B	Lt RN	01-Sep-05	ENG	TM	DNR RCHQ NORTH	HMS CALEDONIA
Armour, Graeme A.	Lt Col	30-Jun-06	RM	GS	NATO BRUSSELS	BRUSSELS
Armstrong, Alison C	SLt	01-Nov-11	WAR	HM	BRNC DARTMOUTH	
Armstrong, Christopher T	Capt	01-Sep-09	RM	GS	3 CDO BDE RM	PLYMOUTH
Armstrong, Colin D.	Lt RN	01-Sep-00	WAR	PWO	NAVY MCTA PORTSMOUTH	HMNB PORTSMOUTH
Armstrong, David M	Lt Cdr	01-Oct-12	WAR	MCD	HMS MONTROSE	
Armstrong, Nicholas P.	Lt Cdr	01-Oct-96	WAR	O MER	RNAS CULDROSE	
Armstrong, Paul	Lt RN	01-Apr-12	WAR	P UT	RNAS YEOVILTON	
Armstrong, Paul C	Lt RN	13-Jul-12	ENG	WE	HMS SOMERSET	
Armstrong, Rory J	Lt Cdr	01-Oct-12	WAR	MCD	HMS KENT	
Armstrong, Sally	Lt RN	09-Apr-04	WAR	MEDIA OPS	UK MCC	BAHRAIN
Armstrong, Scott T.	Lt Cdr	01-Oct-04	WAR	P SK4	771 SQN	RNAS CULDROSE
Armstrong, Stuart M.	Lt Cdr	01-Oct-07	WAR	SM(CQ)	DEFAC JSCSC ACSC	SHRIVENHAM
Arnold, Lee J.	Lt RN	01-Sep-11	ENG	MESM	HMS VANGUARD	
Arr Woodward, Robert W	Surg Lt RN	01-Aug-12	MED	MEDICAL	BRNC DARTMOUTH	
Arscott, James S.	2Lt	01-Sep-13	RM	N/A	CTCRM OFFICERS	EXMOUTH
Arthur, Calum H C	Surg Lt Cdr	01-Aug-06	MED	T&O	INM ALVERSTOKE	GOSPORT
Asbridge, Jonathan I	Cdr	30-Jun-08	LOGS	L SM	ACDS	MAIN BUILDING LONDON
Ash, Timothy C V	Cdr	30-Jun-08	WAR	MW	DES/COMFLEET	HMS NELSON
Ashby, Maxine	Lt RN	01-Dec-00	LOGS	L	RNAS CULDROSE - CA	RNAS CULDROSE

Person Name	Substantive Rank	Seniority	Branch	Specialisation	Organisation	Location
Ashcroft, Adam C	Capt RN	30-Jun-08	WAR	P LYNX	ATTACHE/ADVISER TOKYO	JAPAN
Ashcroft, Benjamin J	Capt	01-Sep-09	RM	GS	CTCRM	EXMOUTH
Ashley, Elizabeth A	Surg Lt RN	01-Aug-12	MED	MEDICAL	BRNC DARTMOUTH	
Ashley, Scott M	Capt	18-Jul-08	RM	SCC	NCHQ CNPERS	NCHQ
Ashley, Stephen J	Lt RN	01-Sep-08	ENG	WE	UKRBATSTAFF	HMNB PORTSMOUTH
Ashley-Smith, Richard	Lt RN	01-Mar-09	ENG	ME	DES/COMFLEET	ABBEY WOOD,BRISTOL
Ashlin, James M	Lt Cdr	01-Oct-12	WAR	P SK4	750 SQN SEAHAWK	RNAS CULDROSE
Ashman, Rodney G	Cdr	30-Jun-07	LOGS	L C	FLEET SPT LOGS	NCHQ
Ashton, James	Lt Cdr	01-Mar-10	ENG	MESM	HMS VICTORIOUS	
Ashton, Karl	Lt RN	01-Jan-12	LOGS	L	COMPORFLOT WLSG	HMNB PORTSMOUTH
Ashton, Megan E	Lt RN	01-Mar-09	ENG	AE	DCDS PERS TRG	MAIN BUILDING LONDON
Asker, Tristan	SLt	01-Sep-11	ENG	WE	MWS COLLINGWOOD	HMS COLLINGWOOD
Askham, Mathew T	Lt RN	01-Jun-06	WAR	P MER	814 SQN	RNAS CULDROSE
Aspden, Andrew M	Capt RN	21-Oct-08	WAR	O SK6	FLEET FOST ACOS	NCHQ
Asquith, Simon P OBE	Cdr	30-Jun-08	WAR	SM(CQ)	OPS DIR	MAIN BUILDING LONDON
Astley, Daniel	Lt RN	01-Sep-13	ENG	WE	HMS LANCASTER	
Astley, William E	Lt RN	23-Jul-13	ENG	ME	HMS NELSON	
Aston, James A	Lt RN	01-Aug-10	ENG	TM	FOST FAS SHORE	HELENSBURGH
Aston, Mark W	Surg Cdr (D)	30-Jun-97	DENTAL	GDP	RNAS YEOVILTON	
Atherton, Bruce W	Maj	01-Oct-04	RM	P LYN7	CAREER TRAINING	IPSWICH
Atherton, Martin J	Capt RN	30-Jun-03	LOGS	N/A	FLEET FOSNNI	LONDON
Atkins, Ian	Cdr	30-Jun-09	ENG	ME	DES/COMFLEET	ABBEY WOOD BRISTOL
Atkinson, Andrew W	Capt	21-Mar-13	RM	SCC	HMS BULWARK	
Atkinson, David	Capt	21-Mar-13	RM	GS	NCHQ	
Atkinson, James D	Lt RN	26-Feb-06	WAR	OP INT (RES)	NATO ACO	NORTHWOOD
Atkinson, Kevin A	Mid	01-Nov-13	ENG	WE	BRNC DARTMOUTH	
Atkinson, Mark	Cdr	30-Jun-08	WAR	MCD PWO(A)	FLEET CAP	NCHQ
Atkinson, Neil C	Maj	01-May-06	RM	GS	OPS DIR	MAIN BUILDING LONDON
Atkinson, Richard J	Cdr	30-Jun-13	WAR	AAWO	FLEET CAP SSM	NCHQ
Attrill, Jonathan D	Capt	01-Sep-13	RM	GS	40 CDO RM	TAUNTON
Attwater, Richard P	Lt RN	01-Jan-05	WAR	PWO	HMS DUNCAN	
Attwood, Keith A	Lt RN	01-Sep-04	WAR	P LYNX	815 SQN FLT	RNAS YEOVILTON
Atwal, Kamaldip	Lt RN	01-Jan-02	ENG	TM	JFC - DCTS (H)	RAF HALTON
Atwill, John W O	Cdr	30-Jun-11	LOGS	L BAR	MOD CNS/ACNS	MAIN BUILDING LONDON
Aujla, Pavandip S	SLt	08-Dec-12	WAR	GSX	HMS ARGYLL	
Auld, Douglas	Lt Cdr	01-Oct-06	ENG	MESM	DES/COMFLEET	WASHINGTON USA
Austin, Peter Nigel	Lt Cdr	01-Oct-07	ENG	WESM	DES/COMFLEET	HMNB DEVONPORT
Avison, Christopher J	SLt	01-Apr-12	WAR	P UT	RNAS YEOVILTON	RNAS YEOVILTON
Ayers, Oliver R B	Lt RN	01-Nov-06	WAR	GSX	MWS COLLINGWOOD	
Aylmer, Matthew A	SLt	01-Apr-11	WAR	ATC	RNAS CULDROSE	
Ayrton, Robert E	Lt RN	01-Dec-02	WAR	HM(AS)	HMS ENTERPRISE	
Ayto, Lydia Jane	SLt	08-Oct-12	WAR	GSX	MWS COLLINGWOOD	

B

Back, Charles P	Capt	01-Sep-13	RM	GS	43 CDO	HMNB CLYDE
Backhouse, Jonathan R	RN Chpln	03-Sep-07	Ch S		HMS NELSON	HMNB PORTSMOUTH
Bacon, David Ross	Lt RN	09-Apr-12	LOGS	L	HMS DAUNTLESS	
Bacon, Thomas Giles	Capt	01-Sep-08	RM	GS	HQ 3 CDO BDE RM	PLYMOUTH
Baddeley, James	Lt RN	01-Sep-13	ENG	ME	HMS DUNCAN	
Baggaley, Jason A L	Cdr	30-Jun-11	ENG	WE	MWS COLLINGWOOD	
Bagnall, Sally-Anne E	Cdr	06-Aug-12	QARNNS	Nurse Officer	DMS WHITTINGTON	LICHFIELD
Bagshaw, James R W	Lt Cdr	01-Oct-08	WAR	PWO(A)	FASLANE	HELENSBURGH
Bailes, Kenneth	Lt Cdr	01-Oct-10	WAR	PWO	RN EXCHANGE AUSTRALIA	CANBERRA
Bailey, Andrew Paul	Lt RN	01-Apr-11	WAR	O SKW	857 NAS	RNAS CULDROSE
Bailey, David James	Lt RN	01-Oct-09	WAR	MW	MCM2 CREW 1	PORTSMOUTH
Bailey, Ian John	Lt Cdr	01-Oct-10	ENG	WE	HMS ARGYLL	
Bailey, Jeremy J	Cdr	30-Jun-09	ENG	ME	FLEET CAP RCAP DIVISION	NCHQ
Bailey, Jonathan	Lt RN	01-Sep-10	ENG	WESM(TWS)	FLEET COMOPS	FAREHAM
Bailey, Michael	Lt Cdr	01-Oct-10	WAR	INT	JFIG - JT IP	RAF WYTON
Bailey, Sian	Lt RN	01-Aug-99	ENG	TM	OCLC NCH	MANCHESTER
Bailey, Simon	Lt Cdr	01-Oct-11	WAR	PWO	HMS RALEIGH	
Baillie, Robbie W	Lt Cdr	01-Oct-11	ENG	TM	CTCRM	EXMOUTH

Person Name	Substantive Rank	Seniority	Branch	Specialisation	Organisation	Location
Bainbridge, John R	Lt Cdr	01-Oct-07	WAR	MCD	HMS COLLINGWOOD	
Bainbridge, Paul A	Lt Cdr	01-Oct-11	LOGS	L	OCLC PETERBRGH	PETERBOROUGH
Bainbridge, Stuart D	Lt Cdr	01-Oct-08	WAR	P MER	FLEET AV CU	RNAS CULDROSE
Baines, David M L	Cdr	30-Jun-10	ENG	IS	NCHQ - NAVY CMD SEC	NCHQ
Baines, Gary A	Maj	01-Oct-06	RM	SCC	CTCRM	EXMOUTH
Baines, Liam P	Lt RN	01-Sep-12	ENG	WESM	HMS TIRELESS	
Bains, Baldeep S	Surg Lt Cdr	01-Aug-06	MED	GMP	FLEET AV HENLOW	RAF HENLOW
Baker, Adrian B	Surg Capt RN	17-Feb-09	MED	Occ Med	INM ALVERSTOKE	GOSPORT
Baker, Adrian P	Cdr	30-Jun-13	WAR	O LYNX	FOST DPORT SHORE	HMNB DEVONPORT
Baker, James E G	Lt Cdr	01-Oct-10	WAR	PWO	HMS DEFENDER	
Baker, James K	Lt RN	01-May-06	WAR	P SK4	AACEN 7 (TRG) REGT	STOCKBRIDGE
Baker, James O	Surg Lt RN	01-Mar-08	MED	GDMO	HMS ILLUSTRIOUS	
Baker, Kyle L	Lt RN	01-Sep-13	ENG	MESM	DCEME SULTAN	
Baker, Luke D	Surg Lt RN	03-Aug-11	MED	GDMO	HMS DARING	
Baker, Mark A	Lt RN	08-Dec-09	LOGS	L SM	COMDEVFLOT WLSG	
Baker, Michael	Maj	01-Oct-05	RM	P LYN7	HQ JHC	ANDOVER
Baker, Michael	Lt Cdr	01-Jun-98	ENG	WE	HMS NELSON	
Baker, Nicholas	Lt Cdr	01-Oct-05	LOGS	L	HMS RALEIGH	
Bakewell, Emma C	Lt RN	01-Jan-07	ENG	ME	HMS NELSON	
Bakewell, Timothy D	Lt Col	30-Jun-12	WAR	HW	ATTACHE/ADVISER RONIA	BUCHAREST
Bakker-Dyos, Joshua J	Surg Lt RN	01-Aug-12	MED	MEDICAL	BRNC DARTMOUTH	
Balcam, Jonathan E	SLt	01-May-12	LOGS	L	BRNC DARTMOUTH	
Baldie, Steven A	Lt Cdr	01-Oct-11	WAR	P CDO	CHF(MERLIN)	RAF BENSON
Baldwin, Christopher M	Cdr	30-Jun-11	WAR	MCD PWO(A)	DSEA DST	PORTSMOUTH
Balfour, Ross D	Lt Cdr	01-Oct-12	WAR	MCD	RN EXCHANGE USA	WASHINGTON
Balhetchet, Adrian S	Cdr	30-Jun-09	ENG	AE	STABILISATION UNIT	MAIN BUILDING LONDON
Ball, Ian N	SLt	01-Sep-13	WAR	SM(X)	HMS IRON DUKE	
Ball, Jacob	Lt RN	01-Sep-12	WAR	SM(X)	HMS VIGILANT	
Ball, Liam	SLt	01-Sep-12	ENG	AE	BRNC DARTMOUTH	
Ball, Matthew P	Lt Cdr	01-Oct-08	ENG	MESM	DES/COMFLEET	HMNB CLYDE
Ball, Samuel P	Mid	01-May-13	WAR	O UT	BRNC DARTMOUTH	
Ball, William J E	Lt Cdr	01-Oct-09	ENG	ME	FOST DPORT SEA	HMNB DEVONPORT
Ballantyne, Craig	Lt Cdr	25-Jun-13	WAR	SM(CQ)	WMO DEVONPORT	HMNB DEVONPORT
Ballard, Adam P V	Lt Cdr	01-Oct-12	WAR	PWO(N)	HMS PROTECTOR	
Ballard, Danelle R	Lt Cdr	01-Oct-12	WAR	PWO(N)	HMS NELSON	
Ballard, Mark L	Cdr	30-Jun-11	ENG	WESM	COMFASFLOT	HMNB CLYDE
Balletta, Rene J	Lt Cdr	01-Nov-04	WAR	PWO(C)	RN EXCHANGE FRANCE	PARIS
Balls, Christopher F	Lt RN	01-Sep-11	ENG	WESM	HMS TRIUMPH	
Balmer, Guy A	Maj	24-Apr-02	RM	GMP	NAVY CORE TRG HQ	HMNB DEVONPORT
Balmond, Samuel J	Lt RN	01-Feb-11	ENG	TM	HMS SULTAN	
Bamber, Michael S	Surg Lt Cdr (D)	05-Jul-12	DENTAL	GDP	RNAS CULDROSE	
Bambro, Calum A	SLt	01-Feb-12	WAR	GSX	BRNC DARTMOUTH	
Bamford, Alexander	Surg Lt RN	07-Aug-13	MED	MEDICAL	BRNC DARTMOUTH	
Bamforth, Christian J	Cdr	30-Jun-13	ENG	WESM(TWS)	ACNS SPT	NCHQ
Bance, Nicholas D	Lt Cdr	01-Oct-04	WAR	P LYNX	LHF 702 SQN	RNAS YEOVILTON
Band, James W	Cdr	30-Jun-04	ENG	AE	NCHQ CNPERS	PORTSMOUTH
Band, Sir Jonathon, GCB, DL	Adm	02-Aug-02				
Bane, Nicholas St John	Lt Cdr	01-Oct-13	WAR	P SK4	RAF SHAWBURY	SHREWSBURY
Banfield, Steven D	Lt Cdr	01-Oct-10	WAR	PWO	NCHQ CNPERS	PORTSMOUTH
Bannister, Jonathan	Lt Cdr	01-Oct-12	WAR	PWO	RN EXCHANGE AUSTRALIA	CANBERRA AUSTRALIA
Banyard, Adelaide C	Mid	01-Nov-13	WAR	HM	BRNC DARTMOUTH	
Barber, Alexander S L	Lt RN	01-Jan-05	WAR	INT	FLEET COMOPS NWD	HMS COLLINGWOOD
Barber, Christopher J	Lt Cdr	01-Oct-07	WAR	O SKW	750 SQN SEAHAWK	RNAS CULDROSE
Barber, Christopher J	Lt RN	01-Apr-11	WAR	GSX	MWS DDS	DDS PORTSMOUTH
Barber, Mark	Lt RN	01-Sep-03	WAR	P SK6	DEF HELI FLYING SCH	RAF SHAWBURY
Barber, Max A	SLt	01-Sep-13	WAR	GSX	HMS DARING	
Barber, Ralph W	RN Chpln	31-Mar-08	Ch S	Chaplain	FWO PORTS SEA - ACOS	HMNB PORTSMOUTH
Barber, Thomas E	Capt	01-Sep-10	RM	GS	RMR MERSEYSIDE	LIVERPOOL
Barclay, Alastair J	Lt RN	21-Jun-96	WAR	ATC	RNAS CULDROSE - ATC	RNAS CULDROSE
Barden, Paul E	Maj	01-Oct-10	RM	SCC	40 CDO RM	TAUNTON
Barfoot, Peter M	Lt Cdr	01-Oct-10	WAR	PWO	HMS DARING	
Barham, Edward	Lt RN	01-Sep-06	WAR	O LYNX	MOD CNS/ACNS	MAIN BUILDING LONDON

Person Name	Substantive Rank	Seniority	Branch	Specialisation	Organisation	Location
Bark, James S	Lt Cdr	01-Sep-96	WAR	SM(CQ)	DES/COMFLEET	HELENSBURGH
Barker, Helen A	Lt RN	01-Sep-07	LOGS	L	FLEET ACOS(RP)	ABBEY WOOD BRISTOL
Barker, Paul D	Lt Cdr	01-Apr-08	ENG	AE	848 SQN	RNAS YEOVILTON
Barker, Peter R	Lt RN	01-Jan-07	LOGS	L BAR	DCDS PERS - SPA	RAF NORTHOLT
Barker, Piers T	Cdr	30-Jun-05	WAR	SM(CQ)	COMFASFLOT	HMNB CLYDE
Barker, William G	Lt RN	16-Mar-13	ENG	MESM	DCEME SULTAN	HMS SULTAN
Barkey, Barry J	Lt RN	01-Sep-11	WAR	P UT	824 SQN	RNAS CULDROSE
Barks, Nicholas	Capt	30-Mar-12	RM	GS	NCHQ	
Barley, Andrew G	SLt	01-Feb-12	LOGS	L	BRNC DARTMOUTH	DARTMOUTH
Barlow, Jay P	Lt RN	05-Aug-11	ENG	WE	HMS SOMERSET	
Barlow, Leonard J	Lt RN	30-Jul-10	ENG	WESM	HMS VIGILANT	
Barlow, Martin J	Cdr	30-Jun-12	WAR	O SKW	HQ AIR - COS(OPS)	RAF HIGH WYCOMBE
Barlow, Matthew J	Capt	01-Aug-07	RM	GS	HMS DRAKE	
Barlow, Paul R	Lt RN	01-Sep-12	ENG	WESM	HMS VICTORIOUS	
Barnard, Edward B G	Surg Lt Cdr	04-Aug-09	MED	EM	INM ALVERSTOKE	GOSPORT
Barnbrook, Jeremy C	Lt Cdr	16-Dec-96	WAR	P SKW	771 SQN	RNAS CULDROSE
Barnes, David C	Lt RN	01-Sep-09	ENG	WE	MWS COLLINGWOOD	
Barnes, Paul F	Lt RN	14-Aug-07	ENG	TM	NETS (OPS)	HMS DRAKE
Barnes, Thomas M	Lt RN	01-May-13	WAR	GSX	HMS NORTHUMBERLAND	
Barnes-Yallowley, Jonathan	Lt Cdr	16-Jul-92	WAR	P SK6	RN EXCHANGE USA	WASHINGTON USA
Barnett, Caila	Lt RN	01-Sep-06	ENG	TM	MOD CNS/ACNS	MAIN BUILDING LONDON
Barnett, Christopher J	Lt RN	01-Apr-12	LOGS	L	DES/COMFLEET	HELENSBURGH
Barnick, Sebastian J	SLt	08-Mar-13	WAR	GSX	MCM2 CREW 7	PORTSMOUTH
Barnicoat, Karen	Lt RN	01-Jan-06	WAR	O MER	829 SQN FLT 05	RNAS CULDROSE
Barnwell, Alan F	Capt	21-Jul-01	RM	P SK4	CHFHQ (SEA)	RNAS YEOVILTON
Barr, Andrew R	SLt	01-Feb-11	WAR	SM(X)	MWS COLLINGWOOD	HMS COLLINGWOOD
Barr, Derek D	Lt RN	01-Apr-02	ENG	AE	RNAS CULDROSE - ETS	RNAS CULDROSE
Barr, Simon J C	Lt RN	09-Apr-10	ENG	MESM	HMS VIGILANT	
Barrand, Stuart M	Cdr	30-Jun-02	WAR	AAWO	NCHQ CNPS	NCHQ
Barratt, Stephen	Lt Cdr	01-Oct-02	LOGS	L	LSP ON	MUSCAT (BOX 014)
Barrett, Benjamin T	Lt RN	01-Aug-04	WAR	HM	PJHQ	NORTHWOOD
Barrett, Scott	Lt RN	01-Jan-04	WAR	INT	FLEET COMOPS NWD	HUNTINGDON
Barrie, Stuart	Lt Cdr	01-Oct-10	ENG	WESM	FOST SM SEA	FASLANE HELENSBURGH
Barritt, Oliver D	Lt Cdr	01-Oct-07	WAR	HM (H CH)	HMS ECHO	
Barron, Jeremy M	Lt Cdr	01-Oct-13	ENG	WESM	DES/COMFLEET	ABBEY WOOD BRISTOL
Barron, Philip R	Lt Cdr	01-Oct-13	WAR	O LYNX	HMS OCEAN	
Barron-Robinson, David P	Lt Cdr	01-Oct-07	ENG	WESM	DES/COMJE/ISS	CORSHAM
Barrow, Charles M	Lt Cdr	01-Oct-09	WAR	PWO(U)	UKRBATSTAFF	HMNB PORTSMOUTH
Barrowclough, William G	Lt RN	01-Nov-12	WAR	GSX	PORTSMOUTH GSP SEA	HMNB PORTSMOUTH
Barrows, David M	Lt Cdr	01-Oct-03	ENG	WE	HQNATO - UKMILREP	BRUSSELS
Barry, Emma Louise	Lt RN	31-Jan-12	ENG	TM	FLEET HQ	NCHQ
Barry, John P	Lt Cdr	01-Oct-02	WAR	PWO(U)	FOST DPORT SEA	HMNB DEVONPORT
Bartlett, David L	Lt RN	01-Sep-07	ENG	AE	DES/COIR/CA/LIGHTNING	ARLINGTON USA
Bartlett, David S	Capt RN	01-Jul-12	ENG	AE	MOD CNS/ACNS	RNAS YEOVILTON
Bartlett, Ian D	Cdr	30-Jun-08	ENG	MESM	DES/COMFLEET	HMNB DEVONPORT
Bartlett, Marie-Claire	Lt RN	01-Sep-07	ENG	AE	HMS NELSON	
Bartlett, Simon	Lt RN	01-Apr-11	ENG	ME	DES/COMFLEET/NAG	ABBEY WOOD BRISTOL
Barton, Hannah J	SLt	01-Sep-12	MED	MS(EHO)	BRNC DARTMOUTH	
Barton, Jenny	SLt	01-May-12	MED	MEDICAL	BRNC DARTMOUTH	
Barton, Keith J	Lt Cdr	01-Oct-08	ENG	AE	814 SQN	RNAS CULDROSE
Barton, Mark A	Cdr	30-Jun-13	ENG	ME	NCHQ CNPS	NCHQ
Barton, Peter G	Cdr	30-Jun-99	ENG	WE	UKTI - DSO	LONDON
Barton, Sarah J	Surg Lt Cdr	04-Aug-04	MED	GMP	DES/COMFLEET	HMS DRAKE
Bartram, Caroline P	Lt Cdr	01-Oct-12	ENG	AE	DES/COMJE/HELS	ABBEY WOOD,BRISTOL
Bartram, Gregory J	Lt Cdr	01-Oct-12	ENG	WE	DCD - MODSAP KSA	RIYADH (MODSAP)
Bartram, Richard	Lt Cdr	01-Oct-12	WAR	P LYN7	HQ JHC	ANDOVER
Basketfield, Wayne	Lt RN	17-Dec-09	WAR	INT	UKRBATSTAFF	PLYMOUTH
Bass, Andrew G	Lt RN	01-May-13	LOGS	L	RNAS YEOVILTON	
Bass, Emma	Lt Cdr	01-Oct-09	ENG	WE	OCLC NCH	MANCHESTER
Bass, Paul W	Lt Cdr	01-Oct-09	ENG	WESM(TWS)	FOST SM SEA	HELENSBURGH
Bassett, Daniel S	Lt RN	01-Sep-13	WAR	O SKW	857 NAS	RNAS CULDROSE
Bassett, Dean A	Capt RN	09-Sep-13	WAR	PWO(A)	MWS COLLINGWOOD	

Person Name	Substantive Rank	Seniority	Branch	Specialisation	Organisation	Location
Bassett, Nicole	Lt Cdr	01-Oct-13	LOGS	L	DEFAC JSCSC	SHRIVENHAM SWINDON
Basson, Andrew	Cdr	30-Jun-00	ENG	TM	LSP ON	MUSCAT (BOX 014)
Bastiaens, Paul A	Lt Cdr	01-Oct-13	ENG	AE	DES/COMJE/HELS	YEOVIL
Bate, Christopher	Lt RN	20-May-10	WAR	SM(X)	HMS TALENT	
Bate, David I G	Lt Cdr	01-Oct-95	WAR	MCD	MWS COLLINGWOOD	
Bates, Nicholas	Lt Cdr	01-Oct-12	WAR	O MER	829 SQN HQ	RNAS CULDROSE
Bates, Oliver J	Capt	01-Sep-09	RM	P UT	RAF SHAWBURY	
Bateson, Timothy N	Lt RN	01-Sep-11	ENG	WESM(TWS)	HMS ASTUTE	
Bath, Edward G	Lt Cdr	27-Dec-95	WAR	AAWO	MWS COLLINGWOOD	
Bath, Michael A W	Cdre	01-Jul-12	LOGS	L SM	DCDS PERS TRG	MAIN BUILDING LONDON
Batham, Donald R	Surg Cdr	01-Sep-04	MED	GMP	NCHQ MEDDIV	NCHQ
Bathurst, Benjamin G	2Lt	01-Sep-11	RM	GS	40 CDO RM - DGHR(O)	TAUNTON
Batsford, Gareth E	Lt RN	13-Jun-08	ENG	MESM	HMS TRIUMPH	
Batten, Nicholas J	Capt	01-Sep-12	RM	GS	NCHQ	
Baugh, Adrian J E	Lt RN	01-Feb-06	ENG	WESM	FLEET CAP SSM DIVISION	NCHQ
Baum, Stuart R	Capt RN	30-Jun-06	WAR	SM(CQ)	FOSNNI NRC NEE - LIV	LIVERPOOL
Baverstock, Andrew P	Lt Cdr	01-Oct-09	WAR	INT	JFC HOC C4ISR	NORTHWOOD
Baxendale, Robert F	Lt Col	30-Jun-08	RM	GS	HQ 3 CDO BDE RM	PLYMOUTH
Baxter, Arran C	Lt RN	01-May-02	ENG	MESM	HMS TURBULENT	
Baxter, Iain M	Cdr	30-Jun-10	ENG	AE	RNAS YEOVILTON	
Baybutt, Thomas J	Capt	01-Sep-11	RM	GS	42 CDO RM - K COY	HMNB DEVONPORT
Baylis, Matthew F	Capt	01-Sep-08	RM	GS	HMS ILLUSTRIOUS	
Bayliss, Annabel M	Lt Cdr	16-Mar-12	WAR	ATC	FLEET AV VL - ACOS(AV)	RNAS YEOVILTON
Bayliss, James E L	Lt RN	01-Jan-08	WAR	P LYNX	LHF 702 SQN	RNAS YEOVILTON
Bayliss, James P	Lt RN	01-Apr-09	WAR	P SK4	CHFHQ (SEA)	RNAS YEOVILTON
Beacham, Philip R	Lt Cdr	01-Jul-03	WAR	P MER	824 SQN CULDROSE	RNAS CULDROSE
Beacham, Sophie R	Lt RN	01-Jun-08	LOGS	L	MWS COLLINGWOOD	
Beadnell, Robert M	Lt Cdr	01-Jan-04	ENG	TM	NCHQ CNPERS	HMNB PORTSMOUTH
Beale, David J	Capt	01-Sep-12	RM	GS	40 CDO RM	TAUNTON
Beale, Joshua L	SLt	01-Feb-12	WAR	GSX	BRNC DARTMOUTH	
Beale, Joshua D	Lt Cdr	01-Oct-07	WAR	MCD	MWS DDS	DDS PORTSMOUTH
Bean, Edward C	Lt RN	09-Apr-10	LOGS	L	HMS ST ALBANS	
Beaney, Jonathan M	2Lt	02-Sep-13	RM	GS	CTCRM OFFICERS	EXMOUTH
Beanland, Peter L	Lt Cdr	01-Oct-10	WAR	PWO(C)	COMUKTG SEA	PLYMOUTH
Beard, David J	Surg Lt Cdr	01-Aug-06	MED	Anaes	RCDM	BIRMINGHAM
Beard, Hugh D	Capt RN	03-Jan-12	WAR	SM(CQ)	HMS WESTMINSTER	
Beardall, Michael J D	Capt RN	27-Jun-11	WAR	PWO(A)	DMC	MAIN BUILDING LONDON
Beardall-Jacklin, Paul A	SLt	01-Nov-11	WAR	SM(X)	BRNC DARTMOUTH	DARTMOUTH
Beardsley, Nigel A	RN Chpln	03-May-05	Ch S		CTCRM	EXMOUTH
Beaton, Iain	Lt RN	24-Dec-07	WAR	INFO OPS	UKRBATSTAFF	HMNB PORTSMOUTH
Beattie, Paul	Cdr	30-Jun-08	WAR	AAWO	DSP	MAIN BUILDING LONDON
Beaumont, Alan J	Lt RN	09-Apr-09	ENG	ME	DES/COMFLEET	ABBEY WOOD BRISTOL
Beaumont, Richard	Lt RN	01-Sep-08	ENG	AE P	820 SQN	RNAS CULDROSE
Beaver, Robert M S	Lt Cdr	01-Oct-06	ENG	ME	FLEET COMOPS NWD	NORTHWOOD
Bebbington, David M	Lt RN	17-Feb-06	WAR	C	DES/COMJE	CORSHAM
Beck, Andrew J	Lt RN	01-May-07	WAR	SM(N)	RN EXCHANGE NLANDS	DEN HELDER
Becker, Robert K	Lt Cdr	01-Oct-13	WAR	INT	PJHQ (UK) J3	NORTHWOOD
Becker, Thomas O	Lt RN	01-Sep-06	WAR	HM	HMS SEVERN	
Beckett, Keith A	Cdre	24-Aug-10	ENG	MESM	DES/COMFLEET	HELENSBURGH
Bedford, Daniel J	Capt	01-Sep-11	RM	GS	CTCRM - CTW	EXMOUTH
Bedford, Jonathan	Surg Lt Cdr	01-Jul-00	MED	GMP	NORTHWOOD HQ - PERS	NORTHWOOD
Beech, Christopher M Psc(J), Pce	Cdr	30-Jun-11	WAR	PWO(C)	NATO - BRUSSELS - IMS	BRUSSELS
Beeching, Lee G	Lt RN	20-Oct-06	WAR	MCD	MCM1 CREW 3	FASLANE
Beesley, Christopher A	Capt	01-Sep-08	RM	GS	OCLC LONDON	LONDON
Beete, Jon Edward	Capt	01-Aug-07	RM	GS	OCLC BIRMINGHAM	BIRMINGHAM
Behan, Oliver M	Lt RN	01-Jul-11	WAR	GSX	HMS IRON DUKE	
Bekier, Oliver	Lt RN	01-Sep-12	WAR	GSX	HMS LANCASTER	
Bell Williamson, T	SLt	01-Nov-11	WAR	GSX	BRNC DARTMOUTH	
Bell, Catriona M	Lt Cdr	01-Oct-08	WAR	PWO(N)	HMS BULWARK	
Bell, Charlotte S	Surg Lt Cdr	02-Aug-11	MED	GMP	HQBF GIBRALTAR - MEDIC	HMS ROOKE
Bell, David	Lt RN	01-Feb-10	LOGS	L	HMS SULTAN - CS	HMS SULTAN
Bell, Jeffrey Mark	Cdr	24-Jun-13	ENG	AE	NATO - BRUSSELS - IMS	BRUSSELS

Person Name	Substantive Rank	Seniority	Branch	Specialisation	Organisation	Location
Bell, Lewis G	Lt RN	01-Feb-06	WAR	HM	HMS EXAMPLE	
Bell, Michael H	Capt	16-Apr-10	RM	SCC	30 CDO IX GP RM	PLYMOUTH
Bell, Nicholas Andrew G	Lt RN	01-May-04	WAR	P MER	DEF HELI FLYING SCH	RAF SHAWBURY
Bell, Richard J Ba	Lt RN	01-May-06	WAR	O LYNX	815 SQN	RNAS YEOVILTON
Bell, Robert D	Lt Cdr	01-Mar-97	WAR	MCD PWO	FASLANE	
Bell, Scott W	Lt Cdr	01-Oct-07	LOGS	L SM	DES/COMLAND	ABBEY WOOD BRISTOL
Bell, Tristan A	SLt	01-Jul-12	WAR	GSX	HMS MONTROSE	
Bellfield, Robert J A	Capt RN	27-Sep-11	WAR	PWO(U)	UK MCC	BAHRAIN
Benbow, James A K	Lt RN	01-May-04	WAR	P LYNX	815 SQN FLT	RNAS YEOVILTON
Benbow, Melanie	Lt RN	01-Feb-09	WAR	GSX	FOST DPORT SHORE	HMNB DEVONPORT
Benbow, William	Lt RN	01-Feb-09	WAR	GSX	OP ATALANTA	UK
Bence, David E	Cdr	30-Jun-08	WAR	MCD PWO(C)	UK MCC	BAHRAIN
Bending, Shaun P	Lt RN	01-Mar-13	WAR	P UT	RNAS YEOVILTON	
Benfell, Niall A	Cdr	30-Jun-13	LOGS	L	FLEET SPT LOGS	NORTHWOOD
Benmayor, Dinah E	Lt RN	24-Feb-08	WAR	HUMINT	NPT RES MOBILISATION	UK
Bennet, Matthew J	Capt	01-Sep-12	RM	GS	40 CDO RM	TAUNTON
Bennet, Niall	Lt RN	22-Nov-04	WAR	INFO OPS	FLEET FOSNNI - NRC	HMS CALEDONIA
Bennett, Ashley S	Mid	01-Nov-13	WAR	GSX	BRNC DARTMOUTH	
Bennett, Brian	Lt RN	01-Nov-01	ENG	TM	JFC - DCTS (H)	RAF HALTON
Bennett, Christopher	Lt Cdr	01-Oct-09	WAR	P LYN7	HQ JHC	ANDOVER
Bennett, Elizabeth C	Lt RN	01-Jan-08	LOGS	L	MCM1 FAS SEA1	HELENSBURGH
Bennett, Graham	Lt Cdr	01-Jul-93	WAR	PWO(U)	HMS VIVID	PLYMOUTH
Bennett, Ian James	Lt RN	01-Sep-07	WAR	O MER	820 SQN	RNAS CULDROSE
Bennett, Joseph P	Capt	01-Sep-12	RM	GS	CTCRM - CTW	EXMOUTH
Bennett, Mark A	Lt Cdr	01-Oct-10	ENG	WESM(SWS)	HMS RALEIGH	
Bennett, Oliver F	Lt RN	01-Jan-12	LOGS	L	NCHQ - CNLS	NCHQ
Bennett, Paul OBE	R Adm	04-Feb-13	WAR	PWO(A)	JFC HQ	NORTHWOOD
Bennett, Philippa	Surg Lt RN	03-Aug-11	MED	GDMO	HMS DIAMOND	
Bennett, William E	Lt Cdr	01-Oct-07	ENG	ME	DES/DGRES	ABBEY WOOD BRISTOL
Bennett-Smith, Paula	Lt RN	31-Jul-09	WAR	C	UK MCC	BAHRAIN
Benney, Jordon R	Mid	01-Sep-13	WAR	SM(X)	BRNC DARTMOUTH	
Benson, Adam D	SLt	01-Feb-11	ENG	WESM	HMS VANGUARD	
Benstead, Neil	Lt Cdr	01-Oct-04	ENG	ME	DEFAC JSCSC	SHRIVENHAM SWINDON
Bentley, Grant	Lt RN	01-Aug-06	WAR	GSX	PJHQ (UK) J6	NORTHWOOD
Benton, Angus M	Lt Cdr	01-Sep-96	WAR	MCD	UK MCC	BAHRAIN
Benton, Peter J	Surg Capt RN	31-Dec-08	MED	Occ Med	DES/COMFLEET	HMS DRAKE
Benton, Simon Al	Lt RN	01-Apr-08	ENG	TM	HMS SULTAN	
Benton, William A	Lt RN	06-Apr-07	WAR	AV	RNAS CULDROSE	
Benzie, Andrew	Lt RN	23-Oct-08	WAR	SM(N)	HMS AMBUSH	BARROW IN FURNESS
Berger, Angus E	Capt	01-Sep-13	RM	GS	42 CDO RM	
Bernacchi, Jonathan P	Lt RN	15-Apr-11	ENG	WESM(TWS)	HMS VIGILANT	
Bernau, Jeremy C	Lt Cdr	01-Nov-91	WAR	SM(CQ)	COMFASFLOT	HMNB CLYDE
Berridge, Matthew J	SLt	01-May-11	WAR	SM(X)	MCM2 CREW	HMNB PORTSMOUTH
Berrill, Simon Peter	Mid	01-Nov-12	WAR	GSX	BRNC DARTMOUTH	
Berry, David H	Lt RN	01-Jun-07	WAR	FC	RNAS YEOVILTON	
Berry, Ian MBE Rd	Cdr	30-Jun-13	WAR	MW (RES)	FLEET CMR	NCHQ
Berry, Thomas P	2Lt	01-Sep-13	RM	N/A	CTCRM OFFICERS	EXMOUTH
Berry, Timothy J	Lt Cdr	01-Oct-06	WAR	PWO(N)	HMS SEVERN	
Bessant, Matthew	Lt RN	01-Apr-05	WAR	GSX	HMS ILLUSTRIOUS	
Bessell, David A	Lt Cdr	01-Jun-01	WAR	SM(CQ)	FOST SM SEA	HELENSBURGH
Best, Alexander	Lt RN	01-Jan-11	WAR	O MER	820 SQN	RNAS CULDROSE
Best, Hannah Jane	Lt RN	01-Sep-12	WAR	O MER	814 SQN	RNAS CULDROSE
Best, Paul Neil	Maj	01-Oct-13	RM	SCC	HQ LWC	BATH
Best, Robert M	Lt Cdr	01-Oct-13	ENG	MESM	HMS TALENT	
Beswick, Mark D	Lt RN	03-May-13	MED	MS(CDO)	DMSTG	ALDERSHOT
Betchley, James W	Lt RN	01-May-05	WAR	PWO(SM)	HMS TORBAY	
Bethwaite, Jonathan	SLt	18-Oct-12	WAR	GSX	HMS PORTLAND	
Betteridge, Carol Ann OBE	Capt RN	26-Feb-13	QARNNS	OT (C&S)	DMS WHITTINGTON	
Bettles, John	Lt Cdr	25-Nov-11	WAR	PWO	MWS COLLINGWOOD	
Betton, Andrew OBE	Capt RN	05-Jan-10	WAR	O LYNX	DOC	MAIN BUILDING LONDON
Betts, Andrew T	Lt RN	01-Sep-06	ENG	AE	DES/COMFLEET	ABBEY WOOD BRISTOL
Betts, Peter R	Lt RN	01-Sep-06	ENG	WESM(TWS)	FLEET COMOPS NWD	NORTHWOOD

Person Name	Substantive Rank	Seniority	Branch	Specialisation	Organisation	Location
Bevan, Jeffrey R MBE	Lt Cdr	01-Oct-10	WAR	P MER	CAREER TRAINING WATTISHAM	IPSWICH
Beveridge, Simon A R	RN Chpln	28-Apr-93	Ch S		NEPTUNE 2SL/CNH - CHAP	HELENSBURGH
Beverley, Andrew P	Lt RN	01-Feb-03	ENG	IS	DES/COMJE/ISS	NORTHWOOD
Beverstock, Mark A	R Adm	23-Jul-12	ENG	WESM(SWS)	DES/COMFLEET	ABBEY WOOD BRISTOL
Bevis, Timothy J	Brig	21-Feb-11	RM	GS	OPS DIR	MAIN BUILDING LONDON
Bewley, Geoffrey Rd	Cdr	28-Oct-08	WAR	MW (RES)	NATO ACO	NORTHWOOD
Bicker, Richard E	Lt RN	09-Apr-09	ENG	WESM(SWS)	HMS VICTORIOUS	
Bickley, Gary N	Lt RN	01-Jan-03	WAR	PWO(N)	GIBRALTAR PBS	HMS ROOKE
Bicknell, Benjamin S	Lt RN	08-Dec-13	WAR	GSX	CREW 3	HELENSBURGH
Bicknell, James	Lt RN	20-Aug-09	WAR	SM(X)	FLEET HQ 6	NCHQ
Bicknell, Neil D	Lt RN	12-Jul-13	ENG	WE	MWS COLLINGWOOD	
Biddlecombe, Hugh R	Lt RN	01-Apr-11	LOGS	L	HMS ILLUSTRIOUS	
Biddulph, Andrew R	Lt RN	15-Apr-11	WAR	INT	FLEET COMOPS NWD	HMS COLLINGWOOD
Biggs, David M	Lt Cdr	01-Oct-96	WAR	O SKW	849 SQN	RNAS CULDROSE
Biggs, William	Capt RN	27-Aug-13	ENG	WE	FLEET CAP RCAP DIVISION	NCHQ
Bignell, Stephen	Lt Cdr	01-Apr-00	ENG	WE	DES/COMLAND	ABBEY WOOD BRISTOL
Billam, David A	Lt RN	01-Apr-13	WAR	FC	UKRBATSTAFF	HMNB PORTSMOUTH
Billings, Andrew J	Lt Cdr	01-Oct-13	WAR	REG	NPM WESTERN	HMS DRAKE
Bilson, Gavin	Lt RN	01-May-06	ENG	IS(SM)	NATO-ACO-SHAPE	CASTEAU BRUSSELS
Bing, Neil Adrian	Lt Cdr	01-Oct-05	WAR	P GR7	HQ AIR - COS(CAP)	HIGH WYCOMBE
Bingham, Alexander A	Lt Cdr	01-Oct-11	ENG	ME	HMS SUTHERLAND	
Bingham, David S	Lt Cdr	01-Mar-99	WAR	AAWO	FLEET CSAV	NCHQ
Binns, James B	Lt RN	01-Sep-06	ENG	MESM	DES/COMFLEET	ABBEY WOOD BRISTOL
Binns, John R	Lt Cdr	01-Oct-09	ENG	WE	COMDEVFLOT	HMS DRAKE
Binns, Jon F	Lt Cdr	01-Oct-08	WAR	INT	FLEET COMOPS NWD	NORTHWOOD
Birbeck, Keith	Lt Cdr	01-Oct-98	ENG	WESM(TWS)	OCLC PLYMOUTH	BRISTOL
Birch, Peter L	Lt Cdr	01-Oct-13	WAR	P LYNX	HMS DEFENDER	
Birchall, James	Lt Cdr	01-Oct-08	WAR	P LYN7	HQ JHC	ANDOVER
Bird, Andrew W	Lt RN	01-Sep-04	WAR	P MER	824 SQN - TU	RNAS CULDROSE
Bird, Gary M	Lt Col	30-Jun-13	RM	GS	DCLC RN	SHRIVENHAM SWINDON
Bird, Jonathan M	Lt Cdr	01-Oct-03	WAR	O MER	UKRBATSTAFF	HMNB PORTSMOUTH
Bird, Matthew G	Lt Cdr	01-Nov-02	ENG	AE	ABBEY WOOD BRISTOL	
Bird, Michael P	Lt RN	01-Jan-06	WAR	GSX	MWS COLLINGWOOD	HMS COLLINGWOOD
Bird, Richard A J	Cdr	30-Jun-11	WAR	HM (H CH)	HMS PROTECTOR	
Bird, Timothy M	Lt RN	01-Jun-06	LOGS	L	FLEET SPT LOGS	NCHQ
Birkby, Christina	Lt Cdr	01-Oct-13	WAR	PWO	HMS DUNCAN	
Birley, Jonathan H	Lt Cdr	01-May-95	WAR	PWO(U)	FLEET COMOPS NWD	NORTHWOOD
Birrell, Stuart DSO	Brig	14-Jun-13	RM	GS	HQ 3 CDO BDE RM	PLYMOUTH
Birse, Gregor J	Cdr	30-Jun-13	WAR	HM (M CH)	DI - ICSP	LONDON
Birt, David J	Surg Cdr	30-Jun-01	MED	Anaes	MDHU DERRIFORD	PLYMOUTH
Bisson, Ian J P	Capt RN	01-Jul-08	ENG	WE	DEFAC RCDS	LONDON
Black, Charlotte J	Lt RN	01-Mar-04	ENG	IS	FLEET FOST TBTU	HMS COLLINGWOOD
Black, Dominic J	Lt RN	01-Sep-12	LOGS	L	UKRBATSTAFF	HMNB PORTSMOUTH
Black, Edward J	Lt Cdr	01-Oct-12	WAR	MCD	LSP ON	MUSCAT (BOX 014)
Black, Joanna M	Lt Cdr	01-Oct-12	WAR	PWO	MWS COLLINGWOOD	
Black, Kenneth J	Lt RN	01-Mar-08	LOGS	L	MWS COLLINGWOOD	
Black, Malcolm D	Lt RN	09-Apr-12	ENG	MESM	HMS VANGUARD	
Blackbourn, Stephen A	Lt RN	27-Jul-07	ENG	WE	FOST DPORT SEA	HMNB DEVONPORT
Blackburn, Andrew R	Lt Cdr	01-Oct-06	ENG	AE	HMS QUEEN ELIZABETH	ROSYTH
Blackburn, Craig J	Lt RN	01-Sep-04	WAR	GSX	FOST MPV SEA	HELENSBURGH
Blackburn, Emma C	Lt Cdr	01-Oct-09	ENG	AE	HMS OCEAN	
Blackburn, Ewan J	Mid	01-Sep-13	ENG	WE	BRNC DARTMOUTH	
Blackburn, Lee R	Lt Cdr	01-Sep-08	ENG	ME	RNSME HQ & ATG	HMS SULTAN
Blackburn, Stephen A	Lt Cdr	01-Mar-98	ENG	ME	DES/COMFLEET	ABBEY WOOD BRISTOL
Blackburn, Stuart J	Lt Cdr	25-Jun-13	WAR	SM(CQ)	HMS VANGUARD	
Blackburn, Thomas E	Lt RN	01-Sep-11	ENG	AE	814 SQN	RNAS CULDROSE
Blackett, William P H	Lt Cdr	01-Oct-12	WAR	PWO	HMS DARING	
Blackledge, Benjamin P	Lt RN	01-Jan-12	ENG	TM	CTCRM - TDRPC	EXMOUTH
Blackman, Nicholas T OBE	Capt RN	25-Jan-11	ENG	AE	FLEET CSAV	NCHQ
Blackmore, Andrew M	Lt Cdr	01-Oct-13	ENG	WESM(TWS)	DES/COMFLEET	ABBEY WOOD BRISTOL
Blackmore, James	Lt Cdr	01-Oct-07	WAR	P GR7	FLEET CSAV	WASHINGTON
Blackmore, Mark S	Cdr	30-Jun-02	WAR	O SK6	FLEET CSAV	NORFOLK USA

Person Name	Substantive Rank	Seniority	Branch	Specialisation	Organisation	Location
Blackwell, Mark E	Lt RN	01-Sep-08	LOGS	L BAR	NCHQ - CNLS	HELENSBURGH
Blackwell, Richard E	Cdr	30-Jun-09	LOGS	L SM	IPP	MAIN BUILDING LONDON
Bladen, Christopher S	Lt RN	01-May-04	WAR	P SK4	DEF HELI FLYING SCH	RAF SHAWBURY
Blagden, Laura Jane	SLt	01-Mar-11	ENG	AE	DCEME SULTAN	HMS SULTAN
Blair, Duncan G S	Surg Cdr	30-Jun-03	MED	GMP (C&S)	NCHQ MEDDIV	NCHQ
Blake, Jeremy G	2Lt	02-Sep-12	RM	N/A	CTCRM OFFICERS	EXMOUTH
Blake, Matthew G	Lt RN	01-May-05	WAR	O MER	MWS COLLINGWOOD	
Blakeman, Philip M	Lt RN	01-Aug-08	ENG	WE	FOST DPORT SEA	HMNB DEVONPORT
Blanchford, Daniel	Lt Col	30-Jun-10	RM	GS	NCHQ	
Bland, Christopher D	Lt Cdr	01-Oct-08	ENG	WESM(SWS)	FOST SM SEA	HELENSBURGH
Bland, Steven Aaron	Surg Cdr	07-Aug-07	MED	EM	MDHU PORTSMOUTH	HMNB PORTSMOUTH
Blatcher, David J	Lt RN	01-Sep-08	ENG	ME	DES/COMFLEET	ABBEY WOOD BRISTOL
Blatchford, Timothy P	Lt RN	08-Apr-05	ENG	AE	824 SQN - TU	RNAS CULDROSE
Bleasdale, Daniel R	Lt Cdr	01-Oct-12	ENG	TM	HMS ILLUSTRIOUS	
Blenkinsop, Graham J	Lt RN	02-May-07	WAR	HM	RNAS YEOVILTON	
Blethyn, Catherine	Lt Cdr	01-Oct-12	ENG	TM	HMS NELSON	HMS NELSON
Blethyn, Hugh P	Lt Cdr	01-Oct-11	ENG	IS	FLEET CISSU	PORTSDOWN HILL
Blick, Graham M	Lt RN	30-Jul-10	WAR	AV	RNAS CULDROSE	
Blick, Sarah L	Lt RN	01-Jan-02	LOGS	L	AIB	HMS SULTAN
Bligh, Sarah L	Lt RN	01-May-04	WAR	FC	NCHQ CNPERS	PORTSMOUTH
Blight, Phillip R R	Lt RN	03-May-13	ENG	WESM	HMS RALEIGH	
Block, Andrew W G	Cdr	30-Jun-10	WAR	PWO(A)	HMS KENT	
Blois, Simon D	Lt Cdr	01-Oct-09	ENG	WE	NAVY MCTA PORTSMOUTH	HMNB PORTSMOUTH
Bloor, Thomas W	2Lt	01-Sep-10	RM	GS	40 CDO RM	TAUNTON
Blount, Keith E OBE	Cdre	27-Aug-13	WAR	P SK6	UK MCC	BAHRAIN
Blower, Amy	Lt RN	01-Sep-12	WAR	GSX	HMS MERSEY	
Blowers, Michael D	Cdr	31-Dec-00	WAR	O LYNX	NCHQ CIT	NCHQ
Blunden, Jeremy J F L	Cdre	22-Oct-12	WAR	PWO(N)	UKRBATSTAFF	HMNB PORTSMOUTH
Blunden, Katie L	SLt	07-Aug-13	LOGS	L	824 SQN - TU	RNAS CULDROSE
Blythe, James	Lt Cdr	01-Oct-09	WAR	PWO	HMS DAUNTLESS	
Blythe, Paul C	Cdr	30-Jun-09	WAR	SM(CQ)	CBRN POL	MAIN BUILDING LONDON
Blythe, Tom Stuart	Lt Col	30-Jun-09	RM	LC	DEFENCE ACADEMY	SHRIVENHAM SWINDON
Boaden, Christopher S	Lt RN	19-Feb-09	WAR	O LYNX	815 SQN FLT	RNAS YEOVILTON
Boak, Charlotte L	Mid	01-Feb-13	WAR	GSX	BRNC DARTMOUTH	DARTMOUTH
Boak, Philip R	Lt RN	01-Apr-11	WAR	HM	HMS ECHO	
Boakes, Philip J	Lt Cdr	01-Oct-09	ENG	ME	FLEET CAP SSM DIVISION	NCHQ
Boal, Michael A	Lt Cdr	02-Jun-06	WAR	MW (RES)	NPT RES MOBILISATION	HMNB PORTSMOUTH
Boarder, Richard J	Lt RN	01-Sep-10	ENG	MESM	HMS ASTUTE	
Boardman, Andrew	Lt RN	01-Sep-08	ENG	MESM	DGHR CS - DBR DEF SY	MAIN BUILDING LONDON
Boardman, Daniel	SLt	01-Sep-12	ENG	AE	BRNC DARTMOUTH	DARTMOUTH
Boast, Rachel	Lt RN	22-Oct-12	WAR	O SKW	857 NAS	RNAS CULDROSE
Boddington, Hannah	Lt RN	01-Jan-12	WAR	GSX	HMS KENT	
Boddington, Jeremy D L	Cdr	30-Jun-07	WAR	P MER	FLEET CSAV	NCHQ
Bodkin, Lee	Lt RN	01-Jul-09	ENG	ME	RNLA	HMS COLLINGWOOD
Bodman, Simon A	Lt Cdr	01-Oct-09	WAR	PWO(C)	HMS NORTHUMBERLAND	
Boeckx, Thomas J F	Lt Cdr	01-Oct-07	WAR	PWO(N)	HMS PROTECTOR	
Bolam, Samuel P	Capt	08-Jun-13	RM	GS	MED SQN CDO LOG REGT	BARNSTAPLE
Bolland, Amy	Lt RN	01-Mar-13	ENG	ME	HMS DIAMOND	
Bollen, Johanna M	Lt Cdr	01-Oct-03	LOGS	L	DES/COMLAND	ABBEY WOOD
Bolton, James D	Lt RN	01-Aug-10	WAR	SM(X)	CAREER TRAINING	HMS RALEIGH
Bolton, Jonathan P	Cdr	30-Jun-10	ENG	ME	COMDEVFLOT SEA	HMNB DEVONPORT
Bolton, Matthew T W	Cdr	30-Jun-08	ENG	ME	FLEET CAP SSM DIVISION	NCHQ
Bolton, Stephen J	Cdr	30-Jun-13	WAR	P LYNX	HQ AIR - COS(TRG)	ABBEY WOOD
Bomby, Ross A	2Lt	02-Sep-13	RM	N/A	CTCRM OFFICERS	EXMOUTH
Bond, Frances	Lt RN	01-Nov-10	WAR	HM	HMS PROTECTOR	
Bond, Ian	Lt RN	19-Dec-08	ENG	WESM(SWS)	HMS SULTAN - SEC	HMS SULTAN
Bond, Nigel D MBE	Cdr	31-Dec-00	LOGS	L	NCHQ CNPERS	NCHQ
Bond, Robert D	Lt Cdr	01-Oct-11	WAR	P SK4	HQ JHC	ANDOVER
Bond, Robert J	Lt RN	01-Apr-06	WAR	P MER	814 SQN	RNAS CULDROSE
Bond, Stuart John	SLt	01-Apr-12	WAR	GSX	CAREER TRAINING	HMS DRAKE
Bone, Darren N	Capt RN	01-Jul-09	WAR	PWO(A)	DEFAC RCDS	LONDON
Bone, Jonathan D	Surg Lt RN	07-Aug-13	MED	MEDICAL	BRNC DARTMOUTH	

Person Name	Substantive Rank	Seniority	Branch	Specialisation	Organisation	Location
Bone, Louise	Lt RN	01-Sep-13	WAR	HM	CAREER TRAINING	HMS DRAKE
Bone, Matthew	Lt RN	01-Sep-10	ENG	AE	HMS SULTAN	HMS SULTAN
Bone, Richard C	Cdr	30-Jun-08	ENG	TM(SM)	DES/COMFLEET	ABBEY WOOD BRISTOL
Bonnar, John A	Cdr	30-Jun-12	ENG	WE	FLEET SPT FGEN DIVISION	NCHQ
Bonner, Daniel	Lt RN	27-Jul-07	ENG	AE	DES/COMJE/HELS	YEOVIL
Bonner, Timothy J	Surg Lt Cdr	09-Aug-06	MED	T&O	INM ALVERSTOKE	GOSPORT
Boon, Gareth	Lt Cdr	01-Oct-07	WAR	HM (M CH)	HQ ICG	ABBEY WOOD BRISTOL
Boon, Simon E	Lt Cdr	01-Oct-10	LOGS	L SM	JFLogC	NORTHWOOD
Boot, Stephen	Lt Cdr	01-Oct-09	LOGS	L	HMS RALEIGH - INT R	HMS RALEIGH
Booth, Alan K	Lt RN	01-Sep-07	WAR	P MER	814 SQN	RNAS CULDROSE
Booth, Anthony R	Lt RN	01-Mar-12	WAR	O UT	RNAS CULDROSE	
Booth, Ben	Surg Lt RN	01-Aug-12	MED	MEDICAL	BRNC DARTMOUTH	
Booth, Diccon P P	Lt RN	01-Sep-01	ENG	TM	Op LANSBURY	AFGHANISTAN
Booth, Rachael M	Surg Lt Cdr	02-Aug-11	MED	GMP	DPHC SW	RNAS YEOVILTON
Boothroyd-Gibbs, Adam P	Lt RN	01-Jan-08	WAR	O MER	820 SQN	RNAS CULDROSE
Borbone, Nicholas	Cdr	30-Jun-11	WAR	AAWO	CAREER TRAINING	CANADA
Boreham, Daniel J	Lt RN	01-Sep-13	ENG	MESM	DCEME SULTAN	HMS SULTAN
Borland, Kate E	Lt RN	01-May-13	WAR	GSX	MWS COLLINGWOOD	
Borland, Stuart A	Capt RN	10-Jan-11	ENG	WE	FLEET ACOS(RP)	NCHQ
Borrett, John E	Lt RN	01-Jul-05	WAR	INT	RN REAPER - 39 SQN	RAF WADDINGTON
Borthwick, Christopher D	Mid	01-May-12	WAR	ATC UT	RNAS CULDROSE	
Boston, Justin	Lt Cdr	01-Jan-05	ENG	TM	BRITISH MILITARY MISSION	
Bosustow, Antony M	Cdr	30-Jun-07	ENG	WE	NCHQ CNPS	PORTSMOUTH
Boswell, Emma Jane	Lt RN	30-Jul-10	MED	MS	DES/COMFLEET	ABBEY WOOD BRISTOL
Boswell, Laura Jane	Lt RN	29-Jan-07	QARNNS	ITU	HMS DRAKE	
Botham, Adrian M	Lt RN	16-Dec-05	ENG	WE	NAVY MCTA PORTSMOUTH	HMNB PORTSMOUTH
Botterill, Hugh W S	Lt Cdr	01-Oct-10	WAR	AWO(U)	DEFAC JSCSC ICSCM	SHRIVENHAM SWINDON
Botting, Neil A	Lt Cdr	01-Oct-10	WAR	SM(CQ)	HMS TALENT	
Botwood, Tudor J MBE BD	RN Chpln	09-Sep-02	Ch S		CTCRM	EXMOUTH
Boucher, Jonathan R	Capt	01-Sep-10	RM	GS	42 CDO RM	HMNB DEVONPORT
Boucher, Peter J	2Lt	02-Sep-13	RM	N/A	CTCRM OFFICERS	EXMOUTH
Boud, Colin S	Lt RN	01-Jan-04	ENG	MESM	DES/COMFLEET	HMNB CLYDE
Boughton, Jonathan A L	Lt Cdr	01-Oct-10	ENG	WE	MWS COLLINGWOOD	
Boulding, Andrew D	Lt RN	13-Jun-08	ENG	MESM	DES/COMFLEET	HELENSBURGH
Boulind, Matthew A	Lt Cdr	01-Oct-11	WAR	O LYNX	FLEET CSAV	NCHQ
Boulton, David S	Lt RN	01-Sep-05	ENG	IS(SM)	CBRN POL	MAIN BUILDING LONDON
Boulton, Graham R	Lt RN	01-Jan-05	WAR	MW	MWS COLLINGWOOD	
Bourn, Sebastian J N	Surg Lt Cdr	31-Jul-12	MED	Anaes	INM ALVERSTOKE	GOSPORT
Bourne, Ashley Eric	Capt	03-Apr-09	RM	SCC	DHU	SHEFFORD
Bouyac, David R L	Lt Cdr	01-Oct-13	WAR	P GR7	736 NAS	RNAS CULDROSE
Bovill, Christopher	Lt Cdr	31-Jul-03	ENG	AE	UKLTT	AFGHANISTAN KABUL
Bowbrick, Richard C MCGI	Cdr	30-Jun-05	WAR	AAWO	NCHQ CNPERS	NCHQ
Bowden, Matthew Jon	SLt	01-May-11	WAR	GSX	HMS BULWARK	
Bowden, Matthew T E	Lt RN	30-Jun-12	WAR	PWO(C)	HMS COLLINGWOOD	
Bowen, Nigel T	Cdr	30-Jun-05	WAR	O LYNX	LOAN DSTL - P&CSD	FAREHAM
Bowen, Richard J	Lt Cdr	01-Oct-12	ENG	WE	PJHQ (UK) J2	NORTHWOOD
Bower, Andrew J OBE	Cdr	30-Jun-08	WAR	SM(CQ)	MOD NSD	MAIN BUILDING LONDON
Bower, Dean A	Lt RN	09-Apr-09	ENG	ME	MWS EXCELLENT	
Bower, Nigel S	Cdr	30-Jun-05	WAR	SM(CQ)	HMS ARTFUL	BARROW IN FURNESS
Bowerman, James W	Capt	01-Sep-09	RM	P	848 SQN YEOVILTON	RNAS YEOVILTON
Bowers, John P	Cdr	30-Jun-09	WAR	O LYNX	PJHQ (UK) J3	NORTHWOOD
Bowers, Keith James	Lt Cdr	01-Oct-12	ENG	WE	DES/COMJE/ISS	CORSHAM
Bowers, Mark R	Lt RN	01-Aug-03	ENG	IS	NC PSYA	HMNB PORTSMOUTH
Bowers, Thomas M	SLt	01-Nov-11	ENG	WE	HMS COLLINGWOOD	
Bowes, Nigel E	Capt	01-Sep-06	RM	GS	NCHQ	
Bowgen, John	Capt	16-Apr-10	RM	MLDR (SCC)	CTCRM (SEA)	EXMOUTH
Bowhay, Simon	Lt Cdr	01-May-99	ENG	WESM(TWS)	NAVY MCTA PORTSMOUTH	HMNB PORTSMOUTH
Bowie, Alan Nivan	Surg Cdr	28-Oct-05	MED	GMP	MEDICAL CENTRE	RNAS CULDROSE
Bowie, Richard	Lt Cdr	01-Oct-10	ENG	WESM(TWS)	HMS TIRELESS	
Bowker, Geoffrey N	Cdr	30-Jun-08	WAR	ATC	ABBEY WOOD	
Bowler, James R	Lt RN	01-Apr-11	ENG	MESM	HMS AMBUSH	
Bowler, Thomas	Lt RN	01-Sep-10	ENG	ME	HMS BULWARK	

Person Name	Substantive Rank	Seniority	Branch	Specialisation	Organisation	Location
Bowles, Daniel J	Lt RN	01-Nov-10	WAR	SM(X)	HMS VICTORIOUS	
Bowman, Dean E	Lt RN	01-Sep-07	ENG	MESM	DES/COMFLEET	THURSO
Bowman, Robert	Cdr	30-Jun-13	ENG	AE	NATO-ACT-HQ SACT	NORFOLK USA
Bowman, Simon K J	Lt RN	01-Jun-05	WAR	ATC	RNAS YEOVILTON - AS	RNAS YEOVILTON
Bowmer, Christopher J	Lt RN	01-Sep-08	ENG	MESM	DES/COMFLEET	ABBEY WOOD BRISTOL
Bowness, Zoe Jane	SLt	01-Jan-12	WAR	ATC UT	RNAS YEOVILTON	
Bowra, Mark A MBE	Lt Col	30-Jun-11	RM	SBS	OPS DIR	MAIN BUILDING LONDON
Bowser, Nicholas J	Lt Cdr	01-Oct-05	ENG	AE	HMS SULTAN - RNAESS	HMS SULTAN
Bowyer, Richard	Maj	10-Oct-06	RM	GS (RES)	RN EXCHANGE AUSTRALIA	CANBERRA AUSTRALIA
Boyall, Duane R	Lt RN	01-Jun-09	ENG	TM(SM)	DES/COMFLEET	ABBEY WOOD BRISTOL
Boyce, the Lord, KG, GCB, OBE, DL	Adm	25-May-95				
Boyd, Elaine M	Lt Cdr	01-Oct-11	LOGS	L	HMS MONTROSE	
Boyd, Nicholas Psc(J)	Cdr	30-Jun-05	ENG	ME	FLEET CAP SSM DIVISION	NCHQ
Boyes, Martyn K	Surg Lt RN	05-Aug-09	MED	Med	INM ALVERSTOKE	GOSPORT
Boyes, Martyn R	Cdr	30-Jun-13	ENG	MESM	DES/COMFLEET	ABBEY WOOD BRISTOL
Boyes, Richard A	Lt Cdr	01-Oct-06	WAR	P MER	771 SQN	RNAS CULDROSE
Bradbury, Simon	RN Chpln	18-Sep-96	Ch S		DEFENCE ACADEMY	ANDOVER
Bradford, Malcolm H	Capt	01-Sep-04	RM	P SK4	4 REGT AAC	IPSWICH
Brading, Roland D	Maj	01-Oct-10	RM	GS	43 CDO	HMNB CLYDE
Bradley, Alan C	Lt RN	15-Apr-07	WAR	CIS (RES)	JFCIS	AFGHANISTAN
Bradley, Matthew	Lt Cdr	01-May-02	WAR	PWO(U)	COMUKTG SEA	PLYMOUTH
Bradley, Rupert	Lt Cdr	01-Oct-10	WAR	P SKW	UK MCC	BAHRAIN
Bradley, Trevor A	Lt Cdr	01-Oct-09	ENG	WE	COMPORFLOT ESG	PORTSMOUTH
Bradshaw, James P	Lt RN	01-Oct-09	WAR	SM(N)	HMS VANGUARD	
Bradshaw, Kieran J	SLt	01-Sep-11	ENG	AE	DCEME SULTAN	HMS SULTAN
Brady, Matthew V	Lt RN	01-Nov-06	WAR	ATC	RAF SHAWBURY - CATCS	RAF SHAWBURY
Brady, Sean E	Cdr	30-Jun-08	WAR	PWO(U)	NCHQ CNPERS	PORTSMOUTH
Brady, Sean P	Lt Col	30-Jun-12	RM	GS	FLEET CAP LLM & DRM DIVISION	NCHQ
Braham, Stephen W	Cdre	27-May-11	ENG	ME	DES/COMFLEET	LONDON
Brain, Brandon J	Mid	01-Nov-13	WAR	P UT	BRNC DARTMOUTH	
Brain, Terri	Lt RN	01-Mar-12	ENG	WE	HMS DIAMOND	
Brain, William Ja	Maj	01-Oct-06	RM	GS	OPS DIR	MAIN BUILDING LONDON
Braithwaite, Geoffrey C	Lt Cdr	01-Oct-12	ENG	ME	HMS BULWARK	
Brand, Simon	Capt RN	08-Sep-08	WAR	P LYNX	ATTACHE/ADVISER CAIRO	
Brann, Robert W	Lt Cdr	01-Oct-10	WAR	PWO(A)	HMS PORTLAND	
Brannighan, David M	Lt RN	01-Sep-08	WAR	SM(N)	FOST FAS SHORE	HELENSBURGH
Brannighan, Ian D	Lt RN	01-Sep-04	WAR	P LYNX	815 SQN FLT	RNAS YEOVILTON
Bratt, James R	Lt RN	01-Nov-08	WAR	SM(N)	MWS COLLINGWOOD	
Bravery, Martin A	Cdr	30-Jun-10	WAR	P MER	PJHQ (UK) J3	NORTHWOOD
Bray, Andrew	Lt Cdr	01-Oct-13	LOGS	L	HMS DRAGON	
Bray, Matthew	Lt RN	24-Feb-11	WAR	FC	HMS DEFENDER	
Bray, Michael A	Lt RN	09-Apr-10	ENG	WE	HMS COLLINGWOOD	
Bray, Michael P	SLt	01-Sep-11	ENG	WESM	HMS RALEIGH	
Braycotton, Edward J	Lt RN	22-Mar-08	WAR	P MER	814 SQN	RNAS CULDROSE
Brayson, Mark	Lt Cdr	01-Oct-05	WAR	P LYNX	NO 3 FTS/UAS - JEFTS	
Brazenall, Benjamin C	Lt RN	01-Jan-04	WAR	P SK4	CHFHQ (SEA)	RNAS YEOVILTON
Breach, Charles E	Maj	01-Oct-10	RM	GS	FLEET SPT LOGS INFRA	NCHQ
Breach, Pamela	Lt Cdr	01-Oct-09	WAR	ATC	RAF SHAWBURY	
Breaks, James	SLt	01-May-11	WAR	GSX	BRNC DARTMOUTH	
Breckenridge, Iain G OBE	Cdr	30-Jun-04	WAR	SM(CQ)	HMS DRAKE	
Breckenridge, Robert J	Lt RN	01-Oct-07	WAR	P SK6	854 NAS	RNAS CULDROSE
Bree, Stephen E P	Surg Capt RN	01-Jul-11	MED	Anaes	MDHU DERRIFORD	PLYMOUTH
Breen, John E	Lt Cdr	01-Oct-10	ENG	AE	AWC BSD - RW TES	RAF BOSCOMBE DOWN
Breen, Paul R	Lt RN	15-Apr-11	ENG	AE	857 NAS	RNAS CULDROSE
Breet, Max W	Capt	01-Sep-12	RM	GS	43 CDO FPGRM S SQN	HMNB CLYDE
Brehaut, John R	Lt RN	01-Apr-13	LOGS	L	CHFHQ (SEA)	RNAS YEOVILTON
Brenchley, Nigel G	Cdr	30-Jun-08	LOGS	L	DES/COMLAND/LCS	BICESTER
Brennan, John P	Lt Cdr	01-Oct-12	ENG	WE	HMS PORTLAND	
Brennan, Paul A	Lt Cdr	01-Oct-06	ENG	MESM	DES/COMFLEET	HMS DRAKE
Brennan, Richard D	Mid	01-Sep-13	ENG	ME	BRNC DARTMOUTH	
Brereton, Charles	SLt	01-Nov-11	WAR	GSX	BRNC DARTMOUTH	
Brettell, Jeremy D	Lt Cdr	01-Oct-13	WAR	PWO(N)	CAREER TRAINING	HMS COLLINGWOOD

Person Name	Substantive Rank	Seniority	Branch	Specialisation	Organisation	Location
Bretten, Nicholas J	Lt RN	01-Jul-06	WAR	INT	UK MCC	BAHRAIN
Breward, Daniel P	Lt RN	01-Jan-10	WAR	O SKW	857 NAS	RNAS CULDROSE
Brewer, Christopher E	Lt Cdr	01-Oct-06	WAR	SM(AWC)	COMDEVFLOT SHORE	HMNB DEVONPORT
Brian, Neil	Lt Cdr	01-Oct-02	WAR	O MER	829 SQN EFP	RNAS CULDROSE
Brian, Stephen	Lt RN	01-Sep-07	WAR	PWO(SM)	HMS TALENT	
Briant-Evans, Zoe A	Lt Cdr	01-Oct-06	WAR	GSX	BRNC DARTMOUTH	DARTMOUTH
Bridge, James G	Lt RN	15-Apr-11	WAR	HM	FLEET HM UNIT	HMNB DEVONPORT
Bridges, John M	RN Chpln	02-Jul-05	Ch S		CHAPLAIN OF THE FLEET	PORTSMOUTH
Bridson, Andrew	Capt	28-Jul-06	RM	LC (SCC)	6 OPS SQN HMS ALBION	PLYMOUTH
Brierley, Natalie L	Mid	01-Sep-13	WAR	ATC UT	BRNC DARTMOUTH	
Brierley, Simon P J	Lt Cdr	01-Oct-09	ENG	AE	RAF BENSON	
Briers, Matthew P	Capt RN	21-Sep-09	WAR	P SK4	CHFHQ (SEA)	RNAS YEOVILTON
Briggs, Cathryn S	Lt Cdr	01-Oct-04	QARNNS	OT (C&S)	DMS WHITTINGTON	LICHFIELD
Briggs, Christopher J	Lt RN	16-Dec-11	ENG	WESM(SWS)	HMS VANGUARD	
Briggs-Mould, Timothy P	Lt Cdr	16-Mar-99	ENG	WE	DES/COMJE/ISS	EPISKOPI
Brighouse, Neil G	Maj	24-Apr-02	RM	P SK4	RNAS YEOVILTON - ADHQ	RNAS YEOVILTON
Bright, Amanda C	Lt Cdr	01-Oct-12	WAR	REG	RNP SIB EASTERN	HMS NELSON
Bright, Jack	Lt RN	01-Sep-09	LOGS	L	HQ 3 CDO BDE RM	PLYMOUTH
Brindley, Alice E	Lt RN	10-Nov-13	ENG	WE	HMS DEFENDER	
Brindley, Mark W	Lt Cdr	01-Oct-10	ENG	WE	HMS EXCELLENT	
Briscoe, Daniel A	Lt RN	01-Jan-09	WAR	GSX	UKRBATSTAFF	HMNB PORTSMOUTH
Briscoe, James W A	Lt Cdr	01-Oct-12	ENG	WE	HMS COLLINGWOOD	HMS COLLINGWOOD
Bristow, Paul D	Lt Cdr	01-Oct-12	ENG	TM	NCHQ	
Bristowe, Paul A	Cdr	30-Jun-10	WAR	P SKW	FLEET ACOS(RP)	NCHQ
Britten, Benjamin T	Lt RN	01-Sep-08	WAR	P UT	BDS WASHINGTON	WASHINGTON USA
Britton, Gemma L	Lt RN	01-Apr-08	WAR	GSX	MWS COLLINGWOOD	
Broad, Annabel E	SLt	01-May-13	WAR	GSX	HMS OCEAN	
Broad, James W	Mid	01-Sep-12	WAR	GSX	HMS TYNE	
Broadbent, Nicholas J	Capt	18-Jul-08	RM	SCC	FLEET SPT LOGS INFRA	PORTSMOUTH
Broadley, Kevin J	Cdr	30-Jun-00	WAR	P SK6	NATO - BRUSSELS	
Brock, Danny R	Lt RN	20-Jul-12	LOGS	L	HMS ASTUTE	
Brock, Mathew J	Lt RN	01-Jan-02	WAR	MCD	UK MCC	BAHRAIN
Brock, Matthew T	Lt RN	01-Dec-08	WAR	SM(X)	FLEET COMOPS NWD	NORTHWOOD
Brockie, Alan F	Lt Cdr	01-Oct-13	QARNNS	OT	UK MED GP (AFG)	AFGHANISTAN BASTION
Brocklehurst, Judith E	Lt Cdr	01-Oct-09	QARNNS	ITU	HMS NELSON	
Brodie, Duncan J	Lt Cdr	01-Oct-10	ENG	AE	DES/COMJE	BRISTOL
Brodie, Stephen D	Lt Cdr	01-Oct-09	QARNNS	EN (C&S)	HQ RC(SW)	AFGHANISTAN BASTION
Brogden, Thomas G	Surg Lt Cdr	02-Aug-11	MED	GS	INM ALVERSTOKE	GOSPORT
Brokenshire, Matthew W	Capt	01-Mar-09	RM	GS	HQ BRUNEI GAR	SERIA
Bromage, Kenneth	RN Chpln	02-Aug-92	Ch S		HMS DRAKE - CHAP	HMS DRAKE
Brook, Sophie A	SLt	01-Sep-13	WAR	SM(X)	MWS COLLINGWOOD	HMS COLLINGWOOD
Brooking, Gary N	Lt RN	12-Jul-11	QARNNS	ITU	NCHQ	
Brooks, Alexandra L	Lt Cdr	01-Oct-11	WAR	MEDIA OPS	NCHQ - NAVY CMD SEC	NCHQ
Brooks, Gary	Cdr	30-Jun-08	WAR	HM (H CH)	DEFENCE ACADEMY	SHRIVENHAM SWINDON
Brooks, Nicholas R	Lt Cdr	01-Oct-09	ENG	MESM	DES/COMFLEET	ABBEY WOOD
Brooks, Paul Neil	Lt Cdr	01-Oct-09	ENG	WE	HMS WESTMINSTER	
Brooksbank, Oliver	Lt RN	01-Nov-10	WAR	P	815 SQN	RNAS YEOVILTON
Broster, Lee J	Lt RN	01-Jul-04	ENG	WE	NATO - BRUSSELS - IMS	BRUSSELS
Brotherton, John D	Lt Cdr	16-Apr-02	WAR	P MER	854 NAS	RNAS CULDROSE
Brotton, Peter J	Lt Cdr	01-Apr-06	WAR	PWO(C)	MWS COLLINGWOOD	
Broughton, Arron M	Capt	01-Sep-13	RM	GS	CTCRM - CTW	EXMOUTH
Broughton, Jack E	Capt	03-Apr-09	RM	SCC	CTCRM - CTW	EXMOUTH
Browett, Jon J	Lt Cdr	01-Oct-12	WAR	PWO	HMS MONMOUTH	
Brown, Alastair D	Lt Cdr	01-Oct-12	ENG	ME	1 ASSLT GROUP RM (HQ)	HMNB DEVONPORT
Brown, Andrew	Surg Cdr	20-Jul-10	MED	GMP (C&S)	RM LYMPSTONE	EXMOUTH
Brown, Andrew	Lt Cdr	01-Dec-04	ENG	WE	2 SQN	AYIOS CYPRUS
Brown, Andrew S	Lt Cdr	01-Oct-08	WAR	PWO	MWS COLLINGWOOD	
Brown, Benjamin E	Lt RN	01-Feb-12	WAR	MCD	MCM2 CREW 5	PORTSMOUTH
Brown, Harry G	Mid	01-Sep-13	WAR	SM(X)	BRNC DARTMOUTH	
Brown, James A	Lt Cdr	01-Oct-10	WAR	HM	COMDEVFLOT SHORE	HMNB DEVONPORT
Brown, James A	Lt Cdr	01-Oct-11	ENG	WESM(TWS)	HMS AMBUSH	
Brown, Joe Henry	2Lt	02-Sep-13	RM	N/A	CTCRM OFFICERS	EXMOUTH

Person Name	Substantive Rank	Seniority	Branch	Specialisation	Organisation	Location
Brown, Joshua	SLt	01-Sep-12	MED	MEDICAL	BRNC DARTMOUTH	
Brown, Leonard A MBE	Lt Col	30-Jun-09	RM	P LYN7	OPS DIR	MAIN BUILDING LONDON
Brown, Lynda E	Lt Cdr	01-Oct-13	LOGS	L	HMS PROTECTOR	
Brown, Marc A	Lt RN	11-Apr-08	WAR	O SKW	849 SQN	RNAS CULDROSE
Brown, Matthew O	Lt RN	01-Sep-13	WAR	GSX	MWS COLLINGWOOD	
Brown, Michael A	Lt RN	01-Sep-05	WAR	P SK4	848 SQN	RNAS YEOVILTON
Brown, Nathan D	2Lt	01-Sep-12	RM	GS	42 CDO RM	HMNB DEVONPORT
Brown, Neil Logan	Cdre	01-Jul-10	LOGS	L BAR	MOD NSD	MAIN BUILDING LONDON
Brown, Nigel	Col	30-Jun-06	RM	C	NATO - BRUSSELS - IMS	BRUSSELS
Brown, Oliver G	SLt	01-May-13	WAR	GSX	FLEET HQ	NCHQ
Brown, Peter S J	Lt Cdr	01-Jun-95	ENG	MESM	NATO-ACO-JFC HQ	NAPLES
Brown, Rebecca K	Lt RN	01-Apr-12	WAR	GSX	HMS DARING	
Brown, Scott J	Chpln of the Fleet	01-Nov-10	Ch S		CHAPLAIN OF THE FLEET	NCHQ
Brown, Simon J	Lt RN	28-Jul-06	ENG	AE	DES/COMJE	YEOVIL
Brown, Simon J	Cdr	16-Jun-87	WAR	PWO(U)	DMS WHITTINGTON	LICHFIELD
Brown, Stephen H	Lt Cdr	15-Jan-01	WAR	MCD PWO(U)	NCHQ CNPERS	PORTSMOUTH
Brown, Steven	Lt RN	01-Mar-11	ENG	MESM	HMS VIGILANT	
Brown, William C	Cdr	30-Jun-03	WAR	AAWO	STRIKFORNATO - LISBON	PORTUGAL
Browne, Kevin M	Lt Cdr	01-Oct-13	WAR	INT	SCU SHORE	HMS COLLINGWOOD
Bruce, Robin P	Capt	01-Sep-12	RM	GS	ARMOURED SUPPORT GROUP	RNAS YEOVILTON
Bruford, Robert M C	Cdr	30-Jun-10	WAR	AAWO	ATTACHE/ADVISER RIYADH	SAUDI ARABIA
Brunsden-Brown, Sebastian E	Lt Cdr	01-Oct-01	WAR	P MER	824 SQN - CTT	RNAS CULDROSE
Brunton, Steven B	R Adm	24-Feb-12	ENG	WESM(TWS)	DES/COMFLEET	ABBEY WOOD
Bruzon, Charles	RN Chpln	01-Sep-04	Ch S	Chaplain	HMS RALEIGH	
Bryan, Rory J OBE	Cdr	30-Jun-08	WAR	PWO(U)	OPS DIR	MAIN BUILDING LONDON
Bryant, Nathan C	SLt	01-May-12	ENG	WE	BRNC DARTMOUTH	
Bryce, Andrew A	Capt	01-Sep-13	RM	GS	43 CDO	HMNB CLYDE
Bryce, Graeme E	Surg Lt Cdr (D)	29-Jun-05	DENTAL	GDP	INM ALVERSTOKE	GOSPORT
Bryce, Jenny E	SLt	01-Feb-11	WAR	GSX	CREW 8	HELENSBURGH
Bryce-Johnston, Fiona L	Lt RN	16-Jul-01	QARNNS	Nursing Officer	NORTHWOOD HQ	NORTHWOOD
Bryden, David G	Lt RN	01-Sep-07	WAR	GSX	HMS EXPLORER	
Bryers, Matthew Paul	Lt RN	01-Jan-13	WAR	GSX	MWS DDS	DDS PORTSMOUTH
Bubb, Jonathan David	Lt Col	30-Jun-12	RM	C	FMC - STRAT N	MAIN BUILDING LONDON
Buchan, James	Lt RN	01-Apr-11	WAR	GSX	43 CDO	HMNB CLYDE
Buchan, Sarah R	Lt RN	01-May-98	ENG	TM	NCHQ CNPERS	HMNB PORTSMOUTH
Buchan-Steele, Mark A	Cdr	31-Dec-00	LOGS	L SM	FLEET FOSNNI - NRC	HMS CALEDONIA
Buck, James E	Cdr	30-Jun-13	WAR	PWO(N)	FLEET CAP SSM DIVISION	NCHQ
Buck, Thomas A	2Lt	01-Sep-11	RM	GS	CTCRM OFFICERS	EXMOUTH
Buckenham, Peter J	Lt Cdr	01-Oct-08	ENG	ME	NCHQ CNPERS	PORTSMOUTH
Buckland, Christopher S	Capt	17-Dec-12	RM	GS (RES)	Op LANSBURY	AFGHANISTAN
Buckle, Iain L	Cdr	30-Jun-05	ENG	WE	FMC - NAVY	MAIN BUILDING LONDON
Buckley, James D	Capt	01-Mar-10	RM	GS	NCHQ	
Buckley, Phillip J A	Capt RN	30-Jun-05	WAR	SM(CQ)	DES/COMFLEET	HMS NELSON
Bucknall, Robin J	Lt Col	30-Jun-09	RM	HW	IPP - MENA	MAIN BUILDING LONDON
Bugg, Christopher G	Lt RN	01-May-13	WAR	O UT	RNAS CULDROSE	
Bugg, Jennifer	Lt RN	01-Oct-08	WAR	GSX	HMS OCEAN	
Bukhory, Hamesh	Lt Cdr	01-Oct-12	ENG	AE	DES/COMLAND/JSC	ABBEY WOOD
Bulgin, Martin R	Lt RN	01-Jan-05	WAR	ATC	HMS ILLUSTRIOUS	
Bull, Christopher M	Cdr	30-Jun-04	ENG	WESM(TWS)	DES/COMFLEET	FASLANE
Bull, Louis P	Lt Cdr	01-Oct-09	WAR	SM(AWC)	HMS AMBUSH	
Bullock, James	Lt RN	01-Aug-02	WAR	P SK4	202 SQN - E FLT	HULL
Bullock, John B	Lt Cdr	01-Oct-10	ENG	ME	HMS DUNCAN	
Bullock, Michael P MBE	Cdre	04-Jul-11	LOGS	L SM	FLEET SPT LOGS	NCHQ
Bullock, Robert A	Lt Cdr	01-Oct-11	WAR	PWO(C)	HQBF GIBRALTAR - OPS	HMS ROOKE
Bulmer, Renny John MBE	Maj	01-Oct-00	RM	SCC	FLEET CMR	NCHQ
Bundock, Oliver J	SLt	01-Apr-11	WAR	P UT	702 SQN	RNAS YEOVILTON
Burbeck, Leslie R	SLt	01-Nov-11	WAR	O UT	BRNC DARTMOUTH	
Burbidge, Kay	Lt Cdr	01-Oct-10	WAR	O MER	MWS COLLINGWOOD	
Burbidge, Richard L	SLt	01-May-11	WAR	GSX	HMS DIAMOND	
Burcham, Jason R	Maj	01-Oct-09	RM	BS	RM BAND PLYMOUTH	HMS RALEIGH
Burge, Roger	Cdr	30-Jun-11	ENG	WESM(SWS)	DES/COMFLEET	ABBEY WOOD
Burgess, Andrew J	Surg Capt RN	17-Apr-07	MED	Anaes	MDHU DERRIFORD	PLYMOUTH

Person Name	Substantive Rank	Seniority	Branch	Specialisation	Organisation	Location
Burgess, Mark J	Capt	01-Apr-03	RM	P LYN7	RNAS CULDROSE - EXEC	RNAS CULDROSE
Burgess, Maxine J	Lt RN	11-Dec-09	WAR	AV	HMS OCEAN	
Burgess, Philip G	Lt Cdr	01-Oct-13	ENG	ME	FOST DPORT SEA	HMNB DEVONPORT
Burgess, Thomas A	Mid	01-Sep-13	ENG	AE	BRNC DARTMOUTH	
Burghall, Rebecca C	Lt Cdr	01-Oct-13	WAR	HM(AS)	LOAN HYDROG.- DGHR(N)	TAUNTON
Burgoyne, William	Lt RN	01-May-06	WAR	PWO(SM)	CAREER TRAINING	HMS RALEIGH
Burke, Helen E	Lt RN	01-Sep-12	ENG	ME	HMS WESTMINSTER	
Burke, Michael C	Lt Cdr	01-Sep-95	WAR	SM(X)	FLEET FOST ACOS(Trg)	NCHQ
Burke, Paul D OBE	Capt RN	28-May-10	WAR	SM(CQ)	MOD NSD	MAIN BUILDING LONDON
Burkin, Craig R	Capt	01-Sep-11	RM	GS	43 CDO	HMNB CLYDE
Burlingham, Alexander C R	Lt RN	01-Aug-03	ENG	TM	NCHQ	
Burlingham, Brett L	Cdr	30-Jun-03	ENG	ME	NAVY MCTA PORTSMOUTH	HMNB PORTSMOUTH
Burlton, Patrick	2Lt	06-Jun-12	RM	GS	42 CDO RM	PLYMOUTH
Burnell, Jeremy	Lt Col	31-Dec-00	RM	GS	ATTACHE/ADVISER KIEV	UKRAINE
Burness-Smith, Oliver N	Lt RN	01-Mar-12	WAR	GSX	LOAN NEW ZEALAND	WELLINGTON
Burnett, Daniel D	Lt RN	09-Apr-12	WAR	P UT	RNAS YEOVILTON	
Burnett, Paul H	Lt Cdr	01-Oct-09	MED	MS	DMS WHITTINGTON	LICHFIELD
Burningham, Michael R	Capt RN	12-Mar-12	LOGS	L SM	FLEET SPT LOGS INFRA	NCHQ
Burns, Adrian C	Cdr	30-Jun-10	LOGS	L SM	RNAS YEOVILTON - SA	RNAS YEOVILTON
Burns, Amy	SLt	01-Sep-12	ENG	ME	BRNC DARTMOUTH	
Burns, Andrew P Rcds(S)	Capt RN	03-Jan-12	WAR	PWO(A)	HMS BULWARK	
Burns, David I	Capt RN	02-Jul-13	WAR	PWO(C)	FLEET COMOPS NWD	NORTHWOOD
Burns, David M	Capt	01-Sep-09	RM	GS	DEF SCH OF LANG	WILTON PARK
Burns, Natalie J	Lt RN	01-Jan-12	WAR	GSX	HMS DUNCAN	
Burns, Richard	SLt	01-Sep-12	ENG	WE	BRNC DARTMOUTH	
Burns, Richard J	Lt RN	01-Sep-12	WAR	GSX	MCM2 CREW 2	PORTSMOUTH
Burns, Ruth M	Surg Lt Cdr (D)	24-Jun-10	DENTAL	GDP	HMS NELSON	HMS NELSON
Burr, Christopher J	Maj	01-Oct-13	RM	GS	DEFAC JSCSC	SHRIVENHAM
Burrell, David J	Lt Cdr	01-Oct-11	WAR	SM(AWC)	HMS TRIUMPH	
Burrows, James R	Lt RN	01-Apr-12	WAR	GSX	HMS NELSON	
Burrows, Oliver R	Mid	01-Sep-13	ENG	AE	BRNC DARTMOUTH	
Burrows, Thomas G	Lt RN	01-Sep-08	WAR	P SK4	RS SANDHURST GP	CAMBERLEY
Burton, Alex	Lt Cdr	01-Nov-08	WAR	PWO(U) FC	PJHQ (UK) J3	NORTHWOOD
Burton, Alexander J	Cdre	18-Sep-12	WAR	PWO(U)	FLEET CAP RCAP	NCHQ
Burton, James H	Lt RN	01-Jan-06	WAR	PWO(SM)	HMS ASTUTE	
Burvill, Justin Paul	Cdr	30-Jun-12	ENG	MESM	DES/COMFLEET	USA
Bush, Alexander J T	Lt Cdr	01-Jun-99	WAR	MCD PWO(U)	FOST MPV SEA - S/P O	HELENSBURGH
Butcher, Mark W	Lt RN	01-Sep-08	WAR	HM	MCM1 CREW 5	FASLANE
Butler, Adam	Lt RN	01-Oct-10	WAR	HM	CAREER TRAINING	HMS DRAKE
Butler, James M	Lt RN	17-Dec-10	LOGS	L	UK MCC	BAHRAIN
Butler, Jonathon E	Lt Cdr	01-Oct-11	ENG	WESM(TWS)	FOST FAS SHORE	HELENSBURGH
Butler, Philip M	Lt Cdr	01-Oct-13	WAR	P SK4	845 SQN	RNAS YEOVILTON
Buttar, Daniel M	SLt	01-May-12	WAR	GSX	BRNC DARTMOUTH	
Butterworth, Chester O	SLt	01-Sep-13	WAR	GSX	MWS COLLINGWOOD	
Butterworth, Leslie MBE	Lt RN	16-Jan-99	LOGS	L FS	FLEET ACOS	PORTSMOUTH
Butterworth, Sophie	Surg Lt RN	04-Aug-10	MED	GDMO	HMS DARING	
Buttery, Stephanie A	SLt	01-Sep-11	WAR	GSX	DEF SCH OF LANG	BEACONSFIELD
Buxton, Joshua L	2Lt	02-Sep-12	RM	N/A	CTCRM OFFICERS	EXMOUTH
Buxton, Peter OBE	Surg Cdre	15-Aug-11	MED	Radiologist	DMS WHITTINGTON	LICHFIELD
Bye, Ashley	Lt RN	01-Oct-08	WAR	P SK4	HMS ILLUSTRIOUS	
Bye, Kyo	SLt	01-Feb-12	MED	MEDICAL	BRNC DARTMOUTH	
Byrd, Liam	Lt Cdr	01-Oct-13	LOGS	L	HQ JHC	ANDOVER
Byron, Douglas C	Lt Cdr	01-Oct-12	LOGS	L	DES/COMFLEET	HELENSBURGH
Byron, James D DSC	Cdr	30-Jun-13	WAR	PWO(U) MW	MCM1 FAS SEA1	HELENSBURGH

C

Cabot, Thomas L	2Lt	01-Mar-11	RM	GS	43 CDO FPGRM O SQN	HMNB CLYDE
Cackett, Thomas E R	Lt RN	01-May-06	WAR	P SK4	845 SQN	RNAS YEOVILTON
Caddick, Andrew	Lt RN	01-Sep-03	ENG	MESM	COMDEVFLOT	HMS DRAKE
Caddy, Paul D	Lt RN	01-Sep-08	WAR	GSX	NCHQ CNPERS	HMNB PORTSMOUTH
Cahill, Karen A	Lt Cdr	01-Aug-03	WAR	GSX	COMPORFLOT SEA	HMNB PORTSMOUTH
Cain, John David	2Lt	01-Sep-11	RM	GS	CTCRM	EXMOUTH

Person Name	Substantive Rank	Seniority	Branch	Specialisation	Organisation	Location
Cairns-Holder, Declan P.	Lt RN	20-Aug-10	ENG	WE	HMS OCEAN	
Calder, Thomas A.	Lt RN	01-Mar-12	ENG	AE	820 SQN	RNAS CULDROSE
Caldwell, Daniel J.	Maj	01-Oct-09	RM	GS	45 CDO RM	DUNDEE
Calhaem, Richard T.	Lt Cdr	01-Oct-08	WAR	P SK4	771 SQN	RNAS CULDROSE
Callaghan, John J.	Surg Lt RN	01-Aug-12	MED	MEDICAL	BRNC DARTMOUTH	
Callear, Ben.	SLt	01-May-12	ENG	WE	BRNC DARTMOUTH	
Callender, James T	Lt RN	01-Apr-12	WAR	GSX	HMS ILLUSTRIOUS	
Callis, Gregory J	Lt RN	01-Sep-02	ENG	ME	HMS SULTAN	
Calvert, Lauren J	Lt RN	01-Apr-10	WAR	GSX	HMS DRAKE	
Cambrook, Laura	Lt RN	01-Sep-09	WAR	O LYNX	815 SQN FLT	RNAS YEOVILTON
Cameron, Alastair J.	Capt	01-Sep-13	RM	GS	42 CDO RM	PLYMOUTH
Cameron, Fiona	Lt Cdr	01-Oct-08	ENG	TM	USSC JERUSALEM	ISRAEL
Cameron, Fraser I.	Mid	01-Sep-13	WAR	GSX	BRNC DARTMOUTH	
Cameron, Mark J.	Capt RN	06-Nov-12	WAR	WE	FLEET FOSNNI - CNR	HMNB PORTSMOUTH
Cameron, Peter S OBE	Col	30-Jun-08	RM	GS	MOD NSD - HDS	MAIN BUILDING LONDON
Cameron, Sam.	Lt RN	01-Mar-10	ENG	MESM	HMS ASTUTE	
Campbell, Alastair	Lt RN	01-May-04	WAR	P CDO	CHF(MERLIN)	RAF BENSON
Campbell, Colin	Lt RN	01-Jan-09	WAR	SM(X)	HMS VIGILANT	
Campbell, David C	SLt	01-Nov-11	WAR	GSX	BRNC DARTMOUTH	
Campbell, Edward J	Lt RN	01-Jul-11	WAR	P UT	RAF SHAWBURY	
Campbell, Felicity	Cdr	01-Jul-12	QARNNS	Nursing Officer	RCDM	BIRMINGHAM
Campbell, Jonathan G	Lt RN	01-Sep-07	WAR	MCD	MCM2 CREW 7	PORTSMOUTH
Campbell, Michael M Rd*	Maj	01-Nov-04	RM	GS (RES)	FLEET CAP IS DIVISION	NCHQ
Campbell, Robin D.	Cdr	30-Jun-07	ENG	WESM(TWS)	DES/COMJE	ABBEY WOOD BRISTOL
Campbell, Scott L.	Mid	01-Nov-13	WAR	P UT	BRNC DARTMOUTH	DARTMOUTH
Campbell, Thomas C.	Lt	01-Sep-12	RM	GS	RN EXCHANGE NETHERLANDS	DEN HELDER
Campbell, Timothy R.	Lt RN	01-Jun-00	WAR	INT	FLEET COMOPS NWD	NORTHWOOD
Campbell-Baldwin, James W	Lt RN	01-May-03	WAR	PWO	HMS ILLUSTRIOUS	
Camplisson, Owen G	Lt RN	01-Jul-06	WAR	P SK4	DEF HELI FLYING SCH	RAF SHAWBURY
Canale, Andrew J.	Lt Cdr	01-Oct-05	WAR	PWO(U)	DCDS PERS TRG	MAIN BUILDING LONDON
Cane, Jonathan.	Lt RN	01-Aug-08	LOGS	L	101 LOG BDE J	ALDERSHOT
Cannell, Graham M	Lt RN	01-Nov-99	WAR	P SK4	848 SQN	RNAS YEOVILTON
Canning, Christopher P MBE	Cdr	30-Jun-13	WAR	O SK6	A EXEC GP LONDON	MAIN BUILDING LONDON
Canosa, Luis Joseph	Lt RN	01-Jan-12	LOGS	L	RNAS YEOVILTON	
Cantellow, Stuart J.	Lt Cdr	01-Jun-09	ENG	AE	771 SQN	RNAS CULDROSE
Cantillon, Lloyd M.	Lt RN	16-Jun-08	QARNNS	ITU	DEFAC JSCSC	SHRIVENHAM
Cantrill, Richard John MC	Lt Col	30-Jun-11	RM	MLDR	MTM STONEHOUSE	PLYMOUTH
Canty, Thomas A.	Lt Cdr	01-Feb-10	ENG	ME	HMS KENT	
Capes, Stuart G	Cdr	30-Jun-08	WAR	SM(CQ)	FMC - NAVY	MAIN BUILDING LONDON
Capewell, David A OBE	Lt Gen	01-Dec-11	RM	GS	PJHQ (UK) CMD GP	NORTHWOOD
Caple, Jonathan	Lt Cdr	01-Oct-05	LOGS	L	PJHQ (UK) J1/J4	NORTHWOOD
Capps, James A	Lt RN	01-Jan-05	WAR	P SK4	DEFAC JSCSC	SHRIVENHAM
Carbery, Stephen	Lt Cdr	01-Oct-09	ENG	WE	DES/COMJE/ISTAR	ABBEY WOOD
Carden, Peter D	Cdr	30-Jun-99	WAR	O SK6	AIB	HMS SULTAN
Cardy, Lloyd E	Lt RN	01-Apr-12	WAR	GSX	HMS WESTMINSTER	
Carey, Trevor	Lt RN	01-May-02	ENG	ME	DEFAC	SHRIVENHAM
Carlisle, Jack C.	Mid	01-Nov-13	WAR	P UT	BRNC DARTMOUTH	
Carlton, Paul D	Lt RN	01-May-06	ENG	MESM	DES/COMFLEET	ABBEY WOOD
Carman, Felix.	Lt RN	01-Dec-04	WAR	HM	CAREER TRAINING	HMS DRAKE
Carne, Richard J.	Lt Cdr	01-Oct-08	WAR	O MER	829 SQN HQ	RNAS CULDROSE
Carnell, Richard P.	Lt Cdr	01-Oct-09	QARNNS	EN	JFHQ	NORTHWOOD
Carnew, Sean F.	Lt RN	01-Sep-03	WAR	O MER	RNAS CULDROSE - MHFHQ	RNAS CULDROSE
Carney, Joseph.	SLt	01-May-12	WAR	O UT	BRNC DARTMOUTH	
Carnie, Christopher	Lt RN	01-May-13	LOGS	L	FLEET CAP IS DIVISION	NCHQ
Carnie, Manson J.	Cdr	30-Jun-13	WAR	P LYNX	LHF 815 SQN HQ	RNAS YEOVILTON
Carns, Alistair Scott MC	Maj	01-Oct-10	RM	GS	NCHQ	
Carpenter, Bryony H.	Lt Cdr	01-Oct-04	ENG	TM	COMPORFLOT FPS SEA	HMNB PORTSMOUTH
Carpenter, Gary John	Lt Cdr	01-Oct-12	ENG	WESM(SWS)	CAREER TRAINING	HMS RALEIGH
Carpenter, James E.	Lt RN	01-Jun-11	WAR	GSX	MWS DDS 1	DDS PORTSMOUTH
Carpenter, Neil P.	Lt RN	01-Apr-11	LOGS	L	BRNC DARTMOUTH	
Carr, David J.	Lt Cdr	01-Oct-13	WAR	PWO	HMS ILLUSTRIOUS	
Carr, Stephen A	Mid	01-Nov-13	WAR	GSX	BRNC DARTMOUTH	

Person Name	Substantive Rank	Seniority	Branch	Specialisation	Organisation	Location
Carrick, James P	Lt RN	01-Sep-98	WAR	SM(N)	HMS VENGEANCE	
Carrick, Richard J	Capt RN	06-Sep-11	ENG	MESM	DES/COMFLEET	HMNB DEVONPORT
Carrigan, Jonathan A	Cdr	30-Jun-12	LOGS	L	FLEET SPT LOGS INFRA	NCHQ
Carrioni-Burnett, Ivana M	Lt RN	20-Oct-12	WAR	H	HMS ECHO	
Carroll, Paul C	Cdr	30-Jun-09	ENG	ME	NCHQ CNPERS	PORTSMOUTH
Carroll, Stephen	Lt Cdr	01-Oct-08	ENG	AE	DES/COIR	ARLINGTON USA
Carter Quinn, Michael G	Lt Cdr	01-Oct-09	WAR	AAWO	MOD DEFENCE STAFF	LONDON
Carter, Andrew John M	Lt RN	01-May-07	WAR	O MER	824 SQN	RNAS CULDROSE
Carter, Christopher	Lt RN	18-Feb-05	WAR	GSX	1 ASSLT GROUP RM	HMS RALEIGH
Carter, Holly	Lt RN	01-Apr-09	WAR	ATC	RNAS CULDROSE	
Carter, Jonathon Mark	Lt Cdr	01-Jun-96	ENG	WESM(SWS)	DES/COMFLEET	ABBEY WOOD
Carter, Kevin	Lt Cdr	27-Aug-02	WAR	GSX	HMS DRAKE	
Carter, Kevin C GM	Maj	01-Oct-13	RM	SBS(SCC)	NCHQ	
Carter, Laura Jayne	Lt RN	08-Jul-10	LOGS	L	HMS PROTECTOR	
Carter, Paul	Lt Cdr	01-Oct-06	ENG	WESM(TWS)	FLEET ACOS(RP)	NCHQ
Carter, Sean M	RN Chpln	25-Aug-08	Ch S		COMPORFLOT SEA	HMNB PORTSMOUTH
Carter, Simon N	Capt RN	07-Sep-11	LOGS	L SM	PJHQ (UK) J1/J4	NORTHWOOD
Carter, Simon P	Lt Cdr	01-Oct-04	LOGS	L	DCDS PERS TRG	MAIN BUILDING LONDON
Carthew, Richard J	Lt Cdr	01-Oct-09	LOGS	L SM	FOST SM SEA	FASLANE
Carthey, Ben	Lt RN	01-Jan-09	WAR	P SK6	854 NAS	RNAS CULDROSE
Cartwright, Darren OBE	Cdr	30-Jun-05	WAR	O SK6	OPS DIR	MAIN BUILDING LONDON
Carty, Michael G	Capt	01-Sep-05	RM	P GR7	BDS WASHINGTON	USA
Carver, Charles A	Lt RN	01-May-06	LOGS	L	HMS NELSON	
Carver, James D	Lt RN	01-Nov-10	WAR	P UT	71 SQN CULDROSE	RNAS CULDROSE
Carvill, Joe J	Capt	01-Sep-13	RM	GS	42 CDO RM - DGHR(O)	PLYMOUTH
Cary, Matthew R	Lt RN	01-Sep-13	WAR	GSX	MWS COLLINGWOOD	HMS COLLINGWOOD
Case, Alexander C	Lt Col	01-Jun-06	RM	GS	NATO-ACT-HQ SACT	NORFOLK
Cash, Rupert	Lt RN	19-Nov-10	WAR	HM	FLEET HM UNIT	HMNB DEVONPORT
Cassar, Adrian	Capt RN	30-Jun-08	WAR	MCD PWO(U)	DEFENCE ACADEMY	SHRIVENHAM
Cassells, Benjamin T	Capt	01-Sep-08	RM	GS	NCHQ	
Cassidy, Stuart M	Lt RN	01-Sep-03	WAR	P SK4	HMS GANNET SAR FLT	PRESTWICK
Casson, Paul R	Capt RN	10-May-10	ENG	ME	DES/COMFLEET	ABBEY WOOD BRISTOL
Castle, Alastair S	Lt Cdr	01-Dec-01	WAR	P MER	824 SQN - TU	RNAS CULDROSE
Castle, Colin	Lt Cdr	01-Oct-06	WAR	AAWO	RN EXCHANGE FRANCE	PARIS
Castledine, Benjamin C	Surg Lt RN	03-Feb-09	MED	GMP	INM ALVERSTOKE	GOSPORT
Castleford, Lauren J	Lt RN	01-Oct-09	LOGS	L	DES/COMFLEET	ABBEY WOOD
Castrinoyannakis, Timothy	Lt RN	01-Oct-08	WAR	MCD	MCM1 CREW 7	FASLANE
Caswell, Neil C	Lt Cdr	01-Oct-13	LOGS	L	RNLA	HMS COLLINGWOOD
Cataffo, Paul J	SLt	01-Apr-12	WAR	O UT	849 SQN	RNAS CULDROSE
Catchpole, Andrew D	Capt	21-Mar-13	RM	SCC	SQN CDO LOG REGT RM	RMB CHIVENOR
Cator, Benjamin H	Lt RN	03-Sep-13	ENG	WE	HMS LANCASTER	
Cattanach, James I	Lt RN	01-May-08	WAR	SM(X)	HMS AMBUSH	
Catton, Innes C	Maj	01-Oct-10	RM	GS	40 CDO RM - A COY	TAUNTON
Cave, George	SLt	01-Sep-11	ENG	ME	DCEME SULTAN	HMS SULTAN
Cave, Simon J	Lt RN	09-Apr-10	ENG	ME	HMS SULTAN	
Cave, William	Lt RN	01-Jun-13	ENG	WE	HMS DAUNTLESS	
Cavendish, Gavin W	Lt RN	11-Oct-13	WAR	INT	FLEET COMOPS NWD	RNAS CULDROSE
Cavill, Niki R MBE	Lt Col	30-Jun-13	RM	GS	DCDS MIL STRAT OPS	MAIN BUILDING LONDON
Chadfield, Laurence J	Lt Cdr	01-Oct-04	WAR	PWO(C)	DCOG OGD LONDON	LONDON
Chadwick, Kara	Lt Cdr	01-Oct-08	LOGS	L BAR	STRAT ACDS DC&D	SHRIVENHAM SWINDON
Challans, Benjamin	Lt RN	01-Mar-12	ENG	ME	HMS DRAGON	
Chalmers, Donald P	Cdr	31-Dec-99	WAR	PWO(U)	NATO - BRUSSELS	BRUSSELS
Chambers, Christopher P	Lt RN	01-Dec-99	WAR	P LYNX	RNAS YEOVILTON	RNAS YEOVILTON
Chambers, Harry	Capt	01-Sep-09	RM	GS	RMB STONEHOUSE	PLYMOUTH
Chambers, Joanne	Lt RN	01-Jan-09	ENG	WE	HMS SULTAN	
Chambers, Luke	Lt RN	01-Mar-13	WAR	SM(X)	CREW 8 OFFICERS	FASLANE
Chambers, Mark W	Lt RN	13-Apr-12	MED	MS(SM)	COMDEVFLOT ESG	HMS DRAKE
Chambers, Richard	Lt Cdr	01-Oct-10	WAR	PWO(C)	UKRBATSTAFF	HMNB PORTSMOUTH
Chambers, William J	Cdr	30-Apr-94	WAR	MCD	DCDS PERS TRG-TESRR	MAIN BUILDING LONDON
Chan, Deona Mei Lam	Surg SLt	29-Jul-13	MED	MEDICAL	BRNC DARTMOUTH	
Chandler, Philip	Lt RN	01-Sep-00	ENG	TM	HQ JHC	ANDOVER
Chandler, Rory G	Lt RN	01-Sep-13	ENG	MESM	DCEME SULTAN	

Person Name	Substantive Rank	Seniority	Branch	Specialisation	Organisation	Location
Chandler, Russell S	Lt RN	01-Apr-09	WAR	O LYNX	LHF 815 SQN FLT 215	RNAS YEOVILTON
Chang, Christopher J	Lt Cdr	01-Oct-09	LOGS	L	FOST DPORT SEA	HMNB DEVONPORT
Chang, Hon W	Lt RN	01-Aug-02	ENG	TM	CHAPLAIN OF THE FLEET	NCHQ
Chapman, Charles L MCGI	Cdr	30-Jun-10	ENG	WESM(TWS)	NCHQ CNPERS	PORTSMOUTH
Chapman, Christopher	Lt RN	01-Sep-12	WAR	GSX	HMS WESTMINSTER	
Chapman, James L J	Lt Cdr	01-Oct-09	WAR	HM(AS)	HMS SCOTT	
Chapman, Martin S	Lt Cdr	01-Oct-08	LOGS	L C	HMS IRON DUKE	
Chapman, Nicholas J	Lt Cdr	01-May-90	WAR	SM(CQ)	NCHQ	
Chapman, Peter	Cdr	30-Jun-12	ENG	WE	DES/COMJE	CORSHAM
Chapman, Simon	Lt Col	30-Jun-07	RM	GS	CTCRM	EXMOUTH
Chapman, Simon J	Lt Cdr	01-Apr-98	WAR	AAWO	FLEET ACOS(RP)	NCHQ
Chappell, Benjamin J	Capt	01-Sep-10	RM	GS	CTCRM - ISC	EXMOUTH
Charles, Steven R	Lt RN	19-Dec-08	LOGS	L	NCHQ CNPS	PORTSMOUTH
Charlesworth, Graham	Capt RN	19-Apr-10	ENG	WESM(TWS)	DES/COMFLEET	WASHINGTON DC
Charlesworth, Nicholas J	Lt RN	01-Jan-09	WAR	P SK4	845 SQN	RNAS YEOVILTON
Charlton, Andrew R	Lt RN	01-Jan-12	WAR	P UT	RNAS YEOVILTON	RNAS YEOVILTON
Charlton, Kevin William	Cdr	06-Aug-13	QARNNS	Nursing Officer	NCHQ MEDDIV	NCHQ
Charnley, David John	Capt	01-Sep-12	RM	GS	INFANTRY BATTLE SCHOOL	BRECON
Charnock, Simon James	Lt Cdr	01-Oct-12	LOGS	L	NCHQ CNPS	MAIN BUILDING LONDON
Charters, Emma	Lt RN	01-Sep-13	LOGS	L	COMPORFLOT ESG	PORTSMOUTH
Chaston, Stephen P	Lt Cdr	01-Mar-01	WAR	SM(AWC)	NATO-ACO-JFC HQ	NAPLES
Chatterjee, Shatadeep	Lt Cdr	01-Oct-10	ENG	ME	HMS DARING	
Chatterley-Evans, Dawn A	Lt RN	01-Oct-11	LOGS	L	BRNC DARTMOUTH	
Chatwin, Nicholas J OBE	Cdr	30-Jun-05	WAR	P LYNX	FLEET FOSNNI	LONDON
Chawira, Denis	Lt Cdr	01-Oct-10	WAR	MCD	DEODS	ANDOVER
Cheal, Andrew John	Lt RN	01-Apr-02	ENG	TM	HMS NELSON	
Cheema, Sukhdev Singh	Lt RN	01-Jul-04	ENG	WESM(TWS)	DES/COMJE	CORSHAM
Cheesman, Daniel MBE	Lt Col	30-Jun-10	RM	C	45 CDO RM	DUNDEE
Chenery, Alexander C	SLt	01-Sep-11	ENG	ME	DCEME SULTAN	HMS SULTAN
Cheshire, Thomas E	Cdr	30-Jun-12	ENG	MESM	DES/COMFLEET	ABBEY WOOD BRISTOL
Cheshire, Thomas S	Lt RN	01-Jan-07	WAR	GSX	BRNC DARTMOUTH	
Chestnutt, James	Cdr	30-Jun-13	ENG	AE P	DEFAC JSCSC ACSC	SHRIVENHAM SWINDON
Chew, Christopher	Lt RN	20-May-13	WAR	GSX	HMS NORTHUMBERLAND	
Cheyne, Rory Paul	SLt	01-Feb-12	WAR	P UT	BRNC DARTMOUTH	DARTMOUTH
Chick, Stephen CBE	Cdre	03-Feb-09	WAR	PWO(A)	ACDS (POL) USA - NORFOLK	NORFOLK
Chidley, Timothy J	Capt RN	08-Jan-09	ENG	ME	DES/COMFLEET	ABBEY WOOD
Child, William M	SLt	01-Sep-12	ENG	WE	BRNC DARTMOUTH	
Childs, David G	Capt RN	26-Apr-10	ENG	AE P	DES/COMJE/HELS	ABBEY WOOD
Childs, John R	Lt Cdr	01-Apr-02	WAR	AAWO	NCHQ CNPS	NCHQ
Chin, Henry R	Lt RN	01-Mar-12	ENG	WESM(TWS)	HMS ASTUTE	
Chirnside, Gabriella F	Surg Cdr	30-Jun-06	MED	GMP	DMS WHITTINGTON	
Chisholm, David C	Lt RN	07-Apr-06	ENG	WE	DES/COMFLEET	HMS DRAKE
Chisholm, David T	Lt RN	01-May-06	ENG	MESM	FOST SM SEA	HELENSBURGH
Chisholm, Philip J H	Lt RN	01-Jul-05	WAR	PWO(C)	HMS DRAGON	
Chittick, William	Surg Lt Cdr (D)	10-Jul-02	DENTAL	GDP	ROYAL BRUNEI	SERIA
Chitty, Jack E	2Lt	02-Sep-13	RM	N/A	CTCRM OFFICERS	EXMOUTH
Chivers, Paul A OBE	Cdre	10-May-11	WAR	O LYNX	ABBEY WOOD	BRISTOL
Choules, Barrie	Lt Cdr	01-Sep-02	ENG	TM(SM)	FOST FAS SHORE - RNSSS	HELENSBURGH
Christie, Andrew J	Lt RN	14-Aug-11	ENG	TM	RAF HALTON	
Christie, Laura	Lt RN	01-Jul-11	LOGS	L	COMPORFLOT SHORE	HMNB PORTSMOUTH
Christie, Rhys L	Mid	17-Nov-12	WAR	SM(X)	BRNC DARTMOUTH	DARTMOUTH
Christie, Tom C	2Lt	01-Mar-11	RM	GS	42 CDO RM - J COY	PLYMOUTH
Chudley, Ian V	Lt RN	01-May-03	WAR	P SKW	849 SQN	RNAS CULDROSE
Church, Simon J	Lt RN	01-Sep-06	ENG	MESM	DES/COMFLEET	ABBEY WOOD BRISTOL
Churcher, Jeremy E	Cdr	30-Jun-06	WAR	HM (H CH)	FOST HM	HMS DRAKE
Churchward, Matthew J	Maj	01-Oct-04	RM	LC	COMUKAMPHIBFOR	HMNB PORTSMOUTH
Ciaravella, Timothy J	Lt Cdr	01-Oct-13	ENG	ME	ACDS DEFLOGPOL	ABBEY WOOD BRISTOL
Clague, John J	Lt Cdr	01-Oct-06	WAR	PWO(U)	HMS MONTROSE	
Clapham, Grantley T	Lt RN	01-Apr-01	ENG	IS	NATO-NCSA-NCSA	STAVANGER
Clapham, Philip A	SLt	03-Jul-13	DENTAL	GDP(VDP)	BRNC DARTMOUTH	
Clare, Jonathan F	Maj	01-Oct-04	RM	MLDR (SCC)	43 CDO	HMNB CLYDE
Clare, Katharine	Lt Cdr	01-Oct-05	ENG	IS	DES/COMJE/ISS	CORSHAM

Person Name	Substantive Rank	Seniority	Branch	Specialisation	Organisation	Location
Claridge, Alexander M	Lt Cdr	01-Oct-13	QARNNS	OT (C&S)	MDHU DERRIFORD	PLYMOUTH
Claringbold, Neill R	SLt	01-Nov-11	WAR	ATC UT	BRNC DARTMOUTH	
Clark, Alan Mcmi	Lt Cdr	01-Oct-03	WAR	SM(C)	RN EXCHANGE AUSTRALIA	CANBERRA
Clark, Allan J	Lt RN	09-Apr-09	ENG	MESM	NBC CLYDE BABCOCK	HELENSBURGH
Clark, Benjamin	SLt	01-Sep-12	ENG	AE	BRNC DARTMOUTH	
Clark, Craig S	Lt RN	01-Sep-13	WAR	GSX	HMS ARGYLL	
Clark, David John	Lt RN	11-Apr-08	ENG	WE	DES/COMLAND	ABBEY WOOD
Clark, Gary R	SLt	01-Jan-12	WAR	P UT	RNAS YEOVILTON	
Clark, Gordon D	Lt RN	08-Jul-10	LOGS	L	DEFAC JSCSC	SHRIVENHAM
Clark, Ian D	Cdr	30-Jun-03	ENG	MESM	HMS NELSON	
Clark, James C	SLt	01-Jan-13	WAR	O UT	RNAS CULDROSE	
Clark, Matthew H	Lt RN	01-Sep-11	WAR	P UT	RAF SHAWBURY	
Clark, Matthew T	Capt RN	02-Oct-12	LOGS	L	102 LOG BDE	GUTERSLOH
Clark, Michael H	Lt Cdr	01-Mar-04	WAR	AAWO	MWS COLLINGWOOD	
Clark, Oliver R	Lt RN	01-Jan-08	LOGS	L	CAREER TRAINING	HMS NELSON
Clark, Paul A	Lt RN	01-Jan-04	ENG	TM(SM)	BRNC DARTMOUTH	DARTMOUTH
Clark, Paul A	Lt Col	30-Jun-10	RM	SCC	DIU	ANDOVER
Clark, Philip J	Lt RN	01-Sep-05	WAR	O SKW	PJHQ (UK) J6	NORTHWOOD
Clark, Rachael H	SLt	01-May-12	WAR	GSX	BRNC DARTMOUTH	•DARTMOUTH
Clark, Russell A	Lt Cdr	01-Aug-08	WAR	O LYNX	FLEET CSAV	NCHQ
Clark, Simon	Cdr	30-Jun-05	LOGS	L C	DCDC	SHRIVENHAM
Clark, Stephen M	Lt Cdr	01-Oct-10	LOGS	L C	HMS EXCELLENT - CO	PORTSMOUTH
Clark, Stephen R	Lt Cdr	01-Oct-06	ENG	TM	HMS SULTAN - RNSME TTG	HMS SULTAN
Clarke, Adam G	Lt Cdr	01-Oct-07	ENG	IS	FLEET CISSU	PORTSDOWN HILL
Clarke, Andrew P MBE	Lt Cdr	01-Oct-00	WAR	P SK4	848 SQN	RNAS YEOVILTON
Clarke, Benjamin J	Mid	01-Sep-13	ENG	ME	BRNC DARTMOUTH	
Clarke, Charles M L OBE	Capt RN	01-Jul-09	WAR	PWO(U)	NCHQ CNPS	MAIN BUILDING LONDON
Clarke, Daniel	Cdr	30-Jun-12	WAR	SM(CQ)	HMS TRIUMPH	
Clarke, David W	Maj	01-Oct-12	RM	GS	COMUKAMPHIBFOR	HMNB PORTSMOUTH
Clarke, Ian	Cdr	30-Jun-10	WAR	PWO(A)	DEFENCE ACADEMY	SHRIVENHAM
Clarke, James P	Lt RN	01-Sep-07	ENG	WE	MWS COLLINGWOOD	
Clarke, John	Surg Cdr	30-Jun-02	MED	Occ Med	RN EXCHANGE USA - BDS	WASHINGTON
Clarke, Marcus	SLt	01-Sep-12	MED	MEDICAL	BRNC DARTMOUTH	
Clarke, Matthew	Lt RN	01-Jan-02	WAR	PWO	MWS COLLINGWOOD	
Clarke, Matthew D	Lt Cdr	01-Oct-07	ENG	TM	MWS COLLINGWOOD	
Clarke, Paul A	Lt RN	21-Feb-09	WAR	SM(X)	NATO COMND HQ	NORTHWOOD
Clarke, Peter M	Maj	01-Oct-09	RM	P SK4	847 SQN - AE	RNAS YEOVILTON
Clarke, Richard	Lt RN	01-Mar-10	ENG	MESM	HMS VANGUARD	
Clarke, Richard	Cdr	30-Jun-07	ENG	TM	NCHQ CNPERS	PORTSMOUTH
Clarke, Richard A	Lt RN	20-Oct-06	ENG	MESM	FLEET CAP SSM DIVISION	NCHQ
Clarke, Richard	Cdr	30-Jun-11	ENG	AE	DES/COIR/CA/LIGHTNING/USA	WASHINGTON
Clarke, Robert W	Lt RN	01-Nov-12	ENG	MESM	DCEME SULTAN	HMS SULTAN
Clarke, Steven P	Lt RN	01-Nov-08	WAR	SM(X)	CTCRM	EXMOUTH
Clarke, William	Lt Cdr	31-Mar-00	WAR	MW (RES)	JFC HQ	NORTHWOOD
Clarkson, Andrew	Lt Cdr	01-Oct-09	QARNNS	EN (C&S)	DMS WHITTINGTON SJC	LICHFIELD
Clarkson, Antony M	Lt Cdr	01-Oct-10	ENG	WE	MWS COLLINGWOOD - WE TG	HMS COLLINGWOOD
Clarkson, Paul J I	Lt RN	01-Aug-08	WAR	INT	UK MCC	BAHRAIN
Clasby, Lorraine	Lt RN	21-Aug-09	WAR	GSX	HMS DIAMOND	
Claxton, Alistair	2Lt	01-Sep-10	RM	GS	40 CDO RM - DGHR(O)	TAUNTON
Claxton, Andrew G D	Lt RN	01-Apr-04	WAR	HM	FLEET COMOPS NWD	NORTHWOOD
Clay, Toby	Lt Cdr	01-Oct-08	WAR	P LYNX	DEFAC JSCSC ACSC	SHRIVENHAM
Clayton, Andrew M	Mid	01-Sep-13	ENG	ME	BRNC DARTMOUTH	
Clayton, David H	SLt	01-May-11	ENG	WE	MWS COLLINGWOOD	
Clayton, John D	Lt RN	01-Mar-11	WAR	O SKW	857 NAS	RNAS CULDROSE
Clayton, Peter L	Lt RN	01-Feb-09	WAR	GSX	RN EXCHANGE FRANCE	PARIS
Clear, Nichola J	Lt Cdr	01-Oct-09	ENG	ME	COMPORFLOT ESG EDG COM	PORTSMOUTH
Cleary, Christopher M	Lt Cdr	01-Oct-08	LOGS	L	COMDEVFLOT WLSG FGEN	HMS DRAKE
Cleaves, Richard A	Lt RN	19-Oct-07	WAR	C	PJHQ (UK) J6	NORTHWOOD
Clee, James S	Lt Cdr	01-Oct-12	WAR	HM(AM)	HMS OCEAN	
Clegg, Ross E	Lt RN	03-May-13	ENG	AE	CULDROSE	RNAS CULDROSE
Clements, Elizabeth J	Lt Cdr	01-Oct-07	LOGS	L	RNAS CULDROSE - UPO	RNAS CULDROSE
Cleminson, Mark D	Lt Cdr	01-Feb-05	ENG	MESM	COMFASFLOT	HMNB CLYDE

Person Name	Substantive Rank	Seniority	Branch	Specialisation	Organisation	Location
Clifford, Stephen D	Lt RN	13-Jul-12	WAR	INT	RNU RAF DIGBY	LINCOLN
Clingo, Thomas W	Surg Lt RN	01-Mar-13	MED	MEDICAL	BRNC DARTMOUTH	
Clink, Adam D	Cdr	30-Jun-11	WAR	P GR7	FLEET AV CRANWELL	RAF CRANWELL
Clink, John R	Cdre	25-Apr-11	WAR	PWO(N)	HQBF GIBRALTAR - CBF	HMS ROOKE
Clissold, Patrick	Lt RN	20-Sep-10	ENG	ME	HMS NELSON	
Clough, Christopher R	Capt RN	12-Apr-10	ENG	WE	ATTACHE/ADVISER - PARIS	PARIS
Clough, Warren S	Lt RN	19-Dec-08	WAR	INT	CAREER TRAINING	SHEFFORD
Clow, Jennifer	SLt	24-Jul-13	DENTAL	GDP(VDP)	BRNC DARTMOUTH	
Clow, Thomas W	Capt	03-Apr-09	RM	LC (SCC)	CTCRM - CORPS COL	EXMOUTH
Coackley, Jane	Lt Cdr	01-Oct-10	ENG	TM	BRNC DARTMOUTH	
Coaker, Stewart	Lt RN	02-Nov-02	WAR	OP INT (RES)	MTM NPT RES MOBILISATION	HMNB PORTSMOUTH
Coatalen-Hodgson, Ryan	Lt RN	01-Sep-06	WAR	INT	DEF SCH OF LANG	BEACONSFIELD
Coates, Aaron	Mid	01-Sep-13	ENG	ME	BRNC DARTMOUTH	
Coates, Adam J	Lt Cdr	01-Oct-11	ENG	WE	CIO-DSAS-JSYCC	CORSHAM
Coates, James T	SLt	01-Mar-13	MED	MEDICAL	BRNC DARTMOUTH	
Coates, Jonathan R	Lt RN	17-Dec-10	MED	MS	HQ JMC - COMD AND ADMIN	LICHFIELD
Coates, Philip J B	Surg Cdr	06-Dec-10	MED	Radiologist	MDHU DERRIFORD	PLYMOUTH
Coates, Thomas M	Lt RN	01-Sep-11	LOGS	L	HMS ENTERPRISE	
Coatsworth, Robert W	Lt RN	07-Jan-12	WAR	GSX	MCM2 CREW 3	PORTSMOUTH
Cobbett, James F	Lt Cdr	01-Oct-03	WAR	P SK4	FLEET AV VL - RNFSC	RNAS YEOVILTON
Cobley, Simon D	Mid	01-May-13	WAR	GSX	BRNC DARTMOUTH	
Cochrane, Christopher D	Lt RN	01-Sep-05	ENG	MESM	DES/COMFLEET	ABBEY WOOD
Cochrane, Matthew	Lt RN	01-Jan-13	ENG	AE	DTOEES TYPHOON AND THUNDERER	SOUTHAMPTON
Cochrane, Michael OBE (The Hon Michael Cochrane)	Cdre	25-Nov-08	WAR	PWO(N)	COMPORFLOT SEA	HMNB PORTSMOUTH
Cockcroft, Kim M	Lt RN	16-Jun-06	QARNNS	PHC	DEFAC JSCSC ICSCM	SHRIVENHAM SWINDON
Cocks, Anthony	Lt RN	01-Oct-07	ENG	AE	DES/COIR/CA/LIGHTNING	ARLINGTON USA
Codd, Justin S	Cdr	30-Jun-13	WAR	SM(CQ)	HMS AMBUSH	
Codling, Steven Jon	Lt RN	20-Oct-06	WAR	C	FLEET CAP IS DIVISION	NCHQ
Coe, Ian Lowrey	Lt RN	01-Jan-13	ENG	WESM	HMS VENGEANCE	
Coetzee, Rikus H	Surg Cdr	01-Jul-13	MED	Psych	DPHC SOUTH - DCMH	PORTSMOUTH
Coffey, Ralph B	Lt Cdr	01-Oct-12	ENG	MESM	DES/COMFLEET	ABBEY WOOD
Cogan, Robert	Lt Cdr	01-Oct-04	LOGS	L	101 LOG BDE JFSP	ALDERSHOT
Cogdell, Michael R	Lt RN	01-Sep-13	ENG	WESM	HMS RALEIGH	
Coghill, Adrian	Lt Cdr	01-Oct-13	WAR	INT	ATTACHE/ADVISER MOSCOW	
Colarusso, Barry L	Capt	30-Mar-12	RM	SCC	CDO LOG REGT RM	BARNSTAPLE
Cole, Claire V	Surg Lt Cdr (D)	29-Jun-05	DENTAL	GDP	HMS NELSON	HMS NELSON
Cole, Michael D	Capt	01-Sep-13	RM	GS	LFSS CDO LOG REGT RM	BARNSTAPLE
Cole, Simon Philip	Cdr	30-Jun-08	ENG	WE	DCD - MODSAP LONDON	LONDON
Coleman, Alexander P G	Lt RN	01-Jul-07	WAR	GSX	MCM2 CREW 6	PORTSMOUTH
Coleman, Gareth W	Lt RN	01-Sep-07	LOGS	L SM	DES/COMFLEET	ABBEY WOOD
Coleman, James M	Lt RN	01-Nov-05	WAR	P CDO	RAF SHAWBURY	
Coleman, Joseph M	SLt	15-Aug-12	WAR	SM(X)	MCM1	FASLANE
Coles, Adam J	Lt Cdr	01-Oct-13	WAR	HM(AS)	HMS GLEANER	
Coles, Andrew L OBE	Cdr	30-Jun-03	WAR	SM(CQ)	DES/COMFLEET	HMS DRAKE
Coles, Christopher	Lt Cdr	01-May-08	ENG	AE	HQ JHC	ANDOVER
Coles, Christopher J	Cdr	30-Jun-06	ENG	MESM	DES/COMFLEET	HMS DRAKE
Coles, Simon P	Lt Cdr	01-Oct-10	ENG	TM	FLEET FOST TBTU	HMS COLLINGWOOD
Coles-Hendry, Frances A	Lt Cdr	01-Oct-12	LOGS	L	CAREER TRAINING	HMS NELSON
Coles-Hendry, Hamish R	Lt RN	20-Oct-08	WAR	P SK4	NO 3 FTS/UAS - JEFTS	
Collacott, Jonathan	Lt Cdr	01-Oct-05	LOGS	L SM	DES/COMFLEET	ABBEY WOOD
Collen, Sara J	Lt Cdr	01-Dec-09	WAR	MEDIA OPS	FLEET CMR	NCHQ
Collett, Stuart M	Surg Cdr	14-Dec-09	MED	GMP (C&S)	DPHC SOUTH	HMS COLLINGWOOD
Colley, Ian P	Lt Cdr	01-Oct-11	ENG	WESM(TWS)	HMS TRIUMPH	
Collie, James A	Lt Cdr	01-Oct-13	WAR	PWO(SM)	HMS VANGUARD	
Collier, James R	Lt RN	01-Sep-07	ENG	MESM	HMS SULTAN - ND	HMS SULTAN
Collin, Martin E	Lt Col	30-Jun-12	RM	GS	STRIKFORNATO LISBON	LISBON
Collings, Antony B	SLt	01-May-13	WAR	C	BRNC DARTMOUTH	
Collins, Andrew C	Lt Cdr	01-Oct-13	WAR	O LYNX	AWC BSD - RW TES	RAF BOSCOMBE DOWN
Collins, Charles A	Lt RN	01-Nov-06	WAR	GSX	MWS COLLINGWOOD	
Collins, Christopher J	Lt RN	09-Apr-12	WAR	SM(X)	HMS VANGUARD	
Collins, Dale A	Lt Cdr	01-Oct-08	ENG	AE	RNAS CULDROSE - AED HQ	RNAS CULDROSE
Collins, David	Lt Cdr	01-Oct-09	ENG	TM	JFC - DCTS (H)	RAF HALTON

Person Name	Substantive Rank	Seniority	Branch	Specialisation	Organisation	Location
Collins, David I	Lt Cdr	01-Oct-12	LOGS	L	FLEET SPT LOGS INFRA DIVISION	NORTHWOOD
Collins, Jason D	Lt RN	11-Oct-13	WAR	SM(X)	CAREER TRAINING	HMS RALEIGH
Collins, John	Maj	01-Oct-06	RM	GS	EXCHANGE OFFICERS AUSTRALIA	
Collins, Lorna Jane	Lt RN	01-Mar-02	ENG	TM	FLEET FOSNNI - CNR	PORTSMOUTH
Collins, Mark	Lt RN	01-May-04	ENG	TM	MWS COLLINGWOOD - TS	HMS COLLINGWOOD
Collins, Paul	Lt Cdr	01-Sep-95	ENG	WESM(SWS)	DES/COMFLEET	WASHINGTON
Collins, Peter S	Mid	19-Apr-13	LOGS	L	BRNC DARTMOUTH	DARTMOUTH
Collins, Richard D	Lt RN	07-Aug-13	ENG	ME	HMS DEFENDER	
Collins, Simon H	Lt RN	01-Jan-11	WAR	GSX	30 CDO IX GP RM	PLYMOUTH
Collins, Simon J P	Lt Cdr	01-Oct-09	WAR	O LYNX	LHF 700W SQN	RNAS YEOVILTON
Collins, Stephen J	Lt RN	01-Nov-08	WAR	P GR7	FLEET CSAV	WASHINGTON
Collins, Tamar L	Lt Cdr	01-Oct-07	ENG	IS	FLEET FOST ACOS(Trg)	NCHQ
Collis, Martin J	Lt Cdr	01-Oct-09	ENG	ME	COMPORFLOT ESG	PORTSMOUTH
Colman, Adam J	Lt RN	01-Apr-12	WAR	GSX	MCM1 CREW 3	FASLANE
Colohan, Sam C	Lt RN	01-Sep-13	WAR	O UT	RNAS CULDROSE	
Colthart, Lee	SLt	01-Apr-12	WAR	GSX	HMS PROTECTOR	
Coltman, Timothy P	Surg Cdr	08-Oct-08	MED	T&O	MDHU PORTSMOUTH	PORTSMOUTH
Colvin, Michael A T	Lt RN	01-May-04	WAR	GSX	MWS COLLINGWOOD	
Concarr, David T	Lt RN	19-Sep-99	CS	CS	FOSNNI NRC NEE - NEW	NEWCASTLE UPON TYNE
Congreve, Steven C	Maj	01-May-00	RM	GS	CTCRM - CW	EXMOUTH
Conlin, John	Lt Cdr	01-Oct-08	WAR	PWO(U)	RN EXCHANGE USA - BDS	WASHINGTON
Connaughton, Mark A	SLt	14-Aug-11	ENG	WESM	RALEIGH	HMS RALEIGH
Conneely, Steven	Lt Cdr	01-Oct-07	ENG	WE	RN EXCHANGE USA - BDS	WASHINGTON
Connell, Martin J	Capt RN	05-Sep-11	WAR	O LYNX	CDS	MAIN BUILDING LONDON
Connolly, Christopher J	Cdr	31-Dec-00	WAR	PWO(A)	HMS NELSON	
Connolly, Michael H	Lt RN	20-Oct-97	CS	CS	FLEET FOSNNI - CNR	HMNB PORTSMOUTH
Connolly, Sean P	Capt	01-Sep-09	RM	GS	OPTAG HQ - I&STAT	FOLKESTONE
Connor, Daniel J	Surg Cdr	30-Jun-04	MED	Anaes	MDHU PORTSMOUTH	PORTSMOUTH
Conran, Nicholas W	Lt RN	01-Jan-03	LOGS	L SM	ACDS DEFLOGPOL	ABBEY WOOD
Conroy, David A	RN Chpln	24-Sep-00	Ch S		HMS ILLUSTRIOUS	
Considine, Keith J	Lt RN	01-Feb-00	WAR	P SK4	NO 3 FTS/UAS - JEFTS	
Constable, Thomas	Lt RN	01-Sep-08	ENG	AE	'ABBEY WOOD BRISTOL	
Conway, Keith A Rd	Lt Cdr	31-Mar-99	WAR	MW (RES)	FLEET FOSNNI - NRC	HMS CALEDONIA
Conway, Suzy H	Lt Cdr	01-Mar-07	LOGS	L	DMLS	HMS RALEIGH
Coogan, Thomas	Lt RN	09-Jun-06	ENG	MESM	HMS VANGUARD	
Cook, Christopher B	Cdr	30-Jun-08	ENG	IS	NCHQ CNPS	PORTSMOUTH
Cook, David J	Lt Cdr	01-Oct-97	WAR	O SK6	HQ AIR - COS(TRG) - DFT	ABBEY WOOD
Cook, Gordon E	Lt Cdr	01-Oct-00	WAR	O LYNX	815 SQN B SECTION	RNAS YEOVILTON
Cook, Myles F	Lt Col	30-Jun-07	RM	C	STRAT ACDS DC&D	SHRIVENHAM SWINDON
Cook, Timothy A	Lt Col	30-Jun-08	RM	C	NATO - BRUSSELS - NSA	BRUSSELS (MONS)
Cooke, Benjamin R	Lt RN	01-Apr-10	ENG	WESM(TWS)	MWS COLLINGWOOD	
Cooke, Graham S	Lt Cdr	01-Oct-04	WAR	O LYNX	750 SQN SEAHAWK	RNAS CULDROSE
Cooke, James R	Lt RN	01-Apr-12	LOGS	L	847 SQN - AE	RNAS YEOVILTON
Cooke, Joanne M	Surg Lt Cdr	02-Aug-05	MED	GS	INM ALVERSTOKE	GOSPORT
Cooke, Jonathan E	Cdr	30-Jun-12	WAR	PWO(U)	FLEET CAP RCAP DIVISION	NCHQ
Cooke, Stephen N	Lt RN	01-Jan-02	WAR	P LYNX	AWC BSD - RW TES	RAF BOSCOMBE DOWN
Cooke, Stuart Luke	SLt	01-Feb-12	WAR	O UT	BRNC DARTMOUTH	
Cooke-Priest, Nicholas	Cdr	30-Jun-10	WAR	O LYNX	FMC - NAVY	MAIN BUILDING LONDON
Cooley, Jeannine	Lt RN	01-May-04	WAR	PWO	HMS ARGYLL	
Coomber, Jonathan M	Maj	01-Sep-01	RM	MLDR	HMS ILLUSTRIOUS	
Coombes, George W	SLt	01-May-12	LOGS	L	BRNC DARTMOUTH	
Coomer, Adam	Mid	01-Nov-13	LOGS	L	BRNC DARTMOUTH	
Coope, Philip J	Lt Cdr	01-Mar-03	ENG	WE	FLEET ACOS(RP)	ABBEY WOOD
Cooper, Charlotte E	Lt RN	01-May-13	LOGS	L	HMS ILLUSTRIOUS	
Cooper, Darren T	Lt RN	01-Nov-07	WAR	MCD	MCM2 CREW 4	PORTSMOUTH
Cooper, Edwin	Lt Cdr	01-Oct-13	WAR	O MER	829 SQN FLT 01	RNAS CULDROSE
Cooper, Jack W	Lt RN	01-Sep-10	WAR	GSX	DEF LANG SCHOOL	BEACONSFIELD
Cooper, Janette L	Lt Cdr	01-Oct-11	QARNNS	PHC	HMS NELSON	
Cooper, John C	Lt RN	09-Apr-09	ENG	MESM	HMS TALENT	
Cooper, John D	Lt RN	09-Apr-09	LOGS	L	845 SQN	RNAS YEOVILTON
Cooper, Mark A	Capt RN	11-Oct-11	WAR	SM(CQ)	NATO COMND HQ	NORTHWOOD
Cooper, Michael A	Lt RN	01-Feb-09	WAR	P MER	829 SQN FLT 04	RNAS CULDROSE

Person Name	Substantive Rank	Seniority	Branch	Specialisation	Organisation	Location
Cooper, Michael P.	Maj	01-Oct-12	RM	SCC	NCHQ CNPERS	PORTSMOUTH
Cooper, Neil	Maj	01-Oct-05	RM	SCC	CTCRM - CORPS COL	EXMOUTH
Cooper-Simpson, Roger J	Lt Col	30-Jun-07	RM	C	DIRECTOR (JW)	NORTHWOOD
Copeland, Niall	Lt RN	01-Sep-10	ENG	WE	MWS COLLINGWOOD	HMS COLLINGWOOD
Copeland, Stephen N.	Cdr	30-Jun-11	ENG	AE	DES/COIR/DAT/ABW	ABBEY WOOD
Copinger-Symes, Rory S	Col	14-Sep-09	RM	HW	STRIKFORNATO - LISBON	LISBON
Coppin, Nigel J	Lt RN	01-Jan-03	LOGS	L SM	AIR 22GP - LYNEHAM	RAF LYNEHAM
Copsey, Nicholas R B	Maj	01-Oct-10	RM	GS	43 CDO	HMNB CLYDE
Corbett, Andrew S	Cdr	30-Jun-03	WAR	SM(CQ)	NATO - BRUSSELS	
Corbett, Thomas J.	Lt Cdr	01-Oct-05	WAR	AAWO	UKRBATSTAFF	HMNB PORTSMOUTH
Corbidge, Stephen J MBE	Lt Col	30-Jun-07	RM	SCC	STONEHOUSE	PLYMOUTH
Corden, Adam	Lt RN	01-Jan-12	WAR	GSX	HMS CLYDE	
Corder, Ian F Cb	V Adm	30-May-13	WAR	SM(CQ)	NATO - BRUSSELS	BRUSSELS
Corderoy, John	Cdre	02-Sep-13	ENG	MESM	DES/COMFLEET	BRISTOL
Core, Emily E	Lt RN	01-Apr-13	WAR	HM	CTF 150	HMNB PORTSMOUTH
Cormack, Andrew	Surg Cdr	01-Jul-10	MED	GMP (C&S)	HQ 3 CDO BDE RM	PLYMOUTH
Cornell, Jonathan D	Surg Lt RN	07-Aug-13	MED	MEDICAL	BRNC DARTMOUTH	
Corness, Andrew S	RN Chpln	06-Sep-04	Ch S			HMS COLLINGWOOD
Cornford, Marc	Lt Cdr	01-Oct-10	WAR	P LYN7	CHFHQ (SEA)	RNAS YEOVILTON
Cornhill, Sharon T	Lt RN	12-Jul-10	QARNNS	Infection C	DMSTG	BIRMINGHAM
Corps, Stephen	Lt Cdr	11-Nov-98	ENG	WE	COMPORFLOT	PORTSMOUTH
Corrigan, Niall R.	Capt RN	30-Jun-06	WAR	PWO(A)	NATO-NCSA-NCSA HQ	BRUSSELS
Corrin, Colby St John	Lt Col	30-Jun-10	RM	MLDR	RN EXCHANGE USA	WASHINGTON
Cory, Nicholas John	Lt Cdr	01-Oct-10	WAR	INT	JSSU CH - HQ	CHELTENHAM
Coryton, Oliver C	Maj	01-Oct-09	RM	GS	42 CDO RM - L COY	PLYMOUTH
Coryton, Sophie C	Lt Cdr	01-Oct-10	LOGS	L	HMS NELSON	
Cosby, Max A.	Lt RN	01-Sep-12	WAR	O UT	RNAS CULDROSE	
Costley-White, Benjamin M	Lt RN	01-Jul-11	WAR	GSX	HMS KENT	
Cottee, Benjamin R J	Lt Cdr	01-Sep-06	WAR	ATC	D AIR P	LONDON
Cotterill, Bruce M.	Cdr	30-Jun-11	ENG	WESM(TWS)	DES/COMLAND	USA
Cottis, Mathew C	Cdr	30-Jun-13	LOGS	L SM	DES/COMLAND	ABBEY WOOD
Cotton, Alan	Capt	18-Jul-08	RM	C (SCC)	42 CDO RM - COMD COY	PLYMOUTH
Cottrell, Ralph	Maj	01-Oct-13	RM	GS	DEFAC JSCSC ICSCL A S	SHRIVENHAM SWINDON
Coughlin, Emma J	Lt RN	18-Jan-05	WAR	HM	RNAS CULDROSE	RNAS CULDROSE
Coughlin, Peter J.	Lt RN	01-Oct-05	WAR	O MER	814 SQN	RNAS CULDROSE
Coulson, Neil A	RN Chpln	01-Jul-08	Ch S	Chaplain	FWO PORTS SEA	HMNB PORTSMOUTH
Coulson, Peter	Capt RN	18-Oct-11	ENG	WE	COMDEVFLOT ESG	HMS DRAKE
Coultas, Daniel	Lt RN	01-Sep-13	WAR	SM(X)	HMS CLYDE OFFICERS	PORTSMOUTH
Coulthard, Adrian J	Lt Cdr	11-May-03	ENG	TM	HQ DISC	SHEFFORD
Counter, Paul R	Surg Cdr	01-Aug-09	MED	ORL	MDHU NORTHALLERTON	NORTHALLERTON
Court, Matthew R.	Lt RN	01-Nov-07	WAR	PWO(SM)	HMS TRIUMPH	
Court, Nicholas J.	Lt RN	01-Jan-09	WAR	MW	MCM1 CREW 2	FASLANE
Court, Shane J	Lt RN	24-Oct-08	ENG	AE	OCLC PLYMOUTH	BRISTOL
Courtier, Robert N.	Capt	01-Mar-11	RM	GS	43 CDO FPGRM S SQN	HMNB CLYDE
Courtney, Timothy	Lt RN	01-May-03	ENG	MESM	HMS SULTAN	HMS SULTAN
Coutts, Maxwell G	Lt RN	22-Mar-10	LOGS	L	FLEET SPT LOGS INFRA	NCHQ
Coutts, Phoebe H.	SLt	01-Feb-11	WAR	HM	HMS SOMERSET	
Couzens, Robert F	Lt RN	01-Sep-08	WAR	GSX	HMS WESTMINSTER	
Coventry, Andrew J	Capt	16-Apr-09	RM	SCC	CTCRM - CTW	EXMOUTH
Coverdale, Paul	Lt Cdr	01-Oct-06	WAR	PWO HM	HMS COLLINGWOOD	
Cowan, Christopher D	Lt RN	01-May-13	WAR	GSX	HMS MERSEY	
Cowan, Peter W	Lt Cdr	20-Jul-13	WAR	GSX	RN EXCHANGE NETHERLANDS	DEN HELDER
Coward, Suzanne L	Surg Lt RN (D)	29-Jun-09	DENTAL	GDP	DEFENCE DENTAL SERVS	HMNB PORTSMOUTH
Cowie, Andrew D	Lt Cdr	01-Oct-12	ENG	WE	DES/COMLAND	ABBEY WOOD
Cowie, Michael	Lt RN	19-Oct-07	WAR	INT	NATO-ACO-JFC HQ	NAPLES
Cowlishaw, Nicholas D	Lt RN	01-Jul-04	WAR	ATC	HMS BULWARK	
Cox, David J	Cdr	30-Jun-09	ENG	WE	DCDS PERS TRG	MAIN BUILDING LONDON
Cox, David W.	Capt	01-Sep-12	RM	GS	CHFHQ (SEA)	RNAS YEOVILTON
Cox, Mark A	Capt	28-Jul-06	RM	GS	NCHQ	
Cox, Mark B.	Cdr	30-Jun-13	LOGS	L	NCHQ CNPS	MAIN BUILDING LONDON
Cox, Matthew J	Lt Cdr	01-Oct-13	ENG	WE	FLEET CAP IS DIVISION	NCHQ
Cox, Michael	Lt Cdr	01-Oct-10	WAR	INT	JFIG - JT OPS	RAF WYTON

Person Name	Substantive Rank	Seniority	Branch	Specialisation	Organisation	Location
Cox, Pieter W S	Cdr	30-Jun-93	ENG	WESM(SWS)	CBRN POL	MAIN BUILDING LONDON
Cox, Rex J	Cdr	30-Jun-09	WAR	AAWO	FMC - STRAT N	MAIN BUILDING LONDON
Cox, Sean Adrian J	Lt Cdr	01-Oct-05	WAR	P LYN7	HMS OCEAN	
Cox, Simon James	Lt Cdr	01-Oct-11	WAR	PWO	FLEET COMOPS NWD	NORTHWOOD
Cox, Simon T	Maj	01-Oct-13	RM	GS	DEFAC JSCSC	SHRIVENHAM SWINDON
Cox, Stephen	Capt	16-Apr-10	RM	SCC	CTCRM - MTS	EXMOUTH
Coyle, Gavin J	Cdr	30-Jun-12	WAR	PWO(U)	HMS NELSON	
Coyle, Ross D	Lt RN	01-May-02	ENG	WE	DES/COMFLEET	ABBEY WOOD BRISTOL
Coyne, Paul E	SLt	03-Jan-12	WAR	SM(X)	BRNC DARTMOUTH	
Cozens, Christopher J	Lt RN	01-Sep-08	ENG	ME	HMS PROTECTOR	
Crabb, Antony J	Lt Cdr	01-Oct-04	WAR	PWO(U)	UKRBATSTAFF	HMNB PORTSMOUTH
Cragg, Richard D	Lt Cdr	01-Oct-04	ENG	MESM	COMDEVFLOT SHORE	HMNB DEVONPORT
Craig, Alexander P	Lt RN	01-May-09	WAR	P SK4	845 SQN	RNAS YEOVILTON
Craig, David	Lt RN	19-Oct-07	WAR	C	NATO-ACT-HQ SACT	NORFOLK
Craig, John	Cdr	30-Jun-09	WAR	MCD PWO(U)	RN EXCHANGE USA	WASHINGTON
Craig, Kenneth M	Maj	01-May-01	RM	HW	NATO-ACT-HQ SACT	NORFOLK
Craig, Michael J	Lt RN	01-May-03	WAR	P SK4	CHFHQ (SEA)	RNAS YEOVILTON
Crallan, Alexander	Mid	01-Sep-13	WAR	GSX	BRNC DARTMOUTH	
Crane, Danielle L	Surg Lt RN	04-Aug-10	MED	GDMO	HMS DRAKE	
Crane, Oliver R	Lt RN	01-Oct-98	WAR	P SK4	COMUKTG SEA	PLYMOUTH
Craner, Matthew MB	Surg Cdr	30-Jun-04	MED	Neurology	MDHU FRIMLEY PARK	FRIMLEY
Craven, Dale	Lt Cdr	01-Oct-09	ENG	WESM(SWS)	NBC CLYDE	HELENSBURGH
Craven, Martin W	Lt Cdr	01-Oct-09	WAR	P LYNX	LHF 702 SQN	RNAS YEOVILTON
Craven, Oliver E	Lt Cdr	01-Oct-13	WAR	GSX	HMS NELSON	HMS NELSON
Crawford, Alistair A	Lt RN	01-Nov-07	WAR	P LYNX	LHF 815 SQN FLT 239	RNAS YEOVILTON
Crawford, Jonathan B	Lt RN	11-Apr-08	WAR	AV	RNAS YEOVILTON	
Creaney, Anthony P	Capt	16-Apr-10	RM	SCC	NCHQ CNPERS	PORTSMOUTH
Crease, David A	Lt RN	09-Apr-09	ENG	ME	HMS SCOTT	
Crease, Peter S	Lt RN	01-Apr-13	WAR	P UT	RFA SHAWBURY	
Creasey, Andrew D	Capt	01-Sep-10	RM	GS	SFSG C COY	RAF ST ATHAN
Cree, Andrew	Capt RN	03-Jan-12	ENG	TM	JFC - DCTS (H)	RAF HALTON
Cree, Malcolm C	R Adm	07-Oct-13	WAR	PWO(A) AAWO		NAVY ICP NCHQ
Creedon, Timothy D	Mid	01-Nov-13	WAR	O UT	BRNC DARTMOUTH	DARTMOUTH
Creek, Stephen B	Lt RN	01-Jan-02	ENG	WESM(TWS)	DES/COMFLEET	HMS DRAKE
Cresdee, Samuel	SLt	01-Sep-13	WAR	SM(X)	MWS COLLINGWOOD	HMS COLLINGWOOD
Crew, Julian M	Lt RN	01-Jan-00	WAR	P LYNX	WMO YEOVILTON	RNAS YEOVILTON
Crewdson, Robert P	Lt RN	01-Feb-09	WAR	O MER	820 SQN	RNAS CULDROSE
Crichton, Gary S	Lt Cdr	01-Oct-11	WAR	PWO	DI - CA	LONDON
Criddle, Gary D MBE	Cdr	30-Jun-12	WAR	O LYNX	CAREER TRAINING	FRANCE
Crier, Matthew J	SLt	01-May-12	WAR	O UT	BRNC DARTMOUTH	
Cripps, Michael J	Lt Cdr	01-Oct-12	ENG	AE	RN EXCHANGE CANADA	OTTAWA 1
Cripps, Nicola	Lt RN	01-Jan-04	ENG	TM	JFC - DCTS (H)	RAF HALTON
Crispin, Toby A B	Lt Cdr	01-Apr-94	WAR	O SK6	AWC BSD - RW TES	RAF BOSCOMBE DOWN
Critchley, Ian J	Lt Cdr	01-Oct-13	WAR	PWO(SM)	HMS CHARGER	
Critchlow, Angela J	Surg Lt RN (D)	27-Jul-09	DENTAL	GDP	MDHU PORTSMOUTH	PORTSMOUTH
Crockatt, Stephen R J	Lt Cdr	01-Oct-03	WAR	P LYNX	AWC BSD - TEST & EVALUATION	RAF BOSCOMBE DOWN
Crofts, David J	Lt Cdr	01-Feb-99	ENG	WE	EU OHQ	BRUSSELS
Crombie, Stuart	Lt RN	01-Sep-05	WAR	O LYNX	NATO-ACO-JFC HQ	NAPLES
Cromie, John M	Lt Cdr	01-Oct-08	WAR	AAWO	MWS COLLINGWOOD	
Crompton, Lynne	Lt Cdr	01-Oct-13	WAR	ATC	HMS ILLUSTRIOUS	
Crompton, Philip J	Lt RN	01-Nov-00	WAR	P LYNX	LHF HQ	RNAS YEOVILTON
Crook, Daniel S	Lt RN	09-Apr-13	ENG	WE	HMS ST ALBANS	
Crook, Richard	Lt RN	01-Sep-07	ENG	MESM	DES/COMFLEET	ABBEY WOOD
Crooks, Charles S	Lt RN	01-Mar-11	ENG	MESM	HMS ASTUTE	
Cropper, Martin A K	Lt Cdr	16-May-90	LOGS	L SM	FLEET HQ	NCHQ
Crosbie, Donald E F	Cdr	30-Jun-09	WAR	MCD PWO(U)	FDS HQ	PORTSMOUTH
Crosby, David W M	Lt Cdr	01-Oct-11	WAR	SM(CQ)	HMS TRIUMPH	
Cross, Aaron	Lt RN	01-Jun-12	WAR	P SK4	845 SQN	RNAS YEOVILTON
Cross, Alexander	Lt Cdr	01-Oct-05	ENG	WESM(TWS)	FLEET CAP SSM DIVISION	NCHQ
Cross, Andrew G	Maj	01-Oct-08	RM	SCC	STRIKFORNATO - LISBON	LISBON
Cross, Eric John	Capt	01-Jan-02	RM	P SK4	771 SQN	RNAS CULDROSE
Cross, Nicholas	Lt RN	01-Jul-02	ENG	IS	FLEET CISSU	NCHQ

Person Name	Substantive Rank	Seniority	Branch	Specialisation	Organisation	Location
Crossey, Matthew D	Lt Cdr	01-Oct-13	ENG	TM	FOST DPORT SHORE	HMNB DEVONPORT
Crossley, Heather C	Mid	01-Sep-13	ENG	ME	BRNC DARTMOUTH	DARTMOUTH
Crosswood, Barry T	Lt RN	01-Jan-12	WAR	GSX	MCM2 CREW 2	PORTSMOUTH
Crouch, Benjamin R	Lt RN	01-May-10	LOGS	L	DES/COMFLEET	HMNB PORTSMOUTH
Crow, Jonathan G	Capt	01-Sep-11	RM	GS	SFSG C COY	RAF ST ATHAN
Crowley, James R	Lt	01-Sep-12	RM	GS	42 CDO RM	PLYMOUTH
Crowsley, Francesca C	Lt RN	01-Sep-12	WAR	HM	CAREER TRAINING	HMS DRAKE
Crowson, Elizabeth	Surg Cdr	04-Aug-08	MED	GMP (C&S)	DEFAC JSCSC ACSC	SHRIVENHAM SWINDON
Croxton, Damien P	Lt Cdr	01-Oct-13	LOGS	L	PJHQ (UK) J6	NORTHWOOD
Crozier, Stuart R	Cdr	30-Jun-01	LOGS	L BAR	DCDS PERS - SPA	RAF NORTHOLT
Crump, Alexander I	Capt	01-Sep-09	RM	GS	COMUKAMPHIBFOR	HMNB PORTSMOUTH
Crundell, Richard	Lt Cdr	01-Jul-00	ENG	WE	DES/COMLAND	ABBEY WOOD
Cryar, Timothy M C	Cdr	30-Jun-05	WAR	AAWO	UK MCC	BAHRAIN
Cuff, Samuel H	Lt RN	01-Sep-08	ENG	AE	WMF SHORE	RNAS YEOVILTON
Cull, Iain	Cdr	30-Jun-09	WAR	PWO(N)	NCHQ CNPERS	PORTSMOUTH
Cullen, Donna M	Lt RN	01-Sep-08	WAR	GSX	DCSU	RAF HENLOW
Cullen, Matthew R	Lt RN	01-May-13	LOGS	L	DES/COMFLEET	HMS DRAKE
Cullen, Nicola L	Lt Cdr	01-Oct-06	ENG	TM	RNCR BOVINGTON	WAREHAM
Cullingford, Richard M	Lt RN	01-Jan-13	WAR	P UT	RNAS YEOVILTON	RNAS YEOVILTON
Culwick, Peter F	Surg Capt RN (D)	07-Mar-11	DENTAL	GDP(C&S)	DMS WHITTINGTON	LICHFIELD
Cumming, Frazer S	Lt RN	01-Sep-03	WAR	O SKW	RNAS CULDROSE	
Cummings, Alan	Cdr	30-Jun-07	WAR	O SK6	SHRIVENHAM	
Cummings, Darren	Lt Cdr	01-Oct-13	MED	MS(SM)	COMDEVFLOT	HMS DRAKE
Cummings, David J	Lt Cdr	01-Nov-02	ENG	WE	HMS NELSON	
Cunane, John Ri	Lt Cdr	01-Oct-98	LOGS	L SM	DES/COMLAND	ABBEY WOOD BRISTOL
Cunnell, Rachael L	Lt Cdr	01-Oct-10	LOGS	L	RNAS YEOVILTON	
Cunningham, Dexter A	Lt RN	01-Sep-13	ENG	WE	NCHQ	
Cunningham, John	Cdr	30-Jun-03	WAR	O LYNX	DEFENCE ACADEMY	SHRIVENHAM SWINDON
Cunningham, Matthew S	Mid	01-May-13	LOGS	L	BRNC DARTMOUTH	
Cunningham, Nigel J W	Lt Cdr	01-Oct-03	WAR	O LYNX	RNAS YEOVILTON	RNAS YEOVILTON
Cunningham, Rachel A	Lt RN	01-Jan-03	ENG	WE	FLEET CMR	NCHQ
Curd, Michael C	Lt RN	01-Jan-05	WAR	O LYNX	LHF 815 SQN HQ	RNAS YEOVILTON
Curnock, Timothy C	Lt RN	01-Jan-07	WAR	O SKW	849 SQN	RNAS CULDROSE
Currass, Timothy	Cdr	30-Jun-07	ENG	WE	DES/COMFLEET	ABBEY WOOD BRISTOL
Currie, Duncan G	Lt Cdr	16-Dec-01	WAR	P SKW	771 SQN	RNAS CULDROSE
Currie, Michael J	Lt Cdr	01-Oct-08	WAR	O MER	814 SQN	RNAS CULDROSE
Currie, Stephen	Lt RN	01-Sep-09	ENG	TM	HMS SULTAN - STG	HMS SULTAN
Currie, Stuart M	Cdr	30-Jun-12	ENG	MESM	COMFASFLOT	HMNB CLYDE
Currie, Victor A	Lt RN	08-Dec-12	WAR	P UT	RNAS YEOVILTON	
Currin, Joseph M	Lt RN	01-Apr-12	WAR	FC	HMS ILLUSTRIOUS	
Curry, Philip David	Lt RN	01-Mar-09	WAR	O SKW	857 NAS	RNAS CULDROSE
Curry, Robert E	Cdr	30-Jun-11	WAR	PWO(C)	JFC HOC C4ISR	NORTHWOOD
Cursiter, John D	Lt RN	12-Jun-05	WAR	PWO(SM)	HMS VIGILANT	
Curtis, Peter J MBE	Capt	24-Jul-04	RM	BS	RM BAND COLLINGWOOD	HMS COLLINGWOOD
Curtis, Rebecca	Lt RN	01-Sep-11	LOGS	L	NC PSYA	HMNB PORTSMOUTH
Curtis, Suzannah	Lt Cdr	01-Oct-06	LOGS	L	JFLogC	NORTHWOOD
Curwood, Jenny E	Lt Cdr	01-Oct-06	LOGS	L	COMPORFLOT WLSG SS	HMNB PORTSMOUTH
Cusack, Michael K	Lt RN	09-Apr-13	WAR	SM(X)	MWS COLLINGWOOD	HMS COLLINGWOOD
Cuthbert, Glen	Lt RN	01-May-04	ENG	TM	FOST DPORT SEA	HMNB DEVONPORT
Cutler, Andrew R	Lt Cdr	01-Oct-07	WAR	PWO	HMS KENT	
Cutler, David T	Lt RN	01-May-04	ENG	ME	HMS PROTECTOR	
Cutler, Liam Gary	Capt	01-Mar-11	RM	GS	SFSG F COY	RAF ST ATHAN

D

Person Name	Substantive Rank	Seniority	Branch	Specialisation	Organisation	Location
Dabell, Guy Lester	Capt RN	01-Oct-12	ENG	MESM	DES/COMFLEET	ABBEY WOOD
Dack, Simon B	Capt	01-Apr-11	RM	SCC	FLEET HQ 6	NCHQ
Dailey, Paul	Capt RN	27-Aug-10	ENG	WESM	DES/COMFLEET	ABBEY WOOD
Dainton, Steven CBE	Capt RN	26-Apr-10	WAR	PWO(C)	MWS COLLINGWOOD	
Dale, Alistair	Lt Cdr	01-Feb-06	WAR	ATC	RNAS YEOVILTON	
Dale, Jamie R	Lt RN	01-Apr-07	WAR	ATC	LATCC(MIL) AT SWANWICK	SOUTHAMPTON
Dale, Nathan A	Lt Cdr	01-Oct-13	WAR	P SK4	CHFHQ (SEA)	RNAS YEOVILTON
Dale, Rebecca A	SLt	01-Sep-13	QARNNS	Nursing Officer	BRNC DARTMOUTH	

Person Name	Substantive Rank	Seniority	Branch	Specialisation	Organisation	Location
Dale-Smith, Victoria G.	Lt Cdr	15-Mar-05	WAR	P SK4	849 SQN	RNAS CULDROSE
Dalgleish, Grant A.	Lt RN	01-May-04	WAR	PWO(N)	HMS ARGYLL	
Dalglish, Kenneth M	Lt RN	01-Sep-06	WAR	PWO(C)	JFC HOC C4ISR	NORTHWOOD
Dallamore, Rebecca A	Lt RN	01-Jan-01	WAR	INFO OPS	DCSU	RAF HENLOW
Dallas, Lewis I	Lt RN	01-Sep-05	ENG	MESM	NBC CLYDE BABCOCK	HELENSBURGH
Dalrymple, James	Lt RN	01-Apr-10	WAR	SM(N)	HMS TORBAY	
Dalton, Ebony	Lt RN	01-May-09	WAR	INT	FLEET COMOPS NWD	HMS COLLINGWOOD
Dalton, Mark F.	RN Chpln	12-Jan-03	Ch S		NEPTUNE 2SL/CNH - CHAP	HELENSBURGH
Dalton, Sally A	Lt RN	01-Oct-08	WAR	TM	FLEET FOST ACOS(Trg)	ABBEY WOOD
Daly, Christopher D	Lt RN	01-Jun-08	WAR	GSX	HMS RICHMOND	
Danbury, Ian Gerald	Cdr	30-Jun-98	ENG	WE	DI - CA	LONDON
Dando, Benjamin J	Lt RN	01-Sep-09	WAR	O LYNX	LHF 815 SQN HQ	RNAS YEOVILTON
Dando, Jonathon N.	Lt Cdr	01-Aug-00	WAR	PWO(A)	FLEET COMOPS NWD	NORTHWOOD
Daniel, Benjamin J E	Lt Cdr	01-Oct-12	WAR	P SK4	RNAS YEOVILTON	
Daniell, Christopher J	Lt Cdr	01-Oct-95	WAR	O SKW	750 SQN SEAHAWK	RNAS CULDROSE
Daniels, Josh	Mid	01-Nov-13	WAR	SM(X)	BRNC DARTMOUTH	DARTMOUTH
Daniels, Stuart P.	Lt Cdr	01-Oct-08	WAR	GSX	NATO-ACO-SHAPE	CASTEAU
Danks, Jonathan A.	Mid	01-Sep-13	ENG	AE	BRNC DARTMOUTH	
Darcy, John D	Lt RN	01-Nov-07	WAR	P SK4	845 SQN	RNAS YEOVILTON
D'Arcy, Paul A.	Lt Cdr	01-Oct-02	WAR	O LYNX	MOD DEFENCE STAFF	LONDON
Dare, Clifford R MBE	Maj	16-May-06	RM	GS (RES)	FLEET FOSNNI - NRC EE	LONDON
Darkins, Colin R	Lt Cdr	01-Oct-10	ENG	TM	NAVY CORE TRG HQ	HMNB DEVONPORT
Darley, Matthew E.	Maj	01-Oct-10	RM	P LYN7	DEFAC JSCSC	SHRIVENHAM SWINDON
Darlington, Alan	Lt RN	01-Sep-04	WAR	INT	FLEET COMOPS MDC	GIBRALTAR
Darlington, Mark R	Cdre	03-Feb-09	WAR	PWO(A)	DCDS PERS TRG-TESRR	MAIN BUILDING LONDON
Darlow, Paul R	Lt Cdr	01-Oct-02	LOGS	L	MWS COLLINGWOOD	
Dart, Duncan J	Lt RN	01-Sep-04	WAR	P CDO	CHF(MERLIN)	RAF BENSON
Dart, Michael P	Lt RN	01-Sep-08	WAR	ATC	RAF SHAWBURY	
Darwell, Joseph F	SLt	01-Sep-12	WAR	GSX	BRNC DARTMOUTH	
Dathan, Timothy J.	Cdr	30-Jun-08	ENG	ME	DES/COMFLEET	ABBEY WOOD BRISTOL
Daveney, David	Lt Cdr	01-Oct-05	WAR	SM(CQ)	RN EXCHANGE USA	WASHINGTON
Davey, Alistair J	Lt RN	08-Jul-11	ENG	MESM	HMS AMBUSH	
Davey, Andrew J	Lt RN	01-Jan-12	WAR	GSX	HMS TYNE	
Davey, Kelly L	Surg Lt Cdr	02-Aug-10	MED	GMP	HMS NELSON	
Davey, Timothy	Lt Cdr	01-Oct-06	WAR	MCD PWO(U)	DEFAC JSCSC ACSC	SHRIVENHAM SWINDON
David, Ian	Lt RN	01-Aug-08	WAR	INT	JFIG - JT IP	RAF WYTON
David, Simon E J	Cdr	30-Jun-03	LOGS	L	2SL CNPT	NCHQ
Davidson, Gregor J	Lt RN	01-Jan-08	ENG	ME	CFPS SQUAD	HMNB PORTSMOUTH
Davidson, Mark R.	RN Chpln	01-May-07	Ch S	Chaplain	45 CDO RM	DUNDEE
Davidson, Matthew J	Lt	01-Sep-11	RM	GS	NCHQ	
Davidson, Neil R.	Lt Cdr	01-Oct-03	WAR	P CDO	CHF(MERLIN)	RAF BENSON
Davidson, Serena R	Lt RN	01-Oct-08	WAR	O SKW	857 NAS	RNAS CULDROSE
Davies, Alex	Lt RN	01-Jan-08	ENG	ME	HMS CLYDE	
Davies, Andrew C	Lt RN	15-Apr-11	ENG	ME	HMS DEFENDER	
Davies, Christopher J.	Cdr	30-Jun-02	WAR	MCD PWO(U)	FLEET CAP SSM DIVISION	NCHQ
Davies, Christopher R.	Maj	01-Oct-04	RM	GS	FLEET CAP LLM	NCHQ
Davies, Darren J	Lt Cdr	01-Oct-11	LOGS	L	HMS MONMOUTH	
Davies, Gary P.	Lt RN	12-Aug-90	ENG	MESM	FLEET SPT LOGS	NCHQ
Davies, Geraint W T	Lt Cdr	01-Oct-08	WAR	AAWO	HMS COLLINGWOOD	
Davies, Hazel	Lt RN	01-Sep-06	ENG	AE	RNAS YEOVILTON	
Davies, Huan C	Lt Col	30-Jun-13	RM	MLDR	43 CDO FPGRM COMD SQN	HMNB CLYDE
Davies, James S	Lt RN	01-Sep-06	ENG	AE	FLEET CSAV	YEOVIL
Davies, Jason L	Cdr	16-Jul-12	MED	MS	MED OP CAP	NORTHWOOD
Davies, John P	Lt RN	16-Dec-11	ENG	WE	HMS ILLUSTRIOUS	
Davies, Julia	Lt RN	01-Apr-10	WAR	P SK4	845 SQN	RNAS YEOVILTON
Davies, Lee	Lt Cdr	01-Jan-02	WAR	P LYNX	DMC	MAIN BUILDING LONDON
Davies, Lloyd R.	Mid	19-Apr-13	WAR	GSX	BRNC DARTMOUTH	
Davies, Luke M	Maj	01-Oct-11	RM	LC	HMS BULWARK	
Davies, Mark B.	Cdr	30-Jun-06	WAR	O LYNX	NATO-ACO-JFC HQ	NAPLES
Davies, Nathan R.	SLt	01-Nov-11	WAR	GSX	BRNC DARTMOUTH	
Davies, Neil	Lt RN	08-Feb-13	WAR	C	DES/COMJE/ISS	CORSHAM
Davies, Nicholas M S	Lt Cdr	01-Oct-08	WAR	HM	FLEET COMOPS NWD	NORTHWOOD

Person Name	Substantive Rank	Seniority	Branch	Specialisation	Organisation	Location
Davies, Ross	Capt	01-Sep-12	RM	GS	DHU - D COY	CHICKSANDS
Davies, Sarah J	Lt Cdr	01-Oct-12	WAR	PWO	MWS COLLINGWOOD	
Davis, Carl B	Mid	01-Feb-13	WAR	O UT	BRNC DARTMOUTH	
Davis, Edward G CBE	j Gen	28-Nov-11	RM	SBS	COMUKAMPHIBFOR	HMNB PORTSMOUTH
Davis, Ian P	Capt	03-Apr-09	RM	BS	HQ BAND SERVICE	HMS NELSON
Davis, Mark John	Lt RN	01-Sep-08	ENG	AE	849 SQN	RNAS CULDROSE
Davis, Mark S	Lt RN	27-Jul-07	ENG	AE	RNAS YEOVILTON - AED	RNAS YEOVILTON
Davis, Peter H	Lt RN	01-Sep-02	ENG	IS	NATO - BRUSSELS	BRUSSELS
Davis, Peter H	Lt RN	01-Sep-04	WAR	MCD	SDU 1	HMS DRAKE
Davis, Richard	Lt Cdr	01-Oct-13	ENG	WESM	DES/COMFLEET	ABBEY WOOD BRISTOL
Davis, Stephen R	Lt Cdr	01-Oct-05	ENG	WESM	FOST SM SEA	HELENSBURGH
Davison, Warren M	Lt RN	01-Jun-08	WAR	P CDO	CHF(MERLIN)	RAF BENSON
Daw, Arthur B	Lt RN	01-Feb-09	WAR	P MER	820 SQN	RNAS CULDROSE
Daw, Simon J	Lt Cdr	01-Oct-97	WAR	O SK6	771 SQN	RNAS CULDROSE
Daws, Richard P A	Capt RN	30-Jun-08	ENG	WESM	ACDS (POL) USA	NEBRASKA USA
Dawson, Alan	Lt Cdr	01-Oct-03	ENG	WESM	RNSMS	HMS RALEIGH
Dawson, Kris A	Capt	01-Sep-12	RM	GS	40 CDO RM	TAUNTON
Dawson, Nigel J F	Lt Cdr	01-Oct-03	ENG	TM	UNPOS	UGANDA
Dawson, Paul	Lt Cdr	01-Oct-06	ENG	MESM	HMS CALLIOPE	GATESHEAD
Dawson, William	Lt Cdr	01-Nov-98	WAR	AAWO	BFSAI - HQBFSAI	FALKLAND ISLANDS
Day, Anthony	Lt Cdr	01-Oct-09	WAR	REG	RNP - HQ PMN	HMS EXCELLENT
Day, Benjamin	Lt Cdr	01-Oct-12	WAR	HM	JFIG - IS	RAF WYTON
Day, Michael K	Lt Cdr	01-Oct-06	WAR	P SK4	848 SQN	RNAS YEOVILTON
Day, Paul A	Lt RN	27-May-10	WAR	GSX	HMS NELSON	
Day, Richard J	Lt RN	21-Dec-09	MED	MS(SM)	FLEET CAP SSM	NCHQ
De La Rue, Michael	Lt RN	01-Sep-13	WAR	SM(X)	MWS COLLINGWOOD	
De Reya, Anthony L	Lt Col	30-Jun-08	RM		JCTTAT HQ JCTTAT	FOLKESTONE
De Silva, Oliver A	Lt RN	01-Sep-07	LOGS	L SM	HMS NELSON	
De Velasco, Mari L	Lt Cdr	01-Oct-12	WAR	INT	HMS NELSON	
Deacon, Stephen	Cdr	01-Jun-07	WAR	O MER	HMS OCEAN	
Deakin, Johanna		30-Jun-13	ENG	AE	DCTT HQ	HMS SULTAN
Deakin, Scott M	Lt Cdr	01-Oct-13	ENG	WE	DES/COMFLEET	ABBEY WOOD
Deal, Charlotte	Lt Cdr	01-Oct-08	ENG	WE	FLEET CAP SSM	NCHQ
Dean, Adam C	Lt RN	01-Jun-10	WAR	P SK4	845 SQN	RNAS YEOVILTON
Dean, James R OBE	Cdr	30-Jun-09	LOGS	L	NCHQ CNPERS	PORTSMOUTH
Dean, Natasha C	SLt	01-Jun-13	MED	MEDICAL	BRNC DARTMOUTH	
Dean, Simon I R	Maj	01-Oct-09	RM	GS	42 CDO RM	HMNB DEVONPORT
Dean, Timothy	Surg Lt Cdr (D)	22-Jul-02	DENTAL	GDP	HMS RALEIGH	
Deaney, Mark N	Capt RN	16-Dec-11	ENG	AE	ABBEY WOOD BRISTOL	
De-Banks, Kyle	Lt RN	01-Sep-12	WAR	GSX	MCM1 CREW 5	FASLANE
Dechow, William E	Brig	21-Jun-11	RM	GS	NCHQ	
Deeks, Peter J	Lt Cdr	01-Oct-06	ENG	MESM	DES/COMFLEET	ABBEY WOOD
Deighton, Derek S	Lt Cdr	01-May-92	WAR	AAWO	DEFENCE ATTACHE FREETOWN	SIERRA LEONE
Deighton, Graeme	Lt Cdr	01-Oct-12	WAR	AW (RES)	HMS CALLIOPE	GATESHEAD
Dekker, Barrie J	Surg Cdr	30-Jun-06	MED	Anaes	MDHU PORTSMOUTH	PORTSMOUTH
Delahay, Jonathon E	Maj	01-Oct-08	RM		NCHQ CNPERS	PORTSMOUTH
Deller, Stephen A	Cdr	30-Jun-05	WAR	P SK6	FLEET HQ	NCHQ
De'Maine, Robert	Lt RN	01-Sep-07	WAR	P MER	829 SQN FLT 05	RNAS CULDROSE
Dempsey, Sean P	Lt Cdr	01-Feb-06	WAR	PWO(N)	FOST DPORT SEA	HMNB DEVONPORT
Dennard, Kieron J	Lt Cdr	01-Oct-13	ENG	ME	HMS OCEAN	
Denning, Oliver W	Maj	01-Oct-12	RM	GS	COMNDER FIELD ARMY	HMNB PORTSMOUTH
Dennis, Holly Anne	Lt RN	01-Nov-07	LOGS	L	HMS WESTMINSTER	
Dennis, James A	Maj	01-Oct-05	RM	C	PJHQ (UK) J5	NORTHWOOD
Dennis, Matthew J	Cdr	30-Jun-12	WAR	SM(CQ)	HMS VIGILANT	
Dennis, Philip MBE	Lt Cdr	01-Oct-13	WAR	AAWO	PJHQ (UK) J3	NORTHWOOD
Denniss, Jack A	2Lt	02-Sep-13	RM	N/A	CTCRM OFFICERS	EXMOUTH
Denny, Philip M	Lt RN	01-Apr-13	WAR	SM(X)	CAREER TRAINING	HMS RALEIGH
Dent, James Ian	Lt RN	01-Apr-13	WAR	SM(X)	CAREER TRAINING	HMS RALEIGH
Denyer, Alistair C	Lt RN	01-Jun-11	WAR	SM(N)	HMS TRIUMPH	
Deppe, Garth A	Lt RN	01-Sep-12	WAR	O UT	RNAS CULDROSE	
Derbyshire, Faye M	Lt RN	01-Sep-13	ENG	AE	FLEET HQ 6	NCHQ
Derrick, Matthew	Lt RN	01-Dec-99	ENG	TM	DEODS TRG	ANDOVER

Person Name	Substantive Rank	Seniority	Branch	Specialisation	Organisation	Location
De-Saint-Bissix-Croix, Anna Marie	Lt RN	13-Apr-10	QARNNS	OT	MDHU PORTSMOUTH	PORTSMOUTH
Desmond, Jake O	Lt RN	01-Sep-12	WAR	P UT	RNAS YEOVILTON	RNAS YEOVILTON
Despres, Julian Arrc	Lt Cdr	01-Oct-12	QARNNS	EN (C&S)	DMS WHITTINGTON	BIRMINGHAM
Devereux, Michael E	Maj	01-Sep-03	RM	P LYN7	849 SQN	RNAS CULDROSE
Devine, Alison	Lt RN	12-Feb-07	QARNNS	OT	HMS NEPTUNE	HELENSBURGH
Devine, Edward	Lt RN	09-Apr-13	WAR	O UT	MCM1 CREW 4	HELENSBURGH
Devlin, Craig	Lt RN	01-Jan-04	ENG	IS	ACNS CAP	NCHQ
Devonport, Sean S	Lt RN	01-Sep-10	ENG	AE	HMS SULTAN - ATG	HMS SULTAN
Dew, Anthony M	Surg Cdr	17-Jul-12	MED	GMP	HMS ILLUSTRIOUS	
Dewar, Duncan A	Col	31-Aug-09	RM	GS	NCHQ CNPERS	NCHQ
Dewey, Sarah E	Lt RN	01-Mar-06	QARNNS	EN	FLEET FOSNNI - CNR	HMNB PORTSMOUTH
Dewing, William T	SLt	01-Sep-11	WAR	GSX	BRNC DARTMOUTH	DARTMOUTH
Dewis, Ben M D	SLt	01-Sep-11	ENG	ME	DCEME SULTAN	HMS SULTAN
Dewynter, Alison	Surg Lt Cdr	06-Aug-09	MED	GMP	HMS RALEIGH	HMS RALEIGH
Di Maio, Mark D	Lt Cdr	01-Oct-09	LOGS	L C	UKRBATSTAFF	HMNB PORTSMOUTH
Diaper, Kevin S	SLt	01-Apr-11	WAR	FC	HMS DEFENDER	
Dible, James	Cdr	30-Jun-04	WAR	P LYNX	ATTACHE/ADVISER ROME	ROME ITALY
Dick, Colin M	Lt RN	01-Apr-00	WAR	PWO(SM)	HMS ASTUTE	
Dickie, Andrew K	Surg Lt Cdr	02-Aug-11	MED	GMP	DES/COMFLEET	FASLANE
Dickinson, Philip N	Lt Cdr	01-Jul-82	WAR	O SK6	NCHQ - CNLS	NCHQ
Dickson, Eric	SLt	01-May-12	WAR	SM(X)	BRNC DARTMOUTH	DARTMOUTH
Dickson, James I	Lt Cdr	01-Aug-02	LOGS	L SM	DES/COMFLEET	HMNB PORTSMOUTH
Dickson, Stuart J	Surg Cdr	30-Jun-07	MED	Med	MDHU DERRIFORD	PLYMOUTH
Dietz, Laura M	Lt RN	01-Sep-08	ENG	AE	DES/COMJE	YEOVIL
Dillon, Ben	Lt RN	01-Apr-03	ENG	WE	RAF WITTERING	RAF WITTERING
Dilloway, Philip J	Lt RN	07-Dec-96	QARNNS	RGN	MDHU PORTSMOUTH	PORTSMOUTH
Dimmock, Guy N	Lt RN	01-Jan-08	ENG	ME	HMS QUEEN ELIZABETH	ROSYTH
Dineen, John M G	Lt Cdr	01-Apr-02	WAR	AAWO	MWS COLLINGWOOD	
Dinsmore, Simon	Maj	01-Oct-12	RM	HW	HQ 3 CDO BDE RM	PLYMOUTH
Disney, Luke	Capt	01-Sep-09	RM	GS	FOST DPORT SEA	HMNB DEVONPORT
Disney, Peter W	Lt Cdr	01-Oct-94	WAR	O MER	FOST DPORT SEA	HMNB DEVONPORT
Dixon, Mark E	Lt RN	01-Jan-04	ENG	MESM	FLEET COMOPS NWD	NORTHWOOD
Dixon, Richard A	Lt RN	01-Jan-01	WAR	P LYNX	815 SQN FLT 226	RNAS YEOVILTON
Dixon, Robert	Lt RN	01-Sep-05	WAR	P LYNX	815 SQN FLT 202	RNAS YEOVILTON
Dixon, Simon J	Lt RN	01-Jan-05	WAR	P LYNX	815 SQN	RNAS YEOVILTON
Dobbins, Stuart J	Lt RN	07-Jul-97	LOGS	L	FLEET FOSNNI - CNR	LONDON
Dobbs, Helen A	Lt RN	01-Sep-13	ENG	AE	RNAS CULDROSE	
Dobie, Graham	Capt	18-Jul-08	RM	GS	NCHQ	
Dobner, Paul C	Capt	30-Mar-12	RM	GS	NCHQ	
Dobson, Richard E	Lt RN	17-Dec-10	WAR	GSX	HMS MONMOUTH	
Dobson, William J	SLt	01-Nov-11	WAR	SM(X)	BRNC DARTMOUTH	
Docherty, Zoe	Lt RN	01-Apr-11	LOGS	L	HMS VENGEANCE	
Dockerty, Neil C	Lt RN	01-Apr-09	WAR	O LYNX	815 SQN B SECTION	RNAS YEOVILTON
Dodd, Craig	Lt RN	31-Jul-09	MED	MS	DMS WHITTINGTON DMICP	LICHFIELD
Dodd, Kevin M	Cdr	30-Jun-08	WAR	O MER	RNAS CULDROSE	RNAS CULDROSE
Dodd, Nicholas C	Lt Cdr	30-Jun-07	LOGS	L	DES/COMLAND	ABBEY WOOD
Dodd, Shaun	Lt RN	01-Sep-09	WAR	MCD	MCM1 CREW 4	HELENSBURGH
Dodds, Matthew L	Lt Cdr	01-Oct-06	WAR	PWO(C) MW	FLEET COMOPS NWD	HMS COLLINGWOOD
Dodds, Nicholas L	Surg Lt Cdr	01-Nov-11	MED	Anaes	INM ALVERSTOKE	GOSPORT
Dodds, Stephen	Lt RN	12-Aug-05	ENG	WE	OCLC BIRMINGHAM	BIRMINGHAM
Doggart, Adam J	SLt	01-Sep-11	WAR	GSX	HMS TYNE	
Doherty, Bethany C	Mid	01-Nov-13	WAR	GSX	BRNC DARTMOUTH	
Doherty, Melanie	Surg Cdr (D)	03-Sep-12	DENTAL	GDP	DMS WHITTINGTON	LICHFIELD
Doig, Barry	Lt Cdr	01-Oct-06	WAR	INT	UK MCC	BAHRAIN
Dominy, David J	Cdr	30-Jun-06	WAR	AAWO	MOD CNS/ACNS	MAIN BUILDING LONDON
Dominy, Victoria L	Lt RN	01-Jul-02	ENG	TM	HMS SULTAN	
Donaghey, Mark	Maj	01-Oct-13	RM	SCC	42 CDO RM	HNMB DEVONPORT
Donaldson, Andrew M	Lt Cdr	30-Jun-12	ENG	WE	NCHQ	
Donaldson, Stuart	Lt Cdr	01-Sep-91	WAR	SM(CQ)	RN EXCHANGE USA	WASHINGTON
Donbavand, David W	Lt RN	11-Dec-09	LOGS	L	HMS IRON DUKE	
Doney, Nicholas J	Lt RN	01-Mar-13	ENG	MESM	DCEME SULTAN	HMS SULTAN
Donnelly, James S OBE	Cdr	30-Jun-09	ENG	AE	RNAS YEOVILTON	

Person Name	Substantive Rank	Seniority	Branch	Specialisation	Organisation	Location
Donohue, Paul	Lt RN	13-Feb-07	WAR	OP INT	DI - SA	MAIN BUILDING LONDON
Donovan, Robin J	Cdr	30-Jun-13	LOGS	L SM	MWS COLLINGWOOD	
Donworth, Desmond	Lt Cdr	01-Oct-05	WAR	PWO(N)	FLEET COMOPS NWD	NORTHWOOD
Doran, Catherine M	Surg Cdr	03-Sep-12	MED	GS	RCDM	BIRMINGHAM
Doran, Iain A	Lt Cdr	01-Oct-04	WAR	AAWO	HMS DUNCAN	
Doran, Shane E	Cdr	30-Jun-13	ENG	ME	DCEME SULTAN	HMS SULTAN
Dore, Christopher	Lt RN	01-Sep-07	WAR	SM(N)	HMS VIGILANT	
Dorman, Thomas R	Lt RN	01-Jan-06	ENG	IS	MWS COLLINGWOOD	HMS COLLINGWOOD
Dorrington, Benjamin R	Lt RN	01-Oct-10	WAR	GSX	HMS KENT	
Doubleday, Steven	Lt Cdr	01-Oct-07	WAR	P SK4	CHFHQ (SHORE)	RNAS YEOVILTON
Dougan, David Steven	Lt Cdr	01-Oct-13	WAR	AV	RNAS CULDROSE	
Doughty, Stephen W	Lt RN	09-Apr-12	WAR	P UT	RNAS YEOVILTON	
Douglas, Jason	Lt RN	31-Jul-09	ENG	AE	FLEET AV PHOT SEA	NCHQ
Douglas, Patrick J	Cdr	30-Jun-09	WAR	P SKW	MOD NSD - HDS	MAIN BUILDING LONDON
Doull, Donald J M	Cdr	30-Jun-09	ENG	MESM	DES/COMFLEET	USA
Douthwaite, Stuart J	Lt RN	01-Oct-09	WAR	SM(N)	HMS ASTUTE	
Dow, Andrew J	Maj	01-Oct-11	RM	GS	42 CDO RM	PLYMOUTH
Dow, Clive S	Cdr	30-Jun-10	LOGS	L BAR	FLEET COMNDER DCNS	NCHQ
Dowd, Jonathan W	Lt Col	30-Jun-10	RM	GS	RMR MERSEYSIDE	LIVERPOOL
Dowdell, Robert E J	Lt Cdr	01-Oct-94	WAR	P LYNX	AWC BSD - RW TES	RAF BOSCOMBE DOWN
Dowding, Craig	Lt RN	12-Jul-13	LOGS	L	HMS MONTROSE	
Dowell, Paul H N	Cdr	30-Jun-05	ENG	WE	NCHQ CNPS	NCHQ
Dowling, Andrew J	Lt Cdr	01-Oct-12	WAR	O LYNX	UKRBATSTAFF	PLYMOUTH
Downie, David R	Lt Cdr	01-Oct-10	ENG	AE	FLEET CSAV	NCHQ
Dowse, Andrew R	Lt RN	01-Sep-09	ENG	WE	MWS COLLINGWOOD	
Dowsett, Patrick G	Cdr	30-Jun-09	WAR	PWO(C)	JFHQ	NORTHWOOD
Doyle, Gary	Capt RN	20-Oct-08	WAR	O LYNX	NCHQ CNPS	PORTSMOUTH
Doyle, James R	Lt RN	01-Sep-12	ENG	AE	RNAS CULDROSE	RNAS CULDROSE
Doyle, Michael J	Lt RN	01-Sep-13	ENG	AE	LHF 815 SQN HQ	RNAS YEOVILTON
Drake, Roderick	Lt Cdr	31-Mar-98	WAR	MTO N	NATO ACO	NORTHWOOD
Dransfield, Joseph A J	Lt Cdr	01-Oct-09	WAR	O LYNX	LHF 815 SQN HQ	RNAS YEOVILTON
Draper, Mark Philip	2Lt	02-Sep-13	RM	N/A	CTCRM OFFICERS	EXMOUTH
Draper, Stephen	Cdr	30-Jun-08	WAR	PWO(A)	NATO-ACO-JFC HQ	BRUNSSUM
Dray, Jake M	Lt Cdr	01-Oct-09	WAR	PWO(U)	HMS DRAKE	
Dreaves, Christopher R	Mid	01-Sep-13	ENG	ME	BRNC DARTMOUTH	DARTMOUTH
Dreelan, Michael J	Cdr	30-Jun-07	WAR	PWO(U)	HG	AFGHANISTAN
Drennan, David G	Lt RN	01-Sep-07	WAR	P SK4	DEF HELI FLYING SC	RAF SHAWBURY
Drew, Daniel Mark	Lt RN	21-Mar-13	LOGS	L	NORTHWOOD HQ	NORTHWOOD
Drewett, Brian J	Lt Cdr	01-Oct-13	WAR	GSX	MWS COLLINGWOOD	
Drinkall, Kathryn M	Lt RN	01-Jan-06	ENG	TM	FLEET FOST ACOS(Trg)	ABBEY WOOD
Drinkwater, Ross MBE	Maj	01-Oct-12	RM	GS	43 CDO FPGRM	HMNB CLYDE
Driscoll, Adrian	Lt RN	01-Mar-11	ENG	WE	MWS COLLINGWOOD	
Driscoll, Robert	Lt Cdr	01-Oct-05	ENG	TM	HMS SULTAN	
Drodge, Andrew P F	Lt Cdr	01-Oct-02	WAR	O SK6	GANNET SAR FLT	HMS GANNET
Drodge, Kevin N	Lt Cdr	01-Oct-11	WAR	P SKW	FLEET CSAV	NCHQ
Droog, Sarah J	Surg Lt Cdr	02-Aug-11	MED	Anaes	INM ALVERSTOKE	GOSPORT
Drummond, Anthony S	Lt RN	01-May-08	WAR	SM(N)	HMS VIGILANT	
Drummond, Karl B	Surg Cdr (D)	01-Jul-13	DENTAL	GDP	INM ALVERSTOKE	GOSPORT
Dry, Ian	Lt Cdr	01-Oct-12	ENG	IS	DES/COMJE/ISS	CORSHAM
Drysdale, Robert T	SLt	01-Mar-11	WAR	SM(X)	MCM2 CREW	PORTSMOUTH
Drysdale, Steven R	Cdr	30-Jun-06	WAR	SM(CQ)	FLEET FOST ACOS(Trg)	HELENSBURGH
Drywood, Tobias	Lt Cdr	30-Jun-12	ENG	ME	DES/COMFLEET	ABBEY WOOD
D'Silva, Daniel	Cdr	30-Jun-13	ENG	WE	HERRICK AMN SECRETARIAT	MONS (CASTEAU)
Dubois, Carina	Lt RN	01-Apr-12	WAR	O MER	814 SQN	RNAS CULDROSE
Duby, Alon	Surg Cdr	30-Jun-07	MED	EM	RCDM	BIRMINGHAM
Duce, Matthew	Lt RN	01-May-01	WAR	PWO(N)	1 ASSLT GROUP RM (HQ)	PLYMOUTH
Duckitt, Jack	Maj	01-Oct-11	RM	C	COMUKAMPHIBFOR	HMNB PORTSMOUTH
Dudley, James	Mid	01-Sep-13	ENG	WE	BRNC DARTMOUTH	
Dudley, Stephen	Lt Cdr	01-Jan-99	LOGS	L	ACDS MIL STRAT	MAIN BUILDING LONDON
Du-Feu, Robert J	Lt RN	01-Sep-12	ENG	AE	848 SQN	RNAS YEOVILTON
Duffell, Glyn T	Lt RN	01-May-13	WAR	GSX	MCM2 CREW 4	PORTSMOUTH
Duffin, Colin J	Lt RN	01-Jul-08	WAR	INT	COMUKAMPHIBFOR	HMNB PORTSMOUTH

Person Name	Substantive Rank	Seniority	Branch	Specialisation	Organisation	Location
Duffin, Lee-Anne	Lt RN	01-Jan-05	WAR	MW	HMS COLLINGWOOD	
Duffy, Andrew J	Lt RN	01-Sep-13	WAR	SM(X)	HMS COLLINGWOOD	
Duffy, Henry	Capt RN	06-Dec-11	WAR	PWO(C)	COMPORFLOT SEA	HMNB PORTSMOUTH
Duffy, James C	Lt RN	01-Dec-04	WAR	PWO(SM)	HMS VICTORIOUS	
Duffy, Mark	SLt	01-Sep-12	ENG	WE	BRNC DARTMOUTH	
Dufosee, Sean W	Lt Cdr	08-Apr-02	WAR	P CDO	RNAS YEOVILTON	RNAS YEOVILTON
Duke, Adam J	Lt RN	01-Sep-05	ENG	AE	1710 NAS	PORTSMOUTH
Duke, Jonathan A	Lt RN	01-Oct-08	WAR	P SK6	854 NAS	RNAS CULDROSE
Duke, Karen D	Lt Cdr	01-Oct-09	MED	MS	MDHU PORTSMOUTH	PORTSMOUTH
Dunbar, Ross	Lt RN	01-Sep-08	ENG	AE	FLEET CSAV	NCHQ
Dunbar, Samantha	Lt Cdr	01-Oct-06	ENG	TM	NCHQ CNPERS	PORTSMOUTH
Duncan, Colin J	Lt RN	01-Sep-93	WAR	P LYNX	LHF 700W SQN	RNAS YEOVILTON
Duncan, Giles S	Maj	01-May-04	RM	GS	CTCRM	EXMOUTH
Duncan, Ian S	Cdr	30-Jun-05	RM	MESM	DES/COMFLEET	ABBEY WOOD
Duncan, Jeremy	Lt Cdr	01-Oct-01	WAR	P MER	824 SQN - TU	RNAS CULDROSE
Duncan, Kathryn C	Surg Lt Cdr	03-Apr-13	MED	GDMO	HMS MONTROSE	
Duncan, Ross D	Lt RN	01-Sep-10	ENG	WE	FOST DPORT SEA	HMNB DEVONPORT
Duncan, Rowan J	SLt	01-Sep-12	WAR	P UT	RNAS YEOVILTON	
Dunham, Mark W OBE	Brig	21-Apr-08	RM	HW	FLEET CAP LLM & DRM DIVISION	NCHQ
Dunham, Thomas W	2Lt	02-Sep-13	RM	N/A	CTCRM OFFICERS	EXMOUTH
Dunlop, Joanne	Lt Cdr	30-Mar-07	WAR	INFO OPS	FLEET CMR	NCHQ
Dunn, Anthony	Lt Cdr	01-Oct-08	WAR	AV	DSTO	RAF ST MAWGAN
Dunn, Ashley J	Lt RN	03-May-13	MED	MS	CAREER TRAINING	HMS RALEIGH
Dunn, Charles R	Capt	01-Sep-12	RM	GS	DCSU	RAF HENLOW
Dunn, Gary R	Lt Cdr	01-May-98	ENG	WESM(TWS)	DES/COMFLEET	ABBEY WOOD
Dunn, Giles	Lt RN	01-Sep-07	ENG	IS	DES/COMJE/ISS	CORSHAM
Dunn, Paul Edward OBE	Cdr	30-Jun-06	WAR	SM(CQ)	HMS NELSON	
Dunn, Robert P OBE	Cdr	30-Jun-04	WAR	SM(CQ)	COMDEVFLOT SHORE	HMNB DEVONPORT
Dunning, Stephen T	Lt RN	01-Oct-08	ENG	TM	45 CDO RM	DUNDE
Dunning, Timothy J	Lt RN	01-Nov-13	WAR	GSX	FLEET HQ 6	NCHQ
Dunthorne, Matthew S	Lt RN	13-Apr-12	ENG	ME	HMS NORTHUMBERLAND	
Durbin, Philip John	Lt RN	01-Aug-07	LOGS	L SM	HMS RALEIGH	
Durbin, William John	Lt RN	01-Sep-10	WAR	GSX	FLEET HQ	NCHQ
Durbridge, Joel J	Capt	01-Sep-10	RM	GS	40 CDO RM - B COY	TAUNTON
Durham, Paul C	Lt Cdr	18-May-03	ENG	AE	OP ATALANTA	NORTHWOOD
Durkin, Mark T G	Capt RN	19-Oct-09	WAR	MCD PWO(A)	NCHQ CNPERS	PORTSMOUTH
Durrant, Frederick	Lt RN	01-Oct-11	WAR	P SK4	CHF(MERLIN)	RAF BENSON
Durup, Jason M	Maj	01-Oct-06	RM	LC	HQ 3 CDO BDE RM	PLYMOUTH
Duthie, Andrew G	Lt Cdr	01-Oct-12	ENG	AE	A	ABBEY WOOD
Dutt, James E	SLt	08-Dec-11	WAR	SM(X)	MCM2 CREW 7	PORTSMOUTH
Dutton, David OBE	Cdre	30-Sep-13	WAR	PWO(C)	FLEET ACOS(RP)	NCHQ
Dutton, James	Capt	01-Sep-09	RM	GS	NCHQ	
Duxbury, Katrina J	Mid	01-Nov-13	WAR	GSX	BRNC DARTMOUTH	
Dyer, Martin L	Lt RN	01-Sep-11	ENG	MESM	HMS VANGUARD	
Dyer, Michael D J	Capt RN	04-Jan-11	ENG	WESM(TWS)	CIO-J6	MAIN BUILDING LONDON
Dyer, Shani D	Lt RN	01-Sep-06	WAR	PWO(N)	HMS BULWARK	
Dyer, Timothy A	2Lt	01-Sep-11	RM	N/A	CTCRM OFFICERS	EXMOUTH
Dyke, Christopher	Cdr	30-Jun-03	WAR	PWO(C)	BDS WASHINGTON	WASHINGTON
Dyke, Kenneth A	Lt Cdr	01-Oct-00	ENG	MESM	DES/COMFLEET/SM	THURSO
Dymock, Craig H	Mid	01-Sep-13	ENG	WE	BRNC DARTMOUTH	
Dymond, Justin	Lt RN	01-Sep-03	ENG	WE	DEFENCE ACADEMY	SHRIVENHAM
Dynes, Oliver G	Lt RN	01-May-13	WAR	SM(X)	HMS VANGUARD	

E

Person Name	Substantive Rank	Seniority	Branch	Specialisation	Organisation	Location
Eacock, Jason P	Lt Cdr	01-Oct-11	WAR	PWO	FLEET COMOPS NWD	NORTHWOOD
Eames, Jonathan R	Surg Lt Cdr	01-Dec-12	MED	GMP	INM ALVERSTOKE	GOSPORT
Earle-Payne, Gareth E	Lt RN	01-Sep-03	ENG	MESM	HMS VICTORIOUS	
Early, Thomas W	2Lt	02-Sep-13	RM	N/A	CTCRM OFFICERS	EXMOUTH
Eastaugh, Andrew C	Cdr	30-Jun-06	ENG	IS (RES)	NC PSYA	PORTSMOUTH
Eastburn, Jonathan L	Lt RN	01-May-13	WAR	GSX	MCM2 CREW 1	PORTSMOUTH
Easterbrook, Christopher	Lt RN	01-Sep-04	WAR	P LYNX	815 SQN	RNAS YEOVILTON
Easterbrook, Kevin I	Cdr	30-Jun-13	ENG	WE	HMS OCEAN	

Person Name	Substantive Rank	Seniority	Branch	Specialisation	Organisation	Location
Eastham, Allan M Rd	Lt Cdr	31-Mar-94	WAR	MTO N	MWS COLLINGWOOD	
Eaton, Daniel T	Capt	01-Aug-08	RM	GS	NCHQ	
Eaton, David C	Lt RN	01-Jan-02	WAR	ATC	RNAS CULDROSE	
Eaton, Max H	SLt	01-May-12	WAR	GSX	BRNC DARTMOUTH	
Eaton, Paul G	Lt Cdr	01-Jun-94	WAR	HM (M CH)	NATO-ACO-SHAPE	CASTEAU
Ebbitt, Henry	Lt RN	01-Apr-12	WAR	GSX	HMS ILLUSTRIOUS	
Eccles, Matthew P	Lt RN	01-Sep-11	WAR	O SKW	854 NAS	RNAS CULDROSE
Eddy, Charlotte R	Mid	01-Sep-12	WAR	GSX	HMS WESTMINSTER	
Eden, Christopher J	Capt	01-Sep-06	RM	P SK4	845 SQN	RNAS YEOVILTON
Eden, Jeremy R H	Lt Cdr	01-Oct-13	MED	MS	NCHQ MEDDIV	NCHQ
Eden, Philip Mark	Lt RN	08-Dec-13	ENG	MESM	DCEME SULTAN	HMS SULTAN
Edey, Michael J	Lt Cdr	01-Dec-01	WAR	PWO(U)	MWS COLLINGWOOD	
Edgar, Iain A	Surg Lt Cdr	06-Aug-13	MED	EM	INM ALVERSTOKE	GOSPORT
Edge, John H	Cdr	30-Jun-04	LOGS	L SM	DES/COMLAND/JSC	RAF BOSCOMBE DOWN
Edmonds, Jon S	Lt RN	01-Jun-10	WAR	HM	HMS PROTECTOR	
Edmondson, Mark	Lt Cdr	01-Oct-12	WAR	SM(AWC)	CBRN POL	MAIN BUILDING LONDON
Edmondson, Simon P	Lt Col	30-Jun-13	RM	P GAZ	DIRECTOR (JW)	NORTHWOOD
Edney, Andrew	Capt RN	30-Jun-07	WAR	P LYNX	HMS NELSON	HMS NELSON
Edward, Amanda M	Surg Lt Cdr	07-Aug-07	MED	Anaes	INM ALVERSTOKE	GOSPORT
Edward, Gavin	Cdr	30-Jun-11	ENG	WE	HMS BULWARK	
Edwards, Andrew	Lt RN	01-Jan-13	WAR	O UT	RNAS CULDROSE	RNAS CULDROSE
Edwards, Cassandra J	Lt RN	01-Feb-10	WAR	ATC	OCLC LONDON	LONDON
Edwards, Charles J	Surg Cdr	31-Dec-97	MED	Anaes	RCDM	BIRMINGHAM
Edwards, Gareth B	Capt	01-Sep-09	RM	GS	45 CDO RM - COMD COY	DUNDEE
Edwards, Gavin R	Lt RN	01-Sep-07	ENG	AE	DES/COIR	ABBEY WOOD
Edwards, Helen Marie	Lt RN	08-Feb-13	WAR	ATC	RNAS CULDROSE - ATC	RNAS CULDROSE
Edwards, James	Lt Cdr	01-Oct-11	ENG	TM	GIBRALTAR SVCS EDUCATION CENTRE	GIBRALTAR
Edwards, James Eustice	Lt Cdr	01-Oct-05	ENG	WE	DES/COMFLEET	ABBEY WOOD
Edwards, John David	Lt RN	01-Sep-09	WAR	P SK4	RAF SHAWBURY	
Edwards, Luke	Lt RN	01-Sep-08	WAR	P LYNX	RAF CRANWELL	
Edwards, Neal P	Lt RN	17-Dec-10	LOGS	L	COMDEVFLOT ESG	HMS DRAKE
Edwards, Rhydian Owen	Lt RN	01-Mar-11	WAR	P UT	RAF SHAWBURY	
Edwards, Rhys G	Lt RN	01-Sep-13	ENG	AE	RNAS CULDROSE	RNAS CULDROSE
Edwards, Sharon P	Lt Cdr	01-Oct-13	QARNNS	EN	MDHU DERRIFORD	PLYMOUTH
Edwards, Tom H H	Lt Cdr	01-Oct-12	WAR	PWO	MWS COLLINGWOOD	
Edwards-Bannon, William J	Lt RN	01-Nov-07	WAR	GSX	ACDS C FD	MAIN BUILDING LONDON
Edwins, Mark R	Lt Cdr	01-Oct-07	ENG	ME	NAVY MCTA PORTSMOUTH	HMNB PORTSMOUTH
Edye, Robin	Maj	01-Oct-06	RM	GS	AIB	HMS SULTAN
Eedle, Richard	Lt Cdr	01-Mar-91	WAR	SM(AWC)	RN EXCHANGE FRANCE	PARIS
Eeles, Thomas D	Lt RN	01-Sep-13	ENG	AE	RNAS CULDROSE	RNAS CULDROSE
Egeland-Jensen, Finn A MBE	Lt Cdr	01-Apr-95	WAR	PWO(N)	HMS COLLINGWOOD	
Eglinton, Benjamin R	Lt RN	01-Sep-13	ENG	ME	HMS ARGYLL	
Eldridge, Stephen J	Lt Cdr	01-Oct-10	ENG	TM	DCDS PERS TRG	MAIN BUILDING LONDON
Elford, David G	Cdre	01-Jul-13	ENG	AE	DCTT HQ	HMS SULTAN
Ellera, Richard O	Capt	01-Sep-10	RM	GS	DEF SCH OF LANG	BEACONSFIELD
Ellerton, Paul	Lt Cdr	01-Oct-10	WAR	P LYNX	815 SQN	RNAS YEOVILTON
Ellicott, Matthew J	Lt RN	01-May-06	WAR	FC	MWS COLLINGWOOD	
Elliman, Simon	Cdr	30-Jun-07	WAR	PWO(U)	RN EXCHANGE FRANCE	PARIS
Ellingham, Richard E	RN Chpln	17-Apr-96	Ch S		HMS NELSON	HMNB PORTSMOUTH
Elliot-Smith, Teilo J	Lt Cdr	01-Oct-09	WAR	AAWO	HMS DARING	
Elliott, David J	Lt RN	01-Oct-10	ENG	TM	Op LANSBURY	AFGHANISTAN
Elliott, Jamie A	Lt Cdr	01-Oct-09	ENG	AE	RNAS YEOVILTON - AED	RNAS YEOVILTON
Elliott, Mark F	Maj	01-Oct-09	RM	GS	PJHQ (UK) J3	NORTHWOOD
Elliott, Stephen P	Lt Cdr	01-Oct-10	ENG	WE	HMS NORTHUMBERLAND	
Elliott, Timothy D	Lt RN	01-Sep-04	WAR	O LYNX	MWS COLLINGWOOD	
Ellis, David F	Lt Cdr	01-Oct-05	ENG	IS	DES/COMFLEET/SHIPS	BRISTOL
Ellis, James	Lt Cdr	01-Oct-04	ENG	ME	RN EXCHANGE CANADA	OTTAWA 1
Ellis, James W	2Lt	02-Sep-13	RM	N/A	CTCRM OFFICERS	EXMOUTH
Ellis, Nicholas M	Lt Cdr	18-Jul-97	WAR	N/A	NCHQ CNPERS	PORTSMOUTH
Ellis, William J	Lt RN	09-Apr-12	WAR	P UT	RNAS YEOVILTON	
Ellison, Peter J P	Lt RN	01-Jan-06	WAR	GSX	MWS COLLINGWOOD	HMS COLLINGWOOD
Elmer, Timothy B	Surg Cdr (D)	30-Jun-02	DENTAL	Dent	SGD - DSC	LICHFIELD

Person Name	Substantive Rank	Seniority	Branch	Specialisation	Organisation	Location
Elsey, David C	SLt	01-Feb-11	WAR	SM(X)	HMS BULWARK	
Elsey, David J	Lt Cdr	01-Oct-05	ENG	TM	MWS COLLINGWOOD	
Elston, Luke R	Lt RN	13-Apr-12	ENG	AE	CHF(MERLIN)	RAF BENSON
Elvin, Andrew J OBE	Cdr	30-Jun-06	WAR	MCD PWO(A)	HMS NELSON	HMS NELSON
Elvy, Susan D	Lt RN	01-Jun-10	LOGS	L	ESG EJSU SHAPE	MONS
Embleton, Alison	Lt RN	09-Jun-06	QARNNS	OT	RCDM	BIRMINGHAM
Emery, Christian S	Lt RN	01-May-03	ENG	WE	MCM1 FAS SEA1	HELENSBURGH
Emery, David Gareth	Lt RN	01-Apr-11	WAR	O MER	814 SQN	RNAS CULDROSE
Emmerson, David I	SLt	01-Nov-11	WAR	SM(X)	BRNC DARTMOUTH	
Emptage, Christopher J	Capt	01-Sep-08	RM	GS	COMUKAMPHIBFOR	HMNB PORTSMOUTH
Emptage, Michael A	Lt RN	01-Sep-10	ENG	AE	HMS SULTAN - STG	HMS SULTAN
Enever, Shaun A	Lt Cdr	01-Oct-08	WAR	O LYNX	DES/COMLAND	ABBEY WOOD
England, Philip M	Lt Cdr	01-Oct-11	ENG	TM	RNLA	DARTMOUTH
Entwisle, William N OBE MVO	Cdre	30-Apr-13	WAR	P LYNX	MSP	MAIN BUILDING LONDON
Epps, Matthew	Lt RN	17-Jul-99	ENG	IS	CIO-DSAS	CORSHAM
Erhahiemen, Peter E	Lt RN	01-May-07	LOGS	L	COMFASFLOT	HELENSBURGH
Errington, Ridley J B	Lt RN	01-Sep-06	ENG	ME	HMS SCOTT	
Erskine, Dominic S	Capt	21-Mar-13	RM	GS	NCHQ	
Erskine, Peter	Capt RN	08-Jul-08	ENG	ME	LST AUSTRALIA	AUSTRALIA
Esbensen, Kristoffer P	Lt RN	01-Apr-12	LOGS	L	HMS DEFENDER	
Esfahani, Shahrokh	Lt Cdr	31-Mar-02	WAR	INFO OPS (RES)	DCSU	RAF HENLOW
Essenhigh, Angus N P	Cdr	30-Jun-11	WAR	AAWO	HMS DARING	
Essenhigh, Sir Nigel (Richard), GCB, DL	Adm	11-Sep-98				
Ethell, David R	Maj	01-Oct-03	RM	LC	FLEET COMOPS NWD	NORTHWOOD
Etheridge, Anthony C	Lt RN	01-Sep-12	ENG	MESM	HMS TRIUMPH	
Evangelista, Paul G	Lt RN	30-Jul-10	MED	MS	INM ALVERSTOKE2	GOSPORT
Evans, Benjimin G	Lt Cdr	01-Oct-13	WAR	PWO	HMS MONTROSE	
Evans, Charles A	Cdr	30-Jun-09	LOGS	L SM	COMDEVFLOT WLSG	HMS DRAKE
Evans, Charlotte V	Surg Lt Cdr	01-Aug-12	MED	Psych	INM ALVERSTOKE	GOSPORT
Evans, Christian P	Lt RN	01-Jan-03	ENG	TM	BASTION SP GP	AFGHANISTAN BASTION
Evans, Christopher A	Lt RN	01-May-03	WAR	SM(AWC)	HMS COLLINGWOOD	
Evans, Christopher C	Lt Cdr	01-Oct-11	ENG	MESM	HMS VIGILANT	
Evans, David M M	Brig	03-Sep-13	RM	C	FLEET CAP IS DIVISION	NCHQ
Evans, Edward M	Cdr	30-Jun-06	LOGS	L SM	NCHQ CNPERS	PORTSMOUTH
Evans, Gareth C	Surg Cdr	13-Dec-11	MED	GMP (	DES/COMFLEET/NBC	HELENSBURGH
Evans, Giles	Lt Cdr	01-Oct-07	WAR	SM(AWC)	RNSMS	HMS RALEIGH
Evans, Helen J	Surg Lt Cdr	01-Aug-10	MED	GMP	UK MED GP (AFG)	AFGHANISTAN BASTION
Evans, Joshua J	Lt RN	01-Apr-12	ENG	TM	HMS COLLINGWOOD	
Evans, Karl N M	Capt RN	29-Jul-08	WAR	SM(CQ)	CABINET OFFICE	LONDON
Evans, Laura	SLt	01-May-13	WAR	REG (RES)	BRNC DARTMOUTH	
Evans, Laura-Jane	Lt RN	01-Sep-02	WAR	O SKW	854 NAS	RNAS CULDROSE
Evans, Lee S	Lt Cdr	01-Oct-09	WAR	P LYNX	AWC BSD - RW TES	RAF BOSCOMBE DOWN
Evans, Marc D	Cdr	30-Jun-07	LOGS	L	PJHQ (UK) J1/J4	NORTHWOOD
Evans, Martin J	Cdr	30-Jun-06	WAR	PWO(U)	HMS EXCELLENT - CO	PORTSMOUTH
Evans, Martin L	RN Chpln	01-Sep-98	Ch S		RNAS YEOVILTON - CHAP	RNAS YEOVILTON
Evans, Paul J	Lt Cdr	01-Oct-10	ENG	WE	FOST DPORT SEA	HMNB DEVONPORT
Evans, Peter A	Lt RN	01-May-07	WAR	GSX	MWS COLLINGWOOD	HMS COLLINGWOOD
Evans, Robert	Lt Cdr	01-Oct-11	ENG	WE	COMDEVFLOT SEA	HMNB DEVONPORT
Evans, Robert G	Lt RN	08-Apr-05	ENG	AE	BASTION SP GP	AFGHANISTAN BASTION
Evans, Russell F	Lt RN	31-Jul-09	ENG	AE	RNAS CULDROSE	
Evans, Thomas W	Lt RN	01-Sep-06	LOGS	L BAR SM	NATO ACO	NORTHWOOD
Evans, William Q F	Capt RN	08-Jul-13	WAR	PWO(N)	FLEET CAP SSM DIVISION	NCHQ
Evans-Jones, Thomas M	Maj	01-Oct-12	RM	GS	COMUKAMPHIBFOR	HMNB PORTSMOUTH
Everard, Richard F	Lt RN	20-Oct-06	WAR	C	NCHQ	
Evered, Jonathan F	Lt RN	01-May-06	WAR	P SK4	848 SQN	RNAS YEOVILTON
Everest, Becky	Lt RN	01-May-07	ENG	TM	AIB	HMS SULTAN
Everett, Oliver	Lt RN	01-Jun-08	WAR	P SK4	CHFHQ (SEA)	RNAS YEOVILTON
Everitt, Tobyn W	Cdr	30-Jun-12	WAR	P GR7	FLEET CSAV	PETERBOROUGH
Evershed, Marcus C	Surg Capt RN	01-Mar-11	MED	GMP	APHCS SOUTH WEST	HMS DRAKE
Evershed, Rachael E F	Surg Lt Cdr	07-Aug-07	MED	GMP	HMS COLLINGWOOD	
Every, Michael J	SLt	01-Feb-11	WAR	SM(X)	MWS COLLINGWOOD	
Evison, Toby	Lt Cdr	06-Nov-06	ENG	IS	FLEET CAP IS DIVISION	NCHQ

Person Name	Substantive Rank	Seniority	Branch	Specialisation	Organisation	Location
Ewen, Andrew P	Cdr	30-Jun-06	ENG	AE	RNAS CULDROSE	
Exworthy, Damian A MBE	Cdr	30-Jun-13	LOGS	L	FMC - NAVY	MAIN BUILDING LONDON
Eyers, Dale S	SLt	01-Apr-11	WAR	O SKW	854 NAS	RNAS CULDROSE

F

Person Name	Substantive Rank	Seniority	Branch	Specialisation	Organisation	Location
Fabik, Andre N	Lt RN	01-May-01	WAR	HM(AS)	FOST HM	HMS DRAKE
Fagan, Louis V	Lt RN	01-Mar-11	LOGS	L	HMS BULWARK	
Fairbairn, Oliver	Lt RN	07-Jun-11	ENG	ME	HMS OCEAN	
Fairweather, Donell	Lt RN	07-Aug-13	WAR	O UT	RNAS CULDROSE	
Falconer, Paul	Lt RN	24-Oct-08	MED	MS(CDO)	HQ 3 CDO BDE RM	PLYMOUTH
Falk, Benedict H G	Cdr	30-Jun-02	WAR	PWO(A)	NATO	BRUSSELS
Falla, Lindsay	Surg Lt Cdr (D)	27-Jun-08	DENTAL	GDP	ROYAL BRUNEI ARMED FORCES	SERIA
Fallensen, Lloyd A	Lt	01-Sep-11	RM	GS	NCHQ	
Fallows, Lee David	Lt RN	01-Apr-13	WAR	GSX	HMS BULWARK	
Fancy, Robert OBE Adc	Capt RN	01-Mar-10	WAR	SM(CQ)	HMS RALEIGH - EXEC	
Fane-Bailey, Verity M	Lt RN	01-Jun-09	LOGS	L	HMS NELSON	
Fanshawe, Edward	Lt Cdr	01-Oct-13	ENG	WESM(TWS)	DEFENCE ACADEMY	SHRIVENHAM
Farley, Emma Louise	SLt	01-Nov-11	WAR	HM	BRNC DARTMOUTH	
Farmer, Gary Gordon Rd	Lt RN	28-Jun-92	WAR	AW (RES)	DNR RCHQ NORTH	HMS CALEDONIA
Farquharson, Craig I	Lt RN	01-Jan-11	WAR	O LYNX	LHF 815 SQN FLT 202	RNAS YEOVILTON
Farr, Ian R	Lt RN	16-Aug-00	WAR	P MER	829 SQN FLT 04	RNAS CULDROSE
Farrage, Michael E CBE	Cdre	07-Nov-11	ENG	TM	NCHQ CNPERS	NCHQ
Farrant, James D	Lt Cdr	01-Oct-09	LOGS	L BAR	NCHQ - CNLS	USA
Farrant, Sam	Lt RN	01-Nov-05	ENG	WE	COMMANDER OP TRAINING	HMS COLLINGWOOD
Farrington, John	Cdr	30-Jun-10	ENG	WESM(TWS)	RN EXCHANGE AUSTRALIA	CANBERRA
Farrington, Richard CBE	Cdre	26-Mar-13	WAR	PWO(C)	COMDEVFLOT SEA	HMNB DEVONPORT
Farthing, Findlay C	Capt	20-Jul-07	RM	SCC	RMR MERSEYSIDE	LIVERPOOL
Faulkner, Jonathan I J	Lt RN	09-Apr-09	ENG	ME	COMPORFLOT	PORTSMOUTH
Faulkner, Simon	Lt RN	01-Jan-08	ENG	WESM(SWS)	FLEET COMOPS NWD	NORTHWOOD
Faulkner, Stuart	Lt Cdr	01-Oct-10	ENG	AE	829 SQN HQ	RNAS CULDROSE
Fawcett, Benjamin E	Lt RN	01-Nov-10	WAR	INT	FLEET COMOPS NWD	HMS COLLINGWOOD
Fawcett, Stuart	SLt	04-Dec-12	WAR	GSX	MWS COLLINGWOOD	
Faye, Matthew E	Lt RN	13-Jun-08	MED	MS	UKRBATSTAFF	HMNB PORTSMOUTH
Fayers, Samuel R	SLt	01-Sep-11	ENG	MESM	DCEME SULTAN	HMS SULTAN
Fear, Richard K	Cdr	30-Jun-99	ENG	WESM(TWS)	NATO - BRUSSELS	BRUSSELS
Fearn, Daniel C T	Lt RN	01-Feb-10	WAR	INT	OP VOCATE	LIBYA TRIPOLI TRIPOLI
Fearn, Samuel	Maj	01-Oct-13	RM	GS	MTM DEFAC JSCSC	SHRIVENHAM
Fearon, David J	Lt Cdr	01-Oct-09	ENG	WE	HMS NORTHUMBERLAND	
Feasey, Caroline	Lt RN	01-Jun-06	LOGS	L	HMS RALEIGH - INT R	HMS RALEIGH
Feasey, Ian D	Lt Cdr	01-Oct-08	WAR	PWO	FOST DPORT SEA	HMNB DEVONPORT
Feasey, James A	Capt	01-Sep-11	RM	GS	43 CDO	HMNB CLYDE
Febbrarro, Luke N	Lt RN	01-Sep-11	WAR	SM(X)	HMS VIGILANT	
Feeney, Matthew B	Lt Cdr	01-Apr-08	WAR	INT	NORTHWOOD HQ	NORTHWOOD
Fellows, Christopher R	Lt RN	01-Jan-07	WAR	O SKW	849 SQN	RNAS CULDROSE
Felton, Jonathan E	Capt	01-Sep-10	RM	GS	NCHQ	
Fenn, Christopher J	Mid	01-May-12	LOGS	L	DES/COMFLEET	HELENSBURGH
Fenwick, Robin J	Maj	01-Oct-04	RM	P GR7	A AIB FARNBOROUGH	ALDERSHOT
Fenwick, Steven G	Lt RN	01-Sep-07	ENG	WE	DES/COMJE/ISS	CORSHAM
Fergus-Hunt, Gregory	Lt RN	07-Dec-07	LOGS	L	COMDEVFLOT SHORE	HMNB DEVONPORT
Ferguson, Calum	Lt RN	01-Jan-11	WAR	GSX	DHU - C COY	SHEFFORD
Ferguson, Simon	Lt RN	08-Jul-12	WAR	GSX	MWS DDS	PORTSMOUTH
Ferguson, Andrew C	Maj	01-May-99	RM	SBS	DEFENCE ACADEMY	SHRIVENHAM
Fergusson, Iain B	Lt Cdr	01-Oct-12	WAR	SM(AWC)	HMS VIGILANT	
Fergusson, Nigel A	Cdr	30-Jun-10	ENG	WE	FLEET ACOS(RP)	NCHQ
Ferns, Timothy D	Cdr	30-Jun-07	LOGS	L	UK MCC	BAHRAIN
Ferris, Daniel P	Cdr	30-Jun-04	ENG	WE	FMC JOINT	MAIN BUILDING LONDON
Fickling, James W	Lt Cdr	01-Oct-12	ENG	WE	DES/COMFLEET	ABBEY WOOD
Fiddock, Matthew L	Lt Cdr	01-Oct-12	ENG	ME	HMS KENT	
Fidler, John Q	Maj	01-Oct-09	RM	LC	40 CDO RM	TAUNTON
Fielder, Andrew	Lt RN	01-Sep-08	ENG	AE	DEFAC CMT	SHRIVENHAM
Fields, David	Cdr	30-Jun-03	WAR	PWO(A)	ATTACHE/ADVISER MOSCOW	MOSCOW
Fields, Samuel W	Lt RN	01-Nov-13	WAR	GSX	BRNC DARTMOUTH	

Person Name	Substantive Rank	Seniority	Branch	Specialisation	Organisation	Location
Fieldsend, Mark	Cdr	30-Jun-03	ENG	ME	RN EXCHANGE FRANCE	PARIS
Figgins, Adam A	Mid	01-Feb-13	WAR	O UT	BRNC DARTMOUTH	
Filewod, Roger B	Lt RN	01-Aug-08	WAR	GSX	HMS SEVERN	
Filio, Andrew Paul	Lt RN	01-May-13	WAR	SM(X)	HMS VIGILANT	
Fillmore, Guy M	Capt	01-Sep-12	RM	GS	43 CDO FPGRM S SQN	HMNB CLYDE
Fillmore, Raymond J	Lt Cdr	01-Oct-10	WAR	SM(CQ)	FLEET COMOPS NWD	NORTHWOOD
Filshie, Sarah J	Lt Cdr	01-Oct-13	WAR	ATC	HMS OCEAN	
Filtness, David M	Lt Cdr	25-Jun-13	WAR	SM(CQ)	NCHQ CNPERS	PORTSMOUTH
Filtness, Rebecca A	Lt RN	01-Aug-04	WAR	AW (RES)	43 CDO	HMNB CLYDE
Finch, Robert L	Lt Cdr	01-May-97	ENG	ME	DCTT HQ	HMS SULTAN
Finch, Steven	Lt Cdr	01-Oct-08	ENG	AE	RNAS CULDROSE	
Finch, Timothy S A	Lt Cdr	01-Oct-97	LOGS	L	FLEET ACOS(RP)	NCHQ
Fincher, Kevin J	Cdr	30-Jun-10	WAR	PWO(C)	JSSU CH - HQ	CHELTENHAM
Findlay, Hamish R	Lt RN	01-Oct-12	WAR	P SK4	857 NAS	RNAS CULDROSE
Finn, Ivan R	Cdr	30-Jun-07	ENG	AE	BRNC DARTMOUTH	
Finn, James S	Lt RN	01-Jan-01	WAR	P MER	CHF(MERLIN)	OXFORD
Finn, Stuart A	Lt Cdr	01-Sep-08	WAR	O MER	824 SQN	RNAS CULDROSE
Finn, Tristan A	Maj	01-Oct-13	RM	MLDR	DEFAC JSCSC	SHRIVENHAM
Finnie, Anthony M	Lt RN	01-Jan-12	WAR	O UT	702 SQN YEOVILTON	RNAS YEOVILTON
Finnigan, Sebastian	Lt RN	01-Mar-13	ENG	MESM	DCEME SULTAN	HMS SULTAN
Firth, John S	Lt RN	01-May-00	WAR	PWO(A)	UKRBATSTAFF	HMNB PORTSMOUTH
Firth, Nigel R	Lt Cdr	01-Mar-95	WAR	SM(CQ)	PJHQ (UK) CMSA	NORTHWOOD
Fisher, Aaron G	Lt Col	30-Jun-13	RM	LC	BTT - SOUTH AFRICA	PRETORIA
Fisher, Cameron S	Mid	01-May-13	WAR	GSX	BRNC DARTMOUTH	
Fisher, Clayton R	Capt RN	16-Jul-12	LOGS	L	DCDS PERS TRG	MAIN BUILDING LONDON
Fisher, Daniel Alan MC	Capt	30-Mar-12	RM	GS	NCHQ	
Fisher, Luke I	SLt	01-May-13	WAR	GSX	HMS PROTECTOR	
Fitter, Ian S T	Cdr	30-Jun-02	WAR	O SK6	FLEET AV VL - RNFSC	RNAS YEOVILTON
Fitton, Daniel	Lt RN	01-Sep-10	ENG	MESM	HMS VICTORIOUS	
Fitzgibbon, John P	Lt RN	01-Jan-07	WAR	GSX	MWS COLLINGWOOD	
Fitzpatrick, John A J	Lt Cdr	01-Jul-05	WAR	O LYNX	FLEET CSAV	NCHQ
Fitzpatrick, Michael J	Lt RN	01-Jul-09	ENG	WESM(TWS)	NAVY MCTA PORTSMOUTH	HMNB PORTSMOUTH
Fitzpatrick, Neil	Lt Cdr	01-Oct-12	WAR	PWO	RN EXCHANGE AUSTRALIA	CANBERRA
Fitzpatrick, Paul S	Maj	01-Oct-06	RM	SCC	NCHQ CNPERS	PORTSMOUTH
Fitzsimmons, Mark B	Cdr	30-Jun-09	WAR	PWO(A)	UKTI - DSO	LONDON
Flaherty, Christopher L	Lt Cdr	01-Oct-12	WAR	MCD	CSF FASLANE	HELENSBURGH
Flannagan, Bryan A	Lt RN	01-Sep-13	WAR	SM(X)	HMS ASTUTE	
Flannagan, Donna L	Lt Cdr	01-Oct-13	LOGS	L	UK MCC	BAHRAIN
Flannigan, Aiden	Lt RN	01-Sep-06	ENG	MESM	HMS VIGILANT(PORT)	
Flatman, Timothy David	Lt Cdr	01-Oct-09	WAR	P GR7	736 NAS	RNAS CULDROSE
Flatt, Liam B	Lt RN	01-Sep-06	WAR	INT	HMS ILLUSTRIOUS	
Flegg, Kirsty G	Lt Cdr	01-Sep-08	LOGS	L	HMS DEFENDER	
Flegg, Matthew J	Lt Cdr	01-Oct-08	ENG	AE	DES/COMJE/HELS	RNAS YEOVILTON
Flegg, William J	Lt RN	01-Nov-06	WAR	GSX	RNLA	HMS COLLINGWOOD
Fleming, Caroline S E	Lt RN	01-Jan-08	LOGS	L BAR	NCHQ - CNLS	HMNB DEVONPORT
Fleming, David P	Lt RN	01-Sep-04	WAR	P LYNX	815 SQN	RNAS YEOVILTON
Fleming, Kevin P Arcs	Cdr	30-Jun-06	WAR	O LYNX	LHF HQ	RNAS YEOVILTON
Fleming, Ruth E	Lt Cdr	01-Oct-09	LOGS	L	NCHQ CNPS	MAIN BUILDING LONDON
Fleming, Samuel	Lt Cdr	01-Nov-04	WAR	CIS (RES)	NPT RES MOBILISATION	HMNB PORTSMOUTH
Fletcher, Andrew S	Lt RN	01-Sep-06	WAR	GSX	HMS RANGER	
Fletcher, Christopher P	Lt RN	17-Dec-10	ENG	MESM	HMS TIRELESS	
Fletcher, Ian James	Lt Cdr	01-Oct-09	WAR	HM	DI - ICSP	MAIN BUILDING LONDON
Fletcher, Jonathan H G	Lt RN	01-Nov-06	WAR	PWO	HMS OCEAN	
Fletcher, Richard	Lt RN	31-Mar-04	LOGS	L (RES)	DMLS	HMS RALEIGH
Flewitt, Craig	Capt	01-Sep-09	RM	GS	JFACTSU LEEMING - JFACT	NORTHALLERTON
Flint, Grahame	Lt RN	01-Sep-07	WAR	FC	MWS COLLINGWOOD	HMS COLLINGWOOD
Flint, Thomas Alan	SLt	24-Jan-12	ENG	WESM	MWS COLLINGWOOD	HMS COLLINGWOOD
Flitcroft, Michael	Lt RN	01-Jul-04	ENG	WESM(TWS)	RNSMS	HMS RALEIGH
Flower, Neil P	Capt	01-Apr-04	RM	P LYN7	WILDCAT FORCE	RNAS YEOVILTON
Flowers, David J	Lt RN	01-Sep-11	ENG	MESM	HMS VIGILANT	
Floyd, Robert E	Lt RN	01-Jan-03	ENG	TM	NCHQ CNPERS	PORTSMOUTH
Floyer, Hugo G	Lt RN	01-Nov-07	WAR	GSX	HMS SMITER	OXFORD

Person Name	Substantive Rank	Seniority	Branch	Specialisation	Organisation	Location
Flynn, Andrew	Lt Cdr	01-May-04	ENG	AE	ABBEYWOOD	ABBEY WOOD
Flynn, Christopher	Lt RN	01-Jan-10	WAR	O SKW	771 SQN	RNAS CULDROSE
Flynn, Luke M	SLt	11-Apr-12	WAR	SM(X)	BRNC DARTMOUTH	
Flynn, Michael T	Cdr	30-Jun-03	LOGS	L	DCDS PERS TRG-TESRR	MAIN BUILDING LONDON
Flynn, Simon J	Lt Cdr	01-Oct-08	WAR	O SKW	RNAS CULDROSE	
Foden, Jonathan B	Capt	03-Apr-09	RM	SCC	RMR SCOTLAND	HMS CALEDONIA
Fogell, Andrew D	Cdr	30-Jun-11	LOGS	L SM	RNAS CULDROSE - LOGS	RNAS CULDROSE
Foley, Thomas R	Lt RN	01-Sep-12	WAR	GSX	HMS MONMOUTH	HMS MONMOUTH
Follington, Daniel C	Cdr	03-Aug-09	MED	MS	MDHU PORTSMOUTH	PORTSMOUTH
Fornes, Christopher J	Maj	01-Oct-09	RM	LC	1 ASSLT GROUP RM	PLYMOUTH
Fooks-Bale, Matthew E	Lt RN	01-Sep-04	WAR	P GR7	AWC EDW - JSF TES	USA
Foote, Andrew S	Lt Cdr	01-Oct-09	ENG	ME	NCHQ CNPS	PORTSMOUTH
Forbes, Angela J	Lt Cdr	01-Oct-09	LOGS	L BAR	NCHQ - CNLS	NCHQ
Forbes, Duncan	Maj	01-Oct-07	RM		DEFAC JSCSC ACSC	SHRIVENHAM
Forbes, Simon P	SLt	01-Feb-11	ENG	WESM	HMS TRIUMPH	
Forbes, Thomas E	Lt RN	01-Sep-12	WAR	GSX	MCM2 CREW 5	PORTSMOUTH
Force, Rory J	SLt	01-Mar-11	ENG	MESM	DCEME SULTAN	HMS SULTAN
Ford, Brendan R	Lt RN	01-May-10	ENG	TM	40 CDO RM - HR CELL	TAUNTON
Ford, Christopher R	Lt RN	01-Apr-12	WAR	O UT	RNAS CULDROSE	RNAS CULDROSE
Ford, Johnathan V	Capt	28-Jul-06	RM	C (SCC)	30 CDO IX GP RM	PLYMOUTH
Ford, Jonathan R	Lt RN	01-Aug-09	WAR	ATC	CHFHQ (SEA)	RNAS YEOVILTON
Ford, Martin John Afc	Lt Cdr	05-Aug-98	WAR	O SK6	GANNET SAR FLT	PRESTWICK
Forde, Rupert J	SLt	01-Jan-12	WAR	GSX	MCM1 CREW 6	FASLANE
Fordham, Phillip J	SLt	01-Apr-12	WAR	GSX	MCM1 CREW 1	FASLANE
Foreman, John L R	Cdr	30-Jun-01	WAR	PWO(C)	NATO-ACO-JFC HQ NAPLES	NAPLES
Foreman, Louisa	Lt RN	01-Jun-10	WAR	GSX	HMS TEMERAIRE - DNLM	PORTSMOUTH
Foreman, Neil A	Capt	21-Sep-05	RM	GS (RES)	RMR SCOTLAND	HMS CALEDONIA
Foreman, Simon M	Lt Cdr	01-Apr-05	ENG	WE	DES/COMLAND	ABBEY WOOD
Forer, Duncan A	Cdr	30-Jun-05	ENG	TM	NCHQ CNPS	NCHQ
Forer, Jonathon T	Mid	01-Feb-13	WAR	GSX	BRNC DARTMOUTH	
Forge, Stephen	Lt Cdr	01-Oct-06	LOGS	L	FLEET SPT LOGS INFRA	NCHQ
Forrest, Adam	Lt RN	13-Jul-12	WAR	C	RN ACQUAINT CENTRE	HMS COLLINGWOOD
Forrest, David J	Lt RN	01-Jan-08	WAR	P SK4	727 NAS	RNAS YEOVILTON
Forrest, Paul M	Maj	01-Oct-12	RM	GS	FLEET COMOPS NWD	NORTHWOOD
Forrester, Michael A	Lt RN	01-Sep-08	ENG	MESM	HQ ISAF	AFGHANISTAN KABUL
Forse, Ryan Michael	SLt	01-Sep-11	ENG	WE	MWS COLLINGWOOD	
Forster, Christopher R	SLt	14-Dec-13	WAR	GSX	BRNC DARTMOUTH	
Forster, Robin M	Lt Col	30-Jun-05	RM		CTCRM	EXMOUTH
Forster, Thomas W	SLt	01-Apr-11	WAR	GSX	HMS DAUNTLESS	
Forsyth, Adam L	Lt RN	01-Sep-08	ENG	AE	DES/COMJE/HELS	YEOVIL
Fortescue, Robert	Cdr	30-Jun-07	WAR	O LYNX	NATO-ACT-HQ SACT	BRUSSELS
Foster, Adrian A	Capt	16-Apr-10	RM	MLDR (SCC)	30 CDO IX GP RM	PLYMOUTH
Foster, Alan J	Lt Cdr	01-Oct-11	ENG	MESM	DES/COMFLEET	HMS DRAKE
Foster, Benjamin	Lt Col	30-Jun-13	RM	SBS	MOD DEFENCE STAFF	LONDON
Foster, Bruce M T	Maj	07-Dec-98	RM	GS	STRIKFORNATO LISBON	LISBON
Foster, Matthew P	Mid	01-Sep-13	WAR	GSX	BRNC DARTMOUTH	
Foster, Nicholas P	Maj	01-May-06	RM	GS	DEFAC JSCSC ACSC	SHRIVENHAM
Foster, Nicholas P	Lt Cdr	01-Oct-05	WAR	HM (M CH)	DGC(AE) OPS & PLANS DIV	FELTHAM
Foster, Sebastian J	Surg Lt RN	04-Aug-10	MED	GDMO	HMS LANCASTER	
Foulger, Thomas E	Surg Lt Cdr (D)	11-Jun-04	DENTAL	GDP	HMS SULTAN - DENTAL	HMS SULTAN
Foulis, Niall D A	Lt Cdr	01-Mar-03	WAR	HM	RNAS YEOVILTON	
Fowle, Laura Claire	Lt RN	01-Sep-04	WAR	GSX	BRNC DARTMOUTH	
Fowler, Christopher D	Lt RN	16-Dec-05	ENG	WE	MCM1 FAS SEA1	HELENSBURGH
Fowler, Gareth S	Lt RN	15-Apr-11	ENG	ME	HMS DIAMOND	
Fowler, James E	Lt Cdr	01-Oct-12	MED	MS(CDO)	NCHQ MEDDIV	NCHQ
Fowler, Remington	Lt RN	01-Sep-06	ENG	WESM(SWS)	CBRN POL	MAIN BUILDING LONDON
Fox, Christopher J	Lt RN	01-Oct-09	WAR	GSX	HMS SOMERSET	
Fox, David J	Lt Cdr	01-Oct-12	WAR	SM(CQ)	HMS RALEIGH	
Fox, Owen George	SLt	01-Apr-12	WAR	SM(X)	HMS VANGUARD	
Fox, Richard G OBE	Lt Cdr	30-Jun-05	WAR	P SK4	848 SQN	RNAS YEOVILTON
Fox, Trefor M	Lt Cdr	01-Oct-06	WAR	HM (H CH)	DGC(AE) OPS & PLANS DIV	FELTHAM
Fradley, Nicola Ann	SLt	01-Nov-11	WAR	GSX	BRNC DARTMOUTH	

Person Name	Substantive Rank	Seniority	Branch	Specialisation	Organisation	Location
Frame, Wendy	Lt RN	13-Apr-12	ENG	ME	HMS DARING	
Frampton, Charles	Lt RN	01-Sep-09	WAR	GSX	FLEET COMOPS NWD	NORTHWOOD
Francis, James S	RN Chpln	01-Oct-07	Ch S		COMPORFLOT SEA	HMNB PORTSMOUTH
Francis, Steven	Col	14-Feb-11	RM	GS	ATTACHE/ADVISER - ISLABAD	PAKISTAN
Frankham, Peter J	Cdr	31-Dec-00	ENG	WE	DES/COMFLEET	PORTSMOUTH
Franklin, Benjamin J	Cdr	30-Jun-09	WAR	O MER	RNAS CULDROSE - MHFHQ	RNAS CULDROSE
Franklin, Joseph P	2Lt	02-Sep-13	RM	N/A	CTCRM OFFICERS	EXMOUTH
Franks, Christopher	Lt Cdr	01-Feb-98	ENG	WESM(TWS)	NUCLEAR CAPABILITY	MAIN BUILDING LONDON
Franks, Jason A	Lt RN	03-Sep-13	WAR	OP INT (RES)	YEMEN GCT	YEMEN
Fraser, Callum J	SLt	24-Jul-11	ENG	WESM	MWS COLLINGWOOD	HMS COLLINGWOOD
Fraser, Eric	Cdre	01-Jul-07	WAR	PWO(C)	HMS NEPTUNE	HELENSBURGH
Fraser, Gordon A	Lt RN	11-Dec-09	WAR	ATC	UK MCC	BAHRAIN
Fraser, Graeme W	Lt Col	30-Jun-09	RM	LC	JFHQ	NORTHWOOD
Fraser, Ian D	Lt Cdr	01-Jul-02	ENG	AE	RNLA	DARTMOUTH
Fraser, Ian E	Lt Cdr	01-Oct-07	WAR	P MER	NCHQ CNPERS	PORTSMOUTH
Fraser, James M	Lt RN	01-Feb-03	WAR	P LYNX	DEF HELI FLYING SCH - HQSQN	RAF SHAWBURY
Fraser, Michael	Lt RN	01-Sep-01	WAR	HM(AS)	HMS ECHO	
Fraser, Patrick	Lt Cdr	01-Oct-03	ENG	AE	ACDS DEFLOGOPS INTER	MAIN BUILDING LONDON
Fraser, Simon A	Lt RN	01-Sep-13	ENG	WE	HMS PORTLAND	
Fraser, Timothy P	R Adm	16-Jan-12	WAR	PWO(N)	US CENTCOM	USA TAMPA
Fraser-Shaw, Dominic A	Mid	01-Nov-13	LOGS	L	BRNC DARTMOUTH	
Fraser-Smith, Sharron A	Lt Cdr	01-Oct-11	QARNNS	T&O	MDHU DERRIFORD	PLYMOUTH
Frater, Rebecca S	Lt Cdr	01-Oct-10	WAR	P LYNX	DEF HELI FLYING SCH - HQSQN	SHREWSBURY
Frazer, Catherine	Lt Cdr	01-Oct-11	WAR	ATC	RNAS CULDROSE	
Fredrickson, Charlotte A	Lt RN	01-Sep-06	WAR	O SKW	UKRBATSTAFF - COMUKRFOR	PLYMOUTH
Free, Andrew S	Lt Cdr	01-Oct-08	ENG	IS	NCHQ CNPS	PORTSMOUTH
Freeman, David R	Cdr	30-Jun-08	WAR	O LYNX	HMS TEMERAIRE - DNLM	PORTSMOUTH
Freeman, Edmund M R	Lt RN	01-Feb-06	WAR	PWO	HMS DARING	
Freeman, Mark E	Maj	01-Sep-96	RM		CTCRM - ASC	WAREHAM
Freeman, Martin J	Lt Cdr	01-Oct-07	ENG	MESM	HMS AUDACIOUS	BARROW IN FURNESS
Freeman, Matthew J	SLt	01-Mar-11	ENG	WE	MWS COLLINGWOOD	HMS COLLINGWOOD
Freeman, Nicholas H	Capt	01-Sep-12	RM	GS	HQ 3 CDO BDE RM	PLYMOUTH
French, Jeremy	Lt Cdr	01-Oct-12	WAR	P SK4	RN EXCHANGE AUSTRALIA	AUSTRRALIA
French, Matthew P	SLt	01-Apr-12	WAR	GSX	MCM1 CREW 5	FASLANE
French, Megan	Surg SLt	29-Jul-13	MED	MEDICAL	BRNC DARTMOUTH	
French, Paul	Lt Cdr	01-Oct-09	ENG	AE	FLEET CSAV	YEOVIL
French, Rebecca	Lt RN	01-Feb-10	LOGS	L	FOST DPORT SEA	HMNB DEVONPORT
French, Sophie R	SLt	08-Dec-11	WAR	P	YEOVILTON	RNAS YEOVILTON
Freshwater, Dennis A	Surg Cdr	09-Aug-08	MED	Med	RCDM	BIRMINGHAM
Fries, Charles A	Surg Lt Cdr	02-Feb-10	MED	BPS	INM ALVERSTOKE	GOSPORT
Frith, Adele M	Lt Cdr	01-Oct-13	LOGS	L BAR	NORTHWOOD HQ	NORTHWOOD
Frost, Laurence J	Lt RN	01-Jul-04	ENG	WE	NCHQ CNPS	PORTSMOUTH
Frost, Mark A	Lt Cdr	01-Jan-03	ENG	TM	FLEET FOST ACOS(Trg)	NCHQ
Frost, Oliver A	2Lt	01-Apr-13	RM	GS	CTCRM OFFICERS	EXMOUTH
Frost, Robert W	Lt RN	01-Oct-09	WAR	GSX	CDO LOG REGT RM	BARNSTAPLE
Frost, Timothy S	Lt RN	01-May-05	WAR	P SK4	848 SQN	RNAS YEOVILTON
Fry, Jonathan M S	Capt RN	30-Jun-08	ENG	ME	FLEET CAP SSM DIVISION	NCHQ
Fry, Rebecca L	Surg Lt Cdr	06-Aug-13	MED	Anaes	INM ALVERSTOKE	GOSPORT
Fry, Rohan A	2Lt	02-Sep-13	RM	N/A	CTCRM OFFICERS	EXMOUTH
Fry, Stephen P	Surg Lt Cdr	01-May-10	MED	GMP	INM ALVERSTOKE	GOSPORT
Fryer, Adrian C	Cdr	30-Jun-11	WAR	AAWO	HMS DAUNTLESS	
Fryer, Nicholas B	Mid	01-Nov-13	LOGS	L	BRNC DARTMOUTH	DARTMOUTH
Fulker, Edward P	Lt RN	20-Dec-10	WAR	SM(X)	HMS TORBAY	
Full, Richard J	Lt Cdr	01-Oct-10	WAR	O SKW	849 SQN	RNAS CULDROSE
Fuller, Charles	Lt Cdr	01-Oct-07	WAR	P SK6	FLEET CSAV	ABBEY WOOD
Fuller, James A	Capt	01-Sep-09	RM	GS	45 CDO RM - Y COY	DUNDEE
Fuller, James B	Maj	01-Oct-05	RM	LC	30 CDO IX GP RM	PLYMOUTH
Fuller, Lucy Ann	Lt RN	01-Sep-11	WAR	ATC	RNAS CULDROSE	
Fuller, Nicholas M	Lt RN	01-Jan-12	WAR	O UT	849 SQN	RNAS CULDROSE
Fuller, Richard	Lt RN	01-Jul-03	LOGS	L	DCD - MODSAP KSA	RIYADH
Fuller, Stephen P	Lt Cdr	01-Oct-09	ENG	AE	849 SQN	RNAS CULDROSE
Fulton, Craig R	Cdr	31-Dec-00	WAR	SM(CQ)	NOPF DAM NECK	VIRGINIA BEACH

Person Name	Substantive Rank	Seniority	Branch	Specialisation	Organisation	Location
Fulton, David M	Lt RN	01-May-02	ENG	MESM	HMS ARTFUL	BARROW IN FURNESS
Funnell, Lee C	Lt RN	01-Jun-10	WAR	MW	MCM2 CREW 3	PORTSMOUTH
Furneaux, James	Lt RN	21-Mar-10	WAR	HM	HMS SCOTT	
Furniss, Sam	Mid	15-Aug-12	WAR	GSX	HMS ENTERPRISE	
Fyfe, Karen S	Lt Cdr	01-Oct-07	WAR	HM(AS)	HMS ECHO	
Fyfe, Tobias Richard M	Surg SLt (D)	24-Jul-12	DENTAL	GDP(VDP)	HMS SULTAN - DENTAL	HMS SULTAN
Fyfe-Green, Alexa C	Surg Lt Cdr (D)	09-Jun-10	DENTAL	GDP	HMS DRAKE - SDS	HMS DRAKE
Fyfe-Green, Ian A	Lt Cdr	01-Oct-08	WAR	ATC	FLEET CSAV	NCHQ

G

Person Name	Substantive Rank	Seniority	Branch	Specialisation	Organisation	Location
Gabb, John R	Lt RN	01-Apr-13	WAR	SM(X)	HMS TRIUMPH	
Gaffney, Benjamin	Maj	01-Oct-11	RM	GS	CTCRM	EXMOUTH
Gaffney, Francis	Lt RN	16-Apr-08	WAR	OP INT (RES)	NPT RES MOBILISATION	HMNB PORTSMOUTH
Gahan, Richard J	Lt Cdr	01-Oct-11	ENG	WESM(SWS)	HMS VIGILANT	
Gaines, Edwin J	Lt RN	28-Jul-06	ENG	WESM(TWS)	DES/COMFLEET	ABBEY WOOD BRISTOL
Gale, Crystal V	Lt Cdr	24-Dec-00	LOGS	L	HMS PRESIDENT	LONDON
Gale, Mark A	Capt RN	21-Jan-13	ENG	MESM	DES/COMFLEET	BARROW IN FURNESS
Gale, Simon P	Cdr	30-Jun-09	WAR	PWO(U)	DI - FC(A)	MAIN BUILDING LONDON
Gall, Michael Robert C	Surg Capt RN (D)	04-Sep-07	DENTAL	GDP	DMS WHITTINGTON DDS	LICHFIELD
Gallagher, Kieran J	Capt	01-Sep-11	RM	GS	NC PSYA	NORTHWOOD
Gallagher, Michael V	Lt RN	01-Sep-11	LOGS	L	HMS VIGILANT	
Gallagher, Ross C	Lt RN	01-May-13	WAR	GSX	HMS KENT	
Gallimore, Richard M	Lt RN	01-Oct-00	WAR	P GR7	RNAS YEOVILTON - AS	RNAS YEOVILTON
Gamble, Neil	Lt Cdr	01-Oct-10	WAR	P SK6	DEF HELI FLYING SCH - HQSQN	RAF SHAWBURY
Gamble, Phillip	Lt RN	15-May-93	WAR	O SKW	GANNET SAR FLT	PRESTWICK
Gamble, Stephen B	Lt Cdr	01-Oct-10	WAR	P LYNX	FLEET AV VL - OC	RNAS YEOVILTON
Game, Philip G	Cdr	30-Jun-09	ENG	WE	DES/COMFLEET/ABW	ABBEY WOOD
Gamwell, Sebastian P	Lt RN	01-Jun-13	WAR	ATC	RNAS YEOVILTON - AS	RNAS YEOVILTON
Gannon, Dominic R	Capt	24-Jul-04	RM	GS	NCHQ	
Gardiner, Angus P	2Lt	01-Sep-11	RM	GS	40 CDO RM - DGHR(O)	TAUNTON
Gardiner, Christopher A	Lt RN	13-Jul-12	LOGS	L	820 SQN	RNAS CULDROSE
Gardiner, Dermot	Surg Lt Cdr	01-May-09	MED	GMP	INM ALVERSTOKE	GOSPORT
Gardner, Christopher R	Cdre	04-Jan-10	LOGS	L SM	CUSTOMER DESIGN	MAIN BUILDING LONDON
Gardner, John E	Cdr	30-Jun-09	WAR	PWO(A)	JFC HQ	NORTHWOOD
Gardner, Louis P	Lt Cdr	01-Oct-11	WAR	SM(AWC)	HMS TALENT	
Gardner, Michael P	Lt Cdr	01-Oct-08	WAR	PWO	FLEET COMOPS NWD	NORTHWOOD
Gardner, Rachael	Lt RN	01-Apr-11	LOGS	L	DEPT OF THE CGS JSAU (L)	MAIN BUILDING LONDON
Gardner, Sadie J	Lt RN	09-Apr-09	LOGS	L	OCLC LONDON	LONDON
Gardner-Clark, Suzanne L	Lt Cdr	01-Oct-08	QARNNS	EN (C&S)	RCDM	BIRMINGHAM
Gare, Christopher	Lt Cdr	01-Oct-08	WAR	PWO	RN EXCHANGE CANADA	OTTAWA 1
Garland, Andrew N	Maj	01-Oct-05	RM	SCC	CTCRM - ACOS(PERS)	EXMOUTH
Garman, Richard A	Capt	01-Sep-10	RM	GS	CTCRM - CTW	EXMOUTH
Garner, Dominic	Mid	01-Nov-13	WAR	GSX	BRNC D'ARTMOUTH	
Garner, Llyr	Lt RN	01-Jul-12	WAR	O UT	RNAS CULDROSE	
Garner, Michael E	Lt RN	01-Feb-05	WAR	GSX	DEFAC JSCSC I	SHRIVENHAM
Garner, Robert J	Lt RN	01-Sep-09	WAR	GSX	GIBRALTAR PBS	GIBRALTAR
Garner, Sean M	Lt Cdr	01-Aug-06	WAR	ATC	RNAS CULDROSE	
Garratt, John K	Cdr	30-Jun-10	WAR	AAWO	TIO	LONDON
Garratt, Mark David	Capt RN	30-Jun-08	WAR	P LYNX	RNAS CULDROSE - CA	RNAS CULDROSE
Garreta, Carlos E	Lt Cdr	01-Oct-10	WAR	PWO(A)	UK ACC (83 EAG)	QATAR - JOA - AL UDEID
Garrett, Stephen W OBE	Cdre	07-Feb-12	WAR	SM(CQ)	COMFASFLOT	HMNB CLYDE
Garside, Robert J	Capt	01-Sep-09	RM	GS	CDO LOG REGT RM	BARNSTAPLE
Garth, Lee	Lt RN	15-Apr-11	ENG	AE	ABBEY WOOD	
Garton, Hazelle M	Lt RN	01-Sep-10	ENG	AE	HMS SULTAN - RNAESS	HMS SULTAN
Gaskell-Taylor, Hugh M	Lt RN	01-Oct-11	WAR	GSX	HMS DARING	
Gaskin, Alexander E	2Lt	01-Mar-11	RM	N/A	CTCRM OFFICERS	EXMOUTH
Gatenby, Daniel	Lt RN	01-May-07	WAR	FC	MWS COLLINGWOOD	
Gates, Nigel S	Lt Cdr	01-Oct-08	WAR	P SK4	AWC BSD - RW TES	RAF BOSCOMBE DOWN
Gates, William C	RN Chpln	06-Sep-05	Ch S		HMS DRAKE	
Gaught, Edwin L	Lt RN	01-Sep-11	ENG	ME	DEFAC CMT	SHRIVENHAM
Gaunt, Amy V	Lt RN	01-Sep-04	WAR	O MER	820 SQN	RNAS CULDROSE
Gaunt, Emma	Lt RN	01-Feb-13	LOGS	L	MWS COLLINGWOOD	HMS COLLINGWOOD

Person Name	Substantive Rank	Seniority	Branch	Specialisation	Organisation	Location
Gay, David A T	Surg Cdr	01-Jul-09	MED	Radiologist	MDHU DERRIFORD	PLYMOUTH
Gayfer, Mark E	Capt RN	24-Jun-13	ENG	WESM(SWS)	DES/COMFLEET/NBC	HELENSBURGH
Gayle, David Mark	Lt RN	31-May-11	WAR	HM	HMS OCEAN	
Gayson, Christopher P	Lt RN	01-Mar-10	WAR	P SK4	845 SQN	RNAS YEOVILTON
Gaytano, Ronald T M	Lt RN	01-Apr-02	ENG	AE	PJHQ (UK) J6	NORTHWOOD
Gazzard, Julian H	Cdr	30-Jun-10	WAR	PWO(N)	DCMC	MAIN BUILDING LONDON
Gearing, Richard M	Lt Cdr	01-Oct-12	ENG	AE	DES/COMLAND	YEOVIL
Geary, Timothy W	Cdr	30-Jun-05	ENG	ME	HMS OCEAN	
Geddes, Nathaniel C S	Lt RN	01-Sep-11	ENG	ME	HMS SULTAN - RNSME SEG	HMS SULTAN
Gee, Mathew	Lt RN	20-Oct-06	LOGS	L	HMS ILLUSTRIOUS	
Geldard, Michael A	Lt Col	30-Jun-09	RM		CTCRM - CTW	EXMOUTH
Gell, David M	SLt	01-Sep-11	WAR	SM(X)	CAREER TRAINING	HMS RALEIGH
Gell, Thomas	Lt RN	01-Oct-08	WAR	FC	FOST DPORT SEA	HMNB DEVONPORT
Gellender, Paul S MBE	Capt	24-Jul-03	RM	SCC	HMS TEMERAIRE - DNLM	PORTSMOUTH
Geneux, Nicholas	Lt Cdr	01-Oct-09	ENG	TM	RN EXCHANGE USA - BDS	WASHINGTON USA
Gennard, Anthony Psc(J)	Lt Cdr	01-Mar-03	LOGS	L	DCDC	SHRIVENHAM
George, Alan P	Cdr	30-Jun-05	WAR	O LYNX	FLEET FOSNNI - CNR	HMNB PORTSMOUTH
George, David Mark	Cdr	30-Jun-09	WAR	PWO(A)	FMC - NAVY	MAIN BUILDING LONDON
George, James A	Lt RN	01-Feb-08	WAR	MCD	FOST MPV SEA	FASLANE
George, Nicholas D	Maj	01-Oct-10	RM	GS	FLEET COMOPS NWD	NORTHWOOD
George, Seth D	Lt Cdr	01-Oct-09	ENG	TM	FLEET FOST ACOS(Trg)	NCHQ
Gibb, Alexander K	Maj	01-Oct-09	RM	GS	NCHQ	
Gibbons, Nicholas P	Cdr	30-Jun-12	WAR	O SK6	824 SQN - TU	RNAS CULDROSE
Gibbons, Nicola J	Lt RN	01-Jan-13	ENG	WE	HMS BULWARK	
Gibbs, David J	Lt RN	01-Feb-98	WAR	P SK4	NO 3 FTS/UAS - JEFTS	
Gibbs, Emily K	Lt RN	01-Jan-11	WAR	TM	HMS SULTAN - RNSME HQ	HMS SULTAN
Gibbs, Mark P	Lt Cdr	01-Apr-10	ENG	ME	HMS NORTHUMBERLAND	
Gibbs, Neil David	Cdr	30-Jun-06	ENG	ME	DES/DTECH/TECHTD/ABW	ABBEY WOOD
Gibson, Adrian	Lt RN	01-Jan-04	ENG	WE	SCU SHORE	HMS COLLINGWOOD
Gibson, Alastair D	Cdr	30-Jun-06	LOGS	L	ACDS DEFLOGOPS INTER	MAIN BUILDING LONDON
Gibson, Alexander J	Maj	01-May-05	RM	LC	42 CDO RM - COMD COY	PLYMOUTH
Gibson, Andrew	Surg Cdr	30-Jun-07	MED	Ophthal	MDHU NORTHALLERTON	NORTHALLERTON
Gibson, Andrew M	Lt RN	01-Jan-12	LOGS	L	HMS DRAGON	
Gibson, Scott P	SLt	14-Aug-11	ENG	WESM	HMS RALEIGH	
Gibson, Stephen R	Lt Cdr	31-Mar-94	WAR	P MER	824 SQN - TU	RNAS CULDROSE
Gidney, Raymond S	SLt	01-Feb-12	WAR	SM(X)	BRNC DARTMOUTH	DARTMOUTH
Giffin, Iain	Lt RN	01-Oct-08	WAR	FC	NCHQ CNPERS	PORTSMOUTH
Gilbert, Mark	Lt RN	01-Sep-07	WAR	O MER	829 SQN FLT 02	RNAS CULDROSE
Gilbert, Peter D	Cdr	30-Jun-03	ENG	ME	FLEET ACOS(RP)	ABBEY WOOD
Gilbert, Rachel	Lt RN	01-Jan-05	WAR	O LYNX	RNAS CULDROSE	
Gilderthorp, Thomas D	Lt RN	01-Feb-12	WAR	GSX	HMS KENT	
Gilding, Douglas	Maj	01-Sep-98	WAR	HW	DEFENCE ACADEMY	SHRIVENHAM SWINDON
Giles, David W	Cdr	30-Jun-04	ENG	WE	NATO - BRUSSELS	BRUSSELS
Giles, Gary J	Maj	01-Oct-06	RM	SCC	ACDS DEFLOGOPSANDPLANS	MAIN BUILDING LONDON
Giles, Kevin D L	Lt Cdr	01-May-92	WAR	MCD PWO(U)	HMS COLLINGWOOD	
Giles, Simon	Maj	01-Oct-10	RM	SCC	45 CDO RM	DUNDEE
Gill, Adam M	Lt RN	08-Feb-13	WAR	C	DES/COMJE/ISS	ABBEY WOOD
Gill, Christopher D	Lt Cdr	01-Jan-08	WAR	SM(CQ)	HMS TIRELESS	
Gill, Lee	Lt RN	17-Dec-10	WAR	INT	JOINT OPERATIONAL STAFF	N IRELAND
Gill, Mark H	Lt Cdr	01-Jul-02	WAR	O SKW	857 NAS	RNAS CULDROSE
Gill, Martin R	Cdr	30-Jun-09	ENG	MESM	DES/COMFLEET	ABBEY WOOD
Gill, Paul S	Lt Cdr	01-Oct-13	ENG	TM	HQ EUFOR (SAR)	SARAJEVO
Gill, Samuel R	Lt RN	01-Sep-11	ENG	MESM	HMS TRENCHANT	
Gillespie, Benjamin D	Lt RN	01-Jul-11	WAR	SM(X)	HMS VANGUARD	
Gillett, David A	Lt Cdr	01-Nov-06	WAR	O LYNX	MWS COLLINGWOOD	
Gillett, Nathan David	Lt Cdr	01-Oct-10	WAR	AV	HMS QUEEN ELIZABETH	ROSYTH
Gillies, Brett	Lt Cdr	01-Oct-13	ENG	AE P	RNAS YEOVILTON - AED	RNAS YEOVILTON
Gillingham, George	Lt RN	01-Jan-07	WAR	O MER	824 SQN - TU	RNAS CULDROSE
Gillman, Robert N	Mid	01-Sep-13	ENG	AE	BRNC DARTMOUTH	DARTMOUTH
Gilmartin, Kieran P	Surg Lt Cdr	06-Aug-08	MED	GMP	HMS BULWARK	
Gilmore, Amy F	Lt RN	01-Sep-08	WAR	O LYNX	815 SQN YEOVILTON	RNAS YEOVILTON
Gilmore, Jeremy E	Lt RN	01-Sep-03	WAR	P SK4	845 SQN	RNAS YEOVILTON

Person Name	Substantive Rank	Seniority	Branch	Specialisation	Organisation	Location
Gilmore, Martin A	Lt RN	01-Feb-10	WAR	P MER	820 SQN	RNAS CULDROSE
Gilmore, Martin P	Lt Cdr	01-Oct-11	WAR	P LYNX	FLEET AV VL - OC	RNAS YEOVILTON
Gilmore, Steven J	Lt Cdr	01-Oct-09	ENG	WE	HMS MONMOUTH	
Gilroy, Anthony B	SLt	11-Apr-11	ENG	WESM	FASLANE HELENSBURGH	
Ginn, Robert D	Maj	01-Oct-12	RM	GS	FLEET CAP LLM & DRM DIVISION	NCHQ
Ginty, John A	SLt	01-Sep-11	WAR	SM(X)	HMS NORTHUMBERLAND	
Girling, Steven P	Mid	01-Sep-13	WAR	GSX	BRNC DARTMOUTH	
Gladwin, Michael D	Lt Cdr	01-Oct-12	WAR	ATC	RNAS CULDROSE	
Gleave, James	Lt Cdr	31-Mar-04	WAR	INFO OPS (RES)		UK MCC BAHRAIN
Gleave, Robert D	Lt RN	01-Nov-07	WAR	P LYNX	815 SQN FLT	RNAS YEOVILTON
Glendinning, Andreana S	Lt Cdr	01-Oct-09	QARNNS	ITU	DMS WHITTINGTON	LICHFIELD
Glendinning, Robert	Lt RN	19-Mar-08	WAR	AV	SF	RNAS CULDROSE
Glendinning, Vicky L	Lt RN	16-Jan-09	QARNNS	PHC	NCHQ MEDDIV	NCHQ
Glennie, Andrew M	Capt RN	09-Sep-08	ENG	ME	COMPORFLOT ESG	PORTSMOUTH
Glennie, John S	Surg Lt RN	05-Aug-09	MED	EM	INM ALVERSTOKE	GOSPORT
Gloak, James	Capt	01-Aug-07	RM	GS	PJHQ (UK) J2	NORTHWOOD
Glover, Adam	Lt RN	01-Mar-09	ENG	MESM	FLEET FOSNNI - CNR	PORTSMOUTH
Glover, Daniel	Lt RN	01-Sep-13	ENG	ME	HMS LANCASTER	
Glover, Lee N	Lt RN	13-Apr-12	ENG	AE	820 SQN	RNAS CULDROSE
Glover, Thomas F	Capt	01-Sep-09	RM	GS	COMUKAMPHIBFOR	HMNB PORTSMOUTH
Gobbi, Alexander M	Capt	01-Sep-13	RM	GS	40 CDO RM - A COY	TAUNTON
Gobell, Luke	Capt	01-Sep-12	RM	GS	40 CDO RM - COMD COY	TAUNTON
Gobey, Richard	Lt RN	04-Jun-05	WAR	SM(X) (RES)	NCHQ CNPERS	PORTSMOUTH
Goddard, Alexander C	Lt RN	06-Apr-07	ENG	ME	HMS SULTAN	
Goddard, David	Lt Cdr	01-Oct-10	LOGS	L BAR SM	HMS BULWARK	
Goddard, James A	Lt RN	01-Mar-10	ENG	AE	73 AVN COMPANY	IPSWICH
Goddard, Paul	Lt Cdr	01-Oct-09	ENG	WESM(SWS)	HMS VANGUARD	
Godfrey, Matthew F	RN Chpln	03-Jul-04	Ch S	Chaplain	FLEET HM UNIT	HMNB DEVONPORT
Godfrey, Simeon D	Lt Cdr	01-Oct-07	WAR	SM(AWC)	HQBF GIBRALTAR - OPS	HMS ROOKE
Godwin, Christopher A	Cdr	30-Jun-08	WAR	P MER	820 SQN	RNAS CULDROSE
Godwin, Lee D	Lt RN	07-Apr-06	WAR	AV	RNAS CULDROSE - EXEC	RNAS CULDROSE
Gokhale, Stephen G	Surg Lt Cdr	04-Aug-09	MED	GMP	NCHQ	
Golden, Dominic S	Lt Cdr	01-Jun-99	WAR	FC	DIRECTOR (JW)	NORTHWOOD
Goldman, Paul H L	Lt Cdr	01-Apr-99	ENG	WE	FLEET ACOS(RP)	NCHQ
Goldsmith, Darran	Cdr	30-Jun-09	WAR	O MER	ISAF PAK LO	PAKISTAN
Goldsmith, David T	Cdr	30-Jun-13	ENG	WE	FLEET HQ	NCHQ
Goldsmith, Simon	Lt Cdr	01-May-95	WAR	PWO(C)	EXCH AND LO APPTS (USA	WASHINGTON
Goldstone, Richard S	Cdr	30-Jun-12	WAR	AAWO	MWS COLLINGWOOD	HMS COLLINGWOOD
Gomm, Kevin OBE	Cdr	30-Jun-07	WAR	SM(CQ)	RNSMS	HMS RALEIGH
Goodall, Michael A	Lt Cdr	01-May-06	ENG	ME	UKRBATSTAFF	HMNB PORTSMOUTH
Goodall, William C	Lt RN	01-Sep-12	WAR	GSX	HMS TYNE	
Goode, Alun N	Lt Cdr	01-Sep-99	WAR	PWO(A)	FLEET COMOPS NWD	NORTHWOOD
Goodenough, Rory A	Surg SLt	30-Jul-13	MED	MEDICAL	BRNC DARTMOUTH	
Goodley, Ross	Lt RN	01-Oct-11	WAR	GSX	HMS KENT	
Goodman, David F	Lt Cdr	01-Oct-09	WAR	SM(AWC)	DIRECTOR (JW)	NORTHWOOD
Goodman, William	Capt	01-Aug-08	RM	GS	40 CDO RM	TAUNTON
Goodrum, Simon E	Lt Cdr	01-Oct-05	MED	MS	INM ALVERSTOKE2	GOSPORT
Goodsell, Christopher D	Cdr	30-Jun-06	WAR	SM(CQ)	FLEET COMOPS NWD	NORTHWOOD
Goodwin, Aaron K	Lt RN	01-Sep-11	WAR	GSX	HMS DEFENDER	
Goodwin, Lloyd W	Mid	01-Nov-13	WAR	SM(X)	BRNC DARTMOUTH	
Goodwin, Moss A	2Lt	02-Sep-13	RM	N/A	CTCRM OFFICERS	EXMOUTH
Goodwin, Thomas MBE	RN Chpln	05-May-02	Ch S		NEPTUNE 2SL/CNH	HELENSBURGH
Goose, Samuel J	Lt RN	01-Nov-07	WAR	INT	NORTHWOOD HQ	
Goosen, Richard	Lt RN	01-May-04	WAR	HM	HMS DRAKE	
Goram, Malcolm	Lt Cdr	31-Mar-04	WAR	ATC (RES)	RNAS YEOVILTON	
Gordon, Daniel	Lt RN	19-Oct-07	WAR	AV	HMS ILLUSTRIOUS	
Gordon, David	Cdr	30-Jun-01	ENG	TM(SM)	FLEET FOST ACOS(Trg)	NCHQ
Gordon, David E	Lt Cdr	01-Oct-12	ENG	AE	DES/COMJE/HELS	YEOVIL
Gordon, David I	Lt Cdr	01-Oct-11	WAR	HM(AS)	LOAN HYDROG - DGHR(N)	TAUNTON
Gordon, Emily H	SLt	01-Sep-11	WAR	HM	HMS SEVERN	
Gordon, John	Lt Cdr	01-Oct-09	WAR	SM(C)	FLEET COMOPS NWD	NORTHWOOD
Gorman, Darren A	Lt RN	01-Sep-02	WAR	P SK4	DEF HELI FLYING SCH	RAF VALLEY

Person Name	Substantive Rank	Seniority	Branch	Specialisation	Organisation	Location
Gorman, Glenn K	Lt Cdr	01-Oct-12	WAR	PWO	HMS DIAMOND	
Gorst, Joshua R	Lt RN	01-Jan-13	LOGS	L	FLEET FOSNNI	LIVERPOOL
Gosling, Jonathan C	2Lt	02-Sep-13	RM	N/A	CTCRM OFFICERS	EXMOUTH
Gosney, Christopher J	Maj	01-Oct-05	RM	SCC	HMS OCEAN	
Gotke, Christopher T	Lt Cdr	01-Oct-08	WAR	P SHAR	RNAS YEOVILTON - ADHQ	RNAS YEOVILTON
Gott, Stephen B	Lt Cdr	01-Oct-09	LOGS	L	HMS SULTAN - CS	HMS SULTAN
Goudge, Simon D P	Cdr	30-Jun-12	LOGS	L	FLEET FOST ACOS(Trg)	NCHQ
Gough, Christopher M	Lt RN	11-Apr-11	ENG	TM	HMS ARTFUL	BARROW IN FURNESS
Gough, Martyn	RN Chpln	01-Sep-98	Ch S	GS	101 LOG BDE	ALDERSHOT
Goulder, Jonathan D	Lt Cdr	01-Oct-06	WAR	AAWO	FOST DPORT SEA	HMNB DEVONPORT
Gow, Peter Joseph	Lt RN	16-Sep-09	LOGS	L SM	DES/COMFLEET/	FASLANE HELENSBURGH
Gower, John H OBE	R Adm	28-Nov-11	WAR	SM(CQ)	ACDS NUC CB	MAIN BUILDING LONDON
Gowers, Sarah MBE	Lt RN	09-Jun-06	LOGS	L	101 LOG BDE	ALDERSHOT
Gowling, Stephen M	Lt RN	01-Dec-13	WAR	GSX	MWS COLLINGWOOD	HMS COLLINGWOOD
Goy, Sally E	Lt RN	01-Jun-08	LOGS	L BAR	NCHQ - CNLS	HELENSBURGH
Grace, Nicholas J OBE	Lt Col	30-Jun-09	RM	BS	HQ BAND SERVICE	HMS NELSON
Graddon, Giles J	Lt RN	01-Jan-08	WAR	INT	FLEET COMOPS NWD	HMS COLLINGWOOD
Grafton, Joshua T	SLt	01-Feb-11	WAR	SM(X)	MWS COLLINGWOOD	HMS COLLINGWOOD
Graham, Alastair N S MVO	Lt Cdr	01-Aug-01	ENG	WESM	JFC HOC C4ISR	NORTHWOOD
Graham, Benjamin R	Lt RN	01-Sep-07	LOGS	L	HMS ILLUSTRIOUS	
Graham, David W	Capt RN	01-Jul-11	ENG	MESM	DES/COMFLEET	ABBEY WOOD BRISTOL
Graham, Gordon R	Capt RN	03-Mar-09	ENG	WE	LOAN DSTL - FLD	FAREHAM
Graham, James P	Lt RN	20-Oct-06	WAR	AV	DSTO	RAF ST MAWGAN
Graham, Mark A	Lt Cdr	01-Oct-01	WAR	O LYNX	HANDLING SQN - OC	RAF BOSCOMBE DOWN
Grainge, Christopher L	Surg Cdr	03-Aug-12	MED	Med	MDHU PORTSMOUTH	PORTSMOUTH
Grainger, Natalie	Lt RN	01-Feb-13	WAR	P SK4	CHF(MERLIN)	RAF BENSON
Grandy, Mark	Lt RN	01-Sep-10	ENG	WE	NAVY MCTA PORTSMOUTH	HMNB PORTSMOUTH
Grant, Daniel Paul	Mid	24-Jan-13	WAR	O UT	BRNC DARTMOUTH	DARTMOUTH
Grant, David J	Lt Cdr	01-Oct-03	ENG	MESM	NBC CLYDE BABCOCK	HELENSBURGH
Grant, Elizabeth S A	Lt RN	13-Jul-12	WAR	REG	RNP SIB WESTERN	HMS DRAKE
Grant, Gary	Lt RN	12-Jul-13	ENG	WESM	MWS COLLINGWOOD	
Grant, Hugo J	Capt	01-Sep-13	RM	GS	43 CDO	HMNB CLYDE
Grant, Richard	Lt Cdr	01-Oct-11	ENG	ME	DES/COMFLEET/SHIPS	ABBEY WOOD
Grant, Wayne G	Lt Cdr	01-Jun-08	ENG	AE	1710 NAS	PORTSMOUTH
Grantham, Guy J	Lt RN	01-Nov-00	ENG	IS	FLEET CAP IS DIVISION	NCHQ
Grantham, Stephen	Capt RN	01-Jul-13	ENG	MESM	DES/COMFLEET/NBC	HMNB CLYDE
Gray, Antony J	Capt RN	14-Dec-09	ENG	AE	DES/COMJE/HELS	YEOVIL
Gray, David K	Lt Cdr	01-Apr-95	ENG	WE	FOSNNI - YOUTH	HMNB PORTSMOUTH
Gray, Emma J	Lt Cdr	01-Oct-07	LOGS	L	HMS NELSON	PORTSMOUTH
Gray, John A	Lt Cdr	01-Oct-06	WAR	SM(CQ)	COMFASFLOT	HMNB CLYDE
Gray, John Allan	Cdr	30-Jun-06	WAR	AAWO	FLEET FOSNNI - NRC	HELENSBURGH
Gray, Karl D	Maj	01-May-06	RM	C	40 CDO RM	TAUNTON
Gray, Martina E	Lt RN	24-Aug-92	LOGS	L	NCHQ CNPERS	PORTSMOUTH
Gray, Matthew S	Capt	30-Mar-12	RM	SCC	HQ SQN CDO LOG	RMB CHIVENOR
Gray, Michael J H	Lt Cdr	01-Oct-08	WAR	INT	FLEET CAP IS DIVISION	NCHQ
Gray, Nathan J	Lt Cdr	01-Oct-10	WAR	P GR7	CAREER TRAINING	RAF BOSCOMBE DOWN
Gray, Oliver W	Capt	01-Sep-06	RM	LC	FLEET CAP LLM & DRM DIVISION	NCHQ
Gray, Paul R	Cdr	30-Jun-12	WAR	P MER	FLEET MARITIME WARFARE	HMS COLLINGWOOD
Gray, Richard G	Lt RN	01-Sep-11	ENG	WESM(SWS)	HMS VIGILANT	
Gray, Richard L	Lt Cdr	01-Oct-12	WAR	PWO	HMS PORTLAND	
Gray, Samuel D	Lt RN	01-Aug-04	WAR	GSX	HMS MERSEY	
Gray, Simon A	Maj	01-Oct-08	RM	C	PJHQ (UK) CMD GP	NORTHWOOD
Grayland, Andrew	Lt RN	01-Jan-09	ENG	WE	HMS DEFENDER	
Grayson, Stephen	Lt Cdr	01-Oct-12	LOGS	L SM	UK MCC	BAHRAIN
Greason, Paul A	Lt RN	01-Aug-08	ENG	WE	DES/COMLAND/WPNS	ABBEY WOOD
Greaves, Joshua B	2Lt	02-Sep-13	RM	N/A	CTCRM OFFICERS	EXMOUTH
Greaves, Michael	Lt RN	01-Sep-08	ENG	WESM(TWS)	RNSMS	HMS RALEIGH
Greaves, Timothy M GCGI	Lt RN	01-Sep-06	WAR	ATC	RNAS CULDROSE - ATC	RNAS CULDROSE
Green, Andrew J	Cdr	30-Jun-08	ENG	TM(SM)	DES/COMFLEET	HMS NELSON
Green, Andrew M	Lt Cdr	12-May-99	ENG	ME	DIO SAPT	NCHQ
Green, David	Cdr	30-Jun-03	ENG	WESM(TWS)	DES/COMFLEET	ABBEY WOOD
Green, Gareth M	Maj	01-Sep-98	RM		FLEET COMOPS NWD	NORTHWOOD

Person Name	Substantive Rank	Seniority	Branch	Specialisation	Organisation	Location
Green, Gary E	Lt Col	30-Jun-06	RM	SCC	STRIKFORNATO - LISBON	LISBON
Green, Jayne H	Lt Cdr	01-Sep-11	WAR	O LYNX	815 SQN FLT	RNAS YEOVILTON
Green, Jeremy D	Lt RN	01-Sep-13	ENG	WESM	HMS RALEIGH	
Green, Jonathan	Lt Cdr	01-Oct-13	WAR	P SKW	GANNET SAR FLT	HMS GANNET
Green, Jonathan R	Mid	01-Sep-13	ENG	ME	BRNC DARTMOUTH	DARTMOUTH
Green, Joseph R	Lt RN	01-Sep-11	WAR	GSX	UK MCC	BAHRAIN
Green, Leslie D	Lt Cdr	01-Oct-09	ENG	MESM	COMFASFLOT	HMNB CLYDE
Green, Mark D	Lt RN	09-Apr-10	WAR	O LYNX	815 SQN	RNAS YEOVILTON
Green, Natalie M	Surg Lt RN	07-Aug-13	MED	MEDICAL	BRNC DARTMOUTH	
Green, Nicholas D	Lt RN	01-Apr-10	WAR	SM(X)	POLICY & COMMITMENTS	MAIN BUILDING LONDON
Green, Peter J	Cdr	30-Jun-05	WAR	SM(CQ)	NUCLEAR CAPABILITY	MAIN BUILDING LONDON
Green, Philip	Capt	18-Jul-07	RM	C (SCC)	FOSNNI - YOUTH	HMNB PORTSMOUTH
Green, Richard J	SLt	01-Apr-11	WAR	P UT	RAF SHAWBURY	RAF SHAWBURY
Green, Steven P	Capt	21-Mar-13	RM	BS	CTCRM BAND	EXMOUTH
Green, Timothy C	Cdr	30-Jun-09	WAR	PWO(U)	NATO-ACO-SHAPE	CASTEAU
Green, Timothy J	Cdr	31-Dec-98	WAR	SM(CQ)	UKTI - DSO	LONDON
Greenall, Gilbert E	Surg Lt RN	07-Aug-13	MED	MEDICAL	BRNC DARTMOUTH	
Greene, Michael J	Cdr	31-Dec-99	ENG	TM	FOSNNI - YOUTH C	HMNB PORTSMOUTH
Greener, Carl	Cdr	30-Jun-09	ENG	WE	FLEET CAP IS DIVISION	NCHQ
Greenfield, Stuart	Lt RN	01-Sep-11	ENG	AE	845 SQN	RNAS YEOVILTON
Greenhill, Matthew C	Lt RN	01-May-04	WAR	INT	FLEET COMOPS NWD	NORTHWOOD
Greenland, Michael R MVO	Cdr	30-Jun-11	WAR	P LYNX	FLEET CSAV	NCHQ
Greenlees, Iain W	Capt RN	30-Jun-05	WAR	PWO(A)	DES/COMFLEET	HMNB PORTSMOUTH
Greenway, Crendon A	Lt	01-Sep-12	RM	GS	40 CDO RM - D COY	TAUNTON
Greenwood, Daniel A	Lt RN	11-Apr-08	ENG	WESM(SWS)	NBC CLYDE	HELENSBURGH
Greenwood, David R	Lt RN	01-May-10	WAR	GSX	HMS TYNE	
Greenwood, Julia L	Lt RN	01-Feb-10	WAR	GSX	DEFENCE ACADEMY	SHRIVENHAM
Greenwood, Peter	Lt Cdr	01-Oct-12	WAR	P MER	829 SQN HQ	RNAS CULDROSE
Greenwood, Stephen J	Lt RN	01-May-05	WAR	SM(N)	HMS SCOTIA	HMS CALEDONIA
Gregg, Ryan Lee	Lt RN	01-Sep-11	ENG	AE	DES/COMJE/HELS	ABBEY WOOD
Gregory, Alastair S	Cdr	30-Jun-06	ENG	ME	MTM DRAKE 5 TERMINAL	HMS DRAKE
Gregory, Andrew J	Capt	03-Apr-09	RM	BS	RM BAND SCOTLAND	HMS CALEDONIA
Gregory, Anthony E	Surg Lt Cdr	01-Sep-07	MED	GMP (C&S)	FOST SEA - DMO	HMNB DEVONPORT
Gregory, Daniel P	SLt	01-Apr-11	WAR	P UT	824 SQN CULDROSE	RNAS CULDROSE
Gregory, Jonathan E	Lt RN	01-Jan-05	ENG	TM	FOST FAS SHORE - CSSC	HELENSBURGH
Gregory, Samuel G	Lt RN	01-Feb-11	ENG	TM	43 CDO FPGRM COMD SQN	HMNB CLYDE
Greig, Ryan A	Mid	01-Sep-12	WAR	GSX	HMS SEVERN	
Greig, Stuart J	Lt RN	01-May-13	LOGS	L	FOST NWD (JTEPS)	NORTHWOOD
Grenfell-Shaw, Mark	Cdr	30-Jun-05	ENG	WESM(TWS)	DES/COMFLEET/SM/ABW	ABBEY WOOD
Gresswell, Nick A	Lt RN	01-Sep-08	WAR	P LYNX	LHF 815 SQN FLT 206	RNAS YEOVILTON
Greswell, James S	Capt	01-Sep-11	RM	GS	42 CDO RM - DGHR(O)	PLYMOUTH
Grey, Amy C	Lt RN	01-Apr-03	WAR	O LYNX	WMF SHORE	RNAS YEOVILTON
Grey, Christopher S	Lt Cdr	01-Oct-09	WAR	O LYNX	HMS WESTMINSTER	
Grice, Matthew	Lt Cdr	01-Oct-10	ENG	AE	HQ JHC	ANDOVER
Grierson, Andrew D	Lt Cdr	01-Oct-13	ENG	TM	UKRBATSTAFF	HMNB PORTSMOUTH
Griffen, David J	Lt Cdr	01-Oct-10	WAR	PWO MW	UK MCC	BAHRAIN
Griffin, Niall MBE	Capt RN	01-Jul-13	WAR	P SK4	CHFHQ (SEA)	RNAS YEOVILTON
Griffin, Stephen	Lt Cdr	01-Oct-09	WAR	AV	SF	RNAS CULDROSE
Griffith, Phillip B	SLt	01-May-11	LOGS	L	HMS TRENCHANT	
Griffiths, Adam M	Surg SLt	29-Jul-13	MED	MEDICAL	BRNC DARTMOUTH	
Griffiths, Beth	Lt RN	01-Jan-08	ENG	ME	DES/COMFLEET/SHIPS	ABBEY WOOD
Griffiths, Charlotte E	Surg Lt RN	01-Aug-12	MED	GMP	HMS NELSON	HMS NELSON
Griffiths, Colin	Lt Cdr	01-Oct-12	WAR	P SK4	JAG	AFGHANISTAN - BASTION
Griffiths, David A	SLt	01-Jan-12	WAR	GSX	HMS DRAGON	
Griffiths, Francis M	Lt RN	01-Sep-07	ENG	ME	HMS ENTERPRISE	
Griffiths, Gareth	Lt RN	01-Jan-04	WAR	SM(N)	HMS RALEIGH	
Griffiths, Michael O J	Lt Cdr	16-Jan-00	WAR	PWO(U)	RN EXCHANGE NETHERLANDS	DEN HELDER (POSTBUS 10000)
Griffiths, Neil	Lt Cdr	01-Oct-06	WAR	PWO MW	MWS COLLINGWOOD - WTG	HMS COLLINGWOOD
Griffiths, Nicholas A MBE	Lt Col	30-Jun-11	RM	GS	FLEET SPT FGEN DIVISION	NCHQ
Griffiths, Nigel M	Lt RN	01-Jan-04	WAR	C	HMS COLLINGWOOD	HMS COLLINGWOOD
Griffiths, Richard H	Cdr	30-Jun-12	WAR	SM(CQ)	HMS TIRELESS	
Griggs, James K	Lt RN	30-Jul-10	WAR	ATC	RNAS CULDROSE - ATC	RNAS CULDROSE

Person Name	Substantive Rank	Seniority	Branch	Specialisation	Organisation	Location
Grimes, Keith	Lt RN	01-Mar-09	ENG	MESM	DEFAC JSCSC ICSCM	SHRIVENHAM
Grimley, Timothy P	Lt Cdr	01-Oct-13	LOGS	L SM	DEFAC JSCSC ICSCM	SHRIVENHAM
Grimmer, Nicholas G	Lt RN	01-Jan-10	WAR	P MER	820 SQN	RNAS CULDROSE
Grimshaw, Ernest	RN Chpln	02-May-96	Ch S		HMS SULTAN - CHAP	HMS SULTAN
Grindel, David J S	Cdr	30-Jun-02	ENG	TM	DCTT HQ	HMS SULTAN
Grindon, Matthew G	Cdr	30-Jun-09	WAR	P SK4	MWS COLLINGWOOD	
Groom, Ian S MBE	Cdr	30-Jun-07	ENG	ME	FOST DPORT SEA	HMNB DEVONPORT
Grossett, Kelly M	Lt RN	01-Jan-08	WAR	HM(AS)	HMS ENTERPRISE	
Grout, Christopher L	SLt	01-Nov-11	ENG	WESM	MWS COLLINGWOOD	HMS COLLINGWOOD
Grove, Jeremy J	Lt Cdr	01-Oct-12	WAR	HM (H CH)	FOST HM	HMS DRAKE
Groves, Christopher D	SLt	01-Feb-12	LOGS	L	RALEIGH	HMS RALEIGH
Groves, Christopher K	Capt RN	23-Jan-12	WAR	SM(CQ)	FOST SM SEA	HELENSBURGH
Groves, Nicholas J	Mid	01-May-13	WAR	SM(X)	BRNC DARTMOUTH	DARTMOUTH
Gruber, James P	Lt RN	07-Oct-12	ENG	WE	HMS DARING	
Gubby, Adrian W	Lt Cdr	01-May-10	ENG	WE	HMS LANCASTER	
Guest, Craig A	Lt RN	01-Jan-08	WAR	HM	FLEET HM UNIT	HMNB DEVONPORT
Guest, Ruth E	Surg Lt RN	03-Aug-11	MED	GDMO	HMS RICHMOND	
Guild, Ian	Lt RN	01-Sep-06	ENG	WE	FLEET SPT FGEN DIVISION	NCHQ
Gulley, Trevor J	Capt RN	25-Jan-11	ENG	ME	HMS SULTAN - RNSME HQ & ATG	HMS SULTAN
Gulliver, Jeff W	Lt Cdr	21-Nov-10	WAR	PWO	HMS ST ALBANS	
Gunn, William J S	Lt Cdr	01-Nov-94	WAR	HM (M CH)	RNAS YEOVILTON - MET	RNAS YEOVILTON
Gurmin, Stephen	Cdr	30-Jun-03	WAR	PWO(C)	RN EXCHANGE USA - BDS	WASHINGTON
Gurney, Brian D	2Lt	02-Sep-12	RM	N/A	CTCRM OFFICERS	EXMOUTH
Guthrie, Lee D K	Lt RN	17-Dec-10	ENG	WESM(TWS)	HMS TORBAY	
Guy, Charles R	Lt Cdr	01-Oct-07	WAR	AAWO	COMPORFLOT SEA	HMNB PORTSMOUTH
Guy, Elizabeth	Lt RN	01-Sep-07	WAR	INT	PJHQ (UK) J2	NORTHWOOD
Guy, Frances L	Lt RN	01-Jan-07	WAR	INT	CHFHQ (SEA)	RNAS YEOVILTON
Guy, Mark A MBE	Cdr	30-Jun-06	ENG	WE	DES/COMFLEET/SHIPS	ABBEY WOOD BRISTOL
Guy, Thomas J	Capt RN	18-Sep-12	WAR	PWO(U)	COMDEVFLOT SEA	HMNB DEVONPORT
Guyver, Paul M	Surg Lt Cdr	04-Aug-05	MED	T&O	INM ALVERSTOKE	GOSPORT
Gwatkin, Nicholas J	Lt Cdr	01-Oct-09	WAR	MCD	NATO-ACT-NURC	NAPLES
Gwilliam, Benjamin	Mid	01-Sep-13	WAR	GSX	BRNC DARTMOUTH	
Gwilliam, Richard J	Lt RN	15-Apr-11	WAR	INT	UK MCC	BAHRAIN
Gwinnutt, Oliver F	SLt	01-Sep-11	WAR	GSX	HMS MERSEY	

H

Person Name	Substantive Rank	Seniority	Branch	Specialisation	Organisation	Location
Hackland, Andrew S	Lt RN	01-Apr-03	WAR	ATC	HMS ILLUSTRIOUS	
Hackman, James D	Lt Cdr	01-Oct-10	LOGS	L SM	HMS DARING	
Hadland, Giles	Lt Cdr	01-Oct-08	WAR	INT	DEFAC JSCSC ACSC	SHRIVENHAM
Hadley, Clive M	Lt RN	08-Apr-05	ENG	WESM(TWS)	DES/COMFLEET/SM	ABBEY WOOD BRISTOL
Haggo, Jamie R	Lt RN	16-Apr-98	WAR	P LYNX	RAF LINTON-ON-OUSE	RAF LINTON ON OUSE
Haigh, Alastair J	Cdr	30-Jun-11	WAR	P LYNX	815 SQN HQ	RNAS YEOVILTON
Haigh, Julian J	Lt Cdr	01-Oct-05	LOGS	L SM	FLEET SPT LOGS INFRA DIVISION	PORTSMOUTH
Haigh, Thomas J	Surg SLt	30-Jul-13	MED	MEDICAL	BRNC DARTMOUTH	
Haines, Paul R	Cdr	30-Jun-01	ENG	WE	DMC	MAIN BUILDING LONDON
Hains, Justin	Lt Cdr	01-Apr-04	WAR	MCD PWO	DEFAC JSCSC ACSC	SHRIVENHAM
Hairsine, William	Lt RN	01-Jul-05	WAR	MW	MWS COLLINGWOOD	
Halahan, Miles D	SLt	01-Feb-11	WAR	GSX	CREW 5 OFFICERS	PORTSMOUTH
Hale, Alexandra L	Surg Lt Cdr	06-Aug-13	MED	GMP	INM ALVERSTOKE	GOSPORT
Hale, Amanda D	Lt RN	01-Nov-04	ENG	TM	DCAE COSFORD - JTDT	WOLVERHAMPTON
Hale, John N	Maj	27-Apr-02	RM	LC	1 ASSLT GROUP RM (HQ)	PLYMOUTH
Hale, Stuart D	Lt RN	01-Apr-05	QARNNS	ITU	FLEET FOSNNI - CNR	HMNB PORTSMOUTH
Hales, Martin	Lt RN	01-Jan-13	WAR	O LYNX	LHF 815 SQN FLT 203	RNAS YEOVILTON
Haley, Christopher J	Lt Cdr	01-Oct-11	WAR	INT	RNU RAF DIGBY	RAF DIGBY
Halford, John A	Lt RN	01-Mar-13	ENG	AE	CULDROSE	RNAS CULDROSE
Halford, Mark L	Lt RN	01-Jun-09	WAR	P SK4	CAREER TRAINING	RAF BENSON
Halford, Patrick	Capt	01-Sep-12	RM	GS	DCSU	RAF HENLOW
Hall, Allan J	Lt RN	01-Sep-08	LOGS	L	COMPORFLOT WLSG	HMNB PORTSMOUTH
Hall, Barry J	Cdr	30-Jun-06	ENG	MESM	NUCLEAR CAPABILITY	MAIN BUILDING LONDON
Hall, Christopher	Lt RN	16-Dec-11	WAR	INT	JCU (CH)	CHELTENHAM
Hall, Christopher L	Lt Cdr	01-Oct-10	ENG	MESM	DES/COMFLEET	THURSO
Hall, Christopher M MBE	Maj	01-Oct-07	RM		FOST DPORT SEA	HMNB DEVONPORT

Person Name	Substantive Rank	Seniority	Branch	Specialisation	Organisation	Location
Hall, Daniel	Lt RN	01-Jan-09	ENG	MESM	DEFAC CMT	SHRIVENHAM
Hall, David J	Surg Capt RN (D)	25-Mar-13	DENTAL	GDP(C&S)	DDS PLYMOUTH PDO	HMS DRAKE
Hall, Edward C	Maj	01-Oct-11	RM	GS	45 CDO RM	DUNDEE
Hall, Graham W	Lt Cdr	01-Oct-10	WAR	HM (M CH)	BRNC DARTMOUTH	
Hall, James E	Lt Cdr	01-Oct-10	WAR	O SKW	849 SQN	RNAS CULDROSE
Hall, Jessica M	Surg Lt Cdr (D)	14-Jul-13	DENTAL	GDP	NCHQ	
Hall, Kilian J D	Lt RN	01-May-01	WAR	FC	RNAS YEOVILTON - RNFS	RNAS YEOVILTON
Hall, Megan E	Lt RN	01-Apr-12	LOGS	L	HMS RICHMOND	HMS RICHMOND
Hall, Nicola E	Mid	01-Nov-13	WAR	GSX	BRNC DARTMOUTH	
Hall, Penelope M	Lt RN	01-Jul-08	WAR	GSX	BRNC DARTMOUTH	
Hall, Richard J	Lt RN	22-Oct-12	WAR	O SKW	857 NAS	RNAS CULDROSE
Hall, Simon C	Lt RN	01-Jan-12	WAR	P UT	CAREER TRAINING	RAF SHAWBURY
Hall, Stephen J	Lt RN	01-Sep-08	WAR	SM(N)	CBRN POL	MAIN BUILDING LONDON
Hall, Victoria J	Lt RN	16-Jun-10	WAR	GSX	HMS TEMERAIRE - DNLM	PORTSMOUTH
Hall, William J	Capt	01-Sep-11	RM	GS	43 CDO FPGRM S SQN	HMNB CLYDE
Hallam, Stuart P	RN Chpln	05-May-02	Ch S		CHFHQ (SEA)	RNAS YEOVILTON
Hallatt, Nicholas E	Lt RN	01-Sep-08	WAR	P SK4	845 SQN	RNAS YEOVILTON
Hallett, Daniel J	Lt Cdr	01-Oct-13	ENG	TM	AIR 22GP - LYNEHAM	RAF LYNEHAM
Hallett, Simon John MA	Lt Cdr	01-Mar-01	LOGS	L	US CENTCOM	USA TAMPA
Halliday, Alexander W	Lt RN	08-Dec-12	ENG	AE	RNAS CULDROSE	
Halliwell, Leon M	Mid	01-Nov-13	WAR	P UT	BRNC DARTMOUTH	
Hallsworth, Kay	Lt Cdr	01-Oct-12	MED	MS	BFGib	GIBRALTAR
Hally, Philip J	Cdr	30-Jun-08	LOGS	L C	HMS ILLUSTRIOUS	
Halsted, Benjamin E MBE	Maj	01-Oct-07	RM	GS	NCHQ	
Halton, Paul V OBE	Capt RN	11-Jan-10	WAR	SM(CQ)	DI - FC(A)	MAIN BUILDING LONDON
Hamblin, Paul A	Lt RN	01-May-06	WAR	GSX	HMS MONTROSE	HMS MONTROSE
Hamer, Scott A	Lt RN	01-Feb-10	WAR	MCD	MCM2 CREW 2	PORTSMOUTH
Hamilton, Graham D	Lt Cdr	01-Oct-08	ENG	AE	A AIB FARNBOROUGH	ALDERSHOT
Hamilton, John R	Lt RN	01-Mar-12	ENG	WE	HMS ILLUSTRIOUS	
Hamilton, Mark	Lt Cdr	01-Oct-08	ENG	ME	DEFAC JSCSC ACSC	SHRIVENHAM
Hamilton, Sean M	Surg Lt Cdr (D)	26-Jun-06	DENTAL	GDP	INM ALVERSTOKE	GOSPORT
Hamlyn, Jonathan D	Lt RN	20-Oct-10	WAR	P	815 SQN	RNAS YEOVILTON
Hammock, Simon G	Lt Cdr	01-Oct-11	WAR	P SK4	848 SQN	RNAS YEOVILTON
Hammon, Mark A	Lt Cdr	01-Oct-08	WAR	AAWO	MCM1 CREW 7	FASLANE
Hammond, Christopher R	Lt Cdr	01-Oct-13	LOGS	L	HMS IRON DUKE	
Hammond, James A	SLt	09-Apr-12	WAR	SM(X)	HMS AMBUSH	
Hammond, Mark C DFC	Maj	01-May-00	RM	P LYN7	4 REGT AAC	IPSWICH
Hammond, Meirion M	Lt RN	01-Apr-00	WAR	P SKW	854 NAS	RNAS CULDROSE
Hammond, Paul A	Cdre	19-Jul-12	ENG	AE	DES/COMFLEET	ABBEY WOOD
Hammond, Paul	Cdr	30-Jun-12	WAR	PWO(U)	HMS ARGYLL	
Hammond, Sean J	Lt RN	01-Jun-08	WAR	SM(N)	FLEET COMOPS NWD	NORTHWOOD
Hammond, Tregaron	Lt RN	15-Apr-11	WAR	INT	FOST DPORT SEA	HMNB DEVONPORT
Hampshire, Tony	Lt Cdr	01-Oct-07	WAR	MCD	HMS NEPTUNE	HELENSBURGH
Hampson, Alexander G	Lt RN	01-Jan-05	WAR	P SK4	CHF(MERLIN)	RAF BENSON
Hanan, William Mark	Surg Lt RN	07-Aug-13	MED	MEDICAL	BRNC DARTMOUTH	
Hancock, Andrew P	Cdr	30-Jun-13	WAR	PWO(U)	RN GLOBAL	CHILE
Hancock, David Paul	SLt	01-Sep-11	WAR	GSX	MCM1 CREW	FASLANE
Hancock, James H	Lt Cdr	01-Oct-11	WAR	INT	DCSU	RAF HENLOW
Hancock, Robert T A	Lt Cdr	01-Oct-01	ENG	WE	LOAN DSTL - IMD	SALISBURY
Hand, Christopher J	Surg Cdr	30-Jun-03	MED	T&O	MDHU PORTSMOUTH	PORTSMOUTH
Handoll, Guy N G	Lt Cdr	01-Apr-10	ENG	MESM	HMS VANGUARD	
Hands, Anthony J	Surg Cdr (D)	23-Sep-13	DENTAL	GDP	HMS COLLINGWOOD	
Hands, Edward W	Capt	01-Sep-06	RM	GS	RNLA	
Hankey, Mark Rd	Lt Cdr	26-Feb-13	WAR	MEDIA OPS	NPT RES MOBILISATION	HMNB PORTSMOUTH
Hanks, Oliver T	Lt Cdr	01-Oct-12	LOGS	L	HMS ILLUSTRIOUS	
Hanks, Richard M	Lt RN	11-Dec-09	WAR	GSX	MWS COLLINGWOOD	
Hanley, Peter H	Lt RN	01-Nov-12	ENG	MESM	DCEME SULTAN	HMS SULTAN
Hannaby, Philippa B	Lt RN	01-Mar-08	LOGS	L	MOD CNS/ACNS	MAIN BUILDING LONDON
Hannah, Edward C	Lt RN	01-Apr-11	LOGS	L	HMS VICTORIOUS	
Hannam, Darrell B	Lt Cdr	01-Oct-12	WAR	O SKW	HMS COLLINGWOOD	
Hannigan, Jason D	Lt RN	17-Feb-06	WAR	PWO	HMS DARING	
Harcombe, Andrew	Lt Cdr	01-Oct-11	WAR	P LYN7	847 SQN - AE	RNAS YEOVILTON

Person Name	Substantive Rank	Seniority	Branch	Specialisation	Organisation	Location
Harcourt, Robert	Cdr	30-Jun-11	WAR	PWO(U)	RNLO JTF4	KEY WEST
Hardern, Simon P	Cdre	01-Jul-13	WAR	PWO(U)	NATO - BRUSSELS	BRUSSELS
Hardiman, Nicholas A	Lt Cdr	01-May-03	ENG	MESM	DES/COMFLEET	HMS DRAKE
Harding, Daniel L	Lt RN	01-Sep-09	WAR	GSX	HMS PROTECTOR	
Harding, David V	Lt Cdr	01-Oct-12	ENG	WESM(SWS)	CAREER TRAINING	
Harding, Gary Alan	Cdr	30-Jun-09	ENG	WE	DES/COMFLEET	ABBEY WOOD
Harding, Georgina E	Lt RN	08-Jul-12	WAR	GSX	HMS RICHMOND	
Harding, Ian R	Lt RN	13-Jul-12	ENG	WE	HMS IRON DUKE	
Harding, Matthew J	Lt RN	01-Dec-09	WAR	P SK4	845 SQN	RNAS YEOVILTON
Harding, Russell G OBE	R Adm	28-Feb-11	WAR	O SK6	FLEET COS AVN	NCHQ
Harding, Scott R	Lt RN	08-Feb-13	WAR	AV	RNAS CULDROSE	
Hardinge, Christopher MBE	Cdr	30-Sep-05	WAR	SM(X) (RES)	NORTHWOOD HQ	
Hardman, Matthew J	Lt Cdr	01-Oct-07	WAR	GSX	HMS OCEAN	
Hardwick, Mark J	Lt Cdr	01-Oct-05	LOGS	L SM	HMS COLLINGWOOD	
Hardy, Lee Charles	Cdr	30-Jun-02	WAR	AAWO	BF BIOT	DIEGO GARCIA
Hardy, Leslie B	Lt Cdr	01-Oct-06	WAR	PWO(U)	FLEET SPT LOGS INFRA	NCHQ
Hardy, Robert J	Lt Cdr	01-Oct-08	ENG	ME	DES/COMFLEET	ABBEY WOOD
Hardy-Hodgson, David N	Lt RN	01-Jul-04	ENG	AE	DES/COMFLEET	ABBEY WOOD
Hare, Nigel J	Cdr	30-Jun-02	WAR	PWO(N)	DES/COMFLEET	PORTSMOUTH
Harfield, Sarah J	Lt RN	01-Jan-99	ENG	IS	NC PSYA	PORTSMOUTH
Harkin, James P	Lt RN	01-Feb-08	WAR	PWO	HMS NORTHUMBERLAND	
Harman, Stephen J	Lt Cdr	01-Oct-08	LOGS	L SM	PJHQ (UK) J1/J4	NORTHWOOD
Harmer, Deborah D	Lt RN	01-May-09	ENG	TM	NCHQ CNPERS	PORTSMOUTH
Harper, James A	Lt Cdr	01-Oct-97	WAR	O LYNX	815 SQN	RNAS YEOVILTON
Harper, Jovin H	Lt RN	01-Apr-12	WAR	P UT	RNAS YEOVILTON	RNAS YEOVILTON
Harper, Kevan James	Lt RN	01-May-06	WAR	O SKW	849 SQN	RNAS CULDROSE
Harper, Nicholas J	Lt RN	30-Jul-10	WAR	C	DES/COMJE	CORSHAM
Harper, Philip R	Lt Cdr	01-Oct-04	WAR	PWO(N)	MSP	MAIN BUILDING LONDON
Harradine, Sam A	Lt RN	01-Sep-11	WAR	GSX	MWS COLLINGWOOD	
Harrap, Nicholas OBE	Capt RN	30-Jun-04	WAR	SM(CQ)	BDS WASHINGTON - BDILS	WASHINGTON
Harriman, Peter	Lt Cdr	01-Oct-06	WAR	C	HMS NELSON	
Harrington, Lee	Lt Cdr	01-Mar-06	ENG	ME	DCD - MODSAP KSA	SAUDI ARABIA
Harris, Alexandra K	Lt RN	01-Jun-10	WAR	GSX	STRIKFORNATO - LISBON	LISBON
Harris, Andrew I	Capt RN	20-Jul-10	WAR	O LYNX	FLEET CSAV	MAIN BUILDING LONDON
Harris, Carl Christian MBE	Lt Col	30-Jun-09	RM	GS	CTCRM - ISC	EXMOUTH
Harris, Christopher G	Lt RN	01-Jun-08	WAR	ATC	FOST DPORT SHORE	HMNB DEVONPORT
Harris, Hugh J L	Lt Cdr	01-Oct-12	WAR	GSX	MWS COLLINGWOOD	
Harris, Keri J	Cdr	30-Jun-05	WAR	O SK6	HMS ILLUSTRIOUS	
Harris, Linda E	Lt RN	01-Jan-08	ENG	TM	FLEET FOST ACOS(Trg)	NCHQ
Harris, Martyn J	SLt	01-Jan-12	WAR	GSX	MCM1 CREW 7	FASLANE
Harris, Michael B	Lt RN	31-Jul-09	ENG	AE	HMS SULTAN - ATG	HMS SULTAN
Harris, Michael T	Cdr	30-Jun-08	LOGS	L	DSPA	WINCHESTER
Harris, Neil Peter	Lt RN	13-Apr-12	WAR	AV	RNAS CULDROSE	
Harris, Richard A	Lt Cdr	01-Oct-11	ENG	WE	HMS DRAGON	
Harris, Richard P	Cdr	30-Jun-09	LOGS	L	DMLS	HMS RALEIGH
Harris, Robert	Lt RN	01-Sep-06	ENG	AE	1710 NAS	PORTSMOUTH
Harris, Robert C	SLt	01-May-13	WAR	P UT	BRNC DARTMOUTH	
Harris, Samuel	SLt	01-Sep-11	WAR	SM(X)	HMS VANGUARD	
Harris, Tristan MBE	Lt Col	30-Jun-10	RM	GS	1 ASSLT GROUP RM	PLYMOUTH
Harrison, Andrew D	Lt Cdr	01-Oct-08	ENG	AE	FLEET AV VL - RNFSC	RNAS YEOVILTON
Harrison, Anthony	Lt RN	25-Jun-05	WAR	AV	FLEET FOST ACOS	NCHQ
Harrison, Ellen	Lt RN	24-Oct-08	WAR	AV	RNAS CULDROSE - SFDO	RNAS CULDROSE
Harrison, Ian	Lt RN	01-Oct-02	WAR	O LYNX	NCHQ CNPERS	PORTSMOUTH
Harrison, James C	Surg Cdr	01-Jul-07	MED	Psych	HMNB DEVONPORT	
Harrison, Laura	Lt RN	20-Jul-07	WAR	MEDIA OPS	NPT RES MOBILISATION	UK
Harrison, Leigh E	Lt Cdr	01-Oct-11	WAR	FC	OCLC NCH	MANCHESTER
Harrison, Mark A	Lt Cdr	01-Oct-05	ENG	WESM	COMFASFLOT	HMNB CLYDE
Harrison, Mark C	Lt RN	01-Jan-13	WAR	O	RNAS CULDROSE	RNAS CULDROSE
Harrison, Matthew S OBE	Capt RN	03-Nov-08	ENG	WE	DES/COMFLEET	BRISTOL
Harrison, Paul D MBE	Cdr	30-Jun-12	WAR	O SKW	AWC BSD - RW TES	RAF BOSCOMBE DOWN
Harrison, Peter M	Lt Cdr	26-Mar-12	RNR		NCHQ - NAVY CMD SEC	NCHQ
Harrison, Richard S MBE	Cdr	30-Jun-11	WAR	P SK4	FLEET CAP LLM & DRM DIVISION	NCHQ

Person Name	Substantive Rank	Seniority	Branch	Specialisation	Organisation	Location
Harrison, Thomas A	Lt RN	01-Feb-13	WAR	HM	HMS SCOTT	HMS SCOTT
Harrison, Thomas I'Anson	Lt Cdr	01-Oct-06	ENG	TM(SM)	DEF BD SEC	MAIN BUILDING LONDON
Harrison-Jones, Stuart	Lt RN	01-Jan-03	ENG	TM	JFC - DCTS (H)	RAF HALTON
Harrisson, Lucas T	Mid	01-Feb-13	WAR	GSX	BRNC DARTMOUTH	
Harrop, Ian	Cdr	30-Jun-05	ENG	MESM	HMS SULTAN	
Harry, Stephen J	Lt RN	01-Sep-13	WAR	P UT	RNAS YEOVILTON	RAF LINTON ON OUSE
Harsent, Paul M	Mid	01-Nov-13	WAR	GSX	BRNC DARTMOUTH	
Hart, Daniel A	Lt RN	01-Mar-09	ENG	WESM	MWS COLLINGWOOD	
Hart, Stephen J	Maj	01-Sep-05	RM	GS	DEFAC JSCSC ACSC	SHRIVENHAM
Hart, Steven D	Lt Cdr	01-Oct-08	WAR	PWO(C)	HMS DIAMOND	
Hartley, Andrew P	Lt Cdr	02-Mar-00	ENG	ME	DES/COMFLEET	ABBEY WOOD
Hartley, David	Capt	16-Apr-10	RM	SCC	CTCRM - CW	EXMOUTH
Hartley, James	Lt RN	01-May-98	ENG	TM	DEFENCE ACADEMY HQ	SHRIVENHAM
Hartley, John L	Lt Cdr	01-Oct-99	WAR	P LYNX	RNAS YEOVILTON - LSF	RNAS YEOVILTON
Hartley, Solomon J	SLt	24-Jan-12	LOGS	L	HMS RALEIGH	
Harvey, Ben P	Mid	03-May-13	WAR	GSX	BRNC DARTMOUTH	
Harvey, Colin A	Cdr	30-Jun-00	ENG	MESM	DES/COMFLEET	HMNB CLYDE
Harvey, Graham A	Lt Cdr	01-Oct-09	ENG	WE	FLEET CAP SSM DIVISION	NCHQ
Harvey, Isha S	Lt RN	01-Apr-12	LOGS	L	HMS ECHO	
Harvey, Martin T	2Lt	02-Sep-13	RM	N/A	CTCRM OFFICERS	EXMOUTH
Harvey, Matthew D	Lt RN	01-Oct-09	WAR	GSX	HMS DEFENDER	
Harvey, Paul G	Lt RN	01-Jan-04	ENG	WE	FLEET CAP IS DIVISION	NCHQ
Harvey, Robert	Cdr	30-Jun-03	WAR	AAWO	DEFENCE ACADEMY JSCSC	SHRIVENHAM
Harwood, Carl D	Lt RN	27-Jul-07	ENG	AE	HMS OCEAN	
Harwood, David Philip A	Lt RN	01-Jul-11	WAR	P UT	CAREER TRAINING	RAF SHAWBURY
Haseldine, Stephen G	Lt Cdr	01-Feb-98	WAR	ATC	FLEET AV VL - JSATO	RNAS YEOVILTON
Haskins, Benjamin S	Lt Cdr	01-Oct-13	WAR	PWO(SM)	FOST FAS SHORE	HELENSBURGH
Hassall, Ian	Lt Cdr	01-Oct-05	ENG	ME	HMS QUEEN ELIZABETH	ROSYTH
Hassett, Justin G	Surg Lt Cdr	01-Jul-10	MED	Occ Med	INM ALVERSTOKE	GOSPORT
Hastings, Craig S	Lt RN	01-Jun-08	LOGS	L	FLEET FOSNNI - NRC EE	LONDON
Hastings, Richard C	Capt	01-Sep-08	RM	GS	COMUKAMPHIBFOR	HMNB PORTSMOUTH
Hastings, Thomas	2Lt	02-Sep-13	RM	N/A	CTCRM	EXMOUTH
Hastings, Thomas H	Lt RN	01-Jan-12	WAR	GSX	MCM1 CREW 8	FASLANE
Hatch, Giles W H	Cdr	31-Dec-98	WAR	PWO(A)	FLEET COMOPS NWD	NORTHWOOD
Hatchard, Pollyanna	Lt Cdr	01-Oct-07	ENG	AE	LHF HQ	RNAS YEOVILTON
Hatcher, Rhett S	Capt RN	26-Sep-11	WAR	P LYNX	HMS PROTECTOR	
Hattle, Prideaux M	Lt Cdr	01-Oct-08	WAR	PWO(U) MW	MWS COLLINGWOOD	
Havers, Luke C	2Lt	02-Sep-13	RM	N/A	CTCRM OFFICERS	EXMOUTH
Havis, Gareth J	Capt	01-Sep-09	RM	GS	HQ 3 CDO BDE RM	PLYMOUTH
Haw, Christopher E MC	Lt Col	30-Jun-12	RM	MLDR	COMUKTG SEA	PLYMOUTH
Haward, Tom A	Capt	01-Sep-13	RM	GS	45 CDO RM - Y COY	DUNDEE
Hawkes, Sophie P	Surg Lt RN	01-Aug-12	MED	MEDICAL	BRNC DARTMOUTH	
Hawkings, Tom	Mid	01-Sep-13	ENG	ME	BRNC DARTMOUTH	
Hawkins, Daniel M	Surg Lt RN	03-Aug-11	MED	GDMO	RNAS CULDROSE	
Hawkins, Emma Louise	Lt RN	01-Jan-05	LOGS	L	DES/COMLAND	ABBEY WOOD
Hawkins, James S	Cdr	30-Jun-06	WAR	O LYNX	LOAN DSTL - NSD	FAREHAM
Hawkins, Martin	Cdr	30-Jun-03	WAR	O SKW	ABBEYWOOD	
Hawkins, Michael J	SLt	01-May-11	LOGS	L	829 SQN HQ	RNAS CULDROSE
Hawkins, Robert MBE	Lt Cdr	01-Oct-07	WAR	MCD PWO(A)	HQ INTER AIR	KUALA LUMPAR
Hawkins, Stephen	Lt Cdr	01-Oct-10	WAR	REG	RNP - HQ PMN	PORTSMOUTH
Hawthorn, Simon	SLt	01-Sep-12	ENG	ME	BRNC DARTMOUTH	
Hawthorne, Michael J	Capt RN	30-Jun-05	WAR	SM(CQ)	JCU (CH)	CHELTENHAM
Hay, James Donald	Cdre	21-Dec-11	ENG	WE	DES/COMJE	CORSHAM
Hay, Michael	Lt Cdr	01-Mar-06	ENG	WE	NCHQ CNPERS	PORTSMOUTH
Hay, Phillip William	Lt RN	30-Jul-10	WAR	INT	JIEDAC	LONDON
Hay, Richard H I	Lt RN	01-Jul-05	WAR	HM	MWS COLLINGWOOD	
Hayashi, Luke R	Lt Cdr	01-Oct-07	WAR	AAWO	FOST DPORT SEA	HMNB DEVONPORT
Haycock, Timothy P	Cdr	30-Jun-05	WAR	O LYNX	UKTI - DSO	LONDON
Hayden, Timothy W	Lt Cdr	01-Oct-08	WAR	P MER	824 SQN - TU	RNAS CULDROSE
Hayes, Brian R	Maj	01-Oct-13	RM	MLDR (SCC)	CTCRM - S	EXMOUTH
Hayes, James V	Capt RN	01-Aug-08	ENG	WESM(SWS)	DEFAC RCDS	LONDON
Hayes, Leigh C	Lt RN	01-Aug-08	ENG	WE	NAVY MCTA PORTSMOUTH	HMNB PORTSMOUTH

Person Name	Substantive Rank	Seniority	Branch	Specialisation	Organisation	Location
Hayes, Mark A	Lt Cdr	01-Oct-13	WAR	PWO	HMS KENT	
Hayes, Matthew P	Lt RN	12-Jul-13	LOGS	L	HMS DARING	
Hayes, Paul	Lt RN	01-May-09	WAR	SM(X)	HMS VANGUARD	
Hayes, Stuart J	Cdr	30-Jun-00	WAR	MCD PWO(A)	DSEA MARITIME	ABBEY WOOD
Hayle, James	Cdr	30-Jun-05	LOGS	L SM	LSP ON	MUSCAT
Haynes, Fiona J	Lt RN	01-Sep-05	ENG	ME	COMDEVFLOT	HMS DRAKE
Haynes, John G	Lt Cdr	01-Oct-13	WAR	HM	FOST DPORT SEA	HMNB DEVONPORT
Haynes, Samuel	Lt RN	01-Apr-08	WAR	O LYNX	LHF 700W SQN	RNAS YEOVILTON
Haynes, Warren E	Lt RN	18-Dec-08	MED	MS(EHO)	NCHQ MEDDIV	NCHQ
Hayton, Stephen R	Lt Cdr	01-Oct-05	WAR	O MER	824 SQN - TU	RNAS CULDROSE
Hayward, Clive E W	Lt Cdr	01-Jun-96	WAR	SM(AWC)	FLEET FOSNNI - HQ	HELENSBURGH
Hayward, Geoffrey MBE	Lt Cdr	01-Oct-03	WAR	O SKW	HMS COLLINGWOOD	
Hayward, John W	Maj	01-Oct-09	RM	GS	FLEET CAP LLM & DRM DIVISION	NCHQ
Haywood, Andrew J	Lt RN	01-Nov-05	WAR	ATC	RAF LINTON-ON-OUSE	
Haywood, Guy	Cdr	30-Jun-02	WAR	P LYNX	NCHQ CNPERS	PORTSMOUTH
Haywood, Peter	Lt Cdr	01-Oct-03	WAR	P MER	DEFAC JSCSC ACSC	SHRIVENHAM
Hazard, Lee MBE	Lt Cdr	01-Oct-10	MED	MS	DMS WHITTINGTON	MAIN BUILDING LONDON
Hazel, Thomas W	Lt RN	01-Apr-11	WAR	GSX	MWS DDS	PORTSMOUTH
Hazell, Emma V	Lt RN	01-May-08	WAR	HM	FLEET HM UNIT	HMNB DEVONPORT
Hazell, Thomas E	SLt	01-Sep-13	WAR	SM(X)	BRNC DARTMOUTH	
Hazelwood, Graeme	Lt RN	01-Oct-08	WAR	FC	RNAS YEOVILTON - RNFS	RNAS YEOVILTON
Hazelwood, Steve	Lt Cdr	01-Oct-12	WAR	C	CIO-CTO	MAIN BUILDING LONDON
Hazledine, Oliver W	Lt RN	08-Dec-12	WAR	GSX	HMS SEVERN	
Head, Matthew A	SLt	01-Feb-11	ENG	ME	DCEME SULTAN	HMS SULTAN
Head, Steven A	Lt Cdr	01-Mar-01	ENG	WE	JFC HOC C4ISR	NORTHWOOD
Headley, Mark J	Lt Cdr	01-Oct-09	WAR	PWO(A)	MWS COLLINGWOOD	
Heal, Thomas M	2Lt	01-Sep-11	RM	GS	CTCRM OFFICERS	EXMOUTH
Healey, Mark Jon	Lt Cdr	01-Oct-07	ENG	AE	CUSTOMER DESIGN	MAIN BUILDING LONDON
Healey, Nicholas J	Surg Lt RN	01-Feb-11	MED	GDMO	40 CDO RM - LOG COY	TAUNTON
Heames, Richard M	Surg Cdr	30-Jun-06	MED	Anaes	MDHU PORTSMOUTH	PORTSMOUTH
Heaney, Martin J	Lt Cdr	01-Oct-09	WAR	O MER	MWS COLLINGWOOD	
Heap, Graham G	Lt Cdr	01-Oct-10	ENG	MESM	DES/COMFLEET	HMS DRAKE
Heap, Matthew J	Lt RN	20-May-09	LOGS	L	RNAS CULDROSE - UPO	RNAS CULDROSE
Heap, Steven A MBE	Lt Cdr	01-Oct-10	ENG	MESM	FLEET CAP SSM DIVISION	NCHQ
Hearn, Samuel P	Lt RN	25-Jun-03	WAR	MEDIA OPS	NCHQ CNPERS	PORTSMOUTH
Hearnden, Simon T	Lt RN	11-Dec-09	ENG	WE	MWS COLLINGWOOD	
Heath, Benjamin	Lt RN	01-Jan-12	WAR	FC	HMS DAUNTLESS	
Heathcote, James E	Lt RN	08-Jul-13	WAR	SM(X)	HMS VANGUARD	
Heatly, Robert J	Lt Col	31-Dec-95	RM	GS	FLEET FOSNNI - NRC	HELENSBURGH
Heaton, Henry G	Lt Cdr	01-Oct-11	WAR	HM(AS)	DI - ICSP	LONDON
Heaton, Oliver H	Lt RN	01-Apr-13	WAR	GSX	HMS WESTMINSTER	
Heaton, Roxane M	Lt RN	01-Apr-05	ENG	TM	FLEET FOST ACOS(Trg)	NCHQ
Heaton, Sean	Lt RN	16-Feb-07	WAR	MCD	FDU2	PORTSMOUTH
Heaver, John D	Capt	01-Sep-09	RM	GS	CTCRM - CW	EXMOUTH
Hecks, Ian J	Maj	01-Oct-08	RM	GS	45 CDO RM - W COY	DUNDEE
Hedgecox, David C	Lt Cdr	01-Jun-04	ENG	WE	FOST DPORT SEA	HMNB DEVONPORT
Hedgecox, Philip R	Lt RN	08-Dec-11	ENG	AE	LHF 702 SQN	RNAS YEOVILTON
Hedges, Justin W OBE	Col	27-Aug-13	RM	GS	DEFENCE ACADEMY	SHRIVENHAM
Hedworth, Anthony	Lt RN	01-Jun-94	WAR	P LYNX	RN EXCHANGE DENMARK	DENMARK
Heenan, Martyn	Capt	01-Apr-05	RM	SCC	HMS RALEIGH	
Hefford, Christopher	Lt Cdr	01-Oct-05	LOGS	L	DCDC	SHRIVENHAM
Heil, Kieran	SLt	01-Sep-13	MED	MEDICAL	BRNC DARTMOUTH	
Heirs, Gavin G	Lt Cdr	01-Oct-12	WAR	P SKW	MWS COLLINGWOOD	HMS COLLINGWOOD
Heley, David N	Capt RN	30-Jun-08	WAR	PWO(U)	NATO-ACO-JFC HQ	NAPLES
Heller, Mark	Lt RN	07-Nov-13	WAR	GSX	MWS COLLINGWOOD	
Helliwell, Thomas P	Lt RN	01-Dec-08	WAR	P SK4	854 NAS	RNAS CULDROSE
Helm, James G	Mid	01-Sep-13	ENG	WE	BRNC DARTMOUTH	
Hember, Marcus	Lt Cdr	01-Oct-06	WAR	PWO(C)	DEFAC JSCSC ACSC	SHRIVENHAM
Hembury, Lawrence	Maj	01-Oct-09	RM	C (SCC)	RM BICKLEIGH	PLYMOUTH
Hemingway, Ross	Surg Lt Cdr	07-Aug-07	MED	GMP	PJHQ (UK) J1/J4	NORTHWOOD
Hems, Wendy Louise	Lt RN	01-Jul-11	WAR	HM	HMS ENTERPRISE	
Hemsworth, Kenneth J	Cdr	30-Jun-06	ENG	ME	COMPORFLOT ESG	PORTSMOUTH

Person Name	Substantive Rank	Seniority	Branch	Specialisation	Organisation	Location
Henaghen, Stephen J	Lt Cdr	01-Oct-07	WAR	PWO(A)	BRNC DARTMOUTH	
Henaghen, Wayne D	SLt	01-Feb-12	WAR	O UT	BRNC DARTMOUTH	
Henderson, Andrew G	Lt RN	01-Jan-07	WAR	O LYNX	LHF 702 SQN	RNAS YEOVILTON
Henderson, Arthur H	Surg Lt Cdr	06-Aug-13	MED	GS	INM ALVERSTOKE	GOSPORT
Henderson, Katy	SLt	01-May-13	WAR	GSX	HMS DIAMOND	
Henderson, Shaun M	Capt	01-Apr-11	RM	SCC	40 CDO RM - LOG COY	TAUNTON
Henderson, Simon A	Lt RN	01-Jun-11	WAR	GSX	HMS NORTHUMBERLAND	
Henderson, Stuart Philip	Cdr	30-Jun-09	ENG	ME	FMC - STRAT N	MAIN BUILDING LONDON
Hendra, Allan J	Lt RN	09-Apr-10	ENG	AE	RNAS YEOVILTON - AED	RNAS YEOVILTON
Hendrickx, Christopher J	Lt Cdr	01-Jan-04	ENG	WE	DES/COMJE/ISS/NET	CORSHAM
Hendrickx, Sarah	Lt RN	01-Feb-08	ENG	TM	FLEET FOST ACOS(Trg)	ABBEY WOOD
Hendry, Alan	SLt	01-Aug-13	WAR	GSX	MWS COLLINGWOOD	
Hennah, Garry	Lt RN	01-Jan-13	WAR	SM(X)	HMS TRIUMPH	
Henning, Daniel C W	Surg Lt Cdr	19-Sep-08	MED	EM	UK MED GP (AFG)	AFGHANISTAN BASTION
Henrickson, Beau	SLt	01-Feb-12	WAR	GSX	BRNC DARTMOUTH	
Henry, David T	Lt RN	01-Apr-11	WAR	GSX	CAREER TRAINING	SHEFFORD
Henry, Mark	Surg Cdr	09-Mar-10	MED	GMP	NCHQ CNPERS	PORTSMOUTH
Henry, Timothy M	Capt RN	09-Sep-13	WAR	PWO(U)	HMS OCEAN	
Henton, James M	Lt RN	01-Sep-10	ENG	MESM	HMS TRENCHANT	
Hepplewhite, Mark B	Lt Cdr	01-Oct-09	ENG	AE	1710 NAS	PORTSMOUTH
Hepworth, Andrew W	Lt Cdr	01-May-98	ENG	IS	DES/COMFLEET	ABBEY WOOD
Hepworth, Nicholas P	Lt RN	20-Oct-08	WAR	SM(N)	RN EXCHANGE NLANDS SEA	DEN HELDER
Herbert, Jack A	Lt RN	09-May-13	WAR	SM(X)	HMS RALEIGH	
Heritage, Francis	Lt RN	01-Jun-10	WAR	FC	DEFAC JSCSC	SHRIVENHAM
Hernon, Robert T B	Lt RN	06-Apr-07	ENG	WE	DES/COMJE	FAREHAM
Herod, Thomas P	Surg Lt Cdr	01-Aug-12	MED	GMP	INM ALVERSTOKE	GOSPORT
Herridge, Daniel J	Lt Cdr	01-Oct-12	WAR	MCD	MWS COLLINGWOOD	HMS COLLINGWOOD
Herrington, Robert J	Lt RN	08-Jun-07	ENG	MESM	DCEME SULTAN	
Herzberg, Mark J	Lt Cdr	08-Apr-05	ENG	WE	UKTI - DSO	LONDON
Heselton, Peter B	Lt RN	01-Apr-12	WAR	SM(X)	FLEET FOSNNI	HELENSBURGH
Hesketh, John J	Lt Cdr	01-Oct-12	WAR	O LYNX	FOST DPORT SEA	HMNB DEVONPORT
Hesling, Gary	Cdr	30-Jun-08	WAR	HM (H CH)	FLEET CAP SSM DIVISION	NCHQ
Hesse, Peter J	SLt	01-Feb-12	WAR	SM(X)	BRNC DARTMOUTH	
Hetherington, Thomas A	Lt RN	01-Dec-03	ENG	ME	NAVY MCTA PORTSMOUTH	HMNB PORTSMOUTH
Heward, Mark G	Lt Cdr	01-Oct-13	WAR	PWO(N)	MWS COLLINGWOOD	
Hewitson, David R	Mid	01-Nov-13	WAR	GSX	BRNC DARTMOUTH	
Hewitson, Jonathan G	Lt RN	01-Aug-00	WAR	MW	HMS HIBERNIA	LISBURN
Hewitt, Adrian J	Lt RN	24-Oct-08	ENG	AE	FLEET FOSNNI - NRC EE	PETERBOROUGH
Hewitt, Clara J	Lt RN	01-Aug-06	WAR	MW	BRNC DARTMOUTH	
Hewitt, David L	Cdr	30-Jun-07	WAR	AAWO	RNEAWC - SNO	LINCOLN
Hewitt, Lloyd	Cdr	30-Jun-09	LOGS	L	RN EXCHANGE AUSTRALIA	CANBERRA
Hewitt, Mark J	Lt Cdr	01-Oct-07	ENG	ME	HQ CFC(A)	AFGHANISTAN KABUL
Hewitt, Nigel William	Lt RN	08-Apr-05	ENG	AE	ABBEY WOOD	
Hewitt, Richard P	Lt Cdr	01-Oct-10	WAR	PWO(N)	HMS ILLUSTRIOUS	
Hewitt, Simon D	SLt	01-Jul-12	WAR	SM(X)	HMS ASTUTE	
Hewlett, Philip J E	Lt RN	01-Nov-05	ENG	WESM	FLEET CAP SSM DIVISION	NCHQ
Heywood, Robert H	Lt RN	01-Sep-06	ENG	MESM	HMS VIGILANT	
Hibberd, Nicholas J	Cdr	30-Jun-04	WAR	SM(CQ)	FLEET COMOPS NWD	NORTHWOOD
Hibbert, Andrew	Lt RN	01-Sep-11	WAR	P UT	RAF SHAWBURY	
Hibbert, Martin C	Lt Cdr	01-Nov-96	WAR	GSX	HMS VIVID	PLYMOUTH
Higgins, Alex P B	Lt Cdr	01-Oct-13	ENG	WE	HMS KENT	
Higgins, Andrew J	Lt RN	13-Jun-05	WAR	P CDO	CHF(MERLIN)	OXFORD
Higgins, Carla L	Lt RN	01-Feb-08	WAR	GSX	HMS DRAGON	
Higgins, Edward	Lt RN	01-Sep-09	ENG	MESM	HMS SULTAN	
Higgins, Peter AFC	Lt RN	01-Oct-11	WAR	P LYNX	HMS TYNE	
Higham, James G OBE	Capt RN	07-Mar-11	ENG	WE	DES/DGRES	ABBEY WOOD
Higham, Stephen	Lt Cdr	01-Oct-04	WAR	AAWO	DEFAC JSCSC ACSC	SHRIVENHAM
Higson, Glenn R	Lt Cdr	01-Oct-12	WAR	INT	PJHQ (UK) J2	NORTHWOOD
Hilder, Harold R	Capt	01-Sep-08	RM	GS	CTCRM	EXMOUTH
Hill, Adrian J	Lt Cdr	01-Oct-08	WAR	O SKW	EMBED FRANCE	TOULON
Hill, Antony P	Maj	01-Oct-13	RM	SCC	40 CDO RM - LOG COY	TAUNTON
Hill, Christopher	Lt RN	01-Apr-04	WAR	SM(AWC)	RNSMS	HMS RALEIGH

Person Name	Substantive Rank	Seniority	Branch	Specialisation	Organisation	Location
Hill, Christopher J	Maj	01-Oct-11	RM	SCC	RM NORTON NOR	TAUNTON
Hill, David	Cdr	30-Jun-07	ENG	AE	HMS ILLUSTRIOUS	
Hill, David E	Lt RN	01-Mar-12	ENG	ME	HMS ILLUSTRIOUS	
Hill, Giulian F	Cdr	30-Jun-04	ENG	ME	HQ RC(SW)	AFGHANISTAN
Hill, Graham A	Surg Capt RN	01-Jul-11	MED	T&O	MDHU PORTSMOUTH	PORTSMOUTH
Hill, Jamie B	Lt RN	01-Mar-11	ENG	MESM	HMS TORBAY	
Hill, Jonathan P	Lt Col	30-Jun-13	RM	GS	JCU (CH)	CHELTENHAM
Hill, Mark R	Lt Cdr	22-Jun-96	WAR	P SK6	WILDCAT FORCE	RNAS YEOVILTON
Hill, Michael J	Surg Lt RN	04-Aug-10	MED	GDMO	HMS VIGILANT	HMS VIGILANT
Hill, Nicholas P	Capt	01-Sep-10	RM	GS	43 CDO	HMNB CLYDE
Hill, Oliver W	Lt RN	01-Sep-11	WAR	P MER	820 SQN	RNAS CULDROSE
Hill, Philip J	Capt RN	15-Aug-11	ENG	WESM(TWS)	DES/COMJE/ISS	CORSHAM
Hill, Rory	Mid	01-Nov-13	WAR	GSX	BRNC DARTMOUTH	DARTMOUTH
Hill, Ross	Lt RN	01-Sep-08	WAR	O SKW	854 NAS	RNAS CULDROSE
Hill, Thomas	Lt RN	01-May-03	WAR	O SKW	854 NAS	RNAS CULDROSE
Hillard, Christopher	Lt RN	01-Sep-08	ENG	AE	854 NAS	RNAS CULDROSE
Hillier, Andrew	RN Chpln	13-Sep-05	Ch S		RN EXCHANGE USA	WASHINGTON
Hillman, Christopher M	Surg Lt Cdr	03-Aug-09	MED	EM	INM ALVERSTOKE	GOSPORT
Hills, Anthony A	Lt Cdr	01-Dec-94	WAR	P LYNX	RNAS CULDROSE - ADM	RNAS CULDROSE
Hills, Matthew	Capt	01-Aug-07	RM	MLDR	30 CDO IX GP RM - SR SQN	PLYMOUTH
Hills, Michael John MBE	RN Chpln	21-Apr-98	Ch S	GS	NCHQ	
Hilson, Steven M	Lt Cdr	01-Oct-04	WAR	O LYNX	LHF HQ	RNAS YEOVILTON
Hilton, Michael	Lt RN	23-Apr-06	ENG	TM	DES/COMJE	ABBEY WOOD
Hilton, Simon T	Lt Cdr	01-Oct-10	WAR	O LYNX	FLEET CSAV	NCHQ
Hind, Joshua	Mid	01-Sep-13	ENG	ME	BRNC DARTMOUTH	DARTMOUTH
Hindle, Christopher K	SLt	24-Jan-12	WAR	P UT	BRNC DARTMOUTH	DARTMOUTH
Hine, Michael J	Lt Cdr	01-Oct-11	LOGS	L SM	ACDS DEFLOGPOL	ABBEY WOOD
Hine, Nicholas W	Capt RN	30-Jun-08	WAR	SM(CQ)	FMC - STRAT N	MAIN BUILDING LONDON
Hine, Thomas P	Mid	01-Sep-13	WAR	GSX	BRNC DARTMOUTH	DARTMOUTH
Hinton, Oliver J	Lt RN	05-Aug-11	LOGS	L	FLEET ACOS(RP)	NCHQ
Hirons, Francis D	Lt Cdr	01-Oct-06	WAR	PWO(C)	HMS SOMERSET	
Hiscock, Stephen R	Lt Cdr	01-Oct-09	ENG	WE	HMS SUTHERLAND	
Hislop, Scott G	Lt RN	28-Jul-06	ENG	AE	DES/COMLAND	ABBEY WOOD
Hitchings, Michael J	Lt RN	01-Sep-06	ENG	MESM	HMS ARTFUL	BARROW IN FURNESS
Hitchman, Stuart M	Capt	18-Jul-08	RM	GS	NCHQ	
Hoar, Mark Edward	Lt RN	01-Apr-11	WAR	P UT	702 SQN	RNAS YEOVILTON
Hoare, Peter J E	Cdr	30-Jun-10	WAR	O LYNX	FLEET COMOPS NWD	NORTHWOOD
Hoather, Martin S	Lt Cdr	01-Oct-05	ENG	WE	DI - CA	LONDON
Hobbs, Richard	Capt RN	22-Sep-08	ENG	WE	NAVY MCTA PORTSMOUTH	HMNB PORTSMOUTH
Hobbs, Thomas P	Lt Cdr	01-Oct-13	WAR	AWO(U)	FOST DPORT SEA	HMNB DEVONPORT
Hobby, David William	Lt RN	01-May-13	WAR	SM(X)	HMS VIGILANT	
Hobin, Daniel Charles	Lt RN	01-Sep-13	ENG	MESM	DCEME SULTAN	HMS SULTAN
Hobley, Christopher J	2Lt	02-Sep-13	RM	N/A	CTCRM OFFICERS	EXMOUTH
Hocking, John Adam	Lt RN	01-Sep-09	ENG	AE	RNAS YEOVILTON	
Hocking, Mark John	Lt Cdr	01-Oct-07	ENG	WE	DES/COMFLEET	ABBEY WOOD
Hocking, Roger C	Lt RN	11-Oct-13	WAR	C	DES/COMJE/ISS	CORSHAM
Hockley, Christopher J	R Adm	09-Sep-11	ENG	ME	FLEET FOSNNI	HELENSBURGH
Hodder, Gregory L	SLt	01-Nov-11	WAR	SM(X)	BRNC DARTMOUTH	
Hodge, Christopher M	Lt Cdr	01-Oct-04	ENG	MESM	DES/COMFLEET	ABBEY WOOD
Hodges, Philip Robin	Lt RN	01-Sep-07	ENG	MESM	DCDS PERS TRG-RFC	MAIN BUILDING LONDON
Hodgkins, Jonathan C	Cdr	30-Jun-02	WAR	O LYNX	NCHQ - NAVY CMD SEC	NCHQ
Hodgkinson, Samuel P	Lt RN	01-Sep-04	WAR	P CDO	CHF(MERLIN)	OXFORD
Hodgkiss, James E	Lt RN	01-Apr-12	WAR	GSX	HMS BULWARK	
Hodgson, Katie J	SLt	01-Sep-11	ENG	ME	DCEME SULTAN	HMS SULTAN
Hodgson, Laura	Lt Cdr	01-Oct-04	ENG	ME	HMS MONMOUTH	
Hodgson, Timothy C	Cdre	04-Sep-12	ENG	MESM	DES/COMFLEET	ABBEY WOOD
Hodkinson, Christopher B	Capt RN	04-Sep-12	WAR	PWO(A)	FLEET CAP LLM & DRM DIVISION	NCHQ
Hofman, Alison Jayne RRC	Cdr	27-Jul-10	QARNNS	Nursing Officer	RCDM	LICHFIELD
Hogben, Andrew L	Cdr	30-Jun-07	WAR	AAWO	HMS COLLINGWOOD	
Hogg, Adam James	Lt Cdr	01-Oct-11	WAR	P GR7	DES/COIR	ABBEY WOOD
Hogg, Christopher W	Lt Cdr	01-Mar-97	WAR	PWO(A)	FOST DPORT SHORE	HMNB DEVONPORT
Hogg, Theodore J	Capt	01-Sep-13	RM	GS	40 CDO RM	TAUNTON

Person Name	Substantive Rank	Seniority	Branch	Specialisation	Organisation	Location
Holborn, Lee James	Lt RN	01-Nov-10	WAR	P LYNX	RNAS YEOVILTON	
Holbrook, Simon J	Lt RN	01-Feb-08	WAR	FC	RNAS YEOVILTON	RNAS YEOVILTON
Holburt, Richard M	Lt RN	01-Nov-06	LOGS	L	RNAS YEOVILTON	
Holdcroft, Luke J	SLt	01-Aug-11	WAR	SM(X)	BRNC DARTMOUTH	
Holden, Paul A	Lt Cdr	01-Oct-02	ENG	AE	FLEET CSAV	NCHQ
Holden, Robert J	Lt Cdr	01-Oct-99	WAR	O SKW	857 NAS	RNAS CULDROSE
Holden, Simon W	Lt RN	01-May-13	WAR	GSX	MWS COLLINGWOOD	HMS COLLINGWOOD
Holder, John	Lt Cdr	01-Oct-09	WAR	P MER	RN EXCHANGE USA - BDS	WASHINGTON
Hole, Joseph S I	Lt RN	01-Apr-09	WAR	P UT	824 SQN	RNAS CULDROSE
Holford, Kane	Capt	01-Sep-10	RM	GS	45 CDO RM	DUNDEE
Holgate, James A	Lt Cdr	01-Oct-11	ENG	WE	HMS MONMOUTH	
Holland, Amanda	Lt Cdr	01-Nov-04	QARNNS	Nursing Officer	HMS RALEIGH	
Holland, Charlotte C	Lt Cdr	01-Oct-08	LOGS	L	RNAS YEOVILTON	
Holland, Edward R	Lt RN	01-Apr-08	WAR	O MER	829 SQN FLT 04	RNAS CULDROSE
Holland, Emma E	Surg Lt RN (D)	04-Jul-11	DENTAL	GDP	RNAS YEOVILTON	
Holland, Fergus W	SLt	14-Aug-12	WAR	GSX	BRNC DARTMOUTH	
Holland, Paul Eric	Lt RN	01-Jul-11	LOGS	L	FLEET SPT LOGS	NCHQ
Holland, Richard	Lt RN	01-May-08	WAR	SM(X)	FLEET COMOPS NWD	NORTHWOOD
Holland, Steven W	Lt Cdr	01-Oct-13	ENG	AE	DES/COIR	ABBEY WOOD
Holliehead, Craig	Lt RN	01-Jan-02	WAR	P LYNX	RN EXCHANGE USA	WASHINGTON
Hollingworth, Christopher R	Lt Cdr	01-Oct-13	WAR	PWO	HMS MONMOUTH	
Hollingworth, Eleanor	Lt RN	01-Sep-08	WAR	FC	HMS DARING	
Hollins, Rupert	Capt RN	01-Jul-09	LOGS	L BAR	ATTACHE/ADVISER BEIJING	PEKING
Holloway, Benjamin S V	Lt RN	01-May-07	LOGS	L SM	HQ BFC J1	EPISKOPI CYPRUS
Holloway, Jonathan T	Capt RN	30-Jun-02	ENG	MESM	FOSNNI - YOUTH C	HMNB PORTSMOUTH
Holloway, Steven A	Lt Cdr	01-Oct-03	WAR	PWO(U)	LSP OMAN	OMAN
Hollyfield, Peter	Lt RN	01-May-00	ENG	IS	CIO-DSAS	CORSHAM
Holmes, Christopher	Lt Cdr	01-Oct-12	ENG	ME	HMS LANCASTER	
Holmes, Christopher J	Lt Col	30-Jun-06	RM	C	FLEET CAP IS DIVISION	NCHQ
Holmes, Matthew DSO	Brig	19-Mar-13	RM	GS	DCDC	SHRIVENHAM
Holmes, Patrick J M	Lt RN	01-May-02	WAR	P MER	HMS NELSON	HMS NELSON
Holmes, Robert	Cdr	25-Feb-96	WAR	PWO (RES)	FLEET CMR	NCHQ
Holmwood, Mark A G	Lt Cdr	01-Aug-11	ENG	ME	RMR MERSEYSIDE	LIVERPOOL
Holroyd, Jason Heath	Lt RN	27-Jul-07	ENG	WE	OCLC NCH	MANCHESTER
Holroyd, Jonathon E J	Lt Cdr	01-Oct-08	WAR	O MER	FLEET CSAV	NCHQ
Holt, Christopher J	SLt	01-Sep-11	ENG	AE	DCEME SULTAN	HMS SULTAN
Holt, John D	Lt RN	01-May-00	ENG	IS(SM)	RNEAWC - SNO	LINCOLN
Holt, Justin Sefton MBE	Lt Col	30-Jun-05	RM	LC	OP VOCATE	LIBYA TRIPOLI
Holt, Laura	Lt RN	01-Jun-10	LOGS	L	DES/COMFLEET	HMNB PORTSMOUTH
Holt, Steven	Capt RN	12-Dec-12	WAR	PWO(N)	UKRBATSTAFF	HMNB PORTSMOUTH
Holvey, Paul J	Lt RN	01-Apr-01	ENG	MESM	DES/COMFLEET	HMS DRAKE
Honey Morgan, J	RN Chpln	01-Sep-03	Ch S		RNAS YEOVILTON	
Honnoraty, Mark R	Cdr	30-Jun-05	WAR	SM(CQ)	COMFASFLOT	HMNB CLYDE
Hood, Kevin C	Capt RN	08-Dec-11	LOGS	L	NCHQ CNPS	MAIN BUILDING LONDON
Hood, Kevin Michael	Lt Cdr	01-Apr-98	ENG	MESM	DES/COMFLEET	ABBEY WOOD
Hood, Matthew John	Maj	25-Apr-96	RM	GS	HMS DRAKE	
Hook, David A CBE	Maj Gen	03-Oct-11	RM	C	HNMB DEVONPORT	PLYMOUTH
Hooper, Christopher C	SLt	01-Feb-13	MED	MEDICAL	BRNC DARTMOUTH	
Hooper, Johanna	Cdr	30-Jun-13	LOGS	L	DCDS PERS TRG	MAIN BUILDING LONDON
Hooper, Thomas	Lt RN	01-Jan-05	LOGS	L	NAVY CORE TRG HQ	HMNB DEVONPORT
Hooper, William R	Lt RN	01-Jan-06	WAR	P LYNX	RAF SHAWBURY	
Hope, Karl	Lt Cdr	01-Sep-13	ENG	IS	DCDS(PERS)/SPVA	GOSPORT
Hope, William D	Mid	01-Sep-13	ENG	WE	BRNC DARTMOUTH	
Hoper, Paul Roger	Cdr	30-Jun-07	WAR	O SKW	DMC	MAIN BUILDING LONDON
Hopkins, Danielle	SLt	01-Sep-12	ENG	WE	BRNC DARTMOUTH	
Hopkins, Rhys	Maj	01-Oct-07	RM	GS	NCHQ - CNLS	PLYMOUTH
Hopkins, Richard MBE	Maj	01-Oct-06	RM	GS	FLEET ACOS(RP)	NCHQ
Hopkins, Steven David MBE	Lt Cdr	01-Oct-03	WAR	P SK6	771 SQN	RNAS CULDROSE
Hopkinson, Geoffrey A	Lt	01-Sep-12	RM	GS	43 CDO	HMNB CLYDE
Hopper, Ian	Lt Cdr	09-Apr-02	WAR	PWO(A)	UKRBATSTAFF	HMNB PORTSMOUTH
Hopper, Simon M	Cdr	30-Jun-07	WAR	PWO(A)	OPS DIR	MAIN BUILDING LONDON
Hopton, Fiona C F	Lt Cdr	01-Oct-13	WAR	HM	HMS MONTROSE	

Person Name	Substantive Rank	Seniority	Branch	Specialisation	Organisation	Location
Hopton, Matthew J	Lt Cdr	01-Oct-13	WAR	PWO(SM)	BRNC DARTMOUTH	
Hopwood, Adrian P	Lt RN	17-Dec-04	WAR	GSX	DES/COMFLEET	HMNB PORTSMOUTH
Horlock, Andrew	Lt Cdr	01-Oct-12	MED	MS(SM)	DES/COMFLEET	HMS DRAKE
Horn, Neil Richard	Lt RN	01-Apr-08	ENG	MESM	DES/COMFLEET	ABBEY WOOD
Horn, Peter Barrick MBE	Cdr	30-Jun-99	WAR	PWO(A)	NCHQ CNPS	NCHQ
Horne, Christopher P	Capt	01-Sep-08	RM	GS	NCHQ	
Horne, Jason	Cdr	30-Jun-10	WAR	PWO(U)	BRITISH MILITARY MISSION	KUWAIT
Horne, Nicholas	Lt RN	01-Apr-09	WAR	FC	UK MCC	BAHRAIN
Horne, Simon T	RN Chpln	01-Sep-04	Ch S	Chaplain	HMS SULTAN - CHAP	HMS SULTAN
Horne, Thomas S	SLt	01-Nov-11	WAR	O UT	BRNC DARTMOUTH	
Horne, Timothy G	Cdr	30-Jun-97	WAR	PWO(A)	NCHQ CNPS	PORTSMOUTH
Horner, Patrick A	Lt Cdr	01-Aug-94	WAR	AAWO	HMS BULWARK	
Horsted, James A	Lt Cdr	01-Mar-10	ENG	MESM	HMS AMBUSH	
Horton, James R	Lt Cdr	01-Oct-13	WAR	P LYNX	CAREER TRAINING	RAF BOSCOMBE DOWN
Horton, Simon	Lt RN	11-Dec-05	WAR	INT	FLEET COMOPS NWD	RAF WYTON
Hotchkiss, Jonathan J	Mid	01-Sep-13	WAR	GSX	BRNC DARTMOUTH	DARTMOUTH
Hougham, Thomas Neil	Lt RN	01-Sep-05	WAR	P MER	824 SQN - TU	RNAS CULDROSE
Houghton, Christopher L	Lt RN	01-Nov-13	ENG	WESM	HMS ASTUTE	
Houghton, David G	Lt RN	01-Jun-13	WAR	P SK4	845 SQN	RNAS YEOVILTON
Houghton, James E	Lt	01-Mar-11	RM	GS	43 CDO	HMNB CLYDE
Houghton, Philip J	Lt Cdr	01-Jul-94	WAR	PWO(U)	COMPORFLOT	HMNB PORTSMOUTH
Houlberg, Kenneth M T	Cdr	30-Jun-08	WAR	PWO(A)	COMUKTG SEA	PLYMOUTH
Houlberg, Kristian A N	Surg Cdr	14-Feb-09	MED	Med	MDHU DERRIFORD	PLYMOUTH
Houlston, Ian J	Lt RN	01-Jan-05	WAR	P LYNX	702 SQN	RNAS YEOVILTON
Hounslow, Oliver W	SLt	24-Jul-11	WAR	SM(X)	BRNC DARTMOUTH	DARTMOUTH
Hounsom, Timothy	Lt Cdr	01-Apr-05	WAR	PWO(U)	LSP ON	MUSCAT
Hounsome, Debra M MBE Arrc	Cdr	01-Jul-13	QARNNS	T&O	MDHU DERRIFORD	PLYMOUTH
Hounsome, Jonathan R	Lt RN	01-Jan-04	WAR	O SK6	RNAS CULDROSE - FT	RNAS CULDROSE
House, Andrew L	Lt RN	01-Oct-09	WAR	GSX	HMS SUTHERLAND	
Houston, Darren	Cdr	30-Jun-11	WAR	PWO(N)	RN EXCHANGE USA	WASHINGTON USA
Hovington, Peter A K	Lt RN	01-Sep-12	ENG	ME	HMS MONMOUTH	
Howard, Alexander D	SLt	01-Sep-11	ENG	AE	DCEME SULTAN	HMS SULTAN
Howard, Dale T	Lt RN	01-Sep-13	ENG	WE	HMS ILLUSTRIOUS	
Howard, Daniel G	Cdr	30-Jun-06	WAR	PWO	JOINT HQ - LO-GE	BERLIN
Howard, James W	Lt RN	01-Feb-09	WAR	PWO(SM)	HMS VANGUARD	
Howard, Martin J	Lt RN	01-Sep-07	WAR	O SKW	AWC BSD - RW TES	RAF BOSCOMBE DOWN
Howard, Nicholas H	Cdr	30-Jun-10	ENG	AE	MOD NSD - HDS	MAIN BUILDING LONDON
Howarth, John	Maj	01-Oct-05	RM	SCC	CTCRM	EXMOUTH
Howarth, Michael C	Lt RN	17-Feb-06	LOGS	L SM	JFC GLOBAL ADMIN UNIT	GLASGOW
Howe, Craig M	Lt RN	01-Jul-98	WAR	INT	FLEET COMOPS NWD	RNAS CULDROSE
Howe, David Norman	Lt RN	05-Aug-11	ENG	WE	DES/COMFLEET	ABBEY WOOD
Howe, Jonathan	Lt RN	16-Dec-11	WAR	INT	JOINT OPERATIONAL STAFF	LISBURN NI
Howe, Jonathan	Lt RN	01-Sep-06	ENG	AE	FLEET CSAV	NCHQ
Howe, Julian P	Lt Cdr	01-Oct-01	WAR	PWO(A)	NCHQ CNPERS	PORTSMOUTH
Howe, Michael	Lt RN	01-Sep-08	WAR	P MER	829 SQN FLT 05	RNAS CULDROSE
Howe, Neil David	Lt RN	19-Dec-08	LOGS	L SM	RNAS CULDROSE	
Howe, Nicholas E	SLt	01-Nov-11	WAR	GSX	BRNC DARTMOUTH	
Howe, Thomas	Lt Cdr	01-Nov-05	WAR	PWO(N	MWS COLLINGWOOD	
Howell, Andrew I	Lt RN	01-Aug-08	ENG	WE	COMDEVFLOT	HMS DRAKE
Howell, Michael A	Surg Capt RN	06-May-08	MED	EM	INM ALVERSTOKE	GOSPORT
Howells, Simon M	Lt Cdr	01-Oct-07	WAR	INT	FLEET CAP IS DIVISION	NCHQ
Howes, Daniel Patrick	Lt RN	01-Nov-13	WAR	P SK4	845 SQN	RNAS YEOVILTON
Howes, Francis CB, OBE	Maj Gen	08-Feb-10	RM	MLDR	BDS WASHINGTON	WASHINGTON DC USA
Howes, Richard J	Surg Lt Cdr	02-Aug-11	MED	EM	INM ALVERSTOKE	GOSPORT
Howie, Ian C	Lt RN	01-Mar-12	WAR	P UT	RNAS YEOVILTON	RNAS YEOVILTON
Hubschmid, Spencer R	Lt Cdr	01-Oct-07	ENG	WESM(SWS)	MOD SSPAG	MAIN BUILDING LONDON
Hucker, Oliver	Lt Cdr	01-Oct-13	WAR	GSX	GIBRALTAR PBS	GIBRALTAR
Huckle, Thomas C	Capt	01-Sep-11	RM	GS	CAREER TRAINING	EXMOUTH
Huckstep, Joseph P	Mid	01-Nov-13	WAR	P UT	BRNC DARTMOUTH	
Hudson, Andrew I	Lt RN	01-Oct-02	WAR	SM(AWC)	DEFAC JSCSC ICSCM	SHRIVENHAM
Hudson, Peter D CBE	V Adm	14-Feb-13	WAR	PWO(N)	NATO ACO	NORTHWOOD
Hudson, Richard A	Lt RN	30-Jul-10	ENG	WE	FOST DPORT SEA	HMNB DEVONPORT

Person Name	Substantive Rank	Seniority	Branch	Specialisation	Organisation	Location
Hudson, Tom A J	Lt RN	01-May-04	ENG	TM	MWS COLLINGWOOD	
Huggett, Christopher G	Capt	01-Sep-13	RM	GS	45 CDO RM - W COY	DUNDEE
Huggins, Michael A	Lt RN	01-Apr-11	WAR	GSX	NORTHWOOD HQ	
Hughes, Adam A	Lt RN	01-Mar-11	ENG	MESM	HMS TRIUMPH	
Hughes, Andrew S	Surg Cdre	25-Jul-11	MED	GMP (C&S)	DEFAC RCDS	LONDON
Hughes, Benjamin	Lt Cdr	01-Oct-09	LOGS	L C	HMS QUEEN ELIZABETH	ROSYTH
Hughes, Charlotte L	Surg Lt Cdr	02-Aug-10	MED	GMP	HMS NELSON	
Hughes, Christopher B	Lt Cdr	01-Oct-09	WAR	O SKW	UKRBATSTAFF	HMNB PORTSMOUTH
Hughes, David M	Lt RN	08-Dec-11	ENG	AE	847 SQN - AE	RNAS YEOVILTON
Hughes, Elizabeth E	Lt Cdr	01-Oct-11	ENG	ME	DES/DTECH	ABBEY WOOD
Hughes, Gareth D	Lt Cdr	01-Oct-09	ENG	ME	NAVY MCTA PORTSMOUTH	HMNB PORTSMOUTH
Hughes, Gareth L	Cdr	31-Dec-00	LOGS	L	NCHQ CNPERS	PORTSMOUTH
Hughes, Gary A	Mid	01-May-13	WAR	GSX	BRNC DARTMOUTH	
Hughes, Gary E	Lt Cdr	01-Oct-12	WAR	AV	DES/COMFLEET	BRISTOL
Hughes, Geoffrey	Lt Cdr	01-Oct-13	LOGS	L	AIO PLANNING BLB1	ANDOVER
Hughes, John J	Lt Cdr	01-Oct-10	WAR	P SK4	CHFHQ (SHORE)	RNAS YEOVILTON
Hughes, Matthew J	Capt	30-Mar-12	RM	MLDR	45 CDO RM	DUNDEE
Hughes, Michael I	Mid	01-Nov-13	WAR	GSX	BRNC DARTMOUTH	
Hughes, Nicholas J	Capt RN	13-Oct-09	WAR	SM(CQ)	COMDEVFLOT SHORE	HMNB DEVONPORT
Hughes, Paul A	Surg Capt RN	08-Sep-08	MED	GMP	DMRC HEADLEY COURT	EPSOM
Hughes, Peter LVO	Cdr	06-Feb-88	WAR	PWO(N)	NCHQ CNPS	NCHQ
Hughes, Roger D	Maj	01-Oct-13	RM	SCC	NCHQ CNPERS	PORTSMOUTH
Hughes, Ryan	SLt	01-Sep-12	WAR	GSX	MCM1 CREW 6	FASLANE
Hughes, Samuel E	Capt	01-Aug-07	RM	GS	FLEET DRM	NCHQ
Hughes, Scott M	Lt Cdr	01-Oct-11	WAR	P SKW	ABBEY WOOD	
Hughes, Sean C	Surg Lt Cdr	14-Nov-08	MED	Med (RES)	UK MED GP (AFG)	AFGHANISTAN BASTION
Hughes, Thomas W	Lt RN	01-Jan-04	ENG	MESM	DES/COMFLEET	ABBEY WOOD
Hughesdon, Mark D	Cdr	30-Jun-10	ENG	WE	NAVY MCTA PORTSMOUTH	HMNB PORTSMOUTH
Hull, Thomas Eden	SLt	02-May-12	WAR	SM(X)	BRNC DARTMOUTH	
Hulme, Timothy OBE	Cdr	30-Jun-08	WAR	O LYNX	DEFENCE ACADEMY	SHRIVENHAM
Hulse, Anthony W	Maj	01-Oct-07	RM	C	DEFENCE ACADEMY	SHRIVENHAM
Hulse, Elspeth J	Surg Lt Cdr	06-Aug-08	MED	Anaes	INM ALVERSTOKE	GOSPORT
Hulse, Rebecca J	Lt Cdr	01-Oct-12	LOGS	L	MOD DEFENCE STAFF	LONDON
Hulston, Lauren M	Lt Cdr	01-Oct-11	WAR	O MER	824 SQN	RNAS CULDROSE
Hume, James A	Lt RN	01-Apr-12	WAR	O UT	702 SQN YEOVILTON	RNAS YEOVILTON
Hume, Kenneth J	Lt RN	01-Mar-99	WAR	HM(AM)	FLEET COMOPS NWD	NORTHWOOD
Humphery, Duncan	Lt Cdr	01-Oct-07	ENG	ME	COMDEVFLOT SEA	HMNB DEVONPORT
Humphrey, Darren P	Lt RN	08-Apr-07	QARNNS	MH	RNLA	HMS COLLINGWOOD
Humphrey, Ivor James	Cdr	30-Jun-11	ENG	WE	D STRAT PROG	MAIN BUILDING LONDON
Humphreys, Rhodri H	Lt RN	08-Jul-09	ENG	TM	RNAS YEOVILTON	
Humphries, Graham D	Lt RN	01-May-01	WAR	P SK4	848 SQN	RNAS YEOVILTON
Humphries, Jason E	Lt Cdr	01-Oct-05	WAR	PWO(U)	HMS FORWARD	BIRMINGHAM
Humphries, Mark	Lt RN	01-Jul-00	WAR	P GR7	AWC WAD - PCC	LINCOLN
Hunnibell, John R	Lt Cdr	01-Oct-13	WAR	MCD	BRNC DARTMOUTH	
Hunnybun, Simon P	Lt RN	17-Dec-10	WAR	REG	RNP - HQ PMN	HMS EXCELLENT
Hunt, Ben P	Lt RN	01-Sep-03	WAR	P MER	MWS COLLINGWOOD	
Hunt, Darren	Maj	01-Oct-08	RM	P SK4	845 SQN	
Hunt, Fraser B G	Lt Cdr	01-Oct-03	WAR	P MER	JAG	AFGHANISTAN BASTION
Hunt, Patrick S	Lt Cdr	01-Jan-07	ENG	WE	AIR - OPS2GP - FP OPS	SALISBURY
Hunt, Rachel E	Lt RN	01-Jan-03	WAR	GSX	FLEET FOSNNI - CNR	HMNB PORTSMOUTH
Hunt, Robert Grant	Lt RN	01-Feb-09	WAR	P GR7	FLEET CSAV	WASHINGTON USA
Hunt, Robert James C	Lt Cdr	01-Oct-09	LOGS	L BAR	HMS WESTMINSTER	
Hunt, Stephen	Lt Cdr	01-Oct-03	WAR	AAWO	LOAN DSTL - NSD	FAREHAM
Hunt, Steven D	2Lt	02-Sep-13	RM	N/A	CTCRM OFFICERS	EXMOUTH
Hunter, Cameron M	Lt RN	03-May-13	ENG	ME	DCEME SULTAN	HMS SULTAN
Hunter, Darran J	Lt RN	01-Sep-07	ENG	MESM	DES/COMFLEET	ABBEY WOOD
Hunter, Deryk J C	Lt RN	15-Mar-08	WAR	SM(N)	COMFASFLOT	HMNB CLYDE
Hunter, Guy M	Surg Lt Cdr	03-Aug-11	MED	GDMO	HMS VICTORIOUS	
Hunter, Mitchell	Lt RN	01-Oct-12	ENG	MESM	HMS VIGILANT	
Huntingford, Damian J	Lt Col	30-Jun-13	RM	GS	DCDS MIL STRAT OPS	MAIN BUILDING LONDON
Huntington, Simon P OBE	Capt RN	28-Oct-13	WAR	PWO(U)	JFHQ	NORTHWOOD
Huntley, Genevieve E	Lt RN	01-Jan-10	WAR	GSX	NCHQ	

Person Name	Substantive Rank	Seniority	Branch	Specialisation	Organisation	Location
Huntley, Ian	Brig	15-Aug-11	RM	HW	DEFENCE ACADEMY	SHRIVENHAM
Hurdle, Ian	Capt	28-Jul-06	RM	GS	NCHQ	
Hurley, Karl	Lt Cdr	01-Oct-11	QARNNS	EN	NCHQ MEDDIV	NCHQ
Hurman, Richard N	Lt Cdr	01-Oct-12	WAR	PWO	HMS WESTMINSTER	
Hurry, Andrew P	Lt Cdr	01-Nov-94	WAR	P LYNX	FLEET CSAV	NCHQ
Hurst, Gareth W	Capt	21-Mar-13	RM	SCC	43 CDO FPGRM	HMNB CLYDE
Hurt, Christopher G	Capt	01-Sep-08	RM	GS	30 CDO IX GP RM	PLYMOUTH
Husband, James	Lt RN	01-Jan-07	LOGS	L SM	FLEET SPT LOGS	NCHQ
Hussain, Shayne MBE	Cdr	30-Jun-07	WAR	METOC	NATO DEF COLLEGE	
Hussey, Steven John MBE	Lt Col	30-Jun-08	RM	P SK4	CHFHQ (SEA)	RNAS YEOVILTON
Hutchings, Justin R	Lt Cdr	01-Oct-07	WAR	SM(CQ)	HMS TORBAY	
Hutchings, Richard	Lt Cdr	01-Dec-05	WAR	PWO	DEFAC JSCSC ACSC	SHRIVENHAM
Hutchings, Ross	Capt	01-Sep-12	RM	GS	NCHQ	
Hutchings, Sam D	Surg Cdr	14-Jun-11	MED	Anaes	MDHU PORTSMOUTH	PORTSMOUTH
Hutchins, Richard F	Cdr	30-Jun-11	ENG	MESM	NCHQ CNPERS	PORTSMOUTH
Hutchins, Timothy	Lt Cdr	01-Oct-05	WAR	HM (M CH)	DEFAC JSCSC ACSC	SHRIVENHAM
Hutchinson, Christopher J	Lt Cdr	01-Sep-00	WAR	HM (M CH)	FOST HM	HMS DRAKE
Hutchinson, Gillian P	Lt RN	01-Jun-07	LOGS	L	HMS NELSON	
Hutchinson, Michael R	Lt Cdr	01-Oct-12	WAR	FC	DCDS PERS TRG	MAIN BUILDING LONDON
Hutchinson, Oliver J	Cdr	30-Jun-06	WAR	AAWO	FLEET CAP SSM DIVISION	NCHQ
Hutchinson, Thomas D	Mid	01-Sep-13	ENG	ME	BRNC DARTMOUTH	
Hutchison, Callum R	SLt	01-Apr-12	WAR	SM(X)	HMS VIGILANT	
Hutchison, Paul G	Lt Cdr	01-May-98	ENG	MESM	FOST SM SEA	HMNB DEVONPORT
Hutton, Graham	Lt Cdr	01-Oct-04	WAR	O SKW	NCHQ CNPERS	PORTSMOUTH
Hutton, James OBE	Col	30-Jun-07	RM	GS	LST AUSTRALIA	CANBERRA AUSTRALIA
Hutton, Paul R	Lt RN	27-Jul-07	ENG	AE	RNAS YEOVILTON - AED	RNAS YEOVILTON
Huxtable, Mark C	SLt	01-Sep-12	WAR	P UT	RNAS YEOVILTON	RNAS YEOVILTON
Huynh, Cuong	Lt Cdr	01-Oct-10	LOGS	L	UK MCC	BAHRAIN
Hyde, James W	Lt Cdr	01-Oct-12	ENG	WE	DES/COMLAND	ABBEY WOOD
Hynde, Claire L	Lt RN	22-Apr-05	LOGS	L	MOD CNS/ACNS	MAIN BUILDING LONDON

I

Person Name	Substantive Rank	Seniority	Branch	Specialisation	Organisation	Location
Iliffe, David I	Lt Cdr	01-Oct-08	WAR	INT	DCOG NORTHWOOD	NORTHWOOD
Illingworth, Richard A	Lt Cdr	01-Oct-12	WAR	INT	JCU (CH)	CHELTENHAM
Imm, Nicholas D H	Surg Cdr	30-Jul-08	MED	GMP (C&S)	NCHQ MEDDIV	NCHQ
Imrie, Peter B DSM	Lt Cdr	01-Oct-04	WAR	AV	NCHQ CNPERS	PORTSMOUTH
Imrie, Samantha J	Lt Cdr	01-Oct-11	LOGS	L	DES/COMLAND	BICESTER
Ingamells, Stephen D	Lt RN	01-Jan-04	WAR	P SK4	845 SQN	RNAS YEOVILTON
Inge, Daniel J	Lt Cdr	01-Oct-06	WAR	ATC	RNAS YEOVILTON	
Ingham, Andrew R	Cdr	30-Jun-13	WAR	AAWO	HMS DIAMOND	
Ingham, Lee-Anne	Lt RN	01-Sep-01	WAR	HM	RNAS CULDROSE	
Ingham, Maryla K	Lt Cdr	01-Oct-08	WAR	PWO(N) PWO(U)		HMS OCEAN
Inglesby, Paul R	Lt RN	11-Dec-09	WAR	GSX	MWS COLLINGWOOD	
Inglis, David	SLt	01-Feb-13	MED	MEDICAL	BRNC DARTMOUTH	
Inglis, David J	Lt RN	01-Jan-02	WAR	P CDO	CHF(MERLIN)	RAF BENSON
Inglis, Graham D	Lt Cdr	01-Oct-12	WAR	PWO	UK ACC	QATAR JOA AL UDEID
Inglis, William S	Lt RN	01-Jan-07	WAR	SM(N)	HMS DALRIADA	GREENOCK
Ingram, Dean D	Lt RN	20-Jan-07	WAR	PWO(SM)	DEFAC JSCSC ICSCM	SWINDON
Ingram, Richard	Capt RN	07-Sep-09	WAR	PWO(A)	LSP ON	MUSCAT
Inness, Matthew	Lt RN	01-Oct-02	ENG	MESM	FLEET CAP SSM DIVISION	NCHQ
Insley, Carrie A	Lt Cdr	01-Oct-12	LOGS	L	DES/COMFLEET	HELENSBURGH
Instrell, Christopher B	Lt RN	01-Jan-09	ENG	AE	FLEET CSAV	ABBEY WOOD
Ireland, John M	Lt Cdr	01-Oct-02	ENG	MESM	DES/COMFLEET	ABBEY WOOD
Irons, Paul A	Lt Cdr	01-Jul-97	WAR	INT	DI - SA	MAIN BUILDING LONDON
Irons, Rupert	Cdr	30-Jun-11	WAR	PWO(C)	HMS NELSON	
Irving, Luke V	Capt	01-Sep-10	RM	GS	HQ 3 CDO BDE RM	PLYMOUTH
Irving, Paul J	Lt Cdr	01-Oct-12	WAR	P LYNX	HMS RICHMOND	
Irwin, Mark A	Cdr	30-Jun-08	ENG	ME	FOSNNI - YOUTH C	LIVERPOOL
Irwin, Matthew	Lt RN	01-Sep-12	WAR	GSX	MCM2 CREW 6	PORTSMOUTH
Irwin, Steven G	Lt RN	01-Oct-11	WAR	P UT	RNAS YEOVILTON	
Irwin, Stuart G	Lt Cdr	01-Oct-11	WAR	P LYNX	AWC BSD - RW TES	RAF BOSCOMBE DOWN
Isaacs, Nathan J	Lt Cdr	01-Oct-13	WAR	MCD	FDU3	PORTSMOUTH

Person Name	Substantive Rank	Seniority	Branch	Specialisation	Organisation	Location
Isherwood, Carl R	Lt RN	01-May-04	WAR	GSX	CHFHQ (SEA)	RNAS YEOVILTON
Issitt, Barry D	Lt Cdr	01-Oct-12	WAR	P GR7	FLEET CSAV	NCHQ
Isted, Lee R	Lt RN	01-Sep-07	LOGS	L SM	HMS NELSON	
Ives, David J	Lt Cdr	25-Oct-12	WAR	HM(AS)	RN EXCHANGE AUSTRALIA	CANBERRA AUSTRALIA
Ives, Katie M	Lt RN	01-Sep-13	ENG	WE	MWS COLLINGWOOD	
Ivill, Stephen	Lt Cdr	01-Oct-12	WAR	O MER	FLEET AV CU	RNAS CULDROSE
Ivory, Matthew J	Lt RN	01-Sep-11	ENG	ME	BRNC DARTMOUTH	
Ivory, Thomas	Lt RN	01-Nov-05	ENG	WE	DEFENCE ACADEMY	SOUTHAMPTON

J

Person Name	Substantive Rank	Seniority	Branch	Specialisation	Organisation	Location
Jack, Valencera	Lt RN	01-Jul-09	ENG	ME	HMS OCEAN	
Jackman, Andrew W	Cdr	30-Jun-98	WAR	PWO(C)	BFSAI - HQBFSAI	FALKLAND ISLANDS
Jacks, Michael J	Lt RN	01-Sep-11	WAR	HM	FLEET HM UNIT	HMNB DEVONPORT
Jackson, Amie R	Lt RN	01-Jan-08	WAR	GSX	HMS BLAZER	
Jackson, Andrew	Cdr	30-Jun-05	ENG	MESM	FLEET FOST ACOS(Trg)	ABBEY WOOD
Jackson, David	Cdr	30-Jun-10	ENG	AE	HQ JHC	ANDOVER
Jackson, Howard C	Lt RN	01-May-01	WAR	P SK4	CHFHQ (SEA)	RNAS YEOVILTON
Jackson, Ian A	Cdr	30-Jun-08	ENG	ME	FLEET ACOS(RP)	NCHQ
Jackson, Mark H	RN Chpln	19-Apr-83	Ch S		RN GIBRALTAR - CHAP	GIBRALTAR
Jackson, Matthew J DSO	Col	05-Nov-13	RM	GS	DEF BD SEC	MAIN BUILDING LONDON
Jackson, Thomas	SLt	10-Nov-11	WAR	GSX	BRNC DARTMOUTH	
Jackson-Spence, Nicholas J	SLt	01-May-12	WAR	P UT	BRNC DARTMOUTH	
Jacob, Andrew W	Lt Cdr	01-Oct-09	WAR	HM (M CH)	NCHQ CNPERS	PORTSMOUTH
Jacobs, Joshua B	SLt	01-Sep-12	WAR	P UT	RNAS YEOVILTON	
Jacques, Kathryn	Lt RN	24-May-08	WAR	AW (RES)	HMS SHERWOOD	NOTTINGHAM
Jacques, Marcus J	Cdr	30-Jun-12	WAR	AAWO	YEMEN GCT	YEMEN
Jacques, Michael S	Lt RN	01-Sep-13	ENG	MESM	HMS SULTAN	
Jacques, Nicholas A	Lt Cdr	01-Oct-02	WAR	O LYNX	FLEET AV VL - OC	RNAS YEOVILTON
Jaffier, Robert Rd	Lt Cdr	01-Oct-10	WAR	INFO OPS	DEFAC JSCSC ACSC	SHRIVENHAM
Jaffrey, Heather B	Lt RN	11-Apr-06	QARNNS	EN	DPHC SOUTH	HMS SULTAN
Jaggers, Gary G	Lt Cdr	01-Oct-01	WAR	O MER	824 SQN - TU	RNAS CULDROSE
Jakes, Matthew O	Lt RN	09-Apr-10	ENG	ME	HMS SULTAN	
James, Adam J	Cdr	30-Jun-07	WAR	HM (H CH)	COMDEVFLOT SHORE	HMNB DEVONPORT
James, Andrew G	Lt Cdr	01-Jan-10	ENG	MESM	FLEET CAP SSM DIVISION	NCHQ
James, Christopher I	Lt RN	13-Apr-12	ENG	AE	824 SQN - TU	RNAS CULDROSE
James, Darren Brian	Lt RN	15-Apr-11	ENG	AE	HMS SULTAN - TSG	HMS SULTAN
James, Gareth C M	Lt Cdr	01-Oct-11	LOGS	L	HMS KENT	
James, Katherine J	Lt Cdr	01-Oct-06	QARNNS	Tutor	DMS WHITTINGTON	LICHFIELD
James, Mark	Lt Cdr	01-Oct-08	ENG	WE	DES/COMFLEET	ABBEY WOOD
James, Oliver N	Lt RN	01-Jan-13	ENG	WESM	HMS TRIUMPH	
James, Paul M DSO	Col	22-Aug-11	RM	GS	COMUKAMPHIBFOR	HMNB PORTSMOUTH
James, Robert Ba	Lt RN	01-Jul-04	WAR	AV	DES/COMLAND	ABBEY WOOD
Jameson, Andrew C Rcds	Cdre	01-Jul-11	LOGS	L BAR	FLEET CMR	NCHQ
Jameson, Andrew J	Lt RN	01-Sep-01	WAR	GSX	CFPS SQUAD	HMNB PORTSMOUTH
Jameson, Roger M	Lt Cdr	01-Oct-09	WAR	P LYNX	LHF 815 SQN HQ	RNAS YEOVILTON
Jamieson, Paul A	Lt Cdr	01-Oct-13	WAR	SM(AWC)	HMS TALENT	
Jamieson, Scott M	Lt RN	13-Apr-12	MED	MS(CDO)	MED SQN CDO LOG	BARNSTAPLE
Jamieson, Scott	Surg Lt Cdr	06-Aug-13	MED	GMP	INM ALVERSTOKE	GOSPORT
Jamison, James S	Maj	01-Oct-11	RM	HW	30 CDO IX GP RM	PLYMOUTH
Jane, Samuel C	Lt RN	01-Jul-05	WAR	MCD	MCM2 CREW 6	PORTSMOUTH
Janzen, Alexander N OBE	Lt Col	30-Jun-10	RM	C	40 CDO RM	TAUNTON
Jaques, Simon C D	Surg Lt Cdr	06-Aug-08	MED	Occ Med	INM ALVERSTOKE	GOSPORT
Jardine, Iain	Lt RN	01-May-04	WAR	P MER	DEF HELI FLYING SCH	RAF SHAWBURY
Jarman, Paul R	Lt Cdr	01-Oct-08	ENG	WESM	COMDEVFLOT SHORE	HMNB DEVONPORT
Jarvis, Lawrence R	Cdr	30-Jun-02	ENG	ME	FLEET CAP SSM DIVISION	NCHQ
Jayes, Neil J	Lt Cdr	01-Oct-07	WAR	REG	NPM EASTERN	HMS NELSON
Jefferson, Toby S	Cdr	30-Jun-11	ENG	AE	1710 NAS	PORTSMOUTH
Jeffrey, Ben S	Lt RN	01-May-09	WAR	SM(X)	HMS TALENT	
Jeffrey, Joseph S	Mid	01-May-13	LOGS	L	BRNC DARTMOUTH	DARTMOUTH
Jeffreys, Susan	Lt RN	12-Jul-13	QARNNS	Nursing Officer	MDHU PORTSMOUTH	PORTSMOUTH
Jeffs, Samuel G	Lt RN	01-Nov-09	WAR	SM(N)	FLEET COMOPS NWD	NORTHWOOD
Jenkin, Alastair M H	Capt RN	30-Jun-08	ENG	WE	NCHQ CNPS	PORTSMOUTH

Person Name	Substantive Rank	Seniority	Branch	Specialisation	Organisation	Location
Jenkin, Richard H	Lt RN	01-Sep-12	WAR	P UT	RNAS YEOVILTON	RNAS YEOVILTON
Jenking-Rees, Damian	Lt Cdr	01-Oct-05	LOGS	L	DMLS	HMS RALEIGH
Jenkins, David G	Lt Cdr	25-Jun-13	WAR	SM(CQ)	FOST SM SEA	HELENSBURGH
Jenkins, David Neil	Lt RN	27-Jul-07	ENG	WE	DES/COMJE	ABBEY WOOD
Jenkins, Gareth S	SLt	24-Jan-12	WAR	P UT	BRNC DARTMOUTH	
Jenkins, Gari Wyn	Cdr	30-Jun-03	ENG	WE	DES/COMFLEET	ABBEY WOOD
Jenkins, Gwyn OBE	Col	01-Jul-11	RM	GS	CDS	MAIN BUILDING LONDON
Jenkins, Robert	Lt RN	01-Dec-99	ENG	TM	JFC - DCTS (H)	RAF HALTON
Jenkins, Thomas R	Lt RN	01-Sep-05	WAR	GSX	MWS COLLINGWOOD	
Jenks, Jennifer C B	Surg Lt Cdr (D)	24-Sep-05	DENTAL	GDP	DEFENCE DENTAL SERVS	HMNB DEVONPORT
Jennings, William	Lt Cdr	01-Mar-03	ENG	ME	FOST DPORT SEA	HMNB DEVONPORT
Jepson, Nicholas H	Lt Col	30-Jun-12	RM	C	DEFENCE ACADEMY	SHRIVENHAM
Jermy, Richard	Lt Cdr	31-Mar-04	WAR	HUMINT (RES)	FLEET FOSNNI - NRC NE	HELENSBURGH
Jerrold, William H.	Maj	01-Oct-13	RM	C	SFSG C COY	RAF ST ATHAN
Jervis, Christopher	Surg Lt RN	04-Aug-10	MED	GDMO	SF MEDICA	RNAS CULDROSE
Jess, Aran E	Lt Col	30-Jun-13	RM	MLDR	FLEET CAP RCAP DIVISION	NCHQ
Jess, Ian M	R Adm	03-Jul-12	ENG	ME	ACNS SPT	NCHQ
Jesson, Christopher M	Capt	20-Jul-07	RM	SCC	FLEET SPT LOGS	NCHQ
Jessop, Paul E	Capt RN	08-Mar-10	ENG	MESM	FLEET CAP SSM DIVISION	NCHQ
Jewitt, Charles	Lt Cdr	30-Jun-03	LOGS	L (RES)	FOSNNI - YOUTH C	LINCOLN
Jewson, Benjamin D	Lt RN	01-May-04	WAR	O LYNX	LHF 815 SQN FLT 211	RNAS YEOVILTON
Johansen, Stephen P	Lt Cdr	01-Oct-10	ENG	ME	NAVY MCTA PORTSMOUTH	HMNB PORTSMOUTH
John, Gareth MBE	Cdr	30-Jun-07	ENG	WE	MOD NSD	CANBERRA AUSTRALIA
John, James	Lt RN	01-Apr-11	LOGS	L SM	COMFASFLOT	HELENSBURGH
Johns, Andrew W	Cdr	30-Jun-12	WAR	SM(CQ)	HMS TORBAY	
Johns, Michael	Cdr	30-Jun-10	WAR	O MER	DES/COMFLEET/SHIPS	ABBEY WOOD
Johns, Sarah A B	Cdr	30-Jun-07	ENG	TM	FLEET FOST ACOS	NCHQ
Johnson, Andrew S	Cdr	31-Dec-99	WAR	AAWO	NATO-ACO-JFC HQ	NAPLES
Johnson, Anthony R	Lt Cdr	01-Oct-05	WAR	O LYNX	815 SQN B	RNAS YEOVILTON
Johnson, Chad C	Cdr	30-Jun-12	ENG	AE P	CHFHQ (SEA)	RNAS YEOVILTON
Johnson, Daren	Capt	30-Mar-12	RM	SCC	42 CDO RM	PLYMOUTH
Johnson, Helen E	Lt RN	01-Sep-05	WAR	O MER	814 SQN	RNAS CULDROSE
Johnson, James C	Capt RN	30-Jun-07	ENG	WESM(TWS)	HMS DRAKE	
Johnson, Jeremy D	Lt RN	01-Jan-98	ENG	TM	HMS SULTAN - PT & R	HMS SULTAN
Johnson, Lauren O	Lt Cdr	01-Oct-10	LOGS	L	DES/COMFLEET	HMS DRAKE
Johnson, Mark	Lt Col	30-Jun-13	RM	P SK4	DEFAC JSCSC ACSC	SHRIVENHAM
Johnson, Matthew D	Lt RN	01-Jun-07	WAR	P SK4	CAREER TRAINING	RAF BENSON
Johnson, Matthew J	SLt	01-Apr-11	WAR	P UT	702 SQN	RNAS YEOVILTON
Johnson, Matthew	Lt RN	01-May-13	WAR	GSX	HMS TYNE	
Johnson, Michael I	Lt RN	09-Apr-12	WAR	GSX	HMS DIAMOND	
Johnson, Paul R	Lt Cdr	01-Oct-07	ENG	AE	ABBEY WOOD	BRISTOL
Johnson, Roy L	Lt RN	12-Nov-97	ENG	WESM	HMS SULTAN - CS	HMS SULTAN
Johnson, Scott	Lt Cdr	01-Oct-06	WAR	SM(CQ)	HMS VANGUARD	
Johnson, Thomas	Lt RN	01-Sep-08	WAR	PWO	HMS LANCASTER	
Johnson, Tim P	Lt Cdr	01-Oct-13	WAR	INT	COMUKAMPHIBFOR	HMNB PORTSMOUTH
Johnson, Tobias E	Surg Lt RN	01-Sep-12	MED	MEDICAL	BRNC DARTMOUTH	DARTMOUTH
Johnson, Voirrey	Lt Cdr	01-Oct-06	QARNNS	PHC	BFG HS HQ	RHEINDAHLEN
Johnston, Andrew I	Lt RN	01-May-04	WAR	P SK4	CHFHQ (SEA)	RNAS YEOVILTON
Johnston, Audrey R	Lt RN	19-May-09	QARNNS	ITU	RCDM	BIRMINGHAM
Johnston, David R	Lt Cdr	01-Oct-08	LOGS	L SM	NCHQ CNPERS	PORTSMOUTH
Johnston, David R	Lt RN	11-Apr-08	ENG	WESM(TWS)	DES/COMJE	ABBEY WOOD
Johnston, David S	Capt	01-Sep-11	RM	GS	43 CDO	HMNB CLYDE
Johnston, Gregory P	Lt RN	01-Jul-08	ENG	TM	1 ASSLT GROUP RM	BRNC DARTMOUTH
Johnston, Karl G	Maj	01-Oct-11	RM	GS	CDO LOG REGT RM	BARNSTAPLE
Johnstone, Clive C CBE	R Adm	24-Jul-07	WAR	PWO(A)	MOD CNS/ACNS	MAIN BUILDING LONDON
Johnstone, Neil C	Capt	01-Sep-10	RM	GS	CAREER TRAINING	HMS NELSON
Johnstone-Burt, Charles E	Lt RN	01-Apr-11	LOGS	L	HMS PORTLAND	
Joll, Simon	Cdr	30-Jun-08	LOGS	L SM	BDS WASHINGTON	WASHINGTON USA
Jones, Adam E	Lt Cdr	01-Nov-02	WAR	P SK4	RNAS CULDROSE	
Jones, Aled L	Surg Lt Cdr	06-Aug-08	MED	GS	INM ALVERSTOKE	GOSPORT
Jones, Alun David	Cdr	30-Jun-07	WAR	P LYNX	NCHQ CNPERS	PORTSMOUTH
Jones, Andrew Neil	Capt	01-Sep-11	RM	GS	45 CDO RM	DUNDEE

Person Name	Substantive Rank	Seniority	Branch	Specialisation	Organisation	Location
Jones, Andrew Neil	Capt	01-Sep-10	RM	GS	JCTTAT	FOLKESTONE
Jones Benjamin L	Capt	01-Sep-10	RM	GS	SP WPNS SCHOOL	WARMINSTER
Jones, Benjamin P	Mid	01-Sep-13	WAR	SM(X)	BRNC DARTMOUTH	
Jones, Carolyn	Lt RN	27-Aug-13	WAR	MEDIA OPS (RES)	NCHQ - NAVY CMD SEC	NCHQ
Jones, Carolyn J	Surg Lt Cdr	02-Aug-10	MED	GMP	INM ALVERSTOKE	GOSPORT
Jones, Charmody E	Lt Cdr	01-Oct-10	WAR	PWO(C)	HMS NELSON	
Jones, Cheryl	Lt RN	01-Sep-06	WAR	O SKW	HMS RALEIGH	
Jones, Christopher	Lt RN	01-Sep-10	WAR	O SKW	849 SQN	RNAS CULDROSE
Jones, Christopher	Lt RN	13-Jun-08	WAR	C	11 EOD REGT	COLCHESTER
Jones, Christopher D	Lt RN	07-Apr-06	ENG	ME	FLEET CAP SSM DIVISION	NCHQ
Jones, Darren P	Lt Cdr	01-Oct-13	ENG	AE	DEFAC CMT MBA	SHRIVENHAM
Jones, David	Cdr	30-Jun-12	ENG	MESM	DES/COMFLEET	ABBEY WOOD
Jones, David K	Lt Cdr	01-Oct-09	LOGS	L	HMS DRAKE	
Jones, David M	Lt Cdr	01-Jul-04	ENG	WE	DES/COMFLEET	ABBEY WOOD
Jones, Emmanuel N L	Lt RN	01-Jan-03	WAR	PWO(N)	MWS COLLINGWOOD	
Jones, Gareth David	Lt Cdr	01-Sep-03	ENG	TM	DI - ICSP	LONDON
Jones, Gemma E	Lt RN	01-Oct-09	WAR	GSX	DEF LANG SCHOOL	BEACONSFIELD
Jones, Gordon	Lt RN	01-Sep-03	WAR	HM(AM)	RN EXCHANGE USA	WASHINGTON
Jones, Helen C	Lt Cdr	01-Oct-12	ENG	ME	HMS SUTHERLAND	
Jones, Hugh	Capt	28-Jul-06	RM	SCC	CTCRM - P&R	EXMOUTH
Jones, Ian Michael	Lt Cdr	01-Oct-07	ENG	AE	RNAS CULDROSE - AED HQ	RNAS CULDROSE
Jones, Jason B	Lt RN	13-Jul-12	ENG	WE	HMS ARGYLL	
Jones, Lewis	Mid	01-Sep-13	WAR	SM(X)	BRNC DARTMOUTH	
Jones, Marc R	Lt RN	01-Jan-07	LOGS	L BAR	DMLS	HMS RALEIGH
Jones, Mark	Lt Cdr	01-Oct-07	ENG	WE	DEFAC JSCSC ACSC	SHRIVENHAM
Jones, Mark	Lt RN	01-Jul-04	ENG	WE	DES/COMJE	ABBEY WOOD
Jones, Mark D	Lt Cdr	01-Oct-10	WAR	O LYNX	DES/COMJE	RNAS YEOVILTON
Jones, Mark F	SLt	01-Feb-12	LOGS	L	HMS RALEIGH	
Jones, Mark O	Lt RN	01-Sep-13	ENG	WE	HMS DRAKE	
Jones, Martin C	Cdr	30-Jun-01	WAR	HM (H CH)	DI - ICSP	LONDON
Jones, Morgan	Lt RN	01-Jan-09	WAR	P MER	829 SQN FLT 03	RNAS CULDROSE
Jones, Nicholas H	Lt Cdr	01-Oct-12	ENG	IS	PJHQ (UK) J6	NORTHWOOD
Jones, Paul T	Surg Lt RN	01-Feb-10	MED	GDMO	45 CDO RM	DUNDEE
Jones, Pauline	Lt Cdr	31-Mar-98	LOGS	L (RES)	FLEET CMR	GATESHEAD
Jones, Philip A CBE	V Adm	13-Dec-11	WAR	PWO(C)	FLEET COMNDER DCNS	NCHQ
Jones, Richard L	Lt RN	20-May-12	WAR	GSX	MWS COLLINGWOOD	
Jones, Robert P	Lt RN	01-Dec-13	ENG	ME	HMS MONTROSE	
Jones, Robert P	Maj	01-Sep-09	RM	HW	45 CDO RM - Z COY	DUNDEE
Jones, Robert T	Lt RN	31-Jul-07	ENG	IS	FLEET CISSU	FLEET HQ
Jones, Simon A	Lt RN	01-Nov-13	WAR	P SK4	845 SQN	RNAS CULDROSE
Jones, Stephen	Lt RN	01-May-03	ENG	ME	HMS DRAKE	HMS DRAKE
Jones, Steven F	Lt RN	01-Sep-08	LOGS	L	FLEET SPT LOGS	NCHQ
Jones, Steven K	Lt RN	15-Apr-11	ENG	WE	HMS OCEAN	
Jones, Timothy M	Cdr	21-Jul-13	MED	MS	MDHU DERRIFORD	PLYMOUTH
Jones, Toby	Lt RN	01-Feb-07	WAR	INT	FLEET COMOPS NWD	NORTHWOOD
Jones, Toby W	Capt	01-Sep-09	RM	LC	NCHQ	
Jones, William A	Lt RN	01-Jun-10	ENG	WE	HMS DAUNTLESS	
Jones-Thompson, Michael	Lt Cdr	01-Oct-07	WAR	AAWO	RN EXCHANGE CANADA	OTTAWA CANADA
Jordan, Adrian M	Surg Capt RN (D)	11-Jan-11	DENTAL	GDP(C&S)	DDS PORTSMOUTH PDO	HMNB PORTSMOUTH
Jordan, Andrew A	Capt RN	25-Sep-13	WAR	PWO(U)	FLEET ACOS(RP)	NCHQ
Jordan, Catherine E	Cdr	30-Jun-13	WAR	O LYNX	HMS ST ALBANS	
Jordan, Craig	Lt Cdr	01-Oct-05	ENG	IS	DEFENCE ACADEMY HQ	SHRIVENHAM
Jordan, Craig D	Lt RN	20-May-09	ENG	AE O	857 NAS	RNAS CULDROSE
Jordan, Emma	Lt RN	01-May-97	WAR	HM METOC	RNR AIR BR VL	RNAS CULDROSE
Jose, Steven	Cdr	30-Jun-12	ENG	AE P	RNAS YEOVILTON	RNAS YEOVILTON
Joshi, Cael R	SLt	01-Nov-11	WAR	GSX	BRNC DARTMOUTH	
Joyce, David A	Cdr	30-Jun-10	ENG	WE	MWS COLLINGWOOD	
Joyce, David J	Lt Cdr	01-Oct-13	ENG	ME	HMS DAUNTLESS	
Joyce, Thomas J	Cdr	30-Jun-11	WAR	P LYNX	FLEET CSAV	NCHQ
Juckes, Martin A	Cdr	30-Jun-06	ENG	AE	DES/COMLAND	ABBEY WOOD
Judd, Oliver James	Lt RN	19-Aug-09	ENG	WE	DES/COMFLEET	BRISTOL
Julian, Timothy Mark	Lt Cdr	01-Oct-04	WAR	P SK6	RNAS CULDROSE - FT	RNAS CULDROSE

Person Name	Substantive Rank	Seniority	Branch	Specialisation	Organisation	Location

K

Person Name	Substantive Rank	Seniority	Branch	Specialisation	Organisation	Location
Kadinopoulos, Benjamin A	Lt Cdr	01-Apr-11	ENG	WE	FLEET CAP RCAP DIVISION	NCHQ
Kain, Matthew J	SLt	01-Sep-12	MED	MEDICAL	BRNC DARTMOUTH	
Kane, Anthony P	Lt RN	01-Sep-12	WAR	GSX	HMS ARGYLL	
Kantharia, Paul	Lt RN	25-Jun-05	ENG	MESM	DES/COMFLEET	HMNB DEVONPORT
Kantharia, Richard P	Lt RN	01-Sep-12	WAR	SM(X)	HMS TALENT	
Karavla, Alexandra M I	Lt RN	01-Jan-13	WAR	GSX	HMS SOMERSET	
Karsten, Thomas M	R Adm	14-Dec-12	WAR	PWO(U)	LOAN HYDROG - DGHR(N)	TAUNTON
Kassapian, David L	Col	16-Feb-11	RM	GS	CTCRM	EXMOUTH
Kavanagh, Craig M	SLt	01-Sep-12	WAR	P	RNAS YEOVILTON	
Kay, David Rd	Cdr	01-Jan-02	LOGS	L (RES)	NORTHWOOD HQ	NORTHWOOD
Kay, Paul S	Lt Cdr	01-Oct-08	WAR	SM(CQ)	HMS ASTUTE	
Kay, Victoria J	Lt RN	15-Mar-06	ENG	WE	DES/COMJE/ISS	CORSHAM
Keam, Ian	Lt Cdr	01-Oct-10	ENG	AE	DES/COMJE	YEOVIL
Keane, Brendan M	Lt RN	01-May-03	ENG	WE	DES/COMFLEET	ABBEY WOOD
Keane, Joseph P	Lt RN	01-May-06	WAR	O LYNX	815 SQN FLT 214	RNAS YEOVILTON
Kearsley, Iain P	Lt Cdr	01-Oct-12	LOGS	L	HMS DAUNTLESS	
Keeble, Christopher	SLt	01-May-11	WAR	GSX	HMS MONTROSE	
Keegan, Amanda C	Lt RN	01-Oct-06	WAR	O MER	820 SQN	RNAS CULDROSE
Keeler, Charlotte L	Mid	14-Aug-12	LOGS	L	HMS KENT	
Keeling, Megan	Lt RN	01-Sep-11	ENG	ME	HMS IRON DUKE	
Keenan, Benjamin F	Lt RN	01-Sep-02	ENG	MESM	COMDEVFLOT SHORE	HMNB DEVONPORT
Keenan, Douglas J	Lt RN	01-May-07	WAR	O LYNX	LHF 702 SQN	RNAS YEOVILTON
Keenan, Gregory F	Lt RN	01-Sep-12	ENG	WESM(TWS)	HMS VANGUARD	
Keens, Emma Louise	Lt RN	07-Oct-11	WAR	HM	FLEET HM UNIT	HMNB DEVONPORT
Keillor, Stuart J	Lt Cdr	01-Oct-12	WAR	SM(AWC)	UK MCC	BAHRAIN
Keith, Benjamin C	Lt Cdr	01-Oct-08	WAR	P LYNX	HMS DEFENDER	
Keith, Charles R	Lt RN	01-Feb-10	WAR	INT	PJHQ (UK) J2	NORTHWOOD
Kelday, Alexander W	Lt RN	16-Feb-12	ENG	MESM	BRNC DARTMOUTH	
Kellett, Andrew	Cdr	30-Jun-13	ENG	ME	DES/COMFLEET	ABBEY WOOD
Kelley, Alexandra L	Lt RN	01-Jan-07	WAR	O MER	824 SQN - TU	RNAS CULDROSE
Kelly, Frank A Arrc	Lt RN	01-Feb-02	QARNNS	EN	MDHU DERRIFORD	PLYMOUTH
Kelly, Grant J	Lt Cdr	01-Oct-09	ENG	TM	UK MCC	BAHRAIN
Kelly, Howard C	Lt Cdr	01-Apr-02	ENG	MESM	DES/COMFLEET	BARROW IN FURNESS
Kelly, John	Cdr	30-Jun-06	ENG	ME	BDS WASHINGTON	WASHINGTON
Kelly, Nigel J	RN Chpln	26-May-92	Ch S		HMS NELSON	HMNB PORTSMOUTH
Kelly, Patrick J	Lt RN	01-Jun-07	WAR	HM	HMS ENTERPRISE	
Kelly, Philip M	Lt Col	30-Jun-10	RM	P GR7	FLEET CSAV	WASHINGTON
Kelly, Simon P	Lt Cdr	01-Jul-07	WAR	MCD PWO(A)	MCM1 CREW 5	HELENSBURGH
Kelway, Jenna	Lt RN	01-Jan-08	ENG	ME	RN EXCHANGE NETHERLANDS	DEN HELDER
Kemp, Gillian J	Surg Lt Cdr (D)	19-Jun-07	DENTAL	GDP	RNAS YEOVILTON	
Kemp, Peter	Lt RN	24-Oct-08	WAR	AE	RNAS CULDROSE	RNAS CULDROSE
Kemp, Peter G	Surg Lt Cdr	06-Aug-13	MED	GMP	INM ALVERSTOKE	GOSPORT
Kemp, Peter John	Lt Col	30-Jun-10	RM	MLDR	NATO SCHOOL OBERAMMERGAU	BRUSSELS
Kemp, Richard L	Lt RN	01-Sep-04	WAR	GSX	FASLANE PBS	HELENSBURGH
Kemp, Thomas A	SLt	01-Nov-11	WAR	SM(X)	BRNC DARTMOUTH	
Kempley, Paul S	Lt RN	11-Dec-09	ENG	WE	DES/COMJE	NORTHWOOD
Kenchington, Robin A	Lt RN	01-Nov-09	WAR	O LYNX	NCHQ	
Kendall-Torry, Guyan C	Lt RN	01-Sep-06	ENG	WESM(SWS)	FOST FAS SHORE	HELENSBURGH
Kendrick, Alexander	Lt Cdr	01-Feb-05	ENG	WE	DES/COMFLEET	BRISTOL
Kendry, Adam	SLt	11-May-13	WAR	INFO OPS (RES)	HMS FLYING FOX	BRISTOL
Kenneally, Sean J	Maj	01-Oct-06	RM	GS	NCHQ	
Kennedy, Catheryn H	Lt Cdr	01-Oct-12	QARNNS	ITU	DMS WHITTINGTON	LICHFIELD
Kennedy, Elizabeth H	Lt RN	01-Aug-08	WAR	GSX	FOST DPORT SHORE	HMNB DEVONPORT
Kennedy, Ian C	Lt Cdr	01-Oct-10	QARNNS	MH	HQ DPHC	LICHFIELD
Kennedy, Ian J	Cdr	30-Jun-03	ENG	ME	DES/COMFLEET	ABBEY WOOD
Kennedy, Inga J	Capt RN	21-Nov-11	QARNNS	Tutor (C&S)	NCHQ MEDDIV	NCHQ
Kennedy, Roger J	Lt Cdr	01-Oct-07	WAR	O SKW	HMS ILLUSTRIOUS	
Kennington, Lee A	Lt Cdr	01-Oct-07	WAR	O LYNX	RNAS YEOVILTON - LSF	RNAS YEOVILTON
Kennon, Stanley	RN Chpln	17-Sep-00	Ch S		BRNC DARTMOUTH	
Kent, Andrew G	Lt RN	20-Oct-08	WAR	MCD	MWS DDS	PORTSMOUTH

Person Name	Substantive Rank	Seniority	Branch	Specialisation	Organisation	Location
Kent, Matthew J	Lt Cdr	01-Oct-08	ENG	ME	UK MCC	BAHRAIN
Kent, Robert	Lt RN	12-Feb-08	ENG	WE	LOAN DSTL - ASD	FAREHAM
Kent, Thomas W	SLt	14-Aug-11	WAR	SM(X)	HMS ECHO	
Kenward, Jonathan C	SLt	15-Aug-11	LOGS	L	HMS IRON DUKE	
Kenyon, Adam M	Lt RN	01-Nov-10	WAR	SM(X)	HMS VANGUARD	
Kenyon, Carolyn M	Lt Cdr	01-Oct-07	LOGS	L BAR	DCDS PERS - SPA	RAF NORTHOLT
Ker, Catherine M	Lt RN	01-Jan-08	WAR	MCD	FOST MPV MWOTC	HMS COLLINGWOOD
Ker, Stuart W	Lt RN	01-Sep-08	ENG	WE	FLEET CAP RCAP DIVISION	NCHQ
Kerley, Benjamin J	Lt RN	01-May-03	WAR	P MER	BRNC DARTMOUTH	
Kern, Alastair S	Maj	01-Sep-00	RM	GS	NCHQ	
Kerr, Adrian N	Lt Cdr	01-Jan-01	ENG	WESM(TWS)	DES/COMLAND	ABBEY WOOD
Kerr, Jack	Lt Cdr	06-Feb-00	WAR	GSX	MWS COLLINGWOOD	
Kerr, Martin A	Lt RN	22-Mar-09	WAR	P SK4	202 SQN - AFLT	RAF BOULMER
Kerr, William M	Lt Cdr	09-Apr-90	WAR	MCD PWO(U)	FLEET CAP SSM DIVISION	NCHQ
Kerrigan, Glen	Lt RN	01-Jan-12	ENG	WE	HMS WESTMINSTER	
Kershaw, Neville L	Lt RN	08-Oct-12	WAR	SM(X)	HMS AMBUSH	
Kershaw, Richard J	Surg Lt Cdr	07-Aug-07	MED	GMP	HMS BULWARK	
Kershaw-Yates, Elizabeth H	Surg Cdr	03-Sep-13	MED	GMP	DPHC SW	HMS RALEIGH
Kershaw-Yates, Simon H	Surg Lt Cdr (D)	18-Jul-06	DENTAL	GDP	HMS ILLUSTRIOUS	
Kerslake, Richard	Cdr	30-Jun-09	WAR	P LYNX	HMS NELSON	
Kestle, Mark E	Lt Cdr	01-Oct-09	ENG	ME	DES/COMFLEET	ABBEY WOOD
Kestle, Ryan	Maj	01-Oct-12	RM	MLDR	CTCRM - CTW	EXMOUTH
Kew, Nigel	Lt RN	27-Jul-07	ENG	WESM(TWS)	RNSMS	HMS RALEIGH
Key, Benjamin J	R Adm	29-Apr-13	WAR	O LYNX	FOST DPORT SEA	HMNB DEVONPORT
Key, Matthew P	Lt RN	01-Jan-12	WAR	GSX	HMS DRAKE	
Keyworth, Mark A	Lt RN	01-Aug-08	WAR	C	FOST DPORT SEA	HMNB DEVONPORT
Khan, Mansoor Ali	Surg Lt Cdr	01-Aug-06	MED	GS	UK MED GP (AFG)	AFGHANISTAN BASTION
Kidd, Andrew N	Lt RN	01-Aug-07	WAR	SM(N)	HMS TORBAY	
Kidson, Adam W	2Lt	01-Sep-11	RM	GS	40 CDO RM	TAUNTON
Kiernan, Colin	Lt Cdr	01-Oct-13	WAR	P LYNX	HQ JHC DDEV	ANDOVER
Kierstan, Simon	Lt RN	01-Jan-01	ENG	TM	JFC - DCTS (H)	RAF HALTON
Kies, Lawrence N	Lt Cdr	01-Oct-03	ENG	TM	FLEET FOST ACOS	NCHQ
Kiff, Ian W	Lt Cdr	01-Oct-10	ENG	WE	SCU SHORE	HMS COLLINGWOOD
Kilbane, Liam	Surg Lt Cdr	07-Aug-13	MED	MED	BRNC DARTMOUTH	
Kilbride, Paul	Lt RN	01-Feb-09	WAR	GSX	MCM1 CREW 7	FASLANE
Kilmartin, Steven N	Lt Col	30-Jun-13	RM		CTCRM	EXMOUTH
Kimberley, Robert	Lt Cdr	01-Jul-98	WAR	PWO(U)	RN EXCHANGE USA	WASHINGTON USA
Kime, David	Lt RN	01-May-13	LOGS	L	FLEET CSAV	NCHQ
King, Alexander P	SLt	01-Sep-12	WAR	O UT	702 SQN	RNAS YEOVILTON
King, Charles E W	Capt RN	30-Jun-04	LOGS	L	NCHQ CNPERS	PORTSMOUTH
King, David A	Lt Cdr	01-Oct-12	WAR	PWO	HMS NORTHUMBERLAND	
King, Gordon C	Lt Cdr	01-Oct-03	ENG	MESM	DES/COMFLEET	HELENSBURGH
King, Iain A	Lt RN	01-Sep-02	WAR	P SKW	771 SQN	RNAS CULDROSE
King, Ian	Lt Cdr	01-Oct-08	WAR	OP INT (RES)	HQ UKTF	AFGHANISTAN
King, Ian J	Lt RN	01-Sep-05	ENG	AE	NC PSYA	PORTSMOUTH
King, James M	Lt RN	07-Jan-12	ENG	MESM	DCEME SULTAN	HMS SULTAN
King, Jason M	Lt Cdr	01-Oct-10	ENG	MESM	HMS ARTFUL	BARROW IN FURNESS
King, Katherine L	Surg Lt Cdr	10-Sep-08	MED	GMP	DES/COMFLEET	HMS NELSON
King, Matthew	Lt RN	01-Jun-09	WAR	P GR7	FLEET CSAV	WASHINGTON
King, Michael A	Lt RN	01-Sep-06	ENG	WE	JCU (CH)	CHELTENHAM
King, Nicholas W	Cdr	30-Jun-06	ENG	MESM	HMS NEPTUNE	HELENSBURGH
King, Paul William	Capt	01-Sep-13	RM	GS	45 CDO RM - Y COY	DUNDEE
King, Richard E	Capt	19-Jul-05	RM	SCC	RNLA	DARTMOUTH
King, William R C	Lt Cdr	01-Oct-08	WAR	PWO	MWS COLLINGWOOD	
King, William T	Lt Cdr	01-Oct-10	ENG	MESM	DES/COMFLEET	ABBEY WOOD
Kingdom, Mark A	Lt Cdr	01-Oct-05	ENG	AE	DEFAC JSCSC ACSC	SHRIVENHAM
Kingdon, Samuel R	SLt	01-Sep-11	ENG	AE	DCEME SULTAN	HMS SULTAN
Kingdon, Simon C	Lt RN	01-Jan-02	LOGS	L	OCLC PLYMOUTH	BRISTOL
Kingsley-Smith, Benjamin	SLt	01-Sep-12	MED	MEDICAL	BRNC DARTMOUTH	
Kingston, Carl A	Lt Cdr	01-Oct-13	WAR	P MER	FOST DPORT SEA	HMNB DEVONPORT
Kingwell, John M	R Adm	14-Oct-13	WAR	PWO(U)	STRAT ACDS DC&D	SHRIVENHAM
Kinnear-Mellor, Rex G	Surg Lt Cdr	01-Dec-09	MED	Anaes	INM ALVERSTOKE	GOSPORT

Person Name	Substantive Rank	Seniority	Branch	Specialisation	Organisation	Location
Kinsella, Edward T P	Lt RN	17-Mar-13	ENG	ME	HMS LANCASTER	
Kirby, Benjamin P	Lt RN	01-Apr-08	WAR	GSX	HMS KENT	
Kirk, Adrian C	Lt Cdr	01-May-05	ENG	AE	DES/COMFLEET	ABBEY WOOD
Kirk, David N	Capt	01-Sep-13	RM	GS	42 CDO RM - DGHR(O)	BRNC DARTMOUTH
Kirkup, John P	Cdr	30-Jun-03	ENG	TM	LSP ON	MUSCAT (BOX 014)
Kirkwood, James A D	Lt Cdr	25-Oct-91	WAR	PWO(A)	NATO-NCSA-NCSA	ITALY
Kirkwood, Tristram A	Cdr	30-Jun-13	WAR	PWO(U)	HMS NORTHUMBERLAND	
Kirrage, Charles H	Mid	01-Sep-13	WAR	SM(X)	BRNC DARTMOUTH	
Kissane, Robert E	Capt RN	07-May-13	ENG	WE	JFC HOC C4ISR	NORTHWOOD
Kitchen, Bethan	Lt Cdr	01-Oct-10	ENG	AE	RNAS CULROSE	
Kitching, Paul	Lt RN	01-Sep-12	WAR	GSX	HMS DARING	
Kitson, Matthew	Lt RN	01-Sep-13	WAR	O UT	RNAS CULDROSE	
Kitt, Robert G	Lt Cdr	01-Oct-05	ENG	WE	DES/COMFLEET	ABBEY WOOD
Klein, Michael E	Lt RN	11-Oct-13	WAR	AV	RNAS CULDROSE	
Klidjian, Michael J	Lt Cdr	01-Oct-08	WAR	AAWO	HMS DAUNTLESS	
Kneller, James	Lt RN	01-Sep-10	ENG	AE	DEFAC CMT	SHRIVENHAM
Knibbs, Mark	Capt RN	30-Jun-07	WAR	PWO(U)	DCDS PERS TRG-RFC	MAIN BUILDING LONDON
Knight, Alastair C	Lt RN	01-Mar-94	WAR	P SK6	RNAS CULDROSE	
Knight, Alexander J	Lt RN	01-Feb-09	WAR	GSX	BRNC DARTMOUTH	
Knight, Andrew R	Lt Cdr	01-Oct-01	WAR	P MER	857 NAS	RNAS CULDROSE
Knight, Anthony R	Lt RN	01-Oct-09	WAR	ATC	RAF SHAWBURY	
Knight, Charles E	SLt	01-Jan-13	WAR	O UT	RNAS CULDROSE	
Knight, Damon A	Cdr	30-Jun-01	WAR	AAWO	FLEET FOST ACOS(Trg)	NCHQ
Knight, Daniel S	Lt Cdr	01-Oct-05	WAR	SM(CQ)	FLEET COMOPS NWD	NORTHWOOD
Knight, David W	Lt Cdr	01-Dec-00	WAR	AAWO	MWS COLLINGWOOD	
Knight, James MC	Maj	01-Oct-12	RM	GS	BDS WASHINGTON	WASHINGTON USA
Knight, Jonathan M	Lt RN	01-Jan-06	WAR	ATC	RNAS CULDROSE	RNAS CULDROSE
Knight, Paul R	Cdr	30-Jun-03	ENG	MESM	NATO-ACO-JFC HQ	NAPLES ITALY
Knight, Richard J	Lt RN	01-Sep-08	WAR	P MER	820 SQN	RNAS CULDROSE
Knight, Richard J	Lt RN	01-Oct-09	WAR	P SK4	845 SQN	RNAS YEOVILTON
Knock, Gareth P	Cdr	30-Jun-13	LOGS	L SM	FLEET FOSNNI	HELENSBURGH
Knott, Clive	Lt Cdr	29-May-07	WAR	P LYNX	WMF SHORE	RNAS YEOVILTON
Knott, Michael B	Cdr	30-Jun-10	WAR	PWO(N)	FLEET ACOS(RP)	NCHQ
Knott, Thomas M	Lt Cdr	01-Oct-13	WAR	GSX	DEFAC JSCSC	SHRIVENHAM
Knowles, Christopher J	Lt Cdr	01-Oct-11	WAR	P MER	FLEET CSAV	NCHQ
Knowles, David	Lt RN	01-Sep-04	WAR	PWO(N)	MWS COLLINGWOOD	
Knox, Graeme P	Lt Cdr	01-Oct-06	LOGS	L BAR	NCHQ - CNLS	NCHQ
Koheeallee, Mohummed	Lt RN	01-Mar-06	ENG	AE	1710 NAS	PORTSMOUTH
Kohler, Andrew P	Lt Cdr	01-Apr-02	WAR	PWO(A)	DI - CA	LONDON
Kohn, Patricia A	Lt Cdr	01-Jul-08	WAR	PWO	HMS MONMOUTH	
Kromolicki, Matthew J	Mid	01-Nov-13	WAR	SM(X)	BRNC DARTMOUTH	
Krosnar-Clarke, Steven M	Cdr	30-Jun-09	ENG	TM	NCHQ CNPERS	PORTSMOUTH
Kubara, Alex M	Mid	01-Sep-13	WAR	GSX	BRNC DARTMOUTH	
Kumwenda, Temwa	Lt RN	01-Sep-13	WAR	GSX	MWS COLLINGWOOD	HMS COLLINGWOOD
Kutarski, Emily A	Mid	01-Sep-13	ENG	ME	BRNC DARTMOUTH	
Kyd, Jeremy Paul	Capt RN	02-Nov-09	WAR	PWO(N)	BRNC DARTMOUTH	
Kyle, Ryan	Maj	01-Oct-13	RM	GS	NC PSYA	NORTHWOOD
Kyme, Robert	Lt RN	01-Jul-10	WAR	INT	FLEET COMOPS NWD	NORTHWOOD
Kyte, Andrew J	Capt RN	23-Feb-09	LOGS	L	MOD CNS/ACNS	MAIN BUILDING LONDON

L

Person Name	Substantive Rank	Seniority	Branch	Specialisation	Organisation	Location
Lacey, Catherine	Lt Cdr	01-Oct-00	ENG	WE	DEFENCE ACADEMY	SHRIVENHAM
Lacey, Thomas S	Lt RN	01-Sep-12	ENG	WESM(SWS)	HMS VIGILANT	
Lacy, Andrew P	Capt	31-Dec-08	RM	LC	1 ASSLT GROUP RM	
Ladds, Grace	SLt	01-Feb-12	MED	MEDICAL	BRNC DARTMOUTH	
Ladislaus, Cecil J	Lt RN	01-Jan-02	WAR	HM	HMS DRAKE	HMNB DEVONPORT
Ladlow, Michael I	Lt RN	14-Sep-13	ENG	WESM(SWS)	HMS VANGUARD	
Laidlaw, Jonathan M	Lt RN	01-Jan-05	WAR	P SKW	GANNET SAR FLT	HMS GANNET
Laidler, Paul J	Lt Cdr	01-Oct-10	ENG	WE	FLEET CAP IS DIVISION	NCHQ
Lai-Hung, Jeremy J	Lt Cdr	01-Oct-10	LOGS	L SM	DCDS PERS TRG	MAIN BUILDING LONDON
Laing, Iain	Lt Cdr	01-Sep-01	ENG	WE	FLEET CAP IS DIVISION	PORTSMOUTH
Laird, Douglas A	Lt RN	01-Jul-09	WAR	SM(X)	HMS RALEIGH	

Person Name	Substantive Rank	Seniority	Branch	Specialisation	Organisation	Location
Laird, Ellen L	Lt RN	01-Feb-10	LOGS	L	DMLS	HMS RALEIGH
Laird, Iain A	Lt RN	01-Sep-07	WAR	GSX	HMS TYNE	
Laird, Joanne E	Surg Lt RN	03-Aug-11	MED	GDMO	HMS SOMERSET	
Lake, James R	2Lt	02-Sep-12	RM	N/A	CTCRM OFFICERS	EXMOUTH
Lake, Richard J	Capt	18-Jul-08	RM	SCC	RMR BRISTOL	BRISTOL
Lamb, Andrew G OBE	Cdr	30-Jun-10	WAR	PWO(A)	MCM2 POR SEA	HMNB PORTSMOUTH
Lamb, Bryce M	Lt RN	07-Aug-13	ENG	WESM	CAREER TRAINING	HMS RALEIGH
Lamb, Robert J F	Lt Cdr	01-Oct-13	WAR	GSX	MWS COLLINGWOOD	HMS COLLINGWOOD
Lambert, Anthony W OBE	Surg Cdr	30-Jun-99	MED	GS	MDHU DERRIFORD	PLYMOUTH
Lambert, Daniel	Lt RN	11-Oct-13	LOGS	L SM	RALEIGH	HMS RALEIGH
Lambourne, David John	Lt Cdr	01-Oct-97	WAR	P SK6	771 SQN	RNAS CULDROSE
L'Amie, Christopher A	Lt Cdr	01-Oct-12	WAR	PWO(U)	HMS IRON DUKE	
Lamont, Neil J	Lt Cdr	01-Oct-05	WAR	SM(CQ)	UKRBATSTAFF	PLYMOUTH
Lanaghan, Richard	Lt RN	01-Sep-11	WAR	SM(X)	OCLC NCH	MANCHESTER
Lancashire, Antony	Maj	01-Oct-05	RM	LC	DES/COMFLEET	ABBEY WOOD BRISTOL
Lancaster, James H D	Lt Cdr	01-Oct-12	LOGS	L SM	HMS SOMERSET	
Landrock, Graham J	Cdr	30-Jun-10	WAR	MCD PWO(A)	HQ ISAF	AFGHANISTAN KABUL
Lane, Adam J	Lt RN	19-Aug-09	WAR	P MER	814 SQN	RNAS CULDROSE
Lane, Ashley D	Capt	01-Sep-11	RM	GS	NCHQ	
Lane, Harry	Capt	01-Sep-11	RM	GS	CTCRM - CTW	EXMOUTH
Lane, Heather J	Lt Cdr	01-Oct-08	WAR	MEDIA OPS (RES)		FLEET CMR HMS NELSON
Lane, Joseph O	Capt	01-Sep-09	RM	GS	HMS DRAKE	
Lane, Paul V	Lt RN	09-Jul-10	WAR	GSX	CAREER TRAINING	HMS DRAKE
Lane, Peter	Lt RN	01-Sep-11	ENG	MESM	HMS VICTORIOUS	
Lane, Roland J	Lt RN	20-Oct-07	ENG	AE	CHFHQ (SHORE)	RNAS YEOVILTON
Lang, Alasdair J	Lt RN	01-Jan-05	WAR	O LYNX	LHF 815 SQN FLT 208	RNAS YEOVILTON
Lang, Christopher	Lt RN	01-May-13	LOGS	L	CAREER TRAINING	HMS RALEIGH
Lang, Lesley A	Lt RN	01-Jan-05	WAR	ATC	RNAS YEOVILTON	RNAS YEOVILTON
Langford, Joanna P	Lt RN	01-Feb-06	WAR	GSX	HMS NELSON	
Langford, Timothy D	Lt RN	01-May-07	WAR	PWO	HMS ST ALBANS	
Langley, David J	Lt RN	01-Jan-09	WAR	FC	RAF BOULMER	
Langrill, Mark P	Cdr	30-Jun-09	ENG	AE	RNAS YEOVILTON - AED	RNAS YEOVILTON
Lanni, Martin N AFC	Lt Cdr	01-Oct-05	WAR	P SK6	GANNET SAR FLT	HMS GANNET
Lanning, Roderick M	Lt Cdr	01-Oct-09	WAR	AAWO	HMS DEFENDER	
Lappin, Adam J	Lt RN	09-Apr-09	LOGS	L	HMS DARING	
Large, Stephen A	Cdr	30-Jun-11	ENG	ME	HMS BULWARK	
Lasker, Jonathan A	Capt	01-Sep-08	RM	GS	OCLC NCH	MANCHESTER
Latchem, Andrew J	Lt RN	01-Jan-07	WAR	P LYNX	LHF 815 SQN FLT 215	RNAS YEOVILTON
Latham, Daniel G	Lt RN	01-Sep-07	WAR	P GR7	FLEET CSAV	WASHINGTON
Latham, Mark A	Capt	01-Apr-04	RM	SCC	RMB CHIVENOR - BASE	RMB CHIVENOR
Latus, Simon H	Lt Cdr	01-Oct-10	WAR	PWO	MWS COLLINGWOOD	
Latus, William A	Capt	01-Sep-09	RM	GS	1 ASSLT GROUP RM	PLYMOUTH
Lauchlan, Robert A	Cdr	30-Jun-08	ENG	WESM(SWS)	NUCLEAR CAPABILITY	MAIN BUILDING LONDON
Laud, Nicola Jane	Lt RN	01-Apr-11	ENG	ME	RN EXCHANGE NETHERLANDS	DEN HELDER
Laughton, Peter MBE	Cdr	30-Jun-12	WAR	MCD PWO(A)	HMS LANCASTER	
Laurence, Simon T	Lt Cdr	01-Oct-10	WAR	O MER	814 SQN	RNAS CULDROSE
Laverick, Jonathan R	Lt RN	01-Feb-11	WAR	GSX	MSSG ENDURING OP	BLACKWATER
Laverty, Robert E	Lt Cdr	01-Feb-03	WAR	PWO(U)	HMS TYNE	
Law, Benjamin W	Capt	01-Sep-12	RM	GS	4 SCOTS C COY	GERMANY
Law, Michael J	SLt	01-Sep-11	WAR	O UT	702 SQN YEOVILTON	RNAS YEOVILTON
Law, Samuel J	Lt Cdr	01-Oct-09	LOGS	L	CAREER TRAINING	FRANCE
Lawley, Richard J	Capt	03-Apr-09	RM	C (SCC)	BF BIOT	DIEGO GARCIA
Lawrence, Kevin	Lt RN	01-Sep-10	ENG	AE	DES/COMJE/HELS	YEOVIL
Lawrence, Linda J	Lt RN	16-Sep-99	WAR	HM(AM)	RNSMS	HMS RALEIGH
Lawrence, Stuart P	Cdr	30-Jun-11	LOGS	L	COMFASFLOT WLSG	HELENSBURGH
Lawrence-Archer, Sally E	Lt RN	07-Sep-07	WAR	O LYNX	815 SQN HQ	RNAS YEOVILTON
Lawrenson, Timothy A	Lt Cdr	01-Oct-13	ENG	WE	DCCIS CISTU	HMS COLLINGWOOD
Lawson, James M	Capt	01-Sep-08	RM	GS	LAND WARFARE SCHOOL	WARMINSTER
Lawton, Peter MBE	Capt	01-Jan-99	RM	GS	NCHQ	
Lay, Benjamin	SLt	01-Aug-11	LOGS	L	HMS RALEIGH	
Lay, Jack	SLt	01-Apr-11	WAR	SM(X)	HMS TALENT	
Laycock, Antony	Lt Cdr	01-Oct-06	WAR	O LYNX	NCHQ CNPERS	PORTSMOUTH

Person Name	Substantive Rank	Seniority	Branch	Specialisation	Organisation	Location
Layland, Stephen	Cdr	30-Jun-02	WAR	PWO(N)	HMS RALEIGH	
Layton, Christopher	Lt Cdr	01-Oct-10	ENG	MESM	HMS TRIUMPH	
Le Gassick, Peter J	Lt Cdr	01-Oct-04	ENG	TM	FLEET FOST ACOS(Trg)	NCHQ
Le Huray, Jason W	Mid	01-May-13	WAR	O UT	BRNC DARTMOUTH	
Le Poidevin, Ian W	Lt RN	01-Mar-09	ENG	WE	UKRBATSTAFF	HMNB PORTSMOUTH
Lea, Chloe	Lt RN	01-Sep-11	WAR	GSX	HMS MONTROSE	
Lea, John	Cdr	30-Jun-08	WAR	O SKW	RNAS CULDROSE - EXEC	RNAS CULDROSE
Lea, Oliver D	Lt RN	01-Apr-11	WAR	SM(N)	DEF LANG SCHOOL	BEACONSFIELD
Lea, Thomas G	Capt	01-Mar-13	RM	GS	42 CDO RM - DGHR(O)	PLYMOUTH
Leach, Helen	Lt RN	01-Apr-11	ENG	AE	RNAS CULDROSE	
Leach, Sarah J	Cdr	30-Jun-11	ENG	ME	COMDEVFLOT	HMS DRAKE
Leadbeater, Mark K	Lt RN	01-Sep-08	ENG	MESM	HMS AMBUSH	
Leahy, Sam	SLt	01-Sep-12	ENG	AE	BRNC DARTMOUTH	
Leaker, Daniel T	Lt RN	01-May-04	WAR	P SK4	CAREER TRAINING WATTISHAM	IPSWICH
Lear, Stuart F	Lt Cdr	01-Oct-07	LOGS	L	DES/ACDS	MAIN BUILDING LONDON
Leason, Joanna	Surg Cdr	05-Oct-10	MED	Radiologist	RCDM	BIRMINGHAM
Leather, Roger J	Lt Cdr	01-Jun-87	WAR	AW (RES)	MWS COLLINGWOOD	
Leckey, Elizabeth H	Lt RN	01-May-05	ENG	AE	HMS ILLUSTRIOUS	
Leckey, Timothy	Lt RN	01-Sep-09	ENG	TM	NETS (OPS)	HMNB PORTSMOUTH
Lee, Daniel C	Lt RN	01-Jun-10	WAR	GSX	HMS DUNCAN	
Lee, David A	Lt Cdr	01-Oct-13	ENG	IS	HMS NELSON	HMS NELSON
Lee, David M	SLt	01-Sep-12	WAR	GSX	MCM1 CREW 1	FASLANE
Lee, Jonathan J E	Lt RN	01-Sep-12	ENG	ME	FOST MPV SEA	HELENSBURGH
Lee, Martin John	SLt	07-Aug-13	WAR	GSX	MCM2 CREW 8	PORTSMOUTH
Lee, Nicholas F	Lt Cdr	01-Mar-99	WAR	P SK6	RNAS CULDROSE - ADM	RNAS CULDROSE
Lee, Oliver OBE	Col	12-Jan-12	RM		DEFENCE ACADEMY	SWINDON
Lee, Peter A	Lt Cdr	01-Aug-99	ENG	ME	NCHQ CNPERS	PORTSMOUTH
Lee, Raymond A	Lt RN	01-Jan-04	ENG	WESM(TWS)	COMDEVFLOT	HMS DRAKE
Lee, Ross J	Lt RN	01-Apr-09	ENG	ME	RNLA	
Lee, Simon	SLt	01-Sep-12	ENG	WE	BRNC DARTMOUTH	
Lee, Steven E	Lt Cdr	01-Oct-07	ENG	WE	FOST DPORT SEA	HMNB DEVONPORT
Lee, Steven P	Lt Col	30-Jun-09	RM		HMS NELSON	HMS NELSON
Lee, Stuart D	Lt RN	01-Apr-12	WAR	GSX	MCM1 CREW 2	FASLANE
Leeder, Timothy R	Lt Cdr	01-Oct-09	WAR	PWO	FOST DPORT SEA	HMNB DEVONPORT
Leeper, James S	Lt Cdr	01-Oct-12	WAR	PWO	HMS COLLINGWOOD	
Lees, Adrian C	Lt RN	01-Jan-07	ENG	MESM	BRNC DARTMOUTH	
Lees, Christopher M	Lt RN	11-Apr-08	ENG	WE	CTCRM	EXMOUTH
Lees, Claire M	Lt RN	01-May-07	LOGS	L	HMS DRAKE	
Lees, Colin A	Capt	01-Apr-11	RM	MLDR (SCC)	CTCRM - CTW	EXMOUTH
Lees, Edward C	Lt Cdr	01-Feb-99	WAR	PWO(C)	DCOG NORTHWOOD	
Lees, Rachel H	Lt RN	31-Jul-09	LOGS	L	FLEET ACOS(RP)	NCHQ
Leeson, Antony R	Lt Cdr	01-Oct-09	WAR	AAWO	HMS DUNCAN	
Legge, William J	Lt RN	26-Aug-12	WAR	P MER	814 SQN	RNAS CULDROSE
Leidig, George	SLt	01-Sep-13	MED	MEDICAL	BRNC DARTMOUTH	
Leigh-Smith, Simon J	Surg Cdr	30-Jun-04	MED	EM	MDHU NORTHALLERTON	NORTHALLERTON
Leightley, Simon M	Lt Cdr	01-Oct-11	WAR	MCD	MWS COLLINGWOOD	
Leighton, Matthew R	Lt Cdr	01-Oct-07	WAR	P SK4	848 SQN YEOVILTON	RNAS YEOVILTON
Leisk, Oliver L	Mid	01-Feb-13	WAR	P UT	BRNC DARTMOUTH	
Le-Maistre, Matthew R	Lt RN	03-May-13	ENG	AE	RNAS YEOVILTON	RNAS YEOVILTON
Lemkes, Paul D	Capt RN	30-Jun-05	WAR	PWO(A)	ATTACHE/ADVISER - DRID	DRID SPAIN
Lemon, Christopher J	Lt RN	12-Jul-13	WAR	AV	RNAS YEOVILTON - FS	RNAS YEOVILTON
Lennon, Thomas	Lt RN	01-Sep-13	WAR	P UT	RNAS YEOVILTON	RNAS YEOVILTON
Leonard, John F	Surg Cdr	01-Jul-08	MED	Occ Med	DES/COMFLEET	HELENSBURGH
Leonard, Matthew D	Lt RN	01-Nov-13	WAR	P UT	702 SQN	RNAS YEOVILTON
Leonard, Thomas	Lt RN	01-Jul-07	WAR	GSX	DEFAC JSCSC	SHRIVENHAM
Leong, Melvin J	Surg Lt Cdr	06-Feb-13	MED	Anaes	INM ALVERSTOKE	GOSPORT
Leppan, Warren K	Lt RN	01-Nov-12	WAR	O UT	RNAS CULDROSE	RNAS CULDROSE
Leslie, Bruce D	Lt Cdr	01-Oct-13	WAR	O SKW	849 SQN	RNAS CULDROSE
Leslie, Daren J	Lt RN	06-Apr-07	ENG	ME	COMPORFLOT	PORTSMOUTH
Lester, Rodney L MBE	Lt Cdr	01-Oct-08	WAR	INT	HQ DISC	SHEFFORD
Lett, Jonathan D	Cdr	30-Jun-10	WAR	PWO(U)	FLEET CAP RCAP DIVISION	NCHQ
Lett, Timothy J	Lt RN	19-Oct-07	WAR	INT	FLEET COMOPS NWD	NORTHWOOD

Person Name	Substantive Rank	Seniority	Branch	Specialisation	Organisation	Location
Lettington, Paul D W	Lt RN	01-Jan-06	ENG	WE	COMDEVFLOT SHORE	HMS DRAKE
Lever, Thomas J	Lt RN	01-Sep-08	ENG	AE	DES/COMJE/HELS	YEOVIL
Leveridge, Adam M	SLt	01-Mar-11	ENG	WE	MWS COLLINGWOOD	
Lewis, Andrew	Lt Cdr	01-Mar-04	ENG	MESM	DES/COMFLEET	HELENSBURGH
Lewis, Angela B	Lt RN	01-Sep-01	WAR	O SK6	GANNET SAR FLT	PRESTWICK
Lewis, Barry M	Maj	01-Oct-10	RM	GS	42 CDO RM - K COY	HMNB DEVONPORT
Lewis, Benjamin	Lt Cdr	01-Oct-07	WAR	P SK4	DEFAC JSCSC ACSC	SHRIVENHAM
Lewis, Daniel	Lt RN	01-Dec-01	ENG	AE P	848 SQN YEOVILTON	RNAS YEOVILTON
Lewis, David P	2Lt	01-Sep-12	RM	GS	42 CDO RM - K COY	PLYMOUTH
Lewis, George R	SLt	01-May-11	WAR	SM(X)	MCM2 CREW 2	PORTSMOUTH
Lewis, Gethin Huw	SLt	01-Nov-11	MED	MEDICAL	BRNC DARTMOUTH	
Lewis, James A E	Maj	01-Oct-11	RM	GS	42 CDO RM	PLYMOUTH
Lewis, Jonathan M	Lt Cdr	01-Oct-13	WAR	SM(AWC)	HMS VIGILANT	
Lewis, Kay E	Lt Cdr	01-Oct-08	WAR	PWO(A)	HMS COLLINGWOOD	
Lewis, Kieran	Lt RN	03-Aug-11	ENG	WE	DEFAC CMT	SHRIVENHAM
Lewis, Richard QVRM	Lt Cdr	31-Mar-01	WAR	O SKW	849 SQN	RNAS CULDROSE
Lewis, Robert G	Lt RN	01-Sep-07	QARNNS	MH	HMS DRAKE	
Lewis, Scott	Lt RN	01-Dec-11	WAR	MEDIA OPS	NCHQ CNPERS	PORTSMOUTH
Lewis, Stephen R	Capt	16-Apr-10	RM	SCC	45 CDO RM	DUNDEE
Lewis, Stuart D	Lt RN	01-Jan-13	WAR	P	848 SQN	RNAS YEOVILTON
Lewis, Thomas R	SLt	01-Feb-11	WAR	GSX	CREW 7 OFFICERS	FASLANE
Ley, Alastair B	Lt Cdr	01-Nov-03	WAR	SM(AWC)	FLEET COMOPS NWD	NORTHWOOD
Leyshon, Robert J	Surg Cdr (D)	09-Jan-09	DENTAL	GDP	DMS WHITTINGTON DDS	LICHFIELD
Leyson, Rhodri	Mid	01-Nov-13	WAR	P UT	BRNC DARTMOUTH	
Lias, Carl David	Cdr	30-Jun-06	ENG	MESM	DES/COMFLEET	ABBEY WOOD
Lifoda, Charlotte	Surg Lt RN (D)	09-Jul-10	DENTAL	GDP	DDS SCOTLAND	HELENSBURGH
Ligale, Eugene	Lt RN	01-Jan-03	WAR	GSX	MWS COLLINGWOOD	
Lightfoot, Iain M	Lt RN	27-Jul-07	ENG	TM	HMS SULTAN	
Lightfoot, Richard A	Lt RN	16-Feb-01	WAR	O SK6	GANNET SAR FLT	PRESTWICK
Lilley, Benjamin D	SLt	01-Feb-11	WAR	P UT	MWS COLLINGWOOD	HMS COLLINGWOOD
Lillington, Claire	SLt	01-Sep-13	MED	MEDICAL	BRNC DARTMOUTH	
Lilly, David	Lt RN	01-Dec-98	WAR	P LYNX	LOANS TO OTHER GOVTS	OMAN
Lim, Fong Chien	Surg Lt Cdr	01-Sep-10	MED	GMP	DPHC SW	EXMOUTH
Limb, Thomas J	Capt	01-Sep-12	RM	GS	FLEET COMOPS NWD	NORTHWOOD
Linderman, Ian R	Cdr	30-Jun-10	ENG	TM	DCDS PERS TRG-TESRR	MAIN BUILDING LONDON
Lindeyer, Matthew J	Lt RN	01-May-02	WAR	HM(AS)	UK MCC	BAHRAIN
Lindley, Nicholas	Col	15-Dec-08	RM		DEFENCE ACADEMY	SHRIVENHAM
Lindsay, David J	Cdr	30-Jun-09	WAR	P GR7	FLEET CSAV	NCHQ
Lindsay, Irvine G	Cdr	30-Jun-06	WAR	SM(CQ)	FOST SM SEA	HELENSBURGH
Lindsay, James A	Capt	01-Sep-12	RM	GS	CTCRM - CORPS COL	EXMOUTH
Lindsay, Jonathan M	Maj	01-Oct-09	RM	MLDR	HQ ISAF	AFGHANISTAN KABUL
Lindsay, Michael H	Surg Lt Cdr	06-Aug-08	MED	Occ Med	INM ALVERSTOKE	GOSPORT
Lindsey, Thomas S	SLt	01-Sep-11	WAR	GSX	HMS DUNCAN	
Linehan, Paul R	Lt RN	19-Dec-08	LOGS	L	HMS TRIUMPH	
Lines, James M	Capt RN	04-May-09	LOGS		DES/COMLAND	ABBEY WOOD
Ling, Christopher	Cdr	30-Jun-12	ENG	AE	DEFENCE ACADEMY	SOUTHAMPTON
Ling, John W	Lt Cdr	01-Oct-05	WAR	O SKW	854 NAS	RNAS CULDROSE
Ling, Peter A	Lt RN	20-Oct-09	ENG	WE	OCLC ROSYTH	HMS CALEDONIA
Linn, Byron John	Lt RN	01-Jan-13	WAR	GSX	MCM2 CREW 7	PORTSMOUTH
Lipczynski, Benjamin J	Lt RN	01-Nov-05	ENG	WE	MWS COLLINGWOOD	
Lippitt, Benjamin J	Lt RN	01-May-09	WAR	ATC	FOST DPORT SHORE	HMNB DEVONPORT
Lippitt, Simon T	Lt Cdr	01-Apr-10	WAR	ATC	RNAS YEOVILTON - AS	SOUTHAMPTON
Lipscomb, Paul	Cdr	30-Jun-07	ENG	MESM	DES/COMFLEET	ABBEY WOOD
Lishman, Stuart H	Lt RN	09-Apr-09	ENG	WE	DES/COMFLEET	ABBEY WOOD
Lisle, Robert A	SLt	15-Aug-11	WAR	SM(X)	HMS SOMERSET	
Lison, Andrew C	Cdre	01-Jul-13	ENG	AE	DES/COMJE	RNAS YEOVILTON
Lister, Mark	Cdr	30-Jun-04	WAR	SM(CQ)	HMS NEPTUNE	HELENSBURGH
Lister, Matthew J	Lt RN	01-Sep-06	ENG	MESM	HMS ASTUTE	
Lister, Shaun	Lt RN	01-Jan-08	ENG	WE	HMS RALEIGH	
Lister, Simon	Lt Cdr	01-Oct-06	WAR	SM(AWC)	FOST DPORT SHORE	HMNB DEVONPORT
Lister, Simon R OBE	V Adm	27-Nov-13	ENG	MESM	DES/COMFLEET	ABBEY WOOD
Litchfield, Hannah	Mid	01-Sep-13	ENG	ME	BRNC DARTMOUTH	

Person Name	Substantive Rank	Seniority	Branch	Specialisation	Organisation	Location
Litster, Alan OBE	Col	09-May-11	RM	LC	BDS WASHINGTON - NA	WASHINGTON
Little, George J	Maj	01-Oct-12	RM	GS	NCHQ	
Little, Graeme T OBE	Cdre	17-Jul-12	ENG	ME	DES/COMFLEET	HMS DRAKE
Little, Jonathan I	Lt RN	01-Sep-07	ENG	WE	MCM2 POR SEA	HMNB PORTSMOUTH
Little, Matthew I G	Lt Cdr	01-Oct-13	WAR	INT	NORTHWOOD HQ	
Little, Nicola S	Lt RN	01-Jan-05	ENG	TM	MWS COLLINGWOOD	
Little, Philippa C	Mid	01-Nov-12	LOGS	L	HMS WESTMINSTER	
Liva, Anthony J	Maj	01-Oct-08	RM		45 CDO RM	DUNDEE
Livesey, John E	Cdr	30-Jun-11	WAR	SM(CQ)	FOST SM SEA	HELENSBURGH
Livingstone, Alan J MBE	Lt Col	30-Jun-04	RM		OPS DIR	MAIN BUILDING LONDON
Livingstone, Andrew	Lt RN	01-Sep-13	WAR	SM(X)	MWS COLLINGWOOD	
Livingstone, Colin S	Lt RN	06-Apr-07	ENG	ME	HMS ENTERPRISE	
Livingstone, Dana M	Lt RN	07-Aug-13	WAR	GSX	MWS COLLINGWOOD	
Livsey, Andrew E	Lt Cdr	01-Nov-06	WAR	PWO(U)	HMS RICHMOND	
Llewellyn, Jonathan G	Lt Cdr	01-Oct-12	WAR	AV	FLEET CSAV	NCHQ
Lloyd, Jane L	Surg Lt Cdr	02-Aug-10	MED	Occ Med	INM ALVERSTOKE	GOSPORT
Lloyd, Matthew R	Lt RN	01-Sep-02	LOGS	L SM	RNLA	HMS COLLINGWOOD
Loadman, Dougal R	Lt RN	01-Mar-04	ENG	TM	CTCRM	EXMOUTH
Lock, Andrew G	Lt Col	30-Jun-10	RM		CTCRM - CW	EXMOUTH
Lock, William	Lt RN	01-May-02	WAR	O MER	UK MCC	BAHRAIN
Locke, Nicholas M	Lt Cdr	01-Oct-13	ENG	MESM	HMS VIGILANT	
Lockett, Alexander T	Lt RN	13-Feb-08	WAR	P LYN7	771 SQN	RNAS CULDROSE
Lockett, David J	Lt Cdr	01-Apr-04	WAR	PWO(N)	BRNC DARTMOUTH	
Lockhart, John B	Lt Cdr	01-Oct-10	ENG	AE	HMS SULTAN - 764 ITS	HMS SULTAN
Lockley, Simon M	Lt RN	19-Oct-07	LOGS	L	RNAS CULDROSE	
Lofthouse, Thomas D	Lt RN	01-Jan-12	WAR	P UT	RAF SHAWBURY	
Lofts, Anthony J	Lt RN	01-Apr-09	ENG	WE	DES/COMJE	CORSHAM
Loftus, Andrew L	SLt	01-Oct-13	MED	MEDICAL	BRNC DARTMOUTH	
Loftus, Ashley M	Mid	01-May-13	WAR	ATC UT	BRNC DARTMOUTH	
Logan, Joseph M	Lt Cdr	01-Oct-03	WAR	FC	DES/COMFLEET	ABBEY WOOD
Login, Matthew B	2Lt	02-Sep-14	RM	N/A	CTCRM OFFICERS	EXMOUTH
Lomas, Timothy P	Lt RN	09-Oct-10	WAR	GSX	CAREER TRAINING	HMS DRAKE
London, Heidi C	Lt RN	01-Apr-06	WAR	PWO	MWS COLLINGWOOD	
London, Nicholas J	Lt Cdr	01-Oct-12	ENG	WE	MWS COLLINGWOOD	
Long, Adrian J	Lt RN	31-Jul-12	ENG	ME	HMS MONTROSE	
Long, Adrian M	Capt RN	21-Nov-11	ENG	WE	VCDS	MAIN BUILDING LONDON
Long, Michael	Lt Cdr	01-Apr-08	WAR	INT	RN EXCHANGE USA - BDS	WASHINGTON
Long, Richard	Maj	01-Oct-13	RM	BS	HQ BAND SERVICE	HMS NELSON
Long, Simon C	Capt	01-Sep-12	RM	GS	NCHQ	
Long, Stuart G	Lt Cdr	01-Oct-10	WAR	HM(AS)	HMS SCOTT	
Long, Victoria S	Lt Cdr	01-Oct-13	QARNNS	B&P	DMSTG	ALDERSHOT
Longia, Sandeep	Lt RN	01-Sep-10	ENG	AE	1710 NAS	PORTSMOUTH
Longley, Richard J	2Lt	02-Sep-13	RM	N/A	CTCRM OFFICERS	EXMOUTH
Longman, Matthew S	Lt Cdr	01-Oct-13	ENG	ME	DES/COMFLEET	ABBEY WOOD
Longmore, David	Surg Lt Cdr	04-Aug-09	MED	GMP	INM ALVERSTOKE	GOSPORT
Longstaff, Thomas O	Lt RN	20-Jul-11	WAR	O UT	849 SQN	RNAS CULDROSE
Longstaff, Thomas W	Lt Cdr	01-Oct-11	LOGS	L SM	RNAS YEOVILTON - C&SS	RNAS YEOVILTON
Lonsdale, Gavin	Lt RN	01-Sep-10	ENG	ME	HMS RALEIGH - INT R	HMS RALEIGH
Lorenz, Rudi	Lt RN	01-Jun-06	WAR	P LYNX	LHF 815 SQN FLT 210	RNAS YEOVILTON
Loring, Andrew	Cdr	30-Jun-09	ENG	ME	FLEET FOSNNI - NRC WWE	BRISTOL
Louden, Carl A	Lt Cdr	01-Oct-07	WAR	C	HMS KING ALFRED	PORTSMOUTH
Loughran, Oliver A G	Lt RN	01-Feb-08	WAR	GSX	HMS CLYDE	
Loughrey, Neil C	Lt Cdr	01-Oct-08	ENG	AE	DES/COMJE/HELS	RNAS YEOVILTON
Louis, David R A	Lt Cdr	01-Jul-12	WAR	MCD	MWS COLLINGWOOD	
Louw, Len	Lt RN	01-Jan-02	ENG	WESM(SWS)	DES/COMFLEET	ABBEY WOOD
Lovatt, Graham J	Cdr	30-Jun-11	WAR	AAWO	COMPORFLOT FPS SEA	HMNB PORTSMOUTH
Lovatt, Steven	Lt RN	01-Sep-12	ENG	WE	HMS DUNCAN	
Love, John J	Lt RN	04-Jun-03	ENG	TM	HQ EUFOR (SAR)	SARAJEVO
Love, Richard J	Lt Cdr	01-Oct-05	ENG	AE	ABBEY WOOD	
Love, Tristram S	Lt RN	30-Jun-12	ENG	WESM(TWS)	COMDEVFLOT SHORE	HMNB DEVONPORT
Lovegrove, Raymond A	Capt RN	03-Dec-13	ENG	WE	HMS NELSON	
Lovell, Alistair	Surg Lt Cdr (D)	25-Jun-08	DENTAL	GDP	HMS RALEIGH	

Person Name	Substantive Rank	Seniority	Branch	Specialisation	Organisation	Location
Lovell, James E	Lt Cdr	01-Oct-12	WAR	AWO(U)	FOST DPORT SEA	HMNB DEVONPORT
Lovell, James H	Lt RN	01-Sep-09	WAR	O MER	824 SQN - TU	RNAS CULDROSE
Lovell, Jonathan	Lt RN	03-May-13	ENG	ME	HMS DAUNTLESS	
Lovell-Smith, Alexandre R	Lt RN	01-Oct-12	WAR	P LYN7	847 SQN - AE	RNAS YEOVILTON
Lovering, Tristan T MBE	Lt Cdr	01-Oct-04	WAR	INT	EU OHQ	NORTHWOOD
Lovett, Stephen	Lt Cdr	01-Oct-06	WAR	SM(C)	HMS RALEIGH	
Lowe, Christian T Miles	Lt RN	01-May-13	WAR	GSX	HMS PORTLAND	
Lowe, Christopher	Lt Cdr	01-Oct-05	ENG	MESM	DI - CA	LONDON
Lowe, Gavin J	Lt RN	01-May-04	WAR	GSX	MWS COLLINGWOOD	
Lowe, Julian Charles	Cdr	30-Jun-10	ENG	ME	HMS QUEEN ELIZABETH	ROSYTH
Lowe, Stuart M	Lt Cdr	01-Dec-00	ENG	WE	FLEET ACOS(RP)	NCHQ
Lowe, Stuart W	Lt RN	01-Jan-13	WAR	O UT	RNAS CULDROSE	
Lowe, Timothy M	R Adm	17-Sep-12	WAR	PWO(N)	STRIKFORNATO - LISBON	LISBON
Lower, Iain S	Capt RN	10-Sep-12	WAR	PWO(A) AAWO		HMS DRAGON
Lownes, Sarah E	Surg Lt RN	07-Aug-13	MED	MEDICAL	BRNC DARTMOUTH	
Lowther, James	Cdr	30-Jun-07	WAR	PWO(N)	MAIN BUILDING LONDON	
Loxton, Thomas C	Lt RN	01-Sep-11	WAR	GSX	HMS SOMERSET	
Lucas, Darren P	Lt RN	01-May-02	ENG	WE	JFCIS(I)	QATAR - JOA - AL UDEID
Lucas, Simon U	Maj	01-Oct-06	RM	SCC	CTCRM	EXMOUTH
Lucocq, Nicholas J	Lt Cdr	01-Oct-04	WAR	PWO(N)	MWS COLLINGWOOD	
Lucy, Thomas David	Lt	01-Sep-11	RM	GS	NCHQ	
Lugg, John Charles	Maj	01-Oct-04	RM	SCC	DES/COMFLEET	ABBEY WOOD
Luke, Christopher	Lt RN	01-Jan-08	WAR	O MER	820 SQN	RNAS CULDROSE
Lumsden, Gavin T	Lt RN	05-Aug-11	MED	MS	MDHU PORTSMOUTH	PORTSMOUTH
Lundie, Andrew J	Surg Lt RN	05-Aug-09	MED	GMP	INM ALVERSTOKE	GOSPORT
Lunn, Adam C	Lt Cdr	01-Jun-94	WAR	P LYNX	NATO-ACO-JFC HQ NAPLES	
Lunn, Darren A	SLt	01-Sep-11	ENG	MESM	HMS AMBUSH	
Lupini, James M	Lt RN	01-Oct-02	WAR	GSX	RNLA	DARTMOUTH
Luscombe, Michael D	Lt Cdr	01-Oct-99	WAR	P SK6	854 NAS	RNAS CULDROSE
Luxford, Charles A	Lt Cdr	01-Oct-10	WAR	PWO	HMS MONTROSE	
L'Vov-Basirov, Nikolai E	SLt	12-Jan-11	ENG	WESM	HMS TIRELESS	
Lynas, Jonathan F	Lt RN	01-Sep-00	WAR	P SK6	GANNET SAR FLT	PRESTWICK
Lynch, John S	Capt	01-Sep-10	RM	GS	40 CDO RM	TAUNTON
Lynch, Paul Patrick MC	Lt Col	30-Jun-11	RM		SOFS	MAIN BUILDING LONDON
Lynch, Stephen	Cdr	30-Jun-11	WAR	O SKW	DES/COMJE	ABBEY WOOD
Lynn, Ian H	Cdr	30-Jun-10	WAR	PWO(U)	MOD NSD	MAIN BUILDING LONDON
Lynn, James M	Mid	24-Dec-12	WAR	SM(X)	BRNC DARTMOUTH	
Lynn, Sarah Louise	Lt Cdr	01-Oct-11	WAR	O MER	820 SQN	RNAS CULDROSE
Lynn, Steven Robert	Cdr	30-Jun-07	ENG	WE	HMS QUEEN ELIZABETH	ROSYTH
Lyons, Michael J	Lt Cdr	01-Jun-04	ENG	MESM	DCDS(PERS)/SPVA	GLOUCESTER

M

Mabbott, Keith I	Lt Cdr	01-Oct-08	WAR	MCD PWO	UKRBATSTAFF	HMNB PORTSMOUTH
Macartney, Simon G	SLt	01-May-11	ENG	WESM	HMS VANGUARD	
Maccorquodale, Mairi A	Lt Cdr	01-Oct-06	ENG	IS	HMS NELSON	
Maccrimmon, Stuart	Maj	01-Oct-11	RM	GS	RN EXCHANGE USA - BDS	WASHINGTON
Macdonald, Adam	Lt RN	13-Jul-12	ENG	WESM	HMS RALEIGH	
Macdonald, Alasdair I	Capt RN	30-Jun-07	ENG	WE	DIO SAPT	HMS COLLINGWOOD
Macdonald, Alastair J	Lt RN	20-May-08	LOGS	L SM	NCHQ CNPERS	NCHQ
Macdonald, Alastair J	Lt Cdr	01-Sep-02	ENG	WE	CYBER PROGRAMME SUPPORT	MAIN BUILDING LONDON
Macdonald, John R	Cdre	22-Jul-13	ENG	WESM(TWS)	CBRN POL	MAIN BUILDING LONDON
Macdonald, Michael	Maj	01-Oct-12	RM	C	CTCRM - CISTC	EXMOUTH
Macdonald, Stuart	Lt Cdr	01-Oct-07	LOGS	L	RN EXCHANGE USA	WASHINGTON
Macdonald-Robinson, Nicholas U	Cdr	30-Jun-08	WAR	PWO(A)	UK MCC	BAHRAIN
Macdougall, Stewart J	Lt Cdr	01-Oct-03	ENG	WESM(TWS)	DES/COMFLEET	ABBEY WOOD
Mace, Stephen J	Lt RN	01-Sep-10	ENG	AE	DES/COMLAN	ABBEY WOOD
Macfarlane, Gordon T	Surg Lt RN	08-Oct-08	MED	EM	INM ALVERSTOKE	GOSPORT
Macfarlane, Iain St	Lt Cdr	01-Oct-07	WAR	P MER	824 SQN - TU	RNAS CULDROSE
Machin, Matthew P	SLt	01-Nov-11	ENG	WE	HMS BULWARK	
Maciejewski, Luke W	SLt	01-May-13	WAR	O UT	RNAS CULDROSE	
Macindoe, Neil	Lt RN	23-Apr-06	ENG	TM	OP VOCATE	LIBYA TRIPOLI TRIPOLI
Mack, Peter E	SLt	01-Feb-11	ENG	AE	DCEME SULTAN	HMS SULTAN

Person Name	Substantive Rank	Seniority	Branch	Specialisation	Organisation	Location
Mackay, Andrew	Lt Cdr	01-Feb-04	WAR	INT	JFIG - JT OPS	HUNTINGDON
Mackay, Fraser R	Lt RN	01-Sep-11	ENG	WE	HMS DARING	
Mackay, Graeme A	Cdre	22-Aug-11	WAR	O SK6	FLEET CSAV	NCHQ
Mackay, Hugh P	Capt	01-Sep-09	RM	GS	CTCRM	EXMOUTH
Mackay, Peter	Cdr	30-Jun-10	ENG	WE	COMDEVFLOT SEA	HMNB DEVONPORT
Mackay, Richard	Lt RN	01-Sep-10	ENG	AE	DEFENCE ACADEMY	LOUGHBOROUGH
Mackay, Shaun A	Lt RN	01-Sep-12	ENG	MESM	HMS VIGILANT	
Mackay-Brown, Alan L	Surg Lt Cdr	01-Aug-05	MED	Occ Med	RNAS YEOVILTON	
Mackenow, Helen R	Lt Cdr	01-Oct-13	LOGS	L BAR	NCHQ CNPS	MAIN BUILDING LONDON
Mackenzie, Hannah	Lt Cdr	01-Oct-12	WAR	MTO A (RES)	RNLO GULF	DUBAI
Mackey, Martin C	Cdr	30-Jun-08	WAR	MCD PWO(U)	OPS DIR	MAIN BUILDING LONDON
Mackie, David F S	Cdr	30-Jun-11	ENG	WE	HMS BULWARK	
Mackie, Richard P	Capt	01-Sep-10	RM	GS	42 CDO RM - COMD COY	
Mackie, Scott	SLt	01-Mar-11	WAR	GSX	HMS ILLUSTRIOUS	
Mackie, Simon J	Surg Cdr	01-Dec-10	MED	Urol	MDHU PORTSMOUTH	PORTSMOUTH
Mackinnon, Donald J	Cdr	30-Jun-11	WAR	PWO(U)	MSP	MAIN BUILDING LONDON
Mackley-Heath, Megan A	Mid	01-Sep-13	ENG	ME	BRNC DARTMOUTH	
Maclean, Graeme	Lt RN	01-Sep-10	ENG	MESM	HMS VANGUARD	
Maclean, Shamus	Lt Cdr	01-Oct-12	WAR	INT	DI - FC(A) - WYT	RAF WYTON
Maclennan, Neil R	Lt RN	01-Dec-08	LOGS	L BAR	DCDS PERS - SPA	RAF NORTHOLT
Macleod, Alanna M	Surg Lt Cdr (D)	24-Jun-10	DENTAL	GDP	HMS DRAKE	
Macleod, Alastair M	Lt RN	01-Jun-07	WAR	P SK4	RNLA	HMS COLLINGWOOD
Macleod, James N	Capt RN	01-Sep-09	ENG	WE	IPP - MENA	MAIN BUILDING LONDON
Macleod, Mark S	Cdr	30-Jun-11	WAR	P MER	AWC BSD - RW TES	RAF BOSCOMBE DOWN
Macnae, Bridget R	Lt RN	01-Oct-09	WAR	GSX	RN EXCHANGE GERMANY	BERLIN
Macphail, Neil M	Lt Cdr	01-Oct-11	MED	MS(SM)	FLEET CAP SSM DIVISION	NCHQ
Macpherson, Craig A C	Lt RN	01-Jan-03	WAR	FC	RNAS YEOVILTON - RNFS	RNAS YEOVILTON
Macpherson, William G C	Maj	01-Oct-08	RM	SCC	FLEET CAP SSM DIVISION	NCHQ
Macquarrie, Gary A	Lt Cdr	01-Oct-10	ENG	ME	HMS DEFENDER	
Macrae, Kirk	Lt RN	01-Jan-07	WAR	GSX	FOST MPV SEA	HELENSBURGH
Maddick, James J	Lt RN	27-Nov-12	ENG	MESM	HMS ASTUTE	
Maddick, Mark J	Col	26-Sep-11	RM	LC	MISSION TO THE UN	NEW YORK USA
Maddison, Hugh R	Lt Cdr	01-Oct-12	ENG	ME	FLEET CAP SSM DIVISION	NCHQ
Maddison, John D MBE	Lt Col	30-Jun-12	RM	SCC	CTCRM - CORPS COL	EXMOUTH
Maddison, Paul	Lt Cdr	01-Oct-12	ENG	WE	HMS SOMERSET	
Maden, Steven G	Lt RN	08-Apr-05	ENG	WESM(TWS)	DES/COMLAND	ABBEY WOOD BRISTOL
Madgwick, Edward C C	Surg Cdr (D)	14-Oct-08	DENTAL	GDP	HMS DRAKE - SDS	HMS DRAKE
Magan, Michael J C	Capt RN	21-Feb-12	ENG	WE	NC PSYA	PORTSMOUTH
Magill, Alasdair	Lt RN	01-Jul-07	WAR	MCD	RN EXCHANGE AUSTRALIA	CANBERRA
Magill, Hal R	Lt RN	09-Apr-09	ENG	ME	HMS ECHO	
Magill, Michael P	Mid	01-Sep-13	WAR	GSX	BRNC DARTMOUTH	
Magowan, Conor C	Capt	01-Sep-08	RM	GS	NCHQ	
Magowan, Robert A CBE	Brig	18-Mar-13	RM		NCHQ CNPS	NCHQ
Magzoub, Mohayed	Lt RN	01-Sep-06	ENG	ME	OPS DIR	MAIN BUILDING LONDON
Magzoub, Mowafag M	Mid	01-Nov-13	LOGS	L	BRNC DARTMOUTH	
Maher, Michael	Cdr	30-Jun-05	WAR	AAWO	ATTACHE/ADVISER ANKARA	TURKEY
Mahoney, Andrew	Lt RN	01-Jul-05	WAR	PWO	RN EXCHANGE N ZLAND	WELLINGTON
Mahony, David G	Cdr	30-Jun-03	WAR	O SK6	US CENTCOM	TAMPA USA
Mailes, Ian R	Lt Cdr	01-Oct-03	WAR	O MER	HMS COLLINGWOOD	
Main, Matthew	Lt RN	01-Sep-08	ENG	MESM	BDS WASHINGTON	WASHINGTON USA
Mains, Graham	Lt Cdr	01-Oct-11	WAR	O MER	RN EXCHANGE USA	WASHINGTON
Mair, Barbara I	Surg Lt RN (D)	21-Jun-11	DENTAL	GDP	RNAS CULDROSE	
Mair, Joanna	SLt	01-Apr-12	MED	MEDICAL	BRNC DARTMOUTH	
Major, Lee A	Lt RN	01-Sep-13	WAR	GSX	HMS BULWARK	
Major, William	Lt RN	01-Jun-08	WAR	P SK4	RAF ODIHAM	
Makosz, Simon P	SLt	01-Apr-12	WAR	P UT	RNAS YEOVILTON	
Malcolm, Paul	Lt RN	01-Sep-02	WAR	HM	1 GP RHAM	KINGS LYNN
Malcolm, Stephen R OBE	Capt RN	04-May-09	WAR	HM (H CH)	HMS DRAKE	
Malkin, Sharon L	Cdr	30-Jun-11	ENG	AE	DES/COIR/CA	ABBEY WOOD
Mallabone, James J K	Lt Cdr	01-Oct-12	ENG	TM	RNAS YEOVILTON	
Mallalieu, Harry J	2Lt	01-Sep-10	RM	GS	40 CDO RM - DGHR(O)	TAUNTON
Mallard, James	Lt	01-Sep-12	RM	GS	RMR SCOTLAND	HMS CALEDONIA

Person Name	Substantive Rank	Seniority	Branch	Specialisation	Organisation	Location
Mallinson, Laurence J	Lt Cdr	01-Oct-10	LOGS	L	DES/COMFLEET	HMS NELSON
Mallinson, Robert	Cdr	30-Jun-05	ENG	AE O	NCHQ CNPERS	PORTSMOUTH
Mallows, Andy	Maj	01-Oct-12	RM	GS	HQ AIR - COS(OPS) - JALO	RAF HIGH WYCOMBE
Malone, Martin T	Lt Cdr	01-Oct-09	LOGS	L	FOST DPORT SEA	HMNB DEVONPORT
Malone, Roger W	Lt Cdr	01-Oct-13	WAR	HM(AS)	FLEET CAP SSM DIVISION	NCHQ
Malster, Dudley A	Lt RN	01-May-05	WAR	MW	MWS COLLINGWOOD	HMS COLLINGWOOD
Maltby, Richard J	Lt Col	30-Jun-12	RM		HMS BULWARK	
Manders-Trett, Victoria	Lt Cdr	01-Oct-07	LOGS	L	PJHQ (UK) J1/J4	NORTHWOOD
Mandley, Philip J	Lt Cdr	01-May-02	ENG	TM	FLEET FOST ACOS(Trg)	NCHQ
Manger, Garth S C	Col	19-Apr-10	RM	C	1 ASSLT GROUP RM (HQ)	HMNB DEVONPORT
Manktelow, Benjamin T	Lt RN	01-Dec-11	WAR	GSX	HMS NELSON	HMS NELSON
Manning, David Simon	Lt RN	08-May-06	ENG	IS	DES/COMJE	CORSHAM
Manning, Gary P	Lt Cdr	01-Oct-07	LOGS	L	DMLS	HMS RALEIGH
Manning, Leslie G	Capt	21-Mar-13	RM	SCC	MED SQN CDO LOG	BARNSTAPLE
Mannion, Christopher M	Lt RN	01-Sep-09	ENG	AE	LOAN DSTL - NSD	FAREHAM
Mansergh, Michael P CBE	Cdre	01-Sep-08	WAR	PWO(C)	MWS COLLINGWOOD	
Mansfield, Alastair J	RN Chpln	10-Dec-07	Ch S		RNAS CULDROSE	
Mansfield, James A	Lt Cdr	01-Oct-06	WAR	PWO(U)	FLEET CAP WARFARE	NCHQ
Manson, Peter D	Maj	01-Sep-99	RM	P SK4	NCHQ CNPERS	NCHQ
Manson, Robert P	Lt RN	08-Dec-12	ENG	ME	HMS SUTHERLAND	
Manson, Thomas E	Capt RN	02-Jul-13	ENG	AE P	DES/COIR	ABBEY WOOD
Manwaring, Roy G	Cdr	25-Jul-11	MED	MS	DMSTG	ALDERSHOT
Maples, Andrew T	Surg Lt Cdr	01-Aug-06	MED	GMP	DES/COMFLEET	HMS DRAKE
Marden, Tony	Lt Cdr	01-Oct-09	ENG	WE	HMS MONTROSE	
Marder, Michael P	2Lt	02-Sep-13	RM	N/A	CTCRM OFFICERS	EXMOUTH
Mardlin, Stephen A	Cdr	30-Jun-10	LOGS	L C	HQBF GIBRALTAR - OPS	GIBRALTAR
Marfleet, Adam J	SLt	01-Sep-11	ENG	WESM	HMS RALEIGH	
Marin-Ortega, Carl	Lt RN	01-Sep-11	ENG	WE	HMS RICHMOND	
Marjoribanks, Charlotte	Lt RN	01-Sep-03	WAR	P MER	BRNC DARTMOUTH	
Marland, Eunice E	Lt Cdr	01-Oct-08	LOGS	L BAR	NCHQ - CNLS	HMNB DEVONPORT
Marlor, Andrew	Lt Cdr	01-Oct-12	ENG	WESM(TWS)	DI - CA	LONDON
Marlor, Kirsty L	Lt RN	01-Sep-06	ENG	AE	DCAE COSFORD - TES	WOLVERHAMPTON
Marmont, Kerry L	Cdr	31-Dec-00	ENG	WESM(TWS)	DES/COMLAND	ABBEY WOOD
Marr, Stephen	Capt	28-Jul-06	RM	SCC	NCHQ	
Marratt, Richard	Cdr	30-Jun-12	ENG	TM	HMS RALEIGH - INT R	
Marriner, Henry M	SLt	01-Sep-12	WAR	GSX	MCM1 CREW 4	FASLANE
Marriott, Isabella M	Lt RN	01-Dec-08	WAR	MEDIA OPS	NCHQ CNPS	NCHQ
Marriott, Matthew J	Lt Cdr	01-Sep-09	WAR	PWO	HMS RICHMOND	
Marriott, Neil K	Lt Cdr	01-Oct-05	WAR	MCD PWO(U)	HMS NELSON	
Marrison, Andrew C	Lt RN	16-Dec-11	ENG	WE	HMS DARING	
Marsden, Christopher N	Lt RN	01-Jun-10	LOGS	L	UKRBATSTAFF	HMNB PORTSMOUTH
Marsden, Daniel C	Lt RN	01-Apr-11	WAR	GSX	RNP TEAM	RAF NORTHOLT
Marsh, Alexander R	Lt RN	01-Aug-12	ENG	MESM	DCEME SULTAN	HMS SULTAN
Marsh, Ceri	Lt Cdr	01-Oct-12	LOGS	L BAR	HMS DIAMOND	
Marsh, Edward R	Lt RN	01-Apr-11	WAR	GSX	EU OHQ	NORTHWOOD
Marsh, James Paul	Mid	01-Sep-13	WAR	GSX	BRNC DARTMOUTH	
Marsh, Stephen W	Lt Cdr	01-Oct-11	LOGS	L	COMUKAMPHIBFOR	HMNB PORTSMOUTH
Marsh, Stuart D	Lt RN	01-May-02	WAR	HM(AS)	FLEET HM UNIT	HMNB DEVONPORT
Marshall, Alexander J	Lt RN	01-Sep-11	WAR	SM(X)	HMS TALENT	
Marshall, Alistair J	Lt Cdr	01-Oct-08	WAR	SM(CQ)	FLEET COMOPS NWD	NORTHWOOD
Marshall, David S	Lt RN	01-Sep-10	ENG	AE	1710 NAS	PORTSMOUTH
Marshall, Fleur R	Surg Capt RN	20-Aug-13	MED	GMP (C&S)	APHCS SOUTH	ALDERSHOT
Marshall, Gavin P	Lt Cdr	01-Oct-09	ENG	ME	NAVY MCTA PORTSMOUTH	HMNB PORTSMOUTH
Marshall, Leon	Maj	01-Oct-13	RM	LC	DEFAC JSCSC	SHRIVENHAM
Marshall, Paul	Capt RN	01-Jul-12	ENG	ME	JFC HQ	NORTHWOOD
Marshall, Richard G C	Lt Cdr	01-May-95	WAR	PWO(C)	EU OHQ	BAHRAIN
Marshall, Tracey	Lt Cdr	01-Oct-05	WAR	GSX	DEFENCE ESTATES - DHE	RAF BRAMPTON
Marshall, William E	Mid	01-Nov-13	WAR	P UT	BRNC DARTMOUTH	
Martin, Alan F	Lt RN	01-Jul-10	ENG	TM	CDO LOG REGT RM	BARNSTAPLE
Martin, Andrew	Lt RN	01-Nov-10	WAR	GSX	MWS COLLINGWOOD	
Martin, Andrew J	Lt RN	01-Apr-10	WAR	SM(X)	HMS RALEIGH	
Martin, Antoinette	Surg Lt RN	01-Aug-12	MED	MEDICAL	BRNC DARTMOUTH	

Person Name	Substantive Rank	Seniority	Branch	Specialisation	Organisation	Location
Martin, Ben R.	Lt RN	01-May-07	WAR	PWO	HMS DIAMOND	
Martin, Brian H	Lt RN	11-Dec-09	ENG	WESM(TWS)	HMS ARTFUL	BARROW IN FURNESS
Martin, Bruce A	Cdr	30-Jun-05	ENG	MESM	DES/COMFLEET	BARROW IN FURNESS
Martin, David C S	Cdr	30-Jun-13	WAR	PWO	MWS COLLINGWOOD	
Martin, David L	Lt RN	01-Sep-06	WAR	MW	FOST MPV SEA	HELENSBURGH
Martin, Euan A	Lt RN	01-Apr-12	WAR	GSX	MCM2 CREW 2	PORTSMOUTH
Martin, Graham	Lt RN	01-Jul-04	ENG	ME	FLEET FOST TBTU	HMS COLLINGWOOD
Martin, Harry C	Lt RN	01-Sep-08	ENG	AE	FLEET CSAV	NCHQ
Martin, James N	Lt RN	01-Jan-06	WAR	GSX	HMS ARCHER	
Martin, Jamie M	SLt	01-Mar-11	ENG	MESM	DCEME SULTAN	HMS SULTAN
Martin, Neil	Surg Cdr	01-Sep-11	MED	Med	MDHU PETERBOROUGH	PETERBOROUGH
Martin, Nigel	Lt RN	20-Sep-99	WAR	C	NATO-ACO-JFC HQ	BRUNSSUM
Martin, Robert J	Lt Cdr	01-Oct-08	ENG	AE	845 SQN	RNAS YEOVILTON
Martin, Simon J	Cdr	30-Jun-11	ENG	WESM(TWS)	ROYAL BRUNEI	SERIA
Martin, Stephanie	SLt	01-Nov-11	WAR	HM	BRNC DARTMOUTH	
Martin, Stuart A	Lt RN	01-Jul-12	WAR	GSX	HMS PORTLAND	
Martin, Stuart W	Lt Cdr	01-Oct-07	ENG	AE	HMS NEPTUNE	HELENSBURGH
Martyn, Daniel	Lt Cdr	25-Jun-13	WAR	SM(CQ)	FLEET CAP SSM DIVISION	NCHQ
Martyn, Julie M	Lt RN	01-Mar-03	QARNNS	PHC	RNAS YEOVILTON	
Maskell, Bernard M	Lt RN	01-May-04	ENG	WESM(TWS)	MWS COLLINGWOOD	
Maslen, David W J	Capt	16-Apr-10	RM	SCC	30 CDO IX GP RM	PLYMOUTH
Mason, Andrew C	Lt Cdr	01-Oct-06	WAR	PWO(A)	JFC HQ	NORTHWOOD
Mason, Angus E	Lt RN	01-Oct-07	WAR	SM(N)	FLEET COMOPS NWD	NORTHWOOD
Mason, Christopher	Lt RN	01-Dec-08	WAR	P SK4	845 SQN	RNAS YEOVILTON
Mason, Darren J	Lt Cdr	01-Oct-05	WAR	SM(CQ)	DI - ICSP	LONDON
Mason, David	Lt Cdr	01-Oct-13	WAR	MW	MWS COLLINGWOOD	
Mason, Garry	Capt	01-Apr-11	RM	SCC	CHFHQ (SEA)	RNAS YEOVILTON
Mason, Joe W	Lt RN	01-Apr-13	WAR	P UT	RAF VALLEY	HOLYHEAD
Mason, John	Lt RN	01-Apr-11	WAR	GSX	HMS CLYDE	
Mason, Lindsay	Lt Cdr	01-Oct-02	ENG	TM	DEFENCE ACADEMY	SHRIVENHAM
Mason, Mark J	Lt Cdr	01-Oct-09	WAR	PWO(U) MW	HMS DEFENDER	
Mason, Oliver D	Capt	01-Sep-10	RM	GS	CDO LOG REGT RM	BARNSTAPLE
Mason, Richard J	Lt RN	01-May-04	WAR	PWO(SM)	HMS TIRELESS	
Mason, Victoria J	Lt RN	01-Oct-09	LOGS	L	NAVSEC	NCHQ
Massey, Benjamin M	Mid	01-Sep-13	WAR	GSX	BRNC DARTMOUTH	
Massey, Paul	Lt Cdr	05-Dec-02	WAR	AV (RES)	CHFHQ (SHORE)	RNAS YEOVILTON
Masson, Neil G	Lt Cdr	01-Oct-10	WAR	SM(AWC)	HMS TIRELESS	
Masson, Vivienne	Lt RN	01-Apr-08	LOGS	L	1 ASSLT GROUP RM (HQ)	PLYMOUTH
Masters, James C	Cdr	30-Jun-06	WAR	AAWO	FLEET COMOPS NWD	NORTHWOOD
Mather, Christopher J	Lt RN	06-Apr-07	ENG	WESM(SWS)	FLEET COMOPS NWD	NORTHWOOD
Mathers, Fiona C	Lt RN	02-Dec-05	WAR	OP INT (RES)	HQ DISC	SHEFFORD
Matheson, Andrew S	Surg Lt Cdr	01-Nov-11	MED	Path - Micro	HMS NEPTUNE	HELENSBURGH
Mathews, Andrew D	V Adm	05-May-09	ENG	MESM	HMS DRAKE	
Mathieson, Neil B	Lt Cdr	01-Oct-08	ENG	AE	DES/COIR/CA	ABBEY WOOD
Matthews, Christopher L	Lt RN	01-Jan-12	LOGS	L	CDO LOG REGT RM	BARNSTAPLE
Matthews, David W	Cdr	30-Jun-05	ENG	WESM(TWS)	DES/COMJE/ISS	CORSHAM
Matthews, Jonathan J	Surg Cdr	01-Sep-09	MED	T&O	MDHU DERRIFORD	PLYMOUTH
Matthews, Justin	Lt Cdr	01-Oct-09	WAR	O SKW	854 NAS	RNAS CULDROSE
Matthews, Kevin A I	Lt RN	13-Jul-12	MED	MS	INM ALVERSTOKE2	GOSPORT
Matthews, Lucy A	Surg Lt Cdr (D)	19-Jun-13	DENTAL	GDP	MDHU PORTSMOUTH	
Matthews, Paul B	Cdr	30-Jun-09	ENG	TM	NATO-ACO-SHAPE	CASTEAU
Matthews, Paul K	Lt RN	30-Jun-11	LOGS	L	NATO - BRUSSELS	
Mattock, Nicholas J	Lt RN	01-Jan-05	WAR	P GR7	FLEET AV VALLEY	HOLYHEAD
Maude, Colin D	Lt Cdr	01-Oct-11	ENG	AE	LHF 815 SQN HQ	RNAS YEOVILTON
Maumy, Jonathan	Lt RN	01-Jan-10	WAR	P MER	829 SQN FLT 01	RNAS CULDROSE
Maw, Martyn J	Lt Cdr	01-Dec-90	ENG	WESM(TWS)	DES/COMFLEET	ABBEY WOOD BRISTOL
Mawdsley, Gareth R	Lt Cdr	01-Oct-07	LOGS	L	UKRBATSTAFF	HMNB PORTSMOUTH
Mawdsley, Owen R	Lt RN	07-Jun-10	WAR	O SKW	DEFAC JSCSC	SHRIVENHAM
Mawdsley, Richard J	Capt	01-Sep-13	RM	GS	43 CDO	HMNB CLYDE
Maxwell, Emma C	SLt	01-Feb-12	MED	MEDICAL	BRNC DARTMOUTH	
Maxwell, Hamish	Lt RN	01-Oct-10	WAR	SM(X)	HMS VIGILANT	
May, Colin	Lt Cdr	01-Jul-04	WAR	INT	FLEET COMOPS NWD	NORTHWOOD

Person Name	Substantive Rank	Seniority	Branch	Specialisation	Organisation	Location
May, Connor D W R	Lt RN	03-May-13	ENG	WE	MWS COLLINGWOOD	
May, David M	Lt Cdr	01-Oct-08	WAR	REG	RNP - HQ PMN	HMS EXCELLENT
May, Dominic P MBE	Col	06-Mar-12	RM	MLDR	CDO LOG REGT RM	BARNSTAPLE
May, Frederick C	SLt	01-Jul-12	WAR	SM(X)	HMS TORBAY	
May, Nigel Peter	Cdr	30-Jun-06	WAR	P SKW	FLEET CSAV	MAIN BUILDING LONDON
May, Steven	Lt Cdr	01-Jul-03	ENG	ME	HMS SULTAN	
Maybery, James E	Lt Col	30-Jun-05	RM	GS	NCHQ	
Mayell, Julie A	Lt Cdr	01-Oct-02	LOGS	L	NATO	BRUSSELS
Mayes, David John	Mid	11-Apr-12	WAR	GSX	HMNB PORTSMOUTH	
Mayger, Martyn	Lt RN	01-Apr-13	WAR	GSX	HMS PORTLAND	
Maynard, Charles I	Lt Cdr	01-Feb-03	WAR	PWO(A)	UKRBATSTAFF	HMNB PORTSMOUTH
Maynard, Paul A	Maj	01-Oct-07	RM	GS	DEFAC JSCSC ACSC	SHRIVENHAM
McAll, Benjamin J	2Lt	01-Sep-11	RM	GS	40 CDO RM - DGHR(O)	TAUNTON
McAllister, Andrew W	Lt RN	01-Oct-08	WAR	IS	DCMC	MAIN BUILDING LONDON
Mc Allister, Kevin J	Lt RN	17-Dec-10	ENG	WE	OCLC NCH	MANCHESTER
McAllister, Steven E	Lt Cdr	01-Oct-13	WAR	SM(AWC)	CAREER TRAINING	HELENSBURGH
McAlpine, Martin A	Lt RN	08-Jun-07	WAR	C	PJHQ (UK) J6	NORTHWOOD
McAlpine, Paul A OBE	Cdre	08-Feb-11	WAR	MCD PWO(A)	COMUKTG SEA	PLYMOUTH
McAlpine, Rory W	Lt RN	01-Mar-12	WAR	GSX	HMS LANCASTER	
McArdle, Alan D	Surg Lt RN	01-Mar-12	MED	GDMO	RNAS CULDROSE	
McArdle, Christopher J	Capt	01-Sep-09	RM	GS	HMNB DEVONPORT	
McArdle, Martin J	Lt RN	01-Jun-08	WAR	ATC	RNAS YEOVILTON	
McArthur, Calum J	Surg R Adm	08-Oct-12	MED	GMP (C&S)	DMS WHITTINGTON	LICHFIELD
McBarnet, Thomas F	Capt RN	30-Jun-06	WAR	PWO(U)	NATO	BRUSSELS
McBeth, Gary	Lt RN	01-Sep-05	ENG	MESM	DES/COMFLEET	ABBEY WOOD
McBratney, James A	Lt Cdr	01-Nov-04	WAR	SM(AWC)	DI - CA	LONDON
McBride, Shaun P	Mid	01-Nov-12	WAR	P UT	BRNC DARTMOUTH	
McBrierty, Craig J	Lt RN	08-Jul-12	ENG	WE	HMS MONMOUTH	
McCafferty, Lesley F	Surg Lt Cdr (D)	23-Jul-12	DENTAL	GDP	DDS SCOTLAND	HELENSBURGH
McCall, Gary	Lt Cdr	01-Oct-11	WAR	P LYNX	LHF 700W SQN	RNAS YEOVILTON
McCallum, Malcolm D	Lt Cdr	01-Oct-12	WAR	HM(AS)	HMS DRAKE	
McCallum, Neil	Lt Cdr	01-Jun-05	ENG	ME	D CEPP	MAIN BUILDING LONDON
McCamphill-Rose, Paul J	Lt Cdr	01-Oct-11	ENG	WE	FLEET CAP IS DIVISION	NCHQ
McCann, Andrew G	Lt RN	01-Sep-10	WAR	SM(X)	HMS RALEIGH	
McCann, Sally Jane	SLt	24-Jan-12	WAR	HM	BRNC DARTMOUTH	
McCann, Toby	Lt Cdr	01-Dec-06	ENG	AE O	824 SQN - TU	RNAS CULDROSE
McCardle, John A OBE	Col	01-Jul-08	RM	P LYN7	ATTACHE/ADVISER PRETORIA	SOUTH AFRICA
McCarthy, Steven	Cdr	30-Jun-09	ENG	ME	ISAF PAK LO	PAKISTAN
McCaughan, Christopher J	Lt RN	01-Oct-11	ENG	WE	HMS DRAGON	
McCaughey, Vincent J	Lt Cdr	01-Oct-05	ENG	IS	DEFAC	SHRIVENHAM
McCaul, Daniel	Surg Lt RN	01-Aug-12	MED	MEDICAL	BRNC DARTMOUTH	
McCavour, Bryan D	Lt Cdr	01-Sep-05	WAR	INT	HMS MONMOUTH	
McClaren, Ronni	Lt RN	09-Apr-09	WAR	REG	HMS NELSON	HMS NELSON
McClean, Stephen	Lt RN	01-Oct-09	ENG	WESM	DES/COMFLEET	ABBEY WOOD
McCleary, Simon P	Lt Cdr	01-Oct-05	ENG	WESM	COMFASFLOT	HMNB CLYDE
McClelland, Ian	Lt RN	01-Mar-10	WAR	MCD	MCM1 CREW 1	FASLANE
McClelland, Patrick W	Lt RN	07-Jan-07	WAR	AV	RNAS CULDROSE	
McClement, Duncan L	Lt Cdr	01-Jan-07	ENG	MESM	FOST SM SEA	HELENSBURGH
McClintock, Lee R	SLt	01-Feb-13	WAR	SM(X)	HMS DARING	
McClurg, Robert J	Lt Cdr	01-Mar-10	ENG	WE	HMS ST ALBANS	
McCombe, John	Lt Cdr	01-Sep-04	ENG	ME	HMS DRAGON	GLASGOW
McConochie, Andrew D	Lt Cdr	16-Apr-96	LOGS	L	DES/COMFLEET	HMS DRAKE
McCormack, Gary	Lt Cdr	01-Oct-10	ENG	ME	HMS ARGYLL	
McCormick, Emma J	Lt RN	01-Jan-05	WAR	GSX	NCHQ - NAVY CMD SEC	NCHQ
McCrea, Mark J	Lt RN	01-May-05	ENG	ME	HMS QUEEN ELIZABETH	ROSYTH
McCreton, Joshua L	Capt	01-Mar-11	RM	GS	NATO BRUSSELS	BRUSSELS
McCrossan, Amy	Lt RN	01-Aug-09	WAR	GSX	HMS DIAMOND	
McCue, Duncan	Cdr	30-Jun-06	ENG	ME	NCHQ CNPERS	PORTSMOUTH
McCullagh, Timothy AC	Lt RN	11-Oct-13	LOGS	L	HMS RALEIGH	
McCulley, Steven C	Maj	01-Oct-07	RM	GS	HMS DRAKE	
McCullough, Ian Neil	Maj	02-Oct-97	RM	GS (RES)	NCHQ - NAVY CMD SEC	NCHQ
McCullough, Karen M	Lt RN	01-Nov-04	QARNNS	ITU	NCHQ MEDDIV	NCHQ

Person Name	Substantive Rank	Seniority	Branch	Specialisation	Organisation	Location
McCurry, Neill Ian	Capt	30-Aug-12	RM	GS	NCHQ	
McCutcheon, Graeme	Lt Cdr	01-Oct-06	WAR	P LYNX	RNAS YEOVILTON - LSF	RNAS YEOVILTON
McDermott, Owen D	Cdr	30-Jun-10	ENG	WE	DES/COMJE	CORSHAM
McDonald, Andrew W	Lt Cdr	01-Oct-06	ENG	AE	NCHQ CNPERS	PORTSMOUTH
McDonald, Duncan J	Lt Cdr	01-Oct-08	ENG	ME	FLEET CAP SSM DIVISION	NCHQ
McDonald, Morgan J	Lt RN	01-Jan-05	WAR	MW	HMS NEPTUNE	HELENSBURGH
McDonnell, David	Cdr	30-Jun-11	WAR	HM (M CH)	NATO-ACT-HQ SACT	NORFOLK
McDonough, Mark	Lt RN	01-Jan-13	ENG	WESM	HMS VICTORIOUS	
McDougall, James N	Lt RN	01-May-13	ENG	MESM	DCEME SULTAN	HMS SULTAN
McDougall, William	Lt Cdr	02-Oct-10	ENG	MESM	RN EXCHANGE AUSTRALIA	CANBERRA
McElrath, Calum D	SLt	11-Nov-13	WAR	REG (RES)	BRNC DARTMOUTH	
Mcelroy, Paul J	Mid	01-Sep-13	ENG	ME	BRNC DARTMOUTH	
McEllvenny, Joseph P	Capt	01-Sep-09	RM	GS	NCHQ	
McElwaine, Christopher W	Lt RN	08-Dec-11	ENG	WE	DES/COMFLEET	ABBEY WOOD
McEvoy, Jason L	Lt RN	19-Dec-08	ENG	WESM(TWS)	FOST SM SEA	HELENSBURGH
McEvoy, Lee P	Lt Cdr	01-Oct-03	WAR	INT	JMIC	HMS COLLINGWOOD
McEvoy, Thomas P	Capt	01-Sep-13	RM	GS	43 CDO	HMNB CLYDE
McEwan, Rory D	Lt Cdr	01-Oct-10	ENG	WESM(TWS)	HMS ASTUTE	
McFadden, Andrew	RN Chpln	01-Sep-98	Ch S		HMS NELSON - CHAP	HMNB PORTSMOUTH
McFarlane, Daniel	SLt	11-Apr-12	WAR	SM(X)	BRNC DARTMOUTH	
McFarlane, Gregory T	SLt	02-May-12	LOGS	L	BRNC DARTMOUTH	
McGannity, Colin S	Lt Cdr	01-Oct-08	WAR	O SKW	849 SQN	RNAS CULDROSE
McGhee, Craig	Maj	01-Sep-02	RM	P LYN7	CHFHQ (SEA)	RNAS YEOVILTON
McGhie, Ian A	Capt RN	26-Aug-08	WAR	N	COMFASFLOT	HMNB CLYDE
McGill, Gus	Mid	01-Sep-13	WAR	SM(X)	BRNC DARTMOUTH	DARTMOUTH
McGill, Ian	Maj	01-Oct-13	RM	MLDR (SCC)	30 CDO IX GP RM	PLYMOUTH
McGinlay, Matthew J	Mid	01-May-13	WAR	GSX	BRNC DARTMOUTH	
McGinley, Christopher T	Capt	13-Dec-06	RM	GS (RES)	DNR RCHQ NORTH	HMS CALEDONIA
McGivern, Ryan P	Lt RN	01-Sep-04	WAR	P MER	HMS DRAKE	
McGlory, Stephen J	Cdr	30-Jun-13	WAR	PWO(A)	PJHQ (UK) J7	NORTHWOOD
McGreal, Benjamin	Lt Cdr	01-Oct-13	WAR	P CDO	CHF(MERLIN)	RAF BENSON
McGuire, James	Lt Cdr	24-Aug-04	WAR	SM(CQ)	FOST FAS SHORE	HELENSBURGH
McHugh, Richard H	Lt Cdr	01-Mar-05	ENG	ME	NCHQ	
McInally, Mathew	Capt	01-Sep-09	RM	LC	NCHQ	
McInerney, Andrew J	Col	31-Mar-11	RM	GS	FLEET COMOPS NWD	NORTHWOOD
McInerney, David F	Lt Cdr	01-Oct-13	WAR	C	LOAN DSTL - IMD	SALISBURY
McInnes, Allan J	Lt RN	01-Jan-12	WAR	O UT	RNAS CULDROSE	
McInnes, James G	Cdr	30-Jun-05	ENG	WESM(SWS)	DES/COMFLEET	ABBEY WOOD
McInnes, Stephanie	Lt RN	01-Feb-12	WAR	ATC	RNAS YEOVILTON - AS	SOUTHAMPTON
McIntosh, James D	Surg Cdr	10-Sep-08	MED	GMP (C&S)	NCHQ MEDDIV	NCHQ
McIntosh, Simon J	Surg Lt RN	05-Aug-09	MED	GMP	INM ALVERSTOKE	GOSPORT
McKay, Thomas W	Lt Cdr	01-Oct-11	WAR	PWO	FOST NWD	NORTHWOOD
McKechnie, Peter St	Surg Lt RN	01-Jun-11	MED	GS	INM ALVERSTOKE	GOSPORT
McKee, Hamish M	Lt Cdr	01-Oct-09	WAR	O MER	824 SQN - TU	RNAS CULDROSE
McKendrick, Andrew M OBE	Capt RN	01-Jun-09	WAR	SM(CQ)	CBRN POL	MAIN BUILDING LONDON
McKenna, Thomas J	Lt RN	01-Sep-12	ENG	WE	DES/COMFLEET	BRISTOL
McKinlay, Jayne A	Surg Lt RN	01-Feb-10	MED	EM	INM ALVERSTOKE	GOSPORT
McKnight, Derek J S	Lt Cdr	01-Jul-03	WAR	MCD PWO(A)	HMS COLLINGWOOD	
McLachlan, Andrew C	Lt RN	01-Jan-02	ENG	TM	CTCRM - TDRPC	EXMOUTH
McLaren, James P	Lt Col	30-Jun-07	RM	GS	ATTACHE/ADVISER - SOLIA	NAIROBI
McLauchlan, James M	SLt	01-Nov-11	LOGS	L	HMS RALEIGH	
McLaughlan, Christopher T	Lt RN	01-Mar-08	LOGS	L	HMS VANGUARD	
McLaughlin, Ian James	Lt RN	01-Jun-11	ENG	AE	848 SQN	RNAS YEOVILTON
McLaughlin, Steven	Lt Cdr	01-Oct-08	ENG	TM	HMS NELSON	
McLaughlin, Vincent	Lt RN	01-Sep-04	ENG	ME	DCMC	MAIN BUILDING LONDON
McLean, Christopher R	Surg Cdr	01-Jul-10	MED	T&O	MDHU FRIMLEY PARK	FRIMLEY
McLean, David	RN Chpln	18-Sep-96	Ch S		FOST DPORT SEA	HMNB DEVONPORT
McLean, Sean David	Lt RN	01-Jan-13	WAR	MW	FASLANE	HELENSBURGH
McLellan, James D	Cdr	30-Jun-13	ENG	WE	DES/COMFLEET	ABBEY WOOD
McLellan, Moira S	Surg Lt RN	03-Aug-11	MED	GDMO	HMS WESTMINSTER	
McLeman, William P	SLt	01-May-11	WAR	ATC	BRNC DARTMOUTH	
McLennan, Alexander P	Lt RN	01-Sep-12	ENG	ME	HMS OCEAN	

Person Name	Substantive Rank	Seniority	Branch	Specialisation	Organisation	Location
McLennan, Andrew	Lt Cdr	01-Oct-08	WAR	O MER	DEFAC JSCSC ACSC	SHRIVENHAM
McLocklan, Lee Michael	Lt Cdr	01-Oct-06	LOGS	L	MOD DEFENCE STAFF	LONDON
McMahon, Daniel S	Lt RN	01-Jan-04	WAR	HM	RNAS YEOVILTON	
McMenamin, Diarmaid	Surg Lt Cdr	06-Aug-08	MED	GMP	RMB CHIVENOR - BASE	BARNSTAPLE
McMenemy, Louise	Surg Lt RN	03-Aug-11	MED	GDMO	RNAS CULDROSE	
McMichael-Phillips, Scott J	Capt RN	30-Jun-08	WAR	HM (H CH)	LOAN HYDROG	TAUNTON
McMillan, Nelson	Lt Cdr	01-Oct-12	WAR	PWO	HMS SUTHERLAND	
McMonies, Murray J	SLt	01-Feb-12	ENG	MESM	HMS BULWARK	
McMorran, Hannah J	SLt	01-Sep-12	MED	MS(EHO)	BRNC DARTMOUTH	
McMorrow, Kevin M	Lt RN	01-Jun-09	WAR	ATC	HMS ILLUSTRIOUS	
McMorrow, Stephen P	SLt	01-Dec-13	WAR	GSX	HMS MONMOUTH	
McNair, James	Cdr	30-Jun-11	ENG	AE	DES/COMJE	YEOVIL
McNally, Barry J	Lt RN	01-Sep-08	LOGS	L SM	FLEET ACOS(RP)	NCHQ
McNally, Neville	Cdr	30-Jun-10	LOGS	L	DEFENCE ACADEMY	SHRIVENHAM
McNally, Nicholas A	Lt Cdr	01-Oct-13	ENG	ME	CAREER TRAINING	HMS SULTAN
McNally, Peter J	Mid	01-Sep-13	WAR	GSX	BRNC DARTMOUTH	
McNaught, Chilton J	Lt RN	13-Jun-08	WAR	REG	HMS SULTAN - SEC	HMS SULTAN
McNeill Love, Robin M C	Surg Cdre	23-Jul-13	MED		NCHQ MEDDIV	NCHQ
McNicholl, Bruce R	Mid	01-Nov-13	WAR	GSX	BRNC DARTMOUTH	
McPhail, Thomas C	Lt RN	01-May-04	WAR	PWO	HMS DAUNTLESS	
McPhee, Thomas J	Lt RN	17-Dec-09	WAR	INT	HMS TEMERAIRE	PORTSMOUTH
McPherson, Robert B	Capt	01-Sep-10	RM	GS	JCTTAT	FOLKESTONE
McQuaid, Ivor Thomas	Lt RN	12-Aug-05	ENG	WESM(TWS)	DES/COMFLEET	ABBEY WOOD BRISTOL
McQuaker, Stuart R	Capt RN	02-Dec-08	WAR	PWO(N)	CAREER TRAINING	HMS NELSON
McQueen, Jason B	Lt Cdr	01-Oct-03	ENG	TM	JIOTAT	SHRIVENHAM
McQueen, Patrick G	Lt Cdr	01-Oct-13	WAR	MCD	UK MCC	BAHRAIN
McTear, Karen MBE	Cdr	30-Jun-05	ENG	TM	DCLC RN STUDENTS	SHRIVENHAM
McWilliams, Adrian R	Lt Cdr	01-Oct-11	WAR	O LYNX	LHF 700W SQN	RNAS YEOVILTON
McWilliams, Jacqueline E	Lt Cdr	01-Sep-03	WAR	MW	STT	PORTSMOUTH
Meacher, Paul G	Lt Cdr	01-Apr-03	WAR	PWO	NCHQ	
Meachin, Michael C	RN Chpln	07-Jul-97	Ch S		HMS COLLINGWOOD	
Meaden, Alexander P	Lt RN	19-Nov-09	LOGS	L	DES/COMLAND	ABBEY WOOD
Meakin, Brian R	Cdr	30-Jun-03	WAR	O SKW	NATO SCHOOL	OBERAMMERGAU
Mealing, David W	Cdr	30-Jun-13	ENG	AE	DES/COMJE	BRISTOL
Mealing, Steven	Lt Cdr	01-Oct-05	ENG	ME	HQ LAND CTS DIV	ANDOVER
Mearns, Craig M	Cdr	30-Jun-05	LOGS	L	HMS QUEEN ELIZABETH	ROSYTH
Mears, Richard J	Lt Col	30-Jun-13	RM	C	MOD NSD - HDS	MAIN BUILDING LONDON
Medlicott, Nicholas	Lt RN	28-Oct-05	WAR	AV	RNAS CULDROSE - ATC	RNAS CULDROSE
Meeds, Kevin	Lt Cdr	16-Dec-95	WAR	O SK6	LSP ON	MUSCAT
Meehan, Oliver James P	Lt RN	15-Jul-13	LOGS	L	UK MCC	BAHRAIN
Meek, Camilla S	Lt Cdr	01-Mar-02	ENG	ME	HMS NELSON	
Mehsen, Samy	Lt RN	01-Sep-13	ENG	WESM	HMS VENGEANCE	
Mehta, Christopher	Lt RN	19-Feb-10	ENG	MESM	HMS TRIUMPH	
Mehta, Jennifer C	Lt RN	01-Jan-07	ENG	TM	NCHQ - NAVY CMD SEC	NCHQ
Mehta, Kim L	Lt Cdr	01-Oct-06	ENG	TM	NETS (E)	HMNB PORTSMOUTH
Meigh, Peter D	Lt RN	01-Sep-04	WAR	AAWO	HMS DIAMOND	
Melbourne, Steven MBE	Capt	01-Apr-04	RM	SCC	DMC DMOC	RAF HALTON
Meldrum, Richard A	Lt RN	01-Mar-09	ENG	MESM	DEFAC JSCSC	SHRIVENHAM
Melling, Paul G	Lt RN	01-Jun-10	WAR	P LYN7	847 SQN - AE	RNAS YEOVILTON
Mellor, Adrian J	Surg Cdr	30-Jun-03	MED	Anaes	MDHU NORTHALLERTON	
Mellor, Andrew L	Lt RN	16-Dec-11	WAR	INT	UKRBATSTAFF	HMNB PORTSMOUTH
Mellor, Daniel P	Lt RN	01-Sep-05	ENG	MESM	HMS VIGILANT	
Mellows, Christopher R	Mid	01-Nov-13	WAR	SM(X)	BRNC DARTMOUTH	
Melvin, John James	Lt RN	01-Aug-09	LOGS	L	HMS NELSON	
Mendham, Oliver D	Mid	01-Nov-12	WAR	GSX	BRNC DARTMOUTH	
Menzies, Bruce	Lt RN	01-Jul-01	WAR	P LYNX	OCLC ROSYTH	ABERDEEN
Mercer, Simon	Surg Cdr	02-Aug-11	MED	Anaes	RCDM	BIRMINGHAM
Meredith, Nicholas	Cdr	30-Jun-07	WAR	SM(CQ)	NATO-ACO-SHAPE	CASTEAU
Merewether, Henry A H	Cdr	30-Jun-04	WAR	O LYNX	NCHQ CNPS	NCHQ
Merritt, Jonathan J	Cdr	30-Jun-05	ENG	ME	DES/COMFLEET	ABBEY WOOD
Messenger, Gordon K DSO* OBE	Lt Gen	14-Jan-13	RM	MLDR	NATO-ACO-LC-IZMIR	ISTANBUL
Metcalf, Stephen W	Lt Cdr	01-Oct-08	ENG	MESM	DES/COMFLEET	HELENSBURGH

Person Name	Substantive Rank	Seniority	Branch	Specialisation	Organisation	Location
Metcalfe, Anthony P W	Lt Cdr	01-Dec-91	WAR	PWO(U)	LOAN DSTL - P&CSD	FAREHAM
Metcalfe, Liam M	Maj	01-Oct-09	RM	LC	LFSS CDO LOG REGT RM	BARNSTAPLE
Methven, Paul	Capt RN	26-Aug-08	ENG	MESM	DEFAC RCDS	LONDON
Meyer, Alexander J	Lt Cdr	01-Oct-06	WAR	PWO(C)	HMS DIAMOND	
Middleditch, Thomas C	Lt RN	01-Sep-09	ENG	ME	DES/COMFLEET	HNMB PORTMOUTH
Middleton, Christopher S MBE	Lt Col	30-Jun-10	RM	LC	30 CDO IX GP RM	PLYMOUTH
Middleton, Edward J	Capt	01-Sep-08	RM	GS	COMUKAMPHIBFOR	HMNB PORTSMOUTH
Middleton, John R	Capt	01-Sep-08	RM	GS	42 CDO RM	HMNB DEVONPORT
Middleton, Mark A	Lt Cdr	01-Oct-12	MED	MS(CDO)	MED SQN CDO	BARNSTAPLE
Middleton, Shane	Lt RN	30-Jul-10	ENG	WE	DEFENCE	SHRIVENHAM
Middleton, Simon W	Surg Lt Cdr	11-Sep-08	MED	T&O	INM ALVERSTOKE	GOSPORT
Middleton, Wayne T	Lt Cdr	01-Oct-07	LOGS	L	US CENTCOM	USA TAMPA
Midwinter, Mark CBE	Surg Capt RN	01-Sep-07	MED	GS	DMS WHITTINGTON	BIRMINGHAM
Mifflin, Michelle J	Lt RN	01-Jan-05	WAR	PWO	HMS PORTLAND	
Milburn, Philip K	Capt RN	04-Nov-09	WAR	PWO(A)	COMPORFLOT SEA	HMNB PORTSMOUTH
Mildener, Lee D	Capt	30-Mar-12	RM	SCC	45 CDO RM	DUNDEE
Miles, Alexander S	Lt RN	01-Apr-12	WAR	SM(X)	HMS ASTUTE	
Miles, Emma K	Lt RN	01-Apr-12	ENG	ME	HMS ST ALBANS	
Miles, Gary A MBE	Lt RN	11-Apr-08	ENG	ME	COMPORFLOT	HMNB PORTSMOUTH
Miles, Graham J	Lt Cdr	07-Aug-00	ENG	AE	NATO ACO	NORTHWOOD
Miles, Philip	Lt Cdr	01-Oct-06	LOGS	L	PJHQ (UK) J5	NORTHWOOD
Miles, Sean A	Surg Lt Cdr	17-May-07	MED	GMP	NCHQ	
Milkins, Kiel	Lt RN	13-Dec-13	ENG	WE	HMS BULWARK	
Millar, Gary D	SLt	01-Nov-11	WAR	GSX	BRNC DARTMOUTH	
Millar, Jennifer A	Surg Lt Cdr	06-Aug-13	MED	GMP	INM ALVERSTOKE	GOSPORT
Millar, Kevin I	Lt Cdr	01-Oct-07	ENG	MESM	DES/COMFLEET	HELENSBURGH
Millar, Stuart W S	Surg Capt RN	22-Apr-10	MED	GMP (C&S)	DMSTG	ALDERSHOT
Millard, Jeremy	Lt Cdr	01-Oct-07	ENG	ME	LSP ON	MUSCAT (BOX 014)
Millen, Stuart C MBE	Lt Cdr	01-Oct-05	WAR	P SK6	849 SQN	RNAS CULDROSE
Miller, Adam E	Lt RN	09-Apr-10	ENG	AE	RNAS CULDROSE	
Miller, Alexander D	Lt RN	01-May-06	LOGS	L SM	HMS NELSON	
Miller, Andrew J CBE	Capt RN	01-Jun-00	WAR	N/A	FLEET FOSNNI	BRISTOL
Miller, Andrew P	Capt	03-Apr-09	RM	GS	NCHQ	
Miller, Colin R	Cdr	30-Jun-07	WAR	O MER	FLEET COMOPS NWD	NORTHWOOD
Miller, David J	Lt RN	08-Jul-11	ENG	ME	HMS NELSON	HMS NELSON
Miller, Ian	Lt Cdr	01-Jan-08	ENG	MESM	DSEA DNSR	ABBEY WOOD
Miller, Kevin R	Lt Cdr	01-Oct-10	ENG	WE	COMPORFLOT SEA	HMNB PORTSMOUTH
Miller, Mandy C	Lt Cdr	01-Oct-04	ENG	WE	HMS NELSON	
Miller, Paul D	Lt Cdr	01-Feb-01	WAR	INT	UKRBATSTAFF	HMNB PORTSMOUTH
Miller, Rosalyn C	Surg Lt RN	01-Aug-12	MED	MEDICAL	BRNC DARTMOUTH	
Miller, Ross J	Lt RN	01-Sep-12	ENG	MESM	HMS AMBUSH	
Miller, Sasha L	Lt Cdr	01-Oct-12	WAR	INT	PJHQ (UK) J2	NORTHWOOD
Miller, Shane N	Lt RN	24-Nov-09	ENG	AE	PROJECT WINFRA	RNAS YEOVILTON
Milles, Olivia K	Lt RN	16-Aug-01	WAR	P SK4	RAF SHAWBURY	SHREWSBURY
Milligan, Robert J	SLt	19-Jan-11	WAR	SM(X)	HMS PROTECTOR	
Milligan, Robert J	Lt Cdr	01-Oct-08	WAR	O LYNX	ABBEY WOOD	BRISTOL
Mills, Andrew	Lt Cdr	01-May-95	WAR	MEDIA OPS	NPT RES	HMNB PORTSMOUTH
Mills, Gary	Lt Cdr	01-Oct-07	ENG	GSX	NATO-ACT-HQ SACT	NORFOLK
Mills, Gregory	Mid	01-Nov-13	WAR	HM	BRNC DARTMOUTH	
Mills, Scott A	Maj	01-Oct-13	RM	SCC	HASLER COY	HMS DRAKE
Mills, William S	SLt	01-May-11	WAR	HM	HMS DARING	
Millward, Elliott J	Mid	01-Sep-13	ENG	ME	BRNC DARTMOUTH	
Millyard, Matthew	Lt RN	01-Oct-11	WAR	GSX	RN EXCHANGE USA - BDS	WASHINGTON
Miln, David	Lt RN	01-May-11	WAR	GSX	MWS DDS	PORTSMOUTH
Milne, Andre P	Lt Cdr	01-Oct-09	WAR	P LYN7	845 SQN	RNAS YEOVILTON
Milne, Anthony	Capt	18-Apr-07	RM	GS	NCHQ	
Milne, Charlotte L	Lt RN	07-Jun-12	ENG	AE	RNAS YEOVILTON	
Milne, Jason R	Maj	01-Oct-10	RM	MLDR	HQ SQN CDO LOG REGT	BARNSTAPLE
Milne, Roderick M	Lt RN	01-Mar-10	WAR	GSX	HMS ST ALBANS	
Milner, Lisa D	Lt RN	01-Mar-06	ENG	TM	RNAS YEOVILTON	
Milner, Robert A	Surg Cdr	01-Jul-09	MED	Occ Med	NCHQ MEDDIV	NCHQ
Milnes, Grant	SLt	01-Feb-11	WAR	GSX	HMS DEFENDER	

Person Name	Substantive Rank	Seniority	Branch	Specialisation	Organisation	Location
Milsom, Jonathan	Lt Cdr	01-Oct-99	ENG	AE	DSAE COSFORD	WOLVERHAMPTON
Milsom, Matthew L	SLt	01-Sep-11	ENG	AE	DCEME SULTAN	
Milton, Michael E	SLt	22-Apr-12	WAR	GSX	HMS DAUNTLESS	
Mimpriss, Graham D	Cdr	30-Jun-10	WAR	HM (H CH)	DES/COMFLEET	ABBEY WOOD
Minall, Paul A	Surg Cdr (D)	24-Jul-06	DENTAL	GDP	DDS PORTSMOUTH PDO	HMNB PORTSMOUTH
Minns, Robert J	SLt	01-May-12	WAR	GSX	BRNC DARTMOUTH	
Minshall, Darren M	Surg Lt Cdr	02-Aug-10	MED	Psych	INM ALVERSTOKE	GOSPORT
Minty, Darren	Lt Cdr	01-Oct-12	ENG	ME	DCEME SULTAN	
Mion, Jonathan J	Lt RN	01-Sep-11	WAR	GSX	MCM2 CREW 7	PORTSMOUTH
Misiak, Anna L	Lt Cdr	01-Oct-10	LOGS	L	HMS NELSON	
Mitchell, Aleesha W	Lt RN	01-Feb-09	ENG	WE	DES/COMFLEET	ABBEY WOOD
Mitchell, Andrew J	Lt RN	01-Feb-08	WAR	O MER	750 SQN SEAHAWK	RNAS CULDROSE
Mitchell, Hannah M	Lt RN	01-Sep-08	ENG	AE	DES/COMJE/HELS	ABBEY WOOD
Mitchell, Henry	Cdr	30-Jun-01	WAR	P SHAR	DCDC	SHRIVENHAM
Mitchell, James E	Lt RN	01-Oct-11	WAR	GSX	HMS IRON DUKE	
Mitchell, Jamie	Lt Cdr	01-Oct-08	WAR	SM(CQ)	RNSMS	HMS RALEIGH
Mitchell, Paul J	Lt RN	01-May-03	WAR	HM	RNAS YEOVILTON	
Mitchell, Scott C	Lt RN	28-Jul-06	WAR	AE	DES/COMJE	RNAS YEOVILTON
Mitchell, Stephen D	Lt Cdr	01-Oct-01	ENG	MESM	NCHQ CNPERS	PORTSMOUTH
Mitchell, Stuart J	Capt	01-Sep-11	RM	GS	ARMOURED SUPPORT GROUP	RNAS YEOVILTON
Mitchell-Heggs, Hugo C	Lt RN	07-Jun-12	ENG	MESM	DCEME SULTAN	HMS SULTAN
Mittins, Simon	Lt RN	01-May-03	WAR	ATC	RNAS YEOVILTON	
Moat, Richard	Capt	01-Sep-11	RM	GS	45 CDO RM - Z COY	DUNDEE
Mobbs, Thomas	Capt	01-Sep-08	RM	GS	DMC DMOC	RAF HALTON
Moffatt, Neil R	Cdr	30-Jun-02	ENG	MESM	DES/COMFLEET	HMNB DEVONPORT
Moffatt, Roger	Lt Cdr	01-Oct-95	WAR	P MER	824 SQN - CTT	RNAS CULDROSE
Mole, Andrew J	Lt Cdr	01-Oct-11	ENG	MESM	HMS VICTORIOUS	
Molnar, Richard M	Lt Cdr	01-Oct-06	WAR	AAWO	FLEET CAP IS DIVISION	NCHQ
Moloney, Benjamin G	Lt RN	08-Nov-07	WAR	GSX	HMS PORTLAND	
Money, Christopher J	Lt Cdr	01-Oct-10	WAR	HM (M CH)	FLEET COMOPS NWD	NORTHWOOD
Money, John Charles	RN Chpln	12-Aug-13	Ch S	Chaplain	CTCRM	EXMOUTH
Monger, Paul D	Lt Cdr	21-May-95	WAR	HM	RNAS CULDROSE - MET	RNAS CULDROSE
Monnox, Jill	Lt Cdr	01-Oct-08	WAR	PWO(A)	NCHQ CNPS	NCHQ
Montagu, Timothy B	Lt RN	01-Jan-07	WAR	GSX	UKLTT	AFGHANISTAN KABUL
Montgomery, Harvie E	Lt Cdr	01-Oct-13	WAR	TM	HMS QUEEN ELIZABETH	ROSYTH
Moody, Alistair V	Lt Cdr	01-Oct-06	ENG	MESM	DEFAC JSCSC ACSC	SHRIVENHAM
Moody, David C	Cdr	30-Jun-12	ENG	WE	FLEET CISSU	NCHQ
Moore, Aimee C	Lt RN	20-Feb-11	LOGS	L	COMFASFLOT	HMNB CLYDE
Moore, Alison L	Lt RN	20-Oct-06	WAR	PWO	MWS COLLINGWOOD	
Moore, Benjamin A	Capt	01-Apr-11	RM	GS	MOD DEFENCE STAFF	LONDON
Moore, Christopher I	Cdr	30-Jun-99	WAR	AAWO	MWS COLLINGWOOD	
Moore, Christopher J	Capt	01-Aug-07	RM	GS	OCLC ROSYTH	HMS CALEDONIA
Moore, Jonathan P	Lt RN	01-Jun-06	WAR	P SK4	CHF(MERLIN)	RAF BENSON
Moore, Jordan P	Mid	01-Nov-13	WAR	GSX	BRNC DARTMOUTH	
Moore, Martin	Cdr	30-Jun-12	WAR	PWO(U)	NCHQ CNPERS	PORTSMOUTH
Moore, Matthew J	Lt Cdr	01-Oct-08	WAR	MCD PWO	MCM1 CREW 8	FASLANE
Moore, Paul	Surg Cdr (D)	10-Jul-07	DENTAL	GDP	RN GIBRALTAR - SDS	GIBRALTAR
Moore, Piers H G	Cdr	30-Jun-09	WAR	SM(AWC)	NATO-ACO-SHAPE	CASTEAU
Moore, Richard G	Capt	01-Sep-06	RM	P SK4	845 SQN	RNAS YEOVILTON
Moore, Robert W	Lt RN	01-Apr-11	WAR	FC	HMS DIAMOND	
Moore, Sean	Cdr	30-Jun-12	LOGS	L BAR	NCHQ - CNLS	NCHQ
Moore, Suzanne K	Cdr	30-Jun-11	WAR	PWO(U)	COMPORFLOT	HMNB PORTSMOUTH
Moore, William I	Capt	01-Sep-04	RM	P LYN7	847 SQN - AE	RNAS YEOVILTON
Moorey, Christopher	Cdr	30-Jun-07	WAR	PWO(A)	ATTACHE/ADVISE BAHRAIN	
Moorhouse, Edward	Lt Col	30-Jun-11	RM	GS	BDS WASHINGTON - NA	WASHINGTON
Moorhouse, Stephen	Cdr	30-Jun-10	WAR	O SKW	FMC - STRAT N	MAIN BUILDING LONDON
Moran, Benjamin M	Lt Cdr	01-Oct-13	WAR	SM(AWC)	COMFASFLOT	HMNB CLYDE
Moran, Craig A	Lt Cdr	01-Oct-06	WAR	REG	RNP - HQ PMN	PORTSMOUTH
Moran, John-Paul	Lt Cdr	01-Oct-13	ENG	AE	MOD CNS/ACNS	RNAS YEOVILTON
Moran, Julian Toby	Maj	01-Oct-06	RM		DIRECTOR (JW)	NORTHWOOD
Moran, Russell J	Lt Cdr	01-Oct-08	WAR	PWO	MWS COLLINGWOOD	
Moreland, James R	Lt RN	01-Oct-08	ENG	MESM	DES/COMFLEET	ABBEY WOOD BRISTOL

Person Name	Substantive Rank	Seniority	Branch	Specialisation	Organisation	Location
Moreton, Samuel	Capt	01-Sep-13	RM	GS	42 CDO RM	HMNB DEVONPORT
Morey, Kevin N	Lt Cdr	01-Nov-09	WAR	PWO(N)	FOST DPORT SEA	HMNB DEVONPORT
Morgan, Ashley K	Lt RN	01-May-10	WAR	O LYNX	815 SQN B	RNAS YEOVILTON
Morgan, Benjamin P	Lt RN	01-Jan-02	WAR	P MER	824 SQN - TU	RNAS CULDROSE
Morgan, Christopher W	Lt Cdr	01-Oct-11	WAR	SM(AWC)	MWS COLLINGWOOD	
Morgan, David H	Cdr	30-Jun-12	WAR	PWO(U)	FOST NWD	NORTHWOOD
Morgan, Edward J A	Lt Cdr	01-Oct-06	WAR	P SK4	CHFHQ (SEA)	RNAS YEOVILTON
Morgan, Gareth L	Lt RN	01-Sep-04	WAR	P SK4	848 SQN	RNAS YEOVILTON
Morgan, Henry L	Capt	01-Sep-11	RM	GS	CTCRM 6	EXMOUTH
Morgan, Huw L MBE	Maj	01-Oct-07	RM	SRR	DEFAC JSCSC ACSC	SWINDON
Morgan, Hywel R	Lt RN	01-Sep-12	WAR	HM	HMS ENTERPRISE	
Morgan, Michael C	Lt RN	31-Jul-09	ENG	AE	JARTS (RN)	SALISBURY
Morgan, Peter T DSC	Capt RN	30-Jun-06	WAR	PWO(A)	NATO - SHAPE - UKNMR	CASTEAU
Morgan, Stephen	Cdr	30-Jun-07	ENG	WE	LSP ON	MUSCAT (BOX 014)
Morgan, Tony G	Lt RN	01-Sep-12	ENG	WE	HMS DAUNTLESS	
Morgan-Hosey, John N	Lt Cdr	01-Oct-01	ENG	MESM	DES/COMFLEET	HMS DRAKE
Morley, Adrian Mc	Lt Col	30-Jun-12	RM	LC	NCHQ CNPERS	PORTSMOUTH
Morley, David J	Lt RN	11-Dec-09	MED	MS(CDO)	DMSTG	ALDERSHOT
Morley, James	Capt RN	26-Apr-10	WAR	PWO(A)	DEFENCE ACADEMY	SHRIVENHAM
Morley, James I	Lt Cdr	01-Nov-05	ENG	ME	DG FINANCE	MAIN BUILDING LONDON
Morphet, Kathryn	Lt RN	01-Jan-01	ENG	TM	NETS (N)	HELENSBURGH
Morris, Alastair J	Lt RN	27-Feb-11	WAR	INT	DHU	SHEFFORD
Morris, Alistair J	Surg Lt RN	03-Aug-09	MED	GMP	HMS DRAKE	
Morris, Andrew G	Capt	01-Sep-08	RM	GS	NCHQ	
Morris, Anthony M	Lt Cdr	01-Oct-07	WAR	P MER	824 SQN - TU	RNAS CULDROSE
Morris, Ashley R	Mid	01-Nov-13	WAR	P UT	BRNC DARTMOUTH	
Morris, Daniel R	Lt Cdr	01-Oct-11	WAR	MCD	MWS COLLINGWOOD	
Morris, David F	Capt	01-Sep-11	RM	GS	42 CDO RM	HMNB DEVONPORT
Morris, Gavin J	Lt RN	01-May-13	WAR	GSX	RNAS YEOVILTON	RNAS YEOVILTON
Morris, Harriet S	Lt Cdr	01-Oct-08	LOGS	L	DES/COMFLEET	HMNB PORTSMOUTH .
Morris, Harry A	Lt RN	01-Sep-13	WAR	GSX	MWS COLLINGWOOD	
Morris, James A DSO	Col	20-May-10	RM	GS	FMC - NAVY	MAIN BUILDING LONDON
Morris, James E	Maj	01-Oct-13	RM	GS	DEFAC JSCSC ICSCL	SHRIVENHAM
Morris, John O	RN Chpln	06-Oct-92	Ch S		43 CDO FPGRM COMD	HMNB CLYDE
Morris, Jonothan L	Mid	01-Nov-12	WAR	O UT	BRNC DARTMOUTH	
Morris, Joshua T	Lt RN	01-Sep-13	WAR	GSX	MWS COLLINGWOOD	
Morris, Louisa	Surg Lt Cdr	06-Aug-08	MED	GMP	DMS WHITTINGTON	BIRMINGHAM
Morris, Paul	Lt Col	30-Jun-07	RM	P LYN7	DEFENCE ACADEMY	SHRIVENHAM
Morris, Paul J	Lt Cdr	01-Oct-10	WAR	AAWO	HMS DUNCAN	
Morris, Paul W	Lt Cdr	01-Oct-13	WAR	AV	RNAS CULDROSE	
Morris, Richard C	Maj	01-Oct-09	RM	LC	NCHQ	
Morris, Richard J	Cdr	30-Jun-06	WAR	PWO(A)	CAREER TRAINING	SWINDON
Morris, Simon T	Cdr	30-Jun-06	ENG	WESM(TWS)	FLEET CAP SSM DIVISION	NCHQ
Morris, Thomas O	Lt RN	01-Jun-12	WAR	P SK4	845 SQN	RNAS YEOVILTON
Morrison, Alan P	Lt RN	01-May-13	WAR	SM(X)	HMS VANGUARD	
Morrison, Kevin	Lt RN	13-Apr-12	WAR	INT	857 NAS	RNAS CULDROSE
Morrison, Mark J	Lt RN	22-Jul-10	WAR	MCD	MCM1 CREW 2	FASLANE
Morrison, Paul	Lt Cdr	01-Oct-02	WAR	O MER	RN EXCHANGE AUSTRALIA	CANBERRA
Morrison, Philip C	Lt RN	31-Jul-09	LOGS	L	CAREER TRAINING	BEACONSFIELD
Morrison, Richard J	Lt RN	01-Apr-07	ENG	TM(SM)	NCHQ CNPS	PORTSMOUTH
Morrison, Ross	Lt RN	01-Nov-11	ENG	TM	HMS SULTAN - STG	HMS SULTAN
Morrison, Shaun	Lt Cdr	01-Oct-11	ENG	MESM	DSEA DNSR	ABBEY WOOD
Morritt, Dain C	Capt RN	30-Jun-08	ENG	WE	DES/COMFLEET	ABBEY WOOD
Morrow, Laura	Surg Lt RN	01-Aug-12	MED	MEDICAL	BRNC DARTMOUTH	
Morrow, Oliver	Lt RN	01-Jan-07	WAR	PWO(SM)	HMS VANGUARD	
Morse, Andrew C	Lt Cdr	01-Jan-92	WAR	O LYNX	RNAS YEOVILTON	
Morse, James	R Adm	28-Aug-12	WAR	PWO(N)	DEFENCE ACADEMY	SWINDON
Morse, Jeremy	Lt Cdr	01-Oct-09	WAR	P SK4	RNAS YEOVILTON	RNAS YEOVILTON
Mortlock, Philip	Lt Cdr	01-Oct-08	ENG	WESM(SWS)	ACDS (POL) USA	NEBRASKA
Morton, Charles E	Lt RN	01-Jan-13	WAR	SM(X)	HMS TORBAY	
Morton, David	Lt RN	15-Apr-11	ENG	ME	COMDEVFLOT ESG	HMS DRAKE
Morton, Justin	Maj	01-Oct-08	RM	SCC	HQ 3 CDO BDE RM	PLYMOUTH

Person Name	Substantive Rank	Seniority	Branch	Specialisation	Organisation	Location
Morton, Neil	Lt Cdr	01-Oct-13	WAR	INT	JMIC	HMS COLLINGWOOD
Morton, Nigel P	Cdr	30-Jun-99	LOGS	L	FOSNNI - YOUTH C	BRISTOL
Morton-King, Frederick W	SLt	01-May-13	WAR	O UT	HMS DUNCAN	
Moseley, James F	Lt RN	11-Apr-08	WAR	AV	HMS SULTAN - ATG	HMS SULTAN
Moseley, Stephen H	Lt Cdr	01-Oct-11	WAR	P MER	AWC BSD - RW TES	SALISBURY
Moses, Christopher	Capt	01-Aug-07	RM	GS	DES/COMFLEET/NBC	FASLANE
Moss, Jonathan	Lt Cdr	01-Oct-13	LOGS	L	HMS OCEAN	
Moss, Richard A	Cdr	30-Jun-06	WAR	O SK6	MOD NSD	MAIN BUILDING LONDON
Moss, Richard	Lt RN	01-Jan-02	ENG	TM	FLEET FOST ACOS	NCHQ
Moss, Stephanie	SLt	01-Mar-11	WAR	GSX	MCM1 CREW 7	FASLANE
Moss, Stewart J	Lt RN	11-Dec-09	ENG	MESM	HMS VENGEANCE	
Moss, Tyrone James	Mid	01-Nov-12	WAR	P UT	BRNC DARTMOUTH	
Moss-Ward, Edward G	Lt RN	01-Sep-06	WAR	GSX	MWS COLLINGWOOD	
Mould, Christopher W	Lt RN	01-Jan-11	WAR	P GR7	FLEET CSAV	WASHINGTON
Moulding, Mark D	Lt RN	17-Dec-10	ENG	MESM	HMS ARTFUL	BARROW IN FURNESS
Moules, Matthew A J	Lt Cdr	01-Aug-04	WAR	PWO	HMS KENT	
Moulton, Frederick	Col	23-Sep-13	RM	GS (RES)	FLEET CMR	NCHQ
Mounsey, Carl A	Lt RN	01-Jan-08	ENG	WE	HMS ILLUSTRIOUS	
Mount, James	Lt Cdr	01-Oct-12	WAR	P SK6	FLEET AV CU	RNAS YEOVILTON
Mowat, Andrew D J	Lt Cdr	01-Oct-13	LOGS	L	DMLS	HMS RALEIGH
Mowatt, Patrick	Cdr	30-Jun-13	WAR	HM (H CH)	HMS SCOTT	
Mowthorpe, Sarah L	Lt RN	19-Feb-08	WAR	HM	RNAS YEOVILTON - MET	RNAS YEOVILTON
Moxham, Glen A	2Lt	02-Sep-13	RM	N/A	CTCRM OFFICERS	EXMOUTH
Moyies, Scott A	Capt	03-Apr-08	RM	GS	NCHQ	
Moys, Andrew J	Lt Cdr	01-Oct-97	WAR	HM (M CH)	RNAS CULDROSE - MET	RNAS CULDROSE
Muddiman, Andrew R	Lt Col	30-Jun-12	RM	GS	FLEET COMOPS NWD	NORTHWOOD
Mudford, Hugh C	Lt Col	30-Jun-99	RM	GS	SAUDI ARABIA GCT	RIYADH
Mudge, Adrian M	Cdr	30-Jun-13	WAR	O SKW	UKRBATSTAFF	HMNB PORTSMOUTH
Muir, Andrew	Lt RN	01-Feb-06	ENG	ME	NAVY MCTA PORTSMOUTH	HMNB PORTSMOUTH
Muir, Katie M	Lt Cdr	01-Oct-13	WAR	GSX	MWS COLLINGWOOD	
Muir, Keith	Capt RN	18-Jul-11	WAR	O SKW	D CEPP	MAIN BUILDING LONDON
Mulcahy, Oliver J	Lt RN	01-Jul-12	ENG	WE	HMS NORTHUMBERLAND	
Mules, Anthony J	Lt Cdr	01-Mar-98	WAR	HM(AS)	HMS WILDFIRE	NORTHWOOD
Mullin, Laura E	SLt	01-May-11	LOGS	L	FOST DPORT SHORE	HMNB DEVONPORT
Mullins, Andrew D	Lt Cdr	01-Dec-04	ENG	MESM	DES/COMFLEET	HMS DRAKE
Mullis, Geoffrey	Lt RN	01-Jan-07	ENG	WESM(TWS)	RNSMS	HMS RALEIGH
Mulroy, Paul J	Lt RN	18-Feb-05	ENG	MESM	HMS SULTAN	HMS SULTAN
Mulvaney, Paul A	Cdr	30-Jun-08	ENG	AE	DCDS PERS TRG-RFC	MAIN BUILDING LONDON
Muncer, Richard	Maj	01-Oct-06	RM	GS	DEFAC JSCSC	SHRIVENHAM
Munday, Stephen W	Lt Cdr	01-Oct-10	ENG	WE	HMS ILLUSTRIOUS	
Mundy, Alan R	Lt Cdr	01-Oct-08	MED	MS(CDO)	DMSTG	ALDERSHOT
Munn-Bookless, Kerri	Lt RN	01-Feb-08	ENG	TM	BRNC DARTMOUTH	
Munns, Andrew R	Cdr	30-Jun-03	ENG	ME	COMPORFLOT SEA	HMNB PORTSMOUTH
Munns, Edward N	Lt RN	01-Sep-06	WAR	GSX	FASLANE PBS	HELENSBURGH
Munro, Angus R	Lt RN	01-Apr-08	WAR	GSX	HMS RICHMOND	
Munro, Michael	Lt RN	01-Jul-04	WE		HMS QUEEN ELIZABETH	ROSYTH
Munro-Lott, Peter R	Cdr	30-Jun-06	WAR	O MER	RNAS CULDROSE - ADM	RNAS CULDROSE
Munson, Jason S	Lt RN	01-Sep-13	WAR	GSX	MWS COLLINGWOOD	
Murchie, Alistair D	Lt Cdr	01-Oct-03	ENG	ME	AIB	HMS SULTAN
Murchison, Ewen A DSO MBE	Col	04-Sep-12	RM	GS	TIO	LONDON
Murdoch, Andrew W	Cdr	30-Jun-05	ENG	WESM	FLEET CAP SSM DIVISION	NCHQ
Murdoch, Hannah	SLt	01-Apr-12	WAR	GSX	HMS LANCASTER	
Murgatroyd, Jenna C	Surg Lt RN (D)	28-Jul-09	DENTAL	GDP	CDO LOG REGT RM	BARNSTAPLE
Murgatroyd, Kevin J	Lt Cdr	01-Oct-10	WAR	O MER	824 SQN - CTT	RNAS CULDROSE
Murgatroyd, Steven A	Lt RN	31-Jul-09	ENG	AE	HMS SULTAN - ATG	HMS SULTAN
Murphy, Alan J	Lt RN	01-Sep-12	ENG	AE	845 SQN	RNAS YEOVILTON
Murphy, Caroline R	Lt RN	01-Jul-03	ENG	TM	NCHQ CNPERS	HMNB PORTSMOUTH
Murphy, Christian J	Lt Cdr	01-Oct-12	ENG	AE	HQ AIR - HQ 1GP	ABBEY WOOD
Murphy, Christopher M	Lt RN	13-Jun-08	MED	MS(CDO)	MDHU DERRIFORD	PLYMOUTH
Murphy, Dennis E	Lt RN	01-Jan-12	WAR	SM(X)	HMS TIRELESS	
Murphy, Kian S	Maj	01-Oct-05	RM	GS	EXCHANGE - FRANCE	PARIS
Murphy, Martin J	Lt RN	20-Dec-08	LOGS	L SM	FLEET FOSNNI - NRC	HMS CALEDONIA

Person Name	Substantive Rank	Seniority	Branch	Specialisation	Organisation	Location
Murphy, Paul A	Cdr	30-Jun-08	LOGS	L C SM	MOD CNS/ACNS	MAIN BUILDING LONDON
Murphy, Steven R	Lt Cdr	01-Sep-98	WAR	SM(CQ)	DES/COMFLEET	ABBEY WOOD
Murphy, Thomas C	SLt	01-Nov-11	LOGS	L	BRNC DARTMOUTH	
Murray, Alister	Cdr	14-Oct-12	MED	MS	NCHQ CNPERS	PORTSMOUTH
Murray, Andrew S AFC	Lt Cdr	01-Oct-99	WAR	P SK6	857 NAS	RNAS CULDROSE
Murray, Edward A	Lt RN	01-Sep-13	ENG	MESM	DCEME SULTAN	HMS SULTAN
Murray, Grant M	Cdr	30-Jun-10	ENG	WESM(TWS)	PJHQ (UK) CMSA	NORTHWOOD
Murray, Greig M	Lt Cdr	01-Oct-11	WAR	PWO	HMS OCEAN	
Murray, Jamie C	Lt RN	01-May-07	WAR	P SK6	GANNET SAR FLT	PRESTWICK
Murray, Lee Stuart	Capt	01-Apr-11	RM	MLDR (SCC)	LOANS TO OTHER GOVTS	CZECH
Murray, Sara N	Lt RN	15-Apr-11	MED	MS	HMS SULTAN	
Murray, Simon D	Capt	01-Sep-04	RM	P SK4	RNAS CULDROSE	
Murray, Simon O	Lt RN	01-Sep-10	WAR	MESM	HMS TALENT	
Murray, Stephen J OBE	Lt Cdr	02-Nov-89	WAR	O MER	824 SQN - TU	RNAS CULDROSE
Murray, William	Lt RN	01-May-04	WAR	P SK4	RN EXCHANGE GERMANY	BERLIN
Murray, William J	Mid	01-Nov-13	WAR	GSX	BRNC DARTMOUTH	
Murrison, Richard A	Capt RN	16-May-11	LOGS	L	DEFAC RCDS	LONDON
Musgrave, Thomas E	Lt RN	21-Mar-10	WAR	GSX	HMS DRAGON	
Musgrove, Christopher	Lt RN	01-Sep-11	WAR	GSX	CTF 150	HMNB PORTSMOUTH
Musto, Edward C	Lt Col	31-Dec-96	RM	HW	HMS COLLINGWOOD	
Muyambo, Nomalanga N	Lt RN	01-Jan-00	WAR	TM	NCHQ CNPERS	HMNB PORTSMOUTH
Myatt, Richard W	Surg Lt RN	01-Aug-12	MED	MEDICAL	BRNC DARTMOUTH	
Myhill, James E	Lt RN	01-Jan-12	WAR	GSX	MCM2 CREW 1	PORTSMOUTH
Myhill, Johnathen J	Lt RN	19-Dec-08	ENG	AE	CHF(MERLIN)	RAF BENSON

N

Person Name	Substantive Rank	Seniority	Branch	Specialisation	Organisation	Location
Naden, Andrew C	Cdr	30-Jun-02	ENG	ME	DES/COMFLEET	ABBEY WOOD
Napier, Duncan J	SLt	01-May-11	WAR	HM	HMS MONTROSE	
Napier, Gary	Lt RN	08-Jul-11	ENG	WESM(TWS)	HMS TALENT	
Napier, Graham	Cdr	30-Jun-11	ENG	AE	DES/COIR/CA	WASHINGTON
Nash, Ian D E	SLt	01-Feb-12	LOGS	L	HMS RALEIGH	
Nash, Philip D	Cdr	30-Jun-10	WAR	O LYNX	HMS DEFENDER	
Nash, Robin D C	Lt RN	01-Jan-02	WAR	HM(AS)	HMS PROTECTOR	
Nash, Rubin P	Lt RN	01-Jan-02	WAR	PWO	HMS COLLINGWOOD	
Nash, Russell F	Lt Cdr	01-Oct-11	ENG	WESM(TWS)	DES/COMFLEET	ABBEY WOOD
Nason, Thomas J	Lt RN	01-Sep-10	WAR	P SK4	845 SQN	RNAS YEOVILTON
Naylor, Andrew J	Lt Cdr	01-Oct-08	WAR	P MER	814 SQN	RNAS CULDROSE
Neal, Gareth P	Lt RN	01-Sep-12	WAR	O UT	849 SQN	RNAS CULDROSE
Neal, Simon M	Lt Cdr	01-Oct-03	WAR	O MER	NCHQ CNPERS	PORTSMOUTH
Neave, Andrew M	Cdr	30-Jun-13	WAR	ATC	ABBEYWOOD BRISTOL	ABBEY WOOD BRISTOL
Neave, James R	Lt RN	01-Dec-07	WAR	P SK6	771 SQN	RNAS CULDROSE
Necker, Carl D	Cdr	30-Jun-09	WAR	PWO(N)	DES/COMFLEET	HMS DRAKE
Needle, Peter J	Lt RN	01-Oct-10	WAR	GSX	MWS DDS	PORTSMOUTH
Negus, Trystram W	Lt RN	01-Mar-12	WAR	P UT	RNAS YEOVILTON	RNAS YEOVILTON
Neil, Alexander G	Lt RN	20-May-08	WAR	MW	MCM1 CREW 4	FASLANE
Neilan, Samuel J	Lt RN	01-Mar-12	ENG	MESM	BDS WASHINGTON	WASHINGTON
Neild, Timothy	Cdr	30-Jun-12	WAR	PWO(C)	DEFAC CMT	SHRIVENHAM
Neilly, Patrick	Lt RN	01-Sep-12	WAR	SM(N)	HMS VICTORIOUS	
Neilson, Daniel J	Lt RN	22-Jan-13	WAR	MW	MCM1 CREW 3	FASLANE
Neilson, Robert D	Mid	01-Nov-13	WAR	GSX	BRNC DARTMOUTH	
Nekrews, Alan N QGM	Lt Cdr	01-Oct-10	WAR	MCD	DI - CA	LONDON
Nelson, Bartholomew J	Lt RN	01-Sep-09	ENG	MESM	COMDEVFLOT SHORE	HMNB DEVONPORT
Nelson, Christopher S	Lt Cdr	01-Mar-01	WAR	PWO(N)	COMUKTG SEA	PLYMOUTH
Nelson, Matthew R	Lt Cdr	01-Oct-12	WAR	P LYNX	FLEET CSAV	NCHQ
Nelson, Paul M	Lt Cdr	01-Oct-05	ENG	TM	FLEET FOST ACOS	NCHQ
Nelstrop, Andrew	Surg Cdr	11-Feb-11	MED	GMP	DEFAC JSCSC ACSC	SHRIVENHAM
Netherwood, Lyndsey D	Lt Cdr	15-Jan-07	WAR	PWO(U)	HMS IRON DUKE	
Nettleingham, Jamie L	SLt	09-Apr-12	WAR	ATC	903 EAW (BASTION)	AFGHANISTAN BASTION
Neve, Piers	Lt Cdr	11-Feb-94	WAR	SM(CQ)	RN EXCHANGE USA	WASHINGTON USA
New, Christopher M	Cdr	30-Jun-10	ENG	ME	NCHQ CNPS	NCHQ
New, Richard	Lt Cdr	01-Oct-07	LOGS	L SM	DEFAC JSCSC ACSC	SHRIVENHAM
Newall, Paul John	Lt RN	01-Sep-02	ENG	TM	DES/COMFLEET	ABBEY WOOD

Person Name	Substantive Rank	Seniority	Branch	Specialisation	Organisation	Location
Newbury, James S	Lt RN	03-May-13	ENG	AE	RNAS YEOVILTON	RNAS YEOVILTON
Newby, Christopher	Lt RN	01-Jan-05	WAR	O MER	824 SQN - TU	RNAS CULDROSE
Newell, Gary D	Lt Cdr	01-Oct-09	ENG	ME	COMPORFLOT	PORTSMOUTH
Newell, Jonathan M MBE	Cdre	02-Apr-12	ENG	ME	DES/COMFLEET	ABBEY WOOD
Newell, Phillip	Lt Cdr	01-Jun-01	WAR	HM (H CH)	HMS ECHO	
Newlands, Kathryn R	Surg SLt	19-Jul-13	MED	MEDICAL	BRNC DARTMOUTH	
Newlands, Kristoffer G	SLt	27-Jan-12	WAR	FC	MWS COLLINGWOOD	
Newman, Lee	Lt RN	15-Apr-11	WAR	HM	BRNC DARTMOUTH	
Newman, Paul Henry	Lt Cdr	01-May-89	WAR	METOC	RNAS CULDROSE	
Newman, Virginia H	Lt Cdr	01-Oct-09	WAR	MEDIA OPS	OHQ	NORTHWOOD
Newns, Adam David	Lt RN	01-Jul-09	ENG	WE	BRNC DARTMOUTH	DARTMOUTH
Newton, Garry A	Cdr	27-Mar-00	WAR	SM(CQ)	FLEET COMOPS NWD	HUNTINGDON
Newton, James L DFC	Cdr	30-Jun-11	WAR	P SK4	RNAS YEOVILTON	RNAS YEOVILTON
Newton, Nicholas J P	Surg Lt Cdr	06-Aug-08	MED	GS	INM ALVERSTOKE	GOSPORT
Newton, Owen	Lt RN	01-Feb-08	WAR	FC	1 AIR CTRL CENTRE	LINCOLN
Neyland, David A	Lt RN	01-Sep-04	WAR	P LYNX	LHF 700W SQN	RNAS YEOVILTON
Neylen, Serena L	Mid	01-May-13	WAR	GSX	BRNC DARTMOUTH	
Nguyo, David N	Lt RN	01-Sep-02	ENG	WE	DES/COMJE	CORSHAM
Niblock, Gillian	Lt RN	09-Nov-11	WAR	MTO N (RES)	FOSNNI NRC EE - LOND	LONDON
Nicholls, Barry A	Lt Col	30-Jun-11	RM	SCC	FLEET DCS - RNIO	HMS COLLINGWOOD
Nicholls, Edward W	Lt RN	12-Nov-10	WAR	ATC	RNAS YEOVILTON - AS	RNAS YEOVILTON
Nicholls, Larry R	Lt Cdr	01-Oct-11	ENG	WE	MWS COLLINGWOOD	HMS COLLINGWOOD
Nicholson, Brian H	Lt Cdr	01-Oct-09	ENG	AE	DES/COMJE/HELS	RNAS YEOVILTON
Nicholson, Christopher J	Lt RN	31-Jul-09	MED	MS	COMUKTG SEA	PLYMOUTH
Nicholson, David P	Maj	01-Sep-05	RM	LC	DEFAC JSCSC ACSC	SHRIVENHAM
Nicholson, Graeme	Surg Cdr	31-Dec-00	MED	Occ Med	DMS WHITTINGTON	LICHFIELD
Nicholson, Kristin J	Cdr	30-Jun-09	LOGS	L	NCHQ CNPERS	PORTSMOUTH
Nicklin, Gareth	Lt Cdr	01-Oct-08	ENG	MESM	DES/COMFLEET	ABBEY WOOD
Nicoll, Mac A	Lt RN	01-Jan-12	WAR	P UT	RAF SHAWBURY	
Nicolson, Vernon	Lt RN	03-May-05	WAR	OP INT	DEF LANG SCHOOL	BEACONSFIELD
Nielsen, Erik M	Maj	01-Oct-13	RM	SCC	RMB STONEHOUSE	PLYMOUTH
Nielsen, Suzi	Lt Cdr	01-Oct-09	LOGS	L	PJHQ (UK) J1/J4	NORTHWOOD
Nightingale, Christopher J	Capt	01-Sep-11	RM	GS	43 CDO FPGRM S SQN	HMNB CLYDE
Nightingale, Matthew A	Mid	01-Nov-13	WAR	P UT	BRNC DARTMOUTH	
Nightingale, Samuel	Lt RN	01-Jan-05	WAR	GSX	MWS COLLINGWOOD	
Nimmons, Paul MBE	Lt Cdr	01-Oct-05	ENG	MESM	COMDEVFLOT SHORE	HMNB DEVONPORT
Nisbet, James H	Cdr	30-Jun-03	WAR	MCD PWO(U)	DMC	MAIN BUILDING LONDON
Nixon, Alexander J	Capt	01-Aug-08	RM	GS	40 CDO RM	TAUNTON
Nixon, Sebastian W	Surg Lt RN	04-Aug-10	MED	GDMO	MEDICAL	RNAS CULDROSE
Noakes, Kevin M	Lt Cdr	30-Jun-11	ENG	WE	COMPORFLOT SEA	HMNB PORTSMOUTH
Noble, Robert	Lt RN	04-Jun-08	WAR	PWO(SM)	HMS VIGILANT	
Noble, Simon J	Lt RN	01-Jun-13	WAR	ATC	RNAS CULDROSE	RNAS CULDROSE
Noble, Tom M	Maj	01-Oct-12	RM	GS	COMUKAMPHIBFOR	HMNB PORTSMOUTH
Noblett, Peter G A	Lt Cdr	01-Oct-01	WAR	SM(CQ)	DEF SCH OF LANG	BEACONSFIELD
Nokes, Oliver	Lt RN	01-Sep-06	WAR	GSX	MWS COLLINGWOOD	
Nolan, Andrew J	Lt RN	03-May-13	ENG	ME	DCEME SULTAN	HMS SULTAN
Nolan, Paul E MBE	Maj	01-Oct-08	RM	P LYN7	WILDCAT FORCE	RNAS YEOVILTON
Nolan, Samuel T	Lt RN	01-Jun-13	WAR	GSX	MCTC (ARMY)	COLCHESTER
Noon, David MBE	Lt Cdr	01-Oct-03	LOGS	L	NATO-ACO-JFC HQ	NAPLES
Noonan, Charles D	Lt Cdr	01-Oct-10	WAR	MCD	FOST MPV SEA	HELENSBURGH
Norcott, James P	Lt RN	01-Sep-09	ENG	TM	42 CDO RM	
Norcott, William R	Maj	01-Oct-10	RM	HW	SFSG F COY	RAF ST ATHAN
Norgan, David J	Lt Cdr	01-Jul-01	WAR	PWO(C)	FOST NWD	NORTHWOOD
Norgate, Andrew T	Lt Cdr	01-Nov-06	WAR	HM	HMS ENTERPRISE	
Norkett, Luke T	2Lt	02-Sep-13	RM	N/A	CTCRM OFFICERS	EXMOUTH
Norman, Jaimie MDSO	Maj	01-Oct-08	RM	GS	DEFAC JSCSC ACSC	SHRIVENHAM
Norris, Guy P	Lt Cdr	01-Oct-08	WAR	O SK6	771 SQN	RNAS CULDROSE
Norris, James M	SLt	10-Nov-13	WAR	GSX	HMS DEFENDER	
Norris, Paul A MBE MC	Capt	30-Mar-12	RM	GS	NCHQ	
Norris, Richard E	Surg Capt RN (D)	26-Oct-04	DENTAL	GDP(C&S)	HQ DPHC - OVERSEAS	LICHFIELD
Norriss, Mark W	Lt RN	01-Jan-05	WAR	P SK4	18 SQN - OPS	RAF ODIHAM
North, Adam C	Lt Cdr	01-Oct-12	ENG	AE	FLEET CSAV	NCHQ

Person Name	Substantive Rank	Seniority	Branch	Specialisation	Organisation	Location
Northcote, Mark	Lt RN	01-Dec-00	WAR	MCD	RN EXCHANGE AUSTRALIA	CANBERRA AUSTRALIA
Northcott, Philip J	Lt Cdr	20-Apr-10	ENG	MESM	DES/COMFLEET	BARROW IN FURNESS
Northover, Adam F	Lt Cdr	01-Aug-05	WAR	PWO(N)	MWS COLLINGWOOD	HMS COLLINGWOOD
Norton, Ian A	Lt Cdr	01-Oct-11	ENG	AE	RNAS YEOVILTON - AED	RNAS YEOVILTON
Norton, Lee A	Lt RN	01-Oct-08	ENG	TM	RNLA	DARTMOUTH
Notley, Edward J	Lt RN	01-Jan-03	WAR	SM(AWC)	HMS DRAKE	
Nottingham, James M	Lt RN	01-Feb-08	WAR	P LYN7	847 SQN - AE	RNAS YEOVILTON
Nottley, Simon M	Lt Cdr	01-Oct-06	ENG	WESM	FLEET COMOPS NWD	NORTHWOOD
Noyce, Nigel	Lt Cdr	15-Jan-97	WAR	INT	JFIG - JT PLANS & FD	RAF WYTON
Noyce, Roger MBE	Cdr	30-Jun-13	WAR	INT	DCDC	SHRIVENHAM
Nutt, William J	Capt	01-Sep-09	RM	GS	CTCRM	EXMOUTH
Nutting, Christopher J	Capt	01-Sep-13	RM	GS	42 CDO RM - DGHR(O)	NCHQ
Nwokora, Dal	Lt RN	01-Mar-09	ENG	AE P	RNAS YEOVILTON	RNAS YEOVILTON

O

Person Name	Substantive Rank	Seniority	Branch	Specialisation	Organisation	Location
Oakes, Caroline F	Lt RN	01-Sep-11	WAR	O SKW	SF	RNAS CULDROSE
Oakes, Ian J	Lt Cdr	01-Oct-05	WAR	P LYN7	DEF HELI FLYING SCH	RAF SHAWBURY
Oakes, Philippe A	Lt RN	01-Jan-12	WAR	GSX	HMS MERSEY	
Oakey, Dean	Lt RN	08-Jun-07	WAR	REG	HMS COLLINGWOOD	HMS COLLINGWOOD
Oakley, Andrew	Lt Cdr	01-Oct-09	ENG	TM	JFC - DCTS (H)	RAF HALTON
Oakley, Christopher G	Lt RN	01-Nov-12	WAR	SM(X)	HMS ASTUTE	
Oakley, Claire	Lt Cdr	01-Oct-08	WAR	HM(AM)	FOST HM	HMS DRAKE
Oakley, Jonathon	Lt RN	01-Sep-11	WAR	GSX	CDO LOG REGT	BARNSTAPLE
Oakley, Sarah Ellen	Lt Cdr	01-May-05	WAR	PWO(A)	HMS MERSEY	
Oatley, Timothy P	Lt Cdr	01-Oct-05	WAR	O MER	AWC BSD - RW TES	RAF BOSCOMBE DOWN
O'Boy, Thomas J	Capt	01-Sep-10	RM	GS	OPS GP HEADQUARTERS	SHEFFORD
O'Brien, David J	Surg Lt RN	05-Aug-09	MED	Med	INM ALVERSTOKE	GOSPORT
O'Brien, James M	2Lt	01-Sep-11	RM	GS	43 CDO	HMNB CLYDE
O'Brien, Kieran J	Cdr	30-Jun-06	ENG	AE	DES/COMFLEET	ABBEY WOOD
O'Brien, Patrick M C OBE	Capt RN	24-Aug-10	ENG	IS	DCDS(PERS)	GOSPORT
O'Brien, Thomas P	Lt Cdr	01-Oct-11	ENG	WESM	LOAN DSTL - NSD	FAREHAM
O'Byrne, Patrick	Cdr	30-Jun-08	WAR	SM(CQ)	ISAT	FREETOWN
O'Callaghan, Lucy B	Lt RN	01-May-13	WAR	GSX	DDS 1	PORTSMOUTH
O'Callaghan, Patrick	Lt RN	01-May-02	WAR	GSX	HMS EAGLET	LIVERPOOL
O'Callaghan, Philip P	Maj	01-Oct-13	RM	SCC	CTCRM - CTW	EXMOUTH
Ochtman-Corfe, Fergus V	Lt Cdr	01-Oct-10	ENG	ME	HMS MONTROSE	
Ockleton, Christopher D	Lt RN	01-Jun-12	WAR	MCD	MCM1 CREW 8	FASLANE
O'Connell, Daniel	Lt RN	01-Nov-10	WAR	GSX	MCM2 CREW 4	PORTSMOUTH
O'Connell, Heather	Lt RN	01-Jan-10	WAR	HM	HMS ENTERPRISE	
O'Connor, Calum M	SLt	01-Sep-11	WAR	P	CAREER TRAINING	RAF SHAWBURY
O'Connor, David M	Capt	01-Jul-04	RM	C (SCC)	30 CDO IX GP RM	PLYMOUTH
O'Connor, David Paul	Lt Cdr	01-Oct-09	ENG	WESM	DES/COMLAND	ABBEY WOOD
O'Connor, Lucy	Lt RN	01-Jul-05	WAR	GSX	HMS COLLINGWOOD	
O'Dell, Alexander J	SLt	01-Apr-11	WAR	SM(X)	HMS AMBUSH	
O'Donnell, Rory	Mid	01-Sep-13	WAR	GSX	BRNC DARTMOUTH	DARTMOUTH
O'Dooley, Paul	Lt RN	30-Jun-06	WAR	INFO OPS	OPS GP HEADQUARTERS	CHICKSANDS
O'Farrell, Matthew V	Lt RN	01-Sep-12	ENG	WE	HMS BULWARK	
Offord, Matt	Lt Cdr	01-Apr-02	WAR	MCD	FLEET FOSNNI - HQ	HELENSBURGH
Offord, Stephen J	Lt Cdr	01-Oct-13	ENG	AE	DES/COMJE/HELS	YEOVIL
O'Flaherty, Christopher P	Cdr	30-Jun-09	WAR	MCD PWO	HMS NELSON	HMS NELSON
O'Flaherty, John	Cdr	30-Jun-09	ENG	ME	RN EXCHANGE USA - BDS	WASHINGTON
O'Grady, Matthew J	Cdr	30-Jun-01	LOGS	L SM	FLEET SPT LOGS	PORTSMOUTH
O'Hara, Gerard	Maj	01-Sep-03	RM	GS	ATTACHE/ADVISER ALGIERS	ALGIERS
O'Herlihy, Simon I MBE	Lt Col	30-Jun-11	RM	GS	RMR BRISTOL	
O'Kane, Robert J	Lt Cdr	01-Oct-11	WAR	O SK6	771 SQN	RNAS CULDROSE
O'Keefe, Thomas D	Maj	01-Oct-12	RM	GS	HQ 3 (UK) DIV	HMNB PORTSMOUTH
Oldfield, Christian	Lt RN	01-Sep-05	ENG	AE P	LOAN VECTOR	GOSPORT
Oldham, David J	Lt RN	09-Apr-09	ENG	WE	MWS COLLINGWOOD	
Oliphant, Helen	Lt RN	01-Mar-10	WAR	GSX	HMS DRAGON	GLASGOW
Oliphant, William	Capt RN	29-Aug-13	LOGS	L	NATO DEF	ROME
Olive, Peter N OBE	Capt RN	02-Oct-12	WAR	PWO(A)	UKRBATSTAFF	HMNB PORTSMOUTH
Oliver, Graeme J	Lt RN	01-Dec-99	LOGS	L	HMS NELSON	

Person Name	Substantive Rank	Seniority	Branch	Specialisation	Organisation	Location
Oliver, Graham	Lt Cdr	01-May-03	WAR	METOC	FLEET COMOPS NWD	NORTHWOOD
Oliver, Kevin Rcds(S)	Col	22-Feb-11	RM	MLDR	HQ 3 CDO BDE RM	PLYMOUTH
Olle, Andrew R	2Lt	02-Sep-13	RM	N/A	CTCRM OFFICERS	EXMOUTH
Olsson, Alexandra	Lt RN	08-Dec-12	ENG	WESM	HMS VIGILANT	
Olver, Thomas A	Lt RN	10-May-13	ENG	MESM	DCEME SULTAN	HMS SULTAN
O'Malley, James P	Lt RN	11-Dec-09	MED	MS	EU OHQ	NORTHWOOD
O'Neill, Conor M	Lt Cdr	01-Oct-11	WAR	PWO	HMS SOMERSET	
O'Neill, Henry L	Lt RN	01-Jan-03	WAR	P SK4	COMUKAMPHIBFOR	HMNB PORTSMOUTH
O'Neill, James	Lt Cdr	01-Oct-09	WAR	HM (H CH)	HMS SCOTT	
O'Neill, Patrick J	Capt RN	30-Jun-06	ENG	WESM	NUCLEAR CAPABILITY	MAIN BUILDING LONDON
O'Neill, Paul J	Lt Cdr	01-Oct-03	ENG	MESM	DES/COMFLEET	ABBEY WOOD
O'Neill, Timothy J	Lt Cdr	01-Oct-09	WAR	MCD PWO	MCM1 FAS SEA1	HELENSBURGH
Oram, Cemal	Lt RN	01-Jan-11	WAR	P SK4	845 SQN	RNAS YEOVILTON
Orchard, Adrian Pl OBE	Capt RN	19-Apr-12	WAR	P GR7	BDS WASHINGTON	WASHINGTON
Orchard, Jonathan J	Lt RN	01-Sep-09	ENG	AE	FLEET FOSNNI - CNR	HMNB PORTSMOUTH
Ordway, Christopher N	Lt Col	30-Jun-12	RM	GS	COMUKAMPHIBFOR	HMNB PORTSMOUTH
O'Regan, Kyle	SLt	01-Sep-11	WAR	HM	HMS MERSEY	
O'Reilly, Christopher A	Lt Cdr	01-Oct-11	LOGS	L	DES/COMFLEET	HMNB PORTSMOUTH
O'Reilly, Paul A	Lt RN	19-Dec-08	ENG	WESM	NAVY MCTA PORTSMOUTH	BARROW IN FURNESS
Ormrod, Ryan	Mid	01-Nov-13	WAR	SM(X)	BRNC DARTMOUTH	DARTMOUTH
Ormshaw, Martin A	Lt RN	01-Jan-06	WAR	O LYNX	815 SQN FLT	RNAS YEOVILTON
O'Rourke, Richard M	Lt Cdr	01-Oct-08	LOGS	L	DES/COMFLEET	ABBEY WOOD
Orr, Jacqueline M	SLt	01-May-11	WAR	GSX	BRNC DARTMOUTH	DARTMOUTH
Orr, Keith J	Lt Cdr	01-Oct-09	ENG	MESM	FOST SM SEA	HELENSBURGH
Orr, Robert	SLt	01-Sep-11	ENG	MESM	DCEME SULTAN	HMS SULTAN
Orton, David M	Cdr	30-Jun-13	ENG	TM(SM)	FLEET FOST ACOS(Trg)	NCHQ
Orton, Trevellyan	Lt RN	01-Sep-09	ENG	WE	MWS COLLINGWOOD	
Orton, Trevor	Lt RN	01-Oct-04	WAR	MCD	MWS DDS	PORTSMOUTH
Osbaldestin, Richard A	Lt Cdr	01-Oct-06	WAR	MCD	NDG	HELENSBURGH
Osborn, Colvin G	Lt Cdr	01-Jun-02	WAR	INT	HQ RC(SW)	AFGHANISTAN BASTION
Osborn, Richard	Lt Cdr	01-Feb-99	WAR	AAWO	LSP ON	MUSCAT
Osborne, Andrew R	Lt RN	01-May-13	WAR	GSX	HMS ST ALBANS	
Osborne, Connor T	Mid	01-Nov-13	WAR	O UT	BRNC DARTMOUTH	DARTMOUTH
Osborne, John M	Lt RN	01-Oct-99	ENG	TM	HMS SULTAN - STG	HMS SULTAN
Osborne, Matthew A	Surg Lt RN	05-Aug-09	MED	GMP	INM ALVERSTOKE	GOSPORT
Osborne, Oliver J	Capt	01-Sep-08	RM	GS	NCHQ CNPERS	PORTSMOUTH
O'Shaughnessy, Paul	Lt Cdr	01-Oct-06	ENG	WE	DEFAC JSCSC ACSC	SWINDON
O'Shea, Matthew K	Surg Lt Cdr	06-Sep-09	MED	Med	INM ALVERSTOKE	GOSPORT
Osmond, Justin B	Capt RN	03-Sep-12	ENG	AE	DES/COIR	ABBEY WOOD
O'Sullivan, Barrie O	Cdr	30-Jun-09	WAR	P SK4	BDS WASHINGTON	WASHINGTON
O'Sullivan, Daniel A N	Lt RN	01-Apr-08	ENG	WESM	FLEET COMOPS	FAREHAM
O'Sullivan, Luke A	Lt RN	01-Sep-13	WAR	P UT	CAREER TRAINING	IPSWICH
O'Sullivan, Mark	Capt	01-Mar-10	RM	GS	CAREER TRAINING	NCHQ
O'Sullivan, Matthew	Capt	01-Sep-04	RM	P LYN7	RN EXCHANGE USA - BDS	WASHINGTON USA
O'Sullivan, Michael	Cdr	30-Jun-09	WAR	HM	ATTACHE/ADVISER OTTAWA	OTTAWA CANADA
O'Sullivan, Nicholas J	Maj	01-Oct-13	RM	C	NCHQ	
O'Sullivan, Stephen	Capt	16-Apr-09	RM	GS	RMB STONEHOUSE	PLYMOUTH
O'Toole, Mathew C	Lt Cdr	01-Oct-05	ENG	MESM	FLEET CAP SSM DIVISION	NCHQ
O'Toole, Mathew C	Capt	01-Sep-10	RM	GS	CAREER TRAINING	EXMOUTH
Ottaway, Thomas A	SLt	01-Sep-12	MED	MEDICAL	BRNC DARTMOUTH	
Ottewell, Paul S	Lt Cdr	01-Jan-05	WAR	PWO	MCM1 CREW 6	HELENSBURGH
Ottley, Lucy Jane	Lt Cdr	01-Oct-10	LOGS	L	HMS RICHMOND	
Ovenden, Neil S P	Lt Cdr	01-Feb-95	WAR	PWO(U)	FLEET COMOPS NWD	NORTHWOOD
Owen, Christopher R	Lt RN	01-Apr-12	ENG	ME	HMS SOMERSET	
Owen, Douglas P C	Lt RN	01-Sep-02	WAR	PWO	MWS COLLINGWOOD	HMS COLLINGWOOD
Owen, Glyn	Cdr	30-Jun-13	WAR	O LYNX	LHF 702 SQN	RNAS YEOVILTON
Owen, Peter Clive	Lt Cdr	30-Oct-91	WAR	P MER	824 SQN - TU	RNAS CULDROSE
Owen, Robert	Lt RN	01-Jan-13	WAR	O SKW	857 NAS	RNAS CULDROSE
Owen, Samuel T L	Lt Cdr	01-Oct-08	WAR	SM(CQ)	HMS VANGUARD	
Owen, Vincent F	Lt Cdr	01-Oct-12	WAR	O LYNX	HMS DARING	
Owen-Hughes, Daniel	Lt RN	01-Apr-12	WAR	GSX	MCM1 CREW 3	HELENSBURGH
Owens, Daniel T	Lt Cdr	01-Aug-99	ENG	ME	NUCLEAR CAPABILITY	MAIN BUILDING LONDON

Person Name	Substantive Rank	Seniority	Branch	Specialisation	Organisation	Location
Owens, John W	Lt RN	01-Jan-05	LOGS	L	DES/COMLAND	ABBEY WOOD
Oxley, James D	Lt RN	01-May-08	WAR	MCD	MCM2 CREW 3	PORTSMOUTH

P

Person Name	Substantive Rank	Seniority	Branch	Specialisation	Organisation	Location
Packer, Lee James	Lt RN	01-Sep-10	ENG	WE	LOAN DSTL - SD	SALISBURY
Packer, Robert	Lt RN	01-Jul-04	WAR	GSX	HMS RALEIGH - INT R	HMS RALEIGH
Padden, Gregory M	SLt	08-Jul-11	WAR	GSX	HMS ARGYLL	
Paddock, Lee	Lt RN	01-Mar-94	WAR	SM(X) (RES)	HQ 42 (NW) BDE	PRESTON
Page, Christopher A	Lt RN	01-Apr-12	WAR	GSX	HMS IRON DUKE	
Page, David	Capt RN	30-Jun-08	ENG	WE	DEFENCE ACADEMY	SHRIVENHAM
Page, Durward C	Lt Col	30-Jun-08	RM	GS	BDS WASHINGTON - DABS	WASHINGTON
Page, Mark R	Lt RN	01-May-00	WAR	O LYNX	AWC BZN - JADTEU	RAF BRIZE NORTON
Page, Martin J	Capt	21-Mar-13	RM	SCC	40 CDO RM - LOG COY	TAUNTON
Page, Michael	Col	30-Jun-07	RM	LC	ATTACHE/ADVISER BUENOS AIRES	ARGENTINA
Paget, Simon	Lt RN	02-May-00	WAR	GSX	MWS RALEIGH	
Palethorpe, Nicholas	Lt Cdr	01-Oct-07	WAR	PWO	FLEET COMOPS NWD	NORTHWOOD
Palin, Giles R	Lt Cdr	01-Oct-05	WAR	PWO(N)	NCHQ CNPERS	PORTSMOUTH
Pallett, Tony S	Lt RN	01-Jan-06	ENG	IS	HMS RALEIGH - SWPT	HMS RALEIGH
Palmer, Alan C	Surg Cdr	02-Oct-06	MED	GMP	DPHC SOUTH	HMS SULTAN
Palmer, Christopher R	Lt Cdr	01-Oct-07	ENG	MESM	LOAN DSTL - NSD	FAREHAM
Palmer, Matthew L	2Lt	02-Sep-13	RM	N/A	CTCRM OFFICERS	EXMOUTH
Palmer, Michael E	Lt Cdr	01-Nov-01	ENG	WE	NCHQ CNPERS	NCHQ
Palmer, Nicholas J	Lt RN	01-Feb-10	WAR	GSX	HMS WESTMINSTER	
Panic, Alexander	Lt Cdr	01-Oct-05	ENG	TM(SM)	DEFAC JSCSC ACSC	SWINDON
Panther, Andrew	Cdr	30-Jun-10	ENG	WE	DEFENCE ACADEMY	SWINDON
Pariser, Andrew M	Lt RN	01-May-06	WAR	PWO(SM)	HMS TALENT	
Park, Brian C	Lt Cdr	01-Oct-03	LOGS	L	NAVSEC	PORTSMOUTH
Park, Ian D	Lt Cdr	01-Oct-07	LOGS	L BAR	HMS DUNCAN	
Parker, Anthony R	Lt RN	29-Oct-04	LOGS	L	NCHQ CNPS	NCHQ
Parker, Berron M	Lt RN	01-Oct-06	ENG	IS	UK MCC	BAHRAIN
Parker, Daniel J	Lt Cdr	01-Oct-11	LOGS	L SM	FLEET SPT LOGS	PORTSMOUTH
Parker, Darren S	Lt Cdr	01-Oct-11	MED	MS	DMS WHITTINGTON	LICHFIELD
Parker, Henry H	R Adm	06-Feb-12	ENG	WESM	D CEPP	MAIN BUILDING LONDON
Parker, John R	Lt RN	01-Sep-12	ENG	WESM	HMS AMBUSH	
Parker, Jonathan D	Lt RN	01-Apr-03	ENG	WE	DES/COMJE	CORSHAM
Parker, Laura Marie	Lt RN	01-Mar-07	LOGS	L	BRNC DARTMOUTH	
Parker, Luke Rhys	Lt RN	01-Sep-11	ENG	AE	DES/COMJE/HELS	YEOVIL
Parker, Neil A	Lt RN	11-Dec-09	WAR	INT	FLEET COMOPS NWD	HMS COLLINGWOOD
Parker, Richard B	Lt RN	01-Nov-10	WAR	P UT	RAF LINTON-ON-OUSE	YORK
Parker, Sarah E	Lt RN	01-Jan-09	LOGS	L	FLEET SPT LOGS	NCHQ
Parker, Shaun M	Lt RN	03-May-13	ENG	AE	RNAS CULDROSE	
Parker, Simon O	Lt RN	01-Mar-09	ENG	WESM	HMS TRIUMPH	
Parker, Timothy S	Lt Cdr	01-Oct-06	ENG	IS	NCHQ CNPERS	PORTSMOUTH
Parker-Carn, Rebecca L	Lt RN	17-Apr-08	LOGS	L	COMUKTG SEA	PLYMOUTH
Parkin, Brett Ashley	Lt RN	08-Apr-05	ENG	WESM	DES/COMFLEET	ABBEY WOOD
Parkin, James M B	Cdr	30-Jun-11	WAR	PWO FC	HMS MONTROSE	
Parkin, Matthew J	Lt RN	01-Aug-06	WAR	INT	FLEET COMOPS NWD	HMS COLLINGWOOD
Parkinson, Henry M	Lt Cdr	01-Nov-11	ENG	AE P	RNAS CULDROSE	
Parkinson, Nicholas	Lt Cdr	07-Apr-06	WAR	AV	ABBEY WOOD BRISTOL	
Parks, Luke Jethro	Lt RN	01-Sep-11	WAR	HM	HMS ECHO	
Parks, Natasha	Lt RN	01-Jun-10	WAR	HM	RNAS CULDROSE	
Parmar, Bhavna R	Lt RN	01-Nov-07	ENG	TM	NCHQ CNPERS	PORTSMOUTH
Parnell, Daniel C	Lt Cdr	01-Oct-13	ENG	ME	COMDEVFLOT SHORE	HMNB DEVONPORT
Parnell, Terence A MBE	Lt RN	24-Oct-08	WAR	AV	RNAS YEOVILTON - SY	RNAS YEOVILTON
Parr, Matthew J	R Adm	02-Dec-11	WAR	SM(CQ)	FLEET COMOPS NWD	NORTHWOOD
Parr, Michael J E	Lt Cdr	02-Feb-05	WAR	HM	UKRBATSTAFF	HMNB PORTSMOUTH
Parri, Eifion L	Lt RN	01-Apr-08	WAR	P LYNX	815 SQN FLT	RNAS YEOVILTON
Parrock, Neil G	Lt Cdr	01-Oct-09	WAR	P MER	820 SQN	RNAS CULDROSE
Parrott, James P	Lt Cdr	01-Jul-04	WAR	AAWO	FOST DPORT SEA	HMNB DEVONPORT
Parrott, Stuart S	Lt RN	01-Apr-06	WAR	INT	FLEET COMOPS NWD	RNAS CULDROSE
Parry, Alexander K I	Cdr	30-Jun-05	LOGS	L	NAVSEC	NCHQ
Parry, Christopher A	Surg Cdr	12-Aug-09	MED	GS	MDHU DERRIFORD	PLYMOUTH

Person Name	Substantive Rank	Seniority	Branch	Specialisation	Organisation	Location
Parry, Jonathan A	Maj	01-Oct-04	RM	P LYN7	CAREER TRAINING	RAF BENSON
Parry, Mark	Cdr	30-Jun-13	ENG	AE	DEFAC JSCSC ACSC	SWINDON
Parry, Stephen J	Lt RN	01-Jul-06	WAR	ATC	HMS OCEAN	
Parry, Stuart D	Lt Cdr	01-Oct-09	LOGS	L	COMUKAMPHIBFOR	HMNB PORTSMOUTH
Parry-Jones, Alexander	SLt	01-Apr-11	WAR	SM(X)	HMS TIRELESS	
Parsonage, Neil	Lt Cdr	31-Mar-00	WAR	MTO N (RES)	FLEET RCRT	NCHQ
Parsons, Andrew D	Cdr	30-Jun-11	WAR	PWO(C)	FLEET CAP IS DIVISION	NCHQ
Parsons, Brian R	Cdr	31-Dec-00	ENG	AE	DES/COMJE/HELS	YEOVIL
Parsons, Christopher G	Capt RN	15-Jul-08	ENG	WE	DI - ICSP	LONDON
Parsons, Jacob W	Lt	01-Sep-11	RM	GS	NCHQ	
Parsons, Richard G	Lt RN	01-Apr-11	MED	MS(EHO)	DES/COMFLEET/NB	HELENSBURGH
Parsons, Thomas E	SLt	01-Jul-13	WAR	GSX	BRNC DARTMOUTH	
Parsonson, Max E	Lt RN	01-Apr-10	WAR	GSX	HMS DRAKE	
Partridge, Richard W	Lt RN	06-Sep-12	WAR	GSX	BFSAI - HQBFSAI	FALKLAND ISLANDS
Parvin, Philip S	Cdr	30-Jun-11	ENG	MESM	DSEA DNSR	ABBEY WOOD
Parvin, Richard A	Lt Col	30-Jun-11	RM	GS	RMR SCOTLAND	HMS CALEDONIA
Pashneh-Tala, Samira	Lt RN	17-Apr-11	WAR	GSX	HMS PORTLAND	
Passey, David W	Capt	01-Apr-11	RM	SCC	HQ SQN CDO LOG REGT	RMB CHIVENOR
Paston, William A	Lt Cdr	01-Oct-11	WAR	PWO	HMS DRAGON	
Pate, Christopher M	Lt Cdr	01-Oct-11	WAR	PWO	HMS DEFENDER	
Paterson, James M	Lt RN	01-Jan-06	WAR	P MER	814 SQN	RNAS CULDROSE
Paterson, Laura	Surg Lt RN	04-Aug-10	MED	GDMO	HMS NELSON	
Paterson, Mark GCGI	Capt	18-Jul-08	RM	C (SCC)	HQ 3 CDO BDE RM	PLYMOUTH
Paterson, Matthew	Lt RN	09-Mar-07	WAR	MW (RES)	FOSNNI NRC	HMNB PORTSMOUTH
Paterson, Michael	Capt RN	20-Nov-12	WAR	PWO(N)	DCDC	SWINDON
Paterson, Thomas J	Maj	01-Oct-08	RM	MLDR	RM CONDOR	DUNDEE
Paton, Mark W	Lt RN	01-Jan-09	LOGS	L SM	MCM1 FAS SEA1	HELENSBURGH
Patrick, Christopher M	Lt RN	21-Feb-09	WAR	HM	HMS ILLUSTRIOUS	
Patrick, John A	Lt RN	01-Jan-06	WAR	HM	FOST DPORT SEA	HMNB DEVONPORT
Patrick, Thomas D	Lt	01-Sep-11	RM	GS	CTCRM - CTW	EXMOUTH
Patterson, David	Cdr	30-Jun-09	ENG	WE	DES/COMJE/ISS	CORSHAM
Patterson, John	Lt Cdr	01-Aug-04	WAR	PWO(A)	DEFAC JSCSC ACSC	SWINDON
Patterson, Pascal X	Lt RN	01-Jan-07	WAR	INT	FLEET COMOPS NWD	NORTHWOOD
Patterson, Paul	Lt RN	01-Feb-10	LOGS	L	HMS LANCASTER	
Pattinson, Ian H	Capt RN	30-Jun-08	LOGS	L	DES/COMLAND/LCS	ABBEY WOOD
Patton, Stephen T	Lt RN	28-Jul-06	ENG	WE	DHU	SHEFFORD
Paul, Russell W	Lt Col	30-Jun-01	RM	LC	OPS SQN HMS ALBION	HMNB DEVONPORT
Pavie, Richard M	Lt RN	01-Jun-10	WAR	P GR7	FLEET CSAV	WASHINGTON
Pawley, Ross S	SLt	01-Jul-11	WAR	SM(X)	HMS VICTORIOUS	
Pawson, Jonathan	SLt	01-Feb-13	MED	MEDICAL	BRNC DARTMOUTH	DARTMOUTH
Payling, William A	Lt RN	01-May-13	WAR	GSX	HMS OCEAN	
Payne, Christopher	Maj	01-Oct-12	RM	GS	40 CDO RM	TAUNTON
Payne, John D	Cdr	30-Jun-08	WAR	PWO(U)	FLEET COMOPS NWD	NORTHWOOD
Payne, Mathew J	Lt Cdr	01-Oct-03	WAR	PWO(C)	CAREER TRAINING	SPAIN
Payne, Michael	Lt RN	01-Mar-11	LOGS	L	HMS VANGUARD	
Payne, Philip J	Lt Cdr	01-Jul-02	WAR	HM	LOAN HYDROG - DGHR(N)	TAUNTON
Payne, Richard C	Capt RN	01-Jul-09	WAR	P SHAR	HMS NELSON	HMS NELSON
Peace, Richard W	Lt Cdr	02-Jul-97	ENG	MESM	FLEET COMOPS NWD	NORTHWOOD
Peachey, Neil D	Lt RN	07-Apr-06	ENG	WE	MCM2 POR SEA	HMNB PORTSMOUTH
Peachey, Richard M	Lt RN	01-Nov-94	WAR	P SK4	847 SQN - AE	RNAS YEOVILTON
Peachey, Sarah Louise	Lt RN	01-Apr-08	LOGS	L	HMS NELSON	
Peacock, Anouchka	Lt RN	01-Dec-05	WAR	OP INT (RES)	DEFENCE LANGUAGE SCHOOL	BEACONSFIELD
Peacock, Joanna R	Mid	01-Sep-13	WAR	GSX	BRNC DARTMOUTH	
Peacock, Laura G J	Lt RN	01-May-07	LOGS	L	FLEET COMOPS NWD	NORTHWOOD
Peacock, Timothy J	Capt RN	10-Dec-12	WAR	P SK6	FOST DPORT SEA	HMNB DEVONPORT
Peake, Stephen P	Lt RN	01-Jul-04	MED	MS	NCHQ MEDDIV	NCHQ
Pearce, Christopher J	SLt	01-Mar-11	ENG	AE	DCEME SULTAN	HMS SULTAN
Pearce, Jonathan	Lt Cdr	01-Oct-10	ENG	WE	HMS DEFENDER	
Pearce, Robert	Lt Cdr	01-Oct-11	WAR	PWO(N)	RN EXCHANGE AUSTRALIA	CANBERRA AUSTRALIA
Pearce, Sarah L	Lt RN	01-Sep-05	WAR	INT	DI - CDI	MAIN BUILDING LONDON
Pearce, Stephen F	Lt RN	01-Nov-10	WAR	P	848 SQN	RNAS YEOVILTON
Pearch, Sean M	Lt Cdr	01-Oct-10	WAR	ATC	DES/COMFLEET	ABBEY WOOD BRISTOL

Person Name	Substantive Rank	Seniority	Branch	Specialisation	Organisation	Location
Pearmain, Stephanie R	Lt Cdr	01-Oct-10	ENG	TM	FLEET FOST ACOS	NCHQ
Pears, Ian James MBE	Cdr	30-Jun-12	ENG	IS	JFC HOC C4ISR	NORTHWOOD
Pearson, Alan J	Lt RN	01-Jan-05	WAR	O SKW	854 NAS	RNAS CULDROSE
Pearson, Andrew C	Lt RN	08-Jun-07	LOGS	L	HQ BFC J4	CYPRUS
Pearson, Christopher	Surg Cdr	30-Jun-02	MED	ORL	MDHU CLINICAL DIVISION	FRIMLEY
Pearson, Edward T	SLt	01-Sep-13	WAR	GSX	HMS LANCASTER	
Pearson, Ellis	Lt RN	31-Jul-09	ENG	WE	DES/COMFLEET/SHIPS	ABBEY WOOD
Pearson, Ian T	Lt RN	01-Sep-04	ENG	AE P	RNAS YEOVILTON - AED	RNAS YEOVILTON
Pearson, James C	Lt Cdr	01-Oct-08	WAR	MCD	DCD - MODSAP LONDON	HMS COLLINGWOOD
Pearson, Liam M	Lt RN	20-Oct-06	LOGS	L	DES/COMLAND/JSC	ABBEY WOOD
Pearson, Michael	Lt Cdr	01-Mar-01	WAR	O SK6	DEFENCE ACADEMY	SWINDON
Pearson, Sarah I	Lt RN	01-Jan-07	LOGS	L	HMS NELSON	
Pearson, Stephen	Capt RN	07-Jan-11	WAR	O SKW	NATO-ACT-HQ SACT	NORFOLK
Pease, Catherine A	SLt	16-Feb-11	LOGS	L	HMS DIAMOND	
Peattie, Ian W	Lt Cdr	01-Oct-08	LOGS	L	FLEET SPT LOGS	NCHQ
Peck, Simon R	Lt Cdr	01-Mar-10	ENG	AE	DEFAC CMT MBA	SHRIVENHAM SWINDON
Pedler, Mark D	Cdr	30-Jun-13	WAR	P SK4	CHFHQ (SEA)	RNAS YEOVILTON
Pedre, Robert G	Cdr	30-Jun-10	WAR	PWO(A)	HMS RICHMOND	
Pedrick, Amelia	Surg Lt Cdr (D)	11-Jul-13	DENTAL	GDP	42 CDO RM - SDS	PLYMOUTH
Peek, Samuel Richard	Capt	01-Sep-13	RM	GS	43 CDO FPGRM O	HMNB CLYDE
Pelham Burn, Alexander	Lt RN	01-Jun-10	LOGS	L	HMS TIRELESS	
Pellecchia, Daniel N	Lt RN	01-Sep-07	WAR	INT	JFIG - JT OPS	MAIN BUILDING LONDON
Pelly, Gilbert Ralph	Maj	24-Apr-96	RM	GS	NATO-ACT-JWC	STAVANGER (BODO)
Penfold, Andrew J	Lt RN	01-Sep-08	WAR	MCD	MCM1 CREW 6	HELENSBURGH
Penfold, Daniel B	Lt RN	01-May-11	ENG	MESM	HMS TALENT	
Pengelley, Tristan A H	Maj	01-Oct-11	RM	C	30 CDO IX GP RM	PLYMOUTH
Pengelly, Michael	Mid	01-May-13	WAR	P UT	BRNC DARTMOUTH	
Pengelly, Steven P	Surg Lt Cdr	06-Aug-08	MED	GS	INM ALVERSTOKE	GOSPORT
Penkman, William	Maj	01-Sep-04	RM	P LYN7	847 SQN - AE	RNAS YEOVILTON
Pennant, Marcus A	Lt RN	01-Apr-12	WAR	O LYNX	LHF 815 SQN FLT 210	RNAS YEOVILTON
Penn-Barwell, Jowan G	Surg Lt Cdr	07-Oct-08	MED	T&O	INM ALVERSTOKE	GOSPORT
Pennefather, Douglas C	Maj	01-Oct-10	RM	GS	NCHQ	
Pennington, Charles E	Maj	01-Oct-07	RM	GS	CTG LAND WARFARE	WARMINSTER
Pennington, Matthew J	SLt	01-Dec-13	WAR	SM(X)	HMS MONMOUTH	
Pentreath, Jonathan OBE	Cdre	16-Jul-12	WAR	P SK4	HQ JHC	ANDOVER
Pepper, Nicholas R	Lt RN	01-Sep-07	LOGS	L SM	DES/COMFLEET/SM	ABBEY WOOD
Pepper, Thomas D	Surg Lt Cdr (D)	13-Jul-09	DENTAL	GDP	INM ALVERSTOKE	GOSPORT
Peppitt, Christopher J	Lt RN	21-Feb-09	WAR	INT	15 (UK) PSY OPS	SHEFFORD
Percival, Fiona	Cdr	30-Jun-12	LOGS	L	UKRBATSTAFF	HMNB PORTSMOUTH
Percival, Victoria H	Lt RN	01-Jan-07	ENG	ME	DES/COMFLEET/CST	ABBEY WOOD
Percy, Nicolas A	Lt Cdr	01-Apr-11	WAR	MCD	FOST MPV SEA	HELENSBURGH
Perham, Nicholas J	Capt	03-Apr-09	RM	SCC	42 CDO RM	HMNB DEVONPORT
Perigo, Oliver F	Surg SLt	30-Jul-13	MED	MEDICAL	BRNC DARTMOUTH	
Perkins-Brown, Ben	Lt Cdr	01-Jul-09	WAR	AE	702 SQN	RNAS YEOVILTON
Perks, Andrew	Lt Cdr	01-Oct-12	ENG	WESM(TWS)	HMS TORBAY	
Perks, James Le Seeleur OBE	Cdr	30-Jun-05	WAR	SM(CQ)	RNP TEAM	RAF NORTHOLT
Perks, Matthew David	Lt RN	01-Sep-09	ENG	MESM	COMFASFLOT	HMNB CLYDE
Perks, Matthew N	Capt	01-Sep-11	RM	GS	45 CDO RM	DUNDEE
Perrett, Luke W	Lt RN	01-Sep-12	WAR	SM(N)	HMS TALENT	
Perrin, Mark S	Maj	01-Oct-07	RM	GS	JFHQ	NORTHWOOD
Perrins, Sam A	Lt RN	01-Apr-12	WAR	GSX	CDO LOG REGT RM	BARNSTAPLE
Perry, Carl S L	Lt RN	01-Mar-05	ENG	TM	RNSME HQ & ATG	HMS SULTAN
Perry, James M	Surg Lt RN	01-Jan-11	MED	GDMO	DCEME SULTAN	
Perry, Jonathan N	Surg Cdr	31-Dec-96	MED	Radiologist	MDHU PETERBOROUGH	
Perry, Kit J	Lt RN	01-Mar-13	ENG	WE	HMS KENT	
Perry, Robert W	Maj	01-Oct-00	RM	GS	NCHQ	
Pershevey, Alistair A	SLt	01-Aug-11	WAR	GSX	BRNC DARTMOUTH	DARTMOUTH
Peskett, Daniel M	Lt Cdr	01-Oct-10	ENG	ME	FOST DPORT SEA	HMNB DEVONPORT
Petch, Alan Napier	Lt RN	01-Sep-03	WAR	P SK4	RAF BENSON	OXFORD
Peters, Colin Sean	Lt RN	01-Oct-09	ENG	TM	RMB STONEHOUSE	PLYMOUTH
Peters, Matthew T	Lt RN	01-May-12	WAR	ATC	RAF SHAWBURY	
Peters, William R	Lt Cdr	01-Mar-04	WAR	PWO(U)	FLEET COMOPS NWD	NORTHWOOD

Person Name	Substantive Rank	Seniority	Branch	Specialisation	Organisation	Location
Peterson, Keith A	Lt RN	01-Sep-03	ENG	WESM(TWS)	CLYDE BABCOCK	HELENSBURGH
Pethick, Ian	Cdr	30-Jun-10	LOGS	L (RES)	FLEET CMR	NCHQ
Pethick, Thomas G	SLt	01-Sep-12	WAR	P UT	RNAS YEOVILTON	
Pethrick, Jerome F	Lt RN	01-Sep-07	ENG	AE	DES/COIR/CA	ABBEY WOOD
Pethybridge, Richard A	Cdr	30-Jun-07	WAR	PWO(N)	OP VOCATE	LIBYA
Petitt, Simon Richard	Capt RN	28-May-12	ENG	WE	HMS QUEEN ELIZABETH	ROSYTH
Petken, Alexander G	Mid	01-Sep-13	ENG	ME	BRNC DARTMOUTH	DARTMOUTH
Pett, Jeremy G	Capt RN	30-Jun-08	ENG	TM	FLEET FOST ACOS(Trg)	ABBEY WOOD
Pettigrew, Thomas R	Lt Cdr	01-Oct-09	ENG	TM(SM)	FOST FAS SHORE	HELENSBURGH
Pettinger, Joseph H	Lt RN	20-Oct-13	WAR	SM(X)	HMS VIGILANT	
Pettitt, Gary W	Capt RN	20-Sep-10	WAR	PWO(U)	DES/COMFLEET	HMS DRAKE
Petty, Darren L	Mid	19-Apr-13	WAR	HM	BRNC DARTMOUTH	
Peyman, Tracy	Lt Cdr	01-Oct-07	LOGS	L	DEFENCE ACADEMY	SWINDON
Phelan, Sean C	Lt RN	01-Jan-09	WAR	SM(N)	HMS VICTORIOUS	
Phelps, Alexander M	Lt RN	01-Aug-13	ENG	WE	HMS COLLINGWOOD	
Phelps, Jonathan J	Capt	01-Sep-10	RM	GS	NCHQ	
Phenna, Andrew	Cdr	30-Jun-01	ENG	WE	HMS COLLINGWOOD	
Philips, Thomas J	Lt RN	01-Jan-06	ENG	ME	DES/COMFLEET	ABBEY WOOD
Philipson, Matthew J	Lt RN	01-Sep-06	ENG	WE	DES/COMJE/ISTAR	FAREHAM
Phillippo, Duncan G	Lt Cdr	01-Oct-12	ENG	MESM	HMS ASTUTE	
Phillips, Edward H L	Lt RN	01-Feb-07	WAR	GSX	HMS MONMOUTH	
Phillips, Ian M	Capt RN	06-Aug-12	MED	MS	MEDDIV	NCHQ
Phillips, James C	Surg Lt Cdr	01-Aug-07	MED	GMP	BRNC DARTMOUTH	
Phillips, Jason Peter OBE	Cdr	30-Jun-09	WAR	O MER	BRNC DARTMOUTH	
Phillips, John Robert	Lt RN	01-Jan-10	WAR	P LYNX	LHF 815 SQN FLT 211	RNAS YEOVILTON
Phillips, Lewis Paul	Mid	11-Apr-12	WAR	ATC UT	RAF SHAWBURY	
Phillips, Matthew R	Lt Cdr	01-Oct-13	LOGS	L BAR SM	EU OHQ	NORTHWOOD
Phillips, Paul J	Lt RN	15-Apr-11	ENG	ME	1 ASSLT GROUP RM	PLYMOUTH
Phillips, Richard E	Lt Cdr	01-Oct-11	WAR	P GR7	CAREER TRAINING	WASHINGTON USA
Phillips, Simon M	Surg Cdr	01-Jul-09	MED	Occ Med	INM ALVERSTOKE2	GOSPORT
Phillips, Stephen John	Lt Col	30-Jun-04	RM	GS	AIB	HMS SULTAN
Phillips, Thomas	Lt RN	01-Dec-12	WAR	GSX	HMS DEFENDER	
Phillips, Thomas Martin J	Capt	01-Sep-11	RM	GS	CTCRM - CTW	EXMOUTH
Philo, Julian Quentin	Cdr	30-Jun-10	ENG	ME	COMPORFLOT ESG	PORTSMOUTH
Philpott, Marcus C	Surg Cdr	01-Jul-12	MED	GMP	MEDICAL CENTRE	RNAS YEOVILTON
Pickard, Stephen Richard	Lt Cdr	01-Oct-10	ENG	AE	DES/COIR/DAT	ABBEY WOOD
Pickering-Wheeler, Christopher	Lt Cdr	01-Oct-05	WAR	SM(AWC)	NATO - COMM	NAPLES ITALY
Pickett, Alexander Paul	Capt	11-Dec-98	RM	GS (RES)	RMR TYNE	NEWCASTLE UPON TYNE
Pickles, David Richard	Lt Cdr	01-Oct-10	WAR	ATC	RNAS YEOVILTON - AS	RNAS YEOVILTON
Pickles, Ian S	Cdr	30-Jun-97	WAR	SM(CQ)	NCHQ CNPS	PORTSMOUTH
Pickles, Martin Richard	Lt RN	01-May-01	WAR	P LYNX	702 SQN	RNAS YEOVILTON
Pickthall, David N	Lt Cdr	31-Dec-97	ENG	WE	NATO - BRUSSELS	
Pierce, Adrian K M	Cdr	30-Jun-08	WAR	PWO(N)	MWS COLLINGWOOD	
Pierson, Matthew F	Col	07-Dec-10	RM	GS	43 CDO FPGRM COMD SQN	HMNB CLYDE
Piggott, Andrew John	Lt RN	08-Jul-11	WAR	P UT	RAF SHAWBURY	
Pike, Robin Timothy	Lt Cdr	01-Oct-10	ENG	WESM(TWS)	DES/COMFLEET	
Pike, Stuart	Lt RN	27-Jul-07	ENG	AE	ABBEY WOOD BRISTOL	
Pilkington, Barry M	Lt RN	01-Feb-07	WAR	P GR7	FLEET CSAV	WASHINGTON
Pillai, Sonia Nandhini	Surg Lt RN	06-Aug-13	MED	GMP	INM ALVERSTOKE	GOSPORT
Pillar, Christopher D	Lt Cdr	01-Mar-95	WAR	PWO(U)	DSTL - NSD	FAREHAM
Pimm, Anthony R	Lt Cdr	01-Oct-13	WAR	PWO	HMS IRON DUKE	
Pinches, Ben M	2Lt	02-Sep-12	RM	N/A	CTCRM OFFICERS	EXMOUTH
Pinder, Aidan O	SLt	01-Feb-11	WAR	GSX	HMS SEVERN	
Pinder, Christopher D	Lt Cdr	01-Oct-04	ENG	TM	OCLC ROSYTH	HMS CALEDONIA
Pine, Paul M	Lt Cdr	01-Oct-07	ENG	TM	FLEET FOST ACOS(Trg)	ABBEY WOOD
Pinhey, Andrew D	Lt Cdr	01-Oct-08	MED	MS(SM)	MDHU DERRIFORD	PLYMOUTH
Pink, Simon E	Lt Cdr	01-Jan-02	WAR	PWO(N)	COMDEVFLOT SEA	HMNB DEVONPORT
Pinney, Jonathan R	Capt	01-Sep-11	RM	GS	NCHQ	
Pinney, Richard F	SLt	01-Sep-12	MED	MEDICAL	BRNC DARTMOUTH	
Piper, Benjamin J	Lt RN	01-May-06	WAR	MCD	HMS NELSON	
Piper, Lee J	Capt	30-Mar-12	RM	GS	NCHQ	
Piper, Neale Derek ARRC	Cdr	05-Sep-11	QARNNS	Nursing Officer	NCHQ CNPERS	PORTSMOUTH

Person Name	Substantive Rank	Seniority	Branch	Specialisation	Organisation	Location
Pipkin, Peter J	Lt Cdr	01-Aug-07	ENG	WE	DES/COMLAND/WPNS	ABBEY WOOD
Pitcher, Paul P	Cdr	30-Jun-10	WAR	PWO(C)	FLEET CAP IS DIVISION	NCHQ
Pitcher, Tim C	2Lt	02-Sep-13	RM	N/A	CTCRM OFFICERS	EXMOUTH
Pitt, David	Lt RN	13-Apr-12	LOGS	L	HMS AMBUSH	
Pitt, Jonathan M	Lt Cdr	17-Feb-99	WAR	SM(AWC)	DES/COMFLEET	ABBEY WOOD
Pittock, Martin W	Lt RN	01-Apr-12	WAR	O UT	849 SQN CULDROSE	RNAS CULDROSE
Pizii, Jane V	Lt RN	01-Aug-08	LOGS	L	NCHQ CNPERS	HMNB PORTSMOUTH
Plackett, Andrew J	Lt Cdr	01-Oct-03	WAR	INT	DCOG CIO	MAIN BUILDING LONDON
Plant, Anna Louise	Lt RN	01-Sep-13	WAR	GSX	HMS ARGYLL	
Plant, Michael J	Lt RN	01-Sep-13	WAR	P UT	RNAS YEOVILTON	
Platt, Andrew J	Lt RN	01-Sep-11	WAR	FC	HMS DIAMOND	
Platt, Jonathan H	Lt Cdr	01-Oct-08	WAR	P SK6	FLEET CSAV	NCHQ
Platt, Maximilian J	Lt RN	01-Jan-10	ENG	MESM	HMS VIGILANT	
Pledger, David	Cdr	30-Jun-10	WAR	AV	DSTO	RAF ST MAWGAN
Plenty, Andrew J	Lt RN	01-Sep-03	WAR	ATC	FLEET CSAV	RNAS YEOVILTON
Plewes, Andrew B	Maj	27-Apr-02	RM	GS	COMD FDT DGLS&E D EQPT	ANDOVER
Plumer, Stephen J	Lt RN	08-Jun-06	LOGS	L	COMDEVFLOT WLSG FGEN	HMS DRAKE
Plunkett, Gareth N	Lt RN	01-Sep-06	WAR	P SK4	CHFHQ (SEA)	RNAS YEOVILTON
Pocock, Oliver R	Lt RN	01-Jun-12	WAR	P GR7	6 SQN TYPHOON	RAF LEUCHARS
Pollard, Alexandra E	Lt Cdr	01-Oct-07	WAR	AAWO	MWS COLLINGWOOD	
Pollard, Jonathan R	Lt Cdr	01-Oct-07	ENG	WE	DES/COMFLEET	ABBEY WOOD
Pollard, Stephen J	Lt RN	01-Dec-13	WAR	SM(X)	HMS DARING	
Polley, Christopher F	Lt RN	01-Sep-09	WAR	SM(X)	HMS VIGILANT	
Pollitt, Alexander W	Lt RN	01-May-06	WAR	P SK6	857 NAS	RNAS CULDROSE
Pollitt, David N A	Lt Cdr	01-Apr-89	WAR	SM(CQ)	FLEET CAP SSM DIVISION	NCHQ
Pollock, Barnaby J	Lt RN	01-Nov-05	WAR	PWO	HMS DEFENDER	
Pollock, David J	Capt RN	01-May-12	WAR	SM(CQ)	FLEET CAP SSM DIVISION	NCHQ
Pomfrett, Nicholas J	Lt Cdr	01-Apr-95	WAR	SM(CQ)	FOST NWD	NORTHWOOD
Pons, Michael D	RN Chpln	01-Jul-06	Ch S	Chaplain	FLEET HM UNIT	PLYMOUTH
Ponsford, Philip K	Cdr	30-Jun-12	WAR	PWO(U)	PJHQ (UK) J2	NORTHWOOD
Poole, Daniel C	Lt RN	01-Sep-05	LOGS	L BAR	UKRBATSTAFF	HMNB PORTSMOUTH
Poole, Jason L	Capt RN	15-Jul-13	WAR	MCD PWO(A)	ATTACHE/ADVISER TRIPOLI	LIBYA
Poole, Timothy J	Lt Cdr	01-Oct-07	WAR	O MER	RNAS CULDROSE	
Pooley, Steven W	Lt Cdr	01-Jul-96	ENG	WESM(TWS)	DES/COMLAND	ABBEY WOOD
Pope, Catherine	Maj	24-Jun-98	WAR	METOC	DEFENCE ACADEMY	SHRIVENHAM
Pope, Kevin David	Lt RN	01-Jan-05	WAR	P MER	RAF SHAWBURY	
Pope, Michelle L	Lt RN	01-Sep-06	ENG	AE P	RNAS YEOVILTON	
Porrett, Johnathan A	Cdr	30-Jun-07	LOGS	L SM	DIO SAPT	NCHQ
Porteous, Cameron	Lt RN	01-Sep-10	ENG	WESM	HMS TALENT	
Porter, Edward J	Capt	01-Sep-11	RM	GS	HMS DRAKE	
Porter, Matthew E CBE	Col	09-Nov-09	RM	GS	STRAT ACDS DC&D	SHRIVENHAM
Porter, Simon P	Capt RN	13-Jul-09	WAR	PWO(A)	NCHQ CNPS	PORTSMOUTH
Postgate, Michael O	Lt RN	01-Oct-13	RM	LC	43 CDO FPGRM COMD	HMNB CLYDE
Potter, David L	Surg Lt Cdr	04-Aug-09	MED	EM	HMS NELSON	
Potter, Ian	Lt RN	08-Jun-07	ENG	MESM	CSF FASLANE	HELENSBURGH
Potter, Stephen R	Lt RN	01-Aug-13	WAR	SM(X)	MWS COLLINGWOOD	
Potts, David A	Lt RN	11-Oct-13	LOGS	L	HMS RALEIGH	
Potts, Duncan L	R Adm	26-Jan-11	WAR	PWO(U)	ACNS CAP	NCHQ
Potts, Kevin M	Lt Cdr	01-Feb-92	WAR	P LYNX	115(R) SQN	RAF CRANWELL
Poulsom, Matthew	SLt	01-May-12	LOGS	L	BRNC DARTMOUTH	DARTMOUTH
Poulson, Christopher	Lt RN	01-Nov-10	WAR	GSX	HMS MONTROSE	
Poundall, Gareth	Mid	01-Sep-13	WAR	GSX	BRNC DARTMOUTH	
Pounder, Richard H	Lt RN	01-Oct-09	WAR	SM(X)	MCM1 CREW 5	HELENSBURGH
Pounds, Alexander N	Maj	01-Oct-13	RM	GS	NCHQ	
Powell, David A	Lt RN	01-Apr-12	WAR	GSX	HMS DAUNTLESS	
Powell, Gregory M J	Lt Cdr	01-Oct-13	WAR	MCD	HMS CLYDE	
Powell, Ian David	Capt	01-Sep-13	RM	GS	45 CDO RM - Y COY	DUNDEE
Powell, Matthew T	SLt	01-Sep-10	WAR	SM(X)	MWS COLLINGWOOD	
Powell, Philip James	Lt RN	01-Jan-07	ENG	TM	HQ DISC	CHICKSANDS
Powell, Richard L OBE	Cdre	10-Sep-12	WAR	P LYNX	HMS NELSON	
Powell, Robert	Lt RN	01-Jun-10	WAR	P SK4	845 SQN	RNAS YEOVILTON
Powell, Steven R	Lt Cdr	01-Jul-98	WAR	PWO(C) MW	UK MCC	BAHRAIN

Person Name	Substantive Rank	Seniority	Branch	Specialisation	Organisation	Location
Powell, William	Lt Cdr	16-Dec-98	WAR	PWO(U)	MWS COLLINGWOOD	
Power, Benjamin	Lt Cdr	01-Oct-13	WAR	FC	HMS EXPRESS	
Powles, Derek A	Lt Cdr	01-Feb-04	ENG	ME	NCHQ CNPS	PORTSMOUTH
Powne, Laura	Lt RN	20-Oct-10	ENG	ME	HMS RALEIGH	
Powne, Simon P W	Lt Cdr	01-Oct-11	ENG	ME	HMS OCEAN	
Powney, Lewis	Mid	01-Sep-13	ENG	WE	BRNC DARTMOUTH	
Prausnitz, Luke	Mid	01-Nov-13	LOGS	L	BRNC DARTMOUTH	
Precious, Angus	Maj	01-Oct-11	RM	MLDR	30 CDO IX GP RM	PLYMOUTH
Preece, David G	Cdr	30-Jun-09	LOGS	L SM	FOST DPORT SEA	HMNB DEVONPORT
Preece, David J	Lt RN	01-Apr-12	WAR	GSX	HMS SEVERN	
Preece, Simon E	Lt RN	01-Sep-04	WAR	GSX	BRNC DARTMOUTH	
Preece, Timothy M	Lt RN	20-Jul-13	WAR	P UT	RAF LINTON-ON-OUSE	YORK
Preedy, Helen C	Surg Lt RN	07-Aug-13	MED	MEDICAL	BRNC DARTMOUTH	
Prescott, Shaun	Capt RN	22-Apr-13	ENG	WE	DI - CA	LONDON
Pressdee, Simon J	Lt Cdr	01-Oct-06	WAR	MCD PWO	MCM2 CREW 6	HMNB PORTSMOUTH
Pressly, James	Lt Col	30-Jun-05	RM	GS	BRITISH MILITARY MISSION	KUWAIT
Prest, Stephen	Cdr	30-Jun-13	ENG	WE	FLEET CAP RCAP DIVISION	NCHQ
Preston, Jacqueline N	Lt RN	30-Jun-06	ENG	TM	DEFENCE LANGUAGE SCHOOL	WILTON PARK
Preston, James M	Lt RN	01-Apr-12	WAR	GSX	DDS	PORTSMOUTH
Prevett, Adam M	Lt RN	01-Apr-09	WAR	O LYNX	815 SQN	RNAS YEOVILTON
Price, Andrew M	Lt Col	30-Jun-06	RM	C	CTCRM	EXMOUTH
Price, David Glyn	Capt	01-Jan-01	RM	P SK4	RAF SHAWBURY	
Price, David J	Lt RN	01-Apr-93	WAR	AAWO	HMS BRISTOL	
Price, Joseph C	Lt Cdr	01-Oct-08	WAR	MCD	FOST NWD (JTEPS)	NORTHWOOD
Price, Martin J	Lt Col	31-Dec-98	RM	MLDR	NCHQ CNPERS	PORTSMOUTH
Price, Matthew W	Lt RN	01-Jan-08	LOGS	L SM	101 LOG BDE JFSP	ALDERSHOT
Price, Raymond T	Maj	01-Oct-08	RM	SCC	CTCRM - CTW	EXMOUTH
Price, Timothy A	Cdr	30-Jun-07	WAR	AAWO	NCHQ CNPERS	PORTSMOUTH
Prichard, Charles H	SLt	09-Apr-10	WAR	GSX	MWS COLLINGWOOD	
Prideaux, Robert J	Lt Cdr	01-Oct-12	ENG	MESM	HMS VIGILANT	
Priest, James E	Lt Cdr	01-Oct-09	WAR	P SK4	DES/COMJE/HELS	ABBEY WOOD
Priest, Rachel E	Lt Cdr	01-Oct-12	ENG	AE	DES/COIR/CA	ABBEY WOOD
Prince, Mark E	Cdr	30-Jun-09	ENG	MESM	FLEET CAP SSM	NCHQ
Printer, Alexander J	SLt	01-Nov-11	ENG	WE	MWS COLLINGWOOD	
Printie, Christopher J	SLt	01-Sep-12	WAR	SM(X)	BRNC DARTMOUTH	DARTMOUTH
Prior, Grant M	Cdr	30-Jun-05	ENG	WE	DES/COMFLEET	ABBEY WOOD
Prior, Kate R	Surg Cdr	22-Sep-10	MED	Anaes	MDHU FRIMLEY PARK	FRIMLEY
Prior, Robert P	SLt	01-Sep-12	WAR	P	RNAS YEOVILTON	
Pritchard, Christopher W	Lt RN	01-Oct-08	WAR	INT	JFIG - JT IP	RAF WYTON
Pritchard, Lloyd B	Maj	01-Oct-12	RM	GS	NCHQ	
Pritchard, Lorna F	SLt	01-Apr-11	WAR	GSX	BRNC DARTMOUTH	
Pritchard, Simon A	Lt Col	30-Jun-06	RM	HW	MWS COLLINGWOOD	
Pritchard, Thomas A	SLt	01-Sep-12	WAR	P	MWS COLLINGWOOD	
Proctor, Paul J R	Lt RN	12-Jul-13	ENG	WE	MWS COLLINGWOOD	
Proctor, William J G	Lt Cdr	01-Mar-02	ENG	WE	FLEET CAP IS DIVISION	NCHQ
Proffitt, Adrian	Surg Lt Cdr	01-Sep-10	MED	Med	INM ALVERSTOKE	GOSPORT
Proffitt, Julia M	Lt Cdr	01-Oct-05	ENG	TM	MSP	MAIN BUILDING LONDON
Prole, Nicholas M	Lt Cdr	01-Oct-07	WAR	P SK4	848 SQN	RNAS YEOVILTON
Prosser, Jason W	Lt RN	01-Aug-08	LOGS	L	RNAS YEOVILTON - SUS	RNAS YEOVILTON
Prosser, Matthew J	Lt RN	01-Aug-01	WAR	MCD	DEMS TRG REGT	BICESTER
Proud, Andrew D	Cdr	30-Jun-09	ENG	AE	ABBEY WOOD BRISTOL	
Proudman, Michael P	Lt RN	01-Aug-06	WAR	FC	MWS COLLINGWOOD	
Prouse, Scott	Lt RN	01-Apr-09	WAR	SM(N)	HMS VIGILANT	
Prowle, Owen T	SLt	09-Apr-12	LOGS	L	43 CDO FPGRM	HMNB CLYDE
Prowse, David J	Lt Cdr	01-Oct-09	ENG	ME	FOST DPORT SEA	HMNB DEVONPORT
Pugh, Geoffrey N J	Lt RN	01-Oct-03	WAR	ATC	RNAS YEOVILTON	
Pugh, James	Lt RN	01-Mar-11	ENG	AE	CHF(MERLIN)	RAF BENSON
Pugh, Jonathan	Lt Cdr	08-Mar-00	ENG	WE	DCTT HQ	HMS SULTAN
Pugsley, Andrew	Capt	30-Jul-09	RM	GS (RES)	COMUKTG SEA	PLYMOUTH
Pullan, Keith J	Lt Cdr	01-Oct-05	WAR	HM (H CH)	HMS SCOTT	
Pulvertaft, Rupert J	Lt Col	30-Jun-03	RM	HW	HMS NELSON	HMS NELSON
Punch, John M	Lt Cdr	01-Oct-10	WAR	P SK4	845 SQN	RNAS YEOVILTON

Person Name	Substantive Rank	Seniority	Branch	Specialisation	Organisation	Location
Purdue, Basil H	SLt	01-Apr-11	WAR	SM(X)	HMS VANGUARD	
Purdy, Richard	Lt Cdr	01-Oct-11	ENG	AE	ACNS CAP	NCHQ
Purser, Lloyd J MBE	Maj	01-Oct-08	RM	GS	NCHQ	
Purvis, Christopher	Lt RN	01-May-13	WAR	SM(X)	HMS ARTFUL	BARROW IN FURNESS
Purvis, David M	Lt Cdr	16-Oct-04	WAR	P LYNX	ABBEY WOOD	ABBEY WOOD
Puxley, Michael E	Lt Cdr	01-Sep-04	ENG	WESM	FOST FAS SHORE	HELENSBURGH
Pye, Paula Jayne	RN Chpln	01-Jul-09	Ch S	Chaplain	HMS RALEIGH - EXEC	HMS RALEIGH
Pyke, Daniel G	Capt	01-Aug-07	RM	C	HQ BFC J3 EPISKOPI	CYPRUS
Pyke, Hazel Josie	Lt RN	01-Mar-07	ENG	ME	HMS DRAKE	

Q

Person Name	Substantive Rank	Seniority	Branch	Specialisation	Organisation	Location
Quade, Nicholas A C	Lt Cdr	01-Oct-05	ENG	MESM	HMS VANGUARD	
Quaite, David G	Lt Cdr	01-Oct-13	WAR	HM	RNAS CULDROSE	
Quant, Jacqueline R	Lt RN	20-Oct-06	WAR	INT	DHU	CHICKSANDS
Quantrill, Steven W	Lt Cdr	01-Oct-05	LOGS	L	DES/COMLAND	ABBEY WOOD
Quayle, Christopher A	Lt RN	01-Jun-12	WAR	ATC	RNAS YEOVILTON	
Quekett, Ian P S	Cdr	30-Jun-13	ENG	WE	NCHQ CNPS	PORTSMOUTH
Quick, Benjamin P	Lt RN	01-Jun-06	WAR	MCD	MCM1 CREW 4	HMNB CLYDE
Quick, Christopher J	Lt	01-Sep-11	RM	GS	43 CDO FPGRM O SQN	HMNB CLYDE
Quilter, Gail	Lt RN	01-Nov-10	WAR	GSX	HMS DAUNTLESS	
Quilter, George	Lt RN	01-Mar-11	WAR	GSX	RNAS YEOVILTON	
Quinn, Antony D	Lt Cdr	01-Oct-10	ENG	TM	FLEET FOST ACOS	NCHQ
Quinn, Mark E	Lt Cdr	01-Oct-09	ENG	IS	HMS RICHMOND	
Quinn, Martin	Cdr	30-Jun-10	WAR	MEDIA OPS	FLEET CMR	NCHQ
Quinn, Michael	Lt RN	01-Oct-11	WAR	MEDIA OPS	EU OHQ	UK
Quinn, Morgan	Surg Lt RN	07-Aug-13	MED	MEDICAL	BRNC DARTMOUTH	
Quinn, Thomas J	Maj	01-Oct-13	RM	GS	42 CDO RM	HMNB DEVONPORT
Quirke, Darren L	Lt RN	01-Jul-12	ENG	TM	HMS SULTAN	
Quirke, Fraser J	Lt RN	31-Jul-09	LOGS	L	RNLA	HMS COLLINGWOOD

R

Person Name	Substantive Rank	Seniority	Branch	Specialisation	Organisation	Location
Race, Nigel	Cdr	31-Dec-99	WAR	PWO(C)	EU OHQ	BAHRAIN
Rackham, Anthony D H	Cdr	30-Jun-10	WAR	PWO(A)	HMS OCEAN	
Rackham, Katharine L M	Lt Cdr	01-Mar-05	WAR	INT	NCHQ CNPERS	PORTSMOUTH
Radakin, Antony D	Cdre	12-Sep-11	WAR	PWO(U)	FMC - STRAT N	MAIN BUILDING LONDON
Radcliffe, Albert P	Lt RN	09-Apr-10	ENG	ME	FOST DPORT SEA	HMNB DEVONPORT
Radcliffe, Gemma L	Lt RN	01-Jan-09	ENG	TM	HMS ILLUSTRIOUS	
Radue, Nicholas K	Lt RN	01-Jul-11	WAR	HM	FLEET HM UNIT	HMNB DEVONPORT
Rae, David M	Lt RN	30-Jul-10	ENG	WE	DES/COMFLEET	ABBEY WOOD
Rae, Derek G	Cdr	30-Jun-12	WAR	HM (H CH)	HMS ENTERPRISE	
Raeburn, Craig	Lt Cdr	01-Sep-08	WAR	PWO(U)	FLEET CAP WARFARE	NCHQ
Raeburn, Mark	Lt Cdr	01-Jul-02	WAR	PWO(N)	FLEET CAP SSM DIVISION	NCHQ
Raffle, Edward J	Lt RN	01-Sep-10	ENG	ME	HMS ILLUSTRIOUS	
Raine, Katherine V	Lt RN	01-Dec-09	WAR	GSX	HMS TYNE	
Raine, Murray S	Lt RN	01-May-13	WAR	SM(X)	HMS AMBUSH	
Raine, Sarah L	Lt RN	01-Sep-06	ENG	WE	NCHQ CNPERS	PORTSMOUTH
Rainey, Owen H	Surg Lt Cdr	02-Aug-10	MED	GMP	HMS PROTECTOR	
Rainford, Jayjay	Mid	01-Sep-13	ENG	WE	BRNC DARTMOUTH	
Raisbeck, Paul T	Lt Cdr	08-Jul-99	WAR	PWO(U)	MWS DDS	PORTSMOUTH
Rake, Rachael	Lt RN	01-Sep-09	ENG	ME	DES/COMFLEET	ABBEY WOOD
Ralls, Damien	Lt Cdr	01-Oct-13	ENG	WESM(TWS)	DEFAC JSCSC ICSCM	SWINDON
Ralston, William A.	Lt RN	01-Jan-02	ENG	TM	DEFENCE CBRN CENTRE	SALISBURY
Ramage, Andrew P	Lt RN	21-Mar-13	LOGS	L	DES/COMLAND/JSC	ABBEY WOOD
Ramaswami, Ravi A	Surg Cdr	27-Jul-06	MED	Occ Med	DES/COMFLEET	HMNB PORTSMOUTH
Ramsay, Alastair J D	Lt RN	01-Jul-02	ENG	TM(SM)	NETS (W)	HMS DRAKE
Ramsay, Brian	Lt Cdr	31-Mar-01	WAR	SM(X) (RES)	FLEET CMR	LONDON
Ramsay, Stuart J	Lt RN	01-Mar-13	ENG	WESM	HMS VANGUARD	
Ramsey, Ryan T	Cdr	30-Jun-08	WAR	SM(CQ)	FOST SM SEA	HELENSBURGH
Rance, Maxwell G W	Cdr	31-May-01	LOGS	L	STRAT DEF RESOURCES	MAIN BUILDING LONDON
Rand, Mark C MBE	Capt	24-Jul-04	RM	GS	NCHQ	
Randall, Richard D	Cdr	30-Jun-03	ENG	MESM	DES/COMFLEET	ABBEY WOOD

Person Name	Substantive Rank	Seniority	Branch	Specialisation	Organisation	Location
Randles, Maxwell E	Mid	01-Feb-13	WAR	GSX	BRNC DARTMOUTH	
Randles, Steven	Lt Cdr	01-Oct-11	WAR	PWO	PJHQ (UK) J6	NORTHWOOD
Rankin, Graham J	Lt Cdr	01-Oct-08	WAR	AAWO	EXCHANGE NETHERLANDS	DEN HELDER
Ranscombe, Robert E	Lt RN	01-Jan-12	WAR	P	RNAS YEOVILTON	RNAS YEOVILTON
Ransom, Benjamin R J	Lt RN	01-Sep-00	WAR	GSX	FLEET FOST ACOS	NCHQ
Raper, Daniel S	Mid	01-Nov-12	WAR	P UT	BRNC DARTMOUTH	DARTMOUTH
Rason, Stuart P	RN Chpln	01-Jan-12	Ch S	Chaplain	CDO LOG REGT RM	BARNSTAPLE
Raval, Vivek	Lt RN	01-Feb-08	WAR	INT	FLEET CAP IS DIVISION	NCHQ
Rawlings, Gary	Lt Cdr	01-Oct-08	ENG	ME	RN EXCHANGE	CANADA
Rawlins, Simon	Lt Cdr	01-Oct-10	WAR	P GR7	RN EXCHANGE USA	WASHINGTON
Rawlinson, Katherine H	Surg Lt RN	04-Aug-10	MED	GDMO	MCM2 POR SEA	HMNB PORTSMOUTH
Rawlinson, Kathryn E	Lt RN	01-May-06	WAR	GSX	HMS NELSON	
Rawlinson, W	Mid	19-Apr-13	WAR	SM(X)	BRNC DARTMOUTH	
Rawson, Scott M	Lt Cdr	01-Apr-03	ENG	MESM	FLEET COMOPS NWD	NORTHWOOD
Ray, Daniel J	SLt	01-Sep-11	WAR	GSX	HMS CLYDE	
Ray, Louise B	Lt RN	01-Aug-04	WAR	PWO	HMS NORTHUMBERLAND	
Ray, Steven P	Lt RN	01-Oct-10	ENG	ME	MWS EXCELLENT	
Raybould, Adrian G	Cdr	30-Jun-01	ENG	WESM(TWS)	DES/COMJE	CORSHAM
Raymont, Edward M	Lt RN	01-Apr-11	WAR	HM	HMS BULWARK	
Rayner, Andrew	Cdr	30-Jun-11	ENG	WE	BDS WASHINGTON	WASHINGTON
Raynor, Sean D	Lt Cdr	01-Oct-05	ENG	WE	MWS COLLINGWOOD	HMS COLLINGWOOD
Read, Alun J	Lt Cdr	01-Oct-04	WAR	P LYNX	815 SQN	RNAS YEOVILTON
Read, Benjamin	Lt RN	01-May-09	WAR	GSX	HMS PROTECTOR	
Read, Clinton Derek	Maj	01-May-06	RM		HMS NELSON	
Read, Edmund A	Lt RN	01-Apr-11	WAR	HM	HMS ENTERPRISE	
Read, Jonathon	Surg Cdr	04-Aug-10	MED	Anaes	MDHU FRIMLEY PARK	FRIMLEY
Read, Matthew C	Lt RN	01-Mar-11	ENG	AE	BRNC DARTMOUTH	
Read, Richard J	Lt Col	30-Jun-11	RM	LC	FMC - NAVY	MAIN BUILDING LONDON
Readwin, Roger	Cdr	30-Jun-10	WAR	MCD PWO(A)	RN EXCHANGE USA	WASHINGTON USA
Reah, Stephen	Lt Cdr	02-May-00	ENG	ME	DES/COMFLEET	HMS DRAKE
Reaves, Charles E	Lt Cdr	01-Oct-09	LOGS	L	FOST DPORT SHORE	HMNB DEVONPORT
Rebbeck, Christopher	Lt RN	01-Oct-08	WAR	P LYNX	815 SQN FLT	RNAS YEOVILTON
Redbourn, James	SLt	01-Sep-11	ENG	MESM	DCEME SULTAN	HMS SULTAN
Redman, Charles J R	Lt Cdr	23-Nov-98	WAR	GSX	HMS ILLUSTRIOUS	
Redman, Christopher D	Surg Cdr (D)	31-Dec-00	DENTAL	GDP	DMS WHITTINGTON DDS	ALDERSHOT
Redmayne, Mark E	Lt Cdr	01-Oct-06	WAR	PWO	MCM1 CREW 1	HELENSBURGH
Redpath, Scott D	Lt RN	20-Oct-08	ENG	MESM	FLEET CAP SSM DIVISION	NCHQ
Reece, Nigel David	Cdr	30-Jun-12	ENG	MESM	DES/COMFLEET	ABBEY WOOD
Reed, Andrew W OBE	Capt RN	25-Sep-12	WAR	PWO(A) AAWO		HMS COLLINGWOOD
Reed, Christopher G QGM	Capt	16-Apr-10	RM	GS	NCHQ	
Reed, Darren K	Cdr	30-Jun-10	LOGS	L BAR	DCDS PERS TRG	MAIN BUILDING LONDON
Reed, Mark	Lt Cdr	01-Oct-98	WAR	HM (M CH)	FLEET COMOPS	NORTHWOOD
Reed, Nicholas	Lt Cdr	01-Oct-04	LOGS	L SM	HQ ISAF	AFGHANISTAN KABUL
Reed, Peter K MBE	Lt RN	01-Sep-08	ENG	TM	HMNB PORTSMOUTH	
Reed, Thomas A	Mid	01-Nov-13	WAR	GSX	BRNC DARTMOUTH	
Reekie, Fraser C	Lt RN	01-May-13	WAR	SM(X)	MWS COLLINGWOOD	
Rees, Adam M	Lt RN	01-Sep-98	ENG	TM	CTCRM	EXMOUTH
Rees, Edward T	Lt RN	01-Nov-10	WAR	GSX	HMS NELSON	
Rees, Karen M	Lt Cdr	01-Oct-07	LOGS	L	PJHQ (UK) J1/J4	NORTHWOOD
Rees, Matthew I	Lt RN	01-Sep-08	LOGS	L SM	HMS NELSON	
Rees, Nathan J	Lt RN	01-Feb-12	WAR	ATC	RNAS YEOVILTON	
Rees, Paul S	Surg Cdr	28-Dec-11	MED	Med	MDHU FRIMLEY PARK	FRIMLEY
Rees, Richard T	Lt Cdr	01-Dec-03	WAR	PWO(N)	MCM2 CREW 5	PORTSMOUTH
Rees, Simon G	Lt Cdr	01-Oct-13	WAR	PWO(SM)	HMS TRIUMPH	
Reese, David M	Lt Cdr	01-Sep-02	WAR	O LYNX	LHF HQ	RNAS YEOVILTON
Rees-Hughes, Victoria L	Lt RN	01-Sep-10	ENG	TM	HMS NELSON	HMS NELSON
Rees-Swindon, Mikaela J	Lt RN	05-Aug-11	LOGS	L	814 SQN	RNAS CULDROSE
Reeve, Jennifer A	Lt RN	28-Nov-03	WAR	INT	FLEET CAP IS DIVISION	NCHQ
Reeves, Andrew P	Lt Cdr	01-Oct-11	WAR	SM(AWC)	HMS ILLUSTRIOUS	
Reeves, Paul K	Lt Cdr	01-Oct-10	ENG	MESM	HMS TRENCHANT	
Reeves, Simon	Capt	20-Jul-07	RM	GS	NCHQ	
Reeves, Simon J	Lt RN	08-Jul-08	WAR	MCD	MCM2 CREW 7	PORTSMOUTH

Person Name	Substantive Rank	Seniority	Branch	Specialisation	Organisation	Location
Regan, Kevin QGM	Lt RN	13-Oct-12	WAR	O UT	RNAS CULDROSE	
Reid, Charles I	Capt RN	10-Jan-11	WAR	SM(CQ)	NATO-ACT-HQ SACT	NORFOLK
Reid, Iain J	SLt	01-Sep-11	WAR	GSX	HMS ENTERPRISE	
Reid, James	Lt RN	07-Feb-08	WAR	SM(N)	HMS RALEIGH	
Reid, James L	Lt Cdr	01-Oct-09	WAR	PWO	MWS COLLINGWOOD	
Reid, Jason C	Cdr	30-Jun-12	ENG	WESM(TWS)	DES/COMFLEET/SM	ABBEY WOOD
Reid, Jenny E	SLt	24-Jan-12	WAR	GSX	BRNC DARTMOUTH	
Reid, Mark R	Capt	01-Apr-11	RM	SCC	40 CDO RM - HR CELL	TAUNTON
Reid, Martyn	Lt Cdr	01-Apr-07	WAR	PWO(C)	RN EXCHANGE CANADA	OTTAWA 1
Reid, Philip A	SLt	01-Sep-13	WAR	O	MCM1 CREW	HELENSBURGH
Reilly, Scott J	Lt RN	01-Apr-13	WAR	P SK4	845 SQN	RNAS YEOVILTON
Reindorp, David P	Capt RN	21-Feb-11	WAR	PWO(N)	DIRECTOR (JW)	NORTHWOOD
Renaud, Gavin A R	Lt Cdr	01-Oct-13	WAR	O LYNX	LHF 702 SQN	RNAS YEOVILTON
Rendell, Derrick J	Lt Cdr	01-Oct-05	ENG	MESM	RN GIBRALTAR - PM(NUC)	HMS ROOKE
Renney, Craig	Maj	01-Oct-12	RM	MLDR (SCC)	HQ 3 CDO BDE RM	PLYMOUTH
Rennie, Richard A	Surg Lt Cdr	01-Aug-12	MED	GMP	INM ALVERSTOKE	GOSPORT
Reston, Samuel C	Surg Cdr	01-Jul-12	MED	T&O	UK MED GP (AFG)	AFGHANISTAN BASTION
Retallick, Katherine A	Lt RN	01-Apr-09	WAR	HM	HMS ENTERPRISE	
Revell, Aaron D	Lt RN	30-Sep-08	WAR	GSX	HMS ILLUSTRIOUS	
Rex, Colin	Lt Cdr	01-Oct-10	WAR	P SK4	HQ JHC	ANDOVER
Reynolds, Andrew C J	Lt Cdr	01-Oct-12	ENG	ME	NCHQ CNPERS	PORTSMOUTH
Reynolds, Ben K	Maj	01-Oct-11	RM	GS	CTCRM - CW	EXMOUTH
Reynolds, Darren P	Lt Cdr	01-Oct-13	WAR	WE	NAVY MCTA PORTSMOUTH	HMNB PORTSMOUTH
Reynolds, Huw F	Lt RN	01-Mar-02	ENG	AE P	RNAS CULDROSE - AED HQ	RNAS CULDROSE
Reynolds, James	Lt Cdr	01-Oct-10	WAR	PWO	HMS BULWARK	
Reynolds, Mark E	Lt Cdr	01-Feb-11	ENG	ME	FOST DPORT SEA	HMNB DEVONPORT
Reynolds, Matthew J	Lt Cdr	01-Oct-10	WAR	PWO(C)	MWS COLLINGWOOD	
Reynolds, Zoe A	Lt RN	01-Dec-03	WAR	INT	DIRECTOR (JW)	NORTHWOOD
Rhodes, Andrew W	Lt Cdr	01-Oct-07	ENG	WE	LOAN DSTL - DD	FARNBOROUGH
Rich, David C	Lt Cdr	20-May-97	WAR	SM(CQ)	NCHQ CNPERS	PORTSMOUTH
Rich, Duncan	Lt RN	19-Feb-08	WAR	SM(N)	HMS TIRELESS	
Richards, Alan D CB	V Adm	19-Jan-12	WAR	P SK6	DI - CDI	LONDON
Richards, Anthony J	Lt Cdr	01-Oct-07	LOGS	L SM	HQ ARRC COMND GROUP	MOENCHENGLADBACH
Richards, Gregor I	Lt RN	20-Jul-10	WAR	MW	MCM1 CREW 6	HELENSBURGH
Richards, Guy R	Lt RN	01-Oct-11	LOGS	L	DES/HR/JSST	ABBEY WOOD BRISTOL
Richards, Jack P	2Lt	01-Sep-12	RM	GS	42 CDO RM	HMNB DEVONPORT
Richards, James I	Cdr	30-Jun-13	ENG	WESM(TWS)	FOST SM SEA	HELENSBURGH
Richards, Jonathan C	Lt RN	01-Jul-11	ENG	MESM	HMS TALENT	
Richards, Nigel A	Lt RN	20-Oct-06	ENG	TM	NETS (E)	HMNB PORTSMOUTH
Richards, Paul	Lt Cdr	01-Oct-07	ENG	ME	FOST DPORT SEA	HMNB DEVONPORT
Richards, Robert D	Lt RN	01-Sep-07	ENG	WESM(TWS)	NAVY MCTA PORTSMOUTH	HMNB PORTSMOUTH
Richards, Simon T	Lt RN	01-Aug-99	WAR	O SKW	AWC BSD - RW TES	RAF BOSCOMBE DOWN
Richards, Stephen W	Lt Col	30-Jun-07	RM	SCC	HMS DRAKE	
Richards, Steven	Lt RN	01-Jan-02	ENG	WE	DES/COMFLEET	ABBEY WOOD
Richards, Steven A	Lt RN	01-Sep-08	ENG	MESM	DES/COMFLEET	ABBEY WOOD
Richards, Thomas M L	Lt RN	01-Jan-12	WAR	P	RAF SHAWBURY	
Richardson, Alexander J	Mid	01-Nov-13	WAR	O	BRNC DARTMOUTH	DARTMOUTH
Richardson, Benjamin F	Maj	01-Oct-13	RM	GS	CTCRM - CTW	EXMOUTH
Richardson, Craig A	SLt	01-Sep-11	ENG	WESM	HMS VIGILANT	
Richardson, Gavin A	Cdr	30-Jun-10	WAR	O MER	NCHQ CNPS	NCHQ
Richardson, Ian D	Lt RN	24-Oct-08	MED	MS	DMS WHITTINGTON	LICHFIELD
Richardson, Ian H	Lt Cdr	01-Oct-08	WAR	MCD	NCHQ	
Richardson, James	Lt RN	01-Jan-09	LOGS	L	HMS MONMOUTH	
Richardson, James A	Lt RN	01-May-13	WAR	SM(X)	HMS COLLINGWOOD	
Richardson, John F	Lt RN	01-Sep-04	WAR	PWO(N)	HMS COLLINGWOOD	
Richardson, Peter S	Capt	30-Jun-11	ENG	WE	UNPOS	KENYA
Richardson, Philip	Lt Cdr	01-Mar-06	WAR	P LYNX	DEFAC JSCSC ACSC	SWINDON
Richardson, Simon J	Capt	19-Jul-05	RM	SCC	HQ 3 CDO BDE RM	PLYMOUTH
Richardson, Stuart	Lt RN	20-Oct-09	ENG	WESM(SWS)	COMFASFLOT	HMNB CLYDE
Riches, Ian C OBE	Cdr	30-Jun-04	WAR	SM(CQ)	DES/COMFLEET	HELENSBURGH
Riches, Joanne C	Lt Cdr	01-Oct-13	ENG	TM	HMS NELSON	
Richmond, David R	2Lt	02-Sep-13	RM	N/A	CTCRM OFFICERS	EXMOUTH

Person Name	Substantive Rank	Seniority	Branch	Specialisation	Organisation	Location
Richmond, Iain J.	Capt RN	30-Jun-06	WAR	P SK6	PJHQ (UK) J5	NORTHWOOD
Richter, Alwyn S	Lt Cdr	01-Sep-00	ENG	WE	FLEET ACOS(RP)	NCHQ
Rickard, James J	Lt RN	01-May-10	WAR	SM(X)	HMS TRIUMPH	
Rickard, Rory F	Surg Cdr	30-Jun-04	MED	BPS	MDHU DERRIFORD	PLYMOUTH
Ricketts, Alex F	SLt	01-Feb-11	WAR	GSX	MWS COLLINGWOOD	
Ricketts, Simon J	Mid	01-Sep-12	WAR	HM	HMS CLYDE	
Riddett, Adam O	Lt Cdr	01-Oct-10	WAR	PWO	HMS RICHMOND	
Rider, John	Lt Cdr	01-Oct-09	WAR	SM(AWC)	BDS WASHINGTON	WASHINGTON
Ridgeway, Adam	Lt RN	01-Apr-12	WAR	P	RNAS YEOVILTON	RNAS YEOVILTON
Ridgwell, Daniel R	Lt Cdr	01-Oct-13	ENG	ME	DES/COMFLEET	ABBEY WOOD
Ridley, George	Lt RN	01-Apr-09	WAR	P MER	829 SQN FLT 02	RNAS CULDROSE
Ridley, Jon	Maj	01-Oct-10	RM	BS	CTCRM RMSOM	HMS NELSON
Rigby, Jeremy C	Cdre	01-Jul-13	LOGS	L	DES/COMFLEET	HMNB PORTSMOUTH
Rigby, Lee A	Lt RN	09-Apr-10	ENG	AE	DES/COMJE/HELS	YEOVIL
Rignall, William J	Lt RN	01-Nov-12	WAR	HM	HMS DRAKE	
Rigsby, David A	SLt	01-May-12	WAR	SM(X)	BRNC DARTMOUTH	
Riley, Neil A	Surg SLt	22-Jul-13	MED	MEDICAL	BRNC DARTMOUTH	
Riley, Ralph A	Lt RN	01-Jun-05	WAR	O MER	MWS COLLINGWOOD	
Rimington, Anthony K	Cdr	30-Jun-11	WAR	P LYNX	LHF 702 SQN	RNAS YEOVILTON
Rimmer, Heather E	Cdr	30-Jun-10	ENG	TM	MWS COLLINGWOOD	
Rimmer, Owen F	Lt Cdr	01-Oct-12	WAR	SM(AWC)	UK MCC	BAHRAIN
Riordan, Shaun	Lt Cdr	01-Oct-12	ENG	WE	DI - CA	LONDON
Ripley, Benjamin E	Cdr	30-Jun-11	WAR	PWO(U) HM	FLEET ACOS(RP)	NCHQ
Ripley, Stephen L	Lt Cdr	01-Oct-13	ENG	WE	UK MCC	BAHRAIN
Rippingale, Stuart N	Cdr	30-Jun-05	ENG	IS	LOAN DSTL - IMD	SALISBURY
Risdall, Jane	Surg Cdr	31-Dec-09	MED	Anaes (C&S)	DMS WHITTINGTON	BIRMINGHAM
Risley, James G	Lt Cdr	01-Oct-08	ENG	MESM	BRNC DARTMOUTH	DARTMOUTH
Ritchie, Douglas B	Lt RN	01-Sep-01	ENG	MESM	HMS TIRELESS	
Ritchie, Iain D	Lt Cdr	01-Oct-10	WAR	HM(AM)	FLEET CAP IS DIVISION	NCHQ
Ritchie, Stuart David	Lt RN	01-Jun-09	LOGS	L	PJHQ (UK) J5	NORTHWOOD
Ritson, Jonathan E	Surg Lt Cdr	01-Aug-12	MED	EM	INM ALVERSTOKE	GOSPORT
Rixon, Thomas M	Lt RN	01-Sep-13	WAR	O SKW	854 NAS	RNAS CULDROSE
Roach, Darren J	Lt RN	01-Jun-10	WAR	INT	COMUKTG SEA	PLYMOUTH
Roach, Lewis G	SLt	24-Nov-11	ENG	AE	DCEME SULTAN	
Robbins, Daniel M	SLt	01-Apr-12	WAR	GSX	RNAS CULDROSE	
Robbins, Harry V	Capt	01-Jan-02	RM	P SK4	771 SQN	RNAS CULDROSE
Roberts, Andrew	Lt RN	23-May-10	WAR	ATC	FOST DPORT SHORE	HMNB DEVONPORT
Roberts, Andrew	Lt RN	16-Feb-07	WAR	SM(X)	FLEET COMOPS	FAREHAM
Roberts, Andrew	Lt Cdr	01-Oct-12	ENG	AE	RN EXCHANGE AUSTRALIA	AUSTRALIA
Roberts, Benjamin	Lt RN	01-Oct-09	LOGS	L	RN EXCHANGE USA	WASHINGTON
Roberts, Charlotte M	Lt RN	01-Sep-12	ENG	AE	771 SQN	RNAS CULDROSE
Roberts, Christopher S	Lt RN	24-Oct-07	WAR	AV	FLEET CSAV	NCHQ
Roberts, David	Lt RN	01-Nov-06	WAR	FC	RN EXCHANGE FRANCE	PARIS
Roberts, David G	Lt RN	01-Sep-10	ENG	MESM	HMS VIGILANT	
Roberts, Dean	Cdr	30-Jun-11	ENG	WE	FOST DPORT SEA	HMNB DEVONPORT
Roberts, Iain G	Lt Cdr	01-Oct-03	ENG	WESM(TWS)	COMDEVFLOT	HMS DRAKE
Roberts, Joel	Lt RN	01-Feb-09	WAR	GSX	HMS KENT	
Roberts, John A	Lt RN	11-Dec-09	MED	MS(SM)	NBC CLYDE	HELENSBURGH
Roberts, Llion G	Mid	01-Nov-13	WAR	GSX	BRNC DARTMOUTH	
Roberts, Martin A	Lt RN	01-Nov-94	WAR	O SKW	854 NAS	RNAS CULDROSE
Roberts, Nicholas S	Cdre	03-Jan-12	ENG	WE	FMC - NAVY	MAIN BUILDING LONDON
Roberts, Nigel D	Lt Cdr	01-Oct-11	WAR	O LYNX	AWC BSD - RW TES	RAF BOSCOMBE DOWN
Roberts, Peter N	Lt RN	09-Apr-10	ENG	AE	1710 NAS	PORTSMOUTH
Roberts, Peter S	Cdr	30-Jun-06	WAR	AAWO	JFC HOC C4ISR	NORTHWOOD
Roberts, Stephen	Lt RN	01-Feb-03	WAR	INFO OPS (RES)		EU OHQ UK
Roberts, Stephen D	Cdr	30-Jun-03	ENG	WE	DES/COMFLEET	ABBEY WOOD
Roberts, Thomas P	Capt	16-Apr-09	RM	MLDR (SCC)	42 CDO RM - LOG COY	HMNB DEVONPORT
Roberts, Thomas R	Lt RN	01-Sep-10	WAR	SM(X)	HMS RALEIGH	
Roberts, Timothy J	Cdr	30-Jun-03	ENG	MESM	COMDEVFLOT SHORE	HMNB DEVONPORT
Robertson, Adam J	Lt Cdr	01-Oct-13	ENG	WE	FLEET CAP	NCHQ
Robertson, David C	Capt RN	17-Sep-13	WAR	HM (H CH)	COMDEVFLOT SHORE	HMNB DEVONPORT
Robertson, Douglas M	Lt Cdr	01-Oct-93	WAR	ATC	FLEET CSAV	LONDON

Person Name	Substantive Rank	Seniority	Branch	Specialisation	Organisation	Location
Robertson, Keith H	Capt	18-Jul-08	RM	SCC	RM CONDOR	DUNDEE
Robertson, Michael G	Cdr	30-Jun-03	WAR	O LYNX	HMS SULTAN - CS	HMS SULTAN
Robertson, Paul N	Lt Cdr	01-Oct-00	WAR	O SK6	771 SQN	RNAS CULDROSE
Robertson, Sean P	SLt	01-Sep-11	ENG	MESM	DCEME SULTAN	HMS SULTAN
Robertson, Stuart T	Lt Cdr	01-Oct-06	LOGS	L SM	JFHQ	NORTHWOOD
Robertson, Thomas A	Lt RN	01-Apr-12	WAR	GSX	HMS DRAGON	
Robey, James C	Lt Cdr	01-Oct-11	WAR	PWO(N)	UK MCC	BAHRAIN
Robin, Christopher C E	Lt Cdr	01-Sep-94	WAR	P LYNX	FLEET CSAV	RNAS YEOVILTON
Robin, Julie I	Surg Cdr	05-Apr-12	MED	Anaes	UK MED GP	AFGHANISTAN BASTION
Robinson, Alan J	Lt RN	16-Dec-11	ENG	MESM	HMS VICTORIOUS	
Robinson, Alex James	SLt	01-Feb-12	WAR	P	BRNC DARTMOUTH	
Robinson, Charles E T	Cdr	30-Jun-99	WAR	PWO(U)	NATO - BRUSSELS	BRUSSELS
Robinson, David	Lt Cdr	01-Oct-08	LOGS	L	NCHQ CNPERS	PORTSMOUTH
Robinson, Guy A OBE	Cdre	03-Sep-13	WAR	PWO(A)	FLEET CAP WARFARE	NCHQ
Robinson, John P	Lt RN	18-May-13	LOGS	L	FOST FAS SHORE	HELENSBURGH
Robinson, Lee D	Lt Cdr	01-Oct-10	ENG	WESM(SWS)	HMS VANGUARD	
Robinson, Lindsy	Lt RN	11-Oct-13	MED	MS	MDHU DERRIFORD	PLYMOUTH
Robinson, Matthew S	Lt RN	01-May-04	WAR	P MER	820 SQN	RNAS CULDROSE
Robinson, Melanie S	Lt Cdr	07-Jun-04	WAR	GSX	NCHQ CNPERS	PORTSMOUTH
Robinson, Michael P	Capt RN	05-Oct-09	ENG	MESM	DSEA DNSR	ABBEY WOOD BRISTOL
Robinson, Michael W	Surg Lt Cdr	06-Aug-13	MED	GS	INM ALVERSTOKE	GOSPORT
Robinson, Nicholas	SLt	01-May-13	ENG	TM	BRNC DARTMOUTH	DARTMOUTH
Robinson, Nicholas P	Lt RN	30-Aug-13	LOGS	L	HMS MONTROSE	
Robinson, Steven L	Lt Cdr	01-Jan-09	ENG	WE	HMS DEFENDER	
Robinson, Timothy	Surg Lt Cdr	02-Aug-10	MED	GMP	DPHC SW	RNAS CULDROSE
Robley, William F	Lt Cdr	01-Oct-06	WAR	P SK6	DEF HELI FLYING SCH	RAF SHAWBURY
Robson, James P	SLt	14-Aug-11	LOGS	L	HMS ILLUSTRIOUS	
Robson, Mark A	Capt	16-Apr-10	RM	GS	NCHQ	
Robus, Keith	RN Chpln	27-Aug-07	Ch S	Chaplain	FLEET HM UNIT	HMNB DEVONPORT
Robus, Lucy Jayne	SLt	01-Apr-11	WAR	GSX	HMS LANCASTER	
Rock, James Andrew	Lt RN	01-Jun-07	WAR	P MER	820 SQN	RNAS CULDROSE
Roddy, Christopher M	Lt RN	31-Jul-09	ENG	AE	MOD CNS/ACNS	NCHQ
Rodgers, Mark A	SLt	01-Sep-11	ENG	MESM	DCEME SULTAN	HMS SULTAN
Roe, Roma Jane	Lt Cdr	01-Oct-11	ENG	AE	DES/COMJE/HELS	RNAS CULDROSE
Roessler, Philippa F	Lt RN	01-Sep-11	WAR	HM	FLEET COMOPS NWD	NORTHWOOD
Roffey, Kevin D	Lt Cdr	01-Oct-13	ENG	AE	DES/COMJE/HELS	YEOVIL
Rogers, Alan	Lt Cdr	25-Dec-02	WAR	AV (RES)	RNAS CULDROSE	
Rogers, Alexander T	Lt Cdr	31-Jul-05	WAR	P LYN7	3 REGT AAC 663 SQN	IPSWICH
Rogers, Andrew	Cdr	30-Jun-07	ENG	WE	NATO-ACO-JFC HQ	BRUSSELS
Rogers, Christopher M	Lt Cdr	01-Jun-00	ENG	WE	ACDS DEFLOGPOL	ABBEY WOOD
Rogers, Clare A	SLt	15-May-13	LOGS	L	HMS DUNCAN	
Rogers, Dominic J J	Capt	01-Sep-09	RM	GS	CAREER TRAINING	NCHQ
Rogers, James	Lt RN	01-Sep-09	ENG	MESM	CAREER TRAINING	HMS SULTAN
Rogers, Jennifer C	Surg Lt RN	01-Aug-12	MED	MEDICAL	BRNC DARTMOUTH	
Rogers, Julia A	Lt Cdr	01-Oct-09	WAR	P SK4	HMS NELSON	
Rogers, Julian C E	Lt Cdr	01-Mar-03	WAR	SM(AWC)	COMFASFLOT	HELENSBURGH
Rogers, Mark D	Lt RN	01-Apr-12	LOGS	L	HMS TORBAY	
Rogers, Philip S	Lt Cdr	01-Oct-06	ENG	TM	DCDS PERS TRG-TESRR	MAIN BUILDING LONDON
Rogers, Phillip R	Lt RN	01-Sep-07	ENG	MESM	DES/COMFLEET	ABBEY WOOD
Rogers, Simon Ja	Lt Cdr	01-Oct-06	WAR	PWO(C)	MCM2 CREW 4	PORTSMOUTH
Rogers, Simon M	Maj	01-Oct-08	RM	GS	NCHQ	
Roissetter, David	RN Chpln	03-Jan-06	Ch S		HMS RALEIGH	
Rolfe, Conrad	Lt RN	01-Sep-12	WAR	GSX	HMS NORTHUMBERLAND	
Rollason, Kristina M	SLt	01-Sep-12	ENG	AE	BRNC DARTMOUTH	
Rollinson, Christopher D	Lt RN	01-May-13	WAR	GSX	MCM2 CREW 8	PORTSMOUTH
Rolls, Edward C	Lt RN	01-Jul-06	WAR	ATC	FLEET CAP SSM DIVISION	NCHQ
Rolph, Andrew P M	Cdr	30-Jun-04	WAR	PWO(C)	DI - ICSP	MAIN BUILDING LONDON
Roocroft, Nathaniel T	Surg SLt	29-Jul-13	MED	MEDICAL	BRNC DARTMOUTH	
Rook, Christopher	Lt RN	30-Jul-10	LOGS	L	NATO-ACO-JFC HQ	BRUSSELS
Rook, Graeme I	Lt Cdr	01-Apr-98	ENG	WE	NATO	BRUSSELS
Rooke, Adam E	Lt RN	01-Sep-06	ENG	MESM	HMS SULTAN	
Rooke, Mark D	Lt RN	01-Apr-12	ENG	TM	HMS SULTAN	

Person Name	Substantive Rank	Seniority	Branch	Specialisation	Organisation	Location
Rooney, Thomas M	Lt RN	08-Apr-05	ENG	WE	COMDEVFLOT ESG	HMS DRAKE
Roper, Jack H	Capt	01-Sep-13	RM	GS	45 CDO RM - X COY	DUNDEE
Roscoe, David	Surg Lt Cdr	04-Aug-09	MED	GMP	INM ALVERSTOKE	GOSPORT
Rose, Alan	Lt Cdr	01-Oct-12	ENG	WESM(TWS)	CAREER TRAINING	HMS RALEIGH
Rose, Andrew D	Cdr	30-Jun-13	WAR	O SKW	RNAS CULDROSE	
Rose, Harry John	2Lt	01-Sep-11	RM	N/A	CTCRM	EXMOUTH
Rose, Ian David	Lt RN	01-Jan-10	ENG	MESM	DES/COMFLEET	BARROW IN FURNESS
Rose, Marcus E	Lt Cdr	01-Oct-13	ENG	WESM	DI - CA	LONDON
Rose, Mark Nigel	Lt RN	30-Nov-06	WAR	P SK6	GANNET SAR FLT	HMS GANNET
Rose, Matthew L	Surg SLt	09-Jul-13	MED	MEDICAL	BRNC DARTMOUTH	
Rose, Michael F	Cdr	30-Jun-08	ENG	ME	FLEET COMOPS NWD	NORTHWOOD
Rose, Simon P	Lt RN	01-Jan-07	ENG	WE	DI - SA - JTAC	LONDON
Rose, Victoria	Lt RN	01-Nov-09	WAR	O MER	820 SQN	RNAS CULDROSE
Rosenberg, Marcel M	Lt Cdr	01-Oct-10	ENG	WE	HMS DARING	
Rosen-Nash, William A	Lt RN	01-Sep-12	ENG	WESM	HMS TORBAY	
Roskilly, Martyn	Capt	01-May-01	RM	P LYN7	771 SQN	RNAS CULDROSE
Ross, Alison Kay	Mid	01-Sep-13	ENG	ME	BRNC DARTMOUTH	
Ross, David C	Lt RN	31-Jul-08	WAR	SM(C)	NATO ACO	NORTHWOOD
Ross, Jamie M	Lt RN	01-Sep-08	WAR	P SK4	GANNET SAR FLT	PRESTWICK
Ross, Paul W	Lt RN	01-Jan-05	ENG	WESM(TWS)	HMS VANGUARD	
Ross, Phillip David	Lt RN	01-Sep-13	WAR	P	771 SQN C	RNAS CULDROSE
Ross, Robert A MBE	Surg Capt RN	16-Sep-08	MED	GMP (C&S)	PJHQ (UK) J1/J4	NORTHWOOD
Ross, Samuel K	Lt RN	01-Jun-12	WAR	ATC	RNAS CULDROSE - ATC	RNAS CULDROSE
Ross, Steven	Lt RN	28-Jul-06	ENG	WESM	DES/COMFLEET	ABBEY WOOD
Roster, Shaun P	Lt Cdr	01-Oct-06	WAR	O LYNX	LOAN VECTOR	GOSPORT
Rostron, David W	Lt Cdr	01-Jan-04	ENG	MESM	HMS TURBULENT	
Rostron, John H	Lt Cdr	01-Oct-09	ENG	WESM	DSEA DNSR	ABBEY WOOD
Rotherham, Dominic L	Lt RN	20-Oct-09	WAR	O	RNAS CULDROSE	RNAS CULDROSE
Rothwell, Christopher D	SLt	01-Apr-11	WAR	GSX	HMS DEFENDER	
Rothwell, Kirsty S	Mid	03-Jul-13	WAR	GSX	BRNC DARTMOUTH	
Rouault, Lewis Dean	SLt	14-Aug-12	WAR	SM(X)	BRNC DARTMOUTH	
Roughton, Joshua N	2Lt	02-Sep-13	RM	N/A	CTCRM OFFICERS	EXMOUTH
Roulston-Eldridge, James W	Lt RN	01-Jan-08	ENG	ME	HMS ILLUSTRIOUS	
Round, Matthew J	Lt RN	01-May-02	WAR	O SKW	750 SQN SEAHAWK	RNAS CULDROSE
Routledge, Ricky J	Lt RN	01-Sep-06	ENG	IS	HMS SULTAN	
Routledge, Rosemary P	Lt RN	01-Nov-09	ENG	GS	NCHQ	
Rowan, Tristian G	Lt RN	01-Sep-12	WAR	P CDO	CHF(MERLIN)	RAF BENSON
Rowberry, Adrian G	Lt Cdr	01-Oct-11	WAR	PWO	FLEET COMOPS NWD	NORTHWOOD
Rowbotham, Mark J	Lt RN	06-Apr-07	WAR	ME	HMS ECHO	
Rowden, Paul C	2Lt	01-Sep-11	RM	GS	CTCRM OFFICERS	EXMOUTH
Rowe, Antony N	Lt RN	06-Apr-07	ENG	WE	SF	RNAS CULDROSE
Rowe, Joanne	Lt RN	01-Sep-11	LOGS	L	FLEET FOSNNI	BRISTOL
Rowe, Kevin C	Lt RN	04-May-01	WAR	O (RES)	849 SQN	RNAS CULDROSE
Rowe, Richard D	RN Chpln	24-Sep-00	Ch S		COMFASFLOT	HMNB CLYDE
Rowe, Warren L	2Lt	01-Sep-12	RM	GS.	CTCRM OFFICERS	EXMOUTH
Rowland, Charles	SLt	01-Sep-11	MED	MEDICAL	BRNC DARTMOUTH	
Rowland, Justin M	Lt RN	13-Apr-12	ENG	AE	LHF 702 SQN	RNAS YEOVILTON
Rowland, Paul N	Cdr	30-Jun-08	ENG	MESM	DES/COMFLEET	BARROW IN FURNESS
Rowland, Steven G	Capt	01-Apr-11	RM	SCC	HQ SQN CDO LOG	BARNSTAPLE
Rowlands, Andrew P	Lt RN	01-Jan-10	WAR	GSX	DEFAC JSCSC I	SHRIVENHAM
Rowlands, Andrew R	Cdr	30-Jun-13	ENG	WE	DES/COMJE/ISS	CORSHAM
Rowlands, Kevin	Cdr	30-Jun-11	WAR	PWO(A) FC	DOC	MAIN BUILDING LONDON
Rowlands, Sarah J	Lt RN	19-Jun-10	ENG	TM	FLEET FOSNNI - CNR	HMNB PORTSMOUTH
Rowley, Thomas P	Lt Cdr	01-Oct-12	WAR	PWO	MWS COLLINGWOOD	
Rowntree, Paul J	Lt RN	01-Jun-07	WAR	INT	904 EAW	AFGHANISTAN
Rowson, Marcus J	Lt Cdr	01-Oct-13	WAR	P SK4	845 SQN	RNAS YEOVILTON
Roy, Christopher A	Lt RN	16-Jun-03	WAR	P GR7	FLEET CSAV	NCHQ
Roy, Sudipta K	Surg Lt Cdr	01-Aug-10	MED	GS	INM ALVERSTOKE	GOSPORT
Royce, Roderick H	Lt RN	01-Feb-06	WAR	P LYN7	CHFHQ (SEA)	PLYMOUTH
Roylance, Jaimie F	Lt Col	30-Jun-09	RM	P LYN7	JAG	AFGHANISTAN BASTION
Royle, Michael	SLt	01-Feb-12	WAR	GSX	BRNC DARTMOUTH	
Royston, James L	Lt RN	01-Sep-03	WAR	PWO(SM)	HMS AMBUSH	

Person Name	Substantive Rank	Seniority	Branch	Specialisation	Organisation	Location
Royston, Sarah L	Lt RN	01-Jan-07	ENG	ME	DES/COMFLEET	HELENSBURGH
Royston, Stuart J	Cdr	30-Jun-10	WAR	PWO(C)	NC PSYA	HMNB PORTSMOUTH
Ruddock, Gordon W D	Cdr	30-Jun-12	WAR	AAWO	HMS MONMOUTH	
Rudkin, Adam L	Lt RN	01-Sep-05	ENG	AE P	LHF 815 SQN FLT 203	RNAS YEOVILTON
Ruffell, Lauren	Lt RN	01-Apr-12	WAR	GSX	HMS IRON DUKE	
Rusbridger, Robert C	Capt RN	30-Jun-03	ENG	ME	AIR 22GP	RAF LYNEHAM
Ruscoe, David I	Lt RN	01-Apr-09	WAR	MW	MCM1 CREW 8	HELENSBURGH
Rushforth, Robert M	SLt	08-Dec-11	WAR	P	RAF SHAWBURY	
Rushton, Emma V	Lt RN	01-Feb-06	ENG	TM	NAVSEC	NCHQ
Rushworth, Benjamin J	Lt Cdr	01-May-06	WAR	PWO(N)	FLEET FOST ACOS	NCHQ
Russell, Bruce	Lt Cdr	01-May-00	ENG	WESM	FLEET CAP RCAP DIVISION	NCHQ
Russell, Katherine E	Lt Cdr	01-Oct-09	WAR	AAWO	HMS NELSON	
Russell, Martin S	Lt Cdr	01-Oct-11	WAR	O SKW	MWS COLLINGWOOD	
Russell, Michael	Surg Lt Cdr	01-Nov-11	MED	GMP	DES/COMFLEET	HELENSBURGH
Russell, Nigel A D	Lt Cdr	01-Oct-04	WAR	PWO(A)	UK MCC	BAHRAIN
Russell, Paul	Cdr	30-Jun-10	WAR	AAWO	FLEET CAP SSM DIVISION	NCHQ
Russell, Philip R	Cdr	30-Jun-05	ENG	ME	DES/COMFLEET	ABBEY WOOD
Russell, Thomas	Cdr	30-Jun-07	WAR	MCD PWO(A)	NATO-ACO-SHAPE	CASTEAU BRUSSELS
Rutherford, Adam T	Maj	01-Oct-10	RM	MLDR (SCC)	CTCRM (SEA)	EXMOUTH
Rutherford, Ian J D	Lt RN	01-Sep-13	ENG	MESM	DCEME SULTAN	HMS SULTAN
Rutter, John Charles	Lt RN	01-Sep-07	WAR	P SK4	TEMPORARY SAAVN	STOCKBRIDGE
Rweyemamu, Anatol M	Lt RN	01-Apr-12	LOGS	L	HMS DUNCAN	
Ryall, Thomas A	Maj	01-Oct-10	RM	GS	NCHQ	
Ryan, John P	Lt Cdr	01-Oct-08	ENG	MESM	HMS TRENCHANT	
Ryan, Kathleen R	Lt RN	12-Jul-10	QARNNS	Infection C	HMS RALEIGH	
Ryan, Paul Justin	Lt Cdr	01-Oct-13	WAR	P MER	824 SQN - TU	RNAS CULDROSE
Ryan, Richard M	Cdr	30-Jun-09	WAR	O LYNX	OPS DIR	MAIN BUILDING LONDON
Ryan, Sean J	Cdr	30-Jun-11	WAR	SM(CQ)	HMS VICTORIOUS	
Ryan, Stephen J	Lt RN	01-Sep-06	ENG	ME	HMS SULTAN	
Rycroft, Alan E	Capt RN	30-Jun-07	WAR	O LYNX	NATO - BRUSSELS	BRUSSELS
Ryde, Emma	SLt	14-Aug-11	LOGS	L	HMS BULWARK	
Ryder, Matthew R	Lt Cdr	01-Oct-12	ENG	WE	LOAN DSTL - NSD	FAREHAM
Rydiard, Michael	Lt RN	01-Apr-11	WAR	GSX	MCM2 CREW 5	PORTSMOUTH
Rylah, Joshua G	Lt RN	01-Sep-12	WAR	GSX	HMS TYNE	
Rylah, Osgar J	Surg Lt RN	04-Aug-10	MED	GDMO	HMS VANGUARD	

S

Person Name	Substantive Rank	Seniority	Branch	Specialisation	Organisation	Location
Sabin, Scott M	Lt RN	01-Jul-13	WAR	GSX	HMS SOMERSET	
Saddleton, Andrew D	Lt Col	30-Jun-05	RM	LC	ISAF PAK LO	PAKISTAN
Sadler, Aimee Rose G	SLt	16-Feb-11	RM	HM	HMS DUNCAN	
Sadler-Smith, Aaron J	Lt	01-May-10	RM	GS	CTCRM OFFICERS	EXMOUTH
Saffin, James R	Surg Lt RN	05-Aug-09	MED	Anaes	INM ALVERSTOKE	GOSPORT
Said, Phillip M	Lt RN	15-Apr-11	ENG	AE	LHF 815 SQN HQ	RNAS YEOVILTON
Salberg, David G	Lt RN	01-Sep-12	WAR	P	RNAS YEOVILTON	
Sales, Adam	SLt	01-Sep-12	MED	MEDICAL	BRNC DARTMOUTH	
Salisbury, David P OBE	Cdr	30-Jun-03	WAR	P LYNX	HMS COLLINGWOOD	
Salisbury, Dominic B A	Lt RN	17-Dec-10	MED	MS	INM ALVERSTOKE2	GOSPORT
Salmon, Michael A	Capt RN	01-Jul-13	WAR	O SKW	HQ AIR - COS(CAP)	HIGH WYCOMBE
Salt, Isaac P	Mid	01-Sep-13	WAR	GSX	BRNC DARTMOUTH	
Salt, Jennifer M	Lt RN	01-May-07	ENG	WE	MWS COLLINGWOOD	
Salter, Jonas A	Capt	01-Sep-10	RM	GS	HMS BULWARK	
Saltonstall, Hugh F R	Lt Cdr	01-Oct-12	WAR	P LYNX	FOST DPORT SEA	HMNB DEVONPORT
Salzano, Gerard M MBE	Brig	04-May-10	RM	GS	NAVY CORE TRG HQ	HMNB DEVONPORT
Sambrooks, Richard J B	Lt Cdr	01-Oct-09	WAR	P SHAR	FLEET AV VL - OC	RNAS YEOVILTON
Sampson, James	Lt Cdr	01-Oct-12	ENG	IS	DES/COMFLEET	ABBEY WOOD BRISTOL
Sampson, James L	Capt	30-Mar-12	RM	GS	NCHQ	
Sampson, Jonathan A	Lt RN	11-Dec-09	WAR	AV	DSTO	RAF ST MAWGAN
Samuel, Ben James	Lt RN	01-Apr-11	LOGS	L	HMS TALENT	
Samuel, Christopher D	Maj	01-Oct-07	RM	C	HMS NELSON	HMS NELSON
Samuels, Nicholas J	Lt Cdr	01-Oct-09	WAR	SM(AWC)	FOST DSTF - CSST	HMNB DEVONPORT
Samwell, Michael G	Lt RN	01-Sep-04	ENG	WESM	CBRN POL	MAIN BUILDING LONDON
Sander, Oliver P	Lt RN	01-Jul-12	ENG	ME	DCEME SULTAN	HMS SULTAN

Person Name	Substantive Rank	Seniority	Branch	Specialisation	Organisation	Location
Sanders, Lee C	Lt RN	19-Apr-12	ENG	AE	FLEET CSAV	RNAS YEOVILTON
Sanderson, Christopher P	Lt Cdr	01-Oct-07	WAR	HM	HMS ENTERPRISE	
Sanderson, Mark A	Capt	20-Jul-07	RM	SCC	HQ SQN CDO LOG	BARNSTAPLE
Sandhu, Jagdeep S	Surg Lt RN	04-Aug-10	MED	GS	NCHQ	
Sandiford, Aran Jamie	Capt	24-Mar-13	RM	GS	40 CDO RM - B COY	TAUNTON
Sandle, Neil D	Lt Cdr	01-Aug-03	ENG	ME	FLEET CAP SSM DIVISION	NCHQ
Sandy, David J	Lt Cdr	01-Oct-12	WAR	PWO(C)	FOST DPORT SEA	HMNB DEVONPORT
Sanguinetti, Hector R	Cdre	06-Jan-12	WAR	PWO(C)	PJHQ (UK) J2	NORTHWOOD
Sankey, Freddie O	2Lt	01-Sep-11	RM	GS	43 CDO	HMNB CLYDE
Sanocki, Anna Marie	Lt RN	01-Apr-10	WAR	GSX	RNAS CULDROSE - MET	RNAS CULDROSE
Sansford, Adrian J	Cdr	30-Jun-07	ENG	MESM	DES/COMFLEET	ABBEY WOOD BRISTOL
Santrian, Karl	Lt Cdr	01-Oct-05	WAR	AV	RNLA	DARTMOUTH
Santrian, Mark	Lt RN	21-Feb-09	WAR	AV	CHFHQ (SEA)	RNAS YEOVILTON
Santrian, Tracey M	Lt RN	26-Oct-09	LOGS	L FS	NCHQ CNPERS	NCHQ
Santry, Patrick J	Lt RN	26-Oct-09	LOGS	L FS	FLEET ACOS(NLM)	NCHQ
Santry, Paul M	Lt Cdr	01-Oct-07	WAR	C	FLEET CAP IS DIVISION	NCHQ
Sargent, David S	Surg Lt Cdr	06-Aug-08	MED	GMP	NCHQ	
Sargent, Lindsay M	Lt Cdr	01-Oct-04	ENG	TM	FLEET FOST ACOS	NCHQ
Sargent, Nicholas M	Lt Cdr	01-Oct-05	ENG	AE	MOD CNS/ACNS	RNAS YEOVILTON
Satterly, Robert J	Lt Cdr	01-Oct-10	ENG	ME	HMS IRON DUKE	
Satterthwaite, Benjamin J	Lt Cdr	01-Oct-06	WAR	INT	DI - FC(A)	MAIN BUILDING LONDON
Saunders, Alexander J	Mid	01-Sep-13	WAR	HM	BRNC DARTMOUTH	
Saunders, Alexander M	SLt	01-Sep-13	MED	MEDICAL	BRNC DARTMOUTH	
Saunders, Alice	Lt Cdr	01-Oct-09	WAR	HM METOC	RNR AIR	YEOVIL
Saunders, Christopher E MBE	Cdr	30-Jun-12	WAR	PWO(C)	HMS BULWARK	
Saunders, Jason	Lt Cdr	01-Oct-06	ENG	TM	DMOC	RAF HALTON
Savage, Alexander F	Lt Cdr	01-Oct-12	LOGS	L	HMS COLLINGWOOD	
Savage, Dominic N	Lt RN	01-Nov-13	WAR	P	848 SQN YEOVILTON	RNAS YEOVILTON
Savage, Mark R OBE	Cdr	30-Jun-07	WAR	PWO(U)	FLEET COMOPS NWD	NORTHWOOD
Saveal, Matthew P	Lt RN	11-Oct-13	MED	MS	DES/COMFLEET	HELENSBURGH
Savery, Stuart L	Lt RN	01-Sep-11	ENG	MESM	HMS VIGILANT	
Savin, David	SLt	01-Sep-12	ENG	WE	BRNC DARTMOUTH	
Saw, Stephen	Lt RN	11-Apr-08	ENG	ME	RN EXCHANGE N ZLAND	NEW ZEALAND
Saward, Justin R E	Lt Cdr	01-Oct-06	ENG	AE	HMS SULTAN - RNAESS	HMS SULTAN
Sawers, John R	Lt RN	09-Apr-13	ENG	WESM	HMS VANGUARD	
Sawyer, Jason L	Lt RN	20-Feb-08	WAR	O SK6	771 SQN	RNAS CULDROSE
Sawyer, Richard C	Lt RN	01-Mar-11	WAR	INT	FLEET COMOPS NWD	HMS COLLINGWOOD
Sawyer, Trevor J	Lt Col	27-Feb-01	RM	GS	FLEET CAP	NCHQ
Sawyers, Daniel	Capt	01-Sep-09	RM	GS	PJHQ (UK) J3	NORTHWOOD
Say, Russell G	Lt RN	01-Jan-04	ENG	WE	MWS COLLINGWOOD	
Sayer, Jamie M	Lt Cdr	01-Oct-05	ENG	AE	DES/COIR/CA	ABBEY WOOD BRISTOL
Sayer, Russell J	Maj	01-Oct-13	RM	GS	CNPERS	NCHQ
Sayer, Timothy J	2Lt	01-Mar-11	RM	GS	42 CDO RM	HMNB DEVONPORT
Saywell-Hall, Stephen E	Lt Cdr	01-Oct-06	ENG	AE	FLEET FOSNNI - CNR	HMNB PORTSMOUTH
Scales, Dean R	Lt RN	18-Feb-05	WAR	PWO	HMS BULWARK	
Scamp, Simon James	Lt RN	01-Oct-10	WAR	FC	HMS DUNCAN	
Scandling, Rachel J	Cdr	30-Jun-11	LOGS	L	JFC HQ	NORTHWOOD
Scanlon, Michael J	Maj	01-Oct-07	RM	GS	CTCRM - CW	EXMOUTH
Scarlett, Christopher J	Lt RN	01-Jan-04	ENG	WESM	NBC CLYDE	HELENSBURGH
Schnadhorst, James C	Lt Cdr	01-May-95	WAR	PWO(U)	NATO ACO	NORTHWOOD
Schnetler, Simon F	Lt RN	01-Oct-10	WAR	O SKW	857 NAS	RNAS CULDROSE
Schofield, Susan R	Surg Cdr	30-Mar-09	MED	GMP	DES/COMFLEET	HMS DRAKE
Scivier, John S	Lt Cdr	01-Oct-01	WAR	ATC	AIB	HMS SULTAN
Scopes, David	Cdr	30-Jun-12	ENG	AE	DES/COIR/CA	ARLINGTON USA
Scorer, Thomas G	Surg Lt Cdr	01-Aug-12	MED	Path Haem	UK MED GP (AFG)	AFGHANISTAN BASTION
Scott, Alexander J	Lt RN	01-May-04	WAR	MCD	MCM2 CREW 8	PORTSMOUTH
Scott, Alexandra	Surg Lt Cdr	01-Aug-13	MED	GMP	INM ALVERSTOKE	GOSPORT
Scott, Andrew R D	Lt RN	01-Sep-09	ENG	WE	NCHQ CNPS	PORTSMOUTH
Scott, Elizabeth K	Lt RN	01-Jul-02	ENG	TM	FLEET FOST ACOS	NCHQ
Scott, James B	Cdr	30-Jun-06	ENG	MESM	DES/COMFLEET	HMS DRAKE
Scott, Jason	Lt RN	08-Jul-11	WAR	ATC	RNAS YEOVILTON	
Scott, Julian V	Lt Cdr	01-Oct-11	WAR	INT	UK MCC	BAHRAIN

Person Name	Substantive Rank	Seniority	Branch	Specialisation	Organisation	Location
Scott, Mark R.	Lt Cdr	01-Oct-04	WAR	P LYNX	NCHQ CNPERS	PORTSMOUTH
Scott, Michael	Cdr	30-Jun-06	ENG	WESM	DES/COMFLEET	HELENSBURGH
Scott, Neil	Lt Cdr	01-Oct-10	WAR	HM	HMS ILLUSTRIOUS	
Scott, Nigel L J	Capt RN	10-Jan-12	ENG	WESM	HMS NELSON	
Scott, Peter D.	Lt RN	01-Feb-07	WAR	ATC	RNAS YEOVILTON	
Scott, Peter J D S OBE	RN Chpln	03-Sep-91	Ch S		HMS DRAKE	
Scott, Richard A.	Lt Cdr	01-Aug-06	ENG	WE	RNEAWC - SNO	LINCOLN
Scott, Robert J	Lt Cdr	02-Mar-98	WAR	O LYNX	HMS COLLINGWOOD	
Scott, Russell B.	Lt Cdr	01-Oct-13	ENG	ME	DES/COMFLEET	HMNB PORTSMOUTH
Scott, Serena C S	Lt RN	01-May-06	ENG	TM	DEFENCE ACADEMY	SHRIVENHAM
Scott, Simon John	Col	14-Oct-13	RM	LC	FMC JOINT	MAIN BUILDING LONDON
Scott, Thomas	Maj	01-Oct-13	RM	HW(M)	NCHQ CNPERS	PORTSMOUTH
Scott, Thomas L	Capt	01-Sep-13	RM	GS	45 CDO RM	DUNDEE
Scott, Timothy E.	Surg Cdr	01-Jul-13	MED	Anaes	MDHU PETERBOROUGH	PETERBOROUGH
Scott, Victoria	Lt RN	01-Aug-06	QARNNS	OT	HMS NELSON	HMS NELSON
Scown, William O	Lt RN	01-Mar-10	WAR	ATC	RNAS CULDROSE - ATC	RNAS CULDROSE
Scraggs, Daniel R	SLt	01-Sep-13	WAR	SM(X)	MWS COLLINGWOOD	
Screaton, Richard M.	Lt Cdr	01-Mar-04	ENG	ME	HQ RC(SW)	AFGHANISTAN BASTION
Screen, James W.	Lt Cdr	01-Oct-11	ENG	WE	HMS QUEEN ELIZABETH	ROSYTH
Scutt, Martin J	Surg Lt Cdr	04-Feb-09	MED	GMP	DPHC SOUTH	PORTSMOUTH
Seabrook, Peter J	Lt RN	01-Nov-13	WAR	SM(X)	HMS AMBUSH	
Seager, Daniel	Lt RN	01-Sep-08	ENG	MESM	DEFENCE ACADEMY	SHRIVENHAM
Seagrave, Suzanna J.	Lt Cdr	01-Nov-08	ENG	ME	RN EXCHANGE CANADA	OTTAWA
Seal, Martin R	Lt RN	01-Apr-06	WAR	MCD	FDU1	PORTSMOUTH
Seal, Michael O.	Lt Cdr	01-Oct-13	WAR	PWO(SM)	HMS VICTORIOUS	
Seaman, Alec L	Lt RN	10-Feb-08	LOGS	L	FLEET FOSNNI - NRC EE	LONDON
Seaman, Gregg P.	Lt RN	01-Sep-09	ENG	WE	NCHQ CNPERS	PORTSMOUTH
Sear, Jonathan J	Lt Col	30-Jun-07	RM	GS	TIO	MAIN BUILDING LONDON
Searight, Mark F	Maj	01-May-97	RM	GS	RN EXCHANGE FRANCE	TOULON FRANCE
Searight, William M	Capt	01-Sep-10	RM	GS	NCHQ	RAF ST ATHAN
Searle, Andrew J A	Lt Cdr	01-Oct-13	ENG	WE	DI - CA	LONDON
Seaton, Samuel	Lt RN	01-Mar-13	ENG	AE	RNAS CULDROSE	
Seddon, Jonathan D.	Lt RN	01-Apr-06	WAR	FC	HMS DEFENDER	
Sedgwick, Hugo.	Lt RN	01-Jan-04	WAR	INT	FLEET COMOPS NWD	NORTHWOOD
Selden, John D.	Lt RN	01-Nov-03	ENG	IS(SM)	DES/COMFLEET	ABBEY WOOD
Sellars, Scott J.	Cdr	30-Jun-12	LOGS	L C	FLEET ACOS(RP)	NCHQ
Sellen, Thomas J	Mid	01-Feb-13	WAR	SM(X)	BRNC DARTMOUTH	
Sellers, Graham.	Lt Cdr	01-Feb-01	ENG	WE	LSP ON	MUSCAT
Selway, Mark A.	Lt Cdr	01-Jul-05	ENG	AE	DES/COMJE/HELS	YEOVIL
Selwood, Benjamin J	SLt	01-Jan-13	WAR	O	RNAS CULDROSE	
Selwood, Peter J	Lt Cdr	01-Oct-08	QARNNS	Tutor	DMS WHITTINGTON	LICHFIELD
Semple, Brian.	Lt Cdr	01-Oct-10	WAR	P GR7	FLEET CSAV	WASHINGTON USA
Sennett, Michael	Lt RN	01-May-02	ENG	TM	HMS SULTAN	
Sercombe, Benjamin	Capt	16-Apr-10	RM	SCC	COMUKAMPHIBFOR	HMNB PORTSMOUTH
Sercombe, Daniel	Lt RN	01-May-11	WAR	GSX	HMS MONTROSE	
Sergeant, Adam H	Surg SLt	20-Jul-13	MED	MEDICAL	BRNC DARTMOUTH	
Sewed, Michael A.	Lt Cdr	01-Oct-94	WAR	O LYNX	LHF 700W SQN	RNAS YEOVILTON
Sewell, Lynsey E	Lt RN	01-Jan-11	WAR	GSX	MCM1 CREW 6	HELENSBURGH
Seymour, Kevin W.	Capt RN	02-Sep-13	WAR	P GR7	FLEET CSAV	NCHQ
Shackleton, Scott	RN Chpln	20-Sep-94	Ch S		DEFAC JSCSC ACSC	SHRIVENHAM
Shakespeare, Christopher A	Lt RN	01-Sep-04	ENG	AE	HQ RC(SW)	AFGHANISTAN BASTION
Shallcroft, John E	Lt Cdr	01-Oct-98	WAR	P MER	750 SQN SEAHAWK	RNAS CULDROSE
Shanahan, Lloyd A	Lt Cdr	01-Oct-12	WAR	P SK4	GANNET SAR FLT	HMS GANNET
Sharkey, Elton R.	Cdr	30-Jun-12	ENG	MESM	FOST SM SEA	HELENSBURGH
Sharkey, Michael	RN Chpln	01-Oct-90	Ch S		PERNENT JOINT HQ - J1	NORTHWOOD
Sharkey, Philip J.	Lt Cdr	01-Oct-13	ENG	ME	HMS DIAMOND	
Sharland, Craig J.	Lt RN	20-Oct-08	ENG	WE	DES/COMFLEET	ABBEY WOOD BRISTOL
Sharland, Simon P.	Maj	01-Sep-90	RM	LC	NCHQ CNPERS	PORTSMOUTH
Sharman, Max C.	Capt	01-Sep-06	RM	GS	43 CDO FPGRM	HMNB CLYDE
Sharp, Andrew P MBE	Lt Cdr	01-Oct-11	ENG	MESM	NCHQ CNPERS	PORTSMOUTH
Sharp, Christopher A	Lt RN	01-Feb-09	WAR	GSX	HMS LANCASTER	
Sharp, Thomas W	SLt	01-Sep-12	WAR	P	RNAS Y	RNAS YEOVILTON

Person Name	Substantive Rank	Seniority	Branch	Specialisation	Organisation	Location
Sharp, William M J	Surg Lt RN	05-Aug-09	MED	GMP	INM ALVERSTOKE	GOSPORT
Sharpe, Benjamin J	Surg SLt	09-Jul-13	MED	MEDICAL	BRNC DARTMOUTH	
Sharpe, Marcus R	Maj	01-Oct-09	RM	SCC	CTCRM - CW	
Sharpe, Thomas G OBE	Cdr	30-Jun-09	WAR	PWO(A)	PJHQ (UK) J5	NORTHWOOD
Sharples, Joseph H	Lt RN	01-Nov-05	WAR	P LYNX	815 SQN	RNAS YEOVILTON
Sharpley, John G	Surg Capt RN	01-Jul-10	MED	Psych	DPHC SOUTH - DCMH	PORTSMOUTH
Sharrott, Christopher	Lt RN	01-Sep-03	WAR	P LYNX	815 SQN B SECTION	RNAS YEOVILTON
Shattock, James D	Lt RN	01-Nov-07	WAR	P SK4	AACEN 7 (TRG) REGT AAC	MIDDLE WALLOP
Shaughnessy, Sophie L	Cdr	30-Jun-12	ENG	ME	DCTT HQ	HMS SULTAN
Shaughnessy, Toby E	Lt Cdr	01-Oct-05	WAR	AAWO	MCM1 CREW 4	HELENSBURGH
Shaves, Thomas D L	Lt RN	01-Sep-07	LOGS	L	DEFAC JSCSC	SWINDON
Shaw, Callam R	Lt RN	01-Jan-06	ENG	MESM	DES/COMFLEET	HELENSBURGH
Shaw, Christopher	Lt RN	16-Dec-11	ENG	WE	HMS DUNCAN	
Shaw, Hannah K	Lt RN	01-Feb-07	LOGS	L	FOST NWD (JTEPS)	NORTHWOOD
Shaw, Kevin	Capt RN	01-Jul-13	ENG	WE	JFIG	RAF WYTON
Shaw, Mark A	Lt Cdr	01-Oct-13	WAR	MCD	MWS DDS	PORTSMOUTH
Shaw, Mathew J C	Lt RN	17-Dec-10	WAR	GSX	HMS BULWARK	
Shaw, Matthew B	Capt	01-Sep-10	RM	GS	RMR BRISTOL	BRISTOL
Shaw, Neil A	Lt Cdr	01-Oct-08	ENG	WE	HMS TEMERAIRE - DNLM	PORTSMOUTH
Shaw, Ramsay	Lt RN	20-Oct-08	ENG	WESM	DES/COMFLEET	ABBEY WOOD
Shaw, Simon J	Lt RN	01-Nov-05	WAR	GSX	HMS EXPLOIT	
Shaw, Steven M	Cdr	30-Jun-01	LOGS	L	NCHQ CNPS	PORTSMOUTH
Shaw, Stewart	Lt RN	01-Jul-05	WAR	P MER	829 SQN FLT 05	RNAS CULDROSE
Shawcross, Paul K OBE	Capt RN	01-May-10	WAR	P SK4	DEF HELI FLYING SCH	RAF SHAWBURY
Shayler, Stephen A	Lt RN	12-Jul-09	WAR	OP INT	UK MCC	BAHRAIN
Shearman, Alexander J	Surg Lt Cdr	06-Aug-08	MED	Anae	INM ALVERSTOKE	GOSPORT
Shearn, Matthew A	Lt RN	01-Apr-00	WAR	HM(AM)	FLEET COMOPS	NORTHWOOD
Shears, Alexandra F	Lt Cdr	01-Oct-11	LOGS	L BAR	HMS WESTMINSTER	
Shears, Gary R	Lt RN	01-Sep-03	WAR	ATC	RNAS YEOVILTON - AS	RNAS YEOVILTON
Sheehan, Thomas J	Lt RN	01-Oct-04	ENG	WESM	DES/COMFLEET	ABBEY WOOD
Shelton, James R	Capt	01-Sep-08	RM	GS	45 CDO RM	DUNDEE
Shenton, Calvin L	Lt RN	13-Apr-11	LOGS	L	BRNC DARTMOUTH	
Shephard, Samuel J	Capt	01-Sep-13	RM	GS	40 CDO RM - DGHR(O)	TAUNTON
Shepherd, Anya C	Lt RN	01-Dec-02	WAR	PWO(C)	NATO SUPPORT	NCHQ
Shepherd, Charles S	Cdr	30-Jun-07	WAR	SM(CQ)	MWS COLLINGWOOD	
Shepherd, Christopher E	Lt Cdr	01-Oct-12	ENG	WESM	HMS TALENT	
Shepherd, Daniel T	Lt RN	07-May-13	WAR	GSX	MWS COLLINGWOOD	
Shepherd, Fiona R	Cdr	30-Jun-12	LOGS	L	FLEET SPT LOGS	NCHQ
Shepherd, Louise C	Lt RN	01-Sep-13	WAR	GSX	MWS COLLINGWOOD	
Shepherd, Martin P	Cdr	30-Jun-13	WAR	P SK6	771 SQN	RNAS CULDROSE
Shepherd, Oliver J	Lt RN	01-Sep-09	WAR	MCD	NDG	HELENSBURGH
Shepherd, Roger G	Lt Cdr	01-May-96	ENG	WESM	DES/COMFLEET	ABBEY WOOD
Shepley, Benjamin J	Lt RN	01-Jan-13	WAR	GSX	HMS RICHMOND	
Sherriff, David A	Lt Cdr	30-Jun-03	WAR	P LYNX	RN EXCHANGE USA	WASHINGTON USA
Sherriff, Jacqueline MBE	Lt Cdr	31-Mar-06	WAR	MEDIA OPS	EU OHQ	NORTHWOOD
Sherwin, Antony J	Lt RN	01-Jan-05	WAR	O MER	814 SQN	RNAS CULDROSE
Sherwood, Gideon A F	Lt Cdr	01-Oct-09	WAR	AAWO	COMUKTG SEA	PLYMOUTH
Shield, Simon J	Cdr	31-Dec-08	WAR	SM(CQ)	FLEET CAP SSM DIVISION	NCHQ
Shine, David J	Lt RN	01-Sep-10	LOGS	L	HMS ILLUSTRIOUS	
Shipperley, Ian	Cdre	28-Aug-12	ENG	ME	FLEET CAP SSM DIVISION	NCHQ
Shirley, Andrew J	Lt Cdr	01-Aug-01	ENG	MESM	DES/COMFLEET	ABBEY WOOD
Shirley, Benjamin	Lt RN	01-Sep-08	ENG	WE	DES/COMJE/ISS	CORSHAM
Shirley, Christopher I	Capt	01-Sep-11	RM	GS	45 CDO RM	DUNDEE
Shirvill, Matthew J	Lt RN	01-Sep-07	ENG	ME	FLEET CAP SSM DIVISION	NCHQ
Shirvill, Victoria L	Lt Cdr	01-Oct-13	ENG	AE	FLEET CSAV	NCHQ
Short, Gavin C	Cdr	30-Jun-00	ENG	WESM	HMS DRAKE	
Short, John J	Cdr	30-Jun-05	ENG	ME	MOD NSD	MAIN BUILDING LONDON
Shortland, Karen	Lt RN	01-Jan-04	LOGS	L	HMS NELSON	HMS NELSON
Shortt, Martin	Lt RN	01-Sep-12	ENG	TM	HMS SULTAN	HMS SULTAN
Shouler, Matthew F	Lt RN	30-Aug-07	WAR	HUMINT	UK MCC	BAHRAIN
Shrestha, Shekhar	Lt Cdr	01-Oct-13	ENG	ME	HMS SOMERSET	
Shrives, James M	SLt	01-Feb-12	WAR	P	BRNC DARTMOUTH	

Person Name	Substantive Rank	Seniority	Branch	Specialisation	Organisation	Location
Shropshall, Helen L	Lt RN	01-Sep-02	ENG	TM	DES/COMFLEET	HMS DRAKE
Shropshall, Ian	Lt RN	01-Sep-03	WAR	PWO(SM)	RNSMS	HMS RALEIGH
Shutt, David	Mid	01-Nov-13	WAR	GSX	BRNC DARTMOUTH	
Shuttleworth, Andrew	Maj	01-Oct-13	RM	SCC	HQ 3 CDO BDE RM	PLYMOUTH
Simmonds, Daniel D H	Lt Cdr	01-Oct-10	WAR	SM(CQ)	HMS VICTORIOUS	
Simmonds, Zoe N.	Lt RN	01-Nov-13	LOGS	L	HMS DAUNTLESS	
Simmonite, Gavin I DFC	Lt Cdr	01-Oct-08	WAR	P SK4	845 SQN	RNAS YEOVILTON
Simmons, Nigel D	Cdr	30-Jun-99	ENG	WESM	DES/DTECH/TECHEG	ABBEY WOOD
Simmons, Paul C	Capt	01-Sep-12	RM	GS	43 CDO	HMNB CLYDE
Simmons, Robert L	Maj	01-Oct-09	RM	LC	ARMOURED SUPPORT GROUP	RNAS YEOVILTON
Simmons, Sarah	Lt RN	01-Sep-10	ENG	AE	HMS ILLUSTRIOUS	
Simpson, Brett R	Lt RN	31-Jul-09	LOGS	L	HMS DARING	
Simpson, Christopher J	Lt RN	01-Jan-04	WAR	P MER	DEF HELI FLYING SCH	RAF SHAWBURY
Simpson, Colin C	Lt Cdr	01-Oct-04	WAR	P LYNX	700W SQN	RNAS YEOVILTON
Simpson, Daley G.	Lt RN	01-Sep-10	WAR	P	HMS DRAKE	
Simpson, Daniel J.	Lt RN	01-Oct-11	WAR	GSX	HMS DAUNTLESS	
Simpson, David J.	RN Chpln	07-Mar-05	Ch S		HMS SULTAN	
Simpson, Erin L	Lt RN	15-Mar-06	ENG	WE	FLEET CISSU	PORTSDOWN HILL
Simpson, John N.	Lt Cdr	01-Oct-13	MED	MS	HQ 2 MED BDE	YORK
Simpson, Jolyon E	Capt	01-Sep-09	RM	GS	HQ 3 CDO BDE RM	PLYMOUTH
Simpson, Matthew A	Surg Lt RN	05-Aug-09	MED	GDMO	INM ALVERSTOKE	GOSPORT
Simpson, Paul G.	Lt RN	09-Apr-09	ENG	MESM	HMS TIRELESS	
Simpson, Paul N.	Capt	20-Jul-07	RM	GS	NCHQ	
Simpson, Scott F	Lt Cdr	01-Oct-10	WAR	O LYNX	PJHQ (UK) J3	NORTHWOOD
Simpson, William J S MBE	Cdr	01-Oct-08	ENG	MESM	HQ ISAF	AFGHANISTAN KABUL
Sims, Alexander R	Lt Cdr	01-Oct-12	WAR	O LYNX	HMS COLLINGWOOD	
Sims, Deborah L	Lt RN	01-Jan-94	WAR	FC (RES)	RNAS YEOVILTON - RNFS	RNAS YEOVILTON
Sinclair, Gregory W	SLt	15-Aug-11	ENG	WE	MWS COLLINGWOOD	
Sindall, Steven D	Capt	21-Mar-13	RM	GS	NCHQ	
Singleton, Mark D.	Lt Cdr	01-Oct-09	WAR	AV	FLEET CSAV	NCHQ
Singleton, Rachel M	Lt Cdr	01-Oct-09	ENG	IS	FLEET CAP IS DIVISION	NCHQ
Sitton, John B	Lt Cdr	01-Oct-05	ENG	MESM	DES/COMFLEET	HMS DRAKE
Skeer, Martyn	Cdr	30-Jun-02	WAR	P SK6	DEFENCE ACADEMY	SWINDON
Skelding, Joshua J	Lt RN	01-Apr-12	LOGS	L	CHFHQ (SEA)	RNAS YEOVILTON
Skelley, Alasdair N M.	Lt Cdr	01-Mar-03	WAR	PWO(U)	JFHQ	NORTHWOOD
Skelley, Julie C.	Surg Cdr (D)	30-Jun-05	DENTAL	GDP	DEFENCE DENTAL SERVS	HMNB PORTSMOUTH
Skelley, Roger.	Lt RN	01-Feb-08	WAR	GSX	HMS DASHER	
Skelton, Michael G.	Lt RN	18-Apr-13	WAR	MTO	RNLO GULF	DUBAI
Skelton, Richard S.	Lt RN	01-Nov-07	WAR	GSX	HMS TYNE	
Skidmore, Christopher M OBE	Capt RN	30-Jun-07	LOGS	L SM	DES/HR/JSST/LDN	MAIN BUILDING LONDON
Skinner, Amy L	Lt RN	01-Feb-07	WAR	GSX	FOST DPORT SHORE	HMNB DEVONPORT
Skinner, Jennifer E.	Lt RN	13-Oct-12	LOGS	L	HMS KENT	
Skinner, Jonathan J	Lt RN	01-May-06	WAR	MW	MCM1 CREW 1	HELENSBURGH
Skinner, Neil D	Lt RN	01-May-07	WAR	GSX	HMS ILLUSTRIOUS	
Skinsley, Terry J.	Lt Cdr	01-Oct-10	WAR	PWO(N)	FOST DPORT SEA	HMNB DEVONPORT
Skirton, Daniel G.	Lt RN	01-Apr-12	ENG	WESM	HMS TRENCHANT	
Skittrall, Steven	Lt RN	15-Oct-05	ENG	AE O	FLEET CSAV	NCHQ
Skorko, Konrad	Surg Lt RN (D)	20-Jul-11	DENTAL	GDP	40 CDO RM - SDS	TAUNTON
Skuse, Matthew	Lt Col	30-Jun-09	RM	MLDR	SERV ATTACHE/ADVISER	OSLO NORWAY
Slack, Jeremy M	Maj	01-May-97	RM	LC	RN EXCHANGE NETHERLANDS	
Slater, Benjamin	SLt	01-Sep-12	ENG	WE	BRNC DARTMOUTH	
Slater, Sir Jock (John Cunningham Kirkwood) GCB, LVO, DL	Adm	29-Jan-91				
Slater, Louis G.	Capt	01-Sep-12	RM	GS	45 CDO RM - X COY	DUNDEE
Slater, William G	Mid	01-Nov-13	WAR	SM(X)	BRNC DARTMOUTH	
Slattery, Damian J.	Lt Cdr	01-Oct-09	WAR	PWO	COMPORFLOT SHORE	HMNB PORTSMOUTH
Slavin, Max	SLt	01-May-11	MED	MEDICAL	BRNC DARTMOUTH	
Slayman, Emily.	Lt RN	01-Sep-06	LOGS	L	COMUKTG SEA	PLYMOUTH
Sleight, Thomas M	Lt RN	01-Sep-13	WAR	GSX	MCM2 CREW 5	PORTSMOUTH
Slight, Oliver W L	Lt Cdr	01-Oct-13	WAR	PWO	HMS NORTHUMBERLAND	
Sloan, Ian A	Lt RN	01-Dec-99	WAR	P GR7	EMBED FRANCE	TOULON
Slocombe, Christopher A OBE	Cdr	30-Jun-06	WAR	P SK4	CHFHQ	RNAS YEOVILTON

Person Name	Substantive Rank	Seniority	Branch	Specialisation	Organisation	Location
Slocombe, Nicholas R	Cdr	30-Jun-11	WAR	ATC	FLEET CSAV	NCHQ
Sloper, Max David	SLt	01-Apr-11	WAR	P	824 SQN	RNAS CULDROSE
Slowther, Stuart J	Lt Cdr	01-Oct-08	ENG	WE	FLEET CAP SSM DIVISION	NCHQ
Small, Richard	Cdr	30-Jun-09	WAR	SM(CQ)	BDS WASHINGTON - NA	WASHINGTON USA
Smalley, Paul J	Lt RN	01-Jan-08	WAR	P SK4	771 SQN	RNAS CULDROSE
Smallwood, Rachel J MBE	Lt Cdr	01-Oct-10	ENG	TM	NETS (OPS)	HMNB PORTSMOUTH
Smart, Tyler M	SLt	01-Jan-12	WAR	GSX	MCM1 CREW 2	
Smedley, Rachel	Lt Cdr	01-Oct-13	LOGS	L	HMS PORTLAND	
Smees, James E	Mid	01-Sep-13	ENG	ME	BRNC DARTMOUTH	
Smillie, Eleanor J	Lt RN	01-Oct-10	ENG	TM	FLEET HQ 6	NCHQ
Smit, Nathan J	Mid	01-Nov-13	LOGS	L	BRNC DARTMOUTH	
Smith, Adrian G	Lt Cdr	01-Feb-99	ENG	WE	DES/COMFLEET	ABBEY WOOD
Smith, Andrew J E	Lt Cdr	01-Oct-08	WAR	PWO	MCM2 CREW 2	PORTSMOUTH
Smith, Ashley	Lt RN	01-Sep-08	WAR	O MER	814 SQN	RNAS CULDROSE
Smith, Austin	Cdr	30-Jun-09	WAR	P SK4	ATTACHE/ADVISER MUSCAT	MUSCAT
Smith, Barry J	Lt RN	31-Jul-09	WAR	AV	FLEET AV PHOT	PORTSMOUTH
Smith, Benjamin	Lt Cdr	01-Oct-12	WAR	PWO(SM)	HMS VANGUARD	
Smith, Benjamin J	SLt	01-Nov-11	WAR	GSX	BRNC DARTMOUTH	
Smith, Benjamin W	Lt RN	01-Apr-11	WAR	GSX	UK MCC	BAHRAIN
Smith, Brian J	Lt Cdr	01-Dec-99	WAR	AAWO	FLEET CAP SSM DIVISION	NCHQ
Smith, Brian S	Surg Cdr (D)	30-Jun-01	DENTAL	GDP	FLEET DENPOL	PORTSMOUTH
Smith, Charles J	Lt Cdr	01-Oct-09	WAR	C	ACNS CAP	NCHQ
Smith, Christian G	SLt	08-Dec-12	WAR	O	RNAS CULDROSE	
Smith, Christopher A	Capt	01-Sep-10	RM	GS	CTCRM	EXMOUTH
Smith, Christopher J H	Lt Cdr	01-Oct-04	ENG	WE	DES/DTECH	WASHINGTON DC USA
Smith, Christopher J	Cdr	30-Jun-06	LOGS	L (RES)	FLEET FOSNNI - NRC	HELENSBURGH
Smith, Craig A	Lt RN	01-Feb-06	ENG	WE	NAVY MCTA	HMNB PORTSMOUTH
Smith, Dale A	Lt RN	01-Mar-09	ENG	MESM	COMFASFLOT	HMNB CLYDE
Smith, David J	Lt RN	01-May-03	WAR	PWO(SM)	HMS AMBUSH	
Smith, David L	Lt Cdr	01-Oct-04	WAR	AAWO	DES/COMFLEET	ABBEY WOOD
Smith, Edwin J	Lt RN	01-Feb-09	WAR	GSX	HMS MERSEY	
Smith, Fiona E	Surg Lt RN	01-Aug-12	MED	GMP	INM ALVERSTOKE	GOSPORT
Smith, Gary John	Lt RN	17-Dec-10	LOGS	L	HMS ARGYLL	
Smith, Graeme D J	Lt Cdr	01-Jan-01	WAR	PWO(C)	HMS ILLUSTRIOUS	
Smith, Gregory C	Cdr	30-Jun-08	WAR	O SKW	AWC BSD - RW TES	RAF BOSCOMBE DOWN
Smith, Gregory K	Cdr	30-Jun-05	ENG	IS	DCOG JPO	CHELTENHAM
Smith, James A	Lt RN	01-Jan-08	WAR	FC	HMS BITER	
Smith, James E	Capt	01-Sep-11	RM	GS	42 CDO RM	HMNB DEVONPORT
Smith, Jason E	Surg Cdr	30-Jun-05	MED	EM	MDHU DERRIFORD	HMNB DEVONPORT
Smith, Jason J	Surg Lt Cdr	07-Aug-01	MED	BPS	MDHU PORTSMOUTH	HMNB PORTSMOUTH
Smith, Jason P	Lt RN	08-Feb-13	ENG	MESM	DCEME SULTAN	HMS SULTAN
Smith, Jeff R	SLt	01-Jan-12	WAR	P	RNAS YEOVILTON	RAF LINTON ON OUSE
Smith, Jennifer	Lt RN	01-Apr-11	WAR	HM	HMS GLEANER	
Smith, Jennifer C	Lt RN	01-Jan-07	WAR	GSX	UKRBATSTAFF	HMNB PORTSMOUTH
Smith, Karly Jane	Lt RN	15-May-06	WAR	ATC	RNAS CULDROSE	
Smith, Keven J	Lt Cdr	01-Oct-95	WAR	P SK4	848 SQN	RNAS YEOVILTON
Smith, Kim Gyles	Lt RN	01-Sep-12	WAR	SM(X)	HMS TALENT	
Smith, Kristian G	Lt RN	30-Jul-10	ENG	WESM	HMS VICTORIOUS	
Smith, Laurence M	Lt RN	01-Sep-09	WAR	P MER	814 SQN	RNAS CULDROSE
Smith, Mark M	Cdr	30-Jun-08	ENG	AE	DES/COMJE/HELS	YEOVIL
Smith, Mark Peter	Cdr	26-Mar-12	MED	MS(CDO)	NATO-ACT-JWC	STAVANGER (BODO)
Smith, Martin Linn MBE	Brig	31-Jan-11	RM	GS	DEFAC RCDS	LONDON
Smith, Martin R K	Cdr	30-Jun-03	WAR	METOC	FLEET COMOPS NWD	NORTHWOOD
Smith, Matthew D	Lt Cdr	01-Oct-13	LOGS	L SM	HMS RICHMOND	
Smith, Matthew J	Mid	01-Sep-12	WAR	GSX	HMS BULWARK	
Smith, Matthew R	Lt RN	01-Oct-05	WAR	INT	854 NAS	RNAS CULDROSE
Smith, Michael D	Cdr	30-Jun-10	WAR	O LYNX	HMS SOMERSET	
Smith, Michael J	Lt Cdr	01-May-04	ENG	WESM	NCHQ CNPERS	PORTSMOUTH
Smith, Nicholas	Lt RN	01-Oct-08	WAR	P GR7	FLEET CSAV	WASHINGTON
Smith, Nigel J	Lt Cdr	01-Jul-91	WAR	PWO(U)	DES/COMJE/ISTAR	ABBEY WOOD
Smith, Oliver H	Lt RN	01-Sep-12	ENG	MESM	HMS TORBAY	
Smith, Owen J	Lt Cdr	01-Oct-11	ENG	ME	COMPORFLOT SEA	HMNB PORTSMOUTH

Person Name	Substantive Rank	Seniority	Branch	Specialisation	Organisation	Location
Smith, Richard J	Lt RN	01-Sep-08	LOGS	L	HMS NELSON	
Smith, Richard W	Lt RN	01-Jan-12	LOGS	L	HMS DIAMOND	
Smith, Robert	Lt Cdr	01-Oct-07	WAR	O MER	RNAS CULDROSE	
Smith, Robert C	Cdr	30-Jun-10	WAR	O LYNX	ABBEY WOOD	ABBEY WOOD
Smith, Scott A	Lt RN	01-Jan-12	WAR	GSX	HMS DEFENDER	
Smith, Shelley J	Lt RN	30-Jul-10	LOGS	L	LHF 702 SQN	RNAS YEOVILTON
Smith, Simon J	Capt	01-Sep-13	RM	GS	40 CDO RM	TAUNTON
Smith, Stephen A	Lt Cdr	31-Mar-07	WAR	INFO OPS	EU OHQ	NORTHWOOD
Smith, Steven L OBE	Cdr	30-Jun-05	WAR	AAWO	CNPS	NCHQ
Smith, Steven R C	Surg Cdr	30-Jun-03	MED	T&O	MDHU DERRIFORD	PLYMOUTH
Smith, Thomas	Lt RN	14-Aug-11	ENG	TM	CAREER TRAINING	RAF HALTON
Smith, Trevor M	Capt	18-Jul-08	RM	GS	1 ASSLT GROUP RM	HMNB DEVONPORT
Smith, William A	Surg SLt	17-Jul-13	MED	MEDICAL	BRNC DARTMOUTH	
Smith, William F	Lt RN	01-Feb-11	ENG	TM	CTCRM - CTW	EXMOUTH
Smithson, James I	Lt RN	11-Dec-09	MED	MS	NCHQ MEDDIV	NCHQ
Smithson, Peter E	Capt RN	30-Jun-08	ENG	AE	RNAS YEOVILTON	
Smye, Malcolm	Lt Cdr	01-Oct-12	ENG	AE	RN EXCHANGE FRANCE	PARIS FRANCE
Smyth, Daniel	SLt	01-Sep-12	ENG	AE	BRNC DARTMOUTH	
Smyth, Duncan R	Lt RN	01-Apr-12	WAR	GSX	HMS IRON DUKE	
Smythe, Sean R	Lt RN	07-Nov-13	WAR	SM(X)	MWS COLLINGWOOD	
Snazell, Matthew A	Lt RN	01-Jan-09	WAR	P MER	814 SQN	RNAS CULDROSE
Sneddon, Russell N	Lt Cdr	01-Oct-01	WAR	P SK6	RAF SHAWBURY	
Snell, Andrew J	Lt Cdr	01-Oct-10	ENG	ME	HMS PORTLAND	
Snell, Daley A	Lt RN	01-Oct-09	WAR	GSX	HMS DARING	
Snelling, Paul D	Cdr	30-Jun-12	ENG	MESM	CBRN POL	MAIN BUILDING LONDON
Snook, Mathew	Capt	01-Sep-12	RM	GS	CTCRM - CTW	EXMOUTH
Soar, Gary	Lt Cdr	01-Oct-02	WAR	O MER	DES/COMJE	BRISTOL
Sobers, Scott	Lt Cdr	01-Oct-12	ENG	MESM	HMS VANGUARD	
Sollitt, Victoria A	Lt Cdr	01-Oct-08	LOGS	L	DES/COMLAND	ABBEY WOOD
Solly, Matthew M	Cdr	30-Jun-12	ENG	TM(SM)	FLEET FOST ACOS	ABBEY WOOD
Soukup, Sebastian A	2Lt	02-Sep-13	RM	N/A	CTCRM OFFICERS	EXMOUTH
Soul, Nicholas J	Lt Cdr	01-Oct-04	WAR	P SK4	Op LANSBURY	AFGHANISTAN
Souter, Alasdair J	SLt	01-Sep-11	WAR	SM(X)	HMS RICHMOND	
South, David J	Lt Cdr	15-Jun-97	WAR	AAWO	FLEET CAP SSM DIVISION	NCHQ
South, Jack W	2Lt	01-Sep-12	RM	GS	43 CDO FPGRM R SQN	HMNB CLYDE
Southall, Nicholas C J	Lt RN	01-Nov-07	WAR	FC	54(R) SQN A FLT	RAF WADDINGTON
Southorn, Bryony J	Surg Lt Cdr (D)	27-Jun-10	DENTAL	GDP	CTCRM - SDS	EXMOUTH
Southorn, Mark D	Cdr	30-Jun-08	WAR	PWO(U)	UKRBATSTAFF	HMNB PORTSMOUTH
Southwood, Shaun C	Lt Cdr	01-Oct-10	ENG	MESM	HMS VENGEANCE	
Southworth, Christopher	Lt RN	01-Jan-06	WAR	P LYNX	815 SQN	RNAS YEOVILTON
Spacey, Craig D	Lt Cdr	01-Oct-13	ENG	MESM	HMS TRENCHANT	
Spackman, Lucy C	Lt RN	19-May-08	WAR	HM	HMS ECHO	
Spalding, Richard E	Capt RN	30-Jun-06	ENG	WE	NCHQ CNPS	NCHQ
Spalton, Gary	Cdr	11-Jun-93	WAR	PWO(U)	DEFENCE ACADEMY	SHRIVENHAM
Spanner, Paul	Maj	01-May-01	RM	GS	FLEET SPT LOGS	NCHQ
Sparkes, Peter J	Capt RN	08-Nov-10	WAR	PWO(C)	PJHQ (UK) J5	NORTHWOOD
Sparkes, Simon N	Cdr	30-Jun-10	WAR	P MER	FLEET CSAV	NCHQ
Sparrow, Mark	Lt Cdr	01-Oct-09	WAR	P GR7	LOAN DSTL - ASD	FAREHAM
Spearpoint, Damon M	Lt Cdr	01-Oct-12	WAR	INT	NATO BRUSSELS	BRUSSELS
Spears, Andrew G	Lt Cdr	01-Oct-12	WAR	SM(AWC)	HMS ARTFUL	BARROW IN FURNESS
Speedie, Alan	Maj	01-Oct-11	RM	GS	MSSG ENDURING OP	WILTSHIRE
Speller, Nicholas S F	Lt Cdr	01-May-88	WAR	GSX	FLEET ACOS(RP)	NCHQ
Spence, Andrei B	Capt RN	10-Feb-09	LOGS	L BAR	NCHQ - CNLS	NCHQ
Spence, Robert G	Lt Cdr	01-Oct-06	WAR	P SK4	847 SQN - AE	RNAS YEOVILTON
Spencer, Ashley C	Lt Cdr	01-Oct-10	WAR	MCD PWO	MCM1 CREW 2	HMS BLYTH
Spencer, Charles M	Capt	01-Sep-11	RM	GS	45 CDO RM	DUNDEE
Spencer, Douglas A	Capt	01-Sep-10	RM	GS	NCHQ	
Spencer, Richard A	Brig	22-Jul-11	RM	C	FLEET HQ	NCHQ
Spencer, Steven J	Cdr	04-Aug-09	QARNNS	Nursing Officer	HQ ISAF	AFGHANISTAN KABUL
Spike, Adam James	Lt RN	01-May-02	WAR	P SK4	CHF(MERLIN)	RAF BENSON
Spillane, Paul W	Lt Cdr	01-Oct-06	WAR	O SKW	FLEET CSAV	NCHQ
Spiller, Stephen N	Lt Cdr	01-Aug-05	ENG	WE	DES/COMLAND/WPNS	ABBEY WOOD

Person Name	Substantive Rank	Seniority	Branch	Specialisation	Organisation	Location
Spink, David A	Maj	01-Oct-08	RM	GS	PJHQ (UK) CMD GP	NORTHWOOD
Spinks, David	Lt Cdr	01-Aug-05	WAR	AAWO	MWS COLLINGWOOD	
Spinks, Robert J	Lt RN	01-May-01	WAR	P LYN7	848 SQN	RNAS YEOVILTON
Spooner, Ross	Cdr	30-Jun-13	WAR	P MER	824 SQN	RNAS CULDROSE
Spoors, Brendan	Lt Cdr	01-Oct-10	WAR	P MER	824 SQN	RNAS CULDROSE
Spreadborough, Philip J	Surg Lt Cdr	01-Aug-12	MED	GS	INM ALVERSTOKE	GOSPORT
Spreckley, Damian R C	Lt RN	09-Apr-09	LOGS	L	CHFHQ (SEA)	RNAS YEOVILTON
Springer, Rory Jay	SLt	01-Sep-11	WAR	P	CAREER TRAINING	RAF SHAWBURY
Springett, Simon P	RN Chpln	10-Sep-91	Ch S		CTCRM	EXMOUTH
Spurdle, Andrew P	Lt Cdr	01-Oct-05	WAR	PWO(A)	FOST DPORT SEA	HMNB DEVONPORT
Squires, Jack Ellis	Mid	19-Apr-13	WAR	GSX	BRNC DARTMOUTH	
Squires, Russell A	Capt	01-Mar-10	RM	GS	40 CDO RM - LOG COY	TAUNTON
St Aubyn, John D	Cdr	30-Jun-01	ENG	WESM	DES/COMFLEET	ABBEY WOOD
St Claire, Christopher	Lt RN	01-Oct-08	WAR	ATC	RAF COLLEGE - OACHQ	RAF CRANWELL
Stace, Ivan Spencer	Capt RN	28-Aug-12	ENG	WESM	DES/COMFLEET	ABBEY WOOD
Stacey, Andrew M	Cdr	30-Jun-08	WAR	PWO(A)	PJHQ (UK) J3	NORTHWOOD
Stacey, Piers	SLt	01-May-13	WAR	INT	BRNC DARTMOUTH	
Stachow, Elizabeth A	Surg Lt RN	03-Aug-11	MED	GDMO	SF MEDICAL	RNAS CULDROSE
Stack, Eleanor F	Lt RN	01-Oct-09	WAR	AAWO	MCM2 CREW 7	PORTSMOUTH
Stackhouse, Martyn C	Lt RN	01-Jan-07	WAR	P MER	824 SQN	RNAS CULDROSE
Stafford, Benjamin R	Lt Cdr	01-Oct-07	ENG	MESM	HMS DRAKE	
Stafford, Derek B MBE	Lt Col	30-Jun-12	RM	P SK4	CHF MERLIN 2	RAF BENSON
Stafford, Wayne	Cdr	30-Jun-13	ENG	WESM	DI - ICSP	LONDON
Stafford-Shaw, Damian	Lt RN	01-Sep-06	ENG	TM	DMC DMOC	RAF HALTON
Stagg, Antony R	Lt Cdr	01-Mar-03	ENG	AE	DES/COMLAND/JSC	ABBEY WOOD
Stait, Benjamin J	Lt Cdr	01-Oct-06	WAR	PWO	JFC HQ	NORTHWOOD
Staley, Simon P L	Cdr	30-Jun-07	WAR	O SKW	DIRECTOR (JW)	NORTHWOOD
Stamper, Jonathan C	Cdr	30-Jun-09	ENG	IS	DES/COMFLEET	HMNB PORTSMOUTH
Stamper, Valerie L	Lt RN	01-Mar-06	LOGS	L	FLEET CMR	NCHQ
Stanbury, David R	Lt RN	19-Oct-07	WAR	MCD	MCM1 CREW 8	FASLANE
Stancliffe, Andrew E ACMI	Lt RN	01-Jul-04	ENG	AE	HMS TEMERAIRE	HMNB PORTSMOUTH
Standen, Gary David	Lt Cdr	01-Oct-09	ENG	AE	DES/COMFLEET	ABBEY WOOD
Stanford, Thomas C	Lt RN	01-Jan-12	ENG	TM	DCDS(PERS) - TDG	RAF HALTON
Stanhope, Sir Mark, GCB, OBE	Adm	10-Jul-04				
Stanistreet, Georgina C	Lt RN	01-May-04	ENG	ME	DCMC	MAIN BUILDING LONDON
Stanley, Nicholas	Capt RN	30-Jun-02	WAR	MCD PWO(U)	HMS NELSON	HMS NELSON
Stanley-Adams, Tony R	Lt RN	29-Oct-12	ENG	WESM	HMS TALENT	
Stanley-Whyte, Berkeley J	Capt RN	01-Jul-11	ENG	WESM(SWS)	DES/COMFLEET/SM	USA
Stannard, Adam	Surg Lt Cdr	02-Aug-05	MED	GS	INM ALVERSTOKE	GOSPORT
Stannard, Joshua N	2Lt	02-Sep-13	RM	N/A	CTCRM OFFICERS	EXMOUTH
Stannard, Mark	Lt Cdr	01-Aug-97	WAR	GSX	RNLT - KFNA	SAUDI ARABIA
Stanning, Alastair J	Surg Lt Cdr	01-Aug-12	MED	GMP	INM ALVERSTOKE	GOSPORT
Stant, Mark S	Lt RN	01-Apr-07	ENG	WE	HMS QUEEN ELIZABETH	ROSYTH
Stanton, Keith V	Maj	01-Oct-09	RM	SCC	CTCRM - ISC	EXMOUTH
Stanton-Brown, Peter J	Lt Cdr	01-Feb-01	WAR	SM(AWC)	DES/COMFLEET	ABBEY WOOD
Stapley, Sarah Ann	Surg Cdr	30-Jun-02	MED	T&O	MDHU PORTSMOUTH	HMNB PORTSMOUTH
Stapley-Bunten, Thomas A	SLt	01-Sep-13	WAR	GSX	HMS RICHMOND	
Stark, Justin R	Lt RN	31-Jul-09	WAR	AV	RNLA	DARTMOUTH
Starkey, David S	Lt RN	01-Feb-06	WAR	MCD	MCM2 CREW 2	HMNB PORTSMOUTH
Starling, Christopher MBE	Maj	01-Oct-12	RM	SCC	NCHQ CNPERS	PORTSMOUTH
Starsmore, Daniel L	Lt RN	01-Dec-09	WAR	P	CAREER TRAINING	WASHINGTON USA
Staunton, Thomas H	Surg Lt RN	04-Aug-10	MED	GDMO	30 CDO IX GP RM	PLYMOUTH
Staveley, Catherine B	Lt RN	01-Jun-10	WAR	GSX	RNP TEAM	HMNB PORTSMOUTH
Stead, Andrew M	Lt Cdr	01-Oct-12	ENG	TM	RNLA	DARTMOUTH
Steadman, Robert J	Lt Cdr	01-May-04	WAR	AAWO	DEFAC JSCSC ACSC	SHRIVENHAM
Steadman, Thomas W	SLt	01-Feb-12	ENG	WESM	MWS COLLINGWOOD	
Steeds, Sean	Capt RN	27-Jun-09	WAR	P LYNX	DCD - MODSAP KSA	RIYADH (MODSAP)
Steel, David G CBE	V Adm	10-Oct-12	LOGS	L BAR	2SL CNPT	NCHQ
Steele, Ashley T	SLt	01-May-13	WAR	O	RNAS CULDROSE	RNAS CULDROSE
Steele, Jason K	Lt RN	31-Jul-09	LOGS	L	ACNS CAP	NCHQ
Steele, Katie	Lt RN	01-Jun-10	LOGS	L	MCM2 POR SEA	HMNB PORTSMOUTH
Steele, Marie L	Lt RN	01-Nov-05	WAR	HM	HMS COLLINGWOOD	

Person Name	Substantive Rank	Seniority	Branch	Specialisation	Organisation	Location
Steele, Matthew E.	Lt RN	09-Apr-10	ENG	ME	COMPORFLOT	HMNB PORTSMOUTH
Steele, Matthew S.	Lt Cdr	01-Oct-13	WAR	HM(AM)	RNAS YEOVILTON - MET	RNAS YEOVILTON
Steele, Nathan C.	SLt	01-Nov-10	WAR	GSX	BRNC DARTMOUTH	
Steen, Kieron M.	Lt Cdr	01-Oct-08	WAR	P GR7	RAF LINTON-ON-OUSE	RAF LINTON ON OUSE
Steiger, Gary J.	Lt RN	17-Dec-10	MED	MS	MDHU DERRIFORD	PLYMOUTH
Stellon, Christopher	Lt RN	02-Apr-09	WAR	O SKW	854 NAS	RNAS CULDROSE
Stembridge, Daniel P T	Cdr	30-Jun-09	WAR	P SHAR	FLEET CSAV	RNAS YEOVILTON
Stemp, Justin E	Maj	01-Sep-04	RM	GM	PJHQ (UK) J3	NORTHWOOD
Stephen, Barry M	Lt Cdr	01-Mar-02	WAR	PWO(N)	FOST MPV SEA	HELENSBURGH
Stephen, Cameron E	Lt RN	01-Sep-07	ENG	AE	DES/COMJE	YEOVIL
Stephen, Nicola	Lt RN	01-Feb-11	WAR	GSX	RNP TEAM	RAF NORTHOLT
Stephens, Brian J	Lt RN	08-Feb-13	WAR	ATC	RNAS YEOVILTON	
Stephens, Carl W	Lt RN	01-Sep-13	WAR	O MER	814 SQN	RNAS CULDROSE
Stephens, Patrick G	Lt RN	01-Jul-05	WAR	SM(N)	NCHQ CIT	NCHQ
Stephens, Samuel J R	Lt RN	01-Jan-06	WAR	GSX	MWS COLLINGWOOD	
Stephenson, Christopher J	Lt RN	01-Apr-03	WAR	MCD	HMS OCEAN	
Stephenson, Fiona	Lt RN	01-Sep-11	WAR	GSX	MCM1 CREW 7	FASLANE
Stephenson, Gavin	SLt	01-Feb-12	MED	MEDICAL	BRNC DARTMOUTH	
Stephenson, John	Lt RN	01-Aug-09	WAR	C	RAF GIBRALTAR - ENG	HMS ROOKE
Stephenson, Keith J M	Cdr	30-Jun-12	ENG	IS	FLEET ACOS(RP)	NCHQ
Stephenson, Philip G	Lt Cdr	01-Oct-03	LOGS	L	HMS NELSON	
Stephenson, Richard J E	Lt RN	08-Apr-05	LOGS	L	RNLA	HMS COLLINGWOOD
Steven, William G	2Lt	01-Sep-11	RM	GS	CTCRM OFFICERS	EXMOUTH
Stevens, Anthony John	Lt Cdr	01-Oct-06	ENG	TM(SM)	BRNC DARTMOUTH	
Stevens, Christopher K	Lt RN	01-Sep-09	WAR	GSX	HMS PUNCHER	
Stevens, Christopher N	Capt	01-Sep-09	RM	GS	42 CDO RM	HMNB DEVONPORT
Stevens, Joseph I	Lt Cdr	01-Oct-11	ENG	AE	DES/COIR	ABBEY WOOD
Stevens, Lisa C	Surg Lt Cdr	02-Aug-10	MED	GMP	RM LYMPSTONE	EXMOUTH
Stevens, Mark	Lt RN	15-Apr-11	WAR	SM(X)	HMS TRIUMPH	
Stevens, Mark J	Lt RN	07-Apr-06	ENG	ME	NCHQ	
Stevenson, Adam	Lt Cdr	01-Oct-13	WAR	GSX	MWS COLLINGWOOD	
Stevenson, Alexander N	Lt RN	06-Apr-07	WAR	O SK6	DEFAC JSCSC	SHRIVENHAM
Stevenson, Charles D	SLt	01-Mar-11	WAR	GSX	HMS WESTMINSTER	
Stevenson, Geoffrey S	Surg Cdr (D)	14-Jan-09	DENTAL	GDP	DDS SCOTLAND	EDINBURGH
Stevenson, Helen L	Lt RN	01-Nov-13	ENG	WE	MWS COLLINGWOOD	
Stevenson, Julian P	Lt Cdr	01-Nov-05	ENG	MESM	SETT	GOSPORT
Stevenson, Simon	Lt Cdr	01-Oct-13	WAR	P MER	829 SQN EFP	RNAS CULDROSE
Stevenson, Thomas E	Surg Lt Cdr	01-Aug-13	MED	GS	INM ALVERSTOKE	GOSPORT
Stewart, Charles H	Lt RN	01-Sep-01	WAR	GSX	NCHQ CNPERS	NCHQ
Stewart, Lee A	Capt	01-Sep-12	RM	GS	CTCRM	EXMOUTH
Stewart, Leonie H	SLt	01-Apr-13	DENTAL	DENTAL	BRNC DARTMOUTH	
Stewart, Nicholas J	Lt RN	01-May-04	WAR	HM	FLEET COMOPS NWD	RAF WYTON
Stewart, Rory W	Lt Cdr	01-Jul-91	ENG	MESM	DES/COMFLEET	THURSO
Stewart, Sean T	Lt RN	09-Jun-06	WAR	REG	NPM NORTHERN	HELENSBURGH
Stewart, Tristan J	Capt	01-Sep-11	RM	GS	40 CDO RM	TAUNTON
Stickland, Charles R OBE	Col	01-Dec-09	RM	LC	JFHQ	NORTHWOOD
Stidston, Ian J	Capt RN	15-Jun-09	ENG	TM	NCHQ NAVY CMD	NCHQ
Stiles, Maxine K	Lt RN	01-Apr-11	LOGS	L	HMS VIGILANT	
Still, James C	SLt	08-Dec-12	WAR	P	RNAS CULDROSE	
Still, Peter A	Lt RN	01-Apr-05	ENG	MESM	NCHQ	
Stilwell, James M	Lt Cdr	01-Oct-06	WAR	SM(AWC)	FOST FAS SHORE	HELENSBURGH
Stinchcombe, Mark E	SLt	01-Nov-11	WAR	GSX	BRNC DARTMOUTH	
Stinton, George T	2Lt	01-Sep-11	RM	GS	CTCRM OFFICERS	EXMOUTH
Stirling, Andrew C	Lt RN	16-Dec-00	WAR	P LYN7	847 SQN - AE	RNAS YEOVILTON
Stitson, Paul	Maj	01-Oct-10	RM	LC	DCBRN CENTRE	SALISBURY
Stock, Christopher M	Cdr	30-Jun-12	WAR	O MER	814 SQN	RNAS CULDROSE
Stockbridge, Antony	Lt Cdr	01-Oct-05	LOGS	L BAR	PJHQ (UK) J9	NORTHWOOD
Stocker, Jeremy	Capt RN	01-Mar-10	WAR	INFO OPS (RES)		FLEET CMR NCHQ
Stockley, Sean A	Lt RN	01-Mar-13	ENG	WESM	HMS VIGILANT	
Stockton, Barry G	Lt RN	27-Jul-07	ENG	WESM(TWS)	DES/COMLAND/WPNS	ABBEY WOOD
Stockton, Kevin G	Lt Cdr	19-Nov-00	WAR	MCD PWO	FDS HQ	PORTSMOUTH
Stoffell, David	Cdr	30-Jun-07	LOGS	L SM	NATO-ACT-HQ SACT	NORFOLK

Person Name	Substantive Rank	Seniority	Branch	Specialisation	Organisation	Location
Stokes, Richard	Cdre	25-Jul-11	ENG	WESM(TWS)	NUCLEAR CAPABILITY	MAIN BUILDING LONDON
Stone, James	Lt Cdr	01-Oct-11	WAR	O SKW	849 SQN	RNAS CULDROSE
Stone, Marc D	Lt RN	20-Aug-12	ENG	AE	845 SQN	RNAS YEOVILTON
Stone, Matthew J	Lt RN	01-Jan-13	ENG	WE	HMS DAUNTLESS	
Stone, Nicholas	Lt Cdr	01-Oct-06	LOGS	L SM	RN EXCHANGE FRANCE	PARIS
Stone, Nicholas S	Lt RN	11-Dec-08	WAR	SM(N)	HMS TIRELESS	
Stone-Ward, Robert O	Lt RN	01-Sep-12	WAR	MCD	MCM2 CREW 6	PORTSMOUTH
Stopps, Gregory A M	Lt RN	01-Jan-08	WAR	SM(N)	FOST FAS SHORE	HELENSBURGH
Storey, Andrew	Lt Cdr	01-Oct-10	WAR	PWO(N)	RN EXCHANGE USA	WASHINGTON USA
Storey, Helen J	Lt Cdr	01-Oct-08	LOGS	L BAR	NORTHWOOD HQ	
Storey, James I	Lt RN	18-Dec-12	ENG	MESM	HMS VICTORIOUS	
Storey, Kristopher J	Lt RN	01-Sep-12	ENG	AE	814 SQN	RNAS CULDROSE
Storey, William	Lt RN	01-Nov-12	ENG	ME	HMS BULWARK	
Storton, George H	Lt Cdr	01-Oct-13	WAR	PWO(N)	MWS COLLINGWOOD	
Stovin-Bradford, Matthew	Col	07-Jan-13	RM	C	NCHQ CNPERS	PORTSMOUTH
Stowell, Perry I M	Cdr	30-Jun-13	WAR	PWO(U)	UK MCC	BAHRAIN
Strachan, Gordon J	SLt	18-Apr-12	WAR	SM(X)	BRNC DARTMOUTH	
Strachan, Robert C	Surg RN	01-Mar-13	MED	MEDICAL	BRNC DARTMOUTH	
Stradling, Duncan E	Lt RN	01-Sep-11	WAR	FC	HMS DARING	
Straker, Peter D	Lt RN	01-Dec-09	WAR	P SK4	845 SQN	RNAS YEOVILTON
Strange, Jamie L	Lt RN	17-Dec-10	WAR	AV	DSTO	RAF ST MAWGAN
Strange, Steven P	Lt Cdr	01-Oct-05	ENG	WESM(TWS)	COMDEVFLOT	HMS DRAKE
Strathern, Roderick J	Lt Cdr	01-Oct-98	WAR	PWO(U) MW	HMS VICTORY	HMNB PORTSMOUTH
Strathie, Gavin S	Lt Cdr	01-Jun-08	WAR	ATC	FLEET CSAV	RNAS YEOVILTON
Stratton, Matthew P	Lt Cdr	01-Oct-08	ENG	WE	DES/COMLAND/WPNS	ABBEY WOOD
Stratton, Nicholas C	Lt Cdr	01-May-12	WAR	INT	FLEET COMOPS NWD	NORTHWOOD
Stratton, Stuart J	Lt Cdr	01-Oct-09	ENG	MESM	HMS SULTAN	
Strawbridge, Chantal M	Lt RN	01-Sep-04	WAR	GSX	HMS EXAMPLE	
Street, Sarah	Lt Cdr	01-Oct-13	LOGS	L	HMS ST ALBANS	
Streeten, Christopher M	Capt RN	01-Jul-13	ENG	WESM(SWS)	NUCLEAR CAPABILITY	MAIN BUILDING LONDON
Streets, Christopher G	Surg Cdr	30-Jun-07	MED	GS	MDHU DERRIFORD	PLYMOUTH
Strickland, Timothy	Lt RN	01-Apr-07	WAR	P MER	829 SQN FLT 02	RNAS CULDROSE
Stride, James A	Cdr	30-Jun-11	WAR	PWO(A) HM	HMS DUNCAN	
Stride, Jamieson Colin	Cdr	30-Jun-13	WAR	O LYNX	AWC WAD - AWG	LINCOLN
Stringer, Graeme E	Lt Cdr	01-Oct-10	WAR	ATC	RNAS YEOVILTON	
Stroude, Paul	Cdr	30-Jun-10	WAR	PWO(U)	DEFENCE ACADEMY	SHRIVENHAM
Strutt, Jason F	Lt Cdr	01-May-00	ENG	WE	FLEET CAP IS DIVISION	NCHQ
Stuart, Euan E	Lt Cdr	01-Oct-04	WAR	AAWO	HMS ARGYLL	
Stuart, Simon A	Lt RN	01-Sep-04	WAR	O LYNX	RNAS YEOVILTON	
Stubbs, Benjamin D	Lt RN	01-Sep-03	WAR	P GR7	RNAS YEOVILTON	
Stubbs, Ian	Lt Cdr	01-Oct-11	ENG	TM	MWS COLLINGWOOD	
Stubbs, Ian	Lt Cdr	01-Oct-09	WAR	O MER	824 SQN - TU	RNAS CULDROSE
Sturgeon, David M	Lt Cdr	01-Oct-08	LOGS	L SM	ACDS LOGCONANDFD	ABBEY WOOD
Sturgeon, Mark	Lt Cdr	01-Oct-12	ENG	WESM(TWS)	HMS TRENCHANT	
Sturman, Andrew J	SLt	01-Nov-11	WAR	GSX	BRNC DARTMOUTH	
Sturman, Richard W	Lt Cdr	01-Oct-11	WAR	P SK4	CHF(MERLIN)	RAF BENSON
Sturt, Ashleigh N	Lt RN	17-Dec-10	WAR	P LYN7	HMS CLYDE	
Stuttard, Mark	Cdr	30-Jun-06	WAR	PWO(A)	RNLO GULF	DUBAI 1
Suckling, Christopher	Lt RN	01-Jun-09	WAR	P MER	829 SQN EFP	RNAS CULDROSE
Suckling, Robin L	Lt Cdr	01-Oct-02	WAR	O SK6	GANNET SAR FLT	HMS GANNET
Sullivan, Mark N	Lt Cdr	01-Oct-05	ENG	ME	FLEET HQ	NCHQ
Summers, Alastair J	Lt RN	01-Dec-00	WAR	P SK6	771 SQN	RNAS CULDROSE
Summers, James A	Maj	24-May-02	RM	GS	LOAN DSTL - NSD	FAREHAM
Sunderland, Scott A	SLt	01-Apr-12	WAR	P	RNAS YEOVILTON	RNAS YEOVILTON
Sutcliff, Jonathan D	Lt RN	01-Nov-05	WAR	WE	MWS COLLINGWOOD	
Sutcliffe, Paul	Lt RN	01-Jan-05	WAR	P MER	829 SQN FLT 01	RNAS CULDROSE
Suter, Francis T	Lt RN	01-Jan-02	WAR	O LYNX	LHF 700W SQN	RNAS YEOVILTON
Sutherland, Iain	Maj	01-Oct-12	RM	GS	FLEET COMOPS	NORTHWOOD
Sutherland, Neil MBE	Lt Col	30-Jun-09	RM	C	42 CDO RM	HMNB DEVONPORT
Sutherland, Oliver	SLt	01-Sep-11	ENG	MESM	DCEME SULTAN	HMS SULTAN
Sutherland, Steven	Maj	01-Oct-13	RM	C (SCC)	45 CDO RM - LOG COY	DUNDEE
Suttle, Celia E	Lt RN	01-Sep-13	WAR	HM	MWS COLLINGWOOD	

Person Name	Substantive Rank	Seniority	Branch	Specialisation	Organisation	Location
Sutton, David MBE	Maj	01-Oct-09	RM	P LYN7	HQ JHC	ANDOVER
Sutton, Gary B	Capt RN	30-Jun-05	WAR	PWO(N)	FLEET HQ 6	NCHQ
Sutton, Richard M J MBE	Cdr	30-Jun-10	WAR	P SK4	848 SQN	RNAS YEOVILTON
Suzuki, Hironobu M	Lt RN	01-Apr-12	WAR	P	RNAS YEOVILTON	
Swain, Andrew V MBE	Cdr	30-Jun-05	WAR	HM (H CH)	LSP ON	MUSCAT
Swain, Cara Simone	Surg Lt RN	07-Aug-13	MED	MEDICAL	BRNC DARTMOUTH	
Swales, Richard	Lt RN	01-Jan-08	WAR	O MER	771 SQN	RNAS CULDROSE
Swan, Anthony M	2Lt	02-Sep-13	RM	N/A	CTCRM OFFICERS	EXMOUTH
Swann, Adam P	Lt RN	01-Apr-08	LOGS	L (RES)	EU OHQ	NORTHWOOD
Swann, James John	SLt	01-May-12	ENG	WE	MWS COLLINGWOOD	
Swannick, Derek J	Cdr	30-Jun-02	WAR	METOC	UKMO	EXETER
Sweeney, Fiona Jane	SLt	01-May-12	MED	MEDICAL	BRNC DARTMOUTH	DARTMOUTH
Sweeney, Keith P M	Cdr	30-Jun-12	ENG	ME	NATO-ACT-JWC	NORWAY
Sweeney, Rachel J	Lt Cdr	01-Oct-13	ENG	AE	HMS ILLUSTRIOUS	
Sweny, Gordon	Maj	01-Oct-12	RM	GS	RN EXCHANGE FRANCE	PARIS FRANCE
Swift, Robert D	Lt RN	01-Sep-04	LOGS	L SM	COMFASFLOT	HELENSBURGH
Swindells, Mark	Lt Cdr	01-Oct-10	WAR	P LYNX	WMF SHORE	RNAS YEOVILTON
Swire, Barry J	Lt RN	26-Jul-02	QARNNS	MH	DPHC SCOTLAND	HELENSBURGH
Swithinbank, George R	Lt RN	01-Sep-11	WAR	SM(X)	HMS TRENCHANT	
Sykes, Leah D	Lt Cdr	01-Oct-04	QARNNS	PHC	HQ DPHC	LICHFIELD
Sykes, Matthew J	Lt Cdr	01-Sep-10	WAR	PWO	HMS SOMERSET	
Sykes, Mitchell C	Lt	01-Sep-12	RM	GS	NCHQ	
Sykes, Robert A	Lt Cdr	01-Oct-96	WAR	O LYNX	DES/COMJE/HELS	RNAS YEOVILTON
Sykes-Popham, Christopher	Capt	01-Sep-13	RM	GS	45 CDO RM	DUNDEE
Sylvan, Christopher A	Maj	01-Oct-13	RM	GS	DEFAC JSCSC ICSCL	SWINDON
Symcox, Charles M	Lt RN	01-Jan-08	WAR	P LYNX	LHF 702 SQN	RNAS YEOVILTON
Syrett, Matthew E	Cdr	30-Jun-10	WAR	HM (H CH)	HMS ECHO	
Syson, Carl F	Lt RN	01-Jan-04	WAR	P GR7	FLEET AV VL - OC	RNAS YEOVILTON
Szweda, Alexander A	Lt RN	01-Nov-10	WAR	GSX	HMS ILLUSTRIOUS	

T

Person Name	Substantive Rank	Seniority	Branch	Specialisation	Organisation	Location
Tabeart, George W	Cdr	30-Jun-10	WAR	HM (H CH)	DI - ICSP	NORTHWOOD
Tabor, James Hugh	RN Chpln	26-Jun-04	Ch S		BRNC DARTMOUTH	
Taborda, Matthew A	Lt RN	01-Sep-05	WAR	GSX	HMS MONMOUTH	
Tacey, Richard	Lt Cdr	01-Dec-07	WAR	PWO(A)	STRIKFORNATO LISBON	LISBON PORTUGAL
Tagg, Peter William	Lt RN	01-Aug-08	MED	MS(EHO)	DES/COMFLEET	HMNB PORTSMOUTH
Tait, Iain Campbell	Capt	03-Apr-09	RM	SCC	CHFHQ (SEA)	RNAS YEOVILTON
Tait, Martyn D	Lt RN	27-Aug-02	ENG	TM(SM)	NCHQ CNPERS	HMNB PORTSMOUTH
Talbot, Edward T	2Lt	02-Sep-13	RM	N/A	CTCRM OFFICERS	EXMOUTH
Talbot, Rebecca J	Lt RN	01-Mar-09	LOGS	L	BRNC DARTMOUTH	
Talbot, Richard J	Lt Cdr	01-Oct-09	WAR	PWO	HMS PORTLAND	
Talbot, Simon J	Lt RN	01-May-05	WAR	FC	HMS DAUNTLESS	
Talbott, Aidan H	Capt RN	01-Jul-13	LOGS	L	DES/COMFLEET	HMNB PORTSMOUTH
Tall, Iain T G	Lt Cdr	01-Oct-10	ENG	WE	HMS DIAMOND	
Talmage, Charles R	Lt RN	01-Apr-08	WAR	P SK4	NO 3 FTS/UAS - JEFTS	
Tamayo, Kieran	SLt	01-Nov-11	LOGS	L	HMS SOMERSET	
Tamlyn, Stephen	Maj	01-Oct-07	RM	GS	DEFENCE ACADEMY	SHRIVENHAM
Tanner, Michael J	Col	16-Dec-13	RM	GS	DES/COMFLEET/NB	HMNB PORTSMOUTH
Tanner, Richard	Cdr	30-Jun-13	WAR	SM(CQ)	HMS VIGILANT	
Tantam, Robert J G	Lt Cdr	01-Oct-09	ENG	MESM	HMS ASTUTE	
Tanzer, William J C E	Surg Lt RN	05-Aug-09	MED	GMP	INM ALVERSTOKE	GOSPORT
Tapp, Steven J	Maj	01-Oct-09	RM	P GAZ	COMUKTG SEA	PLYMOUTH
Tappin, Simon John	Lt Cdr	01-Oct-10	WAR	AWO(U)	HMS WESTMINSTER	
Tarbard, Gavin T	Lt RN	01-May-10	ENG	TM	RNCR BOVINGTON	WAREHAM
Targett, Edward G	Lt RN	01-Sep-10	WAR	O LYNX	815 SQN	RNAS YEOVILTON
Tarnowski, Tomasz A	Maj	12-Nov-04	RM	LC	CAREER TRAINING	PARIS FRANCE
Tarpey, Richard J	SLt	01-Feb-11	WAR	SM(X)	HELENSBURGH	
Tarr, Barry S	Cdr	30-Jun-02	ENG	MESM	DES/COMFLEET	ABBEY WOOD
Tarr, Richard N V	Cdr	30-Jun-04	ENG	MESM	FLEET DCS - RNIO	HMNB PORTSMOUTH
Tarrant, Robert K	R Adm	14-Jan-13	WAR	SM(CQ)	UKRBATSTAFF	HMNB PORTSMOUTH
Tasker, Adam M	Lt RN	01-May-05	WAR	O SKW	PJHQ (UK) CMSA	NORTHWOOD
Tate, David N	Lt RN	01-Apr-13	WAR	GSX	HMS DARING	

Person Name	Substantive Rank	Seniority	Branch	Specialisation	Organisation	Location
Tate, Dennis	SLt	24-May-11	ENG	MESM	BRNC DARTMOUTH	
Tate, Paul A	Lt RN	13-Jul-12	LOGS	L	HQ DCLPA	CAMBERLEY
Tatham, Stephen A	Cdr	30-Jun-10	ENG	TM	RMR LONDON	LONDON
Tayal, Manish	Surg Lt Cdr	01-Aug-09	MED	GMP	BFG HS HQ	NAPLES ITALY
Taylor, Alastair B	SLt	01-Jan-12	WAR	FC	HMS DRAGON	
Taylor, Alexander I	Lt RN	01-Sep-10	WAR	P SK4	CHF(MERLIN)	RAF BENSON
Taylor, Andrew	Lt RN	18-Feb-05	WAR	GSX	NATO ACO	NORTHWOOD
Taylor, Andrew I	Lt Cdr	01-Oct-13	WAR	HM(AM)	MWS COLLINGWOOD	
Taylor, Benjamin G	Lt RN	20-Oct-12	WAR	P SK4	845 SQN	RNAS YEOVILTON
Taylor, Christopher	Lt Cdr	01-Oct-08	ENG	TM(SM)	DEFENCE ACADEMY	SWINDON
Taylor, David R	Lt RN	15-Apr-11	ENG	WE	DES/COMJE/ISS	CORSHAM
Taylor, Dean A	Mid	01-Nov-13	WAR	GSX	BRNC DARTMOUTH	
Taylor, Dominic	SLt	24-Nov-11	WAR	GSX	BRNC DARTMOUTH	
Taylor, Helen M	Lt RN	01-Apr-11	WAR	GSX	HMS MERSEY	
Taylor, Ian K	Lt Cdr	01-Oct-01	LOGS	L	DCDS(PERS)	GLASGOW
Taylor, James E	Lt RN	01-Sep-04	WAR	P MER	RAF SHAWBURY	
Taylor, James T	Lt Cdr	01-Oct-13	WAR	O SKW	EMBED FRANCE	FRANCE
Taylor, Jennifer L	Lt RN	01-May-13	WAR	GSX	MWS COLLINGWOOD	
Taylor, Jonathan P	Lt Cdr	01-Oct-03	WAR	SM(C)	RNU - DAM NECK	NORFOLK
Taylor, Keith M	Lt Cdr	01-Oct-06	ENG	WE	NCHQ CNPERS	PORTSMOUTH
Taylor, Kenneth	Capt RN	30-Jun-07	WAR	O SK6	ADVISER/ADVISER	KUALA LUMPAR
Taylor, Lisa M	Cdr	03-Mar-13	QARNNS	Nursing Officer	MDHU PORTSMOUTH	HMNB PORTSMOUTH
Taylor, Marc Glyn	Lt RN	01-Nov-07	WAR	HM	BRNC DARTMOUTH	
Taylor, Marian C	Lt RN	01-Jan-11	WAR	O SKW	NO 3 FTS/UAS - JEFTS	
Taylor, Mark A	Cdr	30-Jun-09	WAR	P LYNX	DGHR(N)	RNAS YEOVILTON
Taylor, Mark A	Lt RN	11-Apr-08	WAR	ATC	RNAS CULDROSE	
Taylor, Matthew R	Lt RN	01-Nov-07	WAR	P SK6	771 SQN	RNAS CULDROSE
Taylor, Matthew R	Lt RN	01-Nov-10	WAR	GSX	HMS SEVERN	
Taylor, Neil John	Maj	01-Oct-08	RM	GS	NCHQ	
Taylor, Neil R	Lt RN	01-Feb-07	WAR	SM(N)	FLEET COMOPS NWD	NORTHWOOD
Taylor, Nicholas	Lt RN	01-Nov-05	WAR	HM	902 EAW	OMAN JOA MUSANNAH
Taylor, Nicholas F	Lt Cdr	16-Feb-87	WAR	PWO(C)	DES/COMJE/ISS	CORSHAM
Taylor, Oliver L	Lt RN	01-May-13	WAR	GSX	HMS ST ALBANS	
Taylor, Peter G	Col	14-Dec-09	RM	GS	LONDON MAIN BUILDING	
Taylor, Peter J	Surg Cdr	30-Jun-05	MED	GS	MDHU PETERBOROUGH	PETERBOROUGH
Taylor, Rachel S	Lt RN	01-Sep-12	WAR	GSX	RN EXCHANGE ITALY	ROME ITALY
Taylor, Robert	Cdr	30-Jun-10	ENG	WE	HMS ILLUSTRIOUS	
Taylor, Robert A	Capt	01-Sep-10	RM	GS	RMR LONDON	LONDON
Taylor, Robert J	Lt Cdr	01-Oct-05	WAR	O LYNX	WMF SHORE	RNAS YEOVILTON
Taylor, Robert P	Lt RN	01-May-02	WAR	P MER	814 SQN	RNAS CULDROSE
Taylor, Scott A	Lt RN	01-Jun-06	WAR	SM(N)	HMS TALENT	
Taylor, Spencer A	Capt RN	01-Jul-08	ENG	IS	DCDS(PERS)	CENTURION GOSPORT
Taylor, Stephen J	Lt Cdr	01-Oct-01	ENG	WE	HMS CAMBRIA	CARDIFF
Taylor, Stephen R	Lt RN	01-Jun-07	ENG	ME	COMPORFLOT FPS SEA	HMNB PORTSMOUTH
Taylor, Steven	Capt	01-Sep-12	RM	GS	43 CDO	HMNB CLYDE
Taylor, Stuart D	Maj	01-Oct-04	RM	GS	42 CDO RM	HMNB DEVONPORT
Taylor, William OBE	Brig	10-May-10	RM	GS	ATTACHE/ADVISER CANBERRA	AUSTRALIA
Tazewell, Matthew R	Lt Cdr	01-Oct-09	WAR	O LYNX	LHF 702 SQN	RNAS YEOVILTON
Tear, Trevor M	Lt RN	15-Apr-11	ENG	AE	DES/COMLAND	ABBEY WOOD BRISTOL
Teare, Matthew R	Lt RN	01-Jan-10	WAR	MW	MWS COLLINGWOOD	
Teasdale, David A	Cdr	30-Jun-11	WAR	SM(X) (RES)	RNP - HQ PMN	
Teasdale, James P	Lt RN	01-Nov-05	ENG	WE	DCCIS CISTU	HMS COLLINGWOOD
Tebbet, Paul	Cdr	30-Jun-07	WAR	PWO(U)	RNLO SINGAPORE	SINGAPORE
Teece, Nicholas J	Lt RN	01-Apr-11	WAR	P	RAF SHAWBURY	
Teideman, Ian C	Cdr	30-Jun-09	ENG	WE	DCDS PERS TRG	MAIN BUILDING LONDON
Telford, Jonathan	Lt RN	01-Jan-05	ENG	TM	FLEET FOST ACOS	NCHQ
Telford, Steven M	Lt RN	15-Apr-11	MED	MS	DES/COMFLEET	HMS DRAKE
Tennant, Gareth M	Capt	01-Sep-08	RM	GS	30 CDO IX GP RM	PLYMOUTH
Terry, Judith H	Lt Cdr	01-Oct-06	LOGS	L	FLEET COMNDER DCNS	NCHQ
Terry, Michael C	Surg Cdr	30-Jun-03	MED	GS	MDHU PORTSMOUTH	HMNB PORTSMOUTH
Terry, Nigel P	Lt Cdr	01-Oct-05	WAR	P SK6	HMS ILLUSTRIOUS	
Tetchner, David J	Lt RN	01-Nov-05	ENG	WE	HMNB PORTSMOUTH	

Person Name	Substantive Rank	Seniority	Branch	Specialisation	Organisation	Location
Tetley, Mark	Lt Cdr	01-Oct-03	WAR	O MER	824 SQN - TU	RNAS CULDROSE
Tetlow, Hamish S G	Cdr	30-Jun-08	WAR	SM(AWC)	MOD NSD	MAIN BUILDING LONDON
Thackray, Penelope D	Lt RN	01-Apr-05	ENG	TM	HMS VIGILANT	
Thain-Smith, Julie C	Cdr	01-Apr-08	QARNNS	Nursing Officer	HQ ISAF	AFGHANISTAN KABUL
Thatcher, Geraint L	Capt	01-Sep-11	RM	GS	NCHQ	
Theobold, Daniel	Lt RN	01-Sep-13	ENG	WESM	HMS ARTFUL	BARROW IN FURNESS
Thicknesse, Thomas R	SLt	21-Nov-11	WAR	FC	HMS ILLUSTRIOUS	
Thomas, Adam J MBE	Lt Cdr	01-Oct-13	ENG	AE	FLEET CSAV	NCHQ
Thomas, Andrew G	Lt RN	01-Sep-06	ENG	ME	HMS ECHO	
Thomas, Andrew N	RN Chpln	04-Nov-13	Ch S	Chaplain	BRNC DARTMOUTH	DARTMOUTH
Thomas, Charlotte	Lt RN	01-Sep-11	ENG	WE	DHU - E COY	CHICKSANDS
Thomas, Daniel G D	Lt RN	01-Jan-12	LOGS	L	HMS SCOTT	
Thomas, Daniel H	Lt Cdr	01-Oct-06	WAR	P LYNX	HMS CLYDE	
Thomas, David J	Cdr	30-Jun-13	LOGS	L	DES/ACDS	ABBEY WOOD
Thomas, David N	Lt Cdr	01-Oct-11	WAR	P MER	829 SQN HQ	RNAS CULDROSE
Thomas, Duncan J	Lt Cdr	01-Oct-13	WAR	O LYNX	FLEET SPT	NCHQ
Thomas, Emma	Lt RN	26-Jul-86	WAR	N/A	NCHQ CNPS	NCHQ
Thomas, James M	Lt RN	01-Feb-10	WAR	GSX	MCM1 CREW 8	FASLANE
Thomas, Joseph	Lt RN	01-May-04	WAR	P MER	RNAS CULDROSE	
Thomas, Katie J	Lt RN	01-Sep-07	LOGS	L	DES/COMFLEET	HMNB PORTSMOUTH
Thomas, Lynn M	Surg Capt RN	01-Jul-10	MED	Med	NCHQ MEDDIV	NCHQ
Thomas, Mark A	Lt Cdr	01-Oct-11	ENG	WE	COMDEVFLOT	
Thomas, Mark P	Lt RN	01-May-06	WAR	O MER	824 SQN - TU	RNAS CULDROSE
Thomas, Matthew	Lt RN	01-Feb-09	WAR	SM(X)	HMS ASTUTE	
Thomas, Michael J	Lt RN	01-Jun-10	WAR	P SK4	845 SQN	RNAS YEOVILTON
Thomas, Nicholas E	Lt	01-Sep-11	RM	GS	INFANTRY BATTLE SCHOOL	BRECON
Thomas, Owen H	Lt Cdr	01-Oct-10	WAR	INT	PJHQ (UK) CMSA	NORTHWOOD
Thomas, Richard	Lt RN	01-Mar-10	ENG	MESM	HMS TORBAY	
Thomas, Richard	Capt RN	08-Nov-10	WAR	PWO(U)	DEFENCE ACADEMY	SWINDON
Thomas, Richard D	Lt RN	01-Sep-08	LOGS	L	2SL CNPT	NCHQ
Thomas, Robert L	Surg Lt RN	01-Mar-13	MED	MEDICAL	BRNC DARTMOUTH	
Thomas, Ryan C	Surg Lt RN	04-Feb-09	MED	GMP	INM ALVERSTOKE	GOSPORT
Thomas, Stephen	Lt Cdr	01-Oct-06	WAR	P MER	HQBF GIBRALTAR - OPS	HMS ROOKE
Thomas, Stephen	Lt Cdr	01-Jan-01	ENG	ME	ACDS DEFLOGPOL	ABBEY WOOD
Thomason, Michael	Cdr	30-Jun-12	LOGS	L (RES)	FLEET CMR	NCHQ
Thompson, Adam D	Lt RN	07-Aug-13	ENG	WE	HMS DIAMOND	
Thompson, Alastair J	Lt RN	01-Jan-04	WAR	P LYNX	LHF 702 SQN	RNAS YEOVILTON
Thompson, Alexander	Lt RN	14-Sep-13	ENG	ME	HMS IRON DUKE	
Thompson, Andrew	Cdr	30-Jun-02	ENG	AE	DES/DTECH	WASHINGTON DC
Thompson, Andrew R	Lt Cdr	01-Oct-10	WAR	O LYNX	LHF 702 SQN	RNAS YEOVILTON
Thompson, Antony C	2Lt	02-Sep-12	RM	N/A	CTCRM OFFICERS	EXMOUTH
Thompson, Bernard	Cdr	30-Jun-02	WAR	PWO(A)	BRITISH MILITARY MISSION	KUWAIT
Thompson, Claire F	Lt RN	01-Nov-07	WAR	PWO	HMS DRAGON	
Thompson, David A	Lt RN	16-Apr-99	WAR	P LYN7	CHFHQ (SEA)	RNAS YEOVILTON
Thompson, David J	Lt Cdr	01-Oct-11	WAR	AAWO	FOST DPORT SEA	HMNB DEVONPORT
Thompson, Fiona	Cdr	06-Feb-12	QARNNS	Nursing Officer	DMS WHITTINGTON	LICHFIELD
Thompson, George C	Lt RN	01-Sep-06	WAR	P LYNX	RAF SHAWBURY	
Thompson, James	Lt RN	01-May-04	WAR	GSX	MWS COLLINGWOOD	
Thompson, James N	Lt RN	01-May-10	WAR	SM(X)	HMS TALENT	
Thompson, Luke C A	Lt RN	01-May-13	WAR	GSX	HMS SEVERN	
Thompson, Matthew D	SLt	01-Nov-11	WAR	ATC	BRNC DARTMOUTH	
Thompson, Michael J	Cdr	30-Jun-13	ENG	ME	HMS NELSON	HMS NELSON
Thompson, Michael W	Mid	01-Sep-13	ENG	ME	BRNC DARTMOUTH	
Thompson, Michelle E	Lt RN	19-Dec-08	WAR	REG	RNP - HQ PMN	HMS EXCELLENT
Thompson, Neil J OBE	Cdr	30-Jun-06	WAR	P SK4	RNAS YEOVILTON	
Thompson, Peter	SLt	01-Sep-12	ENG	AE	BRNC DARTMOUTH	
Thompson, Peter W	Lt RN	01-Oct-12	WAR	MCD	MCM1 CREW 5	FASLANE
Thompson, Richard C OBE	Cdre	27-Jul-12	ENG	AE	DES/COIR	ABBEY WOOD
Thompson, Robert	Cdr	30-Jun-09	WAR	O MER	RN EXCHANGE USA	WASHINGTON
Thompson, Sam D	Lt RN	01-Jun-09	WAR	P SK6	771 SQN	RNAS CULDROSE
Thompson, Samuel C	SLt	01-Jan-12	WAR	P UT	RNAS YEOVILTON	
Thompson, Sarah K	Lt RN	01-Nov-03	QARNNS	EN	DMRC HEADLEY COURT	EPSOM

Person Name	Substantive Rank	Seniority	Branch	Specialisation	Organisation	Location
Thompson, Sarah L	Lt RN	01-May-03	WAR	GSX	BFSAI - HQBFSAI - J2/J3	FALKLAND ISLANDS
Thompson, Simon C	Lt RN	01-Oct-08	WAR	P SK6	857 NAS	RNAS CULDROSE
Thompson, Simon J	Lt RN	01-Jan-09	LOGS	L	ACNS CAP	NCHQ
Thompson, Stephen J	Capt RN	09-Jan-12	ENG	ME	DES/COMFLEET	ABBEY WOOD
Thompson, William A	Lt Cdr	01-Oct-13	WAR	P LYNX	FOST DPORT SEA	HMNB DEVONPORT
Thompson-Pettit, Richard J	Lt RN	31-Jul-09	ENG	WE	DEFAC JSCSC	SWINDON
Thomsen-Rayner, Lavinia L	Lt Cdr	01-Oct-06	WAR	PWO(C)	BDS WASHINGTON	USA
Thomson, Calum M	Surg Lt RN	07-Aug-13	MED	MEDICAL	BRNC DARTMOUTH	
Thomson, David G	Lt RN	20-Dec-13	WAR	GSX	UK MCC	BAHRAIN
Thomson, Ian W	Lt Cdr	01-Oct-08	ENG	WESM(TWS)	FLEET CAP IS DIVISION	NCHQ
Thomson, James C	Lt Cdr	01-Oct-09	WAR	AAWO	HMS LANCASTER	
Thomson, Jane M	Lt Cdr	01-Oct-13	ENG	TM	DTR LOGS TTT UPAVON	CAMBERLEY
Thomson, Leighton G	Maj	01-Oct-11	RM	GS	NCHQ	
Thomson, Luke I	Maj	01-Oct-13	RM	GS	DEFAC JSCSC	SWINDON
Thomson, Michael L	Lt Cdr	01-Oct-08	ENG	ME	DES/COMFLEET	ABBEY WOOD
Thomson, Paul A	Lt Cdr	01-Oct-12	ENG	AE	AWC EDW - JSF TES	USA
Thomson, Paul D	Lt Cdr	01-Oct-06	ENG	IS	FOST DPORT SEA	HMNB DEVONPORT
Thomson, Roger	Surg Lt RN	05-Nov-03	MED	GMP	DES/COMFLEET	HMS NELSON
Thomson, Susie	Lt Cdr	31-Mar-99	WAR	MEDIA OPS	PJHQ (UK) J9	NORTHWOOD
Thorley, Graham	Lt RN	01-Jan-04	WAR	SM(N)	FLEET COMOPS	FAREHAM
Thorne, Dain MBE	Lt Cdr	01-Mar-05	ENG	AE	DEFAC JSCSC ACSC	SHRIVENHAM
Thorne, Lee J	Lt Cdr	31-Mar-02	WAR	MW (RES)	FLEET FOSNNI	HMNB PORTSMOUTH
Thornhill, Stephen M	Lt Cdr	01-Oct-11	MED	MS(CDO)	MOD DEFENCE STAFF	LONDON
Thornton, Charles A	Lt RN	01-Apr-09	WAR	SM(N)	HMS TRIUMPH	
Thornton, William S	Lt RN	01-Apr-11	WAR	P UT	702 SQN	RNAS YEOVILTON
Thorp, David B	Lt Cdr	01-Mar-06	ENG	WE	CIO-SPP	MAIN BUILDING LONDON
Thorpe, Richard J	Lt RN	01-Sep-08	WAR	O MER	WMO CULDROSE	RNAS CULDROSE
Thorpe, Robert M	Maj	01-Oct-09	RM	GS	30 CDO IX GP RM - Y SQN	PLYMOUTH
Thrippleton, Mark G	Cdr	30-Jun-10	ENG	AE	ABBEY WOOD BRISTOL	
Thurgood, Anthony D	Lt RN	13-Jul-12	MED	MS	DMSTG	ALDERSHOT
Thurstan, Richard W	Lt Col	30-Jun-07	RM	LC	1 ASSLT GROUP RM (HQ)	HMNB DEVONPORT
Thurston, Edward K	Lt RN	01-Jun-10	WAR	P SK6	771 SQN	RNAS CULDROSE
Thurston, Mark S	Lt Cdr	01-Oct-11	WAR	C	DES/COMJE/ISS	CORSHAM
Thwaites, Lindsey W	Lt RN	01-Jul-04	ENG	WESM(TWS)	HMS ARTFUL	BARROW IN FURNESS
Tibballs, Laura R	Lt RN	01-Jul-04	LOGS	L	FLEET SPT LOGS	NCHQ
Tibbitts, James A	Lt RN	01-Sep-08	WAR	GSX	MWS COLLINGWOOD	
Tidball, Ian C	Lt Cdr	01-Oct-04	WAR	P GR7	AWC EDW - JSF TES	LINCOLN
Tidman, Martin D MBE	Capt	10-Sep-01	RM	GS	NCHQ	
Tidswell, Stephen R	Lt RN	13-Apr-12	WAR	INT	HQ RC(SW)	AFGHANISTAN BASTION
Tilden, Philip J E	Lt Cdr	01-Mar-05	WAR	PWO(A)	RN GLOBAL	USA
Tilley, Duncan	Cdr	30-Jun-00	WAR	HM (H CH)	HMS DRAKE	
Tilley, Eleanor V	Lt RN	01-May-13	WAR	GSX	HMS NORTHUMBERLAND	
Timmins, Paul G	Capt	03-Apr-09	RM	LC (SCC)	CTCRM - CTW	EXMOUTH
Timpson, Benjamin H	Lt RN	08-Apr-12	ENG	TM	HMS SULTAN	
Tin, Jennifer Mary J	Lt RN	01-Jan-09	QARNNS	PHC	MEDICAL CENTRE	
Tindal, Nicolas H C	Capt RN	08-Oct-12	WAR	P SK6	OPS DIR	MAIN BUILDING LONDON
Tindle, Jack A	SLt	01-Sep-11	WAR	WESM	HMS RALEIGH	
Tingle, Dawn	Lt RN	01-Jan-09	WAR	ATC UT	RNAS YEOVILTON	
Tinsley, David	Lt RN	01-Sep-13	ENG	WE	OCLC PETERBRGH	PETERBOROUGH
Tippetts, Thomas C M	2Lt	02-Sep-13	RM	N/A	CTCRM OFFICERS	EXMOUTH
Tipping, Anthony	Lt RN	28-Jul-06	MED	MS(CDO)	UK MCC	BAHRAIN
Titcombe, Adam J ACMA	Lt Cdr	01-Oct-07	LOGS	L C	HMS EXCELLENT - CO	
Tite, Matthew W	Lt RN	01-Sep-13	WAR	GSX	MWS COLLINGWOOD	
Titerickx, Andrew T	Maj	01-Oct-10	RM	SCC	42 CDO RM - LOG COY	HMNB DEVONPORT
Titherington, Mark E	Lt RN	01-Apr-12	WAR	HM	HMS SCOTT	
Titmuss, Julian F	Lt Cdr	01-Dec-02	LOGS	L C	ACDS DEFLOGPOL	ABBEY WOOD
Titterton, Phillip J OBE	Capt RN	30-Jun-08	WAR	SM(CQ)	FLEET COMOPS NWD	NORTHWOOD
Tobin, Keith M	Lt RN	01-Sep-13	ENG	ME	HMS KENT	
Todd, James A	SLt	01-May-11	WAR	GSX	BRNC DARTMOUTH	
Todd, Oliver James	Maj	01-Oct-06	RM	MLDR	NATO ACO	NORTHWOOD
Toft, Michael David	Cdr	30-Jun-04	ENG	WE	DES/COMFLEET	ABBEY WOOD
Tolcher, Daniel G	Lt RN	15-Apr-11	WAR	SM(X)	HMS TIRELESS	

Person Name	Substantive Rank	Seniority	Branch	Specialisation	Organisation	Location
Tomasi, Vittorio L	2Lt	01-Sep-11	RM	GS	42 CDO RM - J COY	PLYMOUTH
Tomlin, Ian S	Lt Cdr	01-Oct-11	ENG	WESM(TWS)	HMS COLLINGWOOD	
Tomlinson, Amy R	Lt Cdr	01-Oct-11	LOGS	L	HMS NORTHUMBERLAND	
Tomlinson, Luke M	Lt RN	01-Sep-13	WAR	SM(X)	MWS COLLINGWOOD	
Toms, Nicholas J	Lt RN	01-Jul-11	LOGS	L	HQ 3 CDO BDE RM	PLYMOUTH
Tonge, Malcolm S	Lt Cdr	01-Oct-09	ENG	ME	FOST DPORT SEA	HMNB DEVONPORT
Tonge, Michael	Lt Cdr	09-Jun-06	ENG	MESM	DES/COMFLEET	HMS DRAKE
Toogood, Mark J	Lt RN	11-Apr-08	LOGS	L	MWS COLLINGWOOD	
Toon, Paul G	Lt Cdr	01-Oct-09	WAR	AV	RNAS CULDROSE	
Toone, Stephen A	Lt Cdr	01-Oct-09	ENG	WE	MWS COLLINGWOOD	
Topham, Neil E	Lt RN	01-Feb-01	ENG	TM	NETS (OPS)	HMNB PORTSMOUTH
Torbet, Linda	Lt RN	01-Jan-04	ENG	AE	OCLC LONDON	LONDON
Torney, Colin J	Lt Cdr	01-Oct-06	ENG	MESM	FOST SM SEA	HELENSBURGH
Tortelli, Yasmin	Lt RN	13-Jul-12	LOGS	L	RNAS CULDROSE - UPO	RNAS CULDROSE
Totten, Philip M MBE	Lt Col	30-Jun-12	RM		HQ 3 CDO BDE RM	PLYMOUTH
Tough, Iain S	Lt Cdr	01-Oct-09	ENG	WESM(SWS)	HMS VICTORIOUS	
Towell, Peter J	Cdr	30-Jun-06	ENG	ME	NCHQ CNPERS	PORTSMOUTH
Towler, Alison	Cdr	30-Jun-06	LOGS	L BAR	NCHQ - CNLS	NCHQ
Townend, Henry R	Lt Cdr	01-Sep-10	RM	GS	CDO LOG REGT	RMB CHIVENOR
Towner, Stephen D P	Surg Lt Cdr	06-Aug-13	MED	EM	INM ALVERSTOKE	GOSPORT
Townsend, Anna M	Lt RN	22-Mar-08	WAR	HM	FLEET COMOPS NWD	NORTHWOOD
Townsend, Graham P	Lt Cdr	01-Oct-06	WAR	O SK6	NATO-MOU-NSHQ	CASTEAU
Toy, Malcolm John	Cdre	04-Oct-10	ENG	AE	ABBEY WOOD	
Tracey, Alan David	Cdr	30-Jun-13	ENG	AE	DES/COIR/CA	ABBEY WOOD
Trafford, Michael	Maj	01-Oct-13	RM	C	104 LOG BDE	GLOUCESTERSHIRE
Treanor, Martin A	Cdr	31-Dec-99	ENG	AE	NCHQ CNPS	NCHQ
Tredray, Thomas P	Cdr	30-Jun-13	WAR	AAWO	HMS IRON DUKE	
Tregale, Jamie	Lt RN	01-Apr-04	WAR	HM	FLEET COMOPS NWD	NORTHWOOD
Tregunna, Gary A	Lt Cdr	08-Aug-03	WAR	SM(N)	SETT	GOSPORT
Tremelling, Paul N	Lt Cdr	01-Oct-06	WAR	P GR7	HQ AIR - COS(CAP)	HIGH WYCOMBE
Trent, Thomas	Lt Cdr	01-Oct-11	WAR	PWO	COMPORFLOT SHORE	HMNB PORTSMOUTH
Tretton, Caroline	Lt RN	01-Jan-05	WAR	HM	1 GP RHAM	KINGS LYNN
Tretton, Joseph E	Lt Cdr	01-Oct-13	WAR	HM(AM)	1 GP RHAM	KINGS LYNN
Trevethan, Christopher J	Lt Cdr	01-Oct-13	WAR	PWO	FLEET CAP SSM DIVISION	NCHQ
Trevethan, Sean C	Lt Cdr	01-Oct-13	ENG	WE	DES/COMFLEET	ABBEY WOOD
Trevor-Harris, George G	Mid	01-May-13	WAR	GSX	BRNC DARTMOUTH	
Trewinnard-Boyle, Robin M	Lt Cdr	01-Oct-10	ENG	AE	AWC BSD - RW TES	RAF ROSCOMBE DOWN
Triggol, Martin P	Capt	01-Apr-11	RM	GS	HMNB DEVONPORT	
Trigwell, Simon P	Lt RN	08-Apr-05	ENG	AE	FLEET CSAV	RNAS YEOVILTON
Trim, Brian Joseph	Lt Cdr	01-Jan-07	WAR	PWO(N)	HMS KENT	
Trinder, Stephen	Lt Cdr	01-Oct-08	LOGS	L	DCD - MODSAP KSA	RIYADH (MODSAP)
Tristram, Robert E	Lt RN	01-Nov-10	WAR	GSX	MWS DDS 1	PORTSMOUTH
Tritschler, Edwin L MBE	Capt RN	01-Jul-13	ENG	AE	DES/COMJE/HELS	YEOVIL
Trosh, Nicholas	Lt RN	01-Sep-04	ENG	WE	DES/COMJE/ISS	CORSHAM
Trowman, Oliver S	Lt RN	01-Sep-09	ENG	AE P	CHF (MERLIN) 1	RAF BENSON
Trubshaw, Christopher	Lt Cdr	01-Oct-04	WAR	P SKW	FLEET AV VL - OC	RNAS YEOVILTON
Trudgian, Paul	Lt RN	01-Apr-12	WAR	HM	HMS ECHO	
Truelove, Samantha	Lt Cdr	01-Oct-08	LOGS	L	MOD NSD	MAIN BUILDING LONDON
Truman, Oliver J	Capt	01-Sep-08	RM	GS	MOD DEFENCE STAFF	LONDON
Tucker, Philip J	Lt RN	01-Sep-04	WAR	P SK4	848 SQN	RNAS YEOVILTON
Tucker, Simon J	Maj	01-Oct-08	RM	LC	CTCRM	EXMOUTH
Tuckley, Christopher J	SLt	01-Sep-11	ENG	MESM	DCEME SULTAN	
Tuckwood, Alex I	Lt RN	19-Nov-09	WAR	O LYNX	815 SQN	RNAS YEOVILTON
Tuckwood, Neil E	Lt RN	01-Oct-10	WAR	O SKW	854 NAS	RNAS CULDROSE
Tudor, Owen O	Lt RN	01-May-07	LOGS	L	JFC HQ	NORTHWOOD
Tuhey, James J G	Lt RN	01-Sep-05	ENG	WESM(TWS)	PJHQ (UK) CMSA	NORTHWOOD
Tulloch, Stuart W	Lt Col	30-Jun-13	RM	SCC	CDO LOG REGT RM	RMB CHIVENOR
Tumilty, Kevin	Lt RN	01-Jan-04	ENG	WE	DES/COMFLEET	ABBEY WOOD
Turberville, Christopher T	Lt Cdr	01-Oct-11	LOGS	L	DES/COMFLEET	HMS DRAKE
Turfrey, Matthew	Lt RN	01-Jun-13	ENG	AE	DCEME SULTAN	HMS SULTAN
Turley, Richard A	Lt RN	04-Mar-08	WAR	AW (RES)	FLEET CMR	DARTMOUTH
Turnbull, Graham D	Cdr	30-Jun-02	WAR	HM (H CH)	FLEET FOSNNI	LONDON

Person Name	Substantive Rank	Seniority	Branch	Specialisation	Organisation	Location
Turnbull, Paul S	Surg Cdr	30-Jun-01	MED	Occ Med	NCHQ MEDDIV	NCHQ
Turnbull, Simon J L	Cdr	30-Jun-02	WAR	PWO(U)	HMS COLLINGWOOD	
Turner, Antony R	Lt Col	30-Jun-13	RM	GS	NCHQ	LONDON
Turner, David J	Cdr	30-Jun-12	LOGS	L SM	PJHQ (UK) J1/J4	NORTHWOOD
Turner, David N	Lt Cdr	01-Oct-08	WAR	P LYNX	FLEET COMOPS NWD	NORTHWOOD
Turner, Duncan L	Lt RN	01-Jan-06	ENG	WE	DES/COMFLEET	ABBEY WOOD
Turner, Gareth L	Lt RN	19-Sep-07	LOGS	L	HMS NELSON	
Turner, Gary H	Lt RN	09-Apr-09	LOGS	L	DES/COMLAND	ABBEY WOOD
Turner, Keith J	Lt RN	01-Sep-12	ENG	ME	HMS ILLUSTRIOUS	
Turner, Kevin P	Lt RN	01-Sep-08	ENG	MESM	DES/COMFLEET	BARROW IN FURNESS
Turner, Mathew J	SLt	01-Sep-12	MED	MEDICAL	BRNC DARTMOUTH	
Turner, Matthew	Lt Cdr	01-Oct-13	ENG	ME	HMS ST ALBANS	
Turner, Matthew C	SLt	01-Sep-11	WAR	GSX	HMS ARGYLL	
Turner, Matthew J	Surg Cdr	04-Jan-11	MED	GMP	NCHQ MEDDIV	NCHQ
Turner, Simon A	Lt Col	30-Jun-13	RM	GS	NCHQ	
Turrell, Richard D	Lt RN	17-Dec-10	WAR	AV	HMS ILLUSTRIOUS	
Turrell, Shelly S	Lt RN	08-Dec-12	ENG	ME	HMS RICHMOND	
Tustain, Paul A	Lt RN	09-Jun-06	ENG	MESM	DES/COMFLEET	
Tutchings, Andrew	Lt Cdr	01-Oct-08	WAR	GSX	RN EXCHANGE GERNY	HMNB PORTSMOUTH
Tweed, Jonathan J	Lt RN	01-Sep-08	ENG	ME	HMS SULTAN	
Tweedie, Howard J	Lt Cdr	22-Oct-97	WAR	CIS (RES)	FLEET CAP IS DIVISION	NCHQ
Twigg, Kelly A	Lt RN	01-Aug-05	WAR	ATC	RNAS YEOVILTON	
Twigg, Neil R	Lt Cdr	01-Oct-13	WAR	P GR7	HMS KENT	
Twinn, Richard	Lt RN	01-Mar-11	ENG	MESM	HMS VANGUARD	
Twiselton, Matthew J	Lt Cdr	01-Oct-12	ENG	AE	ABBEY WOOD,BRISTOL	
Twist, Martin T	Maj	01-Sep-01	RM	GS	HQ RC(SW)	AFGHANISTAN BASTION
Tyack, Terence J	Cdr	30-Jun-07	WAR	P SK4	RNAS YEOVILTON - C&SS	RNAS YEOVILTON
Tyacke, Richard S	Lt RN	01-May-06	WAR	FC	RAF BOULMER	
Tyce, David John	Maj	01-Oct-05	RM	SCC	DMC	MAIN BUILDING LONDON
Tyler, Adrian	Lt RN	13-Jun-08	WAR	INT	RN EXCHANGE USA	WASHINGTON
Tyler, Ian Paul	Capt	03-Apr-09	RM	SCC	RMR LONDON	LONDON
Tyler, Jeremy	Lt Cdr	01-Jul-04	WAR	AAWO	RN EXCHANGE USA	WASHINGTON
Tyler, Joseph J	2Lt	01-Sep-11	RM	N/A	CTCRM OFFICERS	EXMOUTH
Tysler, Charlotte G	Lt RN	01-Mar-11	WAR	P UT	RAF SHAWBURY	

U

Person Name	Substantive Rank	Seniority	Branch	Specialisation	Organisation	Location
Ubaka, Philip B N	Capt	24-Jul-04	RM	C (SCC)	43 CDO FPGRM LOG SQN	HMNB CLYDE
Ubhi, Wayne G	Lt Cdr	01-Jun-04	ENG	ME	MOD NSD	MAIN BUILDING LONDON
Uglow, Natalie E	Lt RN	01-Sep-04	ENG	AE	DES/COMJE	RNAS YEOVILTON
Uhrin, Dusan	Capt	01-Sep-12	RM	GS	43 CDO	HMNB CLYDE
Underwood, Michael R	Lt RN	01-Nov-13	ENG	WE	MWS COLLINGWOOD	
Underwood, Richard	Lt Cdr	01-Oct-07	LOGS	L	EXCHANGE FRANCE HOCS	PARIS
Unsworth, Benjamin M	Lt RN	01-Jan-08	WAR	O SKW	849 SQN	RNAS CULDROSE
Unwin, Nicholas R F	Lt Cdr	01-Oct-09	WAR	PWO	MCM1 CREW 3	FASLANE
Uprichard, Andrew J	Maj	01-Oct-10	RM	GS	40 CDO RM - D COY	TAUNTON
Upton, Iain D	Cdr	30-Jun-03	ENG	WE	HMS DRAKE	
Urry, Simon R MBE	Lt Col	30-Jun-12	RM	GS	NCHQ	
Urwin, Stuart J	Lt Cdr	01-Oct-08	WAR	PWO(C)	UKRBATSTAFF	HMNB PORTSMOUTH
Usborne, Neil V	Lt RN	01-May-13	WAR	GSX	MCM2 CREW 6	PORTSMOUTH
Usher, Brian	Maj	01-Oct-08	RM	SCC	1 ASSLT GROUP RM	HMNB DEVONPORT
Ussher, Jeremy H D	Lt Cdr	01-Oct-11	ENG	TM	FLEET FOST ACOS(Trg)	NCHQ
Utley, Michael K	Capt RN	10-Sep-12	WAR	PWO(A)	HMS ILLUSTRIOUS	

V

Person Name	Substantive Rank	Seniority	Branch	Specialisation	Organisation	Location
Vale, Andrew John	Surg Lt Cdr	07-Aug-07	MED	GMP	HQBF GIBRALTAR - MEDIC	HMS ROOKE
Valender, Charles J A	Surg Lt Cdr (D)	16-Jul-12	DENTAL	GDP	DEFENCE DENTAL SERVS	HNMB DEVONPORT
Valvona, Dominic M MBE	Lt RN	06-Apr-06	ENG	ME	MWS DDS	PORTSMOUTH
Van Den Bergh, Mark	Lt Cdr	05-Oct-10	LOGS	L (RES)	EU OHQ	NORTHWOOD
Van Duin, Martin I A	Lt RN	01-Jan-02	WAR	P LYNX	MWS COLLINGWOOD	
Vance, Andrew	Lt RN	01-Sep-12	ENG	AE	829 SQN HQ	RNAS CULDROSE
Vanderpump, David J	Capt RN	10-Sep-12	ENG	ME	DES/COMFLEET	ABBEY WOOD

Person Name	Substantive Rank	Seniority	Branch	Specialisation	Organisation	Location
Vandome, Andrew M.	Cdr	30-Jun-99	ENG	WE	DCMC	MAIN BUILDING LONDON
Vanstone, Sean M.	Surg SLt	29-Jul-13	MED	MEDICAL	BRNC DARTMOUTH	
Varco, Thomas G	Mid	01-Nov-13	LOGS	L	BRNC DARTMOUTH	
Varley, Ian G.	Lt Cdr	01-Jan-01	WAR	P MER	824 SQN - TU	RNAS CULDROSE
Vartan, Mark R.	Lt Cdr	01-Oct-03	WAR	HM(AS)	FLEET CAP IS DIVISION	NCHQ
Varty, Jason A	Lt Cdr	01-Oct-07	WAR	HM (H CH)	HMS PROTECTOR	
Vasey, Owen R	Lt RN	01-Jun-09	LOGS	L	HMS NELSON	
Vassallo, James	Surg Lt RN	04-Aug-10	MED	GDMO	INM ALVERSTOKE2	GOSPORT
Vaughan, Edward A	Lt Cdr	01-Oct-13	WAR	P SK4	HMS ILLUSTRIOUS	
Vaughan, James R.	Lt RN	01-Jun-03	ENG	MESM	DES/COMFLEET	ABBEY WOOD
Vaughan, Jamie B	Lt RN	15-Apr-11	ENG	ME	HMS QUEEN ELIZABETH	ROSYTH
Veacock, Gary T.	Maj	01-Oct-13	RM	SCC	MONUC CONGO	CONGO
Veal, Dominic J	Lt RN	01-May-02	WAR	INT	43 CDO	HMNB CLYDE
Velickovic, Samuel D	Lt RN	01-Apr-12	WAR	GSX	HMS DUNCAN	
Venables, Daniel M	Maj	01-Oct-09	RM	MLDR	CTCRM - CTW	EXMOUTH
Venn, Nicholas S C	Lt Col	30-Jun-12	RM	P LYN7	CHFHQ 6	RNAS YEOVILTON
Vereker, Richard J P.	Lt RN	01-Apr-06	WAR	SM(X)	43 CDO	HMNB CLYDE
Verney, Kirsty H.	Surg Lt Cdr (D)	09-Jul-02	DENTAL	GDP	DCPPA - SDS	HMS DRYAD
Vessey, Lee M.	Lt Cdr	01-Oct-12	WAR	PWO	HMS IRON DUKE	
Veti, Mark A	Lt RN	01-Feb-06	WAR	PWO	HMS DIAMOND	
Vickers, John OBE	Cdr	30-Jun-06	ENG	AE	DES/COMJE	RNAS YEOVILTON
Vickers, Patrick T.	Lt RN	01-Aug-13	ENG	WESM	HMS AMBUSH	
Vickery, Ben R	Lt Cdr	01-Oct-08	WAR	MCD PWO	MCM2 CREW 1	PORTSMOUTH
Viggars, Christopher E	Capt	01-Sep-11	RM	GS	HMS OCEAN	
Vijayan, Deepak	Surg Lt Cdr	01-Nov-11	MED	GS	INM ALVERSTOKE	GOSPORT
Vincent, Christopher	Lt Cdr	01-May-07	WAR	INT	FLEET COMOPS	HMS COLLINGWOOD
Vincent, Daniel	Lt Cdr	01-Oct-04	ENG	TM	AIR 22GP - LYNEHAM	RAF LYNEHAM
Vincent, Peter	Lt RN	01-Mar-12	ENG	MESM	HMS TIRELESS	
Vincent, Stuart M.	Lt RN	01-Jan-06	ENG	TM	NETS (OPS)	HMNB CLYDE
Vines, Adam M	SLt	01-Apr-11	WAR	P UT	RNAS YEOVILTON	RNAS YEOVILTON
Vines, Nicholas O	Lt Cdr	01-Oct-09	MED	MS(EHO)	DES/COMFLEET	
Vines, Sarah Kate	Lt RN	09-Aug-08	ENG	TM	CTCRM - P&R	EXMOUTH
Viney, Peter M	Lt Cdr	01-Oct-07	LOGS	L	LOAN DSTL - P&CSD	PORTSDOWN WEST
Visram, Adrian H.	Lt Cdr	01-Oct-13	WAR	PWO	HMS DRAGON	
Vitali, Robert C	Capt RN	09-Oct-12	WAR	PWO(A)	MOD NSD	MAIN BUILDING LONDON
Vivian, Michael A.	Mid	01-Feb-13	WAR	P UT	BRNC DARTMOUTH	
Vivian, Philip	Lt Cdr	01-Oct-13	LOGS	L	CHFHQ (SEA)	RNAS YEOVILTON
Vogel, Claire L.	Lt Cdr	01-Sep-05	LOGS	L	STABILISATION UNIT	MAIN BUILDING LONDON
Vogel, Lanning D	Cdr	30-Jun-11	LOGS	L SM	NORTHWOOD HQ	
Voke, Christen A.	Lt RN	01-Aug-02	WAR	SM(X)	FLEET COMOPS NWD	NORTHWOOD
Vollentine, Lucy	Cdr	30-Jun-10	LOGS	L	COMPORFLOT WLSG	HMNB PORTSMOUTH
Vout, Debra K	Lt Cdr	01-Oct-08	WAR	C	HMS COLLINGWOOD	
Vowles, Iain R	Lt RN	01-Sep-06	ENG	WESM	DES/COMFLEET	ABBEY WOOD
Vowles, Mitchell J	Lt Cdr	01-Oct-08	WAR	GSX	OCLC LONDON	LONDON
Voyce, John E.	Cdr	30-Jun-09	ENG	ME	HMS ILLUSTRIOUS	
Vuniwaqa, Atunaisa T	Lt RN	01-Sep-10	ENG	ME	HMS NELSON	HMS NELSON

W

Person Name	Substantive Rank	Seniority	Branch	Specialisation	Organisation	Location
Waddington, Andrew	SLt	01-Sep-12	ENG	ME	BRNC DARTMOUTH	
Wade, Frederick O	SLt	01-Aug-11	WAR	GSX	BRNC DARTMOUTH	
Wade, Nicholas J.	Lt RN	30-Jul-09	WAR	C	NATO ACO	NORTHWOOD
Wade, Robert J	SLt	01-Mar-11	ENG	MESM	DCEME SULTAN	HMS SULTAN
Wadsworth, Richard	Lt Cdr	01-Oct-09	ENG	ME	DES/COMFLEET	ABBEY WOOD
Wagstaff, Michael	RN Chpln	31-Mar-08	Ch S	Chaplain	HMS BULWARK	
Wagstaff, Neil	Capt RN	25-Jun-12	MED	MS	DMS WHITTINGTON	LICHFIELD
Wagstaffe, James N G.	Lt RN	01-Sep-11	ENG	WE	MWS COLLINGWOOD	
Wainhouse, Michael J	Capt RN	02-Nov-09	WAR	PWO(A)	PJHQ (UK) J3	NORTHWOOD
Waite, Matthew T.	Maj	01-Oct-08	RM	GS	HIGH COMMISSION	ISLABAD
Waite, Tobias G.	Lt Cdr	01-Oct-08	WAR	PWO(U)	HMS WESTMINSTER	
Wake, Daniel C	2Lt	01-Sep-11	RM	GS	42 CDO RM - L COY	HMNB DEVONPORT
Wakefield, Matthew A.	Lt RN	01-Sep-11	ENG	AE	DES/COMJE	RNAS YEOVILTON
Waldmeyer, Edward	Maj	01-Oct-10	RM	GS	HQ ARRC COMND GROUP	GLOUCESTER

Person Name	Substantive Rank	Seniority	Branch	Specialisation	Organisation	Location
Wale, Alexandra J	Lt RN	01-Mar-13	WAR	GSX	HMS DAUNTLESS	
Wales, Benjamin D	Cdr	30-Jun-11	LOGS	L C	HQ DCLPA AND DEEPCUT	CAMBERLEY
Walker, Alasdair J OBE QHS	Surg Cdre	01-Jul-11	MED	GS	DMS WHITTINGTON	BIRMINGHAM
Walker, Andrew J	Lt Col	30-Jun-12	RM	GS	NATO-ACT-JWC	STAVANGER (BODO)
Walker, Clive L	Cdre	01-Jul-11	LOGS	L	JFLogC	NORTHWOOD
Walker, Daniel H	Lt RN	01-Jan-04	WAR	P	RNAS YEOVILTON	RNAS YEOVILTON
Walker, Daniel J	SLt	01-May-12	LOGS	L	BRNC DARTMOUTH	
Walker, David	Lt Cdr	31-Mar-97	LOGS	L (RES)	HQ TH TPS	SALISBURY
Walker, Fergus S	Lt RN	01-Sep-08	ENG	WESM	FOST DSTF - CSST	HMNB DEVONPORT
Walker, Graeme H	Lt RN	01-Sep-07	ENG	AE P	815 SQN	RNAS YEOVILTON
Walker, Ian M	Lt Cdr	01-Oct-12	ENG	MESM	HMS TRENCHANT	
Walker, James J	Lt RN	01-Jan-04	WAR	O LYNX	MOD NSD	MAIN BUILDING LONDON
Walker, Jamie	Lt RN	01-Jan-03	ENG	ME	COMPORFLOT ESG	
Walker, John	Lt Cdr	01-Oct-13	WAR	INT	PJHQ (UK) J2	NORTHWOOD
Walker, Mark	Lt Cdr	01-Oct-02	ENG	TM	DEFENCE ACADEMY HQ	SHRIVENHAM
Walker, Mark	Cdr	30-Jun-07	WAR	P SK4	HQ JHC	ANDOVER
Walker, Mark J	Lt RN	01-Feb-06	WAR	PWO(SM)	HMS TRIUMPH	
Walker, Martin D J	Lt RN	01-Jan-04	LOGS	L SM	HMS ARTFUL	BARROW IN FURNESS
Walker, Nicholas J	Capt RN	18-Aug-09	ENG	MESM	DES/COMFLEET	ABBEY WOOD
Walker, Nicholas L	Lt Cdr	01-Feb-93	WAR	PWO(U)	COMUKAMPHIBFOR	HMNB PORTSMOUTH
Walker, Nicholas M	Cdr	30-Jun-09	WAR	P SHAR	HMS ILLUSTRIOUS	
Walker, Nicholas	Lt RN	01-Aug-02	WAR	P SK4	FASLANE HELENSBURGH	
Walker, Peter R	Cdr	30-Jun-07	ENG	IS	PJHQ (UK) J6	NORTHWOOD
Walker, Richard P	Lt RN	01-Jul-04	WAR	O MER	814 SQN	RNAS CULDROSE
Walker, Robin	Lt Cdr	01-Oct-08	WAR	MCD	RN EXCHANGE CANADA	OTTAWA 1
Walker, Stephen	Lt Cdr	01-Apr-10	ENG	WESM	DES/COMFLEET	ABBEY WOOD
Walker, Stephen P	Cdr	30-Jun-08	WAR	SM(CQ)	HMS ASTUTE	
Walkley, Kyle J	Lt RN	07-Oct-11	WAR	GSX	MCM2 CREW 3	PORTSMOUTH
Wall, Irene J	Lt Cdr	01-Oct-06	LOGS	L	CHAPLAIN OF THE FLEET	NCHQ
Wall, John H	Capt	01-Sep-09	RM	GS	539 ASSLT SQN	
Wall, Karl	Lt Cdr	01-Oct-11	WAR	PWO(SM)	NCHQ CNPERS	NCHQ
Wall, Samuel J	Lt RN	01-Mar-13	ENG	ME	HMS PORTLAND	
Wall, Steven N	Lt Cdr	01-Oct-07	WAR	AAWO	HMS DARING	
Wall, Thomas C	Lt RN	01-Feb-08	WAR	MW	MCM2 CREW 5	PORTSMOUTH
Wallace, Allan OBE	Cdr	30-Jun-01	WAR	PWO(N)	CIO-J6	MAIN BUILDING LONDON
Wallace, Anthony R	Lt Cdr	01-Oct-10	WAR	PWO MW	HMS LANCASTER	
Wallace, David J	Cdr	30-Jun-11	ENG	IS	DES/COMJE/ISS	CORSHAM
Wallace, Iain S	Lt Cdr	01-Oct-10	ENG	IS	HMS DAUNTLESS	
Wallace, James G	Lt RN	01-Apr-09	WAR	P SK4	848 SQN	RNAS YEOVILTON
Wallace, Josef K	Surg Lt RN	01-Aug-12	MED	MEDICAL	BRNC DARTMOUTH	
Wallace, Kirsty E	Lt RN	01-Sep-07	ENG	IS	DCCIS CISTU	HMS COLLINGWOOD
Wallace, Michael R B CBE	Cdre	29-Jun-09	WAR	PWO(U)	NAVSEC	PORTSMOUTH
Wallace, Nicola K	Lt RN	19-Dec-08	WAR	AE	1710 NAS	HMNB PORTSMOUTH
Wallace, Richard S	Lt Cdr	01-Oct-10	WAR	PWO	FLEET SPT FGEN DIVISION	NCHQ
Wallace, Richard S	Maj	01-Oct-07	RM	GS	45 CDO RM	DUNDEE
Wallace, Ryan P	Lt Cdr	01-Oct-10	ENG	IS	HMS DUNCAN	
Wallace, Scott P	Maj	01-Oct-08	RM	GS	40 CDO RM - COMD COY	TAUNTON
Wallace, Simon J	Cdr	30-Jun-11	WAR	AAWO	FLEET CAP WARFARE	NCHQ
Waller, Bentley R	Surg Lt Cdr	01-Sep-11	MED	Anaes	INM ALVERSTOKE	GOSPORT
Waller, Ramsay	Maj	01-Oct-13	RM	C	DEFAC JSCSC ICSCL	SHRIVENHAM
Waller, Robert	Lt RN	01-Mar-13	ENG	MESM	DCME SULTAN	HMS SULTAN
Waller, Steven	Cdr	30-Jun-07	WAR	SM(CQ)	BDS WASHINGTON - NA	WASHINGTON USA
Walliker, Michael J D OBE	Capt RN	06-Jan-09	WAR	SM(CQ)	NCHQ CNPS	PORTSMOUTH
Wallington-Smith, James	Lt RN	01-Sep-09	WAR	GSX	MWS COLLINGWOOD	
Wallis, Adrian J	Cdr	30-Jun-02	WAR	PWO(C)	SCU SHORE	
Wallis, Thomas D	2Lt	01-Sep-11	RM	GS	43 CDO FPGRM	HMNB CLYDE
Wallis, Thomas O	Lt RN	01-Mar-11	ENG	AE	RNAS YEOVILTON	
Walls, Kevin F	Maj	01-May-00	RM	MLDR	UNMIS SUDAN	SUDAN
Walsh, Kevin M	Lt Cdr	01-Nov-04	WAR	PWO(A)	DES/COMFLEET/SHIPS	ABBEY WOOD
Walters, Cameron F	Mid	01-Nov-13	WAR	SM(X)	BRNC DARTMOUTH	
Walters, Elizabeth	Surg Lt RN	07-Aug-13	MED	MEDICAL	BRNC DARTMOUTH	
Walters, Richard	Lt Cdr	31-Mar-04	WAR	MEDIA OPS	DEFAC JSCSC ACSC	SHRIVENHAM

Person Name	Substantive Rank	Seniority	Branch	Specialisation	Organisation	Location
Walton, Darren J	SLt	01-Nov-11	LOGS	L	HMS NORTHUMBERLAND	
Walton, George J	Lt Cdr	01-Oct-11	WAR	AAWO	HMS ILLUSTRIOUS	
Walton, Stephen D	Lt Cdr	01-Oct-06	WAR	MW	PJHQ (UK) J3	NORTHWOOD
Warburton, Alison M	Lt Cdr	01-Oct-12	QARNNS	OT	DMSTG - DEFENCE SCHOOL	KEOGH BARRACKS
Ward, Alex James	Surg SLt	17-Jul-13	MED	MEDICAL	BRNC DARTMOUTH	
Ward, Alexander J	Lt Cdr	01-Oct-10	LOGS	L BAR	NCHQ - CNLS	NORTHWOOD
Ward, Andrew E	SLt	01-Nov-11	WAR	GSX	BRNC DARTMOUTH	
Ward, Antony J	Lt RN	01-Dec-08	WAR	ATC	RAF LOSSIEMOUTH	
Ward, Douglas J	Lt Cdr	01-Nov-06	LOGS	L BAR SM	UK MCC	BAHRAIN
Ward, Emma J	Lt RN	01-Jan-01	WAR	O SKW	DIRECTOR (JW)	NORTHWOOD
Ward, Gareth J	Lt RN	01-Mar-09	ENG	MESM	DCEME SULTAN	
Ward, Jared M	Lt Cdr	01-Oct-12	LOGS	L	HMS LANCASTER	
Ward, Matthew B	Lt Cdr	01-Oct-12	WAR	P SK4	AWC BSD - RW TES	RAF BOSCOMBE DOWN
Ward, Michelle T	Lt RN	01-Apr-99	WAR	PWO	NATO-ACO-JFC HQ	BRUSSELS
Ward, Nicholas D	SLt	01-Sep-11	WAR	GSX	MCM2 CREW 4	PORTSMOUTH
Ward, Robert A	Lt RN	01-Jul-12	ENG	WESM	HMS VANGUARD	
Ward, Simon	Lt Cdr	01-Sep-05	WAR	PWO(A)	RNAS YEOVILTON - LSF	RNAS YEOVILTON
Ward, Simon	Capt	01-Sep-12	RM	GS	43 CDO COMD SQN	HMNB CLYDE
Ward, Stephen D	Cdr	30-Jun-07	ENG	ME	DES/COMFLEET	ABBEY WOOD
Ward, Steven J	Capt	30-Mar-12	RM	SCC	CTCRM - S	EXMOUTH
Ward, Timothy E	SLt	01-Mar-11	ENG	MESM	HMS SULTAN	
Warden, Sophie	SLt	01-Apr-13	DENTAL	DENTAL	BRNC DARTMOUTH	
Wardill, George	Lt RN	01-Jan-12	WAR	P UT	RAF SHAWBURY	
Wardle, Daniel J	SLt	01-Feb-11	WAR	GSX	HMS ECHO	
Wardle, Gareth S	Lt RN	21-Feb-09	WAR	P SK4	CHFHQ (SHORE)	RNAS YEOVILTON
Wardley, Thomas E	Lt RN	01-Mar-05	QARNNS	EN	MED SQN CDO LOG	BARNSTAPLE
Ware, Andrew T	Lt Cdr	01-Oct-12	WAR	INT	NCHQ CNPERS	PORTSMOUTH
Ware, Peter James	Lt Cdr	01-Oct-13	WAR	PWO(N)	FOST DPORT SEA	HMNB DEVONPORT
Wareham, Michael P	R Adm	30-Sep-13	ENG	MESM	DES/COMFLEET	ABBEY WOOD
Wareham, Sidney J	Lt RN	20-Oct-06	WAR	INT	FLEET CAP IS DIVISION	NCHQ
Waring, John R	Cdr	30-Jun-11	ENG	TM	NATO - BRUSSELS	
Warland, Adam	Lt RN	01-Feb-11	ENG	TM	CTCRM - TDRPC	EXMOUTH
Warner, Philip C	SLt	01-May-11	LOGS	L	RNAS CULDROSE - UPO	RNAS CULDROSE
Warner, Stephen E	Lt RN	01-Jun-09	LOGS	L FS	RNLA	HMS COLLINGWOOD
Warner, Thomas M	SLt	01-Sep-12	WAR	P UT	MWS COLLINGWOOD	
Warnock, Christopher	SLt	01-Dec-12	WAR	GSX	MWS COLLINGWOOD	
Warr, Richard F	Lt Cdr	01-Oct-02	ENG	WESM	DES/COMFLEET	ABBEY WOOD
Warren, Matthew J	Lt RN	01-May-04	WAR	HM	CAREER TRAINING	HMS DRAKE
Warren, Rebecca J	Lt Cdr	01-Oct-13	WAR	HM (M CH)	FLEET HM UNIT	HMNB DEVONPORT
Warren, William J	Lt RN	01-Apr-12	WAR	GSX	HMS MERSEY	
Warrender, William J	Capt RN	26-Apr-11	WAR	PWO(A)	OPS DIR	MAIN BUILDING LONDON
Warwick, Andrew	Lt RN	01-Nov-12	WAR	SM(X)	HMS TRIUMPH	
Warwick, Francesca R	Surg SLt (D)	19-Jul-12	DENTAL	GDP(VDP)	HMS DRAKE	
Warwick, Philip D	Capt RN	06-Jan-09	WAR	PWO(U)	FLEET SPT FGEN DIVISION	NCHQ
Washer, Nicholas B J	Capt RN	17-Sep-13	WAR	PWO(C)	FLEET CAP IS DIVISION	NCHQ
Waskett, Daniel	Lt RN	01-Jan-07	WAR	O MER	820 SQN	RNAS CULDROSE
Waterfield, Simon	Lt Cdr	01-Jun-02	WAR	AAWO	HMS COLLINGWOOD	
Waterhouse, Phillip	Capt RN	03-Sep-13	LOGS	L	FLEET SPT LOGS I	NCHQ
Waterman, Matthew L	Lt RN	01-Sep-12	ENG	WE	FLEET HQ 6	NCHQ
Waters, Michael R	Lt Cdr	01-Oct-13	WAR	GSX	MWS COLLINGWOOD	
Watkin, Paul	Lt RN	01-Sep-10	ENG	WE	HQ JHC	ANDOVER
Watkins, Alun K	Capt	18-Jul-08	RM	SCC	NAVAL OUTDOOR CENTRE	GERMANY
Watkins, Andrew P	Lt Col	30-Jun-11	RM	GS	MIN AF	MAIN BUILDING LONDON
Watkins, Dean T	Maj	01-Oct-10	RM	GS	DES/COMLAND	ABBEY WOOD
Watkins, Jenny	Lt RN	01-Jan-02	ENG	TM	FLEET HQ 6	NCHQ
Watkins, Kevin J	Lt Cdr	01-Oct-06	ENG	ME	HMS ILLUSTRIOUS	
Watkins, Timothy C	Lt Cdr	01-Oct-00	WAR	P SK4	727 NAS	RNAS YEOVILTON
Watkinson, Neil	Lt Col	30-Jun-09	RM	GS	RMR LONDON	LONDON
Watkis, Andrew N	Lt RN	01-Sep-09	ENG	ME	HMS SULTAN	
Watsham, Richard V	Lt RN	20-May-10	WAR	HM	UK MCC	BAHRAIN
Watson, Andrew	Lt Cdr	01-Oct-07	WAR	O MER	DEFAC JSCSC ACSC	SHRIVENHAM
Watson, Bradley L	Lt Cdr	01-Oct-12	WAR	O SKW	857 NAS	RNAS CULDROSE

Person Name	Substantive Rank	Seniority	Branch	Specialisation	Organisation	Location
Watson, Brian R	Capt	01-Jan-02	RM	P LYN7	WILDCAT FORCE	RNAS YEOVILTON
Watson, Graham	Maj	01-Oct-10	RM	SCC	101 LOG BDE	ST OMER BARRACKS
Watson, Ian	Lt Cdr	01-Mar-03	WAR	PWO(A)	MWS COLLINGWOOD	
Watson, James L	Surg Lt RN	01-Aug-12	MED	MEDICAL	BRNC DARTMOUTH	DARTMOUTH
Watson, Joseph M	2Lt	02-Sep-13	RM	N/A	CTCRM OFFICERS	EXMOUTH
Watson, Richard D	Lt Cdr	01-Oct-08	WAR	MCD	DSEA	PORTSMOUTH
Watson, Richard I	Maj	01-Oct-04	RM	GS	NCHQ	
Watson, Richard J	Lt Cdr	01-Aug-89	WAR	SM(AWC)	NCHQ CNPERS	PORTSMOUTH
Watson, Simon C	Lt RN	01-Sep-05	ENG	WE	DES/COMJE	CORSHAM
Watt, Anthony J L OBE	Capt RN	18-Jun-13	WAR	PWO(U)	FOST NWD (JTEPS)	NORTHWOOD
Watt, Fraser J	Lt RN	01-Sep-12	WAR	GSX	MCM1 CREW 4	HELENSBURGH
Watt, Nicholas J	2Lt	02-Sep-13	RM	N/A	CTCRM OFFICERS	EXMOUTH
Watts, Andrew P	Lt Cdr	01-Oct-93	WAR	O SK6	771 SQN	RNAS CULDROSE
Watts, Nicholas A	SLt	01-May-11	LOGS	L	DES/COMLAND	ABBEY WOOD
Watts, Robert	Cdr	30-Jun-13	WAR	SM(CQ)	HMS VANGUARD	
Waud, Deborah	Lt RN	14-Apr-11	MED	MS	DES/COMFLEET	HELENSBURGH
Way, Robert A	Lt Cdr	01-Oct-09	WAR	INT	DI - SA	LONDON
Weal, Gregory R	Lt RN	01-Jan-10	WAR	P MER	814 SQN	RNAS CULDROSE
Weale, John S	Cdre	03-Sep-12	WAR	SM(CQ)	FLEET FOST ACOS	NCHQ
Weare, Jonathan B	Lt Cdr	01-Oct-06	LOGS	L BAR	NCHQ - CNLS	NCHQ
Weatherall, Mark	Lt RN	21-Feb-09	WAR	INT	DEFAC JSCSC ICSCM	SHRIVENHAM
Weaver, Simon	Lt Cdr	01-Oct-05	WAR	HM(AS)	MWS COLLINGWOOD	
Weaver, Thomas H	Lt Cdr	01-Oct-10	WAR	PWO	UKRBATSTAFF	HMNB PORTSMOUTH
Webb, Eleanor	Lt Cdr	01-Oct-08	LOGS	L	DEFAC JSCSC	SHRIVENHAM
Webb, John P	Lt Cdr	01-Oct-12	WAR	GSX	HMS SULTAN	
Webb, Keith W	Lt RN	01-Jan-12	WAR	O UT	702 SQN	RNAS YEOVILTON
Webber, Adam A	RN Chpln	02-Sep-13	Ch S	Chaplain	CTCRM	EXMOUTH
Webber, Christopher A	Capt	01-Sep-11	RM	GS	RS SANDHURST GP	CAMBERLEY
Webber, David James	SLt	01-Sep-11	ENG	ME	DCEME SULTAN	HMS SULTAN
Webber, Joanne P	Lt Cdr	01-Oct-06	WAR	O MER	750 SQN SEAHAWK	RNAS CULDROSE
Webber, Lauren	Mid	01-May-13	WAR	GSX	BRNC DARTMOUTH	
Webber, Richard J	Surg Cdr	01-Jul-09	MED	Occ Med	INM ALVERSTOKE2	GOSPORT
Webster, Andrew J	Lt RN	01-Jan-04	ENG	TM	BRNC DARTMOUTH	
Webster, Craig	Lt RN	05-Oct-00	WAR	O SKW	857 NAS	RNAS CULDROSE
Webster, David R	SLt	01-Feb-12	WAR	GSX	BRNC DARTMOUTH	
Webster, Mark	Lt RN	01-Apr-07	WAR	GSX	FOST MPV SEA	HELENSBURGH
Webster, Matthew P	Capt	01-Sep-11	RM	GS	CTCRM - CTW	EXMOUTH
Webster, Richard	Lt Cdr	01-Oct-07	WAR	PWO(C)	LSP ON	MUSCAT (BOX 014)
Webster, Richard J	Lt Cdr	01-Dec-05	LOGS	L	ACDS	MAIN BUILDING LONDON
Weedon, Christopher R	SLt	01-Sep-12	ENG	AE	BRNC DARTMOUTH	
Weedon, Grant	Lt Cdr	01-Dec-11	ENG	ME	CAREER TRAINING	HMS SULTAN
Weetch, Matthew E	Lt RN	21-Feb-09	WAR	AV	HQ UKTF	AFGHANISTAN BASTION
Weil, Daniel G	Lt Cdr	01-Oct-11	ENG	AE	847 SQN - AE	RNAS YEOVILTON
Weir, Scott D	Cdr	29-Mar-11	ENG	WESM	CBRN POL	MAIN BUILDING LONDON
Weir, Stewart W	Mid	01-Sep-12	WAR	GSX	CREW 4 OFFICERS	HELENSBURGH
Weites, Matthew G	Capt	21-Mar-13	RM	BS	CTCRM RMSOM	HMS NELSON
Welch, Danielle S	Lt RN	01-Mar-10	WAR	P UT	CAREER TRAINING	RAF SHAWBURY
Welch, Harry A	SLt	24-Jan-12	WAR	SM(X)	BRNC DARTMOUTH	
Welch, James F	Surg Lt RN	05-Aug-03	MED	Ophthal	MDHU NORTHALLERTON	
Welch, Joshua J	Lt RN	01-Jul-12	WAR	GSX	HMS SOMERSET	
Welch, Simon	Capt	28-Jul-06	RM	SCC	1 ASSLT GROUP RM	HMNB DEVONPORT
Weldon, Dominic R	Capt	01-Sep-12	RM	GS	43 CDO FPGRM	HMNB CLYDE
Welford, Robert C	Lt Cdr	01-Feb-99	WAR	PWO(C)	FLEET CAP IS DIVISION	NCHQ
Weller, Jamie K	Lt RN	01-Feb-08	ENG	WE	DES/COMFLEET	ABBEY WOOD
Wellington, Laura J	Lt RN	01-Jun-06	LOGS	L	FASLANE HELENSBURGH	
Wellington, Stuart	Lt Cdr	01-Feb-98	ENG	WE	FLEET CAP SSM DIVISION	NCHQ
Wells, Antony E	Lt RN	01-Sep-09	WAR	P	815 SQN	RNAS YEOVILTON
Wells, Barry C	Lt Cdr	01-Oct-02	ENG	WESM	CBRN POL	MAIN BUILDING LONDON
Wells, Jamie D	Lt Cdr	01-Oct-08	WAR	PWO(N)	FOST DPORT SEA	HMNB DEVONPORT
Wells, John P	Surg Lt Cdr	04-Jul-07	MED	OMFS	INM ALVERSTOKE	GOSPORT
Wells, Jonathan M C	Lt Cdr	01-Aug-97	WAR	P MER	A AIB FARNBOROUGH	ALDERSHOT
Wells, Matthew L	SLt	01-May-12	WAR	GSX	BRNC DARTMOUTH	

Person Name	Substantive Rank	Seniority	Branch	Specialisation	Organisation	Location
Wells, Michael J	Lt RN	01-Sep-08	WAR	P LYN7	847 SQN - AE	RNAS YEOVILTON
Wells, Michael P.	Lt Cdr	01-Mar-05	LOGS	L C	FLEET SPT LOGS	NCHQ
Wells, Rory L	2Lt	02-Sep-13	RM	N/A	CTCRM OFFICERS	EXMOUTH
Welsh, John	Lt Cdr	01-Oct-08	ENG	TM	FLEET FOST ACOS	NCHQ
Welsh, Richard M	Lt Cdr	01-Oct-09	ENG	AE	820 SQN	RNAS CULDROSE
West, Darren C	Lt Cdr	01-Oct-05	WAR	MCD PWO	PJHQ (UK) J3	NORTHWOOD
West, David J	Maj	01-Oct-10	RM	P SK4	FLEET AV VL - OC	RNAS YEOVILTON
West, Graham G	Lt Cdr	06-Jun-99	ENG	ME	MWS EXCELLENT	HMNB PORTSMOUTH
West, Hannah R	Lt Cdr	01-Oct-12	ENG	AE	DES/COIR/AS	ABBEY WOOD
West, the Lord, GCB, DSC, PC	Adm	30-Nov-00				
West, Michael W	Lt Cdr	05-Aug-92	WAR	PWO(A)	845 SQN	RNAS YEOVILTON
West, Nicholas K	Lt Cdr	01-Oct-09	LOGS	L C	ESG EJSU SHAPE	MONS BRUSSEL
West, Olivia N	Mid	01-Nov-13	WAR	GSX	BRNC DARTMOUTH	
West, Rory J	Lt Cdr	01-Jun-02	WAR	O SK6	NCHQ CNPERS	PORTSMOUTH
West, Sarah	Cdr	30-Jun-12	WAR	PWO(U)	HMS PORTLAND	
Westbrook, Kevin	Lt RN	01-Sep-06	ENG	AE	LHF 815 SQN HQ	RNAS YEOVILTON
Westlake, Simon	Lt RN	20-Oct-09	WAR	SM(X)	FLEET COMOPS NWD	NORTHWOOD
Westlake, Simon R	Lt Col	30-Jun-13	RM	SCC	COMUKAMPHIBFOR	HMNB PORTSMOUTH
Westley, Alexander	Lt RN	01-Sep-06	ENG	WESM	FOST FAS SHORE	HELENSBURGH
Westley, David R	Lt Cdr	01-Oct-01	WAR	P SK4	847 SQN - AE	RNAS YEOVILTON
Westmas, Timothy J	Lt RN	01-Sep-13	ENG	WE	HMS DEFENDER	
Weston, Antony T	SLt	01-May-12	WAR	GSX	BRNC DARTMOUTH	
Weston, Karl N N	Lt RN	01-Aug-99	WAR	O LYNX	RN EXCHANGE BRAZIL	
Westwood, Amanda J	Surg Lt Cdr (D)	07-Jul-13	DENTAL	GDP	45 CDO RM - SDS	DUNDEE
Westwood, Andrew J	Lt RN	01-Sep-02	WAR	P SK4	DEF HELI FLYING SCH	RAF SHAWBURY
Westwood, Christopher S	Lt RN	01-Sep-13	ENG	AE	RNAS YEOVILTON	
Westwood, Mark R	Cdr	30-Jun-11	ENG	MESM	DES/COMFLEET	ABBEY WOOD
Westwood, Michelle	Lt Cdr	01-Oct-13	LOGS	L	HMS SUTHERLAND	
Westwood, Thomas P	Lt Cdr	01-Oct-11	WAR	PWO	BRNC DARTMOUTH	
Wetherfield, Sarah F	Lt RN	01-May-08	ENG	TM	NETS (OPS)	HMS DRAKE
Whalley, Richard J	Cdr	30-Jun-09	LOGS	L C	COMUKTG SEA	PLYMOUTH
Wharrie, Craig G	Lt Cdr	01-Oct-11	ENG	ME	HMS WESTMINSTER	
Wharry, Douglas F	Lt RN	01-Aug-13	WAR	GSX	HMS DEFENDER	
Wharton, Charles F	Surg Lt RN	02-Aug-11	MED	GDMO	HQ SQN CDO LOG	BARNSTAPLE
Wheal, Adrian	Cdr	30-Jun-10	ENG	MESM	DES/COMFLEET	ABBEY WOOD
Wheatcroft, Ian J	Lt RN	01-Jun-10	LOGS	L SM	DMLS	HMS RALEIGH
Wheatley, Ian J	RN Prncpl Chpln	07-Aug-12	Ch S		CHAPLAIN OF THE FLEET	NCHQ
Wheatley, Nicola S	Lt Cdr	01-Oct-12	WAR	HM(AM)	FLEET COMOPS NWD	NORTHWOOD
Wheaton, Bowden J S	Cdr	30-Jun-10	WAR	O LYNX	FLEET CAP RCAP DIVISION	NCHQ
Wheeler, Luke A	Capt	01-Mar-10	RM	GS	42 CDO RM - COMD COY	HMNB DEVONPORT
Wheeler, Nicholas J	Cdr	30-Jun-10	WAR	SM(CQ)	MOD NSD	MAIN BUILDING LONDON
Wheeler, Robert J	Lt RN	01-Aug-13	ENG	WE	MWS COLLINGWOOD	
Wheen, Charles	Lt Cdr	01-Oct-12	WAR	MCD	HMS ARGYLL	
Wheldon, Adam J	Lt RN	17-Dec-10	LOGS	L	HMS NORTHUMBERLAND	
Whipp, Ian A	SLt	01-Feb-11	WAR	SM(X)	MWS COLLINGWOOD	
Whitby, Oliver	Capt	01-Sep-13	RM	GS	40 CDO RM	TAUNTON
White, Alec John	2Lt	01-Mar-11	RM	GS	40 CDO RM	TAUNTON
White, Alistair J	Lt RN	01-May-04	WAR	P MER	824 SQN	RNAS CULDROSE
White, Andrew J	Lt RN	01-Feb-09	WAR	P LYN7	652 SQN	GUTERSLOH
White, Daniel J	Lt RN	01-Feb-09	WAR	GSX	HMS SEVERN	
White, Douglas	Lt Cdr	01-Oct-10	ENG	WESM	HMS VIGILANT	
White, Haydn J	Col	19-Jul-10	RM	LC	JFC HQ	NORTHWOOD
White, Ian F	Lt Cdr	18-Nov-99	WAR	SM(AWC)	DES/COMFLEET	HELENSBURGH
White, Jason P QGM	Lt Cdr	01-Oct-08	WAR	MCD	MCM2 CREW 8	PORTSMOUTH
White, Jonathan A P	Capt RN	13-Dec-10	WAR	SM(CQ)	CTCRM 6	EXMOUTH
White, Jonathan E	Lt Cdr	01-Nov-02	LOGS	L	HQ DCLPA AND DEEPCUT	CAMBERLEY
White, Kevin F	Lt Cdr	01-Oct-06	ENG	ME	HMS NELSON	
White, Kristopher	Lt RN	01-Nov-07	WAR	SM(N)	HMS RALEIGH	
White, Mark	Lt RN	01-Feb-09	WAR	HM	FLEET HM UNIT	HMNB DEVONPORT
White, Maxwell A	SLt	01-Apr-12	WAR	O UT	RNAS CULDROSE	
White, Paul	Lt RN	01-Dec-09	WAR	GSX	RN EXCHANGE SPAIN	
White, Paul D	Lt RN	01-May-03	WAR	P SK6	857 NAS	RNAS CULDROSE

Person Name	Substantive Rank	Seniority	Branch	Specialisation	Organisation	Location
White, Ross E.	Lt RN	01-May-04	WAR	P MER	824 SQN CULDROSE	RNAS CULDROSE
White, Simon H W	Lt Cdr	01-Oct-10	WAR	P MER	824 SQN - TU	RNAS CULDROSE
White, Stephen J.	Lt Cdr	06-Oct-09	WAR	C	DES/COMJE	ABBEY WOOD BRISTOL
White, Stephen P.	Lt Cdr	01-Oct-11	ENG	IS	JSSU CH - HQ	CHELTENHAM
White, Steven	Lt Cdr	01-Oct-12	WAR	MCD PWO	MCM2 POR SEA	HMNB PORTSMOUTH
White, Thomas G.	Capt	01-Sep-09	RM	GS	CTCRM - CW	EXMOUTH
Whitehall, Sally	Lt Cdr	01-Oct-09	WAR	PWO(C)	FLEET COMOPS NWD	NORTHWOOD
Whitehead, Benjamin J	Lt RN	01-Sep-10	WAR	SM(X)	CAREER TRAINING	HMS RALEIGH
Whitehead, Peter J.	Lt Cdr	01-Oct-11	WAR	O SKW	FLEET CAP IS DIVISION	NCHQ
Whitehead, Steven J	Lt Cdr	01-Mar-00	ENG	AE	CHFHQ (SHORE)	RNAS YEOVILTON
Whitehouse, Andrew P	Lt RN	01-Sep-05	WAR	P LYN7	AACEN 7 (TRG) REGT AAC	STOCKBRIDGE
Whitehouse, David S.	Lt Cdr	01-Oct-08	WAR	SM(AWC)	HMS COLLINGWOOD	
Whitehouse, Niall R.	Lt Cdr	01-Dec-04	ENG	AE P	DES/COMJE/HELS	YEOVIL
Whiteley, Peter	SLt	01-Mar-11	ENG	MESM	DCEME SULTAN	HMS SULTAN
Whiteman, John W.	Capt	01-Aug-07	RM	GS	CTCRM - CW	EXMOUTH
Whitfield, Kenneth D	Cdr	30-Jun-08	ENG	AE	FLEET CSAV	NCHQ
Whitfield, Philip M	Maj	01-Sep-03	RM	GS	DEFENCE ACADEMY	SHRIVENHAM
Whitley, Helen S.	Lt RN	01-Apr-02	ENG	IS	FLEET COMOPS	NORTHWOOD
Whitley, Ian D B	Cdr	30-Jun-10	WAR	PWO(C)	FLEET COMOPS	NORTHWOOD
Whitley, Janine F	Lt RN	08-Feb-13	QARNNS	EN	RCDM	BIRMINGHAM
Whitmarsh, Adam T.	Maj	01-Oct-09	RM	GS	43 CDO	HMNB CLYDE
Whitson-Fay, Craig D	Lt Cdr	01-Oct-09	WAR	O SKW	DES/COIR/CA	ABBEY WOOD
Whittaker, Mark A	Surg Cdr	30-Jun-05	MED	Path	MDHU PORTSMOUTH	PORTSMOUTH
Whittaker, Terry J	Lt RN	01-Sep-11	ENG	ME	NAVY MCTA PORTSMOUTH	HMNB PORTSMOUTH
Whittington, Christopher C.	Lt RN	01-Nov-08	WAR	P SK6	857 NAS	RNAS CULDROSE
Whittles, Gary W	Lt Cdr	01-Oct-12	LOGS	L SM	JFLogC	NORTHWOOD
Whitworth, Robert M.	Lt Cdr	01-Oct-99	WAR	PWO(U)	UK MCC	BAHRAIN
Whybourn, Lesley A.	Surg Cdr	01-Jul-10	MED	Occ Med	INM ALVERSTOKE	GOSPORT
Whyte, Gordon	Lt Cdr	01-Oct-13	ENG	WE	DES/COMFLEET	ABBEY WOOD
Whyte, Iain P	Cdr	30-Jun-09	ENG	TM	NATO-ACT-HQ SACT	NORFOLK
Wick, Harry M.	Lt Cdr	01-Sep-12	WAR	GSX	DNR N IRELAND	BELFAST
Wickett, Richard J	Lt RN	01-Mar-02	ENG	ME	DES/COMFLEET	ABBEY WOOD
Wickham, Robert J.	Lt RN	01-May-01	WAR	PWO(C)	FLEET CAP IS DIVISION	NCHQ
Wicking, Geoffrey S	Lt Cdr	01-Oct-03	ENG	AE	A AIB FARNBOROUGH	ALDERSHOT
Wicks, Sam	Lt RN	01-Apr-13	WAR	INT	UKRBATSTAFF	HMNB PORTSMOUTH
Widdowson, Matthew G.	Lt RN	01-Sep-08	ENG	AE	DES/COIR/CA	ABBEY WOOD
Wielbo, Dominik J.	SLt	01-May-12	WAR	P UT	BRNC DARTMOUTH	
Wielopolski, Mark L	Lt RN	01-May-01	WAR	P SK4	FLEET FOSNNI - NRC	HMS CALEDONIA
Wilcocks, David N	Lt RN	01-Jul-05	WAR	FC	MWS COLLINGWOOD	
Wilcockson, Roy.	Capt	07-May-99	CS	CS	OCLC PLYMOUTH	HMNB DEVONPORT
Wilcox, Christopher	Lt RN	01-Sep-06	WAR	O SKW	RN EXCHANGE USA	WASHINGTON USA
Wild, Gareth	Surg Cdr	10-Sep-12	MED	GMP	NCHQ	
Wild, Richard J.	Lt Cdr	01-Oct-09	LOGS	L C SM	HMS ARGYLL	
Wild, Simon	SLt	01-Apr-11	WAR	FC	HMS ILLUSTRIOUS	
Wildin, Andrew.	Cdr	30-Jun-13	ENG	WE	DES/COMFLEET	ABBEY WOOD
Wilkins, David P.	Lt RN	01-May-01	WAR	SM(AWC)	HMS COLLINGWOOD	
Wilkins, Richard R	Lt Cdr	01-Oct-03	ENG	MESM	DES/COMFLEET	ABBEY WOOD
Wilkins, Robert L.	Lt Cdr	01-Oct-10	ENG	MESM	HMS TORBAY	
Wilkins, Thomas R.	SLt	01-May-12	ENG	WE	BRNC DARTMOUTH	DARTMOUTH
Wilkinson, David H OBE	Cdr	30-Jun-08	WAR	PWO(U)	JFHQ	NORTHWOOD
Wilkinson, John	Lt RN	01-Mar-09	ENG	WESM	FOST FAS SHORE	HELENSBURGH
Wilkinson, John R	Lt Cdr	01-Oct-10	WAR	AV	DSTO	RAF ST MAWGAN
Wilkinson, Lloyd John	SLt	01-May-12	LOGS	L	BRNC DARTMOUTH	
Wilkinson, Matthew J MBE	Capt	30-Mar-12	RM	GS	NCHQ	
Wilkinson, Timothy L	RN Chpln	04-Mar-97	Ch S			RNAS CULDROSE
Wilks, Thomas S.	2Lt	01-Sep-11	RM	N/A	CTCRM OFFICERS	EXMOUTH
Williams, Aaron P.	Lt RN	20-May-13	WAR	SM(N)	HMS ARTFUL	BARROW IN FURNESS
Williams, Amanda L.	Lt RN	20-Jul-10	WAR	ATC	RNAS CULDROSE	
Williams, Andrew F.	Lt RN	09-Apr-10	WAR	REG	RNP - HQ PMN	HMS EXCELLENT
Williams, Anthony DSC	Cdr	31-Dec-00	WAR	MCD PWO(A)	LSP ON	MUSCAT
Williams, Anthony M	Lt RN	01-Sep-04	WAR	GSX	MWS COLLINGWOOD	
Williams, Anthony S	Lt Cdr	01-Sep-06	WAR	PWO FC	MWS COLLINGWOOD	

Person Name	Substantive Rank	Seniority	Branch	Specialisation	Organisation	Location
Williams, Benjamin R.	Surg Lt Cdr (D)	27-Jun-05	DENTAL	GDP	FLEET DENPOL	NCHQ
Williams, Bruce N CBE	R Adm	07-Jul-09	WAR	PWO(U)	NATO	BRUSSELS
Williams, Cassandra L	Lt Cdr	01-Oct-11	ENG	AE	DES/COIR/AS	ABBEY WOOD
Williams, Colin OBE	Cdr	30-Jun-10	WAR	AAWO	FLEET COMOPS	NORTHWOOD
Williams, Daniel L	Lt RN	01-Jan-00	WAR	P LYNX	RAF CRANWELL	
Williams, David B	Lt RN	08-Dec-11	WAR	GSX	MCM2 CREW 1	PORTSMOUTH
Williams, Dylan S	Surg Lt Cdr (D)	25-Aug-09	DENTAL	GDP	JSU NORTHWOOD	NORTHWOOD
Williams, Edward A	Capt	01-Sep-11	RM	GS	CTCRM - CTW	EXMOUTH
Williams, Gareth	Lt RN	01-Sep-11	ENG	WESM	HMS TIRELESS	
Williams, Gareth	Lt RN	01-Apr-11	ENG	MESM	HMS TIRELESS	
Williams, Graeme T	Lt RN	01-May-13	WAR	SM(X)	CAREER TRAINING	HMS RALEIGH
Williams, Huw Rhys	Capt	16-Apr-10	RM	BS	CTCRM BAND	EXMOUTH
Williams, James L	Lt RN	01-Feb-07	WAR	INT	JFIG - JT IP	RAF WYTON
Williams, James P	Lt Cdr	01-Jun-00	WAR	AAWO	FLEET COMOPS	NORTHWOOD
Williams, Jonathan M	Capt	01-Sep-12	RM	GS	CTCRM - CTW	EXMOUTH
Williams, Julian	Lt RN	11-Apr-08	WAR	AV	DSTO	RAF ST MAWGAN
Williams, Justin L	Capt	30-Mar-12	RM	GS	NCHQ	
Williams, Lee J	Lt RN	01-Jul-04	ENG	WESM	HMS TRIUMPH	
Williams, Liam S	Lt RN	01-Apr-12	WAR	GSX	HMS PORTLAND	
Williams, Luke	Lt RN	01-Apr-05	WAR	PWO(SM)	HMS ARTFUL	BARROW IN FURNESS
Williams, Mark A	Cdr	30-Jun-11	WAR	O LYNX	FLEET CAP RCAP	NCHQ
Williams, Martyn J	Capt RN	13-Oct-09	ENG	WESM	DES/COMFLEET	ABBEY WOOD
Williams, Matthew J	Lt RN	01-Jan-10	WAR	GSX	FLEET FOSNNI - HQ	NCHQ
Williams, Matthew R	Lt RN	01-Oct-09	LOGS	L SM	HMS VIGILANT	
Williams, Matthew R	Capt	01-Sep-10	RM	GS	CTCRM - CTW	EXMOUTH
Williams, Neil A	Capt	01-Sep-11	RM	GS	42 CDO RM	HMNB DEVONPORT
Williams, Nicola J	Lt RN	01-Jan-13	WAR	O UT	RNAS CULDROSE	
Williams, Nigel	Lt RN	17-Dec-09	WAR	SM(C)	FLEET CAP IS DIVISION	NCHQ
Williams, Paul A	Lt Cdr	01-Oct-11	ENG	ME	HMS RICHMOND	
Williams, Paul G	Lt Cdr	01-Oct-10	WAR	INT	DI - FC(A) - WYT	RAF WYTON
Williams, Peter L	Capt	01-Sep-08	RM	GS	NCHQ	
Williams, Peter M	Lt Cdr	01-Oct-03	ENG	TM	HMS SULTAN	
Williams, Peter M	Maj	01-Oct-09	RM	GS	45 CDO RM	DUNDEE
Williams, Richard J	Surg Lt Cdr	02-Aug-11	MED	ORL	INM ALVERSTOKE	GOSPORT
Williams, Robert	Lt Cdr	01-Oct-06	WAR	PWO(C)	DEFAC JSCSC ACSC	SHRIVENHAM
Williams, Russell G	Lt RN	16-Feb-07	WAR	GSX	RNLA	BRNC DARTMOUTH
Williams, Simon P	R Adm	17-Sep-12	WAR	PWO(C)	DCDS PERS TRG	MAIN BUILDING LONDON
Williams, Stephen W	Cdr	30-Jun-10	LOGS	I	DES/COMFLEET	ABBEY WOOD
Williams, Thomas J	Capt	01-Sep-08	RM	GS	CTCRM - CW	EXMOUTH
Williams, Zoe E	SLt	01-May-13	WAR	GSX	FLEET HQ 6	NCHQ
Williams-Allden, Lucy A	Lt RN	01-Sep-07	ENG	AE	FLEET AV SEA	NCHQ
Williamson, Ben L	SLt	01-Sep-13	MED	MEDICAL	BRNC DARTMOUTH	
Williamson, Helen M	SLt	08-May-13	LOGS	L	HMS DEFENDER	
Williamson, Peter J	Lt RN	01-Oct-02	WAR	METOC	NATO-ACO-SHAPE	CASTEAU BRUSSELS
Williamson, Simon J	Lt RN	01-Oct-04	ENG	TM	FOST DPORT SHORE	HMNB DEVONPORT
Williamson, Tobias MVO	Cdre	16-Nov-11	WAR	O SK6	MWS COLLINGWOOD	
Williford, Susanna J	Lt RN	01-Sep-11	WAR	GSX	HMS CLYDE	
Willis, Alistair J	Capt RN	07-May-13	LOGS	L	DES/COMFLEET	HELENSBURGH
Willison, Mark G	Capt	01-Sep-11	RM	GS	CTCRM - CTW	EXMOUTH
Wills, Philip	Cdr	30-Jun-12	WAR	O LYNX	DEFENCE ACADEMY	SHRIVENHAM
Wills, Robert H	Lt RN	01-May-03	ENG	MESM	HMS VIGILANT	
Wills, Timothy M	Lt RN	01-Jan-12	WAR	P UT	RAF SHAWBURY	
Willsmore, Stuart A	Lt RN	01-Jul-05	WAR	PWO	HMS KENT	
Wilmot, Max A	Lt RN	01-May-09	WAR	MCD	MWS DDS	DDS PORTSMOUTH
Wilson, Allan J	Cdr	30-Jun-11	WAR	PWO(U)	FMC - NAVY	MAIN BUILDING LONDON
Wilson, Bruce N	Capt	01-Sep-03	RM	GS	43 CDO	HMNB CLYDE
Wilson, Charles B	Lt	01-Sep-11	RM	GS	1 PWRR B COY	PADERBORN
Wilson, Charles K	Lt RN	01-Sep-06	LOGS	L	FLEET ACOS(RP)	NCHQ
Wilson, Christopher J	Cdr	30-Jun-13	ENG	MESM	DES/COMFLEET	ABBEY WOOD
Wilson, David John	Lt RN	01-May-04	ENG	TM	DEFAC JSCSC ICSCM	SHRIVENHAM
Wilson, David R	Cdr	30-Jun-09	WAR	PWO(A)	MWS COLLINGWOOD	
Wilson, David W H	Lt Col	30-Jun-03	RM	GS	DI - SA - JTAC	LONDON

Person Name	Substantive Rank	Seniority	Branch	Specialisation	Organisation	Location
Wilson, Gary P	Lt Cdr	01-Oct-11	WAR	INT	NORTHWOOD HQ 6	NORTHWOOD
Wilson, Iain E	Lt RN	19-Dec-08	WAR	INT	JSSU CH - HQ	CHELTENHAM
Wilson, John	Lt Cdr	01-Oct-08	WAR	P CDO	CHF(MERLIN)	RAF BENSON
Wilson, Kayleigh J	Lt RN	01-Feb-10	LOGS	L	COMFASFLOT	HELENSBURGH
Wilson, Kevin P	Capt RN	30-Jun-05	ENG	WESM	DES/COMJE/ISS/DIST	CORSHAM
Wilson, Lloyd R	SLt	01-Sep-11	WAR	GSX	UK MCC	BAHRAIN
Wilson, Mark J	Lt RN	08-Jun-07	LOGS	L	HMS SOMERSET	
Wilson, Matthew J	Surg Lt RN	12-Jul-10	MED	GDMO	42 CDO RM	HMNB DEVONPORT
Wilson, Neil A	Lt Cdr	01-Oct-13	WAR	PWO(SM)	HMS TORBAY	
Wilson, Nicholas C	Lt RN	19-Nov-09	WAR	FC	HQ AIR - COS(OPS)	SALISBURY
Wilson, Robert N	Lt RN	01-Jan-13	LOGS	L	FLEET FOSNNI - HQ	HELENSBURGH
Wilson, Simon A	Lt RN	01-Jan-04	WAR	P LYNX	LHF 702 SQN	RNAS YEOVILTON
Wilson, Thomas E	Lt RN	01-Sep-13	ENG	WESM	HMS VIGILANT	
Wilson, Thomas R	SLt	01-Sep-11	WAR	O UT	702 SQN	RNAS YEOVILTON
Wilson-Chalon, Louis M	Cdr	30-Jun-09	WAR	P LYNX	MOD.NSD - HDS	MAIN BUILDING LONDON
Wilton, Mark	Lt RN	01-Dec-04	WAR	HM	RN EXCHANGE USA	WASHINGTON USA
Wiltshire, Ross M	Lt RN	01-Mar-12	WAR	P UT	MWS COLLINGWOOD	
Winborn, David J	Lt Cdr	01-Oct-12	ENG	MESM	HMS TRIUMPH	
Winch, Joseph A	Maj	01-Oct-10	RM	GS	40 CDO RM - B COY	TAUNTON
Winch, Michael T	Lt RN	01-May-13	LOGS	L	845 SQN	RNAS YEOVILTON
Windebank, Stephen	Cdr	30-Jun-12	WAR	P MER	829 SQN HQ	RNAS CULDROSE
Windsor, Christopher J	SLt	01-Sep-12	WAR	O UT	RNAS CULDROSE	RNAS CULDROSE
Wingfield, Michael J	Lt Cdr	01-Oct-06	WAR	O LYNX	LHF 700W SQN	RNAS YEOVILTON
Winkle, Sean J	Cdr	30-Jun-05	ENG	TM	HMS TEMERAIRE	HMNB PORTSMOUTH
Winn, John P	Lt Cdr	01-Oct-09	WAR	HM(AS)	COMUKTG SEA	HMNB DEVONPORT
Winning, Robert A	Lt RN	07-Oct-11	LOGS	L	HMS RALEIGH	
Winsor, James	Lt Cdr	01-Oct-09	WAR	HM(AS)	HMS ECHO	
Winstanley, Mark	Maj	01-Oct-13	RM	SCC	DEF SCHOOL OF TRANSPORT	HULL
Winstanley, Robert A	Capt	03-Apr-09	RM	GS	NCHQ	
Winstone, Nigel P	Lt Cdr	01-Oct-13	ENG	MESM	HMS TORBAY	
Winter, Richard J	Cdr	30-Jun-08	ENG	WE	FLEET CAP SSM DIVISION	NCHQ
Winter, Timothy	Cdr	30-Jun-08	ENG	ME	DES/COMFLEET	ABBEY WOOD
Winterbon, Andrew R	Lt Cdr	01-Oct-10	WAR	AAWO	COMUKAMPHIBFOR	HMNB PORTSMOUTH
Winterton, Gemma	Lt RN	01-Nov-10	ENG	TM	BRNC DARTMOUTH	
Winterton, Paul	Lt Cdr	01-Oct-13	WAR	O MER	824 SQN	RNAS CULDROSE
Winterton, Tom R	Capt	01-Sep-11	RM	GS	42 CDO RM	HMNB DEVONPORT
Wintle, Geoffrey L	Cdr	30-Jun-03	LOGS	L SM	BRNC DARTMOUTH	DARTMOUTH
Winwood, Matthew R	Lt RN	01-Apr-10	WAR	GSX	EU OHQ	NORTHWOOD
Wise, Simon D	Capt RN	19-Apr-10	ENG	WE	DES/COMJE/ISS	CORSHAM
Wiseman, Deborah J	Lt RN	01-Mar-12	ENG	TM	FLEET HQ 6	NCHQ
Wiseman, George R	Maj	01-Oct-05	RM	SCC	FLEET SPT LOGS	NCHQ
Wiseman, Hugo	Lt RN	01-Jul-13	WAR	SM(X)	HMS VICTORIOUS	
Wiseman, Ian C	Cdr	30-Jun-11	WAR	PWO(N)	FOST MPV SEA	HELENSBURGH
Wiseman, Neil	Lt Cdr	01-Oct-09	WAR	O LYNX	LHF 702 SQN	RNAS YEOVILTON
Witcher, Emily R	Mid	01-Feb-13	WAR	SM(X)	BRNC DARTMOUTH	
Witham, Brian M	Lt RN	01-Sep-13	WAR	O UT	JFC HQ	NORTHWOOD
Witham, Katharine V	Lt RN	01-Apr-11	WAR	GSX	HMS NORTHUMBERLAND	
Witt, Alister Kevin	Cdr	14-Jan-13	MED	MS(EHO)	HQ DPHC - PLANS	LICHFIELD
Woad, Jonathan P R	Lt RN	01-Nov-01	WAR	MW	MCM2 CREW 5	PORTSMOUTH
Wood, Alexander M	Surg Lt RN	01-Aug-07	MED	T&O	INM ALVERSTOKE	GOSPORT
Wood, Andrew G	Lt Cdr	01-Oct-06	ENG	AE	FLEET CSAV	NCHQ
Wood, Christopher R	Lt Cdr	01-Jan-05	WAR	P MER	FLEET CSAV	NCHQ
Wood, Christopher T	Lt Cdr	01-Oct-12	ENG	TM	NCHQ CNPS	NCHQ
Wood, Craig	Capt RN	18-Nov-13	WAR	PWO(A)	PJHQ (UK) J3	NORTHWOOD
Wood, Frederick J	Lt RN	01-Jan-08	MED	MS(EHO)	DES/COMFLEET	HMNB PORTSMOUTH
Wood, Graham	Lt Cdr	01-Oct-05	LOGS	L	DEFAC JSCSC ACSC	SHRIVENHAM
Wood, Iain M	Surg Lt Cdr	04-Aug-11	MED	GMP	INM ALVERSTOKE	GOSPORT
Wood, Joanne T	Lt RN	01-Jan-02	WAR	ATC	FLEET CSAV	RNAS YEOVILTON
Wood, Joseph A	Lt Cdr	01-Oct-06	WAR	GSX	HMS TEMERAIRE	
Wood, Julian T S	Lt RN	07-Apr-06	ENG	ME	DES/COMFLEET	HMNB PORTSMOUTH
Wood, Michael J	SLt	01-Feb-13	MED	MEDICAL	BRNC DARTMOUTH	
Wood, Michael L	Lt Cdr	01-Dec-04	WAR	PWO(N)	CAREER TRAINING	USA

Person Name	Substantive Rank	Seniority	Branch	Specialisation	Organisation	Location
Wood, Michael W	Lt RN	01-May-04	WAR	PWO(N)	UK MCC	BAHRAIN
Wood, Nicholas R	Lt Cdr	01-Oct-06	WAR	PWO(U)	COMUKAMPHIBFOR	HMNB PORTSMOUTH
Wood, Richard R T	Lt RN	01-Sep-04	WAR	P GR7	736 NAS	RNAS CULDROSE
Wood, Robert	Capt RN	22-Feb-11	LOGS	L BAR	NCHQ - CNLS	NCHQ
Wood, Stephen A H	Lt Cdr	01-Oct-11	WAR	P SK4	7 SQN	RAF ODIHAM
Wood, Thomas D	Lt RN	01-Jan-13	WAR	SM(X)	HMS ASTUTE	
Wood, Uvedale G	Cdr	30-Jun-13	WAR	P GR7	OPS DIR	MAIN BUILDING LONDON
Woodard, Jolyon	Capt RN	09-Sep-13	WAR	P SK4	HQ JHC	ANDOVER
Woodbridge, Richard G	Lt Cdr	01-Aug-04	ENG	ME	FLEET DCS - RNIO	HMS COLLINGWOOD
Woodcock, Keith	Mid	01-Sep-13	ENG	AE	BRNC DARTMOUTH	
Woodcock, Simon J OBE	R Adm	11-Sep-12	ENG	ME	NAVSEC	NCHQ
Woodley, Stephen L	Lt RN	01-Sep-02	ENG	MESM	DES/COMFLEET	ABBEY WOOD
Woodman, Clare F J	Lt Cdr	31-Mar-07	WAR	MEDIA OPS	FOST DPORT SEA	HMNB DEVONPORT
Woodridge, Ryan A	Mid	01-Nov-13	WAR	GSX	BRNC DARTMOUTH	DARTMOUTH
Woodrow, Kevin	Lt Cdr	01-Oct-03	WAR	SM(C)	JFIG - JT OPS	RAF WYTON
Woods, Anna Louise	SLt	01-Sep-11	WAR	GSX	HMS SEVERN	
Woods, James D	Lt RN	01-Jan-08	WAR	P LYNX	LHF 700W SQN	RNAS YEOVILTON
Woods, Jeremy B	Cdr	30-Jun-04	WAR	AAWO	FLEET COMOPS	NORTHWOOD
Woods, Michael J P	Lt Cdr	01-May-09	ENG	WESM	HMS VENGEANCE	
Woods, Roland P	Cdr	31-Dec-98	WAR	PWO(A)	NC PSYA	NORTHWOOD
Woods, Timothy C	Cdr	30-Jun-08	ENG	TM(SM)	KABUL SU	AFGHANISTAN KABUL
Woodward, Alasdair J	Lt RN	01-Feb-08	WAR	P MER	820 SQN	RNAS CULDROSE
Woodward, Guy F	SLt	01-Feb-12	WAR	GSX	BRNC DARTMOUTH	
Woodward, Ian M	Lt RN	03-Oct-10	WAR	INFO OPS	CTF 150	HMNB PORTSMOUTH
Woodward, Mark A	Lt RN	01-Sep-13	WAR	SM(X)	MWS COLLINGWOOD	
Wookey, Mark	Lt Cdr	01-Oct-11	WAR	O LYNX	700W SQN	RNAS YEOVILTON
Woolhead, Andrew L	Lt Cdr	01-Oct-03	WAR	PWO(N)	CYBER POLICY	MAIN BUILDING LONDON
Woolhead, Craig M	Lt Cdr	01-Oct-09	WAR	PWO(U)	FLEET CAP SSM DIVISION	NCHQ
Woollard, Kerry M	SLt	01-Sep-12	WAR	HM	BRNC DARTMOUTH	
Woollcombe-Gosson, David J	Lt Cdr	01-Jun-97	WAR	AAWO	FLEET CAP SSM DIVISION	NCHQ
Wooller, Mark A H	Cdr	30-Jun-10	LOGS	L SM	RNAS YEOVILTON	
Woolley, Stephen	Surg Lt RN	04-Aug-10	MED	GDMO	FWO DEVPT SEA	HMNB DEVONPORT
Woollven, Andrew	Cdr	30-Jun-13	WAR	MCD PWO(U)	CD CS HQ FD TRG	ANDOVER
Woollven, Christopher D	Lt Cdr	01-Oct-10	WAR	O LYNX	LHF HQ	RNAS YEOVILTON
Woolsey, Kevin	Lt Cdr	01-May-07	WAR	ATC	DEFAC JSCSC ACSC	SHRIVENHAM SWINDON
Woosey, Mark	Maj	01-Jun-04	RM	GS	1 ASSLT GROUP RM	BIDEFORD
Wordsworth, Joel K	Lt RN	01-Mar-12	ENG	MESM	HMS VANGUARD	
Wordsworth, Jonathan D	Lt RN	01-Jul-05	WAR	GSX	HMS TRUMPETER	
Work, Judith	SLt	31-Oct-11	WAR	HM	BRNC DARTMOUTH	DARTMOUTH
Workman, Rayner J	Lt RN	01-Sep-03	WAR	HM	FLEET HM UNIT	HMNB DEVONPORT
Worley, Thomas F	Lt RN	01-Jan-03	WAR	MW	HMS SOMERSET	
Worrall, Adam Craig	Lt RN	01-Aug-13	ENG	WESM	HMS VANGUARD	
Wort, Roland S QHC	RN Chpln	28-Jul-89	Ch S		HMS COLLINGWOOD	
Worthington, Jonathan M	Cdr	30-Jun-06	ENG	TM	NMC HQ	NORTHWOOD
Wotton, Alan	Lt RN	01-Jul-04	WAR	P LYN7	RN EXCHANGE USA	WASHINGTON USA
Wotton, Ryan J	Lt RN	01-Jan-08	WAR	P LYNX	815 SQN	RNAS YEOVILTON
Wragg, Gareth T	Lt Cdr	01-Oct-10	WAR	HM	RNAS CULDROSE	
Wraith, Luke	SLt	08-Dec-11	WAR	P UT	RAF SHAWBURY	
Wraith, Neil	Lt Col	30-Jun-11	RM	LC	FOST DPORT SEA	HMNB DEVONPORT
Wray, Philip	Lt RN	01-Oct-10	WAR	P SK4	845 SQN	RNAS YEOVILTON
Wray, Stuart A	SLt	08-Jul-11	WAR	P UT	RAF SHAWBURY	
Wren, Stephen J	Lt Cdr	01-Oct-11	WAR	PWO	COMUKTG SEA	PLYMOUTH
Wrennall, Eric P	Lt Cdr	01-Oct-08	ENG	ME	COMDEVFLOT	HMS DRAKE
Wrigglesworth, Peter J	Surg Lt Cdr	02-Aug-88	MED	GMP	UK MED GP	AFGHANISTAN BASTION
Wright, Christopher	Lt RN	01-Mar-12	ENG	WE	HMS DRAGON	
Wright, Daniel J	Lt Cdr	01-Oct-07	WAR	SM(AWC)	FOST FAS SHORE	HELENSBURGH
Wright, David	Lt Cdr	01-Oct-06	WAR	MCD	DCD - MODSAP KSA	SAUDI ARABIA
Wright, David I	Lt Cdr	01-Sep-04	ENG	WE	FLEET COMOPS	NORTHWOOD
Wright, Gabriel J	Lt RN	01-Nov-05	ENG	WE	DES/COMFLEET	ABBEY WOOD
Wright, Gillian F	Lt Cdr	01-Oct-05	LOGS	L C	DCDS PERS TRG	MAIN BUILDING LONDON
Wright, Helen J	Lt RN	13-Aug-04	LOGS	L	HMS VICTORY	PORTSMOUTH
Wright, James A H	Lt RN	01-Jan-08	WAR	GSX	HMS BULWARK	

Person Name	Substantive Rank	Seniority	Branch	Specialisation	Organisation	Location
Wright, James N	Lt RN	01-May-06	LOGS	L SM	DES/COMFLEET	HMS DRAKE
Wright, James P	Lt RN	01-Jan-12	WAR	P	RAF SHAWBURY	
Wright, Jennifer S	Lt Cdr	01-Oct-13	LOGS	L BAR	NCHQ - CNLS	PORTSMOUTH
Wright, Joseph R	SLt	01-Apr-11	WAR	SM(X)	HMS TIRELESS	
Wright, Justin C	Lt RN	11-Dec-09	ENG	WE	DES/COMJE/ISS	CORSHAM
Wright, Natalie	SLt	11-Apr-11	WAR	HM	HMS DAUNTLESS	
Wright, Neil D MBE	Lt RN	13-Aug-04	ENG	AE	HQ AIR - HQ 1GP	HIGH WYCOMBE
Wright, Nigel S	Cdr	30-Jun-09	ENG	ME	CUSTOMER DESIGN	MAIN BUILDING LONDON
Wright, Paul D	Lt RN	01-Jan-08	ENG	IS	MWS EXCELLENT	PORTSMOUTH
Wright, Stuart H	Cdr	30-Jun-05	LOGS	L BAR	MOD NSD	MAIN BUILDING LONDON
Wright, Timothy M	Cdr	30-Jun-12	LOGS	L	FLEET SPT LOGS	NCHQ
Wright-Jones, Alexandra E	Lt Cdr	01-Oct-12	QARNNS	PHC	TGHQ	AFGHANISTAN
Wrigley, Alexander J	Surg Lt Cdr	03-Aug-09	MED	GMP	HMS PROTECTOR	
Wyatt, Jason R	Lt RN	01-Sep-12	ENG	WE	HMS MONTROSE	
Wyatt, Julian M	Cdr	30-Jun-03	ENG	MESM	FLEET FOST ACOS	NCHQ
Wyatt, Mark Rd	Cdr	30-Sep-99	WAR	MW (RES)	FLEET DCS - RNIO	HMNB PORTSMOUTH
Wylie, David V	RN Chpln	01-Dec-98	Ch S		42 CDO RM	HMNB DEVONPORT
Wylie, Ian C H	Cdr	30-Jun-08	ENG	WESM	DCDS MIL CAP	MAIN BUILDING LONDON
Wylie, Justin J	Lt RN	01-Sep-07	ENG	AE	FLEET CSAV	NCHQ
Wylie, Robert D	Surg Cdr	01-Apr-03	MED	Occ Med	MEDICAL CENTRE	RNAS CULDROSE
Wyness, Caroline J	Lt Cdr	01-Oct-06	WAR	PWO	NORTHWOOD	
Wyness, Roger S	Lt Cdr	13-Dec-05	WAR	P LYNX	NO 3 FTS/UAS - JEFTS	
Wynn, Simon R	Cdr	30-Jun-10	WAR	METOC	HMS NELSON	
Wyper, James	Cdr	30-Jun-13	WAR	SM(CQ)	FLEET HQ 6	NCHQ

Y

Person Name	Substantive Rank	Seniority	Branch	Specialisation	Organisation	Location
Yarham, Emma	Lt RN	01-May-01	ENG	TM	HMS RALEIGH	
Yarker, Sam	Lt RN	01-Jan-11	WAR	O MER	829 SQN FLT 03	RNAS CULDROSE
Yates, David M	RN Chpln	01-Sep-98	Ch S		COMPORFLOT SEA	HMNB PORTSMOUTH
Yates, Neal P	Lt Cdr	01-Jun-89	WAR	O LYNX	FLEET CSAV	RNAS YEOVILTON
Yates, Simon P	Lt RN	01-Sep-07	WAR	O LYNX	815 SQN	RNAS YEOVILTON
Yates, Stuart E	Lt Cdr	01-Oct-06	WAR	AAWO	MCM2 CREW 3	HMNB PORTSMOUTH
Yaxley, Louise	Lt Cdr	01-Oct-08	WAR	MW	DES/COMFLEET	HMNB PORTSMOUTH
Yearling, Emma C	SLt	24-Nov-11	ENG	WESM	MWS COLLINGWOOD	
Yelland, Christopher B	Lt Cdr	01-Oct-01	WAR	O LYNX	LHF 815 SQN HQ	RNAS YEOVILTON
Yemm, Charlotte P	Lt Cdr	01-Oct-04	WAR	PWO(C) HM	FLEET COMOPS NWD	NORTHWOOD
Yemm, Matthew A	Lt RN	01-Feb-06	WAR	HM	FLEET COMOPS NWD	NORTHWOOD
York, George M	Capt	01-Sep-13	RM	GS	40 CDO RM	TAUNTON
Young, Andrew J	Lt RN	28-Jul-06	ENG	AE	DES/COMJE/HELS	RNAS YEOVILTON
Young, Andrew O	Lt RN	01-Nov-07	ENG	TM	HMS RALEIGH	
Young, David A	Lt RN	01-Jul-04	ENG	AE	DES/COMJE/HELS	RNAS YEOVILTON
Young, James A	SLt	01-Sep-11	WAR	GSX	HMS RICHMOND	
Young, Martin J	Mid	11-Apr-12	WAR	P UT	BRNC DARTMOUTH	
Young, Martin N	Lt RN	01-Sep-09	WAR	O MER	824 SQN - TU	RNAS CULDROSE
Young, Michael	Lt RN	20-Oct-08	ENG	WE	JFCIS(I)	QATAR
Young, Michael S MBE	Capt RN	03-Dec-13	ENG	TM	NCHQ CNPERS	
Young, Neil	Lt RN	01-Sep-08	ENG	WE	MWS COLLINGWOOD	
Young, Sean A	Lt RN	01-Oct-11	WAR	O UT	702 SQN	RNAS YEOVILTON
Young, Stephen W	Cdr	30-Jun-07	LOGS	L SM	DCDS PERS TRG	MAIN BUILDING LONDON
Young, William D	Lt Cdr	31-Mar-05	LOGS	L (RES)	DEFENCE LANGUAGE SCHOOL	WILTON PARK
Youngman, Mitchell C	Lt RN	27-Jul-06	WAR	REG	DCPG - DPS	FAREHAM
Youp, Allan	Cdr	30-Jun-13	ENG	TM	JFC - DCTS (H)	RAF HALTON
Yoxall, William Frank	Lt RN	01-Jan-12	WAR	GSX	HMS DUNCAN	

Z

Person Name	Substantive Rank	Seniority	Branch	Specialisation	Organisation	Location
Zambellas, George M Kcb Dsc Adc Dl	Adm	06-Jan-12	WAR	P LYNX	MOD CNS/ACNS	MAIN BUILDING LONDON
Zauchenberger, Michael J	Lt RN	01-Jan-09	LOGS	L SM	BF BIOT	DIEGO GARCIA
Zitkus, John J	Lt RN	01-May-07	ENG	WE	DES/COMJE	ABBEY WOOD

SENIORITY LIST

ADMIRALS OF THE FLEET

(This rank is now held in abeyance in peacetime (1996))
Edinburgh, His Royal Highness The Prince Philip, Duke of, KG, KT, OM, GBE, AC, QSO.......15 Jan 53

Ashmore, Sir Edward (Beckwith), GCB, DSC .... 9 Feb 77
Bathurst, Sir (David) Benjamin, GCB, DL ....10 Jul 95
Wales, His Royal Highness The Prince Charles, Prince of, KG, KT, CGB, OM, AK, QSO, PC, ADC ... 16 Jun 12

ADMIRALS

FORMER CHIEF OF DEFENCE STAFF, FIRST SEA LORD OR VICE CHIEF OF DEFENCE STAFF WHO REMAIN ON THE ACTIVE LIST

Slater, Sir Jock (John Cunningham Kirkwood), GCB, LVO, DL...29 Jan 91
Boyce, the Lord, KG, GCB, OBE, DL...25 May 95
Abbott, Sir Peter (Charles), GBE, KCB, MA .... 3 Oct 95
Essenhigh, Sir Nigel (Richard), GCB, DL .... 11 Sep 98
West, the Lord, GCB, DSC, PC ....30 Nov 00
Band, Sir Jonathon, GCB, DL.. 2 Aug 02
Stanhope, Sir Mark, GCB, OBE ....10 Jul 04

ADMIRAL

Zambellas, Sir George, KCB, DSC, ADC, DL...6 Jan 12
(CHIEF OF NAVAL STAFF AND FIRST SEA LORD APR 13)..

VICE ADMIRALS

Jones, Philip Andrew, CB...13-Dec-11
(FLEET COMMANDER AND DEPUTY CHIEF OF NAVAL STAFF NOV 12)

Richards, Alan David, CB.. 19-Jan-12
(CHIEF OF DEFENCE INTELLIGENCE JAN 12) ....

Steel, David George, CBE...10-Oct-12
(CHIEF OF NAVAL PERSONNEL & TRAINING AND SECOND SEA LORD JUL 10 & CHIEF NAVAL LOGISTICS OFFICER)

Hudson, Peter Derek, CBE..14-Feb-13
(COMMANDER MARITIME COMMAND FEB 13)

Corder, Ian Fergus, CB 30-May-13
(UK MILITARY REPRESENTATIVE TO NATO & THE EU MAY 13)

Lister, Simon Robert, CB, OBE 27-Nov-13
(CHIEF OF MATERIEL (FLEET) & CHIEF NAVAL ENGINEERING OFFICER NOV 13)

REAR ADMIRALS

Williams, Bruce Nicholas Bromley, CBE 7-Jul-09
(DEPUTY DIRECTOR GENERAL EUROPEAN UNION MILITARY STAFF SEP 11)

Potts, Duncan Laurence 26-Jan-11
(ASSISTANT CHIEF OF NAVAL STAFF (CAPABILITY) JAN 13, CHIEF OF STAFF NCHQ, CONTROLLER OF THE NAVY)

Harding, Russell George, OBE 01-Mar-11
(ASSISTANT CHIEF OF NAVAL STAFF (AVIATION & CARRIERS) AND REAR ADMIRAL FLEET AIR ARM SEP12)

Johnstone, Clive Charles Carruthers, CBE 12-Jul-11
(ASSISTANT CHIEF OF NAVAL STAFF (POLICY) MAY 13)

Hockley, Christopher John, CBE 9-Sep-11
(FLAG OFFICER SCOTLAND, NORTHERN ENGLAND & NORTHERN IRELAND/FLAG OFFICER REGIONAL FORCES AND FLAG OFFICER RESERVES SEP 11)

Gower, John Howard James, OBE 28-Nov-11
(ASSISTANT CHIEF OF DEFENCE STAFF NUCLEAR & CHEMICAL, BIOLOGICAL NOV 11)

Parr, Matthew John 2-Dec-11
(COMMANDER OPERATIONS & REAR ADMIRAL SUBMARINES MAY 13)

Fraser, Timothy Peter 16-Jan-12
(ASSISTANT CHIEF OF DEFENCE STAFF (CAPABILITY FORCE DESIGN) JAN 14

Parker, Henry Hardyman 6-Feb-12
(PROGRAMME DIRECTOR CARRIER STRIKE FEB 12)

Brunton, Steven Buchanan 24-Feb-12
(DIRECTOR SHIP ACQUISITION & DEPUTY DIRECTOR SHIPS FEB 12)

Jess, Ian Michael .... 3 Jul 12
(ASSISTANT CHIEF OF NAVAL STAFF (SUPPORT) JUL 12)

Beverstock, Mark Alistair 23-Jul-12
(CHIEF STRATEGIC SYSTEMS EXECUTIVE JUL 12)

Morse, James Anthony 28-Aug-12
(COMMANDANT JOINT SERVICE COMMAND AND STAFF COLLEGE AUG 12)

Woodcock, (Simon) Jonathan, OBE 11-Sep-12
(ASSISTANT CHIEF OF NAVAL STAFF (PERSONNEL) AND NAVAL SECRETARY SEP 12)

Williams, Simon Paul 17-Sep-12
ASSISTANT CHIEF OF DEFENCE STAFF (PERSONNEL) & DEFENCE SERVICES SECRETARY SEP 12)

Lowe, Timothy Miles 17-Sep-12
DEPUTY COMMANDER STRIKE FORCE NATO SEP 12)

Karsten, Thomas Michael 14-Dec-12
(NATIONAL HYDROGRAPHER AND DEPUTY CHIEF EXECUTIVE (HYDROGRAPHY) DEC 12)

Tarrant, Robert Kenneth 14-Jan-13
COMMANDER UK MARITIME FORCES

Bennett, Paul Martin, OBE 04-Feb-13
(CHIEF OF STAFF JOINT FORCES COMMAND SEP 13)

Key, Benjamin John 29-Apr-13
(FLAG OFFICER SEA TRAINING APR 13)

Wareham, Michael Paul 30-Sep-13
(DIRECTOR SUBMARINES SEP 13)

Cree, Malcolm Charles 07-Oct-13
(CHIEF OF STAFF (INTEGRATED CHANGE PROJECT) OCT 13)

Kingwell, John Matthew Leonard 14-Oct-13
(DIRECTOR CONCEPTS & DOCTRINE OCT 13)

Ancona, Simon James 14-Oct-13
(ASSISTANT CHIEF OF DEFENCE STAFF (MILITARY STRATEGY) OCT 13)

Between appointments:
Since the publication of the last Navy List, the following officers have joined, or will be joining the
Retired List:

Vice Admiral C A JOHNSTONE-BURT CB OBE 30-Nov-13
Major General S T CHICKEN OBE 07-Dec-13
Vice Admiral Sir Andrew Mathews KCB 26-Mar-14

COMMODORES

2007

FRASER, ERIC CBE 01-Jul-07

2008

ALBON, ROSS 07-Jul-08
MANSERGH, MICHAEL P CBE 01-Sep-08
COCHRANE, MICHAEL OBE 25-Nov-08

2009

CHICK, STEPHEN CBE 03-Feb-09
DARLINGTON, MARK 03-Feb-09
WALLACE, MICHAEL CBE 29-Jun-09

2010

GARDNER, CHRISTOPHER 04-Jan-10
BROWN, NEIL 01-Jul-10
BECKETT, KEITH 24-Aug-10
TOY, MALCOLM 04-Oct-10

2011

MCALPINE, PAUL OBE 08-Feb-11

CLINK, JOHN 25-Apr-11
CHIVERS, PAUL OBE 10-May-11
BRAHAM, STEPHEN 27-May-11
JAMESON, ANDREW rcds 01-Jul-11
WALKER, CLIVE 01-Jul-11
BULLOCK, MICHAEL MBE 04-Jul-11
STOKES, RICHARD 25-Jul-11
MACKAY, GRAEME 22-Aug-11
RADAKIN, ANTONY 12-Sep-11
FARRAGE, MICHAEL CBE 07-Nov-11
WILLIAMSON, TOBIAS MVO 16-Nov-11
HAY, JAMES DONALD 21-Dec-11

2012

ROBERTS, NICHOLAS S 03-Jan-12
SANGUINETTI, HECTOR R. 06-Jan-12
GARRETT, STEPHEN W OBE 07-Feb-12
NEWELL, JONATHAN MBE 02-Apr-12
BATH, MICHAEL 01-Jul-12
PENTREATH, JONATHAN OBE 16-Jul-12
LITTLE, GRAEME OBE 17-Jul-12
HAMMOND, PAUL 19-Jul-12
THOMPSON, RICHARD OBE 27-Jul-12

SHIPPERLEY, IAN 28-Aug-12
WEALE, JOHN 03-Sep-12
HODGSON, TIMOTHY 04-Sep-12
POWELL, RICHARD OBE 10-Sep-12
BURTON, ALEXANDER 18-Sep-12
BLUNDEN, JEREMY LVO 22-Oct-12
ADAMS, ALISTAIR 05-Nov-12
ALEXANDER, ROBERT OBE 04-Dec-12

2013

FARRINGTON, RICHARD CBE 26-Mar-13
ENTWISLE, WILLIAM OBE MVO 30-Apr-13
ALLEN, RICHARD 01-Jul-13
ELFORD, DAVID 01-Jul-13
HARDERN, SIMON 01-Jul-13
LISON, ANDREW 01-Jul-13
RIGBY, JEREMY 01-Jul-13
BLOUNT, KEITH E OBE 27-Aug-13
ROBINSON, GUY A OBE 03-Sep-13
MACDONALD, JOHN 22-Jul-13
CORDEROY, JOHN 02-Sep-13
DUTTON, DAVID OBE 30-Sep-13

CAPTAINS

2000

MILLER, ANDREW CBE 01-Jun-00

2002

HOLLOWAY, JONATHAN 01-Jul-02
STANLEY, NICHOLAS 01-Jul-02

2003

ATHERTON, MARTIN 30-Jun-03
RUSBRIDGER, ROBERT 30-Jun-03

2004

KING, CHARLES 30-Jun-04
HARRAP, NICHOLAS OBE 30-Jun-04

2005

BUCKLEY, PHILLIP 30-Jun-05
GREENLEES, IAIN 30-Jun-05
HAWTHORNE, MICHAEL 30-Jun-05
LEMKES, PAUL 30-Jun-05
SUTTON, GARY 30-Jun-05
WILSON, KEVIN 30-Jun-05

2006

BAUM, STUART 30-Jun-06
CORRIGAN, NIALL 30-Jun-06
MCBARNET, THOMAS 30-Jun-06
MORGAN, PETER DSC 30-Jun-06
O'NEILL, PATRICK J 30-Jun-06

RICHMOND, IAIN J M. 30-Jun-06
SPALDING, RICHARD E. 30-Jun-06

2007

ALCOCK, CHRISTOPHER 30-Jun-07
KNIBBS, MARK 30-Jun-07
MACDONALD, ALASDAIR 30-Jun-07
RYCROFT, ALAN E 30-Jun-07
SKIDMORE, CHRISTOPHER OBE 30-Jun-07
TAYLOR, KENNETH 30-Jun-07
EDNEY, ANDREW 30-Jun-07
JOHNSON, JAMES 30-Jun-07

2008

ABRAHAM, PAUL CBE 30-Jun-08
ASHCROFT, ADAM 30-Jun-08
DAWS, RICHARD 30-Jun-08
FRY, JONATHAN 30-Jun-08
HELEY, DAVID N 30-Jun-08
JENKIN, ALASTAIR 30-Jun-08
PETT, JEREMY G 30-Jun-08
SMITHSON, PETER 30-Jun-08
HINE, NICHOLAS 30-Jun-08
MORRITT, DAIN 30-Jun-08
TITTERTON, PHILLIP J OBE 30-Jun-08
MCMICHAEL-PHILLIPS, SCOTT 30-Jun-08
GARRATT, MARK 30-Jun-08
PATTINSON, IAN 30-Jun-08
PAGE, DAVID 30-Jun-08
CASSAR, ADRIAN 30-Jun-08
ANDERSON, ROBERT 01-Jul-08

BISSON, IAN 01-Jul-08
TAYLOR, SPENCER 01-Jul-08
ERSKINE, PETER 08-Jul-08
PARSONS, CHRISTOPHER 15-Jul-08
EVANS, KARL 29-Jul-08
HAYES, JAMES 01-Aug-08
MCGHIE, IAN 26-Aug-08
METHVEN, PAUL 26-Aug-08
BRAND, SIMON 08-Sep-08
GLENNIE, ANDREW 09-Sep-08
HOBBS, RICHARD 22-Sep-08
DOYLE, GARY 20-Oct-08
ASPDEN, ANDREW 21-Oct-08
HARRISON, MATTHEW OBE 03-Nov-08
MCQUAKER, STUART 02-Dec-08

2009

WALLIKER, MICHAEL OBE 06-Jan-09
WARWICK, PHILIP 06-Jan-09
CHIDLEY, TIMOTHY 08-Jan-09
SPENCE, ANDREI 10-Feb-09
KYTE, ANDREW 23-Feb-09
GRAHAM, GORDON 03-Mar-09
MALCOLM, STEPHEN OBE 04-May-09
LINES, JAMES 04-May-09
MCKENDRICK, ANDREW OBE 01-Jun-09
STIDSTON, IAN 15-Jun-09
STEEDS, SEAN 27-Jun-09
BONE, DARREN 01-Jul-09
CLARKE, CHARLES OBE 01-Jul-09
PAYNE, RICHARD 01-Jul-09
HOLLINS, RUPERT 01-Jul-09

CAPTAINS

PORTER, SIMON P 13-Jul-09
WALKER, NICHOLAS 18-Aug-09
MACLEOD, JAMES 01-Sep-09
INGRAM, RICHARD 07-Sep-09
BRIERS, MATTHEW 21-Sep-09
ROBINSON, MICHAEL 05-Oct-09
HUGHES, NICHOLAS 13-Oct-09
WILLIAMS, MARTYN 13-Oct-09
DURKIN, MARK T G 19-Oct-09
WAINHOUSE, MICHAEL 02-Nov-09
KYD, JEREMY 02-Nov-09
MILBURN, PHILIP 04-Nov-09
APLIN, ADRIAN T MBE 24-Nov-09
GRAY, ANTONY 14-Dec-09

2010

BETTON, ANDREW OBE 05-Jan-10
HALTON, PAUL OBE 11-Jan-10
ADAMS, ANDREW 18-Jan-10
STOCKER, JEREMY 01-Mar-10
FANCY, ROBERT OBE ADC 01-Mar-10
JESSOP, PAUL 08-Mar-10
CLOUGH, CHRISTOPHER 12-Apr-10
CHARLESWORTH, GRAHAM 19-Apr-10
WISE, SIMON 19-Apr-10
DAINTON, STEVEN CBE 26-Apr-10
MORLEY, JAMES 26-Apr-10
CHILDS, DAVID 26-Apr-10
SHAWCROSS, PAUL OBE 01-May-10
CASSON, PAUL 10-May-10
BURKE, PAUL OBE 28-May-10
AMPHLETT, NIGEL 07-Jun-10
HARRIS, ANDREW 20-Jul-10
O'BRIEN, PATRICK OBE 24-Aug-10
DAILEY, PAUL 27-Aug-10
PETTITT, GARY 20-Sep-10
SPARKES, PETER 08-Nov-10
THOMAS, RICHARD 08-Nov-10
WHITE, JONATHAN 13-Dec-10

2011

DYER, MICHAEL 04-Jan-11
PEARSON, STEPHEN 07-Jan-11
BORLAND, STUART 10-Jan-11
REID, CHARLES 10-Jan-11
BLACKMAN, NICHOLAS OBE 25-Jan-11
GULLEY, TREVOR 25-Jan-11
REINDORP, DAVID 21-Feb-11

WOOD, ROBERT 22-Feb-11
HIGHAM, JAMES OBE 07-Mar-11
WARRENDER, WILLIAM 26-Apr-11
MURRISON, RICHARD 16-May-11
BEARDALL, MICHAEL 27-Jun-11
GRAHAM, DAVID 01-Jul-11
STANLEY-WHYTE, BERKELEY 01-Jul-11
MUIR, KEITH 18-Jul-11
HILL, PHILIP JOHN 15-Aug-11
CONNELL, MARTIN 05-Sep-11
CARRICK, RICHARD 06-Sep-11
CARTER, SIMON 07-Sep-11
HATCHER, RHETT 26-Sep-11
BELLFIELD, ROBERT 27-Sep-11
COOPER, MARK 11-Oct-11
COULSON, PETER 18-Oct-11
KENNEDY, INGA 21-Nov-11
LONG, ADRIAN 21-Nov-11
DUFFY, HENRY 06-Dec-11
HOOD, KEVIN C 08-Dec-11
DEANEY, MARK 16-Dec-11

2012

BURNS, ANDREW rcds(s) 03-Jan-12
BEARD, HUGH 03-Jan-12
CREE, ANDREW 03-Jan-12
THOMPSON, STEPHEN 09-Jan-12
SCOTT, NIGEL 10-Jan-12
GROVES, CHRISTOPHER 23-Jan-12
MAGAN, MICHAEL 21-Feb-12
BURNINGHAM, MICHAEL 12-Mar-12
ORCHARD, ADRIAN OBE 19-Apr-12
POLLOCK, DAVID 01-May-12
PETITT, SIMON 28-May-12
WAGSTAFF, NEIL 25-Jun-12
MARSHALL, PAUL 01-Jul-12
BARTLETT, DAVID 01-Jul-12
FISHER, CLAYTON 16-Jul-12
PHILLIPS, IAN 06-Aug-12
STACE, IVAN 28-Aug-12
OSMOND, JUSTIN 03-Sep-12
HODKINSON, CHRISTOPHER 04-Sep-12
LOWER, IAIN 10-Sep-12
UTLEY, MICHAEL 10-Sep-12
VANDERPUMP, DAVID 10-Sep-12
GUY, THOMAS 18-Sep-12
REED, ANDREW OBE 25-Sep-12
DABELL, GUY 01-Oct-12
CLARK, MATTHEW 02-Oct-12

OLIVE, PETER OBE 02-Oct-12
TINDAL, NICOLAS 08-Oct-12
VITALI, ROBERT 09-Oct-12
CAMERON, MARK 06-Nov-12
PATERSON, MICHAEL 20-Nov-12
PEACOCK, TIMOTHY 10-Dec-12
HOLT, STEVEN 12-Dec-12

2013

ALLEN, STEPHEN 08-Jan-13
GALE, MARK 21-Jan-13
BETTERIDGE, CAROL OBE 26-Feb-13
ANNETT, IAN 11-Mar-13
PRESCOTT, SHAUN 22-Apr-13
GRANTHAM, STEPHEN 01-Jul-13
STREETEN, CHRISTOPHER 01-Jul-13
TRITSCHLER, EDWIN MBE 01-Jul-13
GRIFFIN, NIALL MBE 01-Jul-13
TALBOTT, AIDAN 01-Jul-13
SALMON, MICHAEL 01-Jul-13
SHAW, KEVIN 01-Jul-13
BIGGS, WILLIAM 27-Aug-13
BASSETT, DEAN 09-Sep-13
HENRY, TIMOTHY 09-Sep-13
WOODARD, JOLYON 09-Sep-13
GAYFER, MARK 24-Jun-13
WOOD, CRAIG 18-Nov-13
ACKLAND, HEBER MVO 10-Dec-13
WATT, ANTHONY OBE 18-Jun-13
HUNTINGTON, SIMON OBE 28-Oct-13
ROBERTSON, DAVID 17-Sep-13
WASHER, NICHOLAS 17-Sep-13
KISSANE, ROBERT 07-May-13
WILLIS, ALISTAIR 07-May-13
JORDAN, ANDREW 25-Sep-13
LOVEGROVE, RAYMOND 03-Dec-13
YOUNG, MICHAEL MBE 03-Dec-13
WATERHOUSE, PHILIP 03-Sep-13
BURNS, DAVID 02-Jul-13
MANSON, THOMAS 02-Jul-13
SEYMOUR, KEVIN 02-Sep-13
POOLE, JASON 15-Jul-13
EVANS, WILLIAM 08-Jul-13
OLIPHANT, WILLIAM 29-Aug-13

COMMANDERS

1987

BROWN, SIMON J 16-Jun-87

1988

HUGHES, PETER LVO 06-Feb-88

1993

SPALTON, GARY 11-Jun-93
COX, PIETER 30-Jun-93

1994

CHAMBERS, WILLIAM 30-Apr-94

1996

HOLMES, ROBERT 25-Feb-96

1997

HORNE, TIMOTHY 30-Jun-97
PICKLES, IAN 30-Jun-97
PICKTHALL, DAVID 31-Dec-97

COMMANDERS

1998

POPE, CATHERINE	24-Jun-98
DANBURY, IAN	30-Jun-98
JACKMAN, ANDREW	30-Jun-98
HATCH, GILES	31-Dec-98
SHIELD, SIMON	31-Dec-98
WOODS, ROLAND	31-Dec-98
GREEN, TIMOTHY	31-Dec-98

1999

CARDEN, PETER	30-Jun-99
FEAR, RICHARD K	30-Jun-99
MOORE, CHRISTOPHER	30-Jun-99
ROBINSON, CHARLES	30-Jun-99
VANDOME, ANDREW	30-Jun-99
MORTON, NIGEL	30-Jun-99
BARTON, PETER	30-Jun-99
HORN, PETER MBE	30-Jun-99
SIMMONS, NIGEL	30-Jun-99
WYATT, MARK RD	30-Sep-99
CHALMERS, DONALD P	31-Dec-99
GREENE, MICHAEL J	31-Dec-99
JOHNSON, ANDREW S	31-Dec-99
TREANOR, MARTIN A	31-Dec-99
RACE, NIGEL	31-Dec-99

2000

NEWTON, GARRY	27-Mar-00
BROADLEY, KEVIN	30-Jun-00
HARVEY, COLIN	30-Jun-00
SHORT, GAVIN	30-Jun-00
ALLIBON, MARK	30-Jun-00
TILLEY, DUNCAN	30-Jun-00
HAYES, STUART J	30-Jun-00
BASSON, ANDREW	30-Jun-00
BLOWERS, MICHAEL	31-Dec-00
BOND, NIGEL D MBE	31-Dec-00
CONNOLLY, CHRISTOPHER	31-Dec-00
FRANKHAM, PETER	31-Dec-00
FULTON, CRAIG	31-Dec-00
HUGHES, GARETH	31-Dec-00
WILLIAMS, ANTHONY DSC	31-Dec-00
BUCHAN-STEELE, MARK	31-Dec-00
PARSONS, BRIAN	31-Dec-00
MARMONT, KERRY	31-Dec-00

2001

RANCE, MAXWELL	31-May-01
FOREMAN, JOHN	30-Jun-01
GORDON, DAVID	30-Jun-01
KNIGHT, DAMON	30-Jun-01
O'GRADY, MATTHEW	30-Jun-01
PHENNA, ANDREW	30-Jun-01
SHAW, STEVEN	30-Jun-01
WALLACE, ALLAN OBE	30-Jun-01
ST AUBYN, JOHN	30-Jun-01
RAYBOULD, ADRIAN	30-Jun-01
MITCHELL, HENRY	30-Jun-01
HAINES, PAUL	30-Jun-01

JONES, MARTIN	30-Jun-01
CROZIER, STUART	30-Jun-01

2002

KAY, DAVID RD	01-Jan-02
BARRAND, STUART	30-Jun-02
BLACKMORE, MARK	30-Jun-02
DAVIES, CHRISTOPHER	30-Jun-02
FALK, BENEDICT	30-Jun-02
FITTER, IAN	30-Jun-02
GRINDEL, DAVID	30-Jun-02
HARE, NIGEL	30-Jun-02
HAYWOOD, GUY	30-Jun-02
HODGKINS, JONATHAN	30-Jun-02
JARVIS, LAWRENCE	30-Jun-02
LAYLAND, STEPHEN	30-Jun-02
MOFFATT, NEIL R	30-Jun-02
SWANNICK, DEREK	30-Jun-02
THOMPSON, ANDREW	30-Jun-02
TURNBULL, GRAHAM	30-Jun-02
TURNBULL, SIMON	30-Jun-02
WALLIS, ADRIAN	30-Jun-02
THOMPSON, BERNARD	30-Jun-02
SKEER, MARTYN	30-Jun-02
HARDY, LEE	30-Jun-02
TARR, BARRY	30-Jun-02
NADEN, ANDREW	30-Jun-02

2003

BROWN, WILLIAM	30-Jun-03
BURLINGHAM, BRETT	30-Jun-03
CLARK, IAN	30-Jun-03
COLES, ANDREW OBE	30-Jun-03
CORBETT, ANDREW	30-Jun-03
DAVID, SIMON	30-Jun-03
GILBERT, PETER	30-Jun-03
KIRKUP, JOHN	30-Jun-03
KNIGHT, PAUL	30-Jun-03
MEAKIN, BRIAN	30-Jun-03
MUNNS, ANDREW	30-Jun-03
ROBERTSON, MICHAEL	30-Jun-03
SALISBURY, DAVID OBE	30-Jun-03
SHERRIFF, DAVID	30-Jun-03
SMITH, MARTIN	30-Jun-03
UPTON, IAIN	30-Jun-03
WYATT, JULIAN M	30-Jun-03
MAHONY, DAVID	30-Jun-03
CUNNINGHAM, JOHN	30-Jun-03
ROBERTS, STEPHEN	30-Jun-03
HARVEY, ROBERT	30-Jun-03
GREEN, DAVID	30-Jun-03
FIELDSEND, MARK	30-Jun-03
ROBERTS, TIMOTHY	30-Jun-03
NISBET, JAMES	30-Jun-03
JENKINS, GARI	30-Jun-03
HAWKINS, MARTIN	30-Jun-03
DYKE, CHRISTOPHER	30-Jun-03
KENNEDY, IAN	30-Jun-03
FLYNN, MICHAEL	30-Jun-03
FIELDS, DAVID	30-Jun-03

RANDALL, RICHARD	30-Jun-03
GURMIN, STEPHEN	30-Jun-03
WINTLE, GEOFFREY	30-Jun-03

2004

ABERNETHY, JAMES	30-Jun-04
BAND, JAMES	30-Jun-04
BRECKENRIDGE, IAIN OBE	30-Jun-04
BULL, CHRISTOPHER	30-Jun-04
DUNN, ROBERT P OBE	30-Jun-04
EDGE, JOHN	30-Jun-04
GILES, DAVID	30-Jun-04
HIBBERD, NICHOLAS	30-Jun-04
HILL, GIULIAN	30-Jun-04
LISTER, MARK	30-Jun-04
MEREWETHER, HENRY	30-Jun-04
ROLPH, ANDREW	30-Jun-04
TARR, RICHARD	30-Jun-04
WOODS, JEREMY	30-Jun-04
DIBLE, JAMES	30-Jun-04
FERRIS, DANIEL PETER	30-Jun-04
TOFT, MICHAEL DAVID	30-Jun-04
RICHES, IAN C OBE	30-Jun-04

2005

BARKER, PIERS	30-Jun-05
BOWBRICK, RICHARD	30-Jun-05
BOWEN, NIGEL	30-Jun-05
BOWER, NIGEL	30-Jun-05
BOYD, NICHOLAS, psc(j)	30-Jun-05
CARTWRIGHT, DARREN OBE	30-Jun-05
CHATWIN, NICHOLAS OBE	30-Jun-05
CRYAR, TIMOTHY	30-Jun-05
DELLER, MARK	30-Jun-05
DOWELL, PAUL	30-Jun-05
FORER, DUNCAN	30-Jun-05
GEARY, TIMOTHY	30-Jun-05
GEORGE, ALAN	30-Jun-05
HARRIS, KERI	30-Jun-05
HARROP, IAN	30-Jun-05
HAYCOCK, TIMOTHY	30-Jun-05
HONNORATY, MARK	30-Jun-05
MALLINSON, ROBERT	30-Jun-05
MARTIN, BRUCE	30-Jun-05
MCTEAR, KAREN MBE	30-Jun-05
MURDOCH, ANDREW	30-Jun-05
PARRY, ALEXANDER	30-Jun-05
PERKS, JAMES OBE	30-Jun-05
RIPPINGALE, STUART	30-Jun-05
SHORT, JOHN	30-Jun-05
SMITH, GREGORY	30-Jun-05
SWAIN, ANDREW MBE	30-Jun-05
WINKLE, SEAN	30-Jun-05
WRIGHT, STUART	30-Jun-05
ANSTEY, ROBERT	30-Jun-05
MATTHEWS, DAVID	30-Jun-05
RUSSELL, PHILIP	30-Jun-05
MEARNS, CRAIG	30-Jun-05
GREEN, PETER	30-Jun-05
HAYLE, JAMES	30-Jun-05

COMMANDERS

GRENFELL-SHAW, MARK......................30-Jun-05
MERRITT, JONATHAN...........................30-Jun-05
JACKSON, ANDREW...............................30-Jun-05
BUCKLE, IAIN...30-Jun-05
CLARK, SIMON.......................................30-Jun-05
MCINNES, JAMES...................................30-Jun-05
DUNCAN, IAN..30-Jun-05
MAHER, MICHAEL..................................30-Jun-05
PRIOR, GRANT.......................................30-Jun-05
SMITH, STEVEN L OBE...........................30-Jun-05
HARDINGE, CHRISTOPHER MBE..........30-Sep-05
ALLEN, ELINOR JANE RD.......................30-Jun-05

2006

ALBON, MARK..30-Jun-06
ALLEN, RICHARD...................................30-Jun-06
CHURCHER, JEREMY...............................30-Jun-06
COLES, CHRISTOPHER............................30-Jun-06
DAVIES, MARK.......................................30-Jun-06
DRYSDALE, STEVEN...............................30-Jun-06
DUNN, PAUL OBE..................................30-Jun-06
EASTAUGH, ANDREW.............................30-Jun-06
EVANS, EDWARD....................................30-Jun-06
EVANS, MARTIN.....................................30-Jun-06
FLEMING, KEVIN....................................30-Jun-06
GOODSELL, CHRISTOPHER......................30-Jun-06
HANCOCK, ANDREW...............................30-Jun-06
HAWKINS, JAMES...................................30-Jun-06
HEMSWORTH, KENNETH........................30-Jun-06
HOWARD, DANIEL..................................30-Jun-06
HUTCHINSON, OLIVER............................30-Jun-06
KING, NICHOLAS....................................30-Jun-06
LINDSAY, IRVINE....................................30-Jun-06
MASTERS, JAMES...................................30-Jun-06
MCCUE, DUNCAN...................................30-Jun-06
MORRIS, SIMON.....................................30-Jun-06
ROBERTS, PETER....................................30-Jun-06
SCOTT, JAMES.......................................30-Jun-06
SCOTT, MICHAEL...................................30-Jun-06
SLOCOMBE, CHRISTOPHER OBE...........30-Jun-06
THOMPSON, NEIL OBE..........................30-Jun-06
TOWELL, PETER......................................30-Jun-06
TOWLER, ALISON....................................30-Jun-06
VICKERS, JOHN OBE..............................30-Jun-06
WORTHINGTON, JONATHAN...................30-Jun-06
MOSS, RICHARD.....................................30-Jun-06
MAY, NIGEL...30-Jun-06
DOMINY, DAVID.....................................30-Jun-06
HALL, BARRY..30-Jun-06
GRAY, JOHN...30-Jun-06
O'BRIEN, KIERAN...................................30-Jun-06
KELLY, JOHN..30-Jun-06
EWEN, ANDREW.....................................30-Jun-06
LIAS, CARL DAVID..................................30-Jun-06
GUY, MARK MBE....................................30-Jun-06
GIBSON, ALASTAIR................................30-Jun-06
STUTTARD, MARK...................................30-Jun-06
MORRIS, RICHARD.................................30-Jun-06
MUNRO-LOTT, PETER..............................30-Jun-06
GIBBS, NEIL...30-Jun-06
SMITH, CHRISTOPHER............................30-Jun-06

JUCKES, MARTIN...................................30-Jun-06
ELVIN, ANDREW OBE.............................30-Jun-06
GREGORY, ALASTAIR.............................30-Jun-06

2007

DEACON, STEPHEN.................................01-Jun-07
ASHMAN, RODNEY ACMA.....................30-Jun-07
BODDINGTON, JEREMY.........................30-Jun-07
BOSUSTOW, ANTONY.............................30-Jun-07
CLARKE, RICHARD.................................30-Jun-07
DREELAN, MICHAEL...............................30-Jun-07
EVANS, MARC D.....................................30-Jun-07
FERNS, TIMOTHY D................................30-Jun-07
GOMM, KEVIN OBE...............................30-Jun-07
GROOM, IAN S MBE...............................30-Jun-07
HEWITT, DAVID......................................30-Jun-07
HILL, DAVID..30-Jun-07
HOGBEN, ANDREW................................30-Jun-07
HOPPER, SIMON....................................30-Jun-07
HUSSAIN, SHAYNE MBE........................30-Jun-07
JAMES, ADAM.......................................30-Jun-07
JOHNS, SARAH......................................30-Jun-07
JONES, ALUN...30-Jun-07
LIPSCOMB, PAUL....................................30-Jun-07
MEREDITH, NICHOLAS...........................30-Jun-07
MILLER, COLIN......................................30-Jun-07
PETHYBRIDGE, RICHARD........................30-Jun-07
PORRETT, JOHNATHAN..........................30-Jun-07
PRICE, TIMOTHY....................................30-Jun-07
RUSSELL, THOMAS.................................30-Jun-07
SHEPHERD, CHARLES.............................30-Jun-07
STALEY, SIMON.....................................30-Jun-07
TYACK, TERENCE....................................30-Jun-07
WALKER, PETER.....................................30-Jun-07
YOUNG, STEPHEN..................................30-Jun-07
AHLGREN, EDWARD OBE........................30-Jun-07
FINN, IVAN RICHARD.............................30-Jun-07
CUMMINGS, ALAN.................................30-Jun-07
CURRASS, TIMOTHY..............................30-Jun-07
HOPER, PAUL ROGER.............................30-Jun-07
DODD, NICHOLAS.................................30-Jun-07
WARD, STEPHEN....................................30-Jun-07
LYNN, STEVEN.......................................30-Jun-07
WALLER, STEVEN...................................30-Jun-07
SAVAGE, MARK OBE.............................30-Jun-07
WALKER, MARK.....................................30-Jun-07
FORTESCUE, ROBERT.............................30-Jun-07
TEBBET, PAUL..30-Jun-07
LOWTHER, JAMES..................................30-Jun-07
GILL, MARTIN.......................................30-Jun-07
SANSFORD, ADRIAN..............................30-Jun-07
STOFFELL, DAVID...................................30-Jun-07
CAMPBELL, ROBIN...............................30-Jun-07
ELLIMAN, SIMON..................................30-Jun-07
JOHN, GARETH MBE..............................30-Jun-07
MOOREY, CHRISTOPHER........................30-Jun-07
MORGAN, STEPHEN..............................30-Jun-07
ROGERS, ANDREW.................................30-Jun-07

2008

THAIN-SMITH, JULIE...............................01-Apr-08
ALLEN, PATRICK.....................................30-Jun-08
ASH, TIMOTHY.......................................30-Jun-08
ASQUITH, SIMON OBE..........................30-Jun-08
ATKINSON, MARK..................................30-Jun-08
BARTLETT, IAN.......................................30-Jun-08
BENCE, DAVID.......................................30-Jun-08
BOLTON, MATTHEW...............................30-Jun-08
BOWER, ANDREW OBE..........................30-Jun-08
BRADY, SEAN...30-Jun-08
COLE, SIMON PHILIP.............................30-Jun-08
COOK, CHRISTOPHER.............................30-Jun-08
DODD, KEVIN QCBA..............................30-Jun-08
FREEMAN, DAVID..................................30-Jun-08
GODWIN, CHRISTOPHER........................30-Jun-08
GREEN, ANDREW...................................30-Jun-08
HALLY, PHILIP..30-Jun-08
HESLING, GARY......................................30-Jun-08
HOULBERG, KENNETH...........................30-Jun-08
IRWIN, MARK...30-Jun-08
JACKSON, IAN..30-Jun-08
LEA, JOHN...30-Jun-08
MACDONALD-ROBINSON, NICHOLAS....30-Jun-08
PAYNE, JOHN...30-Jun-08
PIERCE, ADRIAN....................................30-Jun-08
RAMSEY, RYAN.......................................30-Jun-08
ROSE, MICHAEL.....................................30-Jun-08
ROWLAND, PAUL....................................30-Jun-08
SMITH, MARK..30-Jun-08
SOUTHORN, MARK................................30-Jun-08
STACEY, ANDREW..................................30-Jun-08
TETLOW, HAMISH..................................30-Jun-08
WHITFIELD, KENNETH...........................30-Jun-08
WILKINSON, DAVID H OBE.....................30-Jun-08
WINTER, RICHARD.................................30-Jun 08
WOODS, TIMOTHY.................................30-Jun-08
WYLIE, IAN..30-Jun-08
CAPES, STUART.....................................30-Jun-08
HULME, TIMOTHY OBE..........................30-Jun-08
BRYAN, RORY OBE.................................30-Jun-08
BEATTIE, PAUL.......................................30-Jun-08
MURPHY, PAUL......................................30-Jun-08
LAUCHLAN, ROBERT.............................30-Jun-08
JOLL, SIMON...30-Jun-08
MACKEY, MARTIN..................................30-Jun-08
WALKER, STEPHEN................................30-Jun-08
MULVANEY, PAUL..................................30-Jun-08
WINTER, TIMOTHY................................30-Jun-08
ASBRIDGE, JONATHAN...........................30-Jun-08
BROOKS, GARY......................................30-Jun-08
SMITH, GREGORY..................................30-Jun-08
O'BYRNE, PATRICK................................30-Jun-08
BRENCHLEY, NIGEL...............................30-Jun-08
BONE, RICHARD....................................30-Jun-08
DATHAN, TIMOTHY...............................30-Jun-08
DRAPER, STEPHEN.................................30-Jun-08
HARRIS, MICHAEL.................................30-Jun-08
BOWKER, GEOFFREY.............................30-Jun-08
BEWLEY, GEOFFREY RD..........................28-Oct-08

COMMANDERS

2009

ADAM, IAN	30-Jun-09
ATKINS, IAN	30-Jun-09
BAILEY, JEREMY	30-Jun-09
BALHETCHET, ADRIAN	30-Jun-09
BLACKWELL, RICHARD	30-Jun-09
BLYTHE, PAUL	30-Jun-09
BOWERS, JOHN	30-Jun-09
CARROLL, PAUL	30-Jun-09
COX, DAVID	30-Jun-09
COX, REX	30-Jun-09
CROSBIE, DONALD	30-Jun-09
CULL, IAIN	30-Jun-09
DEAN, JAMES OBE	30-Jun-09
DONNELLY, JAMES OBE	30-Jun-09
DOULL, DONALD	30-Jun-09
DOWSETT, PATRICK	30-Jun-09
EVANS, CHARLES	30-Jun-09
GALE, SIMON	30-Jun-09
GARDNER, JOHN	30-Jun-09
GOLDSMITH, DARRAN	30-Jun-09
GREEN, TIMOTHY	30-Jun-09
GREENER, CARL	30-Jun-09
GRINDON, MATTHEW	30-Jun-09
HARRIS, RICHARD	30-Jun-09
KROSNAR-CLARKE, STEVEN	30-Jun-09
LANGRILL, MARK	30-Jun-09
LINDSAY, DAVID	30-Jun-09
LORING, ANDREW	30-Jun-09
MATTHEWS, PAUL	30-Jun-09
MOORE, PIERS	30-Jun-09
NECKER, CARL	30-Jun-09
NICHOLSON, KRISTIN	30-Jun-09
O'FLAHERTY, CHRISTOPHER	30-Jun-09
O'SULLIVAN, BARRIE	30-Jun-09
PATTERSON, DAVID	30-Jun-09
PREECE, DAVID	30-Jun-09
PRINCE, MARK	30-Jun-09
SHARPE, THOMAS OBE	30-Jun-09
STEMBRIDGE, DANIEL	30-Jun-09
TAYLOR, MARK	30-Jun-09
TEIDEMAN, IAN	30-Jun-09
VOYCE, JOHN	30-Jun-09
WALKER, NICHOLAS	30-Jun-09
WHALLEY, RICHARD	30-Jun-09
WHYTE, IAIN	30-Jun-09
WILSON, DAVID	30-Jun-09
WILSON-CHALON, LOUIS	30-Jun-09
WRIGHT, NIGEL	30-Jun-09
DOUGLAS, PATRICK	30-Jun-09
SMALL, RICHARD	30-Jun-09
SMITH, AUSTIN MA	30-Jun-09
CRAIG, JOHN	30-Jun-09
MCCARTHY, STEVEN	30-Jun-09
GAME, PHILIP GORDON	30-Jun-09
STAMPER, JONATHAN	30-Jun-09
ANIYI, CHRISTOPHER	30-Jun-09
O'SULLIVAN, MICHAEL	30-Jun-09
HENDERSON, STUART	30-Jun-09
FRANKLIN, BENJAMIN	30-Jun-09
GEORGE, DAVID	30-Jun-09

RYAN, RICHARD	30-Jun-09
PHILLIPS, JASON OBE	30-Jun-09
PROUD, ANDREW	30-Jun-09
THOMPSON, ROBERT	30-Jun-09
FITZSIMMONS, MARK	30-Jun-09
HEWITT, LLOYD	30-Jun-09
O'FLAHERTY, JOHN	30-Jun-09
HARDING, GARY	30-Jun-09
KERSLAKE, RICHARD	30-Jun-09
FOLLINGTON, DANIEL	03-Aug-09
SPENCER, STEVEN	04-Aug-09
ADAMS, PETER	01-Sep-09

2010

BAINES, DAVID	30-Jun-10
BAXTER, IAIN	30-Jun-10
BLOCK, ANDREW	30-Jun-10
BOLTON, JONATHAN	30-Jun-10
BRAVERY, MARTIN	30-Jun-10
BRISTOWE, PAUL	30-Jun-10
BRUFORD, ROBERT	30-Jun-10
BURNS, ADRIAN	30-Jun-10
CHAPMAN, CHARLES	30-Jun-10
DOW, CLIVE	30-Jun-10
FERGUSSON, NIGEL	30-Jun-10
FINCHER, KEVIN	30-Jun-10
GAZZARD, JULIAN	30-Jun-10
HOARE, PETER	30-Jun-10
HOWARD, NICHOLAS	30-Jun-10
HUGHESDON, MARK	30-Jun-10
JOYCE, DAVID	30-Jun-10
KNOTT, MICHAEL	30-Jun-10
LANDROCK, GRAHAM	30-Jun-10
LETT, JONATHAN	30-Jun-10
LINDERMAN, IAN	30-Jun-10
MACKAY, PETER	30-Jun-10
MURRAY, GRANT	30-Jun-10
NASH, PHILIP	30-Jun-10
NEW, CHRISTOPHER	30-Jun-10
PITCHER, PAUL P.	30-Jun-10
PLEDGER, DAVID	30-Jun-10
RACKHAM, ANTHONY	30-Jun-10
REED, DARREN	30-Jun-10
RICHARDSON, GAVIN	30-Jun-10
RIMMER, HEATHER	30-Jun-10
ROYSTON, STUART	30-Jun-10
RUSSELL, PAUL	30-Jun-10
SMITH, MICHAEL D.	30-Jun-10
SPARKES, SIMON N.	30-Jun-10
SUTTON, RICHARD MBE	30-Jun-10
SYRETT, MATTHEW	30-Jun-10
TABEART, GEORGE	30-Jun-10
TATHAM, STEPHEN	30-Jun-10
TAYLOR, ROBERT	30-Jun-10
VOLLENTINE, LUCY	30-Jun-10
WHEELER, NICHOLAS	30-Jun-10
WHITLEY, IAN	30-Jun-10
WOOLLER, MARK	30-Jun-10
WYNN, SIMON	30-Jun-10
PEDRE, ROBERT	30-Jun-10
COOKE-PRIEST, NICHOLAS	30-Jun-10

STROUDE, PAUL	30-Jun-10
MOORHOUSE, STEPHEN	30-Jun-10
CLARKE, IAN	30-Jun-10
READWIN, ROGER	30-Jun-10
LAMB, ANDREW OBE	30-Jun-10
WILLIAMS, COLIN OBE	30-Jun-10
HORNE, JASON	30-Jun-10
WHEAL, ADRIAN	30-Jun-10
SMITH, ROBERT	30-Jun-10
LYNN, IAN	30-Jun-10
MIMPRISS, GRAHAM	30-Jun-10
PHILO, JULIAN	30-Jun-10
MARDLIN, STEPHEN	30-Jun-10
LOWE, JULIAN	30-Jun-10
GARRATT, JOHN	30-Jun-10
PANTHER, ANDREW	30-Jun-10
JACKSON, DAVID	30-Jun-10
QUINN, MARTIN	30-Jun-10
PETHICK, IAN	30-Jun-10
MCDERMOTT, OWEN	30-Jun-10
MCNALLY, NEVILLE	30-Jun-10
WILLIAMS, STEPHEN	30-Jun-10
FARRINGTON, JOHN	30-Jun-10
JOHNS, MICHAEL	30-Jun-10
THRIPPLETON, MARK	30-Jun-10
HOFMAN, ALISON ARRC	27-Jul-10

2011

WEIR, SCOTT D.	29-Mar-11
ABLETT, ELEANOR	30-Jun-11
AITKEN, ANDREW	30-Jun-11
ATWILL, JOHN	30-Jun-11
BAGGALEY, JASON	30-Jun-11
BALDWIN, CHRISTOPHER	30-Jun-11
BALLARD, MARK	30-Jun-11
BEECH, CHRISTOPHER psc(j), pce	30-Jun-11
BIRD, RICHARD	30-Jun-11
BORBONE, NICHOLAS	30-Jun-11
CURRY, ROBERT	30-Jun-11
ESSENHIGH, ANGUS	30-Jun-11
FRYER, ADRIAN	30-Jun-11
GREENLAND, MICHAEL MVO	30-Jun-11
HAIGH, ALASTAIR	30-Jun-11
HARRISON, RICHARD MBE	30-Jun-11
HUTCHINS, RICHARD	30-Jun-11
JEFFERSON, TOBY	30-Jun-11
JOYCE, THOMAS	30-Jun-11
LARGE, STEPHEN	30-Jun-11
LAWRENCE, STUART	30-Jun-11
LEACH, SARAH	30-Jun-11
LIVESEY, JOHN	30-Jun-11
LYNCH, STEPHEN	30-Jun-11
MACKIE, DAVID	30-Jun-11
MACLEOD, MARK	30-Jun-11
MATTHEWS, PAUL	30-Jun-11
MCNAIR, JAMES	30-Jun-11
MOORE, SUZANNE	30-Jun-11
NEWTON, JAMES DFC	30-Jun-11
NOAKES, KEVIN	30-Jun-11
PARKIN, JAMES	30-Jun-11
PARSONS, ANDREW	30-Jun-11

COMMANDERS

RAYNER, ANDREW	30-Jun-11	HARRISON, PAUL MBE 30-Jun-12	CARNIE, MANSON 30-Jun-13
RICHARDSON, PETER	30-Jun-11	JACQUES, MARCUS 30-Jun-12	CODD, JUSTIN 30-Jun-13
RIMINGTON, ANTHONY	30-Jun-11	JOHNS, ANDREW 30-Jun-12	COX, MARK 30-Jun-13
RIPLEY, BENJAMIN	30-Jun-11	JOSE, STEVEN 30-Jun-12	DEAKIN, JOHANNA 30-Jun-13
ROBERTS, DEAN	30-Jun-11	LAUGHTON, PETER MBE 30-Jun-12	DONOVAN, ROBIN 30-Jun-13
ROWLANDS, KEVIN	30-Jun-11	LING, CHRISTOPHER 30-Jun-12	DORAN, SHANE E 30-Jun-13
RYAN, SEAN J	30-Jun-11	LOVE, TRISTRAM 30-Jun-12	EASTERBROOK, KEVIN 30-Jun-13
SLOCOMBE, NICHOLAS	30-Jun-11	MOODY, DAVID 30-Jun-12	EXWORTHY, DAMIAN MBE 30-Jun-13
STRIDE, JAMES	30-Jun-11	MOORE, MARTIN 30-Jun-12	GOLDSMITH, DAVID 30-Jun-13
TEASDALE, DAVID	30-Jun-11	MOORE, SEAN 30-Jun-12	HOOPER, JOHANNA 30-Jun-13
WALLACE, SIMON	30-Jun-11	MORGAN, DAVID 30-Jun-12	INGHAM, ANDREW 30-Jun-13
WILLIAMS, MARK	30-Jun-11	NEILD, TIMOTHY 30-Jun-12	JORDAN, CATHERINE 30-Jun-13
WISEMAN, IAN	30-Jun-11	PERCIVAL, FIONA 30-Jun-12	KELLETT, ANDREW 30-Jun-13
EDWARD, GAVIN	30-Jun-11	PONSFORD, PHILIP 30-Jun-12	KIRKWOOD, TRISTRAM 30-Jun-13
LOVATT, GRAHAM	30-Jun-11	RAE, DEREK G 30-Jun-12	KNOCK, GARETH 30-Jun-13
WALES, BENJAMIN	30-Jun-11	RUDDOCK, GORDON 30-Jun-12	MARTIN, DAVID 30-Jun-13
CLARKE, RICHARD	30-Jun-11	SAUNDERS, CHRISTOPHER MBE 30-Jun-12	MCGLORY, STEPHEN 30-Jun-13
WILSON, ALLAN	30-Jun-11	SCOPES, DAVID 30-Jun-12	MOWATT, PATRICK 30-Jun-13
MALKIN, SHARON	30-Jun-11	SELLARS, SCOTT 30-Jun-12	MUDGE, ADRIAN 30-Jun-13
HARCOURT, ROBERT	30-Jun-11	SHARKEY, ELTON 30-Jun-12	ORTON, DAVID 30-Jun-13
MACKINNON, DONALD	30-Jun-11	SHAUGHNESSY, SOPHIE 30-Jun-12	OWEN, GLYN 30-Jun-13
CLINK, ADAM	30-Jun-11	SHEPHERD, FIONA 30-Jun-12	PEDLER, MARK 30-Jun-13
FOGELL, ANDREW	30-Jun-11	SNELLING, PAUL 30-Jun-12	QUEKETT, IAN 30-Jun-13
HOUSTON, DARREN	30-Jun-11	SOLLY, MATTHEW 30-Jun-12	RICHARDS, JAMES 30-Jun-13
MARTIN, SIMON	30-Jun-11	STEPHENSON, KEITH 30-Jun-12	STAFFORD, WAYNE 30-Jun-13
COTTERILL, BRUCE	30-Jun-11	SWEENEY, KEITH 30-Jun-12	STOWELL, PERRY 30-Jun-13
SCANDLING, RACHEL	30-Jun-11	THOMASON, MICHAEL 30-Jun-12	STRIDE, JAMIESON 30-Jun-13
MCDONNELL, DAVID	30-Jun-11	TURNER, DAVID 30-Jun-12	THOMAS, DAVID 30-Jun-13
WALLACE, DAVID	30-Jun-11	WEST, SARAH 30-Jun-12	THOMPSON, MICHAEL 30-Jun-13
PARVIN, PHILIP	30-Jun-11	WHEATON, BOWDEN 30-Jun-12	TREDRAY, THOMAS 30-Jun-13
COPELAND, STEPHEN	30-Jun-11	WRIGHT, TIMOTHY 30-Jun-12	WATTS, ROBERT 30-Jun-13
WARING, JOHN	30-Jun-11	WINDEBANK, STEPHEN 30-Jun-12	WILDIN, ANDREW 30-Jun-13
WESTWOOD, MARK	30-Jun-11	HAMMOND, PAUL 30-Jun-12	WOOD, UVEDALE 30-Jun-13
HUMPHREY, IVOR	30-Jun-11	BARLOW, MARTIN 30-Jun-12	PREST, STEPHEN 30-Jun-13
NAPIER, GRAHAM	30-Jun-11	JOHNSON, CHAD 30-Jun-12	SHEPHERD, MARTIN 30-Jun-13
BURGE, ROGER	30-Jun-11	REID, JASON 30-Jun-12	BAMFORTH, CHRISTIAN 30-Jun-13
VOGEL, LANNING	30-Jun-11	WILLS, PHILIP 30-Jun-12	CHESTNUTT, JAMES 30-Jun-13
IRONS, RUPERT	30-Jun-11	COYLE, GAVIN 30-Jun-12	ROSE, ANDREW 30-Jun-13
MANWARING, ROY	25-Jul-11	MARRATT, RICHARD 30-Jun-12	D'SILVA, DANIEL 30-Jun-13
PIPER, NEAL F ARRC	05-Sep-11	REECE, NIGEL 30-Jun-12	MCLELLAN, JAMES 30-Jun-13
		PEARS, IAN MBE 30-Jun-12	MEALING, DAVID 30-Jun-13
2012		STOCK, CHRISTOPHER 30-Jun-12	PARRY, MARK 30-Jun-13
		CHESHIRE, THOMAS 30-Jun-12	ROWLANDS, ANDREW 30-Jun-13
THOMPSON, FIONA	06-Feb-12	GIBBONS, NICHOLAS 30-Jun-12	BOWMAN, ROBERT 30-Jun-13
SMITH, MARK	26-Mar-12	JONES, DAVID 30-Jun-12	BOYES, MARTYN 30-Jun-13
BONNAR, JOHN A	30-Jun-12	CAMPBELL, FELICITY 01-Jul-12	TRACEY, ALAN D 30-Jun-13
BOWDEN, MATTHEW	30-Jun-12	DAVIES, JASON L 16-Jul-12	SPOONER, ROSS 30-Jun-13
BURVILL, JUSTIN	30-Jun-12	BAGNALL, SALLY-ANNE 06-Aug-12	TANNER, RICHARD 30-Jun-13
CARRIGAN, JONATHAN	30-Jun-12	MURRAY, ALISTER 14-Oct-12	WYPER, JAMES 30-Jun-13
CHAPMAN, PETER	30-Jun-12		BIRSE, GREGOR 30-Jun-13
CLARKE, DANIEL	30-Jun-12	**2013**	YOUP, ALLAN 30-Jun-13
COOKE, JONATHAN	30-Jun-12		BOLTON, STEPHEN 30-Jun-13
CRIDDLE, GARY MBE	30-Jun-12	WITT, ALISTER 14-Jan-13	COTTIS, MATHEW 30-Jun-13
CURRIE, STUART	30-Jun-12	TAYLOR, LISA 03-Mar-13	WOOLLVEN, ANDREW 30-Jun-13
DENNIS, MATTHEW	30-Jun-12	HOUNSOME, DEBRA MBE ARRC 01-Jul-13	BERRY, IAN MBE RD 30-Jun-13
DONALDSON, ANDREW	30-Jun-12	ATKINSON, RICHARD 30-Jun-13	WILSON, CHRISTOPHER 30-Jun-13
DRYWOOD, TOBIAS	30-Jun-12	BAKER, ADRIAN P 30-Jun-13	NOYCE, ROGER MBE 30-Jun-13
EVERITT, TOBYN	30-Jun-12	BARTON, MARK 30-Jun-13	NEAVE, ANDREW 30-Jun-13
GOLDSTONE, RICHARD	30-Jun-12	BENFELL, NIALL 30-Jun-13	BELL, JEFFREY 24-Jun-13
GOUDGE, SIMON	30-Jun-12	BUCK, JAMES 30-Jun-13	JONES, TIMOTHY 21-Jul-13
GRAY, PAUL	30-Jun-12	BYRON, JAMES DSC 30-Jun-13	CHARLTON, KEVIN 06-Aug-13
GRIFFITHS, RICHARD	30-Jun-12	CANNING, CHRISTOPHER MBE 30-Jun-13	

LIEUTENANT COMMANDERS

1982

DICKINSON, PHILIP 01-Jul-82

1987

TAYLOR, NICHOLAS 16-Feb-87
LEATHER, ROGER 01-Jun-87

1989

POLLITT, DAVID 01-Apr-89
NEWMAN, PAUL 01-May-89
YATES, NEAL 01-Jun-89
WATSON, RICHARD 01-Aug-89
MURRAY, STEPHEN OBE 02-Nov-89

1990

KERR, WILLIAM 09-Apr-90
CHAPMAN, NICHOLAS 01-May-90
CROPPER, MARTIN 16-May-90
MAW, MARTYN J..................................01-Dec-90

1991

EEDLE, RICHARD..................................01-Mar-91
STEWART, RORY 01-Jul-91
SMITH, NIGEL 01-Jul-91
DONALDSON, STUART..........................01-Sep-91
HAWKINS, ROBERT MBE......................01-Oct-91
KIRKWOOD, JAMES..............................25-Oct-91
OWEN, PETER 30-Oct-91
BERNAU, JEREMY 01-Nov-91
METCALFE, ANTHONY 01-Dec-91

1992

MORSE, ANDREW.................................01-Jan-92
POTTS, KEVIN 01-Feb-92
DEIGHTON, DEREK S............................01-May-92
GILES, KEVIN D L.................................01-May-92
BARNES-YALLOWLEY,JONATHAN 16-Jul-92
WEST, MICHAEL...................................05-Aug-92

1993

WALKER, NICHOLAS.............................01-Feb-93
PRICE, DAVID J....................................01-Apr-93
BENNETT, GRAHAM 01-Jul-93
ROBERTSON, DOUGLAS 01-Oct-93
WATTS, ANDREW P...............................01-Oct-93

1994

NEVE, PIERS 11-Feb-94
EASTHAM, ALLAN MICHAEL RD 31-Mar-94
GIBSON, STEPHEN RICHARD 31-Mar-94
CRISPIN, TOBY 01-Apr-94
ANDREWS, PAUL 01-Jun-94
EATON, PAUL.......................................01-Jun-94
LUNN, ADAM CHRISTOPHER..................01-Jun-94
HOUGHTON, PHILIP 01-Jul-94
HORNER, PATRICK MBA 01-Aug-94
ROBIN, CHRISTOPHER 01-Sep-94

DISNEY, PETER 01-Oct-94
DOWDELL, ROBERT 01-Oct-94
SEWED, MICHAEL 01-Oct-94
GUNN, WILLIAM 01-Nov-94
HURRY, ANDREW 01-Nov-94
HILLS, ANTHONY 01-Dec-94

1995

OVENDEN, NEIL 01-Feb-95
FIRTH, NIGEL 01-Mar-95
PILLAR, CHRISTOPHER 01-Mar-95
EGELAND-JENSEN, FINN MBE................01-Apr-95
GRAY, DAVID 01-Apr-95
POMFRETT, NICHOLAS 01-Apr-95
BIRLEY, JONATHAN 01-May-95
MARSHALL, RICHARD...........................01-May-95
SCHNADHORST, JAMES 01-May-95
GOLDSMITH, SIMON.............................01-May-95
MILLS, ANDREW 01-May-95
MONGER, PAUL 21-May-95
BROWN, PETER 01-Jun-95
BURKE, MICHAEL 01-Sep-95
COLLINS, PAUL 01-Sep-95
BATE, DAVID I G 01-Oct-95
MOFFATT, ROGER 01-Oct-95
SMITH, KEVEN J...................................01-Oct-95
DANIELL, CHRISTOPHER........................01-Oct-95
MEEDS, KEVIN 16-Dec-95
BATH, EDWARD 27-Dec-95

1996

MCCONOCHIE, ANDREW 16-Apr-96
SHEPHERD, ROGER 01-May-96
HAYWARD, CLIVE 01-Jun-96
CARTER, JONATHON 01-Jun-96
HILL, MARK 22-Jun-96
POOLEY, STEVEN 01-Jul-96
BARK, JAMES 01-Sep-96
BENTON, ANGUS 01-Sep-96
SYKES, ROBERT...................................01-Oct-96
ARMSTRONG, NICHOLAS 01-Oct-96
BIGGS, DAVID MICHAEL 01-Oct-96
HIBBERT, MARTIN C 01-Nov-96

1997

NOYCE, NIGEL.....................................15-Jan-97
BELL, ROBERT D 01-Mar-97
HOGG, CHRISTOPHER..........................01-Mar-97
WALKER, DAVID 31-Mar-97
FINCH, ROBERT L 01-May-97
RICH, DAVID C.....................................20-May-97
WOOLLCOMBE-GOSSON, DAVID 01-Jun-97
SOUTH, DAVID J 15-Jun-97
IRONS, PAUL ANDREW 01-Jul-97
PEACE, RICHARD W..............................02-Jul-97
ELLIS, NICHOLAS M 18-Jul-97
WELLS, JONATHAN 01-Aug-97
STANNARD, MARK 01-Aug-97
DAW, SIMON J 01-Oct-97
FINCH, TIMOTHY S A............................01-Oct-97

HARPER, JAMES A 01-Oct-97
LAMBOURNE, DAVID J..........................01-Oct-97
MOYS, ANDREW JOHN.........................01-Oct-97
COOK, DAVID JOHN 01-Oct-97
TWEEDIE, HOWARD J............................22-Oct-97

1998

HASELDINE, STEPHEN G........................01-Feb-98
WELLINGTON, STUART 01-Feb-98
FRANKS, CHRISTOPHER 01-Feb-98
BLACKBURN, STEPHEN 01-Mar-98
MULES, ANTHONY...............................01-Mar-98
SCOTT, ROBERT J 02-Mar-98
CHAPMAN, SIMON J.............................01-Mar-98
ROOK, GRAEME I.................................01-Mar-98
HOOD, KEVIN MICHAEL........................01-Mar-98
HUTCHISON, PAUL G 01-May-98
DUNN, GARY RUSSELL..........................01-May-98
HEPWORTH, ANDREW 01-May-98
BAKER, MICHAEL.................................01-Jun-98
KIMBERLEY, ROBERT 01-Jul-98
POWELL, STEVEN R MDA 01-Jul-98
FORD, MARTIN JOHN AFC 05-Aug-98
MURPHY, STEVEN 01-Sep-98
BIRBECK, KEITH 01-Oct-98
REED, MARK 01-Oct-98
STRATHERN, RODERICK J 01-Oct-98
SHALLCROFT, JOHN 01-Oct-98
CUNANE, JOHN 01-Oct-98
DAWSON, WILLIAM 01-Nov-98
CORPS, STEPHEN 11-Nov-98
REDMAN, CHARLES..............................23-Nov-98

1999

DUDLEY, STEPHEN 01-Jan-99
CROFTS, DAVID 01-Feb-99
LEES, EDWARD C 01-Feb-99
WELFORD, ROBERT 01-Feb-99
SMITH, ADRIAN 01-Feb-99
OSBORN, RICHARD 01-Feb-99
PITT, JONATHAN 17-Feb-99
BINGHAM, DAVID S 01-Mar-99
LEE, NICHOLAS 01-Mar-99
BRIGGS-MOULD, TIMOTHY MCGI.........16-Mar-99
THOMSON, SUSIE 31-Mar-99
CONWAY, KEITH ALEXANDER RD...........31-Mar-99
GOLDMAN, PAUL H L 01-Apr-99
BOWHAY, SIMON 01-May-99
GREEN, ANDREW M 12-May-99
BUSH, ALEXANDER J T..........................01-Jun-99
GOLDEN, DOMINIC S C 01-Jun-99
WEST, GRAHAM 06-Jun-99
RAISBECK, PAUL 08-Jul-99
COLLIS, MARTIN J 01-Aug-99
LEE, PETER A......................................01-Aug-99
OWENS, DANIEL 01-Aug-99
GOODE, ALUN N 01-Sep-99
HARTLEY, JOHN L.................................01-Oct-99
MILSOM, JONATHAN 01-Oct-99
MURRAY, ANDREW AFC MCGI 01-Oct-99

LIEUTENANT COMMANDERS

WHITWORTH, ROBERT M......................01-Oct-99
HOLDEN, ROBERT 01-Oct-99
LUSCOMBE, MICHAEL 01-Oct-99
WHITE, IAN F 18-Nov-99
SMITH, BRIAN 01-Dec-99

2000

GRIFFITHS, MICHAEL
KERR, JACK
WHITEHEAD, STEVEN
HARTLEY, ANDREW 16-Jan-00
PUGH, JONATHAN 06-Feb-00
CLARKE, WILLIAM 01-Mar-00
PARSONAGE, NEIL 02-Mar-00
BIGNELL, STEPHEN...............................08-Mar-00
RUSSELL, BRUCE..................................31-Mar-00
STRUTT, JASON F 31-Mar-00
REAH, STEPHEN...................................01-Apr-00
WILLIAMS, JAMES P 01-May-00
ROGERS, CHRISTOPHER........................01-May-00
CRUNDELL, RICHARD............................02-May-00
DANDO, JONATHON N 01-Jun-00
MILES, GRAHAM J 01-Jun-00
HUTCHINSON, CHRISTOPHER 01-Jul-00
RICHTER, ALWYN S B.............................01-Aug-00
CLARKE, ANDREW P MBE 07-Aug-00
COOK, GORDON E 01-Sep-00
DYKE, KENNETH A.................................01-Sep-00
WATKINS, TIMOTHY C 01-Oct-00
LACEY, CATHERINE...............................01-Oct-00
ROBERTSON, PAUL NOEL 01-Oct-00
STOCKTON, KEVIN G 01-Oct-00
KNIGHT, DAVID W 01-Oct-00
LOWE, STUART M..................................01-Oct-00
GALE, CRYSTAL V 19-Nov-00

2001

SMITH, GRAEME D J 01-Dec-00
VARLEY, IAN G......................................24-Dec-00
THOMAS, STEPHEN
KERR, ADRIAN N...................................01-Jan-01
BROWN, STEPHEN H 01-Jan-01
MILLER, PAUL D 01-Jan-01
SELLERS, GRAHAM psc(j) 01-Jan-01
STANTON-BROWN, PETER J....................15-Jan-01
CHASTON, STEPHEN P 01-Feb-01
NELSON, CHRISTOPHER S 01-Feb-01
HEAD, STEVEN ANDREW 01-Feb-01
PEARSON, MICHAEL..............................01-Mar-01
HALLETT, SIMON JOHN MA.....................01-Mar-01
LEWIS, RICHARD QVRM..........................01-Mar-01
RAMSAY, BRIAN MA ACMA.....................01-Mar-01
BESSELL, DAVID A..................................01-Mar-01
NEWELL, PHILLIP 31-Mar-01
NORGAN, DAVID J 31-Mar-01
GRAHAM, ALASTAIR MVO 01-Jun-01
SHIRLEY, ANDREW 01-Jun-01
LAING, IAIN 01-Jul-01
DUNCAN, JEREMY.................................01-Aug-01
GRAHAM, MARK A 01-Aug-01

HANCOCK, ROBERT 01-Sep-01
HOWE, JULIAN P...................................01-Oct-01
MITCHELL, STEPHEN.............................01-Oct-01
MORGAN-HOSEY, JOHN 01-Oct-01
NOBLETT, PETER...................................01-Oct-01
SCIVIER, JOHN S 01-Oct-01
TAYLOR, STEPHEN 01-Oct-01
WESTLEY, DAVID R.................................01-Oct-01
YELLAND, CHRISTOPHER 01-Oct-01
BRUNSDEN-BROWN, SEBASTIAN.............01-Oct-01
KNIGHT, ANDREW 01-Oct-01
COOKE, GRAHAM 01-Oct-01
SNEDDON, RUSSELL..............................01-Oct-01
JAGGERS, GARY 01-Oct-01
TAYLOR, IAN KENNEDY 01-Oct-01
PALMER, MICHAEL 01-Oct-01
EDEY, MICHAEL J..................................01-Oct-01
CASTLE, ALASTAIR 01-Oct-01
CURRIE, DUNCAN 01-Nov-01

2002

DAVIES, LEE 01-Dec-01
PINK, SIMON E......................................16-Dec-01
MEEK, CAMILLA S
PROCTOR, WILLIAM..............................01-Jan-02
STEPHEN, BARRY M 01-Jan-02
ESFAHANI, SHAHROKH 01-Mar-02
THORNE, LEE J 01-Mar-02
DINEEN, JOHN M G................................01-Mar-02
KELLY, HOWARD C.................................31-Mar-02
OFFORD, MATT.....................................31-Mar-02
KOHLER, ANDREW................................01-Apr-02
CHILDS, JOHN......................................01-Apr-02
DUFOSEE, SEAN W 01-Apr-02
HOPPER, IAN..01-Apr-02
BROTHERTON, JOHN 01-Apr-02
MANDLEY, PHILIP 08-Apr-02
BRADLEY, MATTHEW.............................09-Apr-02
OSBORN, COLVIN G 16-Apr-02
WEST, RORY J 01-May-02
WATERFIELD, SIMON MCGI 01-May-02
FRASER, IAN D......................................01-Jun-02
PAYNE, PHILIP J 01-Jun-02
RAEBURN, MARK..................................01-Jun-02
GILL, MARK HANSEN 01-Jul-02
DICKSON, JAMES..................................01-Jul-02
CARTER, KEVIN 01-Jul-02
CHOULES, BARRIE 01-Jul-02
REESE, DAVID M 01-Aug-02
MACDONALD, ALASTAIR 27-Aug-02
BARRY, JOHN P 01-Sep-02
BRIAN, NEIL 01-Sep-02
DARLOW, PAUL R..................................01-Sep-02
DRODGE, ANDREW 01-Oct-02
HOLDEN, PAUL.....................................01-Oct-02
JACQUES, NICHOLAS A MCGI 01-Oct-02
MAYELL, JULIE 01-Oct-02
MORRISON, PAUL.................................01-Oct-02
SOAR, GARY 01-Oct-02
SUCKLING, ROBIN L..............................01-Oct-02
WELLS, BARRY......................................01-Oct-02

D'ARCY, PAUL 01-Oct-02
WALKER, MARK.....................................01-Oct-02
WARR, RICHARD...................................01-Oct-02
MASON, LINDSAY 01-Oct-02
IRELAND, JOHN....................................01-Oct-02
BARRATT, STEPHEN..............................01-Oct-02
CUMMINGS, DAVID J.............................01-Oct-02
JONES, ADAM E....................................01-Oct-02
BIRD, MATTHEW 01-Oct-02
WHITE, JONATHAN 01-Nov-02
TITMUSS, JULIAN 01-Nov-02
MASSEY, PAUL 01-Nov-02

2003

ALLFREE, JOSEPH 01-Dec-02
FROST, MARK A 05-Dec-02
MAYNARD, CHARLES
LAVERTY, ROBERT 01-Jan-03
COOPE, PHILIP J 01-Jan-03
FOULIS, NIALL D A 01-Feb-03
GENNARD, ANTHONY 01-Feb-03
JENNINGS, WILLIAM 01-Mar-03
ROGERS, JULIAN C E 01-Mar-03
SKELLEY, ALASDAIR 01-Mar-03
WATSON, IAN 01-Mar-03
STAGG, ANTONY ROBERT.......................01-Mar-03
AITCHISON, IAN....................................01-Mar-03
RAWSON, SCOTT 01-Mar-03
HARDIMAN, NICHOLAS 01-Mar-03
OLIVER, GRAHAM..................................31-Mar-03
COULTHARD, ADRIAN 01-Apr-03
DURHAM, PAUL 01-May-03
JEWITT, CHARLES..................................01-May-03
BEACHAM, PHILIP 11-May-03
MCKNIGHT, DEREK 18-May-03
MAY, STEVEN..30-Jun-03
DOVILL, CHRISTOPHER 01-Jul-03
CAHILL, KAREN A 01-Jul-03
SANDLE, NEIL D 01-Jul-03
TREGUNNA, GARY A 31-Jul-03
MCWILLIAMS, JACQUELINE 01-Aug-03
JONES, GARETH....................................01-Aug-03
BARROWS, DAVID 08-Aug-03
BIRD, JONATHAN M...............................01-Sep-03
COBBETT, JAMES 01-Sep-03
CROCKATT, STEPHEN 01-Oct-03
CUNNINGHAM, NIGEL 01-Oct-03
DAWSON, NIGEL J F 01-Oct-03
FRASER, PATRICK 01-Oct-03
GRANT, DAVID J 01-Oct-03
HOLLOWAY, STEVEN 01-Oct-03
HOPKINS, STEVEN MBE 01-Oct-03
HUNT, FRASER 01-Oct-03
KIES, LAWRENCE 01-Oct-03
KING, GORDON 01-Oct-03
MAILES, IAN...01-Oct-03
MCEVOY, LEE 01-Oct-03
MCQUEEN, JASON 01-Oct-03
MURCHIE, ALISTAIR 01-Oct-03
NEAL, SIMON M 01-Oct-03
NOON, DAVID MBE................................01-Oct-03

LIEUTENANT COMMANDERS

PARK, BRIAN	01-Oct-03
PAYNE, MATHEW	01-Oct-03
ROBERTS, IAIN	01-Oct-03
TETLEY, MARK	01-Oct-03
VARTAN, MARK R	01-Oct-03
WICKING, GEOFFREY	01-Oct-03
WILLIAMS, PETER	01-Oct-03
WOOLHEAD, ANDREW	01-Oct-03
HAYWOOD, PETER	01-Oct-03
HAYWARD, GEOFFREY MBE	01-Oct-03
DAVIDSON, NEIL	01-Oct-03
O'NEILL, PAUL	01-Oct-03
PLACKETT, ANDREW	01-Oct-03
WOODROW, KEVIN	01-Oct-03
BOLLEN, JOHANNA	01-Oct-03
WILKINS, RICHARD	01-Oct-03
CLARK, ALAN MCMI	01-Oct-03
DAWSON, ALAN	01-Oct-03
MACDOUGALL, STEWART	01-Oct-03
STEPHENSON, PHILIP	01-Oct-03
LOGAN, JOSEPH	01-Oct-03
HUNT, STEPHEN	01-Oct-03
TAYLOR, JONATHAN	01-Oct-03
LEY, ALASTAIR B	01-Oct-03
REES, RICHARD T	01-Oct-03

2004

BEADNELL, ROBERT	01-Nov-03
ROSTRON, DAVID	01-Dec-03
HENDRICKX, CHRISTOPHER POWLES, DEREK	01-Jan-04
MACKAY, ANDREW	01-Jan-04
CLARK, MICHAEL H	01-Jan-04
PETERS, WILLIAM	01-Feb-04
SCREATON, RICHARD	01-Feb-04
LEWIS, ANDREW	01-Mar-04
GORAM, MALCOLM	01-Mar-04
JERMY, RICHARD	01-Mar-04
WALTERS, RICHARD	01-Mar-04
GLEAVE, JAMES	31-Mar-04
HAINS, JUSTIN	31-Mar-04
LOCKETT, DAVID JOHN	31-Mar-04
FLYNN, ANDREW	31-Mar-04
SMITH, MICHAEL	01-Apr-04
STEADMAN, ROBERT	01-Apr-04
HEDGECOX, DAVID	01-May-04
LYONS, MICHAEL	01-May-04
UBHI, WAYNE G	01-May-04
ROBINSON, MELANIE S	01-Jun-04
MAY, COLIN MCGI	01-Jun-04
PARROTT, JAMES P	01-Jun-04
JONES, DAVID	07-Jun-04
TYLER, JEREMY	01-Jul-04
DENNIS, PHILIP MBE	01-Jul-04
MOULES, MATTHEW	01-Jul-04
WOODBRIDGE, RICHARD	01-Jul-04
PATTERSON, JOHN	01-Jul-04
MCGUIRE, JAMES	01-Aug-04
MCCOMBE, JOHN	01-Aug-04
PUXLEY, MICHAEL E	01-Aug-04
WRIGHT, DAVID	24-Aug-04

AJALA, AHMED	01-Sep-04
ALLEN, PAUL	01-Sep-04
ARMSTRONG, SCOTT	01-Sep-04
BANCE, NICHOLAS	01-Oct-04
CARPENTER, BRYONY	01-Oct-04
CHADFIELD, LAURENCE	01-Oct-04
CRABB, ANTONY	01-Oct-04
CRAGG, RICHARD	01-Oct-04
DORAN, IAIN	01-Oct-04
HILSON, STEVEN	01-Oct-04
HUTTON, GRAHAM	01-Oct-04
LE GASSICK, PETER	01-Oct-04
LOVERING, TRISTAN MBE	01-Oct-04
LUCOCQ, NICHOLAS	01-Oct-04
MILLER, MANDY	01-Oct-04
READ, ALUN J	01-Oct-04
REED, NICHOLAS	01-Oct-04
RUSSELL, NIGEL	01-Oct-04
SARGENT, LINDSAY	01-Oct-04
SCOTT, MARK R	01-Oct-04
SIMPSON, COLIN C	01-Oct-04
SMITH, CHRISTOPHER	01-Oct-04
SOUL, NICHOLAS	01-Oct-04
SYKES, LEAH D	01-Oct-04
TIDBALL, IAN C	01-Oct-04
TRUBSHAW, CHRISTOPHER	01-Oct-04
VINCENT, DANIEL	01-Oct-04
YEMM, CHARLOTTE P	01-Oct-04
HIGHAM, STEPHEN	01-Oct-04
BENSTEAD, NEIL	01-Oct-04
BRIGGS, CATHRYN	01-Oct-04
STUART, EUAN	01-Oct-04
HARPER, PHILIP	01-Oct-04
ELLIS, JAMES	01-Oct-04
SMITH, DAVID	01-Oct-04
COGAN, ROBERT	01-Oct-04
JULIAN, TIMOTHY	01-Oct-04
HODGE, CHRISTOPHER	01-Oct-04
IMRIE, PETER B DSM	01-Oct-04
PINDER, CHRISTOPHER	01-Oct-04
CARTER, SIMON	01-Oct-04
PURVIS, DAVID	01-Oct-04
BALLETTA, RENE J	01-Oct-04
FLEMING, SAMUEL	01-Oct-04
MCBRATNEY, JAMES	16-Oct-04
WALSH, KEVIN	01-Nov-04
HOLLAND, AMANDA	01-Nov-04
BROWN, ANDREW	01-Nov-04
MULLINS, ANDREW	01-Nov-04
WHITEHOUSE, NIALL	01-Nov-04
WOOD, MICHAEL L	01-Dec-04
ANKAH, GREGORY	01-Dec-04
OTTEWELL, PAUL S	01-Dec-04
WOOD, CHRISTOPHER	01-Dec-04

2005

BOSTON, JUSTIN	01-Dec-04
KENDRICK, ALEXANDER	01-Dec-04
CLEMINSON, MARK PARR, MICHAEL J E	01-Jan-05
MCHUGH, RICHARD H	01-Feb-05

RACKHAM, KATHARINE	01-Feb-05
TILDEN, PHILIP J E	02-Feb-05
WELLS, MICHAEL P	01-Mar-05
THORNE, DAIN MBE	01-Mar-05
DALE-SMITH, VICTORIA	01-Mar-05
YOUNG, WILLIAM D	01-Mar-05
AIRD, PAULINE	01-Mar-05
HOUNSOM, TIMOTHY	15-Mar-05
FOREMAN, SIMON	31-Mar-05
OAKLEY, SARAH ELLEN	01-Apr-05
KIRK, ADRIAN	01-Apr-05
MCCALLUM, NEIL	01-Apr-05
FOX, RICHARD OBE	01-May-05
FITZPATRICK, JOHN	01-May-05
SELWAY, MARK	01-Jun-05
ROGERS, ALEXANDER	30-Jun-05
NORTHOVER, ADAM F	01-Jul-05
SPILLER, STEPHEN	01-Jul-05
SPINKS, DAVID	31-Jul-05
VOGEL, CLAIRE	01-Aug-05
WARD, SIMON	01-Aug-05
BOWSER, NICHOLAS	01-Aug-05
BRAYSON, MARK	01-Sep-05
CANALE, ANDREW J	01-Sep-05
CLARE, KATHARINE	01-Oct-05
CORBETT, THOMAS J	01-Oct-05
COX, SEAN ADRIAN J	01-Oct-05
CROSS, ALEXANDER	01-Oct-05
DAVIS, STEPHEN R	01-Oct-05
DRISCOLL, ROBERT	01-Oct-05
ELSEY, DAVID J	01-Oct-05
GOODRUM, SIMON E	01-Oct-05
HAIGH, JULIAN JOSEPH	01-Oct-05
HARDWICK, MARK J	01-Oct-05
HARRISON, MARK	01-Oct-05
HASSALL, IAN	01-Oct-05
HUMPHRIES, JASON	01-Oct-05
JENKING-REES, DAMIAN	01-Oct-05
JOHNSON, ANTHONY	01-Oct-05
JORDAN, CRAIG	01-Oct-05
KNIGHT, DANIEL S	01-Oct-05
LAMONT, NEIL J	01-Oct-05
LANNI, MARTIN NICHOLAS AFC	01-Oct-05
LOWE, CHRISTOPHER	01-Oct-05
MARRIOTT, NEIL KENNETH	01-Oct-05
MCCAUGHEY, VINCENT	01-Oct-05
MCCLEARY, SIMON	01-Oct-05
NELSON, PAUL M	01-Oct-05
NIMMONS, PAUL MBE	01-Oct-05
OATLEY, TIMOTHY	01-Oct-05
O'TOOLE, MATHEW	01-Oct-05
PALIN, GILES	01-Oct-05
PANIC, ALEXANDER	01-Oct-05
PICKERING-WHEELER, CHRISTOPHER	01-Oct-05
PROFFITT, JULIA	01-Oct-05
QUADE, NICHOLAS	01-Oct-05
SANTRIAN, KARL MA	01-Oct-05
SHAUGHNESSY, TOBY	01-Oct-05
SITTON, JOHN B	01-Oct-05
SPURDLE, ANDREW	01-Oct-05
SULLIVAN, MARK N	01-Oct-05

LIEUTENANT COMMANDERS

TAYLOR, ROBERT	01-Oct-05
WEAVER, SIMON	01-Oct-05
WEST, DARREN	01-Oct-05
WRIGHT, GILLIAN	01-Oct-05
MILLEN, STUART MBE	01-Oct-05
WOOD, GRAHAM	01-Oct-05
OAKES, IAN JAMES	01-Oct-05
DAVENEY, DAVID	01-Oct-05
ANDERSON, MARK	01-Oct-05
COLLACOTT, JONATHAN	01-Oct-05
KINGDOM, MARK	01-Oct-05
MASON, DARREN	01-Oct-05
HAYTON, STEPHEN	01-Oct-05
HUTCHINS, TIMOTHY	01-Oct-05
CAPLE, JONATHAN	01-Oct-05
SAYER, JAMIE	01-Oct-05
EDWARDS, JAMES	01-Oct-05
SARGENT, NICHOLAS	01-Oct-05
DONWORTH, DESMOND	01-Oct-05
PULLAN, KEITH JAMES	01-Oct-05
HEFFORD, CHRISTOPHER	01-Oct-05
LOVE, RICHARD JOHN	01-Oct-05
STOCKBRIDGE, ANTONY	01-Oct-05
MEALING, STEVEN	01-Oct-05
LING, JOHN	01-Oct-05
BING, NEIL ADRIAN	01-Oct-05
FOSTER, NICHOLAS	01-Oct-05
QUANTRILL, STEVEN	01-Oct-05
MARSHALL, TRACEY	01-Oct-05
STRANGE, STEVEN	01-Oct-05
BAKER, NICHOLAS	01-Oct-05
ELLIS, DAVID	01-Oct-05
RENDELL, DERRICK	01-Oct-05
HOATHER, MARTIN	01-Oct-05
KITT, ROBERT GEORGE	01-Oct-05
RAYNOR, SEAN	01-Oct-05
SKITTRALL, STEVEN	01-Oct-05
HOWE, THOMAS	01-Oct-05
STEVENSON, JULIAN P	01-Oct-05
MORLEY, JAMES	15-Oct-05
ALLAN, CHRIS R	01-Nov-05
WEBSTER, RICHARD	01-Nov-05
HUTCHINGS, RICHARD	01-Nov-05
WYNESS, ROGER	01-Dec-05

2006

DALE, ALISTAIR	01-Dec-05
DEMPSEY, SEAN	13-Dec-05
HAY, MICHAEL	
THORP, DAVID	01-Feb-06
RICHARDSON, PHILIP	01-Feb-06
HARRINGTON, LEE	01-Mar-06
SHERRIFF, JACQUELINE MBE	01-Mar-06
BROTTON, PETER J	01-Mar-06
GOODALL, MICHAEL	01-Mar-06
RUSHWORTH, BENJAMIN	31-Mar-06
SCOTT, RICHARD	01-Apr-06
GARNER, SEAN	01-May-06
COTTEE, BENJAMIN	01-May-06
WILLIAMS, ANTHONY	01-Aug-06
ALEXANDER, OLIVER	01-Aug-06

BRENNAN, PAUL A	01-Sep-06
BREWER, CHRISTOPHER	01-Sep-06
BRIANT-EVANS, ZOE	01-Oct-06
CARTER, PAUL	01-Oct-06
CLAGUE, JOHN	01-Oct-06
CLARK, STEPHEN	01-Oct-06
COVERDALE, PAUL	01-Oct-06
CULLEN, NICOLA L	01-Oct-06
CURWOOD, JENNY	01-Oct-06
DAWSON, PAUL	01-Oct-06
DAY, MICHAEL	01-Oct-06
DEEKS, PETER	01-Oct-06
DODDS, MATTHEW L	01-Oct-06
DUNBAR, SAMANTHA	01-Oct-06
FORGE, STEPHEN	01-Oct-06
GOULDER, JONATHAN	01-Oct-06
GRAY, JOHN A	01-Oct-06
GRIFFITHS, NEIL	01-Oct-06
HARRIMAN, PETER	01-Oct-06
HIRONS, FRANCIS	01-Oct-06
INGE, DANIEL J	01-Oct-06
JAMES, KATHERINE	01-Oct-06
JOHNSON, SCOTT	01-Oct-06
JOHNSON, VOIRREY	01-Oct-06
KNOX, GRAEME P	01-Oct-06
LAYCOCK, ANTONY	01-Oct-06
LISTER, SIMON	01-Oct-06
MACCORQUODALE, MAIRI	01-Oct-06
MANSFIELD, JAMES	01-Oct-06
MASON, ANDREW	01-Oct-06
MCCUTCHEON, GRAEME	01-Oct-06
MCDONALD, ANDREW	01-Oct-06
MEHTA, KIM L	01-Oct-06
MEYER, ALEXANDER	01-Oct-06
MOLNAR, RICHARD	01-Oct-06
MORAN, CRAIG A	01-Oct-06
MORGAN, EDWARD	01-Oct-06
NOTTLEY, SIMON	01-Oct-06
OSBALDESTIN, RICHARD	01-Oct-06
PARKER, TIMOTHY	01-Oct-06
PRESSDEE, SIMON	01-Oct-06
REDMAYNE, MARK E	01-Oct-06
ROBERTSON, STUART T	01-Oct-06
ROSTER, SHAUN P	01-Oct-06
SATTERTHWAITE, BENJAMIN	01-Oct-06
SAWARD, JUSTIN R E	01-Oct-06
SAYWELL-HALL, STEPHEN	01-Oct-06
SPENCE, ROBERT G	01-Oct-06
SPILLANE, PAUL W	01-Oct-06
STAIT, BENJAMIN G	01-Oct-06
STILWELL, JAMES M	01-Oct-06
TAYLOR, KEITH M	01-Oct-06
TERRY, JUDITH H	01-Oct-06
THOMAS, DANIEL HUW	01-Oct-06
THOMSEN-RAYNER, LAVINIA	01-Oct-06
THOMSON, PAUL D	01-Oct-06
TORNEY, COLIN J	01-Oct-06
TOWNSEND, GRAHAM	01-Oct-06
TREMELLING, PAUL	01-Oct-06
WALL, IRENE J	01-Oct-06
WALTON, STEPHEN	01-Oct-06

WATKINS, KEVIN J	01-Oct-06
WEARE, JONATHAN	01-Oct-06
WHITE, KEVIN F	01-Oct-06
WINGFIELD, MICHAEL	01-Oct-06
WOOD, ANDREW G	01-Oct-06
WOOD, JOSEPH A	01-Oct-06
WOOD, NICHOLAS R	01-Oct-06
YATES, STUART E	01-Oct-06
HEMBER, MARCUS	01-Oct-06
STONE, NICHOLAS	01-Oct-06
ANSELL, CHRISTOPHER	01-Oct-06
CURTIS, SUZANNAH	01-Oct-06
O'SHAUGHNESSY, PAUL	01-Oct-06
AREND, FAYE MARIE	01-Oct-06
MOODY, ALISTAIR	01-Oct-06
DOIG, BARRY	01-Oct-06
DAVEY, TIMOTHY	01-Oct-06
BERRY, TIMOTHY	01-Oct-06
BEAVER, ROBERT	01-Oct-06
BLACKBURN, ANDREW	01-Oct-06
ROGERS, SIMON	01-Oct-06
ROBLEY, WILLIAM	01-Oct-06
THOMAS, STEPHEN	01-Oct-06
WILLIAMS, ROBERT	01-Oct-06
MILES, PHILIP	01-Oct-06
MCLOCKLAN, LEE	01-Oct-06
HARRISON, THOMAS	01-Oct-06
BOYES, RICHARD	01-Oct-06
ROGERS, PHILIP	01-Oct-06
SAUNDERS, JASON	01-Oct-06
FOX, TREFOR	01-Oct-06
AULD, DOUGLAS	01-Oct-06
HARDY, LESLIE B	01-Oct-06
STEVENS, ANTHONY	01-Oct-06
CASTLE, COLIN	01-Oct-06
WRIGHT, DAVID	01-Oct-06
WYNESS, CAROLINE	01-Oct-06
WEBBER, JOANNE	01 Oct 06
LOVETT, STEPHEN	01-Oct-06
GILLETT, DAVID A	01-Oct-06
NORGATE, ANDREW	01-Oct-06
WARD, DOUGLAS	01-Oct-06
LIVSEY, ANDREW	01-Nov-06
EVISON, TOBY	01-Nov-06
MCCANN, TOBY	01-Nov-06

2007

HUNT, PATRICK S	06-Nov-06
MCCLEMENT, DUNCAN	01-Dec-06
TRIM, BRIAN	
NETHERWOOD, LYNDSEY	01-Jan-07
CONWAY, SUZY H	01-Jan-07
REID, MARTYN	01-Jan-07
WOOLSEY, KEVIN	15-Jan-07
KNOTT, CLIVE	01-Mar-07
KELLY, SIMON P	01-Apr-07
PIPKIN, PETER JOHN	01-May-07
ANDERSON, GARRY S	29-May-07
BAINBRIDGE, JOHN R	01-Jul-07
BARRITT, OLIVER D	01-Aug-07
BEALE, MICHAEL D	01-Oct-07

LIEUTENANT COMMANDERS

BLACKMORE, JAMES	FRASER, IAN EDWARD 01-Oct-07	DAVIES, GERAINT W T 01-Oct-08
BLACKMORE, JAMES 01-Oct-07	POOLE, TIMOTHY JAMES 01-Oct-07	DAVIES, NICHOLAS M S 01-Oct-08
BOECKX, THOMAS J F 01-Oct-07	LEWIS, BENJAMIN 01-Oct-07	DEAL, CHARLOTTE 01-Oct-08
CLARKE, ADAM 01-Oct-07	ABEL, NIGEL PHILIP 01-Oct-07	DUNN, ANTHONY 01-Oct-08
CLARKE, MATTHEW 01-Oct-07	CLEMENTS, ELIZABETH 01-Oct-07	FEASEY, IAN D 01-Oct-08
COLLINS, TAMAR L 01-Oct-07	SMITH, ROBERT 01-Oct-07	FINCH, STEVEN 01-Oct-08
CUTLER, ANDREW R 01-Oct-07	HEALEY, MARK 01-Oct-07	FLEGG, MATTHEW 01-Oct-08
EDWINS, MARK R 01-Oct-07	BARBER, CHRISTOPHER 01-Oct-07	FREE, ANDREW S 01-Oct-08
FREEMAN, MARTIN 01-Oct-07	POLLARD, JONATHAN 01-Oct-07	FYFE-GREEN, IAN 01-Oct-08
FYFE, KAREN S 01-Oct-07	WATSON, ANDREW 01-Oct-07	GARDNER, MICHAEL 01-Oct-08
Gray, EMMA J 01-Oct-07	JONES-THOMPSON, MICHAEL 01-Oct-07	GATES, NIGEL S 01-Oct-08
GUY, CHARLES R 01-Oct-07	MILLARD, JEREMY 01-Oct-07	GOTKE, CHRISTOPHER 01-Oct-08
HAMPSHIRE, TONY 01-Oct-07	MORRIS, ANTHONY 01-Oct-07	GRAY, MICHAEL 01-Oct-08
HARDMAN, MATTHEW 01-Oct-07	BELL, SCOTT WILLIAM 01-Oct-07	HAMMON, MARK 01-Oct-08
HATCHARD, POLLYANNA 01-Oct-07	MACFARLANE, IAIN 01-Oct-07	HARMAN, STEPHEN 01-Oct-08
HAYASHI, LUKE R 01-Oct-07	AUSTIN, PETER NIGEL 01-Oct-07	HARRISON, ANDREW 01-Oct-08
HEWITT, MARK J 01-Oct-07	EVANS, GILES 01-Oct-07	HART, STEVEN D 01-Oct-08
HOWELLS, SIMON M 01-Oct-07	CONNEELY, STEVEN 01-Oct-07	HATTLE, PRIDEAUX 01-Oct-08
HUMPHERY, DUNCAN 01-Oct-07	PEYMAN, TRACY 01-Oct-07	HILL, ADRIAN 01-Oct-08
HUTCHINGS, JUSTIN R 01-Oct-07	MILLS, GARY 01-Oct-07	HOLLAND, CHARLOTTE 01-Oct-08
JAYES, NEIL J 01-Oct-07	HOCKING, MARK 01-Oct-07	HOLROYD, JONATHON 01-Oct-08
KENNEDY, ROGER J 01-Oct-07	GODFREY, SIMEON 01-Oct-07	ILIFFE, DAVID 01-Oct-08
KENNINGTON, LEE 01-Oct-07	BOON, GARETH 01-Oct-07	INGHAM, MARYLA 01-Oct-08
LEE, STEVEN E 01-Oct-07	HENAGHEN, STEPHEN 01-Oct-07	JAMES, MARK 01-Oct-08
LEIGHTON, MATTHEW 01-Oct-07	BARRON-ROBINSON, DAVID 01-Oct-07	JARMAN, PAUL 01-Oct-08
LOUDEN, CARL A 01-Oct-07	MARTIN, STUART 01-Oct-07	JOHNSTON, DAVID 01-Oct-08
MANDERS-TRETT, VICTORIA 01-Oct-07	ALDOUS, BENJAMIN 01-Oct-07	KAY, PAUL S 01-Oct-08
MANNING, GARY P 01-Oct-07	TACEY, RICHARD 01-Oct-07	KEITH, BENJAMIN 01-Oct-08
MAWDSLEY, GARETH R 01-Oct-07		KENT, MATTHEW 01-Oct-08
MIDDLETON, WAYNE T 01-Oct-07	**2008**	KING, WILLIAM 01-Oct-08
MILLAR, KEVIN I 01-Oct-07		KLIDJIAN, MICHAEL 01-Oct-08
PALETHORPE, NICHOLAS 01-Oct-07	GILL, CHRISTOPHER 01-Nov-07	LEWIS, KAY E 01-Oct-08
PALMER, CHRISTOPHER R 01-Oct-07	MILLER, IAN 01-Dec-07	LOUGHREY, NEIL 01-Oct-08
PINE, PAUL M 01-Oct-07	BARKER, PAUL D	MABBOTT, KEITH 01-Oct-08
PROLE, NICHOLAS M 01-Oct-07	FEENEY, MATTHEW 01-Jan-08	MARLAND, EUNICE 01-Oct-08
RHODES, ANDREW 01-Oct-07	LONG, MICHAEL 01-Jan-08	MARSHALL, ALISTAIR 01-Oct-08
RICHARDS, PAUL 01-Oct-07	COLES, CHRISTOPHER 01-Apr-08	MARTIN, ROBERT 01-Oct-08
SANDERSON, CHRISTOPHER 01-Oct-07	GRANT, WAYNE G 01-Apr-08	MAY, DAVID 01-Oct-08
SANTRY, PAUL M 01-Oct-07	STRATHIE, GAVIN 01-Apr-08	MCLAUGHLIN, STEVEN 01-Oct-08
STAFFORD, BENJAMIN 01-Oct-07	KOHN, PATRICIA A 01-May-08	MCLENNAN, ANDREW 01-Oct-08
VARTY, JASON A 01-Oct-07	CLARK, RUSSELL A 01-Jun-08	METCALF, STEPHEN 01-Oct-08
VINEY, PETER M 01-Oct-07	BLACKBURN, LEE R 01-Jun-08	MONNOX, JILL 01-Oct-08
WALL, STEVEN N 01-Oct-07	FINN, STUART A 01-Jul-08	MOORE, MATTHEW 01-Oct-08
WRIGHT, DANIEL J 01-Oct-07	FLEGG, KIRSTY G 01-Aug-08	MORAN, RUSSELL 01-Oct-08
UNDERWOOD, RICHARD 01-Oct-07	RAEBURN, CRAIG 01-Sep-08	MORRIS, HARRIET 01-Oct-08
KENYON, CAROLYN MARIE 01-Oct-07	ADAMS, WILLIAM MBE 01-Sep-08	MUNDY, ALAN R 01-Oct-08
DOUBLEDAY, STEVEN 01-Oct-07	AINSLEY, ANDREW 01-Sep-08	OAKLEY, CLAIRE 01-Oct-08
JONES, IAN MICHAEL 01-Oct-07	ALEXANDER, AMY L 01-Sep-08	OWEN, SAMUEL 01-Oct-08
ARMSTRONG, STUART 01-Oct-07	ALLISON, GLENN 01-Oct-08	PEARSON, JAMES 01-Oct-08
JOHNSON, PAUL 01-Oct-07	ANDERSON, STEPHEN 01-Oct-08	PEATTIE, IAN W 01-Oct-08
NEW, RICHARD 01-Oct-07	BAGSHAW, JAMES 01-Oct-08	PINHEY, ANDREW D 01-Oct-08
REES, KAREN 01-Oct-07	BALL, MATTHEW P 01-Oct-08	PLATT, JONATHAN H 01-Oct-08
BENNETT, WILLIAM 01-Oct-07	BELL, CATRIONA M 01-Oct-08	PRICE, JOSEPH C 01-Oct-08
RICHARDS, ANTHONY 01-Oct-07	BINNS, JON F 01-Oct-08	RANKIN, GRAHAM 01-Oct-08
POLLARD, ALEXANDRA 01-Oct-07	BLAND, CHRISTOPHER 01-Oct-08	RICHARDSON, IAN 01-Oct-08
LEAR, STUART 01-Oct-07	BROWN, ANDREW S 01-Oct-08	ROBINSON, DAVID 01-Oct-08
FULLER, CHARLES 01-Oct-07	BUCKENHAM, PETER 01-Oct-08	RYAN, JOHN 01-Oct-08
MACDONALD, STUART 01-Oct-07	CAMERON, FIONA 01-Oct-08	SELWOOD, PETER 01-Oct-08
HUBSCHMID, SPENCER 01-Oct-07	CHADWICK, KARA 01-Oct-08	SIMMONITE, GAVIN IAN DFC 01-Oct-08
TITCOMBE, ADAM ACMA 01-Oct-07	CLEARY, CHRISTOPHER 01-Oct-08	SIMPSON, WILLIAM 01-Oct-08
WEBSTER, RICHARD 01-Oct-07	CROMIE, JOHN M 01-Oct-08	SLOWTHER, STUART 01-Oct-08
JONES, MARK 01-Oct-07	DANIELS, STUART P 01-Oct-08	

LIEUTENANT COMMANDERS

SMITH, ANDREW 01-Oct-08
STOREY, HELEN 01-Oct-08
STURGEON, DAVID 01-Oct-08
THOMSON, IAN 01-Oct-08
TRUELOVE, SAMANTHA 01-Oct-08
TURNER, DAVID 01-Oct-08
TUTCHINGS, ANDREW..........................01-Oct-08
URWIN, STUART J 01-Oct-08
VOUT, DEBRA K 01-Oct-08
VOWLES, MITCHELL J 01-Oct-08
WATSON, RICHARD D.............................01-Oct-08
WELLS, JAMIE D.....................................01-Oct-08
WELSH, JOHN 01-Oct-08
WHITE, JASON P QGM..........................01-Oct-08
WHITEHOUSE, DAVID 01-Oct-08
WILSON, JOHN 01-Oct-08
WRENNALL, ERIC 01-Oct-08
YAXLEY, LOUISE 01-Oct-08
WEBB, ELEANOR....................................01-Oct-08
WAITE, TOBIAS 01-Oct-08
VICKERY, BEN 01-Oct-08
MITCHELL, JAMIE 01-Oct-08
MCGANNITY, COLIN 01-Oct-08
GARE, CHRISTOPHER............................01-Oct-08
CHAPMAN, MARTIN 01-Oct-08
GARDNER-CLARK, SUZANNE 01-Oct-08
MATHIESON, NEIL 01-Oct-08
RISLEY, JAMES G 01-Oct-08
NICKLIN, GARETH 01-Oct-08
CALHAEM, RICHARD 01-Oct-08
HAMILTON, MARK 01-Oct-08
BARTON, KEITH 01-Oct-08
HADLAND, GILES..................................01-Oct-08
CURRIE, MICHAEL.................................01-Oct-08
STEEN, KIERON 01-Oct-08
MCDONALD, DUNCAN 01-Oct-08
MORTLOCK, PHILIP 01-Oct-08
CLAY, TOBY 01-Oct-08
CARROLL, STEPHEN 01-Oct-08
CONLIN, JOHN MA 01-Oct-08
HAYDEN, TIMOTHY 01-Oct-08
THOMSON, MICHAEL 01-Oct-08
NAYLOR, ANDREW 01-Oct-08
BAINBRIDGE, STUART 01-Oct-08
ENEVER, SHAUN 01-Oct-08
STRATTON, MATTHEW..........................01-Oct-08
O'ROURKE, RICHARD 01-Oct-08
NORRIS, GUY..01-Oct-08
MILLIGAN, ROBERT 01-Oct-08
KING, IAN 01-Oct-08
LESTER, RODNEY MBE 01-Oct-08
HARDY, ROBERT 01-Oct-08
FLYNN, SIMON 01-Oct-08
CARNE, RICHARD 01-Oct-08
WALKER, ROBIN....................................01-Oct-08
SOLLITT, VICTORIA 01-Oct-08
COLLINS, DALE 01-Oct-08
TRINDER, STEPHEN 01-Oct-08
HAMILTON, GRAHAM 01-Oct-08
RAWLINGS, GARY..................................01-Oct-08
TAYLOR, CHRISTOPHER.........................01-Oct-08

SHAW, NEIL ANDREW...........................01-Oct-08
LANE, HEATHER 01-Oct-08
BIRCHALL, JAMES 01-Oct-08
BURTON, ALEX 01-Oct-08
SEAGRAVE, SUZANNA 01-Oct-08

2009

ALEXANDER, PHILLIP 01-Nov-08
ROBINSON, STEVEN L............................01-Nov-08
ADAMS, GEORGE
WOODS, MICHAEL 01-Jan-09
CANTELLOW, STUART............................01-Jan-09
PERKINS-BROWN, BEN 01-May-09
MARRIOTT, MATTHEW..........................01-May-09
ADAMS, EDWIN S.................................01-Jun-09
ALDERTON, PAUL A 01-Jul-09
ANDREWS, CHRISTOPHER....................01-Sep-09
BALL, WILLIAM 01-Oct-09
BARROW, CHARLES 01-Oct-09
BASS, PAUL 01-Oct-09
BAVERSTOCK, ANDREW 01-Oct-09
BINNS, JOHN R.....................................01-Oct-09
BLOIS, SIMON 01-Oct-09
BLYTHE, JAMES.....................................01-Oct-09
BOAKES, PHILIP....................................01-Oct-09
BODMAN, SIMON 01-Oct-09
BOOT, STEPHEN 01-Oct-09
BRADLEY, TREVOR 01-Oct-09
BRIERLEY, SIMON P 01-Oct-09
BROCKLEHURST, JUDITH.......................01-Oct-09
BRODIE, STEPHEN 01-Oct-09
BULL, LOUIS P......................................01-Oct-09
BURNETT, PAUL 01-Oct-09
CARNELL, RICHARD 01-Oct-09
CARTER QUINN, MICHAEL 01-Oct-09
CARTHEW, RICHARD 01-Oct-09
CHANG, CHRISTOPHER 01-Oct-09
CHAPMAN, JAMES 01-Oct-09
CLARKSON, ANDREW...........................01-Oct-09
CLEAR, NICHOLA 01-Oct-09
CRAVEN, DALE 01-Oct-09
CRAVEN, MARTIN W..............................01-Oct-09
DAY, ANTHONY 01-Oct-09
DI MAIO, MARK D 01-Oct-09
DRANSFIELD, JOSEPH 01-Oct-09
DRAY, JAKE M.......................................01-Oct-09
DUKE, KAREN D....................................01-Oct-09
ELLIOT-SMITH, TEILO 01-Oct-09
ELLIOTT, JAMIE A 01-Oct-09
EVANS, LEE S 01-Oct-09
FARRANT, JAMES 01-Oct-09
FEARON, DAVID 01-Oct-09
FLEMING, RUTH 01-Oct-09
FOOTE, ANDREW..................................01-Oct-09
FORBES, ANGELA 01-Oct-09
GEORGE, SETH 01-Oct-09
GILMORE, STEVEN 01-Oct-09
GODDARD, PAUL..................................01-Oct-09
GOODMAN, DAVID 01-Oct-09
GORDON, JOHN 01-Oct-09
GOTT, STEPHEN B 01-Oct-09

GREEN, LESLIE D 01-Oct-09
GRIFFIN, STEPHEN................................01-Oct-09
GWATKIN, NICHOLAS............................01-Oct-09
HARVEY, GRAHAM A.............................01-Oct-09
HEADLEY, MARK J.................................01-Oct-09
HEANEY, MARTIN J 01-Oct-09
HEPPLEWHITE, MARK 01-Oct-09
HUGHES, CHRISTOPHER 01-Oct-09
HUGHES, GARETH D.............................01-Oct-09
JACOB, ANDREW W 01-Oct-09
JONES, DAVID 01-Oct-09
KELLY, GRANT J....................................01-Oct-09
LANNING, RODERICK 01-Oct-09
LAW, SAMUEL J 01-Oct-09
LEEDER, TIMOTHY 01-Oct-09
LEESON, ANTONY.................................01-Oct-09
MALONE, MARTIN 01-Oct-09
MASON, MARK 01-Oct-09
MATTHEWS, JUSTIN 01-Oct-09
MILNE, ANDRE P...................................01-Oct-09
MORSE, JEREMY 01-Oct-09
NEWELL, GARY 01-Oct-09
NICHOLSON, BRIAN 01-Oct-09
NIELSEN, SUZI 01-Oct-09
O'NEILL, JAMES 01-Oct-09
O'NEILL, TIMOTHY 01-Oct-09
ORR, KEITH J 01-Oct-09
PARK, IAN 01-Oct-09
PARRY, STUART 01-Oct-09
PETTIGREW, THOMAS...........................01-Oct-09
PROWSE, DAVID 01-Oct-09
REAVES, CHARLES 01-Oct-09
REID, JAMES L......................................01-Oct-09
ROBERTS, BENJAMIN 01-Oct-09
ROGERS, JULIA 01-Oct-09
RUSSELL, KATHERINE 01-Oct-09
SAMBROOKS, RICHARD 01-Oct-09
SAMUELS, NICHOLAS............................01-Oct-09
SHERWOOD, GIDEON 01-Oct-09
SINGLETON, MARK 01-Oct-09
SINGLETON, RACHEL............................01-Oct-09
SLATTERY, DAMIAN 01-Oct-09
SMITH, CHARLES 01-Oct-09
STACK, ELEANOR 01-Oct-09
STRATTON, STUART 01-Oct-09
STUBBS, IAN 01-Oct-09
TALBOT, RICHARD 01-Oct-09
TANTAM, ROBERT 01-Oct-09
TAZEWELL, MATTHEW 01-Oct-09
THOMSON, JAMES 01-Oct-09
TONGE, MALCOLM 01-Oct-09
TOONE, STEPHEN 01-Oct-09
TOUGH, IAIN 01-Oct-09
UNWIN, NICHOLAS...............................01-Oct-09
VINES, NICHOLAS 01-Oct-09
WAY, ROBERT A....................................01-Oct-09
WEST, NICHOLAS K 01-Oct-09
WHITEHALL, SALLY 01-Oct-09
WINN, JOHN P 01-Oct-09
WINSOR, JAMES 01-Oct-09
WOOLHEAD, CRAIG 01-Oct-09

LIEUTENANT COMMANDERS

GENEUX, NICHOLAS	01-Oct-09	
HUGHES, BENJAMIN	01-Oct-09	
RIDER, JOHN	01-Oct-09	
BROOKS, NICHOLAS	01-Oct-09	
COLLINS, SIMON	01-Oct-09	
MARDEN, TONY	01-Oct-09	
GREY, CHRISTOPHER	01-Oct-09	
MARSHALL, GAVIN PETER	01-Oct-09	
QUINN, MARK	01-Oct-09	
WADSWORTH, RICHARD	01-Oct-09	
FLATMAN, TIMOTHY	01-Oct-09	
PRIEST, JAMES	01-Oct-09	
WISEMAN, NEIL	01-Oct-09	
HOLDER, JOHN	01-Oct-09	
BLACKBURN, EMMA	01-Oct-09	
BENNETT, CHRISTOPHER	01-Oct-09	
SPARROW, MARK	01-Oct-09	
JAMESON, ROGER	01-Oct-09	
WELSH, RICHARD GCGI	01-Oct-09	
NEWMAN, VIRGINIA	01-Oct-09	
PARROCK, NEIL	01-Oct-09	
HISCOCK, STEPHEN	01-Oct-09	
KESTLE, MARK	01-Oct-09	
MCKEE, HAMISH	01-Oct-09	
GLENDINNING, ANDREANA	01-Oct-09	
COLLINS, DAVID	01-Oct-09	
ROSTRON, JOHN	01-Oct-09	
FULLER, STEPHEN	01-Oct-09	
BROOKS, PAUL	01-Oct-09	
WHITSON-FAY, CRAIG	01-Oct-09	
SAUNDERS, ALICE	01-Oct-09	
HUNT, ROBERT J	01-Oct-09	
O'CONNOR, DAVID	01-Oct-09	
WILD, RICHARD	01-Oct-09	
STANDEN, GARY	01-Oct-09	
BASS, EMMA	01-Oct-09	
CARBERY, STEPHEN	01-Oct-09	
TOON, PAUL GRAHAM	01-Oct-09	
BREACH, PAMELA	01-Oct-09	
FLETCHER, IAN	01-Oct-09	
FRENCH, PAUL	01-Oct-09	
OAKLEY, ANDREW	01-Oct-09	
WHITE, STEPHEN	01-Oct-09	
MOREY, KEVIN N	01-Oct-09	
COLLEN, SARA J	01-Oct-09	

2010

JAMES, ANDREW	01-Nov-09
CANTY, THOMAS	01-Dec-09
ASHTON, JAMES	
HORSTED, JAMES	01-Jan-10
PECK, SIMON R	01-Feb-10
MCCLURG, ROBERT	01-Mar-10
GIBBS, MARK	01-Mar-10
HANDOLL, GUY	01-Mar-10
LIPPITT, SIMON	01-Mar-10
WALKER, STEPHEN	01-Apr-10
NORTHCOTT, PHILIP	01-Apr-10
ALCINDOR, DAVID	01-Apr-10
GUBBY, ADRIAN	01-Apr-10
SYKES, MATTHEW	20-Apr-10

ADEY, JOANNA LOUISE	22-Apr-10
ALDER, MARK	01-May-10
ANDERSON, ANDREW	01-Sep-10
ANDREWS, LOUISA J	01-Oct-10
BAILEY, MICHAEL	01-Oct-10
BAKER, JAMES E G	01-Oct-10
BANFIELD, STEVEN	01-Oct-10
BARFOOT, PETER	01-Oct-10
BARRIE, STUART	01-Oct-10
BEANLAND, PETER	01-Oct-10
BENNETT, MARK	01-Oct-10
BEVAN, JEFFREY MBE	01-Oct-10
BOON, SIMON E	01-Oct-10
BOTTERILL, HUGH	01-Oct-10
BOTTING, NEIL A	01-Oct-10
BOUGHTON, JONATHAN	01-Oct-10
BOWIE, RICHARD	01-Oct-10
BREEN, JOHN E	01-Oct-10
BRINDLEY, MARK	01-Oct-10
BROWN, JAMES	01-Oct-10
BULLOCK, JOHN	01-Oct-10
BURBIDGE, KAY	01-Oct-10
CHAMBERS, RICHARD	01-Oct-10
CHATTERJEE, SHATADEEP	01-Oct-10
CLARK, STEPHEN M	01-Oct-10
CLARKSON, ANTONY	01-Oct-10
COACKLEY, JANE	01-Oct-10
COLES, SIMON P	01-Oct-10
CORNFORD, MARC	01-Oct-10
CORY, NICHOLAS	01-Oct-10
CUNNELL, RACHAEL	01-Oct-10
DARKINS, COLIN	01-Oct-10
DOWNIE, DAVID	01-Oct-10
ELLERTON, PAUL	01-Oct-10
ELLIOTT, STEPHEN	01-Oct-10
EVANS, PAUL J	01-Oct-10
FILLMORE, RAYMOND J	01-Oct-10
FULL, RICHARD J	01-Oct-10
GAMBLE, NEIL	01-Oct-10
GAMBLE, STEPHEN B	01-Oct-10
GARRETA, CARLOS E	01-Oct-10
GRAY, NATHAN	01-Oct-10
GRIFFEN, DAVID J	01-Oct-10
HACKMAN, JAMES	01-Oct-10
HALL, CHRISTOPHER L	01-Oct-10
HAWKINS, STEPHEN	01-Oct-10
HAZARD, LEE MBE	01-Oct-10
HEAP, GRAHAM	01-Oct-10
HEWITT, RICHARD	01-Oct-10
HILTON, SIMON	01-Oct-10
HUGHES, JOHN	01-Oct-10
JOHANSEN, STEPHEN	01-Oct-10
JOHNSON, LAUREN	01-Oct-10
JONES, CHARMODY	01-Oct-10
JONES, MARK	01-Oct-10
KEAM, IAN	01-Oct-10
KIFF, IAN	01-Oct-10
KING, JASON M	01-Oct-10
KITCHEN, BETHAN	01-Oct-10
LAIDLER, PAUL J	01-Oct-10
LAYTON, CHRISTOPHER	01-Oct-10

LONG, STUART G	01-Oct-10
LUXFORD, CHARLES	01-Oct-10
MACQUARRIE, GARY	01-Oct-10
MASSON, NEIL	01-Oct-10
MCCORMACK, GARY	01-Oct-10
MCEWAN, RORY	01-Oct-10
MILLER, KEVIN	01-Oct-10
MISIAK, ANNA L	01-Oct-10
MONEY, CHRISTOPHER	01-Oct-10
MORRIS, PAUL	01-Oct-10
MUNDAY, STEPHEN	01-Oct-10
NEKREWS, ALAN QGM	01-Oct-10
NOONAN, CHARLES	01-Oct-10
OCHTMAN-CORFE, FERGUS	01-Oct-10
PEARCE, JONATHAN	01-Oct-10
PEARMAIN, STEPHANIE	01-Oct-10
PESKETT, DANIEL GCGI	01-Oct-10
PUNCH, JOHN MATTHEW	01-Oct-10
QUINN, ANTONY D	01-Oct-10
REEVES, PAUL K	01-Oct-10
REYNOLDS, JAMES	01-Oct-10
REYNOLDS, MATTHEW	01-Oct-10
RITCHIE, IAIN D	01-Oct-10
ROBINSON, LEE D	01-Oct-10
ROSENBERG, MARCEL	01-Oct-10
SATTERLY, ROBERT	01-Oct-10
SEMPLE, BRIAN	01-Oct-10
SIMMONDS, DANIEL	01-Oct-10
SIMPSON, SCOTT	01-Oct-10
SKINSLEY, TERRY	01-Oct-10
SMALLWOOD, RACHEL MBE	01-Oct-10
SOUTHWOOD, SHAUN	01-Oct-10
SPENCER, ASHLEY	01-Oct-10
STRINGER, GRAEME	01-Oct-10
SWINDELLS, MARK	01-Oct-10
TALL, IAIN	01-Oct-10
TERRY, NIGEL	01-Oct-10
THOMAS, OWEN	01-Oct-10
THOMPSON, ANDREW	01-Oct-10
TREWINNARD-BOYLE, ROBIN	01-Oct-10
WALLACE, ANTHONY	01-Oct-10
WALLACE, RICHARD S	01-Oct-10
WALLACE, RYAN	01-Oct-10
WARD, ALEXANDER J	01-Oct-10
WEAVER, THOMAS H	01-Oct-10
WHITE, DOUGLAS	01-Oct-10
WHITE, SIMON H W	01-Oct-10
WILKINS, ROBERT L	01-Oct-10
WILKINSON, JOHN R	01-Oct-10
WILLIAMS, PAUL G	01-Oct-10
WINTERBON, ANDREW	01-Oct-10
WOOLLVEN, CHRISTOPHER	01-Oct-10
GRICE, MATTHEW	01-Oct-10
RIDDETT, ADAM	01-Oct-10
LAI-HUNG, JEREMY	01-Oct-10
STOREY, ANDREW	01-Oct-10
HUYNH, CUONG	01-Oct-10
LATUS, SIMON HARRY	01-Oct-10
HALL, JAMES	01-Oct-10
HALL, GRAHAM	01-Oct-10
MALLINSON, LAURENCE	01-Oct-10

LIEUTENANT COMMANDERS

CORYTON, SOPHIE C	01-Oct-10	
TAPPIN, SIMON J	01-Oct-10	
KING, WILLIAM	01-Oct-10	
FAULKNER, STUART	01-Oct-10	
BAILEY, IAN J	01-Oct-10	
WALLACE, IAIN	01-Oct-10	
SCOTT, NEIL	01-Oct-10	
RAWLINS, SIMON	01-Oct-10	
KENNEDY, IAN	01-Oct-10	
SPOORS, BRENDAN	01-Oct-10	
FRATER, REBECCA	01-Oct-10	
MURGATROYD, KEVIN	01-Oct-10	
BAILES, KENNETH	01-Oct-10	
LAURENCE, SIMON	01-Oct-10	
BRADLEY, RUPERT	01-Oct-10	
PICKLES, DAVID	01-Oct-10	
HEAP, STEVEN A MBE	01-Oct-10	
REX, COLIN	01-Oct-10	
CHAWIRA, DENIS	01-Oct-10	
SNELL, ANDREW	01-Oct-10	
BRANN, ROBERT	01-Oct-10	
GODDARD, DAVID	01-Oct-10	
COX, MICHAEL	01-Oct-10	
LOCKHART, JOHN	01-Oct-10	
PEARCH, SEAN	01-Oct-10	
GILLETT, NATHAN	01-Oct-10	
PIKE, ROBIN	01-Oct-10	
JAFFIER, ROBERT RD	01-Oct-10	
OTTLEY, LUCY JANE	01-Oct-10	
BRODIE, DUNCAN	01-Oct-10	
ELDRIDGE, STEPHEN	01-Oct-10	
WRAGG, GARETH	01-Oct-10	
PICKARD, STEPHEN	01-Oct-10	
MCDOUGALL, WILLIAM	01-Oct-10	
VAN DEN BERGH, MARK	01-Oct-10	
GULLIVER, JEFF W	01-Oct-10	

2011

REYNOLDS, MARK E	05-Oct-10	
PERCY, NICOLAS A	21-Nov-10	
KADINOPOULOS, BENJAMIN		
HOLMWOOD, MARK	01-Feb-11	
GREEN, JAYNE	01-Apr-11	
ANDERSON, NEIL	01-Apr-11	
BAILLIE, ROBBIE	01-Aug-11	
BAINBRIDGE, PAUL	01-Sep-11	
BINGHAM, ALEXANDER	01-Oct-11	
BLETHYN, HUGH	01-Oct-11	
BOND, ROBERT	01-Oct-11	
BOULIND, MATTHEW	01-Oct-11	
BOYD, ELAINE	01-Oct-11	
BROWN, JAMES	01-Oct-11	
BURRELL, DAVID	01-Oct-11	
BUTLER, JONATHON	01-Oct-11	
COLLEY, IAN P	01-Oct-11	
COOPER, JANETTE	01-Oct-11	
CRICHTON, GARY	01-Oct-11	
CROSBY, DAVID	01-Oct-11	
DAVIES, DARREN	01-Oct-11	
DRODGE, KEVIN N	01-Oct-11	
EACOCK, JASON P	01-Oct-11	

EDWARDS, JAMES	01-Oct-11
ENGLAND, PHILIP	01-Oct-11
EVANS, CHRISTOPHER	01-Oct-11
FOSTER, ALAN	01-Oct-11
FRASER-SMITH, SHARRON	01-Oct-11
FRAZER, CATHERINE	01-Oct-11
GAHAN, RICHARD	01-Oct-11
GARDNER, LOUIS	01-Oct-11
GILMORE, MARTIN	01-Oct-11
GORDON, DAVID I	01-Oct-11
GRANT, RICHARD	01-Oct-11
HALEY, CHRISTOPHER	01-Oct-11
HAMMOCK, SIMON	01-Oct-11
HANCOCK, JAMES	01-Oct-11
HARCOMBE, ANDREW	01-Oct-11
HARRIS, RICHARD	01-Oct-11
HARRISON, LEIGH	01-Oct-11
HEATON, HENRY	01-Oct-11
HODGSON, LAURA	01-Oct-11
HOLGATE, JAMES	01-Oct-11
HULSTON, LAUREN	01-Oct-11
HURLEY, KARL	01-Oct-11
IRWIN, STUART G	01-Oct-11
JAMES, GARETH	01-Oct-11
KEARSLEY, IAIN P	01-Oct-11
KNOWLES, CHRISTOPHER	01-Oct-11
LEIGHTLEY, SIMON	01-Oct-11
LONGSTAFF, THOMAS	01-Oct-11
MACPHAIL, NEIL	01-Oct-11
MAINS, GRAHAM	01-Oct-11
MARSH, STEPHEN	01-Oct-11
MAUDE, COLIN	01-Oct-11
MCCALL, GARY	01-Oct-11
MCKAY, THOMAS	01-Oct-11
MCWILLIAMS, ADRIAN	01-Oct-11
MOLE, ANDREW	01-Oct-11
MORRIS, DANIEL	01-Oct-11
MORRISON, SHAUN	01-Oct-11
MOSELEY, STEPHEN	01-Oct-11
MURRAY, GREIG	01-Oct-11
NICHOLLS, LARRY	01-Oct-11
O'BRIEN, THOMAS	01-Oct-11
O'NEILL, CONOR	01-Oct-11
O'REILLY, CHRISTOPHER	01-Oct-11
PARKER, DANIEL	01-Oct-11
PASTON, WILLIAM	01-Oct-11
PATE, CHRISTOPHER	01-Oct-11
PHILLIPS, RICHARD	01-Oct-11
POWNE, SIMON	01-Oct-11
RANDLES, STEVEN	01-Oct-11
REEVES, ANDREW	01-Oct-11
ROBERTS, NIGEL	01-Oct-11
ROBEY, JAMES	01-Oct-11
ROWBERRY, ADRIAN	01-Oct-11
RUSSELL, MARTIN	01-Oct-11
SCOTT, JULIAN	01-Oct-11
SHARP, ANDREW MBE	01-Oct-11
SHEARS, ALEXANDRA	01-Oct-11
STUBBS, IAN	01-Oct-11
THOMAS, MARK	01-Oct-11
THOMPSON, DAVID	01-Oct-11

THORNHILL, STEPHEN	01-Oct-11
TOMLIN, IAN S	01-Oct-11
TOMLINSON, AMY	01-Oct-11
TRENT, THOMAS	01-Oct-11
TURBERVILLE, CHRISTOPHER	01-Oct-11
USSHER, JEREMY	01-Oct-11
WALL, KARL	01-Oct-11
WALTON, GEORGE	01-Oct-11
WEIL, DANIEL	01-Oct-11
WHITE, STEPHEN	01-Oct-11
WHITEHEAD, PETER	01-Oct-11
WILSON, GARY	01-Oct-11
WOOD, SIMON	01-Oct-11
WOOKEY, MARK	01-Oct-11
WREN, STEPHEN	01-Oct-11
AMOROSI, RICCARDO	01-Oct-11
PURDY, RICHARD	01-Oct-11
HUGHES, ELIZABETH	01-Oct-11
HOGG, ADAM	01-Oct-11
COATES, ADAM	01-Oct-11
ABBOTTS, MICHAEL	01-Oct-11
COX, SIMON	01-Oct-11
LYNN, SARAH LOUISE	01-Oct-11
HIGGINS, PETER AFC	01-Oct-11
MORGAN, CHRISTOPHER	01-Oct-11
STONE, JAMES	01-Oct-11
WESTWOOD, THOMAS	01-Oct-11
WILLIAMS, PAUL	01-Oct-11
BROOKS, ALEXANDRA	01-Oct-11
MCCAMPHILL-ROSE, PAUL	01-Oct-11
PEARCE, ROBERT	01-Oct-11
ANDREWS, JUSTIN	01-Oct-11
ROE, ROMA JANE	01-Oct-11
O'KANE, ROBERT	01-Oct-11
THOMAS, DAVID	01-Oct-11
SMITH, OWEN	01-Oct-11
BALDIE, STEVEN	01-Oct-11
STURMAN, RICHARD	01-Oct-11
WHARRIE, CRAIG	01-Oct-11
BULLOCK, ROBERT	01-Oct-11
HUGHES, SCOTT	01-Oct-11
NASH, RUSSELL	01-Oct-11
HINE, MICHAEL	01-Oct-11
PARKER, DARREN	01-Oct-11
NORTON, IAN	01-Oct-11
IMRIE, SAMANTHA	01-Oct-11
STEVENS, JOSEPH	01-Oct-11
EVANS, ROBERT	01-Oct-11
THURSTON, MARK	01-Oct-11
BAILEY, SIMON	01-Oct-11
WILLIAMS, CASSANDRA	01-Oct-11
SCREEN, JAMES	01-Oct-11
PARKINSON, HENRY	01-Oct-11
BETTLES, JOHN	01-Oct-11
WEEDON, GRANT	01-Oct-11

2012

BAYLISS, ANNABEL	25-Nov-11
HARRISON, PETER M	01-Dec-11
STRATTON, NICHOLAS	
LOUIS, DAVID R A	16-Mar-12

LIEUTENANT COMMANDERS

WICK, HARRY M	JONES, NICHOLAS 01-Oct-12	HUTCHINSON, MICHAEL 01-Oct-12
ARMSTRONG, DAVID 01-May-12	KEILLOR, STUART J 01-Oct-12	ALMOND, NICHOLAS 01-Oct-12
ARMSTRONG, RORY 01-Jul-12	KENNEDY, CATHERYN 01-Oct-12	BARTRAM, CAROLINE 01-Oct-12
BALFOUR, ROSS D 01-Sep-12	KING, DAVID 01-Oct-12	BOWERS, KEITH 01-Oct-12
BALLARD, ADAM P V 01-Oct-12	L'AMIE, CHRISTOPHER 01-Oct-12	COFFEY, RALPH 01-Oct-12
BALLARD, DANELLE 01-Oct-12	LANCASTER, JAMES 01-Oct-12	FICKLING, JAMES 01-Oct-12
BANNISTER, JONATHAN 01-Oct-12	LEEPER, JAMES 01-Oct-12	FIDDOCK, MATTHEW 01-Oct-12
BARTRAM, GREGORY 01-Oct-12	LLEWELLYN, JONATHAN 01-Oct-12	CARPENTER, GARY 01-Oct-12
BLACK, EDWARD 01-Oct-12	LONDON, NICHOLAS 01-Oct-12	WINBORN, DAVID 01-Oct-12
BLACK, JOANNA 01-Oct-12	LOVELL, JAMES 01-Oct-12	HYDE, JAMES WILLIAM 01-Oct-12
BLACKETT, WILLIAM 01-Oct-12	MADDISON, HUGH 01-Oct-12	WOOD, CHRISTOPHER 01-Oct-12
BLEASDALE, DANIEL 01-Oct-12	MADDISON, PAUL 01-Oct-12	DESPRES, JULIAN ARRC 01-Oct-12
BLETHYN, CATHERINE 01-Oct-12	MALLABONE, JAMES 01-Oct-12	FITZPATRICK, NEIL 01-Oct-12
BOWEN, RICHARD 01-Oct-12	MARLOR, ANDREW 01-Oct-12	WATSON, BRADLEY 01-Oct-12
BRAITHWAITE, GEOFFREY 01-Oct-12	MCCALLUM, MALCOLM 01-Oct-12	FRENCH, JEREMY 01-Oct-12
BRIGHT, AMANDA 01-Oct-12	MCMILLAN, NELSON 01-Oct-12	GREENWOOD, PETER 01-Oct-12
BRISCOE, JAMES 01-Oct-12	MIDDLETON, MARK 01-Oct-12	ASHLIN, JAMES 01-Oct-12
BRISTOW, PAUL 01-Oct-12	MINTY, DARREN 01-Oct-12	MACKENZIE, HANNAH 01-Oct-12
BROWETT, JON J 01-Oct-12	NELSON, MATTHEW 01-Oct-12	BARTRAM, RICHARD 01-Oct-12
BROWN, ALASTAIR 01-Oct-12	NORTH, ADAM 01-Oct-12	MOUNT, JAMES 01-Oct-12
BUKHORY, HAMESH 01-Oct-12	OWEN, VINCENT 01-Oct-12	GRIFFITHS, COLIN 01-Oct-12
BYRON, DOUGLAS 01-Oct-12	PERKS, ANDREW 01-Oct-12	BATES, NICHOLAS 01-Oct-12
CHARNOCK, SIMON 01-Oct-12	PHILLIPPO, DUNCAN 01-Oct-12	GLADWIN, MICHAEL 01-Oct-12
CLEE, JAMES 01-Oct-12	PRIDEAUX, ROBERT 01-Oct-12	DEIGHTON, GRAEME 01-Oct-12
COLES-HENDRY, FRANCES 01-Oct-12	REYNOLDS, ANDREW 01-Oct-12	BRENNAN, JOHN PAUL 01-Oct-12
COLLINS, DAVID 01-Oct-12	RIMMER, OWEN F 01-Oct-12	DUTHIE, ANDREW 01-Oct-12
DANIEL, BENJAMIN 01-Oct-12	ROBERTS, ANDREW 01-Oct-12	FOWLER, JAMES 01-Oct-12
DAVIES, SARAH 01-Oct-12	ROSE, ALAN 01-Oct-12	MURPHY, CHRISTIAN 01-Oct-12
DE VELASCO, MARI 01-Oct-12	ROWLEY, THOMAS P 01-Oct-12	MACLEAN, SHAMUS 01-Oct-12
DOWLING, ANDREW 01-Oct-12	RYDER, MATTHEW R 01-Oct-12	MARSH, CERI 01-Oct-12
DRY, IAN 01-Oct-12	SALTONSTALL, HUGH 01-Oct-12	WHEEN, CHARLES 01-Oct-12
EDMONDSON, MARK 01-Oct-12	SANDY, DAVID 01-Oct-12	HUGHES, GARY 01-Oct-12
EDWARDS, TOM H H 01-Oct-12	SAVAGE, ALEXANDER 01-Oct-12	TWISELTON, MATTHEW 01-Oct-12
FERGUSSON, IAIN 01-Oct-12	SHANAHAN, LLOYD 01-Oct-12	CRIPPS, MICHAEL 01-Oct-12
FLAHERTY, CHRISTOPHER 01-Oct-12	SHEPHERD, CHRISTOPHER 01-Oct-12	MILLER, SASHA LOUISE 01-Oct-12
FOX, DAVID 01-Oct-12	SIMS, ALEXANDER R 01-Oct-12	SMYE, MALCOLM 01-Oct-12
GEARING, RICHARD 01-Oct-12	SMITH, BENJAMIN 01-Oct-12	COWIE, ANDREW 01-Oct-12
GORDON, DAVID 01-Oct-12	SOBERS, SCOTT 01-Oct-12	DAY, BENJAMIN 01-Oct-12
GORMAN, GLENN 01-Oct-12	SPEARPOINT, DAMON 01-Oct-12	IVES, DAVID 01-Oct-12
GRAY, RICHARD L 01-Oct-12	SPEARS, ANDREW 01-Oct-12	
GRAYSON, STEPHEN 01-Oct-12	STEAD, ANDREW 01-Oct-12	**2013**
GROVE, JEREMY 01-Oct-12	STURGEON, MARK 01-Oct-12	ALLEN, JASON L 01-Oct-12
HALLSWORTH, KAY 01-Oct-12	THOMSON, PAUL 01-Oct-12	BARRON, PHILIP 25-Oct-12
HANKS, OLIVER T 01-Oct-12	VESSEY, LEE 01-Oct-12	BASSETT, NICOLE
HANNAM, DARRELL 01-Oct-12	WALKER, IAN 01-Oct-12	BASTIAENS, PAUL 01-Oct-13
HARDING, DAVID 01-Oct-12	WARBURTON, ALISON 01-Oct-12	BECKER, ROBERT 01-Oct-13
HARRIS, HUGH 01-Oct-12	WARD, JARED 01-Oct-12	BEST, ROBERT 01-Oct-13
HAZELWOOD, STEVE 01-Oct-12	WARD, MATTHEW 01-Oct-12	BILLINGS, ANDREW 01-Oct-13
HEIRS, GAVIN G 01-Oct-12	WARE, ANDREW T 01-Oct-12	BIRCH, PETER L 01-Oct-13
HERRIDGE, DANIEL 01-Oct-12	WEBB, JOHN P 01-Oct-12	BIRKBY, CHRISTINA 01-Oct-13
HESKETH, JOHN 01-Oct-12	WHEATLEY, NICOLA 01-Oct-12	BOUYAC, DAVID 01-Oct-13
HIGSON, GLENN R 01-Oct-12	WHITE, STEVEN 01-Oct-12	BRETTELL, JEREMY 01-Oct-13
HOLMES, CHRISTOPHER 01-Oct-12	WHITTLES, GARY 01-Oct-12	BROCKIE, ALAN 01-Oct-13
HORLOCK, ANDREW 01-Oct-12	WINSTONE, NIGEL 01-Oct-12	BROWN, LYNDA 01-Oct-13
HULSE, REBECCA 01-Oct-12	WRIGHT-JONES, ALEXANDRA 01-Oct-12	BROWNE, KEVIN 01-Oct-13
ILLINGWORTH, RICHARD 01-Oct-12	RIORDAN, SHAUN 01-Oct-12	BURGESS, PHILIP 01-Oct-13
INGLIS, GRAHAM 01-Oct-12	SAMPSON, JAMES 01-Oct-12	BURGHALL, REBECCA 01-Oct-13
INSLEY, CARRIE 01-Oct-12	WEST, HANNAH 01-Oct-12	BUTLER, PHILIP 01-Oct-13
ISSITT, BARRY 01-Oct-12	HURMAN, RICHARD 01-Oct-12	CARR, DAVID 01-Oct-13
IVILL, STEPHEN 01-Oct-12	IRVING, PAUL JOHN 01-Oct-12	CLARIDGE, ALEXANDER 01-Oct-13
JONES, HELEN 01-Oct-12	PRIEST, RACHEL 01-Oct-12	COLES, ADAM 01-Oct-13

LIEUTENANT COMMANDERS

COLLIE, JAMES	MCNALLY, NICHOLAS	KNOTT, THOMAS
01-Oct-13	01-Oct-13	01-Oct-13
COLLINS, ANDREW	MCQUEEN, PATRICK	HOPTON, MATTHEW
COX, MATTHEW	MONTGOMERY, HARVIE	RYAN, PAUL JUSTIN
CRAVEN, OLIVER	MORAN, BENJAMIN	COOPER, EDWIN
CRITCHLEY, IAN	MORAN, JOHN-PAUL	WARE, PETER
CROMPTON, LYNNE	MORTON, NEIL	KIERNAN, COLIN
CROSSEY, MATTHEW	MOWAT, ANDREW	BARRON, JEREMY
CROXTON, DAMIEN	MUIR, KATIE M	QUAITE, DAVID
CUMMINGS, DARREN	OFFORD, STEPHEN	STEVENSON, SIMON
DALE, NATHAN	PARNELL, DANIEL	BANE, NICHOLAS
DAVIS, RICHARD	PHILLIPS, MATTHEW	LESLIE, BRUCE
DENNARD, KIERON	PIMM, ANTHONY	TREVETHAN, SEAN
DREWETT, BRIAN	POWELL, GREGORY	MOSS, JONATHAN
EDEN, JEREMY	POWER, BENJAMIN	DOUGAN, DAVID MBA
EDWARDS, SHARON	REES, SIMON G	BRAY, ANDREW
EVANS, BENJIMIN	RENAUD, GAVIN	MCINERNEY, DAVID
FILSHIE, SARAH	REYNOLDS, DARREN	DEAKIN, SCOTT
FLANNAGAN, DONNA	RICHES, JOANNE	SIMPSON, JOHN N
FRITH, ADELE	RIPLEY, STEPHEN	BLACKMORE, ANDREW
GILL, PAUL	ROSE, MARCUS	BYRD, LIAM
GILLIES, BRETT	ROWSON, MARCUS	GRIMLEY, TIMOTHY
GREEN, JONATHAN	SCOTT, RUSSELL	HOLLAND, STEVEN
GRIERSON, ANDREW	SEAL, MICHAEL	RIDGWELL, DANIEL
HALLETT, DANIEL J	SEARLE, ANDREW	SMEDLEY, RACHEL
HAMMOND, CHRISTOPHER	SHARKEY, PHILIP	STREET, SARAH
HASKINS, BENJAMIN	SHAW, MARK	ROBERTSON, ADAM
HAYES, MARK	SHIRVILL, VICTORIA	CASWELL, NEIL
HAYNES, JOHN	SHRESTHA, SHEKHAR	WESTWOOD, MICHELLE
HEWARD, MARK	SLIGHT, OLIVER	STEVENSON, ADAM
HIGGINS, ALEX P	SPACEY, CRAIG	ROFFEY, KEVIN
HOBBS, THOMAS	STEELE, MATTHEW	RALLS, DAMIEN
HOLLINGWORTH, CHRISTOPHER	STORTON, GEORGE	LONGMAN, MATTHEW
HORTON, JAMES R	SWEENEY, RACHEL	SMITH, MATTHEW
HUCKER, OLIVER	TAYLOR, ANDREW	COGHILL, ADRIAN
ISAACS, NATHAN	TAYLOR, JAMES	HUNNIBELL, JOHN R
JAMIESON, PAUL	THOMAS, DUNCAN	CIARAVELLA, TIMOTHY
JOHNSON, TIM	THOMPSON, WILLIAM	THOMAS, ADAM J MBE
JONES, DARREN	THOMSON, JANE	HUGHES, GEOFFREY
JOYCE, DAVID	TRETTON, JOSEPH	ANDREWS, DOMINIC
01 Oct 13		01-Oct 13 (HUGHES)
KINGSTON, EARL	TREVETHAN, CHRISTOPHER	FANSHAWE, EDWARD
LAMB, ROBERT	TURNER, MATTHEW	MORRIS, PAUL
LAWRENSON, TIMOTHY	TWIGG, NEIL R	HOPTON, FIONA
LEE, DAVID	VAUGHAN, EDWARD	BALLANTYNE, CRAIG
LEWIS, JONATHAN	VISRAM, ADRIAN H	BLACKBURN, STUART
LITTLE, MATTHEW	VIVIAN, PHILIP	FILTNESS, DAVID M
LOCKE, NICHOLAS	WALKER, JOHN	JENKINS, DAVID — 25-Jun-13
LONG, VICTORIA S	WARREN, REBECCA	MARTYN, DANIEL — 25-Jun-13
MACKENOW, HELEN	WATERS, MICHAEL	HOPE, KARL — 25-Jun-13
MALONE, ROGER W	WHYTE, GORDON	HANKEY, MARK RD — 25-Jun-13
MASON, DAVID	WILSON, NEIL A	FARMER, GARY RD — 01-Sep-13
MCALLISTER, STEVEN	WINTERTON, PAUL	GRAY, MARTINA E — 26-Feb-13
MCGREAL, BENJAMIN	WRIGHT, JENNIFER	GAMBLE, PHILLIP

All dates 01-Oct-13 unless otherwise noted.

LIEUTENANTS

1992	1993	1994
		PEACHEY, RICHARD 01-Mar-94
		ROBERTS, MARTIN 01-Mar-94
DUNCAN, COLIN J 28-Jun-92	KNIGHT, ALASTAIR 15-May-93	BARCLAY, ALASTAIR 01-Jun-94
PADDOCK, LEE 24-Aug-92	HEDWORTH, ANTHONY 01-Sep-93	

LIEUTENANTS

DILLOWAY, PHILIP 01-Nov-94
JORDAN, EMMA...................................01-Nov-94

1996

DOBBINS, STUART 21-Jun-96
CONNOLLY, MICHAEL...........................07-Dec-96

1997

JOHNSON, ROY 01-May-97
GIBBS, DAVID J.....................................07-Jul-97
HAGGO, JAMIE R...................................20-Oct-97
BUCHAN, SARAH R 12-Nov-97

1998

HARTLEY, JAMES 01-Feb-98
HOWE, CRAIG M...................................16-Apr-98
CARRICK, JAMES P................................01-May-98
REES, ADAM M.....................................01-May-98
CRANE, OLIVER R...................................01-Jul-98
LILLY, DAVID...01-Sep-98
HARFIELD, SARAH J 01-Sep-98
BUTTERWORTH, LESLIE MBE 01-Oct-98
HUME, KENNETH J................................01-Dec-98

1999

WARD, MICHELLE T 01-Jan-99
THOMPSON, DAVID A...........................16-Jan-99
EPPS, MATTHEW 01-Mar-99
BAILEY, SIAN...01-Apr-99
RICHARDS, SIMON T.............................16-Apr-99
WESTON, KARL N N...............................17-Jul-99
LAWRENCE, LINDA J 01-Aug-99
CONCARR, DAVID T...............................01-Aug-99
OSBORNE, JOHN...................................01-Aug-99
CANNELL, GRAHAM M...........................16-Sep-99
CHAMBERS, CHRISTOPHER 19-Sep-99
OLIVER, GRAEME 01-Oct-99
SLOAN, IAN 01-Nov-99
JENKINS, ROBERT.................................01-Dec-99
DERRICK, MATTHEW 01-Dec-99

2000

CREW, JULIAN M 01-Dec-99
WILLIAMS, DANIEL L
MUYAMBO, NOMALANGA
CONSIDINE, KEITH J 01-Jan-00
DICK, COLIN M......................................01-Jan-00
SHEARN, MATTHEW 01-Jan-00
HAMMOND, MEIRION 01-Feb-00
FIRTH, JOHN S......................................01-Apr-00
HOLT, JOHN D......................................01-Apr-00
PAGE, MARK R......................................01-Apr-00
HOLLYFIELD, PETER 01-May-00
PAGET, SIMON 01-May-00
CAMPBELL, TIMOTHY 01-May-00
HUMPHRIES, MARK 01-May-00
HEWITSON, JONATHAN 02-May-00
FARR, IAN...01-Jun-00
ARMSTRONG, COLIN.............................01-Jul-00

LYNAS, JONATHAN 01-Aug-00
RANSOM, BENJAMIN 16-Aug-00
CHANDLER, PHILIP................................01-Sep-00
GALLIMORE, RICHARD 01-Sep-00
WEBSTER, CRAIG...................................01-Sep-00
CROMPTON, PHILIP 01-Sep-00
GRANTHAM, GUY J................................01-Oct-00
ASHBY, MAXINE 05-Oct-00
SUMMERS, ALASTAIR 01-Nov-00
NORTHCOTE, MARK..............................01-Nov-00
STIRLING, ANDREW 01-Dec-00

2001

AITKEN, STEVEN R 01-Dec-00
DIXON, RICHARD A 16-Dec-00
FINN, JAMES S
MORPHET, KATHRYN 01-Jan-01
DALLAMORE, REBECCA 01-Jan-01
KIERSTAN, SIMON..................................01-Jan-01
WARD, EMMA JANE 01-Jan-01
TOPHAM, NEIL E 01-Jan-01
LIGHTFOOT, RICHARD 01-Jan-01
CLAPHAM, GRANTLEY 01-Jan-01
HOLVEY, PAUL J 01-Feb-01
DUCE, MATTHEW 16-Feb-01
FABIK, ANDRE N 01-Apr-01
HALL, KILIAN J D 01-Apr-01
HUMPHRIES, GRAHAM 01-May-01
JACKSON, HOWARD 01-May-01
SPINKS, ROBERT 01-May-01
WICKHAM, ROBERT 01-May-01
WILKINS, DAVID 01-May-01
PICKLES, MARTIN.................................01-May-01
WIELOPOLSKI, MARK 01-May-01
YARHAM, EMMA 01-May-01
MENZIES, BRUCE 01-May-01
PROSSER, MATTHEW 01-May-01
MILLES, OLIVIA KATE 01-May-01
ANDREWS, IAIN 01-Jul-01
BOOTH, DICCON 01-Aug-01
INGHAM, LEE-ANNE 16-Aug-01
JAMESON, ANDREW 01-Sep-01
LEWIS, ANGELA 01-Sep-01
RITCHIE, DOUGLAS B.............................01-Sep-01
FRASER, MICHAEL 01-Sep-01
STEWART, CHARLES 01-Sep-01
WOAD, JONATHAN 01-Sep-01
BENNETT, BRIAN 01-Sep-01
LEWIS, DANIEL......................................01-Sep-01

2002

BLICK, SARAH L 01-Nov-01
BROCK, MATHEW 01-Dec-01
CLARKE, MATTHEW
COOKE, STEPHEN 01-Jan-02
CREEK, STEPHEN..................................01-Jan-02
INGLIS, DAVID J 01-Jan-02
KINGDON, SIMON C 01-Jan-02
LADISLAUS, CECIL J 01-Jan-02
LOUW, LEN 01-Jan-02

MCLACHLAN, ANDREW 01-Jan-02
MOSS, RICHARD M................................01-Jan-02
NASH, ROBIN D C 01-Jan-02
NASH, RUBIN P.....................................01-Jan-02
RALSTON, WILLIAM A.............................01-Jan-02
SUTER, FRANCIS T.................................01-Jan-02
VAN DUIN, MARTIN I A 01-Jan-02
WOOD, JOANNE T.................................01-Jan-02
HOLLIEHEAD, CRAIG..............................01-Jan-02
MORGAN, BENJAMIN 01-Jan-02
WATKINS, JENNY 01-Jan-02
ATWAL, KAMALDIP 01-Jan-02
EATON, DAVID......................................01-Jan-02
RICHARDS, STEVEN...............................01-Jan-02
KELLY, FRANK A ARRC 01-Jan-02
COLLINS, LORNA JANE...........................01-Jan-02
REYNOLDS, HUW 01-Jan-02
WICKETT, RICHARD J.............................01-Feb-02
GAYTANO, RONALD 01-Mar-02
WHITLEY, HELEN 01-Mar-02
CHEAL, ANDREW 01-Mar-02
BARR, DEREK 01-Apr-02
BAXTER, ARRAN C 01-Apr-02
HOLMES, PATRICK 01-Apr-02
LINDEYER, MATTHEW 01-Apr-02
LUCAS, DARREN P 01-May-02
MARSH, STUART D 01-May-02
O'CALLAGHAN, PATRICK 01-May-02
VEAL, DOMINIC J 01-May-02
SPIKE, ADAM JAMES 01-May-02
LOCK, WILLIAM 01-May-02
COYLE, ROSS D 01-May-02
CAREY, TREVOR....................................01-May-02
ROUND, MATTHEW J 01-May-02
FULTON, DAVID M 01-May-02
TAYLOR, ROBERT 01-May-02
SENNETT, MICHAEL..............................01-May-02
CROSS, NICHOLAS.................................01-May-02
DOMINY, VICTORIA L.............................01-May-02
RAMSAY, ALASTAIR 01-May-02
SCOTT, ELIZABETH K 01-Jul-02
SWIRE, BARRY JOHN.............................01-Jul-02
CHANG, HON W....................................01-Jul-02
VOKE, CHRISTEN A 01-Jul-02
WALKER, NICHOLAS 26-Jul-02
BULLOCK, JAMES 01-Aug-02
TAIT, MARTYN D 01-Aug-02
CALLIS, GREGORY J...............................01-Aug-02
GORMAN, DARREN A.............................01-Aug-02
KEENAN, BENJAMIN 27-Aug-02
LLOYD, MATTHEW R.............................01-Sep-02
NEWALL, PAUL JOHN 01-Sep-02
OWEN, DOUGLAS P C 01-Sep-02
SHROPSHALL, HELEN L..........................01-Sep-02
EVANS, LAURA-JANE 01-Sep-02
WESTWOOD, ANDREW 01-Sep-02
MALCOLM, PAUL..................................01-Sep-02
DAVIS, PETER.......................................01-Sep-02
KING, IAIN A...01-Sep-02
WOODLEY, STEPHEN 01-Sep-02
NGUYO, DAVID 01-Sep-02

LIEUTENANTS

HARRISON, IAN.................................01-Sep-02
HUDSON, ANDREW 01-Sep-02
LUPINI, JAMES 01-Sep-02
WILLIAMSON, PETER 01-Oct-02
INNESS, MATTHEW 01-Oct-02
AYRTON, ROBERT 01-Oct-02
SHEPHERD, ANYA 01-Oct-02

2003

BICKLEY, GARY N 01-Dec-02
CUNNINGHAM, RACHEL 01-Dec-02
FLOYD, ROBERT E
HARRISON-JONES, STUART................01-Jan-03
HUNT, RACHEL 01-Jan-03
JONES, EMMANUEL...........................01-Jan-03
LIGALE, EUGENE................................01-Jan-03
MACPHERSON, CRAIG.......................01-Jan-03
NOTLEY, EDWARD 01-Jan-03
O'NEILL, HENRY 01-Jan-03
WALKER, JAMIE 01-Jan-03
WORLEY, THOMAS F...........................01-Jan-03
EVANS, CHRISTIAN 01-Jan-03
COPPIN, NIGEL 01-Jan-03
CONRAN, NICHOLAS.........................01-Jan-03
BEVERLEY, ANDREW 01-Jan-03
FRASER, JAMES 01-Jan-03
ROBERTS, STEPHEN...........................01-Jan-03
MARTYN, JULIE..................................01-Feb-03
DILLON, BEN 01-Feb-03
GREY, AMY.......................................01-Feb-03
HACKLAND, ANDREW 01-Mar-03
MEACHER, PAUL................................01-Apr-03
STEPHENSON, CHRISTOPHER 01-Apr-03
PARKER, JONATHAN...........................01-Apr-03
CAMPBELL-BALDWIN, JAMES 01-Apr-03
CRAIG, MICHAEL 01-Apr-03
EMERY, CHRISTIAN 01-Apr-03
EVANS, CHRISTOPHER 01 May-03
JONES, STEPHEN 01-May-03
MITCHELL, PAUL J..............................01-May-03
MITTINS, SIMON 01-May-03
SMITH, DAVID J 01-May-03
THOMPSON, SARAH 01-May-03
WILLS, ROBERT H 01-May-03
HILL, THOMAS..................................01-May-03
KEANE, BRENDAN 01-May-03
WHITE, PAUL DONALD.......................01-May-03
KERLEY, BENJAMIN 01-May-03
COURTNEY, TIMOTHY.........................01-May-03
CHUDLEY, IAN 01-May-03
VAUGHAN, JAMES 01-May-03
ANDERSON, KEVIN 01-May-03
LOVE, JOHN J....................................01-May-03
ROY, CHRISTOPHER 01-Jun-03
FULLER, RICHARD 01-Jun-03
MURPHY, CAROLINE..........................04-Jun-03
BOWERS, MARK 16-Jun-03
BURLINGHAM, ALEXANDER 01-Jul-03
BARBER, MARK..................................01-Jul-03
CADDICK, ANDREW 01-Aug-03
CARNEW, SEAN.................................01-Aug-03

CASSIDY, STUART..............................01-Sep-03
CUMMING, FRAZER 01-Sep-03
EARLE-PAYNE, GARETH 01-Sep-03
GILMORE, JEREMY.............................01-Sep-03
HUNT, BEN.......................................01-Sep-03
MARJORIBANKS, CHARLOTTE.............01-Sep-03
PETERSON, KEITH..............................01-Sep-03
PLENTY, ANDREW 01-Sep-03
ROYSTON, JAMES...............................01-Sep-03
SHARROTT, CHRISTOPHER 01-Sep-03
SHEARS, GARY R 01-Sep-03
STUBBS, BENJAMIN 01-Sep-03
WORKMAN, RAYNER 01-Sep-03
JONES, GORDON 01-Sep-03
PETCH, ALAN 01-Sep-03
SHROPSHALL, IAN..............................01-Sep-03
DYMOND, JUSTIN 01-Sep-03
PUGH, GEOFFREY 01-Sep-03
THOMPSON, SARAH K.........................01-Sep-03
SELDEN, JOHN D................................01-Sep-03
REEVE, JENNIFER A.............................01-Oct-03
ABBOTT, KATHERINE 01-Nov-03
HETHERINGTON, THOMAS 01-Nov-03
REYNOLDS, ZOE A 28-Nov-03

2004

BARRETT, SCOTT................................01-Dec-03
BOUD, COLIN S 01-Dec-03
BRAZENALL, BENJAMIN
CLARK, PAUL ANTHONY......................01-Jan-04
DIXON, MARK E.................................01-Jan-04
GIBSON, ADRIAN 01-Jan-04
GRIFFITHS, GARETH 01-Jan-04
GRIFFITHS, NIGEL M...........................01-Jan-04
HARVEY, PAUL G 01-Jan-04
INGAMELLS, STEPHEN 01-Jan-04
LEE, RAYMOND 01 Jan-04
MCMAHON, DANIEL..........................01-Jan-04
RICHARDS, GUY B 01-Jan-04
SAY, RUSSELL G 01-Jan-04
SCARLETT, CHRISTOPHER 01-Jan-04
SHORTLAND, KAREN..........................01-Jan-04
SYSON, CARL....................................01-Jan-04
THOMPSON, ALASTAIR 01-Jan-04
THORLEY, GRAHAM...........................01-Jan-04
TORBET, LINDA.................................01-Jan-04
TUMILTY, KEVIN 01-Jan-04
WALKER, DANIEL...............................01-Jan-04
WALKER, JAMES J 01-Jan-04
WALKER, MARTIN..............................01-Jan-04
WILSON, SIMON 01-Jan-04
CRIPPS, NICOLA................................01-Jan-04
DEVLIN, CRAIG.................................01-Jan-04
HOUNSOME, JONATHAN....................01-Jan-04
SIMPSON, CHRISTOPHER 01-Jan-04
SEDGWICK, HUGO 01-Jan-04
WEBSTER, ANDREW J 01-Jan-04
HUGHES, THOMAS W..........................01-Jan-04
LOADMAN, DOUGAL R........................01-Jan-04
BLACK, CHARLOTTE 01-Jan-04
FLETCHER, RICHARD..........................01-Jan-04

CLAXTON, ANDREW 01-Mar-04
TREGALE, JAMIE 01-Mar-04
HILL, CHRISTOPHER 31-Mar-04
BENBOW, JAMES 01-Apr-04
BLIGH, SARAH L................................01-Apr-04
CAMPBELL, ALASTAIR 01-Apr-04
COLLINS, MARK.................................01-May-04
COLVIN, MICHAEL 01-May-04
COOLEY, JEANNINE............................01-May-04
CUTHBERT, GLEN...............................01-May-04
CUTLER, DAVID T...............................01-May-04
DALGLEISH, GRANT A.........................01-May-04
GREENHILL, MATTHEW 01-May-04
HUDSON, TOM A J 01-May-04
ISHERWOOD, CARL 01-May-04
JARDINE, IAIN...................................01-May-04
JEWSON, BENJAMIN 01-May-04
JOHNSTON, ANDREW I 01-May-04
LEAKER, DANIEL THOMAS 01-May-04
LOWE, GAVIN J..................................01-May-04
MASKELL, BERNARD M........................01-May-04
MASON, RICHARD J............................01-May-04
MCPHAIL, THOMAS C 01-May-04
SCOTT, ALEXANDER J 01-May-04
STANISTREET, GEORGINA 01-May-04
STEWART, NICHOLAS J........................01-May-04
THOMPSON, JAMES............................01-May-04
WARREN, MATTHEW J 01-May-04
WOOD, MICHAEL WILLIAM 01-May-04
WILSON, DAVID J...............................01-May-04
WHITE, ROSS ELLIOTT 01-May-04
BLADEN, CHRISTOPHER 01-May-04
THOMAS, JOSEPH..............................01-May-04
MURRAY, WILLIAM 01-May-04
BELL, NICHOLAS A.............................01-May-04
GOOSEN, RICHARD 01-May-04
ROBINSON, MATTHEW S......................01-May-04
WHITE, ALISTAIR J 01-May-04
BROSTER, LEE J 01-May-04
COWLISHAW, NICHOLAS 01-May-04
FLITCROFT, MICHAEL.........................01-May-04
FROST, LAURENCE J 01-Jul-04
JAMES, ROBERT 01-Jul-04
MARTIN, GRAHAM 01-Jul-04
MUNRO, MICHAEL 01-Jul-04
PEAKE, STEPHEN P 01-Jul-04
STANCLIFFE, ANDREW 01-Jul-04
THWAITES, LINDSEY 01-Jul-04
TIBBALLS, LAURA R............................01-Jul-04
WILLIAMS, LEE J 01-Jul-04
YOUNG, DAVID A 01-Jul-04
WOTTON, ALAN 01-Jul-04
JONES, MARK 01-Jul-04
WALKER, RICHARD PAUL 01-Jul-04
AINSWORTH, ALAN 01-Jul-04
PACKER, ROBERT 01-Jul-04
HARDY-HODGSON, DAVID 01-Jul-04
CHEEMA, SUKHDEV 01-Jul-04
BARRETT, BENJAMIN 01-Jul-04
GRAY, SAMUEL D...............................01-Jul-04
RAY, LOUISE B...................................01-Jul-04

LIEUTENANTS

FILTNESS, REBECCA................01-Aug-04	LANG, LESLEY A 01-Jan-05	GOBEY, RICHARD 03-May-05
WRIGHT, HELEN J................01-Aug-04	LITTLE, NICOLA S 01-Jan-05	CURSITER, JOHN D................01-Jun-05
WRIGHT, NEIL DAVID MBE 01-Aug-04	MATTOCK, NICHOLAS 01-Jan-05	HIGGINS, ANDREW J................01-Jun-05
ATTWOOD, KEITH 01-Aug-04	MCCORMICK, EMMA J................01-Jan-05	KANTHARIA, PAUL................04-Jun-05
BLACKBURN, CRAIG 13-Aug-04	MCDONALD, MORGAN J................01-Jan-05	HARRISON, ANTHONY................12-Jun-05
BRANNIGHAN, IAN 13-Aug-04	MIFFLIN, MICHELLE J................01-Jan-05	BORRETT, JOHN E................13-Jun-05
DARLINGTON, ALAN................01-Sep-04	NEWBY, CHRISTOPHER 01-Jan-05	CHISHOLM, PHILIP J H................25-Jun-05
DART, DUNCAN J................01-Sep-04	NORRISS, MARK W................01-Jan-05	HAY, RICHARD H I................25-Jun-05
EASTERBROOK, CHRISTOPHER................01-Sep-04	ROSS, PAUL W 01-Jan-05	JANE, SAMUEL C 01-Jul-05
ELLIOTT, TIMOTHY 01-Sep-04	TELFORD, JONATHAN................01-Jan-05	O'CONNOR, LUCY................01-Jul-05
FLEMING, DAVID P................01-Sep-04	HAMPSON, ALEXANDER 01-Jan-05	STEPHENS, PATRICK G 01-Jul-05
FOOKS-BALE, MATTHEW 01-Sep-04	TRETTON, CAROLINE 01-Jan-05	WILCOCKS, DAVID N................01-Jul-05
KEMP, RICHARD L 01-Sep-04	NIGHTINGALE, SAMUEL................01-Jan-05	WILLSMORE, STUART A 01-Jul-05
KNOWLES, DAVID................01-Sep-04	POPE, KEVIN DAVID 01-Jan-05	WORDSWORTH, JONATHAN 01-Jul-05
MCGIVERN, RYAN P................01-Sep-04	HAWKINS, EMMA LOUISE................01-Jan-05	MAHONEY, ANDREW................01-Jul-05
MCLAUGHLIN, VINCENT................01-Sep-04	ARMAND-SMITH, PENELOPE 01-Jan-05	SHAW, STEWART 01-Jul-05
MEIGH, PETER D 01-Sep-04	SHERWIN, ANTONY 01-Jan-05	HAIRSINE, WILLIAM 01-Jul-05
MORGAN, GARETH L................01-Sep-04	PEARSON, ALAN 01-Jan-05	TWIGG, KELLY A 01-Jul-05
NEYLAND, DAVID A................01-Sep-04	OWENS, JOHN 01-Jan-05	DODDS, STEPHEN 01-Jul-05
PEARSON, IAN T................01-Sep-04	HOULSTON, IAN J 01-Jan-05	MCQUAID, IVOR THOMAS................01-Jul-05
RICHARDSON, JOHN F 01-Sep-04	CAPPS, JAMES A................01-Jan-05	ARMOUR, ANGELA B................01-Aug-05
SAMWELL, MICHAEL G................01-Sep-04	SUTCLIFFE, PAUL................01-Jan-05	BROWN, MICHAEL A 12-Aug-05
SHAKESPEARE, CHRISTOPHER................01-Sep-04	DUFFIN, LEE-ANNE 01-Jan-05	CLARK, PHILIP J................12-Aug-05
STRAWBRIDGE, CHANTAL................01-Sep-04	COUGHLIN, EMMA J................01-Jan-05	CROMBIE, STUART................01-Sep-05
STUART, SIMON A................01-Sep-04	GARNER, MICHAEL E 01-Jan-05	DALLAS, LEWIS I 01-Sep-05
SWIFT, ROBERT 01-Sep-04	MULROY, PAUL J 01-Jan-05	DUKE, ADAM J 01-Sep-05
TROSH, NICHOLAS................01-Sep-04	SCALES, DEAN R................18-Jan-05	HAYNES, FIONA J................01-Sep-05
TUCKER, PHILIP J................01-Sep-04	TAYLOR, ANDREW 01-Feb-05	JENKINS, THOMAS R................01-Sep-05
UGLOW, NATALIE................01-Sep-04	CARTER, CHRISTOPHER 18-Feb-05	KING, IAN J................01-Sep-05
WILLIAMS, ANTHONY................01-Sep-04	PERRY, CARL S L 18-Feb-05	MCBETH, GARY................01-Sep-05
GAUNT, AMY................01-Sep-04	WARDLEY, THOMAS E 18-Feb-05	MCCAVOUR, BRYAN 01-Sep-05
WOOD, RICHARD R T 01-Sep-04	BESSANT, MATTHEW 18-Feb-05	MELLOR, DANIEL 01-Sep-05
TAYLOR, JAMES E 01-Sep-04	HEATON, ROXANE M................01-Mar-05	PEARCE, SARAH L................01-Sep-05
PREECE, SIMON E 01-Sep-04	STILL, PETER A 01-Mar-05	POOLE, DANIEL C 01-Sep-05
DAVIS, PETER HENRY 01-Sep-04	THACKRAY, PENELOPE................01-Apr-05	RUDKIN, ADAM L................01-Sep-05
BIRD, ANDREW................01-Sep-04	HALE, STUART D................01-Apr-05	TABORDA, MATTHEW A 01-Sep-05
HODGKINSON, SAMUEL 01-Sep-04	WILLIAMS, LUKE 01-Apr-05	TUHEY, JAMES 01-Sep-05
FOWLE, LAURA................01-Sep-04	ANGLISS, ROGER J................01-Apr-05	BOULTON, DAVID 01-Sep-05
ORTON, TREVOR................01-Sep-04	EVANS, ROBERT G 01-Apr-05	DAVIDSON, SERENA 01-Sep-05
WILLIAMSON, SIMON 01-Sep-04	ROONEY, THOMAS M................01-Apr-05	WHITEHOUSE, ANDREW 01-Sep-05
SHEEHAN, THOMAS 01-Sep-04	STEPHENSON, RICHARD 08-Apr-05	OLDFIELD, CHRISTIAN 01-Sep-05
PARKER, ANTHONY R 01-Oct-04	TRIGWELL, SIMON P 08-Apr-05	COCHRANE, CHRISTOPHER 01-Sep-05
MCCULLOUGH, KAREN 01-Oct-04	PARKIN, BRETT ASHLEY................08-Apr-05	JOHNSON, HELEN 01-Sep-05
HALE, AMANDA 01-Oct-04	HERZBERG, MARK J................08-Apr-05	HOUGHAM, THOMAS 01-Sep-05
DUFFY, JAMES 29-Oct-04	BLATCHFORD, TIMOTHY................08-Apr-05	WATSON, SIMON 01-Sep-05
WILTON, MARK................01-Nov-04	HADLEY, CLIVE M 08-Apr-05	DIXON, ROBERT 01-Sep-05
CARMAN, FELIX................01-Nov-04	HEWITT, NIGEL W 08-Apr-05	SMITH, MATTHEW 01-Sep-05
HOPWOOD, ADRIAN P................01-Dec-04	MADEN, STEVEN G 08-Apr-05	COUGHLIN, PETER 01-Sep-05
	HYNDE, CLAIRE LOUISE 08-Apr-05	MEDLICOTT, NICHOLAS 01-Sep-05
2005	BETCHLEY, JAMES W................08-Apr-05	ABEL, JAMES 01-Oct-05
	BLAKE, MATTHEW G 08-Apr-05	FARRANT, SAM 01-Oct-05
ATTWATER, RICHARD 17-Dec-04	FROST, TIMOTHY S................22-Apr-05	HAYWOOD, ANDREW J 28-Oct-05
BARBER, ALEXANDER	LECKEY, ELIZABETH H 01-May-05	HEWLETT, PHILIP J E 01-Nov-05
BOULTON, GRAHAM R	MALSTER, DUDLEY A................01-May-05	LIPCZYNSKI, BENJAMIN 01-Nov-05
BULGIN, MARTIN R 01-Jan-05	MCCREA, MARK J 01-May-05	POLLOCK, BARNABY 01-Nov-05
CURD, MICHAEL 01-Jan-05	TALBOT, SIMON J 01-May-05	SHARPLES, JOSEPH H 01-Nov-05
DIXON, SIMON J 01-Jan-05	TASKER, ADAM M 01-May-05	STEELE, MARIE L 01-Nov-05
GILBERT, RACHEL................01-Jan-05	GREENWOOD, STEPHEN 01-May-05	SUTCLIFF, JONATHAN 01-Nov-05
GREGORY, JONATHAN 01-Jan-05	NICOLSON, VERNON................01-May-05	TEASDALE, JAMES 01-Nov-05
HOOPER, THOMAS 01-Jan-05	BOWMAN, SIMON K J 01-May-05	COLEMAN, JAMES................01-Nov-05
LAIDLAW, JONATHAN 01-Jan-05	RILEY, RALPH A 01-May-05	WRIGHT, GABRIEL................01-Nov-05
LANG, ALASDAIR J................01-Jan-05		

LIEUTENANTS

TETCHNER, DAVID	01-Nov-05
TAYLOR, NICHOLAS	01-Nov-05
IVORY, THOMAS	01-Nov-05
SHAW, SIMON JAMES	01-Nov-05
PEACOCK, ANOUCHKA	01-Nov-05
HORTON, SIMON	01-Nov-05
BOTHAM, ADRIAN M	01-Nov-05
FOWLER, CHRISTOPHER	01-Dec-05

2006

ALEXANDER, WILLIAM	16-Dec-05
BIRD, MICHAEL	16-Dec-05
BURTON, JAMES	
DORMAN, THOMAS	01-Jan-06
DRINKALL, KATHRYN	01-Jan-06
ELLISON, PETER	01-Jan-06
LETTINGTON, PAUL	01-Jan-06
MARTIN, JAMES N	01-Jan-06
ORMSHAW, MARTIN A	01-Jan-06
PATRICK, JOHN A	01-Jan-06
SHAW, CALLAM RODERICK	01-Jan-06
SOUTHWORTH, CHRISTOPHER	01-Jan-06
STEPHENS, SAMUEL J R	01-Jan-06
PALLETT, TONY	01-Jan-06
PHILIPS, THOMAS	01-Jan-06
HOOPER, WILLIAM	01-Jan-06
KNIGHT, JONATHAN	01-Jan-06
BARNICOAT, KAREN	01-Jan-06
TURNER, DUNCAN	01-Jan-06
PATERSON, JAMES	01-Jan-06
BELL, LEWIS G	01-Jan-06
FREEMAN, EDMUND	01-Jan-06
LANGFORD, JOANNA	01-Jan-06
MUIR, ANDREW	01-Feb-06
ROYCE, RODERICK	01-Feb-06
RUSHTON, EMMA VICTORIA	01-Feb-06
STARKEY, DAVID S	01-Feb-06
VETI, MARK A GCGI	01-Feb-06
WALKER, MARK J	01-Feb-06
YEMM, MATTHEW A	01-Feb-06
SMITH, CRAIG ADAM	01-Feb-06
BAUGH, ADRIAN	01-Feb-06
HANNIGAN, JASON D	01-Feb-06
HOWARTH, MICHAEL	01-Feb-06
BEBBINGTON, DAVID MARK	01-Feb-06
ATKINSON, JAMES	17-Feb-06
DEWEY, SARAH E	17-Feb-06
KOHEEALLEE, MOHUMMED	17-Feb-06
MILNER, LISA D	26-Feb-06
STAMPER, VALERIE LOUISE	01-Mar-06
SIMPSON, ERIN L	01-Mar-06
KAY, VICTORIA JOANNE	01-Mar-06
LONDON, HEIDI C	01-Mar-06
PARROTT, STUART S	15-Mar-06
SEAL, MARTIN R	15-Mar-06
SEDDON, JONATHAN	01-Apr-06
VEREKER, RICHARD	01-Apr-06
BOND, ROBERT	01-Apr-06
VALVONA, DOMINIC M MBE	01-Apr-06
CHISHOLM, DAVID C	01-Apr-06
JONES, CHRISTOPHER D	01-Apr-06

PARKINSON, NICHOLAS	06-Apr-06
PEACHEY, NEIL D	07-Apr-06
WOOD, JULIAN T	07-Apr-06
STEVENS, MARK J	07-Apr-06
GODWIN, LEE	07-Apr-06
JAFFREY, HEATHER	07-Apr-06
MACINDOE, NEIL	07-Apr-06
HILTON, MICHAEL	07-Apr-06
BELL, RICHARD J	11-Apr-06
BILSON, GAVIN	23-Apr-06
CACKETT, THOMAS E R	23-Apr-06
CARVER, CHARLES A	01-Sep-06
CHISHOLM, DAVID T	01-Sep-06
ELLICOTT, MATTHEW J	01-Sep-06
EVERED, JONATHAN F	01-Sep-06
HAMBLIN, PAUL A	01-Sep-06
KEANE, JOSEPH P	01-Sep-06
PARISER, ANDREW M	01-Sep-06
PIPER, BENJAMIN J	01-Sep-06
RAWLINSON, KATHRYN	01-Sep-06
SKINNER, JONATHAN J	01-Sep-06
THOMAS, MARK P	01-Sep-06
WRIGHT, JAMES N	01-Sep-06
CARLTON, PAUL DAVID	01-Sep-06
BURGOYNE, WILLIAM	01-Sep-06
BAKER, JAMES	01-Sep-06
HARPER, KEVAN	01-Sep-06
SCOTT, SERENA	01-Sep-06
MILLER, ALEXANDER	01-Sep-06
POLLITT, ALEXANDER	01-Sep-06
TYACKE, RICHARD	01-Sep-06
MANNING, DAVID	01-Sep-06
SMITH, KARLY JANE	01-Sep-06
BIRD, TIMOTHY M	01-Sep-06
FEASEY, CAROLINE	08-May-06
LORENZ, RUDI	15-May-06
QUICK, BENJAMIN P	01-Jun-06
TAYLOR, SCOTT A	01-Jun-06
WELLINGTON, LAURA	01-Jun-06
MOORE, JONATHAN	01-Jun-06
ASKHAM, MATHEW	01-Jun-06
PLUMER, STEPHEN J	01-Jun-06
COOGAN, THOMAS	01-Jun-06
STEWART, SEAN T	01-Jun-06
TONGE, MICHAEL	08-Jun-06
TUSTAIN, PAUL A	09-Jun-06
EMBLETON, ALISON	09-Jun-06
GOWERS, SARAH MBE	09-Jun-06
COCKCROFT, KIM M	09-Jun-06
O'DOOLEY, PAUL	09-Jun-06
PRESTON, JACQUELINE	09-Jun-06
BRETTEN, NICHOLAS J	16-Jun-06
ROLLS, EDWARD C	30-Jun-06
PARRY, STEPHEN	30-Jun-06
CAMPLISSON, OWEN	01-Jul-06
YOUNGMAN, MITCHELL	01-Jul-06
BROWN, SIMON J	01-Jul-06
MITCHELL, SCOTT C	01-Jul-06
ROSS, STEVEN	27-Jul-06
YOUNG, ANDREW J	28-Jul-06
PATTON, STEPHEN	28-Jul-06

TIPPING, ANTHONY	28-Jul-06
HISLOP, SCOTT GRAHAM	28-Jul-06
GAINES, EDWIN JOHN	28-Jul-06
HEWITT, CLARA J	28-Jul-06
PARKIN, MATTHEW	28-Jul-06
PROUDMAN, MICHAEL	28-Jul-06
SCOTT, VICTORIA	01-Aug-06
BENTLEY, GRANT	01-Aug-06
BARNETT, CAILA	01-Aug-06
BECKER, THOMAS O	01-Aug-06
BETTS, PETER R	01-Aug-06
COATALEN-HODGSON, RYAN	01-Sep-06
DALGLISH, KENNETH M	01-Sep-06
DAVIES, HAZEL	01-Sep-06
DAVIES, JAMES	01-Sep-06
DYER, SHANI D	01-Sep-06
ERRINGTON, RIDLEY J B	01-Sep-06
EVANS, THOMAS W	01-Sep-06
FLANNIGAN, AIDEN	01-Sep-06
FLATT, LIAM B	01-Sep-06
FLETCHER, ANDREW S	01-Sep-06
FOWLER, REMINGTON	01-Sep-06
FREDRICKSON, CHARLOTTE	01-Sep-06
HARRIS, ROBERT	01-Sep-06
HEYWOOD, ROBERT H	01-Sep-06
HITCHINGS, MICHAEL J	01-Sep-06
KENDALL-TORRY, GUYAN	01-Sep-06
KING, MICHAEL A	01-Sep-06
LISTER, MATTHEW	01-Sep-06
MAGZOUB, MOHAYED	01-Sep-06
MARTIN, DAVID L	01-Sep-06
MOSS-WARD, EDWARD	01-Sep-06
MUNNS, EDWARD N	01-Sep-06
NOKES, OLIVER	01-Sep-06
PHILIPSON, MATTHEW	01-Sep-06
PLUNKETT, GARETH N	01-Sep-06
RAINE, SARAH L	01-Sep-06
ROOKE, ADAM E	01-Sep-06
ROUTLEDGE, RICKY J	01-Sep-06
RYAN, STEPHEN J	01-Sep-06
SLAYMAN, EMILY	01-Sep-06
THOMAS, ANDREW G	01-Sep-06
WESTBROOK, KEVIN	01-Sep-06
WILSON, CHARLES K	01-Sep-06
WILCOX, CHRISTOPHER	01-Sep-06
VOWLES, IAIN ROBERT	01-Sep-06
STAFFORD-SHAW, DAMIAN	01-Sep-06
JONES, CHERYL	01-Sep-06
MARLOR, KIRSTY	01-Sep-06
BARHAM, EDWARD	01-Sep-06
HOWE, JONATHAN	01-Sep-06
GUILD, IAN	01-Sep-06
CHURCH, SIMON	01-Sep-06
BINNS, JAMES	01-Sep-06
GREAVES, TIMOTHY GCGI	01-Sep-06
WESTLEY, ALEXANDER	01-Sep-06
THOMPSON, GEORGE	01-Sep-06
BETTS, ANDREW	01-Sep-06
POPE, MICHELLE LOUISE	01-Sep-06
PARKER, BERRON	01-Sep-06
DALTON, SALLY ANNE	01-Sep-06

LIEUTENANTS

KEEGAN, AMANDA	PILKINGTON, BARRY M 29-Jan-07	POTTER, IAN 01-Jun-07
BEECHING, LEE G 01-Oct-06	SCOTT, PETER D 01-Feb-07	MCALPINE, MARTIN 08-Jun-07
CLARKE, RICHARD A 01-Oct-06	SHAW, HANNAH K 01-Feb-07	WILSON, MARK John 08-Jun-07
GEE, MATHEW 01-Oct-06	SKINNER, AMY L 01-Feb-07	PEARSON, ANDREW 08-Jun-07
GRAHAM, JAMES P 20-Oct-06	TAYLOR, NEIL R 01-Feb-07	COLEMAN, ALEXANDER 08-Jun-07
MOORE, ALISON L 20-Oct-06	WILLIAMS, JAMES 01-Feb-07	MAGILL, ALASDAIR 08-Jun-07
QUANT, JACQUELINE 20-Oct-06	DEVINE, ALISON 01-Feb-07	LEONARD, THOMAS 08-Jun-07
WAREHAM, SIDNEY J 20-Oct-06	HEATON, SEAN 01-Feb-07	HARRISON, LAURA 01-Jul-07
EVERARD, PAUL JULIAN 20-Oct-06	ROBERTS, ANDREW 01-Feb-07	BLACKBOURN, STEPHEN A 01-Jul-07
CODLING, STEVEN 20-Oct-06	WILLIAMS, RUSSELL G 12-Feb-07	BONNER, DANIEL 01-Jul-07
PEARSON, LIAM 20-Oct-06	PYKE, HAZEL JOSIE 16-Feb-07	DAVIS, MARK S MSc 20-Jul-07
RICHARDS, NIGEL 20-Oct-06	PARKER, LAURA MARIE 16-Feb-07	HARWOOD, CARL D 27-Jul-07
ADAM, MURRAY W 20-Oct-06	PATERSON, MATTHEW 16-Feb-07	HUTTON, PAUL R MSc 27-Jul-07
AYERS, OLIVER R B 20-Oct-06	MORRISON, RICHARD 01-Mar-07	LIGHTFOOT, IAIN M 27-Jul-07
COLLINS, CHARLES A 20-Oct-06	WEBSTER, MARK 01-Mar-07	PIKE, STUART 27-Jul-07
FLEGG, WILLIAM 01-Nov-06	DALE, JAMIE 09-Mar-07	HOLROYD, JASON 27-Jul-07
FLETCHER, JONATHAN 01-Nov-06	STANT, MARK SIMON 01-Apr-07	STOCKTON, BARRY 27-Jul-07
HOLBURT, RICHARD M 01-Nov-06	STRICKLAND, TIMOTHY 01-Apr-07	JENKINS, DAVID 27-Jul-07
ROBERTS, DAVID 01-Nov-06	GODDARD, ALEXANDER C 01-Apr-07	KEW, NIGEL 27-Jul-07
BRADY, MATTHEW 01-Nov-06	HERNON, ROBERT T B 01-Apr-07	JONES, ROBERT T 27-Jul-07
ROSE, MARK NIGEL 01-Nov-06	LESLIE, DAREN J 01-Apr-07	DURBIN, PHILIP JOHN 27-Jul-07
	ROWBOTHAM, MARK 06-Apr-07	KIDD, ANDREW N 27-Jul-07
2007	STEVENSON, ALEXANDER 06-Apr-07	BARNES, PAUL F 31-Jul-07
BAKEWELL, EMMA C 01-Nov-06	LIVINGSTONE, COLIN 06-Apr-07	ANDREWS, RICK 01-Aug-07
CHESHIRE, THOMAS 30-Nov-06	ROWE, ANTONY 06-Apr-07	BARKER, HELEN A 01-Aug-07
FITZGIBBON, JOHN P	BENTON, WILLIAM 06-Apr-07	BARTLETT, MARIE-CLAIRE 14-Aug-07
GILLINGHAM, GEORGE 01-Jan-07	ANDERSON, DAVID 06-Apr-07	BOWMAN, DEAN E 01-Sep-07
GUY, FRANCES L 01-Jan-07	MATHER, CHRISTOPHER 06-Apr-07	BRYDEN, DAVID 01-Sep-07
HENDERSON, ANDREW 01-Jan-07	HUMPHREY, DARREN P 06-Apr-07	CAMPBELL, JONATHAN 01-Sep-07
HUSBAND, JAMES 01-Jan-07	BECK, ANDREW 06-Apr-07	CLARKE, JAMES P 01-Sep-07
JONES, MARC 01-Jan-07	ERHAHIEMEN, PETER 06-Apr-07	DE SILVA, OLIVER A 01-Sep-07
LATCHEM, ANDREW 01-Jan-07	EVANS, PETER A 08-Apr-07	GRAHAM, BENJAMIN R 01-Sep-07
MACRAE, KIRK 01-Jan-07	EVEREST, BECKY 01-May-07	GRIFFITHS, FRANCIS M 01-Sep-07
MCALLISTER, ANDREW 01-Jan-07	GATENBY, DANIEL 01-May-07	GUY, ELIZABETH 01-Sep-07
MEHTA, JENNIFER 01-Jan-07	HOLLOWAY, BENJAMIN S V 01-May-07	HOWARD, MARTIN J 01-Sep-07
MONTAGU, TIMOTHY 01-Jan-07	KEENAN, DOUGLAS 01-May-07	ISTED, LEE R 01-Sep-07
PATTERSON, PASCAL X 01-Jan-07	LEES, CLAIRE MARIE 01-May-07	LAIRD, IAIN A 01-Sep-07
PEARSON, SARAH I 01-Jan-07	MARTIN, BEN R 01-May-07	LATHAM, DANIEL G 01-Sep-07
POWELL, PHILIP JAMES 01-Jan-07	MURRAY, JAMIE C 01-May-07	LEWIS, ROBERT G 01-Sep-07
ROYSTON, SARAH L 01-Jan-07	PEACOCK, LAURA 01-May-07	RICHARDS, ROBERT 01-Sep-07
SMITH, JENNIFER C 01-Jan-07	SALT, JENNIFER M 01-May-07	RUTTER, JOHN 01-Sep-07
VINCENT, STUART 01-Jan-07	SKINNER, NEIL D 01-May-07	SHAVES, THOMAS D L 01-Sep-07
WASKETT, DANIEL 01-Jan-07	TUDOR, OWEN J 01-May-07	SHIRVILL, MATTHEW 01-Sep-07
FELLOWS, CHRISTOPHER 01-Jan-07	VINCENT, CHRISTOPHER 01-May-07	STEPHEN, CAMERON E 01-Sep-07
CHATTERLEY-EVANS, DAWN 01-Jan-07	ZITKUS, JOHN JAMES 01-May-07	WALKER, GRAEME H 01-Sep-07
PERCIVAL, VICTORIA 01-Jan-07	CARTER, ANDREW 01-May-07	WALLACE, KIRSTY E 01-Sep-07
KELLEY, ALEXANDRA LOUISE 01-Jan-07	ANDERSON, MICHAEL 01-May-07	WILLIAMS-ALLDEN, LUCY 01-Sep-07
ROSE, SIMON P 01-Jan-07	AITKEN, NEIL Donald 01-May-07	WYLIE, JUSTIN J 01-Sep-07
MULLIS, GEOFFREY 01-Jan-07	LANGFORD, TIMOTHY 01-May-07	YATES, SIMON P 01-Sep-07
MORROW, OLIVER 01-Jan-07	BLENKINSOP, GRAHAM J 01-May-07	DUNN, GILES 01-Sep-07
CURNOCK, TIMOTHY 01-Jan-07	BERRY, DAVID H 01-May-07	DRENNAN, DAVID 01-Sep-07
BARKER, PETER ROY 01-Jan-07	HUTCHINSON, GILLIAN P 01-May-07	PELLECCHIA, DANIEL 01-Sep-07
ALLEN, ALEXANDER PAUL 01-Jan-07	JOHNSON, MATTHEW D 02-May-07	DORE, CHRISTOPHER 01-Sep-07
INGLIS, WILLIAM SINCLAIR 01-Jan-07	KELLY, PATRICK J 01-Jun-07	THOMAS, KATIE 01-Sep-07
STACKHOUSE, MARTYN 01-Jan-07	MACLEOD, ALASTAIR M 01-Jun-07	ROGERS, PHILLIP 01-Sep-07
LEES, ADRIAN 01-Jan-07	ROWNTREE, PAUL J 01-Jun-07	PETHRICK, JEROME 01-Sep-07
MCCLELLAND, PATRICK 01-Jan-07	TAYLOR, STEPHEN R 01-Jun-07	PEPPER, NICHOLAS 01-Sep-07
INGRAM, DEAN D 01-Jan-07	ROCK, JAMES ANDREW 01-Jun-07	LITTLE, JONATHAN 01-Sep-07
BOSWELL, LAURA JANE 01-Jan-07	BRECKENRIDGE, ROBERT 01-Jun-07	HUNTER, DARRAN 01-Sep-07
JONES, TOBY 07-Jan-07	HERRINGTON, ROBERT J 01-Jun-07	HODGES, PHILIP 01-Sep-07
PHILLIPS, EDWARD 20-Jan-07	OAKEY, DEAN 01-Jun-07	FLINT, GRAHAME 01-Sep-07

LIEUTENANTS

FENWICK, STEVEN	01-Sep-07	
EDWARDS, GAVIN	01-Sep-07	
CROOK, RICHARD	01-Sep-07	
COLLIER, DAVID	01-Sep-07	
COLEMAN, GARETH	01-Sep-07	
BRIAN, STEPHEN	01-Sep-07	
BENNETT, IAN JAMES	01-Sep-07	
BARTLETT, DAVID	01-Sep-07	
GILBERT, MARK	01-Sep-07	
BOOTH, ALAN KEVIN	01-Sep-07	
DE'MAINE, ROBERT	01-Sep-07	
LAWRENCE-ARCHER, SALLY	01-Sep-07	
TURNER, GARETH JOHN	01-Sep-07	
MASON, ANGUS E	01-Sep-07	
COCKS, ANTHONY	07-Sep-07	
COWIE, MICHAEL	19-Sep-07	
GORDON, DANIEL	01-Oct-07	
LETT, TIMOTHY J	01-Oct-07	
STANBURY, DAVID R	19-Oct-07	
CRAIG, DAVID	19-Oct-07	
LOCKLEY, SIMON	19-Oct-07	
CLEAVES, RICHARD	19-Oct-07	
LANE, ROLAND	19-Oct-07	
ROBERTS, CHRISTOPHER	19-Oct-07	
ABBOTT, DUNCAN A J	19-Oct-07	
COURT, MATTHEW R	20-Oct-07	
CRAWFORD, ALISTAIR A	24-Oct-07	
DARCY, JOHN D	01-Nov-07	
DENNIS, HOLLY ANNE	01-Nov-07	
EDWARDS-BANNON, WILLIAM	01-Nov-07	
FLOYER, HUGO G	01-Nov-07	
GLEAVE, ROBERT D	01-Nov-07	
GOOSE, SAMUEL J	01-Nov-07	
PARMAR, BHAVNA RAVINDRA	01-Nov-07	
SOUTHALL, NICHOLAS	01-Nov-07	
THOMPSON, CLAIRE F	01-Nov-07	
YOUNG, ANDREW	01-Nov-07	
TAYLOR, MARC GLYN	01-Nov-07	
WHITE, KRISTOPHER	01-Nov-07	
SKELTON, RICHARD	01-Nov-07	
SHATTOCK, JAMES	01-Nov-07	
COOPER, DARREN	01-Nov-07	
TAYLOR, MATTHEW	01-Nov-07	
MOLONEY, BENJAMIN	01-Nov-07	
NEAVE, JAMES ROBERT	01-Nov-07	
FERGUS-HUNT, GREGORY	01-Nov-07	
BEATON, IAIN	08-Nov-07	

2008

BAYLISS, JAMES E L	07-Dec-07	
BENNETT, ELIZABETH C	24-Dec-07	
CLARK, OLIVER R		
DIMMOCK, GUY NEIL	01-Jan-08	
FLEMING, CAROLINE S E	01-Jan-08	
FORREST, DAVID J	01-Jan-08	
GOY, SALLY E	01-Jan-08	
GRADDON, GILES J	01-Jan-08	
GRIFFITHS, BETH	01-Jan-08	
GROSSETT, KELLY M	01-Jan-08	
GUEST, CRAIG A	01-Jan-08	
HARRIS, LINDA E	01-Jan-08	

JACKSON, AMIE R	01-Jan-08
KER, CATHERINE M	01-Jan-08
LISTER, SHAUN	01-Jan-08
MOUNSEY, CARL A	01-Jan-08
PRICE, MATTHEW W	01-Jan-08
ROULSTON-ELDRIDGE, JAMES	01-Jan-08
STOPPS, GREGORY	01-Jan-08
SWALES, RICHARD	01-Jan-08
SYMCOX, CHARLES M	01-Jan-08
WOOD, FREDERICK	01-Jan-08
WOODS, JAMES	01-Jan-08
WOTTON, RYAN J	01-Jan-08
WRIGHT, JAMES A H	01-Jan-08
WRIGHT, PAUL D	01-Jan-08
KELWAY, JENNA	01-Jan-08
BOOTHROYD-GIBBS, ADAM	01-Jan-08
UNSWORTH, BENJAMIN	01-Jan-08
SMITH, JAMES	01-Jan-08
FAULKNER, SIMON	01-Jan-08
DAVIES, ALEX	01-Jan-08
DAVIDSON, GREGOR	01-Jan-08
LUKE, CHRISTOPHER	01-Jan-08
SMALLEY, PAUL	01-Jan-08
GEORGE, JAMES	01-Jan-08
HARKIN, JAMES P	01-Jan-08
HENDRICKX, SARAH	01-Jan-08
HIGGINS, CARLA L	01-Feb-08
HOLBROOK, SIMON J	01-Feb-08
LOUGHRAN, OLIVER A G	01-Feb-08
MUNN-BOOKLESS, KERRI	01-Feb-08
NOTTINGHAM, JAMES	01-Feb-08
RAVAL, VIVEK	01-Feb-08
SKELLEY, ROGER	01-Feb-08
WALL, THOMAS	01-Feb-08
MITCHELL, ANDREW	01-Feb-08
WOODWARD, ALASDAIR	01-Feb-08
WELLER, JAMIE	01-Feb-08
NEWTON, OWEN	01-Feb-08
REID, JAMES	01-Feb-08
SEAMAN, ALEC L	01-Feb-08
KENT, ROBERT	01-Feb-08
LOCKETT, ALEXANDER	07-Feb-08
MOWTHORPE, SARAH	10-Feb-08
RICH, DUNCAN	12-Feb-08
SAWYER, JASON L	13-Feb-08
BLACK, KENNETH	19-Feb-08
MCLAUGHLAN, CHRISTOPHER	19-Feb-08
HANNABY, PHILIPPA	20-Feb-08
HUNTER, DERYK	01-Mar-08
GLENDINNING, ROBERT	01-Mar-08
TOWNSEND, ANNA	01-Mar-08
BRAYCOTTON, EDWARD	15-Mar-08
BRITTON, GEMMA	19-Mar-08
HAYNES, SAMUEL	22-Mar-08
HOLLAND, EDWARD R	22-Mar-08
KIRBY, BENJAMIN P	01-Apr-08
MASSON, VIVIENNE	01-Apr-08
O'SULLIVAN, DANIEL A N	01-Apr-08
PARRI, EIFION L	01-Apr-08
PEACHEY, SARAH LOUISE	01-Apr-08
SWANN, ADAM PETER	01-Apr-08

ADAMS, JOANNE FAITH	01-Apr-08
TALMAGE, CHARLES	01-Apr-08
BENTON, SIMON	01-Apr-08
MUNRO, ANGUS ROSS	01-Apr-08
HORN, NEIL RICHARD	01-Apr-08
CRAWFORD, JONATHAN	01-Apr-08
GREENWOOD, DANIEL A	01-Apr-08
LEES, CHRISTOPHER M	01-Apr-08
MILES, GARY ANTHONY MBE	11-Apr-08
MOSELEY, JAMES F	11-Apr-08
TOOGOOD, MARK J	11-Apr-08
WILLIAMS, JULIAN	11-Apr-08
CLARK, DAVID JOHN	11-Apr-08
JOHNSTON, DAVID	11-Apr-08
TAYLOR, MARK ANDREW	11-Apr-08
SAW, STEPHEN	11-Apr-08
BROWN, MARC ANDREW	11-Apr-08
GAFFNEY, FRANCIS	11-Apr-08
PARKER-CARN, REBECCA	11-Apr-08
CATTANACH, JAMES I	11-Apr-08
DRUMMOND, ANTHONY S	16-Apr-08
HAZELL, EMMA V	17-Apr-08
HOLLAND, RICHARD	01-May-08
OXLEY, JAMES D	01-May-08
WETHERFIELD, SARAH	01-May-08
SPACKMAN, LUCY C	01-May-08
MACDONALD, ALASTAIR	01-May-08
NEIL, ALEXANDER G	01-May-08
BEACHAM, SOPHIE R	19-May-08
EVERETT, OLIVER	20-May-08
HAMMOND, SEAN J	20-May-08
HARRIS, CHRISTOPHER	01-Jun-08
HASTINGS, CRAIG S	01-Jun-08
MAJOR, WILLIAM	01-Jun-08
MCARDLE, MARTIN J	01-Jun-08
DAVISON, WARREN	01-Jun-08
DALY, CHRISTOPHER	01-Jun-08
NOBLE, ROBERT	01-Jun-08
BATSFORD, GARETH E	01-Jun-08
BOULDING, ANDREW D	01-Jun-08
FAYE, MATTHEW E	04-Jun-08
JONES, CHRISTOPHER	13-Jun-08
MCNAUGHT, CHILTON J	13-Jun-08
MURPHY, CHRISTOPHER	13-Jun-08
TYLER, ADRIAN	13-Jun-08
CANTILLON, LLOYD M	13-Jun-08
DUFFIN, COLIN J	13-Jun-08
JOHNSTON, GREGORY	13-Jun-08
HALL, PENELOPE	16-Jun-08
REEVES, SIMON J	01-Jul-08
ROSS, DAVID C	01-Jul-08
AKERMAN, ANDREW	01-Jul-08
BLAKEMAN, PHILIP	08-Jul-08
CLARKSON, PAUL	31-Jul-08
DAVID, IAN	01-Aug-08
FILEWOD, ROGER B	01-Aug-08
HAYES, LEIGH	01-Aug-08
KENNEDY, ELIZABETH	01-Aug-08
KEYWORTH, MARK	01-Aug-08
PIZII, JANE	01-Aug-08
PROSSER, JASON W	01-Aug-08

LIEUTENANTS

TAGG, PETER WILLIAM	01-Aug-08	
HOWELL, ANDREW JOHN	01-Aug-08	
GREASON, PAUL	01-Aug-08	
CANE, JONATHAN	01-Aug-08	
VINES, SARAH KATE	01-Aug-08	
ALLEN, TIMOTHY W	01-Aug-08	
ASHLEY, STEPHEN J	01-Aug-08	
BEAUMONT, RICHARD	09-Aug-08	
BLACKWELL, MARK E	01-Sep-08	
BOARDMAN, ANDREW	01-Sep-08	
BRANNIGHAN, DAVID	01-Sep-08	
BUTCHER, MARK	01-Sep-08	
CADDY, PAUL D	01-Sep-08	
COZENS, CHRISTOPHER	01-Sep-08	
CUFF, SAMUEL	01-Sep-08	
DIETZ, LAURA M	01-Sep-08	
EDWARDS, LUKE	01-Sep-08	
FORRESTER, MICHAEL A	01-Sep-08	
FORSYTH, ADAM L	01-Sep-08	
GRESSWELL, NICK	01-Sep-08	
HALL, ALLAN J	01-Sep-08	
HALLATT, NICHOLAS	01-Sep-08	
JOHNSON, THOMAS	01-Sep-08	
JONES, STEVEN F	01-Sep-08	
KER, STUART W	01-Sep-08	
KNIGHT, RICHARD J	01-Sep-08	
LEADBEATER, MARK K	01-Sep-08	
LEVER, THOMAS	01-Sep-08	
MARTIN, HARRY	01-Sep-08	
MCNALLY, BARRY J	01-Sep-08	
REED, PETER KIRBY MBE	01-Sep-08	
REES, MATTHEW I	01-Sep-08	
ROSS, JAMIE M	01-Sep-08	
SHIRLEY, BENJAMIN	01-Sep-08	
THOMAS, RICHARD D	01-Sep-08	
TIBBITTS, JAMES A	01-Sep-08	
TURNER, KEVIN P	01-Sep-08	
TWEED, JONATHAN J	01-Sep-08	
WALKER, FERGUS S	01-Sep-08	
WELLS, MICHAEL J	01-Sep-08	
YOUNG, NEIL	01-Sep-08	
DART, MICHAEL PAUL	01-Sep-08	
HOWE, MICHAEL	01-Sep-08	
MITCHELL, HANNAH MARY	01-Sep-08	
HOLLINGWORTH, ELEANOR	01-Sep-08	
PENFOLD, ANDREW	01-Sep-08	
SEAGER, DANIEL	01-Sep-08	
GREAVES, MICHAEL	01-Sep-08	
FIELDER, ANDREW	01-Sep-08	
CONSTABLE, THOMAS	01-Sep-08	
HILLARD, CHRISTOPHER	01-Sep-08	
WIDDOWSON, MATTHEW	01-Sep-08	
DUNBAR, ROSS	01-Sep-08	
SMITH, RICHARD JAMES	01-Sep-08	
SMITH, ASHLEY	01-Sep-08	
BURROWS, THOMAS	01-Sep-08	
BLATCHER, DAVID JOHN	01-Sep-08	
MAIN, MATTHEW	01-Sep-08	
GILMORE, AMY F	01-Sep-08	
CULLEN, DONNA Maria	01-Sep-08	
THORPE, RICHARD JAMES	01-Sep-08	

HILL, ROSS	01-Sep-08
BRITTEN, BENJAMIN	01-Sep-08
BOWMER, CHRISTOPHER	01-Sep-08
DAVIS, MARK JOHN	01-Sep-08
COUZENS, ROBERT FARRER	01-Sep-08
RICHARDS, STEVEN	01-Sep-08
REVELL, AARON D	01-Sep-08
BUGG, JENNIFER	01-Sep-08
BYE, ASHLEY	01-Sep-08
CASTRINOYANNAKIS, TIMOTHY	30-Sep-08
DUKE, JONATHAN ALEXANDER	01-Oct-08
DUNNING, STEPHEN	01-Oct-08
GELL, THOMAS	01-Oct-08
GIFFIN, IAIN	01-Oct-08
HAZELWOOD, GRAEME	01-Oct-08
NORTON, LEE A	01-Oct-08
PRITCHARD, CHRISTOPHER	01-Oct-08
REBBECK, CHRISTOPHER	01-Oct-08
ST CLAIRE, CHRISTOPHER	01-Oct-08
THOMPSON, SIMON	01-Oct-08
MORELAND, JAMES	01-Oct-08
SMITH, NICHOLAS	01-Oct-08
HEPWORTH, NICHOLAS	01-Oct-08
KENT, ANDREW G	01-Oct-08
REDPATH, SCOTT D	01-Oct-08
YOUNG, MICHAEL	20-Oct-08
SHARLAND, CRAIG	20-Oct-08
COLES-HENDRY, HAMISH	20-Oct-08
SHAW, RAMSAY	20-Oct-08
BENZIE, ANDREW	20-Oct-08
COURT, SHANE J	20-Oct-08
FALCONER, PAUL	20-Oct-08
HARRISON, ELLEN	23-Oct-08
HEWITT, ADRIAN J	24-Oct-08
KEMP, PETER	24-Oct-08
PARNELL, TERENCE A MBE	24-Oct-08
RICHARDSON, IAN DEREK	24-Oct-08
BRATT, JAMES R	24-Oct-08
CLARKE, STEVEN P	24-Oct-08
COLLINS, STEPHEN J	24-Oct-08
WHITTINGTON, CHRISTOPHER	01-Nov-08
BROCK, MATTHEW	01-Nov-08
MACLENNAN, NEIL	01-Nov-08
MASON, CHRISTOPHER	01-Nov-08
MARRIOTT, ISABELLA	01-Dec-08
WARD, ANTONY JOHN	01-Dec-08
HELLIWELL, THOMAS	01-Dec-08
STONE, NICHOLAS S	01-Dec-08
HAYNES, WARREN	01-Dec-08
BOND, IAN	01-Dec-08
CHARLES, STEVEN	11-Dec-08
CLOUGH, WARREN S	18-Dec-08
LINEHAN, PAUL R	19-Dec-08
MCEVOY, JASON L	19-Dec-08
THOMPSON, MICHELLE E	19-Dec-08
WALLACE, NICOLA	19-Dec-08
WILSON, IAIN E	19-Dec-08
HOWE, NEIL DAVID	19-Dec-08
MYHILL, JOHNATHEN	19-Dec-08
O'REILLY, PAUL A GCGI	19-Dec-08
MURPHY, MARTIN JAMES	19-Dec-08

2009

BRISCOE, DANIEL ALAN	19-Dec-08
CAMPBELL, COLIN	20-Dec-08
CARTHEY, BEN	
CHAMBERS, JOANNE	01-Jan-09
CHARLESWORTH, NICHOLAS	01-Jan-09
COURT, NICHOLAS JOHN	01-Jan-09
GRAYLAND, ANDREW	01-Jan-09
HALL, DANIEL	01-Jan-09
INSTRELL, CHRISTOPHER B	01-Jan-09
LANGLEY, DAVID JAMES	01-Jan-09
PARKER, SARAH ELIZABETH	01-Jan-09
PATON, MARK WILLIAM	01-Jan-09
PHELAN, SEAN C	01-Jan-09
RADCLIFFE, GEMMA LOUISE	01-Jan-09
RICHARDSON, JAMES	01-Jan-09
SNAZELL, MATTHEW	01-Jan-09
THOMPSON, SIMON	01-Jan-09
TIN, JENNIFER MARY	01-Jan-09
TINGLE, DAWN	01-Jan-09
ZAUCHENBERGER, MICHAEL	01-Jan-09
ADLAM, CHARLOTTE	01-Jan-09
JONES, MORGAN MEng	01-Jan-09
GLENDINNING, VICKY LOUISE	01-Jan-09
BENBOW, MELANIE	01-Jan-09
CLAYTON, PETER	01-Jan-09
COOPER, MICHAEL ANDREW	16-Jan-09
DAW, ARTHUR BENJAMIN	01-Feb-09
HOWARD, JAMES	01-Feb-09
HUNT, ROBERT GRANT	01-Feb-09
KILBRIDE, PAUL	01-Feb-09
MITCHELL, ALEESHA	01-Feb-09
ROBERTS, JOEL	01-Feb-09
SHARP, CHRISTOPHER	01-Feb-09
SMITH, EDWIN J	01-Feb-09
THOMAS, MATTHEW	01-Feb-09
WHITE, ANDREW	01-Feb-09
WHITE, MARK	01-Feb-09
CREWDSON, ROBERT	01-Feb-09
KNIGHT, ALEXANDER	01-Feb-09
BENBOW, WILLIAM	01-Feb-09
BOADEN, CHRISTOPHER	01-Feb-09
CLARKE, PAUL	01-Feb-09
PATRICK, CHRISTOPHER	01-Feb-09
SANTRIAN, MARK	19-Feb-09
WARDLE, GARETH STEVEN	21-Feb-09
WEATHERALL, MARK	21-Feb-09
WEETCH, MATTHEW E	21-Feb-09
PEPPITT, CHRISTOPHER	21-Feb-09
ASHLEY-SMITH, RICHARD	21-Feb-09
ASHTON, MEGAN	21-Feb-09
CURRY, PHILIP	21-Feb-09
GLOVER, ADAM	01-Mar-09
GRIMES, KEITH	01-Mar-09
HART, DANIEL ADAM	01-Mar-09
LE POIDEVIN, IAN WESLEY	01-Mar-09
MELDRUM, RICHARD	01-Mar-09
NWOKORA, DAL	01-Mar-09
PARKER, SIMON OWAIN	01-Mar-09
SMITH, DALE AIDEN	01-Mar-09
WARD, GARETH JOHN	01-Mar-09

LIEUTENANTS

WILKINSON, JOHN	...01-Mar-09	
TALBOT, REBECCA	...01-Mar-09	
KERR, MARTIN	...01-Mar-09	
BAYLISS, JAMES P	...01-Mar-09	
CARTER, HOLLY	...01-Mar-09	
CHANDLER, RUSSELL	...22-Mar-09	
DOCKERTY, NEIL	...01-Apr-09	
HALL, STEPHEN JOHN	...01-Apr-09	
HOLE, JOSEPH S I	...01-Apr-09	
HORNE, NICHOLAS	...01-Apr-09	
LEE, ROSS J	...01-Apr-09	
LOFTS, ANTHONY	...01-Apr-09	
PREVETT, ADAM M	...01-Apr-09	
PROUSE, SCOTT	...01-Apr-09	
RETALLICK, KATHERINE	...01-Apr-09	
RUSCOE, DAVID IAN	...01-Apr-09	
THORNTON, CHARLES	...01-Apr-09	
WALLACE, JAMES G	...01-Apr-09	
RIDLEY, GEORGE	...01-Apr-09	
ANDREWS, ALISTAIR JAMES	...01-Apr-09	
STELLON, CHRISTOPHER	...01-Apr-09	
BICKER, RICHARD E	...01-Apr-09	
BOWER, DEAN A MSc	...01-Apr-09	
CLARK, ALLAN J	...02-Apr-09	
COOPER, JOHN C	...09-Apr-09	
COOPER, JOHN DUNCAN	...09-Apr-09	
CREASE, DAVID A	...09-Apr-09	
FAULKNER, JONATHAN	...09-Apr-09	
GARDNER, SADIE J	...09-Apr-09	
LAPPIN, ADAM	...09-Apr-09	
MAGILL, HAL GCGI	...09-Apr-09	
McCLAREN, RONNI	...09-Apr-09	
OLDHAM, DAVID J	...09-Apr-09	
SIMPSON, PAUL G	...09-Apr-09	
SPRECKLEY, DAMIAN R C	...09-Apr-09	
TURNER, GARY HERBERT	...09-Apr-09	
BEAUMONT, ALAN J	...09-Apr-09	
LISHMAN, STUART	...09-Apr-09	
CRAIG, ALEXANDER P	...09-Apr-09	
DALTON, EBONY	...09-Apr-09	
HARMER, DEBORAH	...09-Apr-09	
HAYES, PAUL	...01-May-09	
JEFFREY, BEN STEWART	...01-May-09	
LIPPITT, BENJAMIN	...01-May-09	
READ, BENJAMIN	...01-May-09	
WILMOT, MAX ANDREW	...01-May-09	
JOHNSTON, AUDREY ROSE	...01-May-09	
JORDAN, CRAIG DAVID	...01-May-09	
HEAP, MATTHEW JAMES	...01-May-09	
FANE-BAILEY, VERITY	...19-May-09	
HALFORD, MARK LESLIE	...20-May-09	
KING, MATTHEW	...20-May-09	
MCMORROW, KEVIN M	...01-Jun-09	
RITCHIE, STUART	...01-Jun-09	
THOMPSON, SAM DAVID	...01-Jun-09	
VASEY, OWEN RHYS	...01-Jun-09	
WARNER, STEPHEN E	...01-Jun-09	
SUCKLING, CHRISTOPHER	...01-Jun-09	
BOYALL, DUANE ROBIN	...01-Jun-09	
BODKIN, LEE	...01-Jun-09	
FITZPATRICK, MICHAEL	...01-Jun-09	

JACK, VALENCERA	...01-Jun-09	
LAIRD, DOUGLAS	...01-Jul-09	
NEWNS, ADAM DAVID	...01-Jul-09	
HUMPHREYS, RHODRI	...01-Jul-09	
WADE, NICHOLAS J	...01-Jul-09	
BENNETT-SMITH, PAULA	...01-Jul-09	
DODD, CRAIG	...08-Jul-09	
DOUGLAS, JASON	...30-Jul-09	
HARRIS, MICHAEL B	...31-Jul-09	
LEES, RACHEL H	...31-Jul-09	
MORGAN, MICHAEL C	...31-Jul-09	
MORRISON, PHILIP	...31-Jul-09	
MURGATROYD, STEVEN A	...31-Jul-09	
QUIRKE, FRASER J	...31-Jul-09	
RODDY, CHRISTOPHER M	...31-Jul-09	
SIMPSON, BRETT R	...31-Jul-09	
SMITH, BARRY J	...31-Jul-09	
STARK, JUSTIN R	...31-Jul-09	
STEELE, JASON M	...31-Jul-09	
NICHOLSON, CHRISTOPHER	...31-Jul-09	
ANDERSON, MARTIN	...31-Jul-09	
PEARSON, ELLIS	...31-Jul-09	
THOMPSON-PETTIT, RICHARD	...31-Jul-09	
EVANS, RUSSELL FREDERICK	...31-Jul-09	
FORD, JONATHAN RICHARD	...31-Jul-09	
MELVIN, JOHN JAMES	...31-Jul-09	
STEPHENSON, JOHN	...31-Jul-09	
MCCROSSAN, AMY	...01-Aug-09	
JUDD, OLIVER JAMES	...01-Aug-09	
LANE, ADAM JAMES	...01-Aug-09	
BICKNELL, JAMES	...01-Aug-09	
CLASBY, LORRAINE	...19-Aug-09	
GOW, PETER JOSEPH	...19-Aug-09	
BAILEY, DAVID JAMES	...20-Aug-09	
BRADSHAW, JAMES	...21-Aug-09	
CASTLEFORD, LAUREN	...16-Sep-09	
DOUTHWAITE, STUART	...01-Oct-09	
FOX, CHRISTOPHER	...01-Oct-09	
FROST, ROBERT	...01-Oct-09	
HARVEY, MATTHEW	...01-Oct-09	
KNIGHT, ANTHONY	...01-Oct-09	
KNIGHT, RICHARD	...01-Oct-09	
MACNAE, BRIDGET ROSE	...01-Oct-09	
MASON, VICTORIA	...01-Oct-09	
MCCLEAN, STEPHEN	...01-Oct-09	
PETERS, COLIN SEAN	...01-Oct-09	
POUNDER, RICHARD	...01-Oct-09	
SNELL, DALEY ANDREW	...01-Oct-09	
WILLIAMS, MATTHEW	...01-Oct-09	
HOUSE, ANDREW LESLIE	...01-Oct-09	
JONES, GEMMA	...01-Oct-09	
LING, PETER ALEXANDER	...01-Oct-09	
RICHARDSON, STUART	...01-Oct-09	
ROTHERHAM, DOMINIC	...01-Oct-09	
WESTLAKE, SIMON	...20-Oct-09	
SANTRIAN, TRACEY M	...20-Oct-09	
SANTRY, PATRICK	...20-Oct-09	
JEFFS, SAMUEL G	...20-Oct-09	
KENCHINGTON, ROBIN	...26-Oct-09	
ROSE, VICTORIA	...26-Oct-09	
ROUTLEDGE, ROSEMARY	...01-Nov-09	

MEADEN, ALEXANDER	...01-Nov-09	
TUCKWOOD, ALEX IAN	...01-Nov-09	
WILSON, NICHOLAS C	...01-Nov-09	
MILLER, SHANE ROBERT	...19-Nov-09	
HARDING, MATTHEW	...19-Nov-09	
RAINE, KATHERINE	...19-Nov-09	
STARSMORE, DANIEL	...24-Nov-09	
STRAKER, PETER	...01-Dec-09	
WHITE, PAUL	...01-Dec-09	
ALLAN, JOHN	...01-Dec-09	
BAKER, MARK	...01-Dec-09	
ALLEN, LLOYD N	...01-Dec-09	
BURGESS, MAXINE	...08-Dec-09	
FRASER, GORDON	...08-Dec-09	
HANKS, RICHARD M	...11-Dec-09	
HEARNDEN, SIMON T	...11-Dec-09	
INGLESBY, PAUL R	...11-Dec-09	
KEMPLEY, PAUL S	...11-Dec-09	
MARTIN, BRIAN H	...11-Dec-09	
MORLEY, DAVID J	...11-Dec-09	
MOSS, STEWART J	...11-Dec-09	
O'MALLEY, JAMES	...11-Dec-09	
PARKER, NEIL A	...11-Dec-09	
ROBERTS, JOHN A	...11-Dec-09	
SAMPSON, JONATHAN	...11-Dec-09	
SMITHSON, JAMES I	...11-Dec-09	
DONBAVAND, DAVID	...11-Dec-09	
WRIGHT, JUSTIN CRAIG	...11-Dec-09	
BASKETFIELD, WAYNE	...11-Dec-09	
MCPHEE, THOMAS J	...11-Dec-09	
WILLIAMS, NIGEL	...11-Dec-09	
DAY, RICHARD J	...17-Dec-09	
FLYNN, CHRISTOPHER	...17-Dec-09	
HUNTLEY, GENEVIEVE	...21-Dec-09	

2010

O'CONNELL, HEATHER		
PHILLIPS, JOHN ROBERT	...01-Jan-10	
PLATT, MAXIMILIAN	...01-Jan-10	
ROSE, IAN DAVID	...01-Jan-10	
ROWLANDS, ANDREW	...01-Jan-10	
TEARE, MATTHEW	...01-Jan-10	
WEAL, GREGORY	...01-Jan-10	
WILLIAMS, MATTHEW	...01-Jan-10	
MAUMY, JONATHAN	...01-Jan-10	
BREWARD, DANIEL	...01-Jan-10	
GRIMMER, NICHOLAS	...01-Jan-10	
BELL, DAVID	...01-Jan-10	
EDWARDS, CASSANDRA	...01-Jan-10	
FEARN, DANIEL C T	...01-Jan-10	
FRENCH, REBECCA	...01-Feb-10	
GILMORE, MARTIN	...01-Feb-10	
HAMER, SCOTT	...01-Feb-10	
KEITH, CHARLES	...01-Feb-10	
LAIRD, ELLEN L	...01-Feb-10	
PALMER, NICHOLAS	...01-Feb-10	
PATTERSON, PAUL	...01-Feb-10	
THOMAS, JAMES MICHAEL	...01-Feb-10	
WILSON, KAYLEIGH JAYNE	...01-Feb-10	
GREENWOOD, JULIA LOUISE	...01-Feb-10	
WHITE, DANIEL JULYAN	...01-Feb-10	

LIEUTENANTS

Name	Date
MEHTA, CHRISTOPHER	01-Feb-10
CAMERON, SAM	01-Feb-10
CLARKE, RICHARD	01-Feb-10
GAYSON, CHRISTOPHER	19-Feb-10
GODDARD, JAMES	01-Mar-10
MCCLELLAND, IAN	01-Mar-10
MILNE, RODERICK	01-Mar-10
OLIPHANT, HELEN	01-Mar-10
SCOWN, WILLIAM OLIVER	01-Mar-10
THOMAS, RICHARD	01-Mar-10
WELCH, DANIELLE	01-Mar-10
FURNEAUX, JAMES	01-Mar-10
MUSGRAVE, THOMAS	01-Mar-10
COUTTS, MAXWELL	01-Mar-10
CALVERT, LAUREN	21-Mar-10
COOKE, BENJAMIN ROSS	21-Mar-10
DALRYMPLE, JAMES	22-Mar-10
DAVIES, JULIA	01-Apr-10
GREEN, NICHOLAS	01-Apr-10
MARTIN, ANDREW	01-Apr-10
PARSONSON, MAX EDWARD	01-Apr-10
SANOCKI, ANNA MARIE	01-Apr-10
WINWOOD, MATTHEW	01-Apr-10
ALLEN-SCHOLEY, SPENCER	01-Apr-10
BARR, SIMON J C	01-Apr-10
BRAY, MICHAEL A.	01-Apr-10
CAVE, SIMON J	09-Apr-10
GREEN, MARK D	09-Apr-10
HENDRA, ALLAN J	09-Apr-10
JAKES, MATTHEW OWEN	09-Apr-10
RADCLIFFE, ALBERT P	09-Apr-10
RIGBY, LEE A	09-Apr-10
ROBERTS, PETER N	09-Apr-10
STEELE, MATTHEW E.	09-Apr-10
WILLIAMS, ANDREW F	09-Apr-10
BEAN, EDWARD CHARLES	09-Apr-10
MILLER, ADAM EDWARD	09-Apr-10
DE-SAINT-BISSIX-CROIX, ANNA MARIE	09-Apr-10
CROUCH, BENJAMIN ROBERT	09-Apr-10
FORD, BRENDAN RICHARD	09-Apr-10
GREENWOOD, DAVID ROBERT	13-Apr-10
MORGAN, ASHLEY K	01-May-10
RICKARD, JAMES JOHN	01-May-10
TARBARD, GAVIN THOMAS	01-May-10
THOMPSON, JAMES	01-May-10
BATE, CHRISTOPHER	01-May-10
WATSHAM, RICHARD VICTOR	01-May-10
ROBERTS, ANDREW	01-May-10
DAY, PAUL ANTHONY	20-May-10
DEAN, ADAM C	20-May-10
EDMONDS, JON S	23-May-10
ELVY, SUSAN DAWN	27-May-10
FOREMAN, LOUISA	01-Jun-10
FUNNELL, LEE CLIFFORD	01-Jun-10
HARRIS, ALEXANDRA	01-Jun-10
HERITAGE, FRANCIS	01-Jun-10
HOLT, LAURA	01-Jun-10
JONES, WILLIAM ALBERT	01-Jun-10
LEE, DANIEL CHARLES	01-Jun-10
MARSDEN, CHRISTOPHER	01-Jun-10
MELLING, PAUL GORDON	01-Jun-10
PARKS, NATASHA	01-Jun-10
PAVIE, RICHARD M	01-Jun-10
PELHAM BURN, ALEXANDER	01-Jun-10
POWELL, ROBERT	01-Jun-10
ROACH, DARREN J.	01-Jun-10
STAVELEY, CATHERINE	01-Jun-10
STEELE, KATIE	01-Jun-10
THOMAS, MICHAEL J.	01-Jun-10
THURSTON, EDWARD	01-Jun-10
WHEATCROFT, IAN JAMES	01-Jun-10
MAWDSLEY, OWEN RUPERT	01-Jun-10
HALL, VICTORIA J	01-Jun-10
ROWLANDS, SARAH JANE	01-Jun-10
MARTIN, ALAN FRASER	07-Jun-10
KYME, ROBERT	16-Jun-10
CARTER, LAURA JAYNE	19-Jun-10
CLARK, GORDON DAVID	01-Jul-10
LANE, PAUL V	01-Jul-10
CORNHILL, SHARON T	08-Jul-10
RYAN, KATHLEEN R	08-Jul-10
RICHARDS, GREGOR IAIN	09-Jul-10
WILLIAMS, AMANDA LOUISE	12-Jul-10
MORRISON, MARK J	12-Jul-10
BARLOW, LEONARD J	20-Jul-10
EVANGELISTA, PAUL G	20-Jul-10
HARPER, NICHOLAS	22-Jul-10
HUDSON, RICHARD	30-Jul-10
RAE, DAVID	30-Jul-10
SMITH, KRISTIAN	30-Jul-10
SMITH, SHELLEY A	30-Jul-10
BOSWELL, EMMA JANE	30-Jul-10
HAY, PHILLIP WILLIAM	30-Jul-10
ROOK, CHRISTOPHER	30-Jul-10
GRIGGS, JAMES KEVIN	30-Jul-10
MIDDLETON, SHANE	30-Jul-10
BLICK, GRAHAM	30-Jul-10
ASTON, JAMES	30-Jul-10
BOLTON, JAMES	30-Jul-10
CAIRNS-HOLDER, DECLAN	30-Jul-10
AMOR, MATTHEW	01-Aug-10
BOARDER, RICHARD	01-Aug-10
BONE, MATTHEW	20-Aug-10
BOWLER, THOMAS	01-Sep-10
COOPER, JACK W	01-Sep-10
COPELAND, NIALL	01-Sep-10
DEVONPORT, SEAN	01-Sep-10
DUNCAN, ROSS D	01-Sep-10
DURBIN, WILLIAM JOHN	01-Sep-10
EMPTAGE, MICHAEL	01-Sep-10
FITTON, DANIEL	01-Sep-10
GRANDY, MARK	01-Sep-10
HENTON, JAMES M.	01-Sep-10
JONES, CHRISTOPHER	01-Sep-10
LAWRENCE, KEVIN	01-Sep-10
LONGIA, SANDEEP	01-Sep-10
LONSDALE, GAVIN	01-Sep-10
MACKAY, RICHARD	01-Sep-10
MACLEAN, GRAEME	01-Sep-10
MCCANN, ANDREW	01-Sep-10
MURRAY, SIMON	01-Sep-10
NASON, THOMAS	01-Sep-10
PORTEOUS, CAMERON	01-Sep-10
RAFFLE, EDWARD J	01-Sep-10
REES-HUGHES, VICTORIA	01-Sep-10
ROBERTS, DAVID	01-Sep-10
ROBERTS, THOMAS	01-Sep-10
SHINE, DAVID JOSEPH	01-Sep-10
SIMMONS, SARAH	01-Sep-10
SIMPSON, DALEY	01-Sep-10
TARGETT, EDWARD G	01-Sep-10
VUNIWAQA, ATUNAISA T	01-Sep-10
WHITEHEAD, BENJAMIN	01-Sep-10
GARTON, HAZELLE MARIE	01-Sep-10
PACKER, LEE JAMES	01-Sep-10
KNELLER, JAMES	01-Sep-10
MARSHALL, DAVID	01-Sep-10
WATKIN, PAUL	01-Sep-10
MACE, STEPHEN JAMES	01-Sep-10
TAYLOR, ALEXANDER IAN	01-Sep-10
BAILEY, JONATHAN	01-Sep-10
ABBEY, RACHEL FAYE	01-Sep-10
CLISSOLD, PATRICK	01-Sep-10
BUTLER, ADAM	01-Sep-10
DORRINGTON, BENJAMIN	07-Sep-10
ELLIOTT, DAVID J	20-Sep-10
MAXWELL, HAMISH	01-Oct-10
RAY, STEVEN PETER	01-Oct-10
SCAMP, SIMON JAMES	01-Oct-10
SCHNETLER, SIMON	01-Oct-10
SMILLIE, ELEANOR JANE	01-Oct-10
TUCKWOOD, NEIL ELLIOTT	01-Oct-10
WRAY, PHILIP	01-Oct-10
LOMAS, TIMOTHY	01-Oct-10
HAMLYN, JONATHAN	01-Oct-10
POWNE, LAURA	01-Oct-10
BOND, FRANCES	09-Oct-10
BOWLES, DANIEL JOHN	20-Oct-10
BROOKSBANK, OLIVER	20-Oct-10
FAWCETT, BENJAMIN	01-Nov-10
HOLBORN, LEE JAMES	01-Nov-10
KENYON, ADAM MAXWELL	01-Nov-10
MARTIN, ANDREW	01-Nov-10
O'CONNELL, DANIEL	01-Nov-10
PARKER, RICHARD	01-Nov-10
PEARCE, STEPHEN	01-Nov-10
POULSON, CHRISTOPHER	01-Nov-10
QUILTER, GAIL	01-Nov-10
REES, EDWARD	01-Nov-10
SZWEDA, ALEXANDER	01-Nov-10
TAYLOR, MATTHEW	01-Nov-10
TRISTRAM, ROBERT	01-Nov-10
WINTERTON, GEMMA	01-Nov-10
CARVER, JAMES	01-Nov-10
NICHOLLS, EDWARD	01-Nov-10
CASH, RUPERT	01-Nov-10
BUTLER, JAMES M	01-Nov-10
COATES, JONATHAN R.	12-Nov-10
DOBSON, RICHARD E.	19-Nov-10
EDWARDS, NEAL P.	17-Dec-10
FLETCHER, CHRISTOPHER	17-Dec-10
GUTHRIE, LEE D K	17-Dec-10
HUNNYBUN, SIMON P	17-Dec-10

LIEUTENANTS

MOULDING, MARK D	17-Dec-10
SALISBURY, DOMINIC	17-Dec-10
SHAW, MATHEW	17-Dec-10
STEIGER, GARY	17-Dec-10
STRANGE, JAMIE L	17-Dec-10
STURT, ASHLEIGH	17-Dec-10
TURRELL, RICHARD D	17-Dec-10
WHELDON, ADAM J	17-Dec-10
SMITH, GARY JOHN	17-Dec-10
GILL, LEE	17-Dec-10
MCALLISTER, KEVIN	17-Dec-10
FULKER, EDWARD	17-Dec-10
BEST, ALEXANDER	17-Dec-10
COLLINS, SIMON HEINZ	20-Dec-10

2011

FARQUHARSON, CRAIG	
FERGUSON, CALUM	01-Jan-11
GIBBS, EMILY	01-Jan-11
MOULD, CHRISTOPHER	01-Jan-11
ORAM, CEMAL	01-Jan-11
SEWELL, LYNSEY E	01-Jan-11
TAYLOR, MARIAN	01-Jan-11
YARKER, SAM	01-Jan-11
BALMOND, SAMUEL	01-Jan-11
GREGORY, SAMUEL	01-Jan-11
LAVERICK, JONATHAN	01-Jan-11
SMITH, WILLIAM	01-Feb-11
STEPHEN, NICOLA	01-Feb-11
WARLAND, ADAM	01-Feb-11
MOORE, AIMEE	01-Feb-11
BRAY, MATTHEW	01-Feb-11
MORRIS, ALASTAIR	01-Feb-11
ANDREWS, NICHOLAS	20-Feb-11
BROWN, STEVEN	24-Feb-11
CLAYTON, JOHN DAVID	27-Feb-11
CROOKS, CHARLES	01-Mar-11
DRISCOLL, ADRIAN	01-Mar-11
EDWARDS, RHYDIAN	01-Mar-11
FAGAN, LOUIS	01-Mar-11
HILL, JAMIE	01-Mar-11
HUGHES, ADAM	01-Mar-11
PAYNE, MICHAEL	01-Mar-11
QUILTER, GEORGE	01-Mar-11
READ, MATTHEW	01-Mar-11
SAWYER, RICHARD	01-Mar-11
TWINN, RICHARD	01-Mar-11
TYSLER, CHARLOTTE	01-Mar-11
WALLIS, THOMAS OLIVER	01-Mar-11
PUGH, JAMES	01-Mar-11
BAILEY, ANDREW	01-Mar-11
BARBER, CHRISTOPHER	01-Mar-11
BARTLETT, SIMON	01-Mar-11
BIDDLECOMBE, HUGH	01-Apr-11
BOAK, PHILIP RICHARD	01-Apr-11
BOWLER, JAMES ROBERT	01-Apr-11
BUCHAN, JAMES	01-Apr-11
CARPENTER, NEIL PAUL	01-Apr-11
DOCHERTY, ZOE	01-Apr-11
EMERY, DAVID GARETH	01-Apr-11
GARDNER, RACHAEL	01-Apr-11

HANNAH, EDWARD	01-Apr-11
HAZEL, THOMAS	01-Apr-11
HENRY, DAVID	01-Apr-11
HOAR, MARK	01-Apr-11
HUGGINS, MICHAEL	01-Apr-11
JOHN, JAMES	01-Apr-11
LAUD, NICOLA JANE	01-Apr-11
LEA, OLIVER	01-Apr-11
LEACH, HELEN	01-Apr-11
MARSDEN, DANIEL	01-Apr-11
MARSH, EDWARD	01-Apr-11
MASON, JOHN	01-Apr-11
MOORE, ROBERT	01-Apr-11
PARSONS, RICHARD	01-Apr-11
RAYMONT, EDWARD	01-Apr-11
READ, EDMUND ARTHUR	01-Apr-11
RYDIARD, MICHAEL	01-Apr-11
SAMUEL, BEN JAMES	01-Apr-11
SMITH, BENJAMIN WILLIAM	01-Apr-11
SMITH, JENNIFER	01-Apr-11
STILES, MAXINE KAY	01-Apr-11
TAYLOR, HELEN	01-Apr-11
TEECE, NICHOLAS JOSEPH	01-Apr-11
THORNTON, WILLIAM	01-Apr-11
WILLIAMS, GARETH	01-Apr-11
WITHAM, KATHARINE	01-Apr-11
JOHNSTONE-BURT, CHARLES	01-Apr-11
GOUGH, CHRISTOPHER	01-Apr-11
WAUD, DEBORAH	01-Apr-11
BERNACCHI, JONATHAN P	01-Apr-11
BIDDULPH, ANDREW R	11-Apr-11
BRIDGE, JAMES G	14-Apr-11
DAVIES, ANDREW C	15-Apr-11
FOWLER, GARETH S	15-Apr-11
GARTH, LEE	15-Apr-11
GWILLIAM, RICHARD J	15-Apr-11
JONES, STEVEN K	15-Apr-11
MORTON, DAVID	15-Apr-11
MURRAY, SARA N	15-Apr-11
PHILLIPS, PAUL J	15-Apr-11
SAID, PHILLIP M	15-Apr-11
TELFORD, STEVEN	15-Apr-11
TOLCHER, DANIEL G	15-Apr-11
VAUGHAN, JAMIE B	15-Apr-11
JAMES, DARREN BRIAN	15-Apr-11
STEVENS, MARK	15-Apr-11
TAYLOR, DAVID ROBERT	15-Apr-11
BREEN, PAUL ROBERT	15-Apr-11
TEAR, TREVOR MICHAEL	15-Apr-11
NEWMAN, LEE	15-Apr-11
HAMMOND, TREGARON	15-Apr-11
PASHNEH-TALA, SAMIRA	15-Apr-11
MILN, DAVID (Dave)	15-Apr-11
PENFOLD, DANIEL	15-Apr-11
SERCOMBE, DANIEL	17-Apr-11
GAYLE, DAVID MARK	01-May-11
CARPENTER, JAMES	01-May-11
DENYER, ALISTAIR C	01-May-11
HENDERSON, SIMON A	31-May-11
McLAUGHLIN, IAN JAMES	01-Jun-11
FAIRBAIRN, OLIVER ACGI	01-Jun-11

BEHAN, OLIVER MICHAEL	01-Jun-11
CAMPBELL, EDWARD	01-Jun-11
CHRISTIE, LAURA	07-Jun-11
COSTLEY-WHITE, BENJAMIN	01-Jul-11
GILLESPIE, BENJAMIN	01-Jul-11
HARWOOD, DAVID PHILIP	01-Jul-11
HEMS, WENDY LOUISE	01-Jul-11
HOLLAND, PAUL ERIC	01-Jul-11
RADUE, NICHOLAS	01-Jul-11
RICHARDS, JONATHAN	01-Jul-11
TOMS, NICHOLAS	01-Jul-11
WISEMAN, HUGO	01-Jul-11
DAVEY, ALISTAIR JAMES	01-Jul-11
MILLER, DAVID JAMES	01-Jul-11
NAPIER, GARY	01-Jul-11
PIGGOTT, ANDREW	08-Jul-11
SCOTT, JASON	08-Jul-11
BROOKING, GARY	08-Jul-11
LONGSTAFF, THOMAS	08-Jul-11
LEWIS, KIERAN	08-Jul-11
BARLOW, JAY P	12-Jul-11
HINTON, OLIVER J	20-Jul-11
REES-SWINDON, MIKAELA	03-Aug-11
LUMSDEN, GAVIN TODD	05-Aug-11
HOWE, DAVID	05-Aug-11
ALLEN-WEST, BART	05-Aug-11
CHRISTIE, ANDREW	05-Aug-11
SMITH, THOMAS	05-Aug-11
ADAMS, KEITH JOHN	05-Aug-11
ARNOLD, LEE J	14-Aug-11
BALLS, CHRISTOPHER F	05-Aug-11
BARKEY, BARRY JOHN	01-Sep-11
BATESON, TIMOTHY NIGEL	01-Sep-11
BLACKBURN, THOMAS	01-Sep-11
COATES, THOMAS	01-Sep-11
CURTIS, REBECCA	01-Sep-11
DYER, MARTIN LEWIS	01-Sep-11
ECCLES, MATTHEW	01-Sep-11
FEBBRARRO, LUKE	01-Sep-11
FLOWERS, DAVID J	01-Sep-11
GALLAGHER, MICHAEL	01-Sep-11
GAUGHT, EDWIN	01-Sep-11
GEDDES, NATHANIEL C S	01-Sep-11
GILL, SAMUEL R	01-Sep-11
GOODWIN, AARON K	01-Sep-11
GRAY, RICHARD G	01-Sep-11
GREEN, JOSEPH	01-Sep-11
GREENFIELD, STUART	01-Sep-11
HARRADINE, SAM A	01-Sep-11
HIBBERT, ANDREW	01-Sep-11
HILL, OLIVER WILLIAM	01-Sep-11
IVORY, MATTHEW	01-Sep-11
JACKS, MICHAEL	01-Sep-11
KEELING, MEGAN	01-Sep-11
LANAGHAN, RICHARD	01-Sep-11
LANE, PETER	01-Sep-11
LEA, CHLOE	01-Sep-11
MACKAY, FRASER	01-Sep-11
MARSHALL, ALEXANDER	01-Sep-11
MION, JONATHAN	01-Sep-11
MUSGROVE, CHRISTOPHER	01-Sep-11

LIEUTENANTS

NEEDLE, PETER JOHN	01-Sep-11	
OAKLEY, JONATHON	01-Sep-11	
PARKER, LUKE RHYS	01-Sep-11	
PARKS, LUKE JETHRO	01-Sep-11	
PLATT, ANDREW JAMES	01-Sep-11	
ROESSLER, PHILIPPA	01-Sep-11	
ROWE, JOANNE	01-Sep-11	
SAVERY, STUART LESLIE	01-Sep-11	
STEPHENSON, FIONA	01-Sep-11	
STRADLING, DUNCAN	01-Sep-11	
SWITHINBANK, GEORGE	01-Sep-11	
WAGSTAFFE, JAMES N G	01-Sep-11	
WAKEFIELD, MATTHEW A	01-Sep-11	
WILLIAMS, GARETH	01-Sep-11	
WILLIFORD, SUSANNA J	01-Sep-11	
THOMAS, CHARLOTTE	01-Sep-11	
WHITTAKER, TERRY	01-Sep-11	
GREGG, RYAN LEE	01-Sep-11	
FULLER, LUCY ANN JANE	01-Sep-11	
MARIN-ORTEGA, CARL	01-Sep-11	
LOXTON, THOMAS CHARLES	01-Sep-11	
CLARK, MATTHEW HENRY	01-Sep-11	
OAKES, CAROLINE	01-Sep-11	
DURRANT, FREDERICK	01-Sep-11	
GASKELL-TAYLOR, HUGH	01-Sep-11	
GOODLEY, ROSS	01-Sep-11	
IRWIN, STEVEN	01-Oct-11	
MCCAUGHAN, CHRISTOPHER	01-Oct-11	
MILLYARD, MATTHEW	01-Oct-11	
MITCHELL, JAMES	01-Oct-11	
SIMPSON, DANIEL	01-Oct-11	
YOUNG, SEAN	01-Oct-11	
QUINN, MICHAEL	01-Oct-11	
KEENS, EMMA LOUISE	01-Oct-11	
WALKLEY, KYLE JAMES	01-Oct-11	
WINNING, ROBERT	01-Oct-11	
MORRISON, ROSS	07-Oct-11	
LEWIS, SCOTT	07-Oct-11	
MANKTELOW, BENJAMIN	07-Oct-11	
HEDGECOX, PHILIP	01-Nov-11	
HUGHES, DAVID MICHAEL	01-Dec-11	
MCELWAINE, CHRISTOPHER	01-Dec-11	
WILLIAMS, DAVID	08-Dec-11	
ADKINS, PAUL	08-Dec-11	
BRIGGS, CHRISTOPHER	08-Dec-11	
DAVIES, JOHN P	08-Dec-11	
HALL, CHRISTOPHER	16-Dec-11	
MARRISON, ANDREW	16-Dec-11	
MELLOR, ANDREW L	16-Dec-11	
ROBINSON, ALAN J	16-Dec-11	
SHAW, CHRISTOPHER	16-Dec-11	
HOWE, JONATHAN	16-Dec-11	

2012

ASHTON, KARL	01-Jan-12
BENNETT, OLIVER	01-Jan-12
BLACKLEDGE, BENJAMIN	01-Jan-12
BODDINGTON, HANNAH	01-Jan-12
BURNS, NATALIE	01-Jan-12
CANOSA, LUIS	01-Jan-12
CHARLTON, ANDREW	01-Jan-12

CORDEN, ADAM	01-Jan-12
CROSSWOOD, BARRY	01-Jan-12
DAVEY, ANDREW JAMES	01-Jan-12
FINNIE, ANTHONY MARK	01-Jan-12
FULLER, NICHOLAS MARTIN	01-Jan-12
GIBSON, ANDREW MARK	01-Jan-12
HALL, SIMON CRAIG	01-Jan-12
HASTINGS, THOMAS	01-Jan-12
HEATH, BENJAMIN O'NEIL	01-Jan-12
KERRIGAN, GLEN	01-Jan-12
KEY, MATTHEW	01-Jan-12
LOFTHOUSE, THOMAS	01-Jan-12
MATTHEWS, CHRISTOPHER	01-Jan-12
MCINNES, ALLAN JAMES	01-Jan-12
MURPHY, DENNIS	01-Jan-12
MYHILL, JAMES EDWARD	01-Jan-12
NICOLL, MAC	01-Jan-12
OAKES, PHILIPPE	01-Jan-12
RANSCOMBE, ROBERT	01-Jan-12
RICHARDS, THOMAS	01-Jan-12
STANFORD, THOMAS	01-Jan-12
THOMAS, DANIEL G D	01-Jan-12
WARDILL, GEORGE	01-Jan-12
WEBB, KEITH WILLIAM	01-Jan-12
WILLS, TIMOTHY	01-Jan-12
WRIGHT, JAMES PHILIP	01-Jan-12
YOXALL, WILLIAM	01-Jan-12
SMITH, RICHARD	01-Jan-12
SMITH, SCOTT	01-Jan-12
COATSWORTH, ROBERT	01-Jan-12
KING, JAMES	01-Jan-12
BROWN, BENJAMIN E	01-Jan-12
GILDERTHORP, THOMAS	07-Jan-12
MCINNES, STEPHANIE	07-Jan-12
REES, NATHAN JAMES	01-Feb-12
KELDAY, ALEXANDER	01-Feb-12
BOOTH, ANTHONY	01-Feb-12
BRAIN, TERRI	01-Feb-12
BURNESS-SMITH, OLIVER	16-Feb-12
CALDER, THOMAS	01-Mar-12
CHALLANS, BENJAMIN	01-Mar-12
CHIN, HENRY	01-Mar-12
HAMILTON, JOHN	01-Mar-12
HILL, DAVID	01-Mar-12
HOWIE, IAN	01-Mar-12
MCALPINE, RORY	01-Mar-12
NEGUS, TRYSTRAM	01-Mar-12
NEILAN, SAMUEL	01-Mar-12
VINCENT, PETER	01-Mar-12
WILTSHIRE, ROSS	01-Mar-12
WISEMAN, DEBORAH	01-Mar-12
WORDSWORTH, JOEL	01-Mar-12
WRIGHT, CHRISTOPHER	01-Mar-12
ARMSTRONG, PAUL	01-Mar-12
BARNETT, CHRISTOPHER	01-Mar-12
BROWN, REBECCA	01-Mar-12
BURROWS, JAMES	01-Apr-12
CALLENDER, JAMES	01-Apr-12
CARDY, LLOYD	01-Apr-12
COLMAN, ADAM	01-Apr-12
COOKE, JAMES	01-Apr-12

CURRIN, JOSEPH	01-Apr-12
DUBOIS, CARINA	01-Apr-12
EBBITT, HENRY	01-Apr-12
ESBENSEN, KRISTOFFER	01-Apr-12
EVANS, JOSHUA JOHN	01-Apr-12
FORD, CHRISTOPHER	01-Apr-12
HALL, MEGAN	01-Apr-12
HARPER, JOVIN	01-Apr-12
HARVEY, ISHA	01-Apr-12
HESELTON, PETER	01-Apr-12
HODGKISS, JAMES	01-Apr-12
HUME, JAMES	01-Apr-12
LEE, STUART DAVID	01-Apr-12
MARTIN, EUAN	01-Apr-12
MILES, ALEXANDER	01-Apr-12
OWEN, CHRISTOPHER	01-Apr-12
OWEN-HUGHES, DANIEL	01-Apr-12
PAGE, CHRISTOPHER	01-Apr-12
PENNANT, MARCUS	01-Apr-12
PERRINS, SAM ADAM	01-Apr-12
PITTOCK, MARTIN	01-Apr-12
POWELL, DAVID	01-Apr-12
PREECE, DAVID JOHN	01-Apr-12
PRESTON, JAMES M	01-Apr-12
RIDGEWAY, ADAM	01-Apr-12
ROBERTSON, THOMAS	01-Apr-12
ROGERS, MARK DAVID	01-Apr-12
ROOKE, MARK D	01-Apr-12
RUFFELL, LAUREN	01-Apr-12
RWEYEMAMU, ANATOL	01-Apr-12
SKELDING, JOSHUA	01-Apr-12
SKIRTON, DANIEL	01-Apr-12
SMYTH, DUNCAN	01-Apr-12
SUZUKI, HIRONOBU	01-Apr-12
TITHERINGTON, MARK	01-Apr-12
TRUDGIAN, PAUL	01-Apr-12
VELICKOVIC, SAMUEL	01-Apr-12
WARREN, WILLIAM	01-Apr-12
WILLIAMS, LIAM	01-Apr-12
MILES, EMMA	01-Apr-12
TIMPSON, BENJAMIN	01-Apr-12
BACON, DAVID ROSS	01-Apr-12
BLACK, MALCOLM	01-Apr-12
BURNETT, DANIEL	08-Apr-12
COLLINS, CHRISTOPHER	09-Apr-12
DOUGHTY, STEPHEN	09-Apr-12
ELLIS, WILLIAM	09-Apr-12
JOHNSON, MICHAEL	09-Apr-12
CHAMBERS, MARK W	09-Apr-12
DUNTHORNE, MATTHEW	09-Apr-12
ELSTON, LUKE R	09-Apr-12
FRAME, WENDY	13-Apr-12
JAMIESON, SCOTT	13-Apr-12
MORRISON, KEVIN	13-Apr-12
ROWLAND, JUSTIN	13-Apr-12
TIDSWELL, STEPHEN	13-Apr-12
GLOVER, LEE	13-Apr-12
PITT, DAVID	13-Apr-12
JAMES, CHRISTOPHER	13-Apr-12
HARRIS, NEIL	13-Apr-12
SANDERS, LEE C	13-Apr-12

LIEUTENANTS

PETERS, MATTHEW	13-Apr-12
JONES, RICHARD	13-Apr-12
CROSS, AARON	19-Apr-12
MORRIS, THOMAS OLIVER	01-May-12
OCKLETON, CHRISTOPHER	20-May-12
POCOCK, OLIVER	01-Jun-12
QUAYLE, CHRISTOPHER	01-Jun-12
ROSS, SAMUEL	01-Jun-12
MITCHELL-HEGGS, HUGO	01-Jun-12
MILNE, CHARLOTTE	01-Jun-12
GARNER, LLYR	01-Jun-12
MARTIN, STUART	07-Jun-12
MULCAHY, OLIVER	07-Jun-12
QUIRKE, DARREN L	01-Jul-12
SANDER, OLIVER	01-Jul-12
WARD, ROBERT	01-Jul-12
WELCH, JOSHUA JAMES	01-Jul-12
ALLEN, NICHOLAS	01-Jul-12
FERGUSON, SIMON	01-Jul-12
HARDING, GEORGINA	01-Jul-12
MCBRIERTY, CRAIG	08-Jul-12
CLIFFORD, STEPHEN D	08-Jul-12
FORREST, ADAM	08-Jul-12
GRANT, ELIZABETH S A	08-Jul-12
HARDING, IAN	13-Jul-12
JONES, JASON B	13-Jul-12
MACDONALD, ADAM	13-Jul-12
MATTHEWS, KEVIN	13-Jul-12
THURGOOD, ANTHONY	13-Jul-12
TORTELLI, YASMIN	13-Jul-12
GARDINER, CHRISTOPHER	13-Jul-12
TATE, PAUL ANTHONY	13-Jul-12
ARMSTRONG, PAUL	13-Jul-12
BROCK, DANNY	13-Jul-12
LONG, ADRIAN JOHN	13-Jul-12
MARSH, ALEXANDER	13-Jul-12
STONE, MARC	20-Jul-12
LEGGE, WILLIAM JAMES	31-Jul-12
ADAMS, HENRY	01-Aug-12
ADAMS, VICTORIA	20-Aug-12
BAINES, LIAM P.	26-Aug-12
BALL, JACOB	01-Sep-12
BARLOW, PAUL R	01-Sep-12
BEKIER, OLIVER	01-Sep-12
BEST, HANNAH JANE	01-Sep-12
BLACK, DOMINIC JAMES	01-Sep-12
BLOWER, AMY	01-Sep-12
CHAPMAN, CHRISTOPHER	01-Sep-12
COSBY, MAX	01-Sep-12
CROWSLEY, FRANCESCA	01-Sep-12
DE-BANKS, KYLE	01-Sep-12
DEPPE, GARTH ANDREW	01-Sep-12
DESMOND, JAKE OLIVER	01-Sep-12
DOYLE, JAMES RHYS	01-Sep-12
DU-FEU, ROBERT JAMES	01-Sep-12
ETHERIDGE, ANTHONY C	01-Sep-12
FOLEY, THOMAS RICHARD	01-Sep-12
FORBES, THOMAS	01-Sep-12
GOODALL, WILLIAM	01-Sep-12
HOVINGTON, PETER A K	01-Sep-12
HUNTER, MITCHELL	01-Sep-12

IRWIN, MATTHEW	01-Sep-12
JENKIN, RICHARD HARRY	01-Sep-12
KANTHARIA, RICHARD	01-Sep-12
KEENAN, GREGORY	01-Sep-12
KITCHING, PAUL	01-Sep-12
LACEY, THOMAS S.	01-Sep-12
LEE, JONATHAN J E	01-Sep-12
LOVATT, STEVEN	01-Sep-12
MACKAY, SHAUN A.	01-Sep-12
MCLENNAN, ALEXANDER	01-Sep-12
MILLER, ROSS JOHN	01-Sep-12
MORGAN, HYWEL RHYS	01-Sep-12
MURPHY, ALAN J	01-Sep-12
NEAL, GARETH PETER	01-Sep-12
NEILLY, PATRICK	01-Sep-12
O'FARRELL, MATTHEW	01-Sep-12
PARKER, JOHN	01-Sep-12
PARTRIDGE, RICHARD	01-Sep-12
PERRETT, LUKE WESLEY	01-Sep-12
ROBERTS, CHARLOTTE	01-Sep-12
ROLFE, CONRAD	01-Sep-12
ROSEN-NASH, WILLIAM	01-Sep-12
ROWAN, TRISTIAN	01-Sep-12
RYLAH, JOSHUA	01-Sep-12
SALBERG, DAVID	01-Sep-12
SHORTT, MARTIN	01-Sep-12
SMITH, KIM GYLES	01-Sep-12
SMITH, OLIVER H	01-Sep-12
STONE-WARD, ROBERT	01-Sep-12
STOREY, KRISTOPHER	01-Sep-12
TAYLOR, RACHEL SARAH	01-Sep-12
TURNER, KEITH	01-Sep-12
WATERMAN, MATTHEW L	01-Sep-12
WATT, FRASER JAMES	01-Sep-12
WYATT, JASON R.	01-Sep-12
BURKE, HELEN	01-Sep-12
KANE, ANTHONY	01-Sep-12
VANCE, ANDREW	01-Sep-12
MORGAN, TONY	01-Sep-12
MCKENNA, THOMAS	01-Sep-12
FINDLAY, HAMISH	01-Sep-12
LOVELL-SMITH, ALEXANDRE	01-Sep-12
THOMPSON, PETER	01-Sep-12
GRUBER, JAMES	01-Oct-12
KERSHAW, NEVILLE LUKE	01-Oct-12
ANDREWS, STEVEN J	01-Oct-12
REGAN, KEVIN QGM	07-Oct-12
SKINNER, JENNIFER E	08-Oct-12
CARRIONI-BURNETT, IVANA	13-Oct-12
TAYLOR, BENJAMIN	13-Oct-12
BOAST, RACHEL	13-Oct-12
HALL, RICHARD JAMES	20-Oct-12
STANLEY-ADAMS, TONY	20-Oct-12
BARROWCLOUGH, WILLIAM	22-Oct-12
CLARKE, ROBERT	22-Oct-12
HANLEY, PETER	29-Oct-12
OAKLEY, CHRISTOPHER	01-Nov-12
RIGNALL, WILLIAM	01-Nov-12
STOREY, WILLIAM	01-Nov-12
WARWICK, ANDREW	01-Nov-12
ADCOCK, MARKUS	01-Nov-12

LEPPAN, WARREN	01-Nov-12
MADDICK, JAMES	01-Nov-12
PHILLIPS, THOMAS	01-Nov-12
CURRIE, VICTOR	01-Nov-12
HALLIDAY, ALEXANDER	27-Nov-12
HAZLEDINE, OLIVER	01-Dec-12
OLSSON, ALEXANDRA	08-Dec-12
TURRELL, SHELLY	08-Dec-12
MANSON, ROBERT	08-Dec-12
STOREY, JAMES	08-Dec-12
COE, IAN LOWREY	08-Dec-12
CULLINGFORD, RICHARD	08-Dec-12
GIBBONS, NICOLA	18-Dec-12

2013

HENNAH, GARRY	01-Jan-13
CULLINGFORD, RICHARD	01-Jan-13
KARAVLA, ALEXANDRA	01-Jan-13
WOOD, THOMAS	01-Jan-13
WILSON, ROBERT	01-Jan-13
HARRISON, MARK	01-Jan-13
GORST, JOSHUA	01-Jan-13
MCLEAN, SEAN	01-Jan-13
GIBBONS, NICOLA	01-Jan-13
LEWIS, STUART	01-Jan-13
HALES, MARTIN	01-Jan-13
COE, IAN LOWREY	01-Jan-13
SHEPLEY, BENJAMIN	01-Jan-13
MCDONOUGH, MARK	01-Jan-13
MORTON, CHARLES	01-Jan-13
JAMES, OLIVER	01-Jan-13
WILLIAMS, NICOLA	01-Jan-13
STONE, MATTHEW	01-Jan-13
LINN, BYRON	01-Jan-13
LOWE, STUART	01-Jan-13
COCHRANE, MATTHEW	01-Jan-13
EDWARDS, ANDREW	01-Jan-13
OWEN, ROBERT	01 Jan 13
NEILSON, DANIEL JOHN	22-Jan-13
HARRISON, THOMAS	01-Feb-13
BRADSHAW, EMMA	01-Feb-13
GRAINGER, NATALIE	01-Feb-13
DAVIES, NEIL	08-Feb-13
HARDING, SCOTT	08-Feb-13
STEPHENS, BRIAN J	08-Feb-13
SMITH, JASON P	08-Feb-13
GILL, ADAM MICHAEL	08-Feb-13
EDWARDS, HELEN	08-Feb-13
WHITLEY, JANINE FIONA	08-Feb-13
STOCKLEY, SEAN	01-Mar-13
WALLER, ROBERT	01-Mar-13
BOLLAND, AMY	01-Mar-13
DONEY, NICHOLAS	01-Mar-13
PERRY, KIT	01-Mar-13
SEATON, SAMUEL	01-Mar-13
WALL, SAMUEL	01-Mar-13
WALE, ALEXANDRA	01-Mar-13
FINNIGAN, SEBASTIAN	01-Mar-13
BENDING, SHAUN	01-Mar-13
RAMSAY, STUART	01-Mar-13
HALFORD, JOHN	01-Mar-13

LIEUTENANTS

CHAMBERS, LUKE	01-Mar-13	
DERBYSHIRE, FAYE	01-Mar-13	
BARKER, WILLIAM	16-Mar-13	
RAMAGE, ANDREW	21-Mar-13	
DREW, DANIEL MARK	21-Mar-13	
FALLOWS, LEE DAVID	01-Apr-13	
TATE, DAVID NICHOLAS	01-Apr-13	
GABB, JOHN RICHARD	01-Apr-13	
DENNY, PHILIP MARTIN	01-Apr-13	
WICKS, SAM	01-Apr-13	
BILLAM, DAVID	01-Apr-13	
HEATON, OLIVER	01-Apr-13	
REILLY, SCOTT JAMES	01-Apr-13	
DENT, JAMES IAN	01-Apr-13	
CORE, EMILY ELIZABETH	01-Apr-13	
MASON, JOE	01-Apr-13	
BREHAUT, JOHN	01-Apr-13	
CREASE, PETER	01-Apr-13	
MAYGER, MARTYN	01-Apr-13	
DEVINE, EDWARD	09-Apr-13	
PRICHARD, CHARLES	09-Apr-13	
CUSACK, MICHAEL	09-Apr-13	
CROOK, DANIEL	09-Apr-13	
SAWERS, JOHN	09-Apr-13	
LANG, CHRISTOPHER	01-May-13	
KIME, DAVID	01-May-13	
RICHARDSON, JAMES	01-May-13	
FILIO, ANDREW PAUL	01-May-13	
OSBORNE, ANDREW	01-May-13	
WINCH, MICHAEL	01-May-13	
TAYLOR, JENNIFER	01-May-13	
WILLIAMS, GRAEME	01-May-13	
EASTBURN, JONATHAN	01-May-13	
BARNES, THOMAS	01-May-13	
RAINE, MURRAY	01-May-13	
ROLLINSON, CHRISTOPHER	01-May-13	
HOBBY, DAVID	01-May-13	
PURVIS, CHRISTOPHER	01-May-13	
GALLAGHER, ROSS	01-May-13	
USBORNE, NEIL	01-May-13	
TAYLOR, OLIVER	01-May-13	
LOWE, CHRISTIAN	01-May-13	
COWAN, CHRISTOPHER	01-May-13	
TILLEY, ELEANOR	01-May-13	
JOHNSON, MATTHEW	01-May-13	
DYNES, OLIVER GERARD	01-May-13	
MCDOUGALL, JAMES	01-May-13	
GREIG, STUART	01-May-13	
BASS, ANDREW	01-May-13	
DUFFELL, GLYN	01-May-13	
PAYLING, WILLIAM	01-May-13	
THOMPSON, LUKE	01-May-13	
COOPER, CHARLOTTE	01-May-13	
BUGG, CHRISTOPHER	01-May-13	
REEKIE, FRASER	01-May-13	
BORLAND, KATE	01-May-13	
MORRIS, GAVIN	01-May-13	
MORRISON, ALAN	01-May-13	
HOLDEN, SIMON	01-May-13	
O'CALLAGHAN, LUCY	01-May-13	
CARNIE, CHRISTOPHER	01-May-13	
CULLEN, MATTHEW	01-May-13	
NEWBURY, JAMES	03-May-13	
BLIGHT, PHILLIP	03-May-13	
CLEGG, ROSS	03-May-13	
HUNTER, CAMERON	03-May-13	
NOLAN, ANDREW J.	03-May-13	
PARKER, SHAUN	03-May-13	
MAY, CONNOR	03-May-13	
LOVELL, JONATHAN	03-May-13	
DUNN, ASHLEY	03-May-13	
LE-MAISTRE, MATTHEW	03-May-13	
BESWICK, MARK	03-May-13	
SHEPHERD, DANIEL	07-May-13	
HERBERT, JACK ALBERT	09-May-13	
OLVER, THOMAS	10-May-13	
CHEW, CHRISTOPHER	20-May-13	
WILLIAMS, AARON PETER	20-May-13	
NOBLE, SIMON JAMES	01-Jun-13	
TURFREY, MATTHEW	01-Jun-13	
NOLAN, SAMUEL	01-Jun-13	
BRYERS, MATTHEW	01-Jun-13	
GAMWELL, SEBASTIAN	01-Jun-13	
HOUGHTON, DAVID	01-Jun-13	
CAVE, WILLIAM	01-Jun-13	
SABIN, SCOTT	01-Jul-13	
HEATHCOTE, JAMES	08-Jul-13	
HAYES, MATTHEW	12-Jul-13	
BICKNELL, NEIL	12-Jul-13	
LEMON, CHRISTOPHER	12-Jul-13	
PROCTOR, PAUL	12-Jul-13	
DOWDING, CRAIG	12-Jul-13	
GRANT, GARY	12-Jul-13	
ANDERSON, BRYAN	12-Jul-13	
JEFFREYS, SUSAN	12-Jul-13	
MEEHAN, OLIVER	15-Jul-13	
COWAN, PETER WILLIAM	20-Jul-13	
PREECE, TIMOTHY MARK	20-Jul-13	
ASTLEY, WILLIAM	23-Jul-13	
PHELPS, ALEXANDER	01-Aug-13	
WHARRY, DOUGLAS	01-Aug-13	
POTTER, STEPHEN	01-Aug-13	
WHEELER, ROBERT	01-Aug-13	
WORRALL, ADAM	01-Aug-13	
VICKERS, PATRICK	01-Aug-13	
MORGAN, KELLY	01-Aug-13	
LAMB, BRYCE	07-Aug-13	
THOMPSON, ADAM	07-Aug-13	
FAIRWEATHER, DONELL	07-Aug-13	
COLLINS, RICHARD	07-Aug-13	
JONES, CAROLYN	27-Aug-13	
PLANT, MICHAEL	01-Sep-13	
WESTWOOD, CHRISTOPHER	01-Sep-13	
ALDERSON, STUART	01-Sep-13	
TOMLINSON, LUKE	01-Sep-13	
LENNON, THOMAS	01-Sep-13	
WOODWARD, MARK	01-Sep-13	
DOBBS, HELEN AMY	01-Sep-13	
CHARTERS, EMMA	01-Sep-13	
STEPHENS, CARL	01-Sep-13	
COLOHAN, SAM	01-Sep-13	
RIXON, THOMAS	01-Sep-13	
MURRAY, EDWARD	01-Sep-13
CLARK, CRAIG	01-Sep-13
FLANNAGAN, BRYAN	01-Sep-13
BADDELEY, JAMES	01-Sep-13
IVES, KATIE	01-Sep-13
GREEN, JEREMY	01-Sep-13
TOBIN, KEITH	01-Sep-13
ROSS, PHILLIP	01-Sep-13
BASSETT, DANIEL	01-Sep-13
O'SULLIVAN, LUKE	01-Sep-13
HOBIN, DANIEL	01-Sep-13
SHEPHERD, LOUISE	01-Sep-13
RUTHERFORD, IAN	01-Sep-13
WITHAM, BRIAN	01-Sep-13
MORRIS, JOSHUA	01-Sep-13
PLANT, ANNA LOUISE	01-Sep-13
HARRY, STEPHEN	01-Sep-13
LIVINGSTONE, ANDREW	01-Sep-13
COULTAS, DANIEL	01-Sep-13
CHANDLER, RORY	01-Sep-13
JACQUES, MICHAEL	01-Sep-13
MORRIS, HARRY	01-Sep-13
DUFFY, ANDREW	01-Sep-13
BURNS, RICHARD	01-Sep-13
SLEIGHT, THOMAS	01-Sep-13
WILSON, THOMAS	01-Sep-13
BAKER, KYLE	01-Sep-13
TITE, MATTHEW	01-Sep-13
ROBINSON, NICHOLAS	01-Sep-13
MUNSON, JASON STANLEY	01-Sep-13
CUNNINGHAM, DEXTER	01-Sep-13
CARY, MATTHEW	01-Sep-13
MAJOR, LEE	01-Sep-13
BROWN, MATTHEW	01-Sep-13
BOREHAM, DANIEL	01-Sep-13
EDWARDS, RHYS	01-Sep-13
KUMWENDA, TEMWA	01-Sep-13
EELES, THOMAS	01-Sep-13
BONE, LOUISE	01-Sep-13
SUTTLE, CELIA	01-Sep-13
DE LA RUE, MICHAEL	01-Sep-13
ASTLEY, DANIEL	01-Sep-13
FRASER, SIMON	01-Sep-13
COGDELL, MICHAEL	01-Sep-13
THEOBOLD, DANIEL	01-Sep-13
HOWARD, DALE	01-Sep-13
DOYLE, MICHAEL	01-Sep-13
GLOVER, DANIEL	01-Sep-13
JONES, MARK	01-Sep-13
WESTMAAS, TIMOTHY	01-Sep-13
TINSLEY, DAVID	01-Sep-13
EGLINTON, BENJAMIN	01-Sep-13
MEHSEN, SAMY	01-Sep-13
KITSON, MATTHEW	01-Sep-13
CATOR, BENJAMIN HUGO	03-Sep-13
THOMPSON, ALEXANDER	14-Sep-13
LADLOW, MICHAEL	14-Sep-13
LAMBERT, DANIEL	11-Oct-13
COLLINS, JASON D.	11-Oct-13
KLEIN, MICHAEL	11-Oct-13
MCCULLAGH, TIMOTHY	11-Oct-13

LIEUTENANTS

CAVENDISH, GAVIN W. 11-Oct-13	ANDREWS, LIAM 01-Nov-13	LIVINGSTONE, DANA 07-Nov-13
SAVEAL, MATTHEW P 11-Oct-13	FIELDS, SAMUEL 01-Nov-13	SMYTHE, SEAN 07-Nov-13
POTTS, DAVID 11-Oct-13	SAVAGE, DOMINIC 01-Nov-13	BRINDLEY, ALICE 10-Nov-13
HOCKING, ROGER 11-Oct-13	LEONARD, MATTHEW 01-Nov-13	ROBINSON, JOHN 10-Nov-13
ROBINSON, LINDSY 11-Oct-13	JONES, SIMON 01-Nov-13	GOWLING, STEPHEN 01-Dec-13
PETTINGER, JOSEPH 20-Oct-13	HOWES, DANIEL 01-Nov-13	JONES, ROBERT 01-Dec-13
DUNNING, TIMOTHY 01-Nov-13	UNDERWOOD, MICHAEL 01-Nov-13	EDEN, PHILIP 08-Dec-13
STEVENSON, HELEN 01-Nov-13	HOUGHTON, CHRISTOPHER 01-Nov-13	MILKINS, KIEL 13-Dec-13
SEABROOK, PETER 01-Nov-13	SIMMONDS, ZOE 01-Nov-13	THOMSON, DAVID 20-Dec-13

SUB LIEUTENANTS

2010

PRICHARD, CHARLES 09-Apr-10	
POWELL, MATTHEW 01-Sep-10	
STEELE, NATHAN 01-Nov-10	

2011

L'VOV-BASIROV, NIKOLAI 12-Jan-11	DIAPER, KEVIN 01-Apr-11	KENT, THOMAS 01-Aug-11
MILLIGAN, ROBERT 12-Jan-11	EYERS, DALE SEAN 01-Apr-11	ROBSON, JAMES 14-Aug-11
ALLDRIDGE, GEORGE 12-Jan-11	FORSTER, THOMAS 01-Apr-11	RYDE, EMMA 14-Aug-11
ARMITAGE, DAVID 12-Jan-11	GREEN, RICHARD 01-Apr-11	KENWARD, JONATHAN 14-Aug-11
BARR, ANDREW 19-Jan-11	GREGORY, DANIEL 01-Apr-11	LISLE, ROBERT 14-Aug-11
BENSON, ADAM 01-Feb-11	JOHNSON, MATTHEW 01-Apr-11	SINCLAIR, GREGORY 14-Aug-11
BRYCE, JENNY 01-Feb-11	LAY, JACK 01-Apr-11	ADEKOLUEJO, GBADEBOWALE 15-Aug-11
COUTTS, PHOEBE 01-Feb-11	O'DELL, ALEXANDER 01-Apr-11	ANDREWS, ROBERT 15-Aug-11
ELSEY, DAVID 01-Feb-11	PARRY-JONES, ALEXANDER 01-Apr-11	ASKER, TRISTAN 15-Aug-11
EVERY, MICHAEL 01-Feb-11	PRITCHARD, LORNA 01-Apr-11	BRADSHAW, KIERAN 01-Sep-11
FORBES, SIMON 01-Feb-11	PURDUE, BASIL 01-Apr-11	BRAY, MICHAEL 01-Sep-11
GRAFTON, JOSHUA 01-Feb-11	ROBUS, LUCY 01-Apr-11	BUTTERY, STEPHANIE 01-Sep-11
HALAHAN, MILES 01-Feb-11	ROTHWELL, CHRISTOPHER 01-Apr-11	CAVE, GEORGE 01-Sep-11
HEAD, MATTHEW 01-Feb-11	SLOPER, MAX 01-Apr-11	CHENERY, ALEXANDER 01-Sep-11
LEWIS, THOMAS 01-Feb-11	VINES, ADAM 01-Apr-11	DEWING, WILLIAM 01-Sep-11
LILLEY, BENJAMIN 01-Feb-11	WILD, SIMON 01-Apr-11	DEWIS, BEN M D. 01-Sep-11
MACK, PETER 01-Feb-11	WRIGHT, JOSEPH 01-Apr-11	DOGGART, ADAM 01-Sep-11
MILNES, GRANT 01-Feb-11	GILROY, ANTHONY 01-Apr-11	FAYERS, SAMUEL 01-Sep-11
PINDER, AIDAN 01-Feb-11	WRIGHT, NATALIE 01-Apr-11	FORSE, RYAN MICHAEL 01-Sep-11
RICKETTS, ALEX 01-Feb-11	BERRIDGE, MATTHEW 01-Apr-11	GELL, DAVID MICHAEL 01-Sep-11
TARPEY, RICHARD 01-Feb-11	BOWDEN, MATTHEW 11-Apr-11	GINTY, JOHN 01-Sep-11
WARDLE, DANIEL J. 01-Feb-11	BREAKS, JAMES 11-Apr-11	GORDON, EMILY HYMAN 01-Sep-11
WHIPP, IAN ANDREW 01-Feb-11	BURBIDGE, RICHARD 01-May-11	GWINNUTT, OLIVER 01-Sep-11
PEASE, CATHERINE 01-Feb-11	CLAYTON, DAVID HUW 01-May-11	HANCOCK, DAVID 01-Sep-11
SADLER, AIMEE ROSE 01-Feb-11	GRIFFITH, PHILLIP 01-May-11	HARRIS, SAMUEL 01-Sep-11
BLAGDEN, LAURA JANE 01-Feb-11	HAWKINS, MICHAEL 01-May-11	HODGSON, KATIE 01-Sep-11
DRYSDALE, ROBERT 16-Feb-11	KEEBLE, CHRISTOPHER 01-May-11	HOLT, CHRISTOPHER 01-Sep-11
FORCE, RORY J 16-Feb-11	LEWIS, GEORGE 01-May-11	HOWARD, ALEXANDER 01-Sep-11
FREEMAN, MATTHEW 01-Mar-11	MACARTNEY, SIMON 01-May-11	KINGDON, SAMUEL 01-Sep-11
LEVERIDGE, ADAM 01-Mar-11	MCLEMAN, WILLIAM 01-May-11	LAW, MICHAEL 01-Sep-11
MACKIE, SCOTT 01-Mar-11	MILLS, WILLIAM 01-May-11	LINDSEY, THOMAS 01-Sep-11
MARTIN, JAMIE 01-Mar-11	MULLIN, LAURA 01-May-11	LUNN, DARREN A 01-Sep-11
MOSS, STEPHANIE 01-Mar-11	ORR, JACQUELINE MARIE 01-May-11	MARFLEET, ADAM 01-Sep-11
PEARCE, CHRISTOPHER 01-Mar-11	SLAVIN, MAX 01-May-11	MILSOM, MATTHEW 01-Sep-11
STEVENSON, CHARLES 01-Mar-11	TODD, JAMES 01-May-11	O'CONNOR, CALUM 01-Sep-11
WADE, ROBERT JOHN 01-Mar-11	WARNER, PHILIP 01-May-11	O'REGAN, KYLE 01-Sep-11
WARD, TIMOTHY 01-Mar-11	WATTS, NICHOLAS 01-May-11	ORR, ROBERT 01-Sep-11
WHITELEY, PETER 01-Mar-11	NAPIER, DUNCAN 01-May-11	RAY, DANIEL 01-Sep-11
ALBON, JOSHUA GUY 01-Mar-11	TATE, DENNIS 01-May-11	REDBOURN, JAMES 01-Sep-11
AYLMER, MATTHEW 01-Mar-11	PAWLEY, ROSS 01-May-11	REID, IAIN JAMES 01-Sep-11
BUNDOCK, OLIVER 01-Mar-11	PADDEN, GREGORY 01-May-11	RICHARDSON, CRAIG A 01-Sep-11
	WRAY, STUART 24-May-11	ROBERTSON, SEAN 01-Sep-11
	HOLDCROFT, LUKE 01-Jul-11	RODGERS, MARK 01-Sep-11
	LAY, BENJAMIN 11-May-11	ROWLAND, CHARLES 01-Sep-11
	PERSHEYEV, ALISTAIR 11-Apr-11	SOUTER, ALASDAIR 01-Sep-11
	WADE, FREDERICK 01-Aug-11	SPRINGER, RORY 01-Sep-11
	CONNAUGHTON, MARK 01-Aug-11	SUTHERLAND, OLIVER 01-Sep-11
	GIBSON, SCOTT 01-Aug-11	TINDLE, JACK 01-Sep-11

SUB LIEUTENANTS

TUCKLEY, CHRISTOPHER 01-Sep-11	COYNE, PAUL 01-Jan-12	BALCAM, JONATHAN 01-May-12
TURNER, MATTHEW 01-Sep-11	FLINT, THOMAS 01-Jan-12	WILKINS, THOMAS 01-May-12
WARD, NICHOLAS 01-Sep-11	HARTLEY, SOLOMON 01-Jan-12	COOMBES, GEORGE 01-May-12
WEBBER, DAVID 01-Sep-11	HINDLE, CHRISTOPHER 03-Jan-12	CRIER, MATTHEW 01-May-12
WILSON, LLOYD 01-Sep-11	JENKINS, GARETH 24-Jan-12	WELLS, MATTHEW 01-May-12
WILSON, THOMAS 01-Sep-11	McCANN, SALLY JANE 24-Jan-12	RIGSBY, DAVID 01-May-12
WOODS, ANNA LOUISE 01-Sep-11	REID, JENNY ELLEN 24-Jan-12	CALLEAR, BEN 01-May-12
YOUNG, JAMES 01-Sep-11	WELCH, HARRY 24-Jan-12	WIELBO, DOMINIK 01-May-12
BEARDALL-JACKLIN, PAUL 01-Sep-11	NEWLANDS, KRISTOFFER 24-Jan-12	POULSOM, MATTHEW 01-May-12
BELL WILLIAMSON, ... 01-Sep-11	BAMBRO, CALUM 24-Jan-12	MINNS, ROBERT JOHN 01-May-12
BOWERS, THOMAS 01-Sep-11	BARLEY, ANDREW 24-Jan-12	JACKSON-SPENCE, NICHOLAS 01-May-12
BRERETON, CHARLES 01-Nov-11	BEALE, JOSHUA 27-Jan-12	CARNEY, JOSEPH 01-May-12
BURBECK, LESLIE 01-Nov-11	BYE, KYO 01-Feb-12	CLARK, RACHAEL 01-May-12
CAMPBELL, DAVID 01-Nov-11	CHEYNE, RORY 01-Feb-12	DICKSON, ERIC 01-May-12
CLARINGBOLD, NEILL 01-Nov-11	COOKE, STUART 01-Feb-12	SWANN, JAMES 01-May-12
DAVIES, NATHAN 01-Nov-11	GIDNEY, RAYMOND 01-Feb-12	BARTON, JENNY 01-May-12
DOBSON, WILLIAM 01-Nov-11	GROVES, CHRISTOPHER 01-Feb-12	BELL, TRISTAN 01-May-12
EMMERSON, DAVID I 01-Nov-11	HENAGHEN, WAYNE 01-Feb-12	HEWITT, SIMON 01-May-12
FARLEY, EMMA LOUISE 01-Nov-11	HENRICKSON, BEAU 01-Feb-12	MAY, FREDERICK 01-May-12
FRADLEY, NICOLA ANN 01-Nov-11	HESSE, PETER 01-Feb-12	COLEMAN, JOSEPH 01-Jul-12
GROUT, CHRISTOPHER 01-Nov-11	JONES, MARK FRANK 01-Feb-12	BROWN, JOSHUA 01-Jul-12
HODDER, GREGORY 01-Nov-11	LADDS, GRACE 01-Feb-12	CLARKE, MARCUS 01-Jul-12
HORNE, THOMAS 01-Nov-11	MAXWELL, EMMA 01-Feb-12	HUGHES, RYAN 15-Aug-12
JOSHI, CAEL 01-Nov-11	MCMONIES, MURRAY 01-Feb-12	HUXTABLE, MARK 01-Sep-12
KEMP, THOMAS 01-Nov-11	NASH, IAN 01-Feb-12	JACOBS, JOSHUA 01-Sep-12
LEWIS, GETHIN 01-Nov-11	ROBINSON, ALEX 01-Feb-12	KAIN, MATTHEW 01-Sep-12
MACHIN, MATTHEW 01-Nov-11	ROYLE, MICHAEL 01-Feb-12	KAVANAGH, CRAIG 01-Sep-12
MARTIN, STEPHANIE 01-Nov-11	SHRIVES, JAMES M 01-Feb-12	KING, ALEXANDER 01-Sep-12
MCLAUCHLAN, JAMES 01-Nov-11	STEPHENSON, GAVIN 01-Feb-12	KINGSLEY-SMITH, BENJAMIN 01-Sep-12
MILLAR, GARY 01-Nov-11	WEBSTER, DAVID 01-Feb-12	LEE, DAVID 01-Sep-12
PRINTER, ALEXANDER 01-Nov-11	WOODWARD, GUY 01-Feb-12	MARRINER, HENRY 01-Sep-12
SMITH, BENJAMIN 01-Nov-11	STEADMAN, THOMAS 01-Feb-12	OTTAWAY, THOMAS 01-Sep-12
STINCHCOMBE, MARK 01-Nov-11	AVISON, CHRISTOPHER 01-Feb-12	PETHICK, THOMAS 01-Sep-12
STURMAN, ANDREW 01-Nov-11	BOND, STUART 01-Feb-12	PINNEY, RICHARD 01-Sep-12
TAMAYO, KIERAN 01-Nov-11	CATAFFO, PAUL 01-Feb-12	PRINTIE, CHRISTOPHER 01-Sep-12
WALTON, DARREN 01-Nov-11	COLTHART, LEE 01-Apr-12	PRITCHARD, THOMAS 01-Sep-12
WARD, ANDREW 01-Nov-11	DUNCAN, ROWAN 01-Apr-12	SALES, ADAM 01-Sep-12
MURPHY, THOMAS 01-Nov-11	FORDHAM, PHILLIP 01-Apr-12	SHARP, THOMAS 01-Sep-12
ARMSTRONG, ALISON 01-Nov-11	FOX, OWEN 01-Apr-12	WARNER, THOMAS 01-Sep-12
HOWE, NICHOLAS 01-Nov-11	FRENCH, MATTHEW 01-Apr-12	WINDSOR, CHRISTOPHER 01-Sep-12
THOMPSON, MATTHEW 01-Nov-11	HUTCHISON, CALLUM 01-Apr-12	HOPKINS, DANIELLE 01-Sep-12
JACKSON, THOMAS 01-Nov-11	MAIR, JOANNA 01-Apr-12	BURNS, AMY 01-Sep-12
THICKNESSE, THOMAS 01-Nov-11	MAKOSZ, SIMON 01-Apr-12	ROLLASON, KRISTINA 01-Sep-12
ROACH, LEWIS 01-Nov-11	MURDOCH, HANNAH 01-Apr-12	SAVIN, DAVID 01-Sep-12
TAYLOR, DOMINIC 10-Nov-11	ROBBINS, DANIEL 01-Apr-12	LEAHY, SAM 01-Sep-12
YEARLING, EMMA 21-Nov-11	SUNDERLAND, SCOTT 01-Apr-12	SMYTH, DANIEL 01-Sep-12
DUTT, JAMES 24-Nov-11	WHITE, MAXWELL 01-Apr-12	LEE, SIMON 01-Sep-12
FRENCH, SOPHIE 24-Nov-11	HAMMOND, JAMES 01-Apr-12	HAWTHORN, SIMON 01-Sep-12
RUSHFORTH, ROBERT 24-Nov-11	NETTLEINGHAM, JAMIE LEE 01-Apr-12	WEEDON, CHRISTOPHER 01-Sep-12
WRAITH, LUKE 08-Dec-11	PROWLE, OWEN 01-Apr-12	BALL, LIAM 01-Sep-12
BOWNESS, ZOE JANE 08-Dec-11	FLYNN, LUKE 09-Apr-12	CLARK, BENJAMIN 01-Sep-12
CLARK, GARY 08-Dec-11	MCFARLANE, DANIEL 09-Apr-12	THOMPSON, PETER 01-Sep-12
	MILTON, MICHAEL 09-Apr-12	SLATER, BENJAMIN 01-Sep-12
2012	ADAMS, MEGAN 11-Apr-12	BOARDMAN, DANIEL 01-Sep-12
	BUTTAR, DANIEL 11-Apr-12	BURNS, RICHARD 01-Sep-12
FORDE, RUPERT 01-Jan-12	SWEENEY, FIONA 22-Apr-12	DUFFY, MARK 01-Sep-12
GRIFFITHS, DAVID 01-Jan-12	WALKER, DANIEL 01-May-12	BARTON, HANNAH 01-Sep-12
HARRIS, MARTYN 01-Jan-12	EATON, MICHAEL 01-May-12	MCMORRAN, HANNAH 01-Sep-12
SMART, TYLER MICHAEL 01-Jan-12	WESTON, ANTONY 01-May-12	DARWELL, JOSEPH 01-Sep-12
SMITH, JEFF ROBERT 01-Jan-12	WILKINSON, LLOYD 01-May-12	WOOLLARD, KERRY 01-Sep-12
TAYLOR, ALASTAIR 01-Jan-12	BRYANT, NATHAN 01-May-12	CHILD, WILLIAM 01-Sep-12
THOMPSON, SAMUEL 01-Jan-12		

SUB LIEUTENANTS

PRIOR, ROBERT	01-Sep-12
TURNER, MATHEW	01-Sep-12
WADDINGTON, ANDREW	01-Sep-12
AYTO, LYDIA JANE	01-Sep-12
WARNOCK, CHRISTOPHER	01-Sep-12
FAWCETT, STUART	01-Sep-12
AUJLA, PAVANDIP	08-Oct-12
SMITH, CHRISTIAN	01-Dec-12
STILL, JAMES	04-Dec-12
CLARK, JAMES	08-Dec-12
KNIGHT, CHARLES	08-Dec-12
SELWOOD, BENJAMIN	08-Dec-12

2013

HOOPER, CHRISTOPHER	01-Jan-13
INGLIS, DAVID	01-Jan-13
MCCLINTOCK, LEE	01-Jan-13
PAWSON, JONATHAN	01-Feb-13
WOOD, MICHAEL	01-Feb-13

COATES, JAMES	01-Feb-13
BARNICK, SEBASTIAN	01-Feb-13
STEWART, LEONIE	01-Feb-13
WARDEN, SOPHIE	01-Mar-13
BROAD, ANNABEL	08-Mar-13
BROWN, OLIVER	01-Apr-13
FISHER, LUKE	01-Apr-13
HENDERSON, KATY	01-May-13
MACIEJEWSKI, LUKE	01-May-13
MORTON-KING, FREDERICK	01-May-13
STEELE, ASHLEY	01-May-13
WILLIAMS, ZOE	01-May-13
EVANS, LAURA	01-May-13
HARRIS, ROBERT	01-May-13
COLLINGS, ANTONY	01-May-13
STACEY, PIERS	01-May-13
ROBINSON, NICHOLAS	01-May-13
LOFTUS, ANDREW	01-May-13
KENDRY, ADAM	01-May-13
PARSONS, THOMAS	01-May-13

BARBER, MAX	11-May-13
BROOK, SOPHIE	01-Jul-13
BUTTERWORTH, CHESTER	01-Sep-13
CRESDEE, SAMUEL	01-Sep-13
PEARSON, EDWARD	01-Sep-13
REID, PHILIP ALAN	01-Sep-13
SCRAGGS, DANIEL	01-Sep-13
STAPLEY-BUNTEN, THOMAS	01-Sep-13
HAZELL, THOMAS	01-Sep-13
LEIDIG, GEORGE	01-Sep-13
HEIL, KIERAN	01-Sep-13
LILLINGTON, CLAIRE	01-Sep-13
SAUNDERS, ALEXANDER	01-Sep-13
WILLIAMSON, BEN	01-Sep-13
DALE, REBECCA	01-Sep-13
MAYES, DAVID JOHN	01-Sep-13

MIDSHIPMEN

2012

PHILLIPS, LEWIS PAUL	11-Apr-12
YOUNG, MARTIN J.	11-Apr-12
BORTHWICK, CHRISTOPHER	11-Apr-12
FENN, CHRISTOPHER	11-Apr-12
FURNISS, SAM	11-Apr-12
BROAD, JAMES	01-May-12
EDDY, CHARLOTTE	01-May-12
GREIG, RYAN	15-Aug-12
RICKETTS, SIMON	01-Sep-12
SMITH, MATTHEW	01-Sep-12
WEIR, STEWART	01-Sep-12
BERRILL, SIMON	01-Sep-12
LITTLE, PHILIPPA	01-Sep-12
MCBRIDE, SHAUN	01-Sep-12
MENDHAM, OLIVER	01-Nov-12
MORRIS, JONOTHAN	01-Nov-12
MOSS, TYRONE	01-Nov-12
RAPER, DANIEL	01-Nov-12
LYNN, JAMES	01-Nov-12
GRANT, DANIEL	01-Nov-12
ANDERSON, JOSEPH	24-Dec-12

2013

BOAK, CHARLOTTE	24-Jan-13
DAVIS, CARL	24-Jan-13
FIGGINS, ADAM	01-Feb-13
FORER, JONATHON	01-Feb-13
HARRISSON, LUCAS	01-Feb-13
LEISK, OLIVER	01-Feb-13
RANDLES, MAXWELL	01-Feb-13
SELLEN, THOMAS	01-Feb-13
VIVIAN, MICHAEL	01-Feb-13
WITCHER, EMILY	01-Feb-13
GROVES, NICHOLAS	01-Feb-13
BALL, SAMUEL	01-Feb-13
FISHER, CAMERON	01-Feb-13

LOFTUS, ASHLEY MICHAEL	01-May-13
CUNNINGHAM, MATTHEW	01-May-13
TREVOR-HARRIS, GEORGE	01-May-13
COBLEY, SIMON DAVID	01-May-13
HUGHES, GARY	01-May-13
WEBBER, LAUREN	01-May-13
LE HURAY, JASON	01-May-13
PENGELLY, MICHAEL	01-May-13
JEFFREY, JOSEPH	01-May-13
McGINLAY, MATTHEW	01-May-13
NEYLEN, SERENA	01-May-13
KIRRAGE, CHARLES	01-May-13
SAUNDERS, ALEXANDER	01-May-13
BENNEY, JORDON	01-May-13
GIRLING, STEVEN	01-Sep-13
MASSEY, BENJAMIN	01-Sep-13
PETKEN, ALEXANDER	01-Sep-13
CAMERON, FRASER	01-Sep-13
MARSH, JAMES	01-Sep-13
KUTARSKI, EMILY	01-Sep-13
SMEES, JAMES	01-Sep-13
JONES, BENJAMIN	01-Sep-13
FOSTER, MATTHEW	01-Sep-13
MAGILL, MICHAEL	01-Sep-13
GWILLIAM, BENJAMIN	01-Sep-13
O'DONNELL, RORY	01-Sep-13
KUBARA, ALEX MYKOLA	01-Sep-13
DREAVES, CHRISTOPHER	01-Sep-13
HINE, THOMAS	01-Sep-13
CRALLAN, ALEXANDER	01-Sep-13
SALT, ISAAC	01-Sep-13
BROWN, HARRY	01-Sep-13
HIND, JOSHUA	01-Sep-13
ROSS, ALISON KAY	01-Sep-13
BRIERLEY, NATALIE	01-Sep-13
DANKS, JONATHAN	01-Sep-13
MCGILL, GUS	01-Sep-13
JONES, LEWIS	01-Sep-13

ANDERSON, PETER	01-Sep-13
BURROWS, OLIVER	01-Sep-13
ALLEN, BENJAMIN	01-Sep-13
COATES, AARON	01-Sep-13
HOTCHKISS, JONATHAN	01-Sep-13
PEACOCK, JOANNA	01-Sep-13
WOODCOCK, KEITH	01-Sep-13
MILLWARD, ELLIOTT	01-Sep-13
HOPE, WILLIAM DAVID	01-Sep-13
THOMPSON, MICHAEL	01-Sep-13
MCELROY, PAUL	01-Sep-13
HUTCHINSON, THOMAS	01-Sep-13
MACKLEY-HEATH, MEGAN	01-Sep-13
BURGESS, THOMAS	01-Sep-13
BRENNAN, RICHARD	01-Sep-13
ALLAN, ROBER	01-Sep-13
MCNALLY, PETER J	01-Sep-13
DUDLEY, JAMES	01-Sep-13
HAWKINGS, TOM	01-Sep-13
CLARKE, BENJAMIN	01-Sep-13
GREEN, JONATHAN	01-Sep-13
DYMOCK, CRAIG	01-Sep-13
GILLMAN, ROBERT	01-Sep-13
RAINFORD, JAYJAY	01-Sep-13
CROSSLEY, HEATHER	01-Sep-13
BLACKBURN, EWAN	01-Sep-13
POWNEY, LEWIS	01-Sep-13
HELM, JAMES	01-Sep-13
POUNDALL, GARETH	01-Sep-13
CLAYTON, ANDREW	01-Sep-13
LITCHFIELD, HANNAH	01-Sep-13
SMIT, NATHAN J.	01-Sep-13
MILLS, GREGORY	01-Sep-13
SLATER, WILLIAM	01-Sep-13
GARNER, DOMINIC	01-Nov-13
NEILSON, ROBERT	01-Nov-13
ROBERTS, LLION	01-Nov-13
MELLOWS, CHRISTOPHER	01-Nov-13

DANIELS, JOSH 01-Nov-13	MORRIS, ASHLEY ROBIN 01-Nov-13	HILL, RORY 01-Nov-13
CARR, STEPHEN 01-Nov-13	BRAIN, BRANDON................................01-Nov-13	HEWITSON, DAVID..............................01-Nov-13
HARSENT, PAUL 01-Nov-13	ATKINSON, KEVIN 01-Nov-13	GOODWIN, LLOYD 01-Nov-13
WOODRIDGE, RYAN 01-Nov-13	CARLISLE, JACK 01-Nov-13	REED, THOMAS 01-Nov-13
MAGZOUB, MOWAFAG 01-Nov-13	NIGHTINGALE, MATTHEW 01-Nov-13	CAMPBELL, SCOTT 01-Nov-13
VARCO, THOMAS 01-Nov-13	CREEDON, TIMOTHY 01-Nov-13	SHUTT, DAVID....................................01-Nov-13
WEST, OLIVIA.......................................01-Nov-13	LEYSON, RHODRI.................................01-Nov-13	HUCKSTEP, JOSEPH 01-Nov-13
DOHERTY, BETHANY 01-Nov-13	AINDOW, ALICE LUCY 01-Nov-13	PRAUSNITZ, LUKE 01-Nov-13
HUGHES, MICHAEL 01-Nov-13	MURRAY, WILLIAM 01-Nov-13	DUXBURY, KATRINA............................01-Nov-13
MOORE, JORDAN 01-Nov-13	MARSHALL, WILLIAM 01-Nov-13	BENNETT, ASHLEY..............................01-Nov-13
TAYLOR, DEAN 01-Nov-13	BANYARD, ADELAIDE 01-Nov-13	HALLIWELL, LEON...............................01-Nov-13
ALVEY, JOSHUA 01-Nov-13	OSBORNE, CONNOR 01-Nov-13	FRASER-SHAW, DOMINIC 01-Nov-13
MCNICHOLL, BRUCE............................01-Nov-13	COOMER, ADAM...................................01-Nov-13	KEELER, CHARLOTTE...........................01-Nov-13
FRYER, NICHOLAS BEN 01-Nov-13	KROMOLICKI, MATTHEW 01-Nov-13	ROTHWELL, KIRSTY.............................01-Nov-13
WALTERS, CAMERON 01-Nov-13	HALL, NICOLA EMILY 01-Nov-13	HARVEY, BEN 01-Nov-13
RICHARDSON, ALEXANDER 01-Nov-13	ORMROD, RYAN...................................01-Nov-13	

MEDICAL OFFICERS

SURGEON REAR ADMIRAL

MCARTHUR, CALUM JAMES GIBB 08/10/2012

SURGEON COMMODORES

2011
WALKER, ALASDAIR JAMES OBE 01/07/2011
HUGHES, ANDREW S............................ 25/07/2011
BUXTON, PETER OBE........................... 15/08/2011

2013
MCNEILL LOVE, ROBIN M.................... 23/07/2013

SURGEON CAPTAINS

2007
BURGESS, ANDREW J........................ 17/04/2007
MIDWINTER, MARK CBE.................... 01/09/2007

2008
HOWELL, MICHAEL A.......................... 06/05/2008
HUGHES, PAUL 08/09/2008
ROSS, ROBERT MBE 16/09/2008
BENTON, PETER 31/12/2008

2009
BAKER, ADRIAN B.............................. 17/02/2009

2010
MILLAR, STUART................................ 22/04/2010
SHARPLEY, JOHN 01/07/2010
THOMAS, LYNN 01/07/2010

2011
EVERSHED, MARCUS 01/03/2011

BREE, STEPHEN 01/07/2011
HILL, GRAHAM A............................... 01/07/2011

2013
MARSHALL, FLEUR T.......................... 20/08/2013

SURGEON COMMANDERS

1996
PERRY, JONATHAN............................ 31/12/1996

1997
EDWARDS, CHARLES 31/12/1997

1998
RISDALL, JANE 31/12/1998

1999
LAMBERT, ANTHONY W OBE 30/06/1999

2000
NICHOLSON, GRAEME 31/12/2000

2001
BIRT, DAVID J................................... 30/06/2001
TURNBULL, PAUL S............................ 30/06/2001

2002
STAPLEY, SARAH ANN....................... 30/06/2002
CLARKE, JOHN.................................. 30/06/2002
PEARSON, CHRISTOPHER................... 30/06/2002

2003
WYLIE, ROBERT................................ 01/04/2003
BLAIR, DUNCAN G 30/06/2003
SMITH, STEVEN R.............................. 30/06/2003
TERRY, MICHAEL.............................. 30/06/2003
MELLOR, ADRIAN 30/06/2003
HAND, CHRISTOPHER 30/06/2003
THOMSON, ROGER............................ 05/11/2003

2004
RICKARD, RORY F 30/06/2004
CRANER, MATTHEW.......................... 30/06/2004
CONNOR, DANIEL 30/06/2004
LEIGH-SMITH, SIMON 30/06/2004
BATHAM, DONALD 01/09/2004

2005
SMITH, JASON E 30/06/2005
TAYLOR, PETER J 30/06/2005
WHITTAKER, MARK A......................... 30/06/2005
BOWIE, ALAN N................................ 28/10/2005

2006
CHIRNSIDE, GABRIELLA F................... 30/06/2006
HEAMES, RICHARD M......................... 30/06/2006
DEKKER, BARRIE J 30/06/2006

RAMASWAMI, RAVI A........................ 27/07/2006
PALMER, ALAN C 02/10/2006

2007
DICKSON, STUART J........................... 30/06/2007
DUBY, ALON.................................... 30/06/2007
GIBSON, ANDREW 30/06/2007
STREETS, CHRISTOPHER 30/06/2007
BLAND, STEVEN A............................. 07/08/2007

2008
LEONARD, JOHN F............................. 01/07/2008
IMM, NICHOLAS D 30/07/2008
CROWSON, ELIZABETH...................... 04/08/2008
FRESHWATER, DENNIS 09/08/2008
MCINTOSH, JAMES D 10/09/2008
COLTMAN, TIMOTHY P....................... 08/10/2008

2009
HOULBERG, KRISTIAN A 14/02/2009
SCHOFIELD, SUSAN R......................... 30/03/2009
GAY, DAVID A T................................ 01/07/2009
MILNER, ROBERT A 01/07/2009
PHILLIPS, SIMON M........................... 01/07/2009
WEBBER, RICHARD J.......................... 01/07/2009
COUNTER, PAUL R 01/08/2009
PARRY, CHRISTOPHER A..................... 12/08/2009

SURGEON COMMANDERS

MATTHEWS, JONATHAN J 01/09/2009
COLLETT, STUART M 14/12/2009

2010

HENRY, MARK 09/03/2010
WHYBOURN, LESLEY A 01/07/2010
CORMACK, ANDREW 01/07/2010
MCLEAN, CHRISTOPHER R 01/07/2010
BROWN, ANDREW 20/07/2010
READ, JONATHON 04/08/2010
PRIOR, KATE R 22/09/2010
LEASON, JOANNA 05/10/2010
MACKIE, SIMON J 01/12/2010

COATES, PHILIP J 06/12/2010

2011

TURNER, MATTHEW J 04/01/2011
NELSTROP, ANDREW 11/02/2011
HUTCHINGS, SAM D 14/06/2011
MERCER, SIMON 02/08/2011
MARTIN, NEIL 01/09/2011
EVANS, GARETH C 13/12/2011
REES, PAUL S 28/12/2011

2012

ROBIN, JULIE I 05/04/2012
HARRISON, JAMES C 01/07/2012
PHILPOTT, MARCUS C 01/07/2012
RESTON, SAMUEL C 01/07/2012
DEW, ANTHONY M 17/07/2012
GRAINGE, CHRISTOPHER L 03/08/2012
DORAN, CATHERINE 03/09/2012
WILD, GARETH 10/09/2012
2013
COETZEE, RIKUS 01/07/2013
SCOTT, TIMOTHY E 01/07/2013
KERSHAW-YATES, ELIZABETH H 03/09/2013

SURGEON LIEUTENANT COMMANDERS

2000

BEDFORD, JONATHAN 01/07/2000

2001

SMITH, JASON 07/08/2001

2003

WELCH, JAMES 05/08/2003

2004

BARTON, SARAH J 04/08/2004

2005

MACKAY-BROWN, ALAN 01/08/2005
COOKE, JOANNE 02/08/2005
STANNARD, ADAM 02/08/2005
GUYVER, PAUL M 02/08/2005

2006

ARTHUR, CALUM H C 01/08/2006
BAINS, BALDEEP S 01/08/2006
MAPLES, ANDREW T 01/08/2006
KHAN, MANSOOR ALI 01/08/2006
BEARD, DAVID JOHN 01/08/2006
BONNER, TIMOTHY 09/08/2006

2007

MILES, SEAN A 17/05/2007
WELLS, JOHN P 04/07/2007
WOOD, ALEXANDER M 01/08/2007
PHILLIPS, JAMES 01/08/2007
EDWARD, AMANDA M 07/08/2007
EVERSHED, RACHAEL E 07/08/2007
HEMINGWAY, ROSS 07/08/2007
KERSHAW, RICHARD J 07/08/2007
ALLCOCK, EDWARD 07/08/2007
VALE, ANDREW JOHN 07/08/2007
GREGORY, ANTHONY E 01/09/2007

2008

GILMARTIN, KIERAN P 06/08/2008
HULSE, ELSPETH 06/08/2008
JAQUES, SIMON 06/08/2008
JONES, ALED L 06/08/2008
NEWTON, NICHOLAS J P 06/08/2008
PENGELLY, STEVEN P 06/08/2008
SARGENT, DAVID S 06/08/2008
SHEARMAN, ALEXANDER J 06/08/2008
MORRIS, LOUISA 06/08/2008
LINDSAY, MICHAEL 06/08/2008
MCMENAMIN, DIARMAID 06/08/2008
KING, KATHERINE 10/09/2008
MIDDLETON, SIMON W F 11/09/2008
HENNING, DANIEL C W 11/09/2008
PENN-BARWELL, JOWAN 19/09/2008
MACFARLANE, GORDON 07/10/2008
SCUTT, MARTIN J 08/10/2008

2009

GARDINER, DERMOT 04/02/2009
TAYAL, MANISH 01/05/2009
HILLMAN, CHRISTOPHER M 03/08/2009
MORRIS, ALISTAIR J 03/08/2009
WRIGLEY, ALEXANDER 03/08/2009
BARNARD, EDWARD B G 04/08/2009
GOKHALE, STEPHEN G 04/08/2009
LONGMORE, DAVID 04/08/2009
POTTER, DAVID L 04/08/2009
ROSCOE, DAVID 04/08/2009
DEWYNTER, ALISON 06/08/2009
O'SHEA, MATTHEW K 06/09/2009
ABLETT, DANIEL 01/11/2009
KINNEAR-MELLOR, REX 01/12/2009

2010

MCKINLAY, JAYNE A 01/02/2010
FRIES, CHARLES A 02/02/2010
FRY, STEPHEN PAUL 01/05/2010
HASSETT, JUSTIN 01/07/2010
EVANS, HELEN J 01/08/2010
ROY, SUDIPTA K 01/08/2010
DAVEY, KELLY L 02/08/2010

HUGHES, CHARLOTTE L 02/08/2010
JONES, CAROLYN J 02/08/2010
MINSHALL, DARREN M 02/08/2010
RAINEY, OWEN H 02/08/2010
STEVENS, LISA C 02/08/2010
LLOYD, JANE L 02/08/2010
ROBINSON, TIMOTHY 02/08/2010
LIM, FONG CHIEN 01/09/2010
PROFFITT, ADRIAN 01/09/2010

2011

McKECHNIE, PETER 01/06/2011
BOOTH, RACHAEL M 02/08/2011
BROGDEN, THOMAS G 02/08/2011
DICKIE, ANDREW K 02/08/2011
DROOG, SARAH J 02/08/2011
HOWES, RICHARD J 02/08/2011
WILLIAMS, RICHARD J 02/08/2011
BELL, CHARLOTTE S 02/08/2011
WOOD, IAIN M 01/09/2011
WALLER, BENTLEY 01/11/2011
DODDS, NICHOLAS 01/11/2011
MATHESON, ANDREW 01/11/2011
RUSSELL, MICHAEL 01/11/2011
VIJAYAN, DEEPAK 01/11/2011

2012

BOURN, SEBASTIAN 31/07/2012
EVANS, CHARLOTTE V 01/08/2012
GRIFFITHS, CHARLOTTE 01/08/2012
HEROD, THOMAS P 01/08/2012
RENNIE, RICHARD A 01/08/2012
RITSON, JONATHAN E 01/08/2012
SCORER, THOMAS G 01/08/2012
SMITH, FIONA E 01/08/2012
SPREADBOROUGH, PHILIP 01/08/2012
STANNING, ALASTAIR 01/08/2012
EAMES, JONATHAN R 01/12/2012

2013

LEONG, MELVIN 06/02/2013
DUNCAN, KATHRYN 03/04/2013
SCOTT, ALEXANDRA 01/08/2013

SURGEON LIEUTENANT COMMANDERS

STEVENSON, THOMAS 01/08/2013	JAMIESON, SCOTT MBChB 06/08/2013	TOWNER, STEPHEN D P...................... 06/08/2013
EDGAR, IAIN.................................... 06/08/2013	KEMP, PETER G 06/08/2013	HALE, ALEXANDRA LOUISE BMBS........ 06/08/2013
FRY, REBECCA L.............................. 06/08/2013	MILLAR, JENNIFER A......................... 06/08/2013	PILLAI, SONIA NANDHINI.................... 06/08/2013
HENDERSON, ARTHUR H...................... 06/08/2013	ROBINSON, MICHAEL W 06/08/2013	ANGUS, DONALD J C MBChB.............. 19/08/2013

SURGEON LIEUTENANTS

2008

BAKER, JAMES OLIVER....................... 01/03/2008

2009

CASTLEDINE, BENJAMIN 03/02/2009	
THOMAS, RYAN C 04/02/2009	
AHUJA, VIJAY Y 05/08/2009	
BOYES, GEORGINA K......................... 05/08/2009	
GLENNIE, JOHN S............................. 05/08/2009	
LUNDIE, ANDREW J........................... 05/08/2009	
MCINTOSH, SIMON J 05/08/2009	
O'BRIEN, DAVID J............................. 05/08/2009	
OSBORNE, MATTHEW A 05/08/2009	
SAFFIN, JAMES R............................. 05/08/2009	
SHARP, WILLIAM M J......................... 05/08/2009	
SIMPSON, MATTHEW A 05/08/2009	
TANZER, WILLIAM J C E 05/08/2009	

2010

JONES, PAUL THOMAS........................ 01/02/2010
WILSON, MATTHEW J 12/07/2010
ANDERSON, TIMOTHY J....................... 04/08/2010
BUTTERWORTH, SOPHIE 04/08/2010
CRANE, DANIELLE L 04/08/2010
FOSTER, SEBASTIAN J........................ 04/08/2010
HILL, MICHAEL J 04/08/2010
JERVIS, CHRISTOPHER........................ 04/08/2010
NIXON, SEBASTIAN W......................... 04/08/2010

PATERSON, LAURA............................ 04/08/2010
RAWLINSON, KATHERINE H................. 04/08/2010
RYLAH, OSGAR 04/08/2010
SANDHU, JAGDEEP S 04/08/2010
STAUNTON, THOMAS H....................... 04/08/2010
VASSALLO, JAMES............................. 04/08/2010
WOOLLEY, STEPHEN 04/08/2010

2011

PERRY, JAMES 01/01/2011
HEALEY, NICHOLAS 01/02/2011
WHARTON, CHARLES 02/08/2011
BAKER, LUKE D................................ 03/08/2011
BENNETT, PHILIPPA........................... 03/08/2011
GUEST, RUTH E 03/08/2011
HAWKINS, DANIEL M......................... 03/08/2011
HUNTER, GUY M 03/08/2011
LAIRD, JOANNE E.............................. 03/08/2011
McLELLAN, MOIRA S.......................... 03/08/2011
McMENEMY, LOUISE.......................... 03/08/2011
STACHOW, ELIZABETH A.................... 03/08/2011

2012

ADSHEAD, STEPHEN P 01/03/2012
MCARDLE, ALAN D............................ 01/03/2012
ARR WOODWARD, ROBERT................. 01/08/2012
ASHLEY, ELIZABETH A 01/08/2012
BOOTH, BEN 01/08/2012
CALLAGHAN, JOHN I 01/08/2012

HAWKES, SOPHIE P........................... 01/08/2012
MARTIN, ANTOINETTE 01/08/2012
MCCAUL, DANIEL.............................. 01/08/2012
MILLER, ROSALYN C........................... 01/08/2012
ROGERS, JENNIFER C 01/08/2012
WALLACE, JOSEF K............................ 01/08/2012
WATSON, JAMES L............................. 01/08/2012
BAKKER-DYOS, JOSHUA J.................... 01/08/2012
MORROW, LAURA 01/08/2012
MYATT, RICHARD W 01/08/2012
JOHNSON, TOBIAS E......................... 01/09/2012

2013

CLINGO, THOMAS W.......................... 01/03/2013
STRACHAN, ROBERT C 01/03/2013
THOMAS, ROBERT L........................... 01/03/2013
ALBERTS, IAN.................................. 07/08/2013
BAMFORD, ALEXANDER 07/08/2013
BONE, JONATHAN D 07/08/2013
CORNELL, JONATHAN D 07/08/2013
GREEN, NATALIE M 07/08/2013
GREENALL, GILBERT E........................ 07/08/2013
HANAN, WILLIAM M........................... 07/08/2013
KILBANE, LIAM 07/08/2013
LOWNES, SARAH E 07/08/2013
PREEDY, HELEN C............................. 07/08/2013
QUINN, MORGAN.............................. 07/08/2013
SWAIN, CARA SIMONE 07/08/2013
THOMSON, CALLUM MAXWELL........... 07/08/2013
WALTERS, ELIZABETH......................... 07/08/2013

DENTAL OFFICERS

SURGEON CAPTAINS (D)

1994
NORRIS, RICHARD 26-Oct-04

1997
GALL, MICHAEL 04-Sep-07

2011
JORDAN, ADRIAN 11-Jan-11
CULWICK, PETER 07-Mar-11

2013
HALL, DAVID 25-Mar-13

SURGEON COMMANDERS (D)

1997
ASTON, MARK................................30-Jun-97

2000
REDMAN, CHRISTOPHER................................31-Dec-00

2001
SMITH, BRIAN S 30-Jun-01

2002
ELMER, TIMOTHY 30-Jun-02

2005
SKELLEY, JULIE 30-Jun-05

2006
MINALL, PAUL 24-Jul-06

2007
MOORE, PAUL 10-Jul-07

2008
MADGWICK, EDWARD 14-Oct-08

2009
LEYSHON, ROBERT................................09-Jan-09
STEVENSON, GEOFFREY 14-Jan-09

2012
DOHERTY, MELANIE................................03-Sep-12

2013
DRUMMOND, KARL................................01-Jul-13
HANDS, ANTHONY 23-Sep-13

SURGEON LIEUTENANT COMMANDERS (D)

2002
VERNEY, KIRSTY 09-Jul-02
CHITTICK, WILLIAM 10-Jul-02
DEAN, TIMOTHY................................22-Jul-02

2004
FOULGER, THOMAS................................11-Jun-04

2005
WILLIAMS, BENJAMIN 27-Jun-05
BRYCE, GRAEME 29-Jun-05
COLE, CLAIRE 29-Jun-05
JENKS, JENNIFER 24-Sep-05

2006
HAMILTON, SEAN 26-Jun-06

KERSHAW-YATES, SIMON 18-Jul-06

2007
KEMP, GILLIAN J................................19-Jun-07

2008
LOVELL, ALISTAIR................................25-Jun-08
FALLA, LINDSAY................................27-Jun-08

2009
PEPPER, THOMAS 13-Jul-09
WILLIAMS, DYLAN 25-Aug-09

2010
FYFE-GREEN, ALEXA 09-Jun-10
BURNS, RUTH 24-Jun-10

MACLEOD, ALANNA 24-Jun-10
SOUTHORN, BRYONY 27-Jun-10

2012
BAMBER, MICHAEL 05-Jul-12
VALENDER, CHARLES................................16-Jul-12
MCCAFFERTY, LESLEY................................23-Jul-12

2013
MATTHEWS, LUCY................................19-Jun-13
PEDRICK, AMELIA................................11-Jul-13
HALL, JESSICA 14-Jul-13
WESTWOOD, AMANDA 07-Jul-13

SURGEON LIEUTENANTS (D)

2009
COWARD, SUZANNE 29-Jun-09
CRITCHLOW, ANGELA 27-Jul-09
MURGATROYD, JENNA 28-Jul-09

2010
LIFODA, CHARLOTTE 09-Jul-10

2011
MAIR, BARBARA 21-Jun-11

HOLLAND, EMMA................................04-Jul-11

SKORKO, KONRAD 20-Jul-11

SURGEON SUB LIEUTENANTS (D)

2012

WARWICK, FRANCESCA........................19-Jul-12
FYFE, TOBIAS 24-Jul-12

QUEEN ALEXANDRA'S ROYAL NAVAL NURSING SERVICE

CAPTAINS

2011
KENNEDY, INGA J 21/11/2011

2013
BETTERIDGE, CAROL OBE 26/02/2013

COMMANDERS

2008
THAIN-SMITH, JULIE 01/04/2008

2009
SPENCER, STEVEN J............................. 04/08/2009

2010
HOFMAN, ALISON RRC 27/07/2010

2011
PIPER, NEALE ARRC.......................... 05/09/2011

2012
THOMPSON, FIONA 06/02/2012
CAMPBELL, FELICITY........................... 01/07/2012
BAGNALL, SALLY-ANNE 06/08/2012

2013
TAYLOR, LISA 03/03/2013
HOUNSOME, DEBRA MBE ARRC 01/07/2013
CHARLTON, KEVIN............................. 11/08/2013

LIEUTENANT COMMANDERS

2004
BRIGGS, CATHRYN 01/10/2004
SYKES, LEAH 01/10/2004
HOLLAND, AMANDA........................... 01/11/2004

2006
JAMES, KATHERINE 01/10/2006
JOHNSON, VOIRREY............................ 01/10/2006

2008
GARDNER-CLARK, SUZANNE 01/10/2008
SELWOOD, PETER JOHN..................... 01/10/2008

2009
CARNELL, RICHARD PAUL 01/10/2009
BROCKLEHURST, JUDITH 01/10/2009
CLARKSON, ANDREW......................... 01/10/2009
BRODIE, STEPHEN DAVID 01/10/2009
GLENDINNING, ANDREANA 01/10/2009

2010
KENNEDY, IAN CHRISTOPHER 01/10/2010

2011
HURLEY, KARL 01/10/2011
FRASER-SMITH, SHARRON 01/10/2011
COOPER, JANETTE 01/10/2011

2012
KENNEDY, CATHERYN 01/10/2012
DESPRES, JULIAN ARRC...................... 01/10/2012
WARBURTON, ALISON M...................... 01/10/2012
WRIGHT-JONES, ALEXANDRA 01/10/2012

2013
CLARIDGE, ALEXANDER 01/10/2013
EDWARDS, SHARON P 01/10/2013
BROCKIE, ALAN................................ 01/10/2013
LONG, VICTORIA 01/10/2013

LIEUTENANTS

1996
DILLOWAY, PHILIP 07/12/1996

2001
BRYCE-JOHNSTON, FIONA................... 16/07/2001

2002
KELLY, FRANK A ARRC 01/02/2002
SWIRE, BARRY 26/07/2002

2003
MARTYN, JULIE 01/03/2003
THOMPSON, SARAH 01/11/2003

2004
MCCULLOUGH, KAREN 01/11/2004

2005
WARDLEY, THOMAS E 01/03/2005
HALE, STUART DENNIS....................... 01/04/2005

2006
DEWEY, SARAH E.............................. 01/03/2006
JAFFREY, HEATHER B 11/04/2006
EMBLETON, ALISON........................... 09/06/2006
COCKCROFT, KIM M.......................... 16/06/2006
SCOTT, VICTORIA.............................. 01/08/2006

2007
BOSWELL, LAURA.............................. 29/01/2007
DEVINE, ALISON............................... 12/02/2007
HUMPHREY, DARREN 08/04/2007
LEWIS, ROBERT G 01/09/2007

2008
CANTILLON, LLOYD M........................ 16/06/2008

2009
TIN, JENNIFER MARY.......................... 01/01/2009
GLENDINNING, VICKY........................ 16/01/2009
JOHNSTON, AUDREY 19/05/2009

2010
DE-SAINT-BISSIX-CROIX, ANNA MARIE. 13/04/2010
CORNHILL, SHARON 12/07/2010
RYAN, KATHLEEN R............................ 12/07/2010

2011
BROOKING, GARY 12/07/2011

2013
WHITLEY, JANINE.............................. 08/02/2013
JEFFREYS, SUSAN.............................. 12/07/2013

SUB LIEUTENANTS

2013

DALE, REBECCA ANNE........................ 01/09/2013
ZDRODOWSKI, CRAIG 03/02/2013

CHAPLAINS

CHAPLAIN OF THE FLEET & PRINCIPAL CHURCH OF SCOTLAND AND FREE CHURCHES CHAPLAIN

The Reverend Scott J Brown, QHC, BD .... 01 November 2010

PRINCIPAL ANGLICAN CHAPLAIN

The Venerable Ian Wheatley, QHC, BTh .... 07 August 2012
Deputy Chaplain of the Fleet and Archdeacon for the Royal Navy

CHAPLAINS

1991
Scott PJD .... 03 September 1991

1992
Kelly NJ .... 26 May 1992

1993
Beveridge SAR .... 28 April 1993

1998
Hills MJ .... 21 April 1998
Evans ML .... 01 September 1998
Gough MJ .... 01 September 1998
Wylie DV .... 01 December 1998

2002
Hallam SP .... 05 May 2002

2004
Corness AS .... 06 September 2004

2005
Simpson DJ .... 07 March 2005
Beardsley NA .... 03 May 2005
Bridges JM .... 02 July 2005
Hillier A .... 13 September 2005

2007
Tabor JH .... 16 April 2007
Robus K .... 27 August 2007
Backhouse JR .... 03 September 2007
Francis JS .... 01 October 2007
Mansfield AJF .... 10 December 2007

2008
Barber RW .... 31 March 2008
Wagstaff M .... 31 March 2008

Allsopp MD .... 02 May 2008

2009
Godfrey MF .... 01 September 2009

2010
Andrew PR .... 04 January 2010
Horne ST .... 07 October 2010

2012
Rason SP .... 01 January 2012
Pye P .... 17 July 2012

2013
Money JC .... 12 August 2013
Webber AA .... 02 September 2013

2014
Wills E .... 27 January 2014

PRINCIPAL DENOMINATIONAL ROMAN CATHOLIC CHAPLAIN

Father Andrew McFadden .... 01 September 1998

CHAPLAINS

1990
Sharkey M .... 01 October 1990

1996
Bradbury S .... 18 September 1996
McLean D .... 18 September 1996

1998
Yates DM .... 01 September 1998

2000
Conroy DA .... 24 September 2000

2010
Bruzon CC .... 02 September 2010

CHAPLAINS

CHURCH OF SCOTLAND AND FREE CHURCH CHAPLAINS

1989

Wort RS .... 28 July 1989

1997

Wilkinson TL .... 04 March 1997
Meachin MC .... 07 July 1997

2000

Ellingham RE .... 17 April 2000
Grimshaw E .... 02 May 2000
Kennon S .... 17 September 2000
Rowe RD .... 24 September 2000

2002

Goodwin T .... 05 May 2002

Botwood TJ .... 09 September 2002

2003

Dalton MF .... 12 January 2003

2005

Gates WC .... 06 September 2005

2006

Roissetter DA .... 03 January 2006

2008

Honey Morgan JC .... 11 August 2008
Carter SM .... 25 August 2008

2009

Allcock AJ .... 05 January 2009

2010

Shackleton SJS .... 20 September 2010

2011

Davidson MR .... 01 May 2011

2012

Pons M .... 02 July 2012
Coulson N .... 10 July 2012

NAVAL CAREERS SERVICE OFFICERS

ROYAL NAVY

LIEUTENANTS

1997	1999
Connolly, MH..20-Oct-97	Concarr, DT... 19-Sep-99

ROYAL MARINES

LIEUTENANTS

1999	
Wilcockson, R 07-May-99	

ROYAL MARINES

CAPTAIN GENERAL

His Royal Highness The Prince Philip Duke of Edinburgh, KG, KT, OM, GBE, AC, QSO

HONORARY COLONEL

His Majesty King Harald V of Norway, KG, GCVO

COLONELS COMMANDANT

Major General David Wilson, CB, CBE 01-May-12
(Colonel Commandant Royal Marines)

Major General Jeremy Thomas, CB, DSO 18-May-12
(Representative Colonel Commandant Royal Marines)

LIEUTENANT GENERALS

Capewell, David Andrew, OBE 01-Dec-11
(CHIEF OF JOINT OPERATIONS DEC 11)

Messenger, Gordon K, DSO*, OBE 13-Jan-13
(DEPUTY COMMANDER LAND COMMAND IZMIR JAN 13)

MAJOR GENERALS

Howes, Francis HR, OBE 09-Feb-10
(HEAD OF BRITISH DEFENCE STAFF (UNITED STATES) JAN 12)

Hook, David A, CBE 03-Oct-11
(RM350)

Davis, Edward GM, CBE 28-Nov-11
(COMMANDER UK AMPHIBIOUS FORCES & COMMANDANT GENERAL ROYAL MARINES NOV 11)

Since the publication of the last Navy List, the following officers have joined, or will be joining the Retired List:

Major General A Salmon CMG OBE – 9 Apr 13

Major General S T Chicken OBE - 7 Dec 13

BRIGADIERS

2008

DUNHAM, MARK W OBE........................21-Apr-08

2010

SALZANO, GERARD MBE 04-May-10
TAYLOR, WILLIAM OBE 10-May-10

2011

SMITH, MARTIN MBE.............................31-Jan-11
BEVIS, TIMOTHY J.................................21-Feb-11
DECHOW, WILLIAM E 21-Jun-11
SPENCER, RICHARD 22-Jul-11
HUNTLEY, IAN.......................................15-Aug-11

2013

MAGOWAN, ROBERT CBE 18-Mar-13
HOLMES, MATTHEW DSO...................... 19-Mar-13
EVANS, DAVID 03-Sep-13
BIRRELL, STUART DSO...........................14-Jun-13

COLONELS

2006

BROWN, NIGEL.....................................30-Jun-06

2007

HUTTON, JAMES OBE 30-Jun-07
PAGE, MICHAEL.....................................30-Jun-07

2008

CAMERON, PETER S OBE 30-Jun-08
MCCARDLE, JOHN OBE 01-Jul-08
LINDLEY, NICHOLAS..............................15-Dec-08

2009

DEWAR, DUNCAN A..............................31-Aug-09
COPINGER-SYMES, RORY 14-Sep-09

PORTER, MATTHEW CBE.......................09-Nov-09
STICKLAND, CHARLES RICHARD OBE..... 01-Dec-09
TAYLOR, PETER OBE 14-Dec-09

2010

MANGER, GARTH S C 19-Apr-10
MORRIS, JAMES DSO 20-May-10
WHITE, HAYDN JOHN 19-Jul-10
PIERSON, MATTHEW 07-Dec-10

2011

FRANCIS, STEVEN 14-Feb-11
KASSAPIAN, DAVID L.............................16-Feb-11
OLIVER, KEVIN rcds(s)............................22-Feb-11
MCINERNEY, ANDREW............................31-Mar-11
LITSTER, ALAN OBE 09-May-11

JENKINS, GWYN OBE 01-Jul-11
JAMES, PAUL MELVYN DSO 22-Aug-11
MADDICK, MARK J................................ 26-Sep-11

2012

LEE, OLIVER OBE 12-Jan-12
MAY, DOMINIC MBE 06-Mar-12
MURCHISON, EWEN DSO MBE 04-Sep-12

2013

STOVIN-BRADFORD, MATTHEW 07-Jan-13
MOULTON, FREDERICK 23-Sep-13
HEDGES, JUSTIN WILLIAM OBE 27-Aug-13
JACKSON, MATTHEW DSO 05-Nov-13
TANNER, MICHAEL 16-Dec-13
SCOTT, SIMON 14-Oct-13

LIEUTENANT COLONELS

1996

MUSTO, EDWARD 31-Dec-96

1998

PRICE, MARTIN 31-Dec-98

1999

MUDFORD, HUGH 30-Jun-99

2000

BURNELL, JEREMY.................................31-Dec-00

2001

PAUL, RUSSELL.....................................30-Jun-01

2003

PULVERTAFT, RUPERT 30-Jun-03
WILSON, DAVID W H 30-Jun-03

2004

LIVINGSTONE, ALAN MBE.....................30-Jun-04
PHILLIPS, STEPHEN 30-Jun-04

2005

FORSTER, ROBIN 30-Jun-05
HOLT, JUSTIN SEFTON MBE....................30-Jun-05
MAYBERY, JAMES 30-Jun-05
SADDLETON, ANDREW 30-Jun-05
PRESSLY, JAMES 30-Jun-05

2006

ARMOUR, GRAEME A............................30-Jun-06
CASE, ALEXANDER 30-Jun-06
GREEN, GARY EDWARD.........................30-Jun-06
HOLMES, CHRISTOPHER 30-Jun-06
PRICE, ANDREW M 30-Jun-06
PRITCHARD, SIMON 30-Jun-06

2007

CHAPMAN, SIMON................................30-Jun-07
COOK, MYLES 30-Jun-07
COOPER-SIMPSON, ROGER....................30-Jun-07
CORBIDGE, STEPHEN JOHN MBE 30-Jun-07
MCLAREN, JAMES 30-Jun-07
RICHARDS, STEPHEN 30-Jun-07
SEAR, JONATHAN 30-Jun-07
THURSTAN, RICHARD 30-Jun-07
MORRIS, PAUL 30-Jun-07

2008

BAXENDALE, ROBERT 30-Jun-08
DE REYA, ANTHONY 30-Jun-08
HUSSEY, STEVEN MBE..........................30-Jun-08
PAGE, DURWARD 30-Jun-08
COOK, TIMOTHY...................................30-Jun-08

2009

BLYTHE, TOM 30-Jun-09
BROWN, LEONARD A MBE.....................30-Jun-09
BUCKNALL, ROBIN 30-Jun-09
FRASER, GRAEME 30-Jun-09
GELDARD, MICHAEL.............................30-Jun-09
GRACE, NICHOLAS J OBE 30-Jun-09
HARRIS, CARL MBE 30-Jun-09
LEE, STEVEN 30-Jun-09
ROYLANCE, JAIMIE 30-Jun-09
SKUSE, MATTHEW 30-Jun-09
SUTHERLAND, NEIL MBE 30-Jun-09
WATKINSON, NEIL.................................30-Jun-09

2010

BLANCHFORD, DANIEL 30-Jun-10
CLARK, PAUL 30-Jun-10
CORRIN, COLBY....................................30-Jun-10
DOWD, JONATHAN 30-Jun-10
HARRIS, TRISTAN MBE 30-Jun-10

LIEUTENANT COLONELS

JANZEN, ALEXANDER OBE 30-Jun-10
KELLY, PHILIP..30-Jun-10
KEMP, PETER 30-Jun-10
LOCK, ANDREW GLENN...............................30-Jun-10
MIDDLETON, CHRISTOPHER MBE............30-Jun-10
CHEESMAN, DANIEL MBE.....................30-Jun-10

2011

BOWRA, MARK ANDREW MBE...............30-Jun-11
CANTRILL, RICHARD JOHN MC 30-Jun-11
GRIFFITHS, NICHOLAS A MBE 30-Jun-11
LYNCH, PAUL PATRICK MC.....................30-Jun-11
NICHOLLS, BARRY 30-Jun-11
READ, RICHARD 30-Jun-11
WATKINS, ANDREW.....................................30-Jun-11
WRAITH, NEIL...30-Jun-11
O'HERLIHY, SIMON IAN MBE.................30-Jun-11
MOORHOUSE, EDWARD 30-Jun-11
PARVIN, RICHARD......................................30-Jun-11

2012

BAKEWELL, TIMOTHY 30-Jun-12
BRADY, SEAN P.......................................30-Jun-12
BUBB, JONATHAN DAVID.......................30-Jun-12
COLLIN, MARTIN E.................................30-Jun-12
HAW, CHRISTOPHER MC 30-Jun-12
JEPSON, NICHOLAS HENRY 30-Jun-12
MADDISON, JOHN DAVID MBE 30-Jun-12
MALTBY, RICHARD JAMES.....................30-Jun-12
MORLEY, ADRIAN MC..............................30-Jun-12
MUDDIMAN, ANDREW ROBERT...............30-Jun-12
ORDWAY, CHRISTOPHER 30-Jun-12
STAFFORD, DEREK B MBE 30-Jun-12
TOTTEN, PHILIP MARK MBE 30-Jun-12
URRY, SIMON RICHARD MBE 30-Jun-12
VENN, NICHOLAS S C 30-Jun-12
WALKER, ANDREW J................................30-Jun-12

2013

BIRD, GARY MICHAEL..........................30-Jun-13
DAVIES, HUAN 30-Jun-13
EDMONDSON, SIMON 30-Jun-13
FISHER, AARON G 30-Jun-13
FOSTER, BENJAMIN 30-Jun-13
HILL, JONATHAN PAUL 30-Jun-13
HUNTINGFORD, DAMIAN 30-Jun-13
JESS, ARAN...30-Jun-13
JOHNSON, MARK 30-Jun-13
KILMARTIN, STEVEN 30-Jun-13
MEARS, RICHARD 30-Jun-13
TULLOCH, STUART 30-Jun-13
TURNER, ANTONY R 30-Jun-13
TURNER, SIMON 30-Jun-13
WESTLAKE, SIMON 30-Jun-13
CAVILL, NIKI MBE 30-Jun-13

MAJORS

1990

SHARLAND, SIMON 01-Sep-90

1996

PELLY, GILBERT 24-Apr-96
HOOD, MATTHEW 25-Apr-96
FREEMAN, MARK E................................01-Sep-96

1997

SEARIGHT, MARK...................................01-May-97
SLACK, JEREMY 01-May-97

1998

GREEN, GARETH 01-Sep-98
GILDING, DOUGLAS...............................01-Sep-98
FOSTER, BRUCE 07-Dec-98

1999

FERGUSSON, ANDREW 01-May-99
MANSON, PETER....................................01-Sep-99

2000

CONGREVE, STEVEN 01-May-00
WALLS, KEVIN 01-May-00
HAMMOND, MARK DFC......................01-May-00
KERN, ALASTAIR 01-Sep-00
BULMER, RENNY JOHN MBE 01-Oct-00
PERRY, ROBERT.....................................01-Oct-00

2001

CRAIG, KENNETH...................................01-May-01
SPANNER, PAUL 01-May-01
COOMBER, JONATHAN 01-Sep-01
TWIST, MARTIN 01-Sep-01

2002

BALMER, GUY 24-Apr-02
BRIGHOUSE, NEIL..................................24-Apr-02
HALE, JOHN N 27-Apr-02
PLEWES, ANDREW B 27-Apr-02
SUMMERS, JAMES.................................24-May-02
MCGHEE, CRAIG 01-Sep-02

2003

DEVEREUX, MICHAEL 01-Sep-03
WHITFIELD, PHILIP 01-Sep-03
O'HARA, GERARD.................................01-Sep-03
ETHELL, DAVID R...................................01-Oct-03

2004

DUNCAN, GILES 01-May-04
WOOSEY, MARK MBA............................01-Jun-04
STEMP, JUSTIN 01-Sep-04
PENKMAN, WILLIAM.............................01-Sep-04
ALDERSON, RICHARD 01-Oct-04
ATHERTON, BRUCE 01-Oct-04
CHURCHWARD, MATTHEW....................01-Oct-04
CLARE, JONATHAN 01-Oct-04
DAVIES, CHRISTOPHER..........................01-Oct-04
FENWICK, ROBIN J 01-Oct-04
PARRY, JONATHAN A 01-Oct-04
TAYLOR, STUART DAVID 01-Oct-04
WATSON, RICHARD I 01-Oct-04
LUGG, JOHN CHARLES 01-Oct-04
CAMPBELL, MICHAEL RD* 01-Nov-04
TARNOWSKI, TOMASZ 12-Nov-04

2005

GIBSON, ALEXANDER J 01-May-05
NICHOLSON, DAVID 01-Sep-05
HART, STEPHEN 01-Sep-05
COOPER, NEIL......................................01-Oct-05

DENNIS, JAMES 01-Oct-05
FULLER, JAMES 01-Oct-05
GARLAND, ANDREW 01-Oct-05
GOSNEY, CHRISTOPHER.........................01-Oct-05
HOWARTH, JOHN 01-Oct-05
MURPHY, KIAN 01-Oct-05
TYCE, DAVID 01-Oct-05
WISEMAN, GEORGE 01-Oct-05
LANCASHIRE, ANTONY 01-Oct-05
BAKER, MICHAEL..................................01-Oct-05

2006

ATKINSON, NEIL 01-May-06
FOSTER, NICHOLAS...............................01-May-06
GRAY, KARL D......................................01-May-06
READ, CLINTON 01-May-06
BAINES, GARY 01-Oct-06
COLLINS, JOHN.....................................01-Oct-06
DURUP, JASON 01-Oct-06
FITZPATRICK, PAUL 01-Oct-06
GILES, GARY 01-Oct-06
HOPKINS, RICHARD 01-Oct-06
LUCAS, SIMON 01-Oct-06
TODD, OLIVER 01-Oct-06
MUNCER, RICHARD 01-Oct-06
BRAIN, WILLIAM 01-Oct-06
MORAN, JULIAN 01-Oct-06
KENNEALLY, SEAN.................................01-Oct-06
EDYE, ROBIN..01-Oct-06

2007

HALL, CHRISTOPHER MBE....................01-Oct-07
HALSTED, BENJAMIN MBE 01-Oct-07
HOPKINS, RHYS....................................01-Oct-07
HULSE, ANTHONY 01-Oct-07
MCCULLEY, STEVEN 01-Oct-07
MORGAN, HUW MBE 01-Oct-07
PERRIN, MARK 01-Oct-07

MAJORS

SAMUEL, CHRISTOPHER 01-Oct-07
WALLACE, RICHARD 01-Oct-07
MAYNARD, PAUL 01-Oct-07
FORBES, DUNCAN 01-Oct-07
TAMLYN, STEPHEN.............................01-Oct-07
SCANLON, MICHAEL 01-Oct-07
PENNINGTON, CHARLES 01-Oct-07

2008

ALSTON, RICHARD..............................01-Oct-08
CROSS, ANDREW...............................01-Oct-08
DELAHAY, JONATHON 01-Oct-08
GRAY, SIMON 01-Oct-08
HECKS, IAN 01-Oct-08
HUNT, DARREN.................................01-Oct-08
LIVA, ANTHONY 01-Oct-08
MACPHERSON, WILLIAM.......................01-Oct-08
NOLAN, PAUL E MBE 01-Oct-08
NORMAN, JAIMIE DSO.........................01-Oct-08
PATERSON, THOMAS 01-Oct-08
PRICE, RAYMOND 01-Oct-08
ROGERS, SIMON M 01-Oct-08
SPINK, DAVID 01-Oct-08
TAYLOR, NEIL..................................01-Oct-08
TUCKER, SIMON 01-Oct-08
USHER, BRIAN..................................01-Oct-08
WAITE, MATTHEW...............................01-Oct-08
WALLACE, SCOTT 01-Oct-08
MORTON, JUSTIN...............................01-Oct-08
PURSER, LLOYD MBE 01-Oct-08

2009

JONES, ROBERT.................................01-Sep-09
ABBOTT, GRANT 01-Oct-09
ALLAN, FRASER 01-Oct-09
BURCHAM, JASON 01-Oct-09
CALDWELL, DANIEL 01-Oct-09
CLARKE, PETER 01-Oct-09
DEAN, SIMON 01-Oct-09
ELLIOTT, MARK 01-Oct-09
FIDLER, JOHN..................................01-Oct-09
FOMES, CHRISTOPHER..........................01-Oct-09
GIBB, ALEXANDER 01-Oct-09
HAYWARD, JOHN 01-Oct-09
HEMBURY, LAWRENCE 01-Oct-09
LINDSAY, JONATHAN M 01-Oct-09
METCALFE, LIAM M 01-Oct-09
MORRIS, RICHARD 01-Oct-09
SHARPE, MARCUS 01-Oct-09
SIMMONS, ROBERT 01-Oct-09
SUTTON, DAVID MBE...........................01-Oct-09
TAPP, STEVEN J.................................01-Oct-09
THORPE, ROBERT 01-Oct-09
VENABLES, DANIEL 01-Oct-09
WHITMARSH, ADAM 01-Oct-09
WILLIAMS, PETER...............................01-Oct-09

CORYTON, OLIVER..............................01-Oct-09
STANTON, KEITH................................01-Oct-09

2010

BRADING, ROLAND 01-Oct-10
BREACH, CHARLES..............................01-Oct-10
CARNS, ALISTAIR SCOTT MC 01-Oct-10
CATTON, INNES 01-Oct-10
COPSEY, NICHOLAS 01-Oct-10
GEORGE, NICHOLAS............................01-Oct-10
GILES, SIMON 01-Oct-10
LEWIS, BARRY..................................01-Oct-10
MILNE, JASON 01-Oct-10
PENNEFATHER, DOUGLAS 01-Oct-10
RIDLEY, JON 01-Oct-10
RUTHERFORD, ADAM 01-Oct-10
RYALL, THOMAS 01-Oct-10
STITSON, PAUL.................................01-Oct-10
TITERICKX, ANDREW 01-Oct-10
UPRICHARD, ANDREW 01-Oct-10
WALDMEYER, EDWARD..........................01-Oct-10
WATKINS, DEAN 01-Oct-10
WEST, DAVID J.................................01-Oct-10
DARLEY, MATTHEW 01-Oct-10
BARDEN, PAUL 01-Oct-10
WATSON, GRAHAM 01-Oct-10
WINCH, JOSEPH 01-Oct-10
NORCOTT, WILLIAM 01-Oct-10

2011

ANDERSON, BRUCE 01-Oct-11
DAVIES, LUKE 01-Oct-11
DOW, ANDREW J...............................01-Oct-11
DUCKITT, JACK.................................01-Oct-11
GAFFNEY, BENJAMIN 01-Oct-11
HALL, EDWARD 01-Oct-11
JAMISON, JAMES 01-Oct-11
JOHNSTON, KARL 01-Oct-11
LEWIS, JAMES 01-Oct-11
PENGELLEY, TRISTAN 01-Oct-11
REYNOLDS, BEN................................01-Oct-11
THOMSON, LEIGHTON...........................01-Oct-11
SPEEDIE, ALAN 01-Oct-11
MACCRIMMON, STUART 01-Oct-11
PRECIOUS, ANGUS 01-Oct-11
HILL, CHRISTOPHER 01-Oct-11

2012

CLARKE, DAVID 01-Oct-12
COOPER, MICHAEL.............................01-Oct-12
DENNING, OLIVER 01-Oct-12
DRINKWATER, ROSS MBE.......................01-Oct-12
EVANS-JONES, THOMAS 01-Oct-12
FORREST, PAUL 01-Oct-12
GINN, ROBERT 01-Oct-12
KNIGHT, JAMES MC............................01-Oct-12

LITTLE, GEORGE 01-Oct-12
MALLOWS, ANDY...............................01-Oct-12
NOBLE, TOM 01-Oct-12
RENNEY, CRAIG 01-Oct-12
PAYNE, CHRISTOPHER..........................01-Oct-12
STARLING, CHRISTOPHER MBE 01-Oct-12
SWENY, GORDON...............................01-Oct-12
PRITCHARD, LLOYD 01-Oct-12
KESTLE, RYAN 01-Oct-12
DINSMORE, SIMON.............................01-Oct-12
SUTHERLAND, IAIN.............................01-Oct-12
O'KEEFE, THOMAS..............................01-Oct-12
MACDONALD, MICHAEL 01-Oct-12

2013

BURR, CHRISTOPHER 01-Oct-13
CARTER, KEVIN GM 01-Oct-13
COTTRELL, RALPH 01-Oct-13
COX, SIMON...................................01-Oct-13
DONAGHEY, MARK 01-Oct-13
FINN, TRISTAN 01-Oct-13
HAYES, BRIAN 01-Oct-13
HILL, ANTONY 01-Oct-13
HUGHES, ROGER 01-Oct-13
KYLE, RYAN....................................01-Oct-13
MARSHALL, LEON...............................01-Oct-13
MCGILL, IAN 01-Oct-13
MILLS, SCOTT 01-Oct-13
MORRIS, JAMES 01-Oct-13
NIELSEN, ERIK 01-Oct-13
O'CALLAGHAN, PHILIP 01-Oct-13
O'SULLIVAN, NICHOLAS 01-Oct-13
POSTGATE, MICHAEL 01-Oct-13
POUNDS, ALEXANDER 01-Oct-13
QUINN, THOMAS JAMES 01-Oct-13
RICHARDSON, BENJAMIN.......................01-Oct-13
SCOTT, THOMAS 01-Oct-13
SHUTTLEWORTH, ANDREW 01-Oct-13
SUTHERLAND, STEVEN..........................01-Oct-13
SYLVAN, CHRISTOPHER 01-Oct-13
THOMSON, LUKE 01-Oct-13
TRAFFORD, MICHAEL...........................01-Oct-13
VEACOCK, GARY 01-Oct-13
WALLER, RAMSAY 01-Oct-13
WINSTANLEY, MARK 01-Oct-13
FEARN, SAMUEL 01-Oct-13
SAYER, RUSSELL 01-Oct-13
LONG, RICHARD 01-Oct-13
BEST, PAUL NEIL 01-Oct-13
JERROLD, WILLIAM 01-Oct-13

CAPTAINS

1999

LAWTON, PETER MBE 01-Jan-99
WILCOCKSON, ROY...............................07-May-99

2001

PRICE, DAVID GLYN 01-Jan-01
ROSKILLY, MARTYN.................................01-May-01
BARNWELL, ALAN F.................................21-Jul-01
TIDMAN, MARTIN DAVID MBE...............10-Sep-01

2002

WATSON, BRIAN R.................................01-Jan-02
CROSS, ERIC JOHN 01-Jan-02
ROBBINS, HARRY 01-Jan-02

2003

FLOWER, NEIL P.......................................01-Apr-03
BURGESS, MARK 01-Apr-03
GELLENDER, PAUL MBE.........................24-Jul-03
WILSON, BRUCE 01-Sep-03

2004

LATHAM, MARK 01-Apr-04
MELBOURNE, STEVEN MBE.....................01-Apr-04
O'CONNOR, DAVID 01-Jul-04
CURTIS, PETER J MBE.............................24-Jul-04
GANNON, DOMINIC 24-Jul-04
RAND, MARK MBE..................................24-Jul-04
UBAKA, PHILIP 24-Jul-04
APPS, JULIAN 01-Sep-04
BRADFORD, MALCOLM 01-Sep-04
MOORE, WILLIAM 01-Sep-04
MURRAY, SIMON 01-Sep-04
O'SULLIVAN, MATTHEW 01-Sep-04

2005

HEENAN, MARTYN 01-Apr-05
KING, RICHARD 19-Jul-05
RICHARDSON, SIMON 19-Jul-05
CARTY, MICHAEL 01-Sep-05

2006

BRIDSON, ANDREW 28-Jul-06
COX, MARK...28-Jul-06
FORD, JOHNATHAN 28-Jul-06
HURDLE, IAN 28-Jul-06
JONES, HUGH..28-Jul-06
MARR, STEPHEN 28-Jul-06
WELCH, SIMON 28-Jul-06
BOWES, NIGEL 01-Sep-06
EDEN, CHRISTOPHER 01-Sep-06
GRAY, OLIVER 01-Sep-06
HANDS, EDWARD....................................01-Sep-06
MOORE, RICHARD 01-Sep-06
SHARMAN, MAX 01-Sep-06
MCGINLEY, CHRISTOPHER......................13-Dec-06

2007

MILNE, ANTHONY....................................18-Apr-07
GREEN, PHILIP...18-Jul-07
ADAMS, MATTHEW 20-Jul-07
FARTHING, FINDLAY 20-Jul-07
JESSON, CHRISTOPHER 20-Jul-07
REEVES, SIMON 20-Jul-07
SANDERSON, MARK 20-Jul-07
SIMPSON, PAUL 20-Jul-07
BARLOW, MATTHEW 01-Aug-07
BEETE, JON 01-Aug-07
GLOAK, JAMES...01-Aug-07
HILLS, MATTHEW.....................................01-Aug-07
MOORE, CHRISTOPHER...........................01-Aug-07
MOSES, CHRISTOPHER............................01-Aug-07
PYKE, DANIEL..01-Aug-07
WHITEMAN, JOHN 01-Aug-07
HUGHES, SAMUEL...................................01-Aug-07

2008

MOYIES, SCOTT.......................................03-Apr-08
ASHLEY, SCOTT.......................................18-Jul-08
BROADBENT, NICHOLAS 18-Jul-08
COTTON, STEVEN 18-Jul-08
DOBIE, GRAHAM.....................................18-Jul-08
HITCHMAN, STUART................................18-Jul-08
LAKE, RICHARD 18-Jul-08
PATERSON, MARK GCGI.........................18-Jul-08
ROBERTSON, KEITH.................................18-Jul-08
SMITH, TREVOR M...................................18-Jul-08
WATKINS, ALUN 18-Jul-08
EATON, DANIEL 01-Aug-08
GOODMAN, WILLIAM.............................01-Aug-08
NIXON, ALEXANDER 01-Aug-08
BACON, THOMAS 01-Sep-08
BAYLIS, MATTHEW 01-Sep-08
BEESLEY, CHRISTOPHER 01-Sep-08
CASSELLS, BENJAMIN 01-Sep-08
EMPTAGE, CHRISTOPHER 01-Sep-08
HASTINGS, RICHARD 01-Sep-08
HILDER, HAROLD 01-Sep-08
HORNE, CHRISTOPHER............................01-Sep-08
HURT, CHRISTOPHER...............................01-Sep-08
LASKER, JONATHAN 01-Sep-08
LAWSON, JAMES 01-Sep-08
MAGOWAN, CONOR..............................01-Sep-08
MIDDLETON, EDWARD 01-Sep-08
MIDDLETON, JOHN 01-Sep-08
MOBBS, THOMAS....................................01-Sep-08
MORRIS, ANDREW 01-Sep-08
OSBORNE, OLIVER 01-Sep-08
SHELTON, JAMES 01-Sep-08
TENNANT, GARETH 01-Sep-08
TRUMAN, OLIVER 01-Sep-08
WILLIAMS, PETER.....................................01-Sep-08
WILLIAMS, THOMAS................................01-Sep-08
LACY, ANDREW 31-Dec-08

2009

BROKENSHIRE, MATTHEW 01-Mar-09

BROUGHTON, JACK 03-Apr-09
CLOW, THOMAS 03-Apr-09
DAVIS, IAN PHILIP 03-Apr-09
GREGORY, ANDREW 03-Apr-09
MILLER, ANDREW 03-Apr-09
PERHAM, NICHOLAS 03-Apr-09
TAIT, IAIN CAMPBELL 03-Apr-09
TIMMINS, PAUL.......................................03-Apr-09
TYLER, IAN 03-Apr-09
WINSTANLEY, ROBERT 03-Apr-09
BOURNE, ASHLEY 03-Apr-09
LAWLEY, RICHARD 03-Apr-09
FODEN, JONATHAN 03-Apr-09
COVENTRY, ANDREW 16-Apr-09
O'SULLIVAN, STEPHEN 16-Apr-09
ROBERTS, THOMAS 16-Apr-09
PUGSLEY, ANDREW 30-Jul-09
ABOUZEID, ADAM 01-Sep-09
ARMSTRONG, CHRISTOPHER 01-Sep-09
ASHCROFT, BENJAMIN JOHN 01-Sep-09
BOWERMAN, JAMES 01-Sep-09
BURNS, DAVID 01-Sep-09
CONNOLLY, SEAN 01-Sep-09
CRUMP, ALEXANDER 01-Sep-09
DISNEY, LUKE..01-Sep-09
DUTTON, JAMES 01-Sep-09
EDWARDS, GARETH 01-Sep-09
FULLER, JAMES 01-Sep-09
GARSIDE, ROBERT...................................01-Sep-09
GLOVER, THOMAS...................................01-Sep-09
HAVIS, GARETH 01-Sep-09
HEAVER, JOHN 01-Sep-09
LANE, JOSEPH 01-Sep-09
LATUS, WILLIAM 01-Sep-09
MACKAY, HUGH 01-Sep-09
MCARDLE, CHRISTOPHER 01-Sep-09
McELVENNY, JOSEPH..............................01-Sep-09
MCINALLY, MATHEW 01-Sep-09
ROGERS, DOMINIC 01-Sep-09
SAWYERS, DANIEL 01-Sep-09
SIMPSON, JOLYON 01-Sep-09
WALL, JOHN 01-Sep-09
WHITE, THOMAS 01-Sep-09
JONES, TOBY 01-Sep-09
NUTT, WILLIAM 01-Sep-09
CHAMBERS, HARRY................................01-Sep-09
BATES, OLIVER 01-Sep-09

2010

BUCKLEY, JAMES 01-Mar-10
O'SULLIVAN, MARK 01-Mar-10
SQUIRES, RUSSELL 01-Mar-10
WHEELER, LUKE 01-Mar-10
BELL, MICHAEL 16-Apr-10
BOWGEN, JOHN 16-Apr-10
COX, STEPHEN..16-Apr-10
CREANEY, ANTHONY 16-Apr-10
FOSTER, ADRIAN 16-Apr-10
HARTLEY, DAVID.....................................16-Apr-10
LEWIS, STEPHEN 16-Apr-10
MASLEN, DAVID 16-Apr-10

CAPTAINS

REED, CHRISTOPHER QGM	16-Apr-10	ROWLAND, STEVEN	01-Apr-11	WILKINSON, MATTHEW MBE	30-Mar-12
ROBSON, MARK	16-Apr-10	TRIGGOL, MARTIN P	01-Apr-11	WILLIAMS, JUSTIN	30-Mar-12
SERCOMBE, BENJAMIN	16-Apr-10	HENDERSON, SHAUN	01-Apr-11	MCCURRY, NEILL	30-Aug-12
WILLIAMS, HUW	16-Apr-10	BAYBUTT, THOMAS	01-Sep-11	BATTEN, NICHOLAS	01-Sep-12
ADDISON, TIMOTHY	01-Sep-10	BEDFORD, DANIEL	01-Sep-11	BENNET, MATTHEW	01-Sep-12
ANRUDE, JACK MC	01-Sep-10	BURKIN, CRAIG	01-Sep-11	BENNETT, JOSEPH	01-Sep-12
BARBER, THOMAS	01-Sep-10	CROW, JONATHAN	01-Sep-11	BREET, MAX	01-Sep-12
BOUCHER, JONATHAN	01-Sep-10	FEASEY, JAMES	01-Sep-11	BRUCE, ROBIN	01-Sep-12
CHAPPELL, BENJAMIN	01-Sep-10	GALLAGHER, KIERAN	01-Sep-11	COX, DAVID	01-Sep-12
DURBRIDGE, JOEL	01-Sep-10	GRESWELL, JAMES	01-Sep-11	DAVIES, ROSS	01-Sep-12
ELLERA, RICHARD	01-Sep-10	HALL, WILLIAM	01-Sep-11	DUNN, CHARLES	01-Sep-12
FELTON, JONATHAN	01-Sep-10	HUCKLE, THOMAS	01-Sep-11	FILLMORE, GUY	01-Sep-12
GARMAN, RICHARD	01-Sep-10	JOHNSTON, DAVID	01-Sep-11	FLEWITT, CRAIG	01-Sep-12
HILL, NICHOLAS	01-Sep-10	JONES, ANDREW	01-Sep-11	FREEMAN, NICHOLAS	01-Sep-12
HOLFORD, KANE	01-Sep-10	LANE, ASHLEY	01-Sep-11	GOBELL, LUKE	01-Sep-12
IRVING, LUKE	01-Sep-10	LANE, HARRY	01-Sep-11	HALFORD, PATRICK	01-Sep-12
JOHNSTONE, NEIL	01-Sep-10	MITCHELL, STUART	01-Sep-11	HUTCHINGS, ROSS	01-Sep-12
JONES, ANDREW	01-Sep-10	MOAT, RICHARD	01-Sep-11	LAW, BENJAMIN	01-Sep-12
JONES, BENJAMIN	01-Sep-10	MORGAN, HENRY	01-Sep-11	LIMB, THOMAS	01-Sep-12
LYNCH, JOHN	01-Sep-10	MORRIS, DAVID	01-Sep-11	LONG, SIMON	01-Sep-12
MACKIE, RICHARD	01-Sep-10	NIGHTINGALE, CHRISTOPHER	01-Sep-11	SIMMONS, PAUL	01-Sep-12
MCPHERSON, ROBERT	01-Sep-10	PHILLIPS, THOMAS	01-Sep-11	SLATER, LOUIS	01-Sep-12
O'BOY, THOMAS	01-Sep-10	PINNEY, JONATHAN	01-Sep-11	STEWART, LEE	01-Sep-12
O'TOOLE, MATHEW	01-Sep-10	PORTER, EDWARD	01-Sep-11	TAYLOR, STEVEN	01-Sep-12
PERKS, MATTHEW	01-Sep-10	SHIRLEY, CHRISTOPHER	01-Sep-11	UHRIN, DUSAN	01-Sep-12
PHELPS, JONATHAN	01-Sep-10	SPENCER, CHARLES	01-Sep-11	WARD, SIMON	01-Sep-12
SALTER, JONAS	01-Sep-10	STEWART, TRISTAN	01-Sep-11	WELDON, DOMINIC	01-Sep-12
SEARIGHT, WILLIAM	01-Sep-10	THATCHER, GERAINT	01-Sep-11	WILLIAMS, JONATHAN	01-Sep-12
SHAW, MATTHEW	01-Sep-10	VIGGARS, CHRISTOPHER	01-Sep-11	SNOOK, MATHEW	01-Sep-12
SMITH, CHRISTOPHER	01-Sep-10	WEBBER, CHRISTOPHER	01-Sep-11	BEALE, DAVID	01-Sep-12
SPENCER, DOUGLAS	01-Sep-10	WEBSTER, MATTHEW	01-Sep-11	DAWSON, KRIS	01-Sep-12
STEVENS, CHRISTOPHER	01-Sep-10	WILLIAMS, EDWARD	01-Sep-11	LINDSAY, JAMES	01-Sep-12
TAYLOR, ROBERT	01-Sep-10	WILLIAMS, NEIL	01-Sep-11	CHARNLEY, DAVID	01-Sep-12
WILLIAMS, MATTHEW	01-Sep-10	WILLISON, MARK	01-Sep-11		
CREASEY, ANDREW	01-Sep-10	WINTERTON, TOM	01-Sep-11		
MASON, OLIVER	01-Sep-10	SMITH, JAMES	01-Sep-11		

2011

COURTIER, ROBERT	01-Mar-11
CUTLER, LIAM	01-Mar-11
MCCRETON, JOSHUA	01-Mar-11
ADAMS, LEE M	01-Apr-11
ALTHORPE, DAMIAN	01-Apr-11
DACK, SIMON	01-Apr-11
LEES, COLIN	01-Apr-11
MASON, GARRY	01-Apr-11
MOORE, BENJAMIN	01-Apr-11
MURRAY, LEE	01-Apr-11
PASSEY, DAVID	01-Apr-11
REID, MARK R	01-Apr-11

2012

BARKS, NICHOLAS	30-Mar-12
COLARUSSO, BARRY	30-Mar-12
DOBNER, PAUL	30-Mar-12
FISHER, DANIEL MC	30-Mar-12
GRAY, MATTHEW	30-Mar-12
HUGHES, MATTHEW	30-Mar-12
JOHNSON, DAREN	30-Mar-12
MILDENER, LEE	30-Mar-12
NORRIS, PAUL MBE MC	30-Mar-12
PIPER, LEE	30-Mar-12
SAMPSON, JAMES	30-Mar-12
WARD, STEVEN	30-Mar-12

2013

LEA, THOMAS	01-Mar-13
ATKINSON, DAVID	21-Mar-13
ATKINSON, ANDREW	21-Mar-13
CATCHPOLE, ANDREW	21-Mar-13
ERSKINE, DOMINIC	21-Mar-13
GREEN, STEVEN	21-Mar-13
HURST, GARETH	21-Mar-13
MANNING, LESLIE	21-Mar-13
PAGE, MARTIN	21-Mar-13
SINDALL, STEVEN	21-Mar-13
WEITES, MATTHEW	21-Mar-13

LIEUTENANTS

2011

HOUGHTON, JAMES	01-Mar-11
ADAMS, JONATHAN	01-Sep-11
DAVIDSON, MATTHEW	01-Sep-11
FALLESEN, LLOYD	01-Sep-11
LUCY, THOMAS	01-Sep-11
PARSONS, JACOB	01-Sep-11

PATRICK, THOMAS	01-Sep-11
THOMAS, NICHOLAS	01-Sep-11
WILSON, CHARLES	01-Sep-11

2012

WEBB, ADRIAN	01-Jul-12
BLOOR, THOMAS	01-Sep-12

CAMPBELL, THOMAS	01-Sep-12
CROWLEY, JAMES	01-Sep-12
GREENWAY, CRENDON	01-Sep-12
HOPKINSON, GEOFFREY	01-Sep-12
MALLARD, JAMES	01-Sep-12
SYKES, MITCHELL	01-Sep-12
TOWNEND, HENRY	01-Sep-12

LIEUTENANTS

2013

BONIN-CASEY, PATRICK 01-Jul-13
COOK, PAUL... 01-Jul-13
CURRAN, STEVEN ....,.................. 01-Jul-13

DAVIES, WARREN.................................... 01-Jul-13
FOSTER, DARRYL 01-Jul-13
GROUNSELL, WAYNE 01-Jul-13
HAIRSINE, SAMUEL................................. 01-Jul-13
MOONEY, JOHN....................................... 01-Jul-13

POWELL, DARYL 01-Jul-13
ROWLES, MICHAEL.................................. 01-Jul-13
GOODE, LEE 13-Jan-14
MUDIE, CRAIG A 13-Jan-14
SEANEY, ADAM 13-Jan-14

SECOND LIEUTENANTS

2010

CLAXTON, ALISTAIR.............................. 01-Sep-10
MALLALIEU, HARRY 01-Sep-10

2011

CABOT, THOMAS 01-Mar-11
CHRISTIE, TOM 01-Mar-11
GASKIN, ALEXANDER 01-Mar-11
SAYER, TIMOTHY 01-Mar-11
WHITE, ALEC 01-Mar-11
AINSLEY, ALEX 01-Sep-11
BATHURST, BENJAMIN 01-Sep-11
CAIN, JOHN DAVID 01-Sep-11
DYER, TIMOTHY 01-Sep-11
GARDINER, ANGUS 01-Sep-11
HEAL, THOMAS 01-Sep-11
KIDSON, ADAM 01-Sep-11
MCALL, BENJAMIN 01-Sep-11
ROSE, HARRY 01-Sep-11
ROWDEN, PAUL..................................... 01-Sep-11
STEVEN, WILLIAM 01-Sep-11
TOMASI, VITTORIO 01-Sep-11
TYLER, JOSEPH 01-Sep-11
WAKE, DANIEL 01-Sep-11
WALLIS, THOMAS 01-Sep-11

2012

BLAKE, JEREMY 02-Sep-12
BROWN, NATHAN 01-Sep-12
BURLTON, PATRICK 06-Jun-12
GURNEY, BRIAN 02-Sep-12
RICHARDS, JACK 01-Sep-12
ROWE, WARREN 01-Sep-12
SOUTH, JACK 01-Sep-12

2013

FROST, OLIVER....................................... 01-Apr-13
ARSCOTT, JAMES 01-Sep-13
BERRY, THOMAS 01-Sep-13
ALESSANDRO, SANTINO 01-Sep-13
BEANEY, JONATHAN 02-Sep-13
BOMBY, ROSS.. 02-Sep-13
BOUCHER, PETER 02-Sep-13
CHITTY, JACK 02-Sep-13
DENNISS, JACK 02-Sep-13
DRAPER, MARK 02-Sep-13
DUNHAM, THOMAS 02-Sep-13
EARLY, THOMAS 02-Sep-13
FRANKLIN, JOSEPH 02-Sep-13
FRY, ROHAN 02-Sep-13
GOODWIN, MOSS 02-Sep-13

GOSLING, JONATHAN 02-Sep-13
GREAVES, JOSHUA 02-Sep-13
HARVEY, MARTIN 02-Sep-13
HASTINGS, THOMAS 02-Sep-13
HAVERS, LUKE 02-Sep-13
HOBLEY, CHRISTOPHER 02-Sep-13
HUNT, STEVEN...................................... 02-Sep-13
MARDER, MICHAEL 02-Sep-13
MOXHAM, GLEN 02-Sep-13
OLLE, ANDREW 02-Sep-13
PALMER, MATTHEW 02-Sep-13
PITCHER, TIM.. 02-Sep-13
RICHMOND, DAVID 02-Sep-13
ROUGHTON, JOSHUA 02-Sep-13
SOUKUP, SEBASTIAN............................ 02-Sep-13
STANNARD, JOSHUA 02-Sep-13
SWAN, ANTHONY.................................. 02-Sep-13
TALBOT, EDWARD 02-Sep-13
WATT, NICHOLAS 02-Sep-13
WELLS, RORY ....,.. .... 02-Sep-13

RFA OFFICERS

HONORARY COMMODORE

His Royal Highness Prince Edward, The Earl of Wessex, KG, KCVO, ADC

COMMODORE

Dorey, Robert

COMMODORE (Engineers)

Temporarily filled by T/A Cdre Ian Schumaker

CAPTAINS (Deck)

ALLAN OBE, ROBERT HUGH
BOOTH, SIMON KEIR
BUCK, DAVID JOHN
BUDD, NIGEL ANDREW
CLARKE MBE, CHRISTOPHER GRAHAM
DONKERSLEY, STEPHEN PAUL
EAGLES, DAVID ALEXANDER
FERRIS OBE MVO, ROSS GEOFFREY
HANTON, PHILIP THOMAS
HERBERT, SIMON CHRISTOPHER
HUXLEY, JONATHAN PETER
ILES, TREVOR JOHN

JONES OBE, SHAUN PETER
LAMB, DUNCAN LAWRENCE
MINTER, PAUL BERNARD
NORRIS, STEPHEN JAMES
PATTERSON, GERARD ANTHONY
PILLING, IAN NIGEL
RIMELL, KEVIN DAVID
SELBY, PETER NIGEL
SHATTOCK, GARY CHARLES
SIMMONS, CHARLES FREDERICK
WATTS, KIM

CAPTAINS (ENGINEER)

AMBROSE, MAURICE OSBON
BOWDITCH, ALISTAIR CHARLES
BURKE, NIGEL PATRICK
COLLINS, JAMES EDWARD
DAUNTON, PAUL RALPH
EDWARDS, TERENCE JOHN
FOX, NICHOLAS WALKER
GRAHAM, RICHARD STEPHEN
KING, BRIAN ARTHUR

LAYSON, BARRY SPENCER
PETERS, STUART MICHAEL
RICHARDSON, JOE WILLIAM
SCHUMACKER, IAN
SIM, NIGEL MAYNARD
SMEATON, MALCOLM
SMITH, DAVID BISSETT
STONE, MARTIN JOHN
WARDELL, DAVID ARMSTRONG

CAPTAINS (LS)

HOOD, JOHN

SHIPS OF THE ROYAL FLEET AUXILIARY SERVICE

ARGUS, Aviation Training Ship
BFPO 433

BLACK ROVER, Small Fleet Tanker
BFPO 435

CARDIGAN BAY, Bay Class Landing Ship
BFPO 436

DILIGENCE, Forward Repair Ship
BFPO 438

FORT AUSTIN, Fleet Replenishment Ship
BFPO 439

FORT ROSALIE, Fleet Replenishment Ship
BFPO 441

FORT VICTORIA, Fleet Replenishment Ship
BFPO 442

GOLD ROVER, Small Fleet Tanker
BFPO 443

LYME BAY, Bay Class Landing Ship
BFPO 447

MOUNTS BAY, Bay Class Landing Ship
BFPO 448

ORANGELEAF, Support Tanker
BFPO 449

WAVE RULER, Fast Fleet Tanker
BFPO 431

WAVE KNIGHT, Fast Fleet Tanker
BFPO 432

OFFICERS PRACTISING AS NAVAL BARRISTERS

VICE ADMIRAL

D G Steel CBE RN (David)

COMMODORES

Brown, N L, ADC
Jameson, A C
Spence, A B
(Commodore Naval Legal Services)

CAPTAINS

Hollins, R P
Towler, A
Wood, R

COMMANDERS

Atwill, J W O
Chadwick, K
Dow, C S
Kenyon, C
Knox, G P
Marland, E E
Park, I D
Reed D K
Stockbridge, A J
Storey, H
Teasdale, D
Ward, D J
Wright, S H

LIEUTENANT COMMANDERS/MAJORS

Carver, C
Coles-Hendry, F A
Coryton, S
Farrant, J D
Fleming, C S
Forbes A J
Frith A M
Goddard, D S
Hopkins R (Major)
Hunt, R J C
MacKenow, H R
Marsh, C L
Shears, A F
Ward, A J
Wright J S

LIEUTENANTS

Barker, J
Blackwell, M
De Silva, O A
Evans, T
Fane-Bailey, V
Goy, S
Jones, M R
Maclennan, N
Phillips, M
Poole, D

HONORARY OFFICERS IN THE MARITIME RESERVES

ROYAL NAVAL RESERVE

Rear Admiral HRH Prince Michael of Kent GCVO

Rear Admiral Sir Donald Gosling KCVO (RNR Air Branch)

Rear Admiral The Right Honourable The Lord Sterling of Plaistow GCVO CBE (HMS President)

Commodore Dame Mary Fagan DCVO JP (HMS King Alfred)

Captain Charles Howeson (HMS Vivid)

Captain Robert Woods CBE (HMS President)

Captain Carl Richardson (HMS Forward)

Captain Sir Eric Dancer KCVO CBE JP (HMS Vivid)

Captain Professor Geoffrey Till (HMS King Alfred)

Captain The Earl of Dalhousie (HMS Scotia)

Captain Jan Kopernicki CMG (HMS King Alfred)

Captain Adam Gosling (HMS Wildfire)

Captain Dame Mary Peters DBE (HMS Hibernia)

Commander John Billington (HMS Eaglet)

Commander Anthony Mason (HMS Cambria)

Commander Peter Moore RD* (HMS Sherwood)

Commander Jeremy Greaves (HMS King Alfred)

Commander Dee Caffari (HMS King Alfred)

Commander Christopher Wells (HMS King Alfred)

Commander Anthony Lima MBE RD (Gibraltar)

Commander Stephen Watson (HMS President)

Lieutenant Commander Dan Snow (HMS King Alfred)

Chaplain The Very Rev Dr Houston McKelvey OBE (HMS Hibernia)

Chaplain The Reverend Gordon Warren (HMS President)

Chaplain The Reverend John Williams MBE (HMS Eaglet)

Chaplain The Reverend Canon David Parrott (HMS President)

HONORARY OFFICERS IN THE MARITIME RESERVES

ROYAL MARINE RESERVE

Brigadier Ian Gardiner (RMR Scotland)

Brigadier Tom Lang (RMR Bristol)

Colonel Charles Hillock (RMR Merseyside)

Colonel Mark Hatt-Cook (RMR City of London)

Lieutenant Colonel David Gosling (1 AGRM)

Lieutenant Colonel Bear Grylls (CTCRM)

OFFICERS OF THE ACTIVE LIST
OF THE ROYAL NAVAL RESERVE,
ROYAL MARINES RESERVE THE QUEEN ALEXANDRA'S
ROYAL NAVAL NURSING RESERVE,
SEA CADET CORPS AND COMBINED CADET FORCE

ROYAL NAVAL RESERVE

Name	Rank	Seniority	Brach/Arm/Group	Unit

A

Name	Rank	Seniority	Brach/Arm/Group	Unit
ABBEY, MICHAEL P MBE	Lt Cdr	01-Oct-88	WAR	RNR AIR BR VL
ACKERMAN, RICHARD J	Lt RN	09-May-99	WAR	HMS CAMBRIA
ADAIR, RICHARD	Lt RN	05-May-08	WAR	HMS WILDFIRE
ADAM, PAUL J	SLt	29-Sep-12	WAR	HMS FERRET - RNRIU
AGELOU, RACHEL S	Lt Cdr	01-Oct-12	WAR	HMS VIVID
AITCHISON, IAN (H)	Lt Cdr	31-Mar-03	WAR	RNR MEDIA OPERATIONS
ALCOCK, CHARLES	Lt Cdr	31-Mar-00	WAR	FLEET CMR
ALLEN, ELINOR JANE	Cdr	30-Sep-05	WAR	HMS VIVID
ALLEN, IAN RD	Cdr	01-May-04	WAR	HMS HIBERNIA
ALLINSON, MICHAEL D	Lt RN	01-Mar-07	WAR	HMS KING ALFRED
ALSOP, SWEYN H	Lt RN	01-Dec-98	WAR	RNR AIR BR VL
ANDERSON, JOHN	Lt Cdr	31-Mar-06	WAR	FLEET CMR
ANDERSON, KERRY	Lt Cdr	17-Nov-04	WAR	HMS HIBERNIA
ANDREW, STEPHEN ROBERT	Mid	29-Sep-09	New Entrant	HMS DALRIADA
ANIM, TEKPEKI	OCdt	05-Nov-12	New Entrant	HMS EAGLET
ARBEID, MARK	Lt Cdr	01-Oct-09	WAR	HMS FERRET - RNRIU
ARKLE, NICHOLAS J	Lt RN	01-Sep-98	WAR	RNR AIR BR VL
ARMOUR, TIMOTHY	Lt RN	20-Sep-10	WAR	RNR MEDIA OPERATIONS
ARMSTRONG, SALLY	Lt RN	09-Apr-04	WAR	RNR MEDIA OPERATIONS
ASHPOLE, RICHARD	Surg Cdr	30-Sep-04	MED	HMS SHERWOOD
ATKINSON, JAMES D	Lt RN	26-Oct-07	WAR	HMS FERRET - RNRIU
AUSTIN, ELIZABETH JANE	SLt	10-Feb-11	New Entrant	HMS PRESIDENT
AUSTIN, KEVIN	Cdr	30-Jun-10	WAR	HMS PRESIDENT

B

Name	Rank	Seniority	Brach/Arm/Group	Unit
BAILEY, ANDREW VINCENT	Mid	25-Apr-12	New Entrant	HMS FORWARD
BAINES, ANDREW R	Lt Cdr	01-Oct-09	WAR	RNR AIR BR VL
BAINES, MARK	Lt Cdr	01-Feb-93	WAR	RNR AIR BR VL
BAKEWELL, ROBERT ANDREW	Lt RN	14-Sep-07	WAR	HMS KING ALFRED
BALMAIN, STEPHEN	Lt RN	01-Jul-94	WAR	HMS PRESIDENT
BANCROFT, DAVID	Lt Cdr	31-Mar-05	WAR	HMS CALLIOPE
BANNISTER, MARK	Lt RN	30-Oct-09	LOGS	HMS WILDFIRE
BARKHUYSEN, EDWARD	Lt RN	24-Oct-05	WAR	HMS FLYING FOX
BARNBROOK, JEREMY C	Lt Cdr	16-Dec-96	WAR	RNR AIR BR VL
BARNES, JUDITH	Lt Cdr	01-Oct-08	WAR	HMS EAGLET
BARNES, PATRICK A L	Lt RN	01-Apr-94	WAR	RNR AIR BR VL
BARR, LYNNE	SLt	26-Oct-11	WAR	HMS DALRIADA
BARRATT, STEPHEN	Lt RN	26-May-07	WAR	HMS FORWARD
BARRETT, NANCY LYNN C	OCdt	18-Oct-11	New Entrant	HMS SCOTIA
BARRY, JACQUELINE	Lt RN	25-Sep-05	LOGS	HMS EAGLET

Name	Rank	Seniority	Brach/Arm/Group	Unit
BARTON, NATASHA MELANIE	Lt RN	17-Feb-12	WAR	HMS PRESIDENT
BASSETT, KAREN	OCdt	26-Apr-03	New Entrant	HMS KING ALFRED
BASSETT, NIGEL PETER QVRM	Capt RN	01-Apr-09	WAR	FLEET CMR
BAYNTUN, DAVID	Lt RN	20-Nov-09	WAR	HMS WILDFIRE
BEATON, IAIN	Lt RN	24-Dec-07	WAR	HMS DALRIADA
BEDDING, SIMON W E	Lt Cdr	01-Apr-00	WAR	HMS KING ALFRED
BEIRNE, STEPHEN	Lt Cdr	01-Oct-12	WAR	RNR AIR BR VL
BELLAMY, SIMON	Lt RN	22-Feb-06	WAR	RNR MEDIA OPERATIONS
BENBOW, WILLIAM	Lt RN	01-Feb-09	WAR	HMS VIVID
BENMAYOR, DINAH ELIZABETH	Lt RN	24-Feb-08	WAR	HMS FERRET - RNRIU
BENN, PETER	Lt Cdr	31-Mar-06	WAR	RNR MEDIA OPERATIONS
BENNET, NIALL	Lt RN	22-Nov-04	WAR	HMS SCOTIA
BENTLEY, DAVID	Lt RN	14-May-04	WAR	HMS SCOTIA
BERRY, IAN MBE RD	Lt Cdr	31-Mar-96	WAR	HMS CALLIOPE
BEVAN, ROSS M.	OCdt	05-Jul-12	New Entrant	HMS EAGLET
BEWLEY, GEOFFREY RD	Cdr	30-Jun-08	WAR	HMS KING ALFRED
BHANUMURTHY, SANAPALA	Surg Lt Cdr	03-Jun-03	MED	HMS CAMBRIA
BICKNELL, RICHARD	Lt Cdr	31-Mar-01	WAR	HMS KING ALFRED
BINGHAM, EDWARD J	Lt RN	15-Jul-12	WAR	HMS CALLIOPE
BINGLEY, LEWIS K L	Lt RN	19-Oct-08	Defence Intelligence	HMS FERRET - RNRIU
BISHOP, GEORGE C	Lt RN	27-Jul-95	WAR	RNR AIR BR VL
BISHOP, JONATHAN	Lt Cdr	31-Mar-96	WAR	RNR AIR BR VL
BLAGDEN, DAVID W	Mid	24-Jun-10	New Entrant	HMS WILDFIRE
BOAL, MICHAEL ALEXANDER	Lt Cdr	02-Jun-06	WAR	HMS HIBERNIA
BOLTON, ADAM ROBERT	Lt Cdr	23-Feb-08	WAR	HMS VIVID
BOULD, EMMA LOUISE BE	Lt RN	19-Nov-09	WAR	HMS FLYING FOX
BOWEN, MICHAEL	Surg Cdr	30-Sep-04	MED	HMS PRESIDENT
BOWN, ANTHONY MARK	Lt Cdr	08-Mar-91	WAR	HMS FERRET - RNRIU
BOWN, CAROL DIANE RD	Lt Cdr	31-Mar-03	WAR	HMS FERRET - RNRIU
BOYLE, ABIGAIL Elder	Lt RN	07-Oct-11	WAR	HMS FERRET - RNRIU
BOYLE, KIRK	Lt Cdr	31-Mar-06	WAR	HMS FERRET - RNRIU
BRADBURN, STEPHEN	Lt Cdr	01-Oct-93	WAR	RNR AIR BR VL
BRADLEY, ALAN C	Lt RN	15-Apr-07	WAR	HMS KING ALFRED
BRAILEY, IAN S F	Lt Cdr	24-Jun-07	WAR	RNR AIR BR VL
BRATBY, SIMON P	Lt Cdr	01-Oct-05	WAR	RNR AIR BR VL
BRAYSHAW, TABITHA L	OCdt	04-Jul-12	New Entrant	HMS FORWARD
BREYLEY, NIGEL	Lt Cdr	31-Mar-98	WAR	RNR AIR BR VL
BROGAN, GARY	Lt Cdr	01-Oct-09	WAR	HMS EAGLET
BROOKS, ALEXANDRA L	Lt Cdr	01-Oct-11	WAR	RNR MEDIA OPERATIONS
BROOKS, RICHARD	Lt RN	19-Apr-06	WAR	HMS KING ALFRED
BROOKSBANK, RICHARD J	Lt Cdr	31-Dec-97	WAR	RNR AIR BR VL
BROOMAN, MARTIN	Lt RN	16-Aug-95	WAR	RNR AIR BR VL
BROSTER, MARK	Lt Cdr	01-Oct-09	WAR	HMS KING ALFRED
BROTHWOOD, MICHAEL	Lt Cdr	18-Oct-10	WAR	RNR AIR BR VL
BROWN, ANDREW P	Lt Cdr	13-Aug-06	RNR Air	RNR AIR BR VL
BROWN, SHARON M J	Lt RN	01-Jul-04	LOGS	HMS KING ALFRED
BROWN, THOMAS	Lt Cdr	01-Jul-00	WAR	HMS VIVID
BROWN, TIMOTHY	Lt Cdr	19-Mar-93	WAR	RNR AIR BR VL
BROWNE, ALASTAIR	Lt RN	31-May-07	WAR	HMS SCOTIA
BROWNING, ELEANORE	Lt RN	26-Nov-10	WAR	HMS KING ALFRED
BROWNING, EMMA	Lt Cdr	01-Oct-12	QARNNS	HMS HIBERNIA
BROWNING, JAMES	Lt RN	07-Dec-04	WAR	HMS PRESIDENT
BRYNING, CHRISTOPHER	Lt Cdr	01-Mar-85	WAR	RNR AIR BR VL
BUCHAN, JOHN	Lt RN	28-Mar-00	WAR	HMS FERRET - RNRIU
BUCKLEY, JONATHAN	Lt Cdr	05-Oct-10	WAR	FLEET CMR
BUCKNELL, DAVID	Lt Cdr	01-Jul-96	WAR	HMS FLYING FOX
BULLOCK, STEPHANIE J	OCdt	16-Aug-12	New Entrant	HMS EAGLET
BURDETT, RICHARD WYNDHAM	Lt RN	01-May-06	WAR	HMS FLYING FOX
BURNS, ANDREW J	Lt RN	01-Jan-03	WAR	RNR AIR BR VL
BUSH, ROBERT L	Mid	28-Jul-09	New Entrant	HMS PRESIDENT
BUTTERWORTH, ROBERT G	OCdt	01-Jul-13	New Entrant	HMS PRESIDENT
BUTTON, EDWARD	Lt RN	01-Jul-10	WAR	HMS FERRET - RNRIU

Name	Rank	Seniority	Brach/Arm/Group	Unit

C

Name	Rank	Seniority	Brach/Arm/Group	Unit
CALHAEM, SARAH	Lt RN	28-Jul-07	WAR	HMS FORWARD
CALLAGHAN, PAUL F	Lt Cdr	30-Oct-99	WAR	RNR AIR BR VL
CALLISTER, DAVID R	Lt Cdr	24-Nov-95	WAR	RNR AIR BR VL
CAMERON, ANNE	Lt Cdr	31-Mar-01	WAR	HMS KING ALFRED
CAMERON, IAIN	Lt Cdr	01-Sep-99	WAR	RNR AIR BR VL
CAMERON, SHAUN	Lt RN	16-Jun-07	WAR	HMS EAGLET
CAMPBELL, GRAHAM	Lt Cdr	31-Mar-05	WAR	HMS FORWARD
CAMPBELL, IAIN A	Lt RN	31-Jul-96	WAR	RNR AIR BR VL
CAMPBELL, PETER	Lt Cdr	01-Oct-12	WAR	RNR AIR BR VL
CAMPBELL-BALCOMBE, ANDRE A	Lt RN	18-Sep-02	WAR	HMS WILDFIRE
CANHAM, WENDY	Cdr	30-Jun-09	WAR	HMS SHERWOOD
CAREY, ANDREW	Lt RN	05-Sep-04	WAR	HMS WILDFIRE
CARPENTER, PHILIP	Lt RN	01-Feb-94	WAR	RNR AIR BR VL
CARRETTA, MARK VINCENT OBE	Lt Cdr	30-Jun-06	WAR	RNR AIR BR VL
CARTER, DAVID	Lt RN	22-Mar-99	WAR	HMS EAGLET
CARTER, ROBERT I	Lt Cdr	01-Oct-95	WAR	RNR AIR BR VL
CHAMPION, RICHARD	Lt RN	15-Mar-13	WAR	HMS EAGLET
CHAN-A-SUE, STEPHEN	Lt Cdr	15-Apr-02	WAR	RNR AIR BR VL
CHAPMAN, ANTHONY	Cdr	30-Jun-11	WAR	FLEET CMR
CHAUVELIN, DAVID C W RD	Lt Cdr	01-Oct-11	WAR	HMS SCOTIA
CHEYNE, STEVEN	Cdr	15-May-04	WAR	RNR AIR BR VL
CHICK, NICHOLAS STEVEN	Lt RN	15-Nov-95	WAR	RNR AIR BR VL
CHISHOLM, FELICITY	Lt RN	05-Dec-11	WAR	HMS SCOTIA
CHURCH, ELIZABETH	Lt Cdr	31-Mar-06	WAR	HMS PRESIDENT
CHURCH, STEPHEN C	Lt RN	10-Apr-97	WAR	RNR AIR BR VL
CLARK, SUZANNE	Lt Cdr	31-Mar-97	WAR	RNR AIR BR VL
CLARKE, BERNARD R MBE, QHC	RN Chpln	30-Jun-81	RN Chaplaincy Service	HMS KING ALFRED
CLARKE, LAURENCE	Lt RN	23-Mar-06	WAR	HMS FLYING FOX
CLARKE, NICHOLAS J	Lt Cdr	12-Oct-00	WAR	RNR AIR BR VL
CLARKE, ROGER RD	Lt Cdr	31-Mar-96	WAR	HMS VIVID
CLARKE, WILLIAM	Lt Cdr	31-Mar-00	WAR	HMS HIBERNIA
CLEEVE, FELICITY	Lt RN	01-Sep-06	LOGS	HMS FORWARD
CLEGG, MARTIN L	Lt Cdr	01-Jun-90	WAR	HMS SHERWOOD
CLEGG, TOBY A	SLt	13-Nov-09	New Entrant	HMS PRESIDENT
CLEWS, HARRIET	Lt RN	20-Jun-04	WAR	HMS WILDFIRE
CLINTON, LESLEY	Lt RN	19-Nov-08	WAR	HMS FERRET - RNRIU
CLOKEY, JOHN H E	Lt RN	04-Feb-08	WAR	HMS PRESIDENT
COAKER, STEWART	Lt RN	02-Nov-02	WAR	HMS FERRET - RNRIU
COATS, MARIA	Surg Lt Cdr	23-Jan-12	MED	HMS SCOTIA
COCHRANE, ROSS	Mid	27-May-10	New Entrant	HMS HIBERNIA
CODY, WILLIAM	Lt Cdr	01-Jul-97	WAR	HMS FERRET - RNRIU
COHEN, JAMES SEYMOUR L	Cdr	30-Jun-08	WAR	HMS PRESIDENT
COHEN, OLIVER GEORGE L	OCdt	09-Jun-11	New Entrant	HMS PRESIDENT
COLEY, JENNIFER	Lt Cdr	01-Oct-12	WAR	RNR MEDIA OPERATIONS
COLLEN, SARA J	Lt Cdr	01-Dec-09	WAR	RNR MEDIA OPERATIONS
COLLIER, ANDREW S	Lt Cdr	01-Jun-93	WAR	HMS CALLIOPE
COLLIER, DAVID	Lt RN	30-Jan-06	WAR	HMS SHERWOOD
COLYER, MICHAEL	Lt Cdr	15-Sep-04	WAR	HMS CALLIOPE
COMPAIN, CRAIG H	Lt RN	21-Mar-97	WAR	RNR AIR BR VL
CONNORS, LIAM	OCdt	01-May-13	New Entrant	HMS PRESIDENT
CONWAY, KEITH ALEXANDER RD	Lt Cdr	31-Mar-99	WAR	HMS SCOTIA
COOK, SIMON HUME HUGH	Lt Cdr	01-Oct-08	WAR	HMS WILDFIRE
COOKE, MICHAEL JOHN	Lt Cdr	01-Oct-02	ENG	RNR AIR BR VL
COOPER, ANTHONY	OCdt	01-Nov-12	New Entrant	HMS PRESIDENT
COOPER, DAVID J	Lt Cdr	31-Mar-99	WAR	HMS KING ALFRED
COPELAND-DAVIS, TERENCE	Lt Cdr	31-Mar-03	WAR	RNR AIR BR VL
COSGROVE, ANTHONY	Lt RN	09-Oct-10	WAR	HMS KING ALFRED
COTTAM, SIMON ROSCOE QVRM	Lt Cdr	31-Mar-97	WAR	HMS FLYING FOX
COTTINGHAM, NEIL	Cdr	30-Jun-12	WAR	RNR AIR BR VL
COUGHLAN, SCOTT	Lt RN	01-Sep-03	WAR	HMS FERRET - RNRIU

Name	Rank	Seniority	Brach/Arm/Group	Unit
COULING, MATTHEW JOHN	Mid	01-Nov-12	New Entrant	HMS WILDFIRE
COUPLAND, MARK	Lt RN	01-Mar-89	WAR	RNR AIR BR VL
COURTNEY, KURT	Lt RN	07-Oct-05	WAR	HMS FERRET - RNRIU
COWAN, ANDREW	Cdr	30-Sep-06	WAR	HMS DALRIADA
COWIN, TIMOTHY J	Lt RN	29-May-99	WAR	RNR AIR BR VL
COX, LAURA	OCdt	09-May-12	New Entrant	HMS KING ALFRED
COX, RHODERICK	Lt Cdr	01-Dec-88	WAR	RNR AIR BR VL
COYNE, JOHN	Lt RN	17-Dec-93	WAR	RNR AIR BR VL
CRAWFORD, VALERIE E	Lt RN	01-Apr-02	WAR	HMS FERRET - RNRIU
CROSS, ELIZABETH J C	Lt Cdr	01-Oct-08	WAR	HMS FERRET - RNRIU
CUBBAGE, JOANNA	Lt RN	09-Dec-11	LOGS	HMS SCOTIA
CURTIS, ROGER	Cdr	30-Jun-11	WAR	HMS DALRIADA

D

Name	Rank	Seniority	Brach/Arm/Group	Unit
DACOMBE, CARL A	Lt RN	01-Sep-04	WAR	RNR AIR BR VL
DADY, SIMON	Lt RN	24-Dec-03	WAR	HMS PRESIDENT
DALBY, RUSSELL	Lt RN	24-May-05	WAR	HMS SHERWOOD
DALLAMORE, REBECCA A	Lt RN	01-Jan-01	WAR	HMS KING ALFRED
DANE, RICHARD M H OBE	Lt Cdr	01-Aug-05	WAR	RNR AIR BR VL
DANGERFIELD, CHARLOTTE	Mid	26-Nov-09	New Entrant	HMS PRESIDENT
DANN, ADRIAN	Lt Cdr	01-Oct-98	WAR	HMS KING ALFRED
DARWEN, CLINT	Lt RN	12-Nov-10	LOGS	HMS PRESIDENT
DAVIES, GEORGE	Lt Cdr	31-Mar-03	WAR	RNR AIR BR VL
DAVIES, RICHARD	Lt RN	17-Sep-03	WAR	RNR MEDIA OPERATIONS
DAVIES, SARAH	Lt RN	19-Feb-99	WAR	HMS PRESIDENT
DAVIS, ANDREW	Lt Cdr	02-Oct-94	WAR	RNR AIR BR VL
DAVIS, SERENA	Lt RN	08-Nov-03	WAR	HMS VIVID
DAWSON, MELISSA C	Lt RN	21-Dec-04	WAR	HMS PRESIDENT
DEAN, NICOLA	Surg Lt Cdr	01-Sep-06	MED	HMS CALLIOPE
DEAVIN, MATTHEW J	Lt Cdr	01-Oct-08	WAR	RNR AIR BR VL
DEENEY, STEPHEN	Lt Cdr	01-Oct-99	WAR	RNR AIR BR VL
DEIGHTON, GRAEME	Lt Cdr	01-Oct-12	WAR	HMS CALLIOPE
DEMUTH, ALICE	OCdt	01-Jul-11	New Entrant	HMS FORWARD
DENT, JOHN	Lt RN	22-Oct-08	WAR	HMS SCOTIA
DEVEREESE, GEORGE B	Lt RN	01-Apr-09	WAR	HMS PRESIDENT
DICKENS, CHARLES	Lt Cdr	01-Oct-12	WAR	HMS FERRET - RNRIU
DITTON, NATHAN	Lt Cdr	01-Oct-12	WAR	HMS KING ALFRED
DONALDSON, JAMES W	OCdt	01-Oct-12	New Entrant	HMS PRESIDENT
DONOHUE, PAUL	Lt RN	13-Feb-07	WAR	HMS FERRET - RNRIU
DORMAN, NICHOLAS RD	Capt RN	01-Sep-09	WAR	FLEET CMR
DOVEY, PHILIP ALAN	Lt RN	11-Mar-11	WAR	HMS DALRIADA
DOWNING, CARL	Lt Cdr	16-Nov-92	ENG	RNR AIR BR VL
DOWNING, CHARLOTTE E P	OCdt	22-Oct-09	New Entrant	HMS PRESIDENT
DOWNING, IAN MICHAEL	Lt RN	16-Sep-94	WAR	RNR AIR BR VL
DOWNING, NEIL RD,	Lt Cdr	31-Mar-00	WAR	HMS HIBERNIA
DRAKE, RODERICK	Lt Cdr	31-Mar-98	WAR	HMS FLYING FOX
DRUMMOND, ANDREW	Surg Lt Cdr	08-Aug-08	MED	HMS CALLIOPE
DUFFIELD, GARY	Cdr	30-Sep-06	ENG	RNR AIR BR VL
DUNLOP, JOANNE	Lt Cdr	30-Mar-07	WAR	HMS CAMBRIA
DUNN, EDWARD	Lt RN	11-Dec-11	WAR	HMS WILDFIRE
DUNNE, LAWRENCE JOHN	Lt Cdr	31-Mar-04	WAR	HMS FORWARD
DUNNE, VICTORIA	SLt	02-Mar-10	WAR	HMS PRESIDENT
DUSTAN, ANDREW J	Lt Cdr	15-May-04	ENG	RNR AIR BR VL
DUTHIE, CHARLES	Lt RN	09-Jul-06	WAR	HMS CALLIOPE
DUTHIE, DAVID	Surg Cdr	30-Sep-00	MED	HMS SHERWOOD

E

Name	Rank	Seniority	Brach/Arm/Group	Unit
EALEY, NICHOLAS J	Lt RN	08-Nov-05	WAR	HMS FLYING FOX
EARLE, GARETH DAVID	OCdt	01-Sep-12	New Entrant	HMS FLYING FOX
EASTAUGH, TIMOTHY	Lt Cdr	01-Oct-93	WAR	RNR AIR BR VL
EASTERBROOK, HELEN ANN	Lt RN	19-Jan-11	WAR	HMS WILDFIRE

Name	Rank	Seniority	Brach/Arm/Group	Unit
EASTHAM, ALLAN MICHAEL	Lt Cdr	31-Mar-94	WAR	HMS KING ALFRED
EDWARDS, MATTHEW PAUL	Lt RN	11-Sep-09	WAR	HMS FERRET - RNRIU
EDWARDS, MICHAEL	Surg Cdr	30-Jun-08	MED	HMS SHERWOOD
ELLISON, BRYONY	Lt RN	20-Feb-05	WAR	HMS PRESIDENT
ENGLAND, ROBERT F	Lt RN	30-Aug-96	QARNNS	HMS KING ALFRED
ESFAHANI, SHAHROKH	Lt Cdr	31-Mar-02	WAR	HMS WILDFIRE
EVANS, ALEX	Lt Cdr	31-Mar-99	WAR	RNR AIR BR VL
EVANS, ANN	Lt Cdr	31-Mar-94	WAR	HMS FERRET - RNRIU

F

Name	Rank	Seniority	Brach/Arm/Group	Unit
FARMER, GARY GORDON	Lt Cdr	31-Mar-06	WAR	HMS SCOTIA
FARQUHAR, JAMES	SLt	19-May-12	WAR	HMS CALLIOPE
FEARON, CATHERINE G.	Lt RN	02-May-08	WAR	HMS PRESIDENT
FEDOROWICZ, RICHARD	Lt Cdr	16-Oct-00	WAR	RNR AIR BR VL
FEGAN, PAUL	Lt RN	25-Oct-01	WAR	RNR MEDIA OPERATIONS
FENWICK, ROBIN J	Maj	01-Oct-04	WAR	RNR AIR BR VL
FERRAN, SIMON HAROLD M	Lt RN	17-Jul-07	WAR	HMS HIBERNIA
FERRIE, HEATHER	Lt RN	22-Sep-07	WAR	HMS FERRET - RNRIU
FILOCHOWSKI, KATE	OCdt	01-Jan-13	New Entrant	HMS PRESIDENT
FILTNESS, REBECCA A J	Lt RN	01-Aug-04	WAR	HMS DALRIADA
FISHER, ROBERT J	Lt Cdr	01-Oct-09	WAR	RNR AIR BR VL
FITZGERALD, NICHOLAS	Lt RN	01-Dec-92	WAR	RNR AIR BR VL
FITZPATRICK, DARREN	Lt RN	30-Apr-08	QARNNS	HMS EAGLET
FLANAGAN, MARTIN	Lt Cdr	01-Feb-92	WAR	RNR AIR BR VL
FLEMING, SAMUEL	Lt Cdr	01-Nov-04	WAR	HMS KING ALFRED
FLETCHER, CATRIONA	Lt RN	23-Jun-08	WAR	HMS SCOTIA
FLETCHER, RICHARD	Lt RN	31-Mar-04	LOGS	HMS VIVID
FLINTOFF, SUSAN ELLEN M	Lt RN	29-Jul-02	WAR	HMS DALRIADA
FLYNN, STEPHEN	Lt RN	23-Jan-06	WAR	HMS CALLIOPE
FORBES, MATTHEW P	Lt RN	01-Oct-10	WAR	HMS KING ALFRED
FORBES, PAUL T	Lt RN	16-Jul-96	WAR	RNR AIR BR VL
FOREMAN, TIMOTHY	Lt Cdr	31-Mar-03	WAR	RNR AIR BR VL
FORSTER, RAYMOND A.	Lt Cdr	01-Oct-01	WAR	RNR AIR BR VL
FOSTER, NICHOLAS	Lt RN	13-Jun-08	WAR	HMS CALLIOPE
FOX, RICHARD GEORGE OBE	Lt Cdr	30-Jun-05	WAR	848 SQN
FRANCIS, GARRY	Lt RN	05-Apr-08	WAR	HMS FERRET - RNRIU
FRANKS, JASON A	SLt	01-Sep-96	New Entrant	HMS FERRET - RNRIU
FREEMAN, PAUL	Lt RN	13-Jul-12	WAR	HMS CALLIOPE
FRY, STEPHEN M RD	Lt Cdr	31-Mar-05	WAR	HMS CAMBRIA
FULFORD, MARK	Lt Cdr	01-Jan-96	WAR	RNR AIR BR VL

G

Name	Rank	Seniority	Brach/Arm/Group	Unit
GAFFNEY, FRANCIS	Lt RN	16-Apr-08	WAR	HMS FERRET - RNRIU
GARDINER, GEORGE	Surg Cdr	30-Sep-04	MED	HMS HIBERNIA
GATENBY, CHRISTOPHER	Lt Cdr	31-Mar-07	WAR	HMS EAGLET
GATER, JAMES C	Lt RN	01-Jan-03	WAR	RNR MEDIA OPERATIONS
GAVEY, STEPHEN RD	Lt Cdr	01-Aug-88	WAR	HMS VIVID
GEARY, MICHAEL	Lt Cdr	31-Mar-05	WAR	RNR AIR BR VL
GHOST, RICHARD	Lt RN	01-Nov-07	WAR	HMS FERRET - RNRIU
GIBBS, ANTHONY M	Lt RN	14-Sep-99	WAR	RNR AIR BR VL
GIBSON, PHAEDRA L	Lt Cdr	01-Oct-07	New Entrant Instructor	HMS VIVID
GILBERT, ANTHONY	Lt RN	26-Aug-06	WAR	HMS FLYING FOX
GLEAVE, JAMES	Lt Cdr	31-Mar-04	WAR	HMS DALRIADA
GOBEY, CHRISTOPHER	Lt Cdr	01-Oct-95	WAR	HMS SCOTIA
GOBEY, RICHARD	Lt RN	04-Jun-05	WAR	HMS KING ALFRED
GOLDSWORTHY, ELAINE T	Lt Cdr	01-Oct-04	WAR	RNR MEDIA OPERATIONS
GOODES, SIMON	Lt Cdr	31-Mar-97	WAR	HMS WILDFIRE
GORAM, MALCOLM	Lt Cdr	31-Mar-04	WAR	RNR AIR BR VL
GOWER, BENJAMIN C S	SLt	09-Dec-10	New Entrant	HMS PRESIDENT
GRACEY, PETER	Cdr	30-Jun-09	WAR	FLEET CMR
GRAHAM, RICHARD	Surg Lt Cdr	06-Apr-02	MED	FLEET CMR

Name	Rank	Seniority	Brach/Arm/Group	Unit
GREAVES, CHRISTOPHER	Lt Cdr	01-Oct-95	WAR	RNR AIR BR VL
GREAVES, MICHAEL	Lt Cdr	01-Apr-94	WAR	RNR AIR BR VL
GREEN, CHRISTOPHER THOMAS	OCdt	23-Feb-11	New Entrant	HMS EAGLET
GREENACRE, RICHARD	Lt Cdr	31-Mar-97	WAR	HMS VIVID
GREENE, ALISTAIR	Lt RN	04-Jul-03	LOGS	HMS PRESIDENT
GRIFFIN, DANIELLE	Lt RN	30-Jan-06	WAR	HMS KING ALFRED
GRIFFITHS, CHRISTOPHER PAUL	OCdt	01-Jul-12	New Entrant	HMS CAMBRIA
GRIFFITHS, LINDSAY	Lt RN	01-Mar-13	WAR	HMS FLYING FOX
GRIFFITHS, MICHAEL EDWARD	Lt Cdr	31-Mar-02	WAR	HMS CAMBRIA
GRIST, DAVID	Lt Cdr	05-Oct-10	QARNNS	HMS KING ALFRED

H

Name	Rank	Seniority	Brach/Arm/Group	Unit
HADDOW, TIMOTHY ROWAT	Lt Cdr	01-Mar-05	WAR	HMS SCOTIA
HAFFENDEN, SIMON	Lt Cdr	21-Nov-05	WAR	HMS FLYING FOX
HAIKIN, PETER	Lt RN	02-Feb-96	WAR	HMS FERRET - RNRIU
HAINES, PAUL	OCdt	01-Aug-11	New Entrant	HMS KING ALFRED
HAINSWORTH, ROBIN	Lt RN	22-Aug-11	WAR	HMS CALLIOPE
HALL, NEIL	Lt Cdr	01-Mar-93	WAR	HMS KING ALFRED
HALL, STEPHEN	Lt Cdr	01-Oct-12	WAR	HMS FERRET - RNRIU
HALLIDAY, IAN	Lt Cdr	01-Sep-90	WAR	RNR AIR BR VL
HAMIDUDDIN, IQBAL	Lt RN	01-Feb-04	WAR	HMS PRESIDENT
HAMILTON, IVAN	Lt RN	16-Nov-91	WAR	RNR AIR BR VL
HAMILTON, RICHARD	Lt RN	10-Feb-08	WAR	HMS PRESIDENT
HANCOCK, ANGELA M QVRM	Capt RN	15-Oct-12	WAR	FLEET CMR
HANDLEY, DANE	Lt Cdr	31-Mar-96	WAR	RNR AIR BR VL
HANKEY, HELEN	Lt RN	14-Dec-01	LOGS	HMS PRESIDENT
HANKEY, MARK RD	Lt Cdr	31-Mar-07	WAR	RNR MEDIA OPERATIONS
HANRAHAN, MARTIN	Lt Cdr	01-Jun-01	WAR	RNR AIR BR VL
HARDINGE, CHRISTOPHER MBE	Cdr	30-Sep-05	WAR	HMS PRESIDENT
HARDWICK, LUCY JAYNE	SLt	10-Jun-10	WAR	HMS FERRET - RNRIU
HARGREAVES, NEALE	Lt Cdr	23-May-98	WAR	RNR AIR BR VL
HARGREAVES, SIMON	Cdr	01-Jul-02	WAR	RNR AIR BR VL
HARPER, ALEC	Lt RN	22-Oct-10	WAR	HMS PRESIDENT
HARRIS, ADAM ROBERT LUKE	OCdt	04-Aug-10	New Entrant	HMS PRESIDENT
HARRIS, ADRIAN	Lt Cdr	31-Mar-06	WAR	HMS VIVID
HARRISON, LAURA	Lt RN	20-Jul-07	WAR	RNR MEDIA OPERATIONS
HARRISON, RICHARD W	Surg Lt Cdr	17-May-95	MED	HMS SHERWOOD
HART, PAUL A	Lt Cdr	01-Oct-98	WAR	RNR MEDIA OPERATIONS
HART, SARAH	SLt	08-May-13	WAR	HMS FERRET - RNRIU
HARTLEY, PHILIP	Lt Cdr	16-Dec-88	WAR	HMS FERRET - RNRIU
HAWES, ALISON	Lt Cdr	31-Mar-98	WAR	RNR MEDIA OPERATIONS
HAWKINS, CHRISTOPHER ROY	OCdt	24-May-12	New Entrant	HMS SCOTIA
HAWKINS, JOHN	Lt RN	01-May-01	WAR	HMS KING ALFRED
HAYES, BRIAN J	Lt Cdr	01-Oct-05	Media	HMS CAMBRIA
HAYHURST, JAMIE	Mid	05-Mar-09	New Entrant	HMS CALLIOPE
HAYWARD-RODGERS, DARREN	Lt RN	10-Aug-97	WAR	RNR AIR BR VL
HEARN, SAMUEL P.	Lt RN	25-Jun-03	WAR	RNR MEDIA OPERATIONS
HEIGHWAY, MARTIN R	Lt RN	08-May-00	WAR	HMS KING ALFRED
HELSBY, EDWARD	Lt Cdr	31-Mar-96	WAR	RNR AIR BR VL
HERBERT-BURNS, RUPERT H	Lt RN	27-Nov-10	WAR	HMS FERRET - RNRIU
HERMANSON, STEPHEN	Lt RN	23-Mar-06	WAR	HMS FERRET - RNRIU
HERRIMAN, JOHN ANDREW	Lt Cdr	07-Jul-06	WAR	HMS PRESIDENT
HETHERINGTON, SIMON DF	Lt RN	24-May-07	WAR	HMS PRESIDENT
HEWINS, CLIVE	Lt Cdr	20-May-91	WAR	HMS CALLIOPE
HEYWOOD, ANTHONY J	Lt RN	11-Dec-11	WAR	HMS FERRET - RNRIU
HIGSON, LEE	SLt	18-Oct-05	WAR	HMS EAGLET
HIGSON, RENNIE	Lt RN	05-Oct-07	WAR	HMS SHERWOOD
HILL, PAUL	Capt RN	11-May-12	WAR	FLEET CMR
HODKINSON-WALKER, KRISTA	Lt RN	18-Nov-05	WAR	HMS CAMBRIA
HOGAN, AMBROSE DOMINIC	Lt RN	15-Jul-00	WAR	HMS PRESIDENT
HOLBORN, CARL	Lt Cdr	31-Mar-03	ENG	RNR AIR BR VL
HOLLAND, OLIVER THOMAS P	OCdt	01-Oct-12	New Entrant	HMS PRESIDENT

Name	Rank	Seniority	Brach/Arm/Group	Unit
HOLLEY, STEVEN	Lt RN	28-Mar-07	WAR	HMS KING ALFRED
HOLOHAN, RUAIRI	OCdt	01-Dec-11	New Entrant	HMS HIBERNIA
HOOK, SAMANTHA	Surg Lt Cdr	01-Apr-05	MED	HMS KING ALFRED
HORNE, MARTIN	Lt RN	23-Sep-96	WAR	HMS KING ALFRED
HORNER, BENJAMIN	Lt RN	13-May-02	WAR	HMS PRESIDENT
HORSLEY, JOHN ROBERT	Surg Lt Cdr	21-Mar-07	MED	HMS EAGLET
HOULSTON, CHRISTOPHER CLIVE	OCdt	22-Aug-12	New Entrant	HMS FORWARD
HOWARD-PEARCE, TAMAR A	Lt RN	18-Jun-11	WAR	RNR MEDIA OPERATIONS
HOWITT, SARA L	Lt RN	04-Jan-10	WAR	HMS PRESIDENT
HOYLE, STEPHEN	Lt Cdr	31-Mar-03	WAR	HMS EAGLET
HUBBLE, ROBERT	Lt Cdr	01-Oct-97	WAR	RNR AIR BR VL
HUGHES, JILL	Lt Cdr	31-Mar-95	WAR	HMS HIBERNIA
HUGHES, PETER	Cdr	06-Feb-88	WAR	NCHQ CNPS
HUGHES, SEAN CORIN	OCdt	14-Nov-08	MED	HMS KING ALFRED
HULSE, ROYSTON M	Lt RN	01-Sep-03	WAR	RNR AIR BR VL
HUNWICKS, SARAH E	Lt Cdr	01-Oct-05	ENG	RNR AIR BR VL

I

IRELAND, STEVEN	OCdt	01-Apr-13	New Entrant	HMS HIBERNIA

J

JACQUES, KATHRYN	Lt RN	24-May-08	WAR	HMS SHERWOOD
JAFFIER, ROBERT	Lt Cdr	01-Oct-10	WAR	HMS FORWARD
JAMESON, SUSAN	Cdr	30-Jun-09	WAR	FLEET CMR
JERMY, RICHARD	Lt Cdr	31-Mar-04	WAR	HMS FERRET - RNRIU
JEWITT, CHARLES	Lt Cdr	30-Jun-03	LOGS	FLEET CMR
JOHNSON, ALEX D	Lt RN	01-Jan-99	WAR	RNR AIR BR VL
JONES, ANDREW	Lt Cdr	01-Oct-12	WAR	HMS KING ALFRED
JONES, CAROLYN	Lt RN	04-Jul-95	WAR	RNR MEDIA OPERATIONS
JONES, CHARLES	Lt Cdr	31-Mar-00	WAR	HMS SCOTIA
JONES, IAIN	Lt RN	17-Nov-07	WAR	RNR MEDIA OPERATIONS
JONES, KEITH W	Lt RN	11-Jan-02	LOGS	HMS FORWARD
JONES, LESLIE	Lt Cdr	11-Sep-93	WAR	HMS FERRET - RNRIU
JONES, PAULINE	Lt Cdr	31-Mar-98	LOGS	HMS CALLIOPE
JORDAN, EMMA	Lt RN	01-May-97	WAR	RNR AIR BR VL

K

KAY, DAVID RD	Cdr	01-Jan-02	LOGS	HMS FLYING FOX
KELLY, TIMOTHY	Lt Cdr	21-Mar-88	WAR	RNR AIR BR VL
KELYNACK, MARK T	Lt Cdr	01-Oct-05	WAR	RNR AIR BR VL
KEMP, SIMON M	Lt Cdr	31-Mar-99	WAR	HMS FERRET - RNRIU
KENDRICK, KATHERINE	Lt RN	29-Nov-04	WAR	HMS PRESIDENT
KENDRY, ADAM	SLt	11-May-13	WAR	HMS FLYING FOX
KENT, THOMAS	Cdr	30-Sep-99	WAR	HMS SHERWOOD
KHALEK, ADHAM A A	Surg Lt Cdr	27-May-11	MED	HMS PRESIDENT
KING, ANDREW	Lt Cdr	31-Mar-99	WAR	HMS FERRET - RNRIU
KING, CHARLES	Lt Cdr	31-Mar-02	WAR	HMS KING ALFRED
KING, IAN	Lt Cdr	01-Oct-08	WAR	HMS FERRET - RNRIU
KING, KIMBERLEY JULIE	OCdt	01-Mar-11	New Entrant	HMS KING ALFRED
KIRK, WILLIAM	Lt RN	31-Mar-96	WAR	HMS FORWARD
KNOTT, STEPHEN JAMES M	OCdt	01-Nov-12	New Entrant	HMS PRESIDENT
KNOWLES, DONNA	Lt Cdr	31-Mar-01	WAR	HMS HIBERNIA
KNOWLES, THOMAS	Lt RN	28-Dec-03	WAR	HMS SCOTIA

L

LACEY, DAVID EDWARD	OCdt	01-Apr-13	New Entrant	HMS VIVID
LADISLAUS, PAUL	Lt RN	07-Jul-04	WAR	HMS CALLIOPE
LAMBERT, ALLISON	Lt Cdr	26-Jun-04	WAR	RNR AIR BR VL
LAMONT, CLAIRE ALLISON	Mid	10-Nov-09	New Entrant	HMS PRESIDENT
LANE, HEATHER J	Lt Cdr	01-Oct-08	WAR	RNR MEDIA OPERATIONS

Name	Rank	Seniority	Brach/Arm/Group	Unit
LANGMEAD, CLIVE FRANCIS QVRM	Lt Cdr	01-Jul-90	WAR	HMS FORWARD
LAUSTE, WILLIAM E	Lt Cdr	01-Mar-99	WAR	RNR MEDIA OPERATIONS
LAWRENCE, IAN	Lt RN	05-May-05	WAR	HMS KING ALFRED
LEACH, SIMON	Lt Cdr	31-Mar-06	WAR	RNR AIR BR VL
LEATHER, ROGER J	Lt Cdr	01-Jun-87	WAR	HMS EAGLET
LEAVER, ASHLEY	Lt RN	01-Jul-04	WAR	HMS CAMBRIA
LEE, AI FAI	SLt	08-May-13	WAR	HMS PRESIDENT
LEE, JOSE	Mid	02-Apr-08	New Entrant	HMS PRESIDENT
LEE, MATTHEW M	Lt Cdr	31-Jul-94	WAR	HMS FERRET - RNRIU
LEE, ROBERT	Lt Cdr	31-Mar-02	WAR	RNR AIR BR VL
LEMKES, JAMES	OCdt	01-Nov-11	New Entrant	HMS FORWARD
LEVINE, ANDREW	Lt Cdr	31-Mar-06	WAR	RNR AIR BR VL
LEWIN, PHILLIP J	SLt	22-Mar-12	WAR	HMS SHERWOOD
LEWIS, CATRIN MAIR	Mid	30-Mar-09	New Entrant	HMS CAMBRIA
LEWIS, KATHRYN E RD	Lt Cdr	31-Mar-05	WAR	HMS PRESIDENT
LEWIS, RICHARD QVRM	Lt Cdr	31-Mar-01	WAR	RNR AIR BR VL
LEWIS, SCOTT	Lt RN	01-Dec-11	WAR	RNR MEDIA OPERATIONS
LEWIS, SIMON RD	Lt Cdr	31-Mar-04	LOGS	HMS KING ALFRED
LEWIS, THOMAS ROBERT	SLt	11-May-13	WAR	HMS FLYING FOX
LIGGINS, MICHAEL	Lt Cdr	01-Oct-01	WAR	RNR AIR BR VL
LING, REBECCA	OCdt	10-Feb-11	New Entrant	HMS FLYING FOX
LINTON, ANDREW	Lt RN	02-Nov-05	WAR	HMS EAGLET
LIPPIATT, DAVID	Lt RN	09-Dec-11	WAR	HMS SCOTIA
LITTMAN, JON ALEXANDER	Lt RN	17-Jun-12	WAR	HMS WILDFIRE
LLOYD, DAVID	Lt Cdr	31-Mar-99	WAR	HMS KING ALFRED
LLOYD, GARETH RD	Lt Cdr	31-Mar-98	WAR	HMS FERRET - RNRIU
LLOYD, PETER	Lt Cdr	31-Mar-00	WAR	HMS KING ALFRED
LLOYD, SUSAN JANE	Lt Cdr	31-Mar-04	WAR	RNR MEDIA OPERATIONS
LOGAN, JOHN G	Lt RN	27-Jul-97	QARNNS	HMS KING ALFRED
LONG, CHRISTOPHER L	Lt RN	20-Oct-10	WAR	RNR AIR BR VL
LORT, TIMOTHY	Lt Cdr	01-Oct-95	WAR	RNR AIR BR VL
LOW, SIMEON A S	Lt RN	01-Nov-05	WAR	HMS WILDFIRE
LOWNDES, TIMOTHY P C	SLt	10-Feb-11	WAR	HMS PRESIDENT
LUMLEY, RICHARD	Lt RN	03-Apr-10	WAR	HMS FERRET - RNRIU
LYDON, MICHAEL	Lt RN	30-Sep-96	LOGS	HMS CALLIOPE
LYNAGH, MICHELLE	OCdt	01-Oct-12	New Entrant	HMS DALRIADA
LYNCH, MATTHEW LUCAS	OCdt	28-Jul-10	WAR	HMS KING ALFRED
LYNCH, RORY D F	Lt Cdr	14-Apr-00	WAR	RNR AIR BR VL
LYNCH, SUZANNE	Lt RN	28-Nov-00	LOGS	HMS CAMBRIA

M

Name	Rank	Seniority	Brach/Arm/Group	Unit
MACDONALD, JOSEPH B C	OCdt	22-Mar-11	New Entrant	HMS PRESIDENT
MACDONALD, JULIE	Lt Cdr	01-Oct-09	QARNNS	HMS KING ALFRED
MACKAY, DAVID	Lt Cdr	01-Oct-93	WAR	RNR AIR BR VL
MACKENZIE, HANNAH	Lt Cdr	01-Oct-12	WAR	HMS WILDFIRE
MACKIE, ROBERT C G	Lt RN	14-Dec-01	WAR	HMS FORWARD
MACLEAN, MARJORY	RN Chpln	25-Nov-04	RN Chaplaincy Service	HMS SCOTIA
MACSEPHNEY, TRACY	Lt Cdr	01-Oct-12	WAR	HMS WILDFIRE
MAHONY, CHRISTOPHER D C	Lt Cdr	12-Apr-96	PILOT	RNR AIR BR VL
MALKIN, ROY	Lt Cdr	01-Oct-08	WAR	HMS KING ALFRED
MALLINSON, STUART	Lt RN	31-Dec-95	WAR	HMS PRESIDENT
MANSER, DARREN	Lt Cdr	31-Mar-06	WAR	RNR AIR BR VL
MANSERGH, FRANCES A	Lt RN	30-Jan-99	WAR	RNR MEDIA OPERATIONS
MANTRI, ANAND H	Lt RN	22-Apr-00	WAR	RNR MEDIA OPERATIONS
MARQUIS, ADRIAN C	Lt RN	02-Dec-93	WAR	RNR AIR BR VL
MARRIOTT, ISABELLA MARIA C	Lt RN	01-Dec-08	WAR	RNR MEDIA OPERATIONS
MARSDEN, SIMON ALEXANDER	Lt RN	25-Nov-11	WAR	HMS PRESIDENT
MARSHALL, COLIN G	Lt RN	01-May-05	WAR	RNR MEDIA OPERATIONS
MARTIN, JAMES HOPE	Lt RN	16-Oct-10	WAR	HMS DALRIADA
MASSEY, PAUL	Lt Cdr	05-Dec-02	WAR	RNR AIR BR VL
MASSEY, STEVEN	Lt Cdr	31-Mar-02	WAR	RNR AIR BR VL
MASTERS, SIMON	Mid	22-Sep-09	New Entrant	HMS FLYING FOX

Name	Rank	Seniority	Brach/Arm/Group	Unit
MATHERS, FIONA C	Lt RN	02-Dec-05	WAR	HMS FERRET - RNRIU
MAWHINNEY, ABIGAIL	OCdt	15-Sep-08	MED	HMS HIBERNIA
MCARDELL, STEVEN	Lt Cdr	31-Mar-04	WAR	RNR AIR BR VL
MCCARTNEY, WILLIAM	Lt RN	26-Jan-02	LOGS	HMS PRESIDENT
MCDADE, CHRISTOPHER G	SLt	19-Nov-09	New Entrant	HMS DALRIADA
MCGINLEY, MARK	Lt RN	09-Aug-95	WAR	HMS KING ALFRED
MCHALE, GARETH J	Lt Cdr	01-Dec-91	WAR	RNR AIR BR VL
MCINTYRE, ALASTAIR W.	Lt Cdr	01-Oct-04	WAR	HMS FERRET - RNRIU
MCKEATING, JOHN	Surg Cdr	31-Dec-99	MED	HMS SHERWOOD
MCKEE, ROBERT W.	Lt RN	01-May-04	WAR	RNR AIR BR VL
MCKENZIE, GARY	Lt Cdr	01-Oct-09	WAR	HMS CAMBRIA
MCKINLEY, MAIRI	Lt RN	06-Aug-05	QARNNS	HMS SCOTIA
MCKINTY, GARETH	Lt RN	12-Jun-07	WAR	HMS FERRET - RNRIU
MCLAVERTY, KAREN	Lt Cdr	17-Mar-99	WAR	HMS HIBERNIA
MCLUNDIE, WILLIAM M.	SLt	18-Feb-12	WAR	HMS FORWARD
MCMAHON, CHRISTOPHER T	OCdt	24-Apr-13	New Entrant	HMS EAGLET
MCMURRAN, ROBERT CAMPBELL	Lt Cdr	17-Nov-04	WAR	HMS FERRET - RNRIU
MCNAUGHT, EDWARD RD	Cdr	30-Jun-08	WAR	FLEET CMR
MCWILLIAMS, BARRY JOHN	OCdt	22-Jan-10	New Entrant	HMS HIBERNIA
MEADOWS, BRIAN MBE	Lt Cdr	01-Oct-98	WAR	RNR MEDIA OPERATIONS
MEHARG, NEIL RD	Lt Cdr	31-Mar-06	WAR	HMS HIBERNIA
MEIKLE, STUART A	Lt Cdr	01-Oct-07	ENG	RNR AIR BR VL
MELHUISH, DAVID ROY	SLt	23-Feb-13	WAR	HMS SCOTIA
MEROPOULOS, JOHN	Lt RN	16-Sep-02	WAR	HMS FERRET - RNRIU
MESTON, JOHN MUNRO	Lt Cdr	10-Apr-00	WAR	RNR AIR BR VL
MILES, CHRISTOPHER A	OCdt	27-Jun-12	New Entrant	HMS EAGLET
MILLER, DAVID	Lt Cdr	01-Apr-95	WAR	RNR AIR BR VL
MILLER, IAN	SLt	18-Jun-11	WAR	HMS CAMBRIA
MILLER, ROY	Lt RN	04-Dec-07	LOGS	HMS EAGLET
MILLS, ANDREW	Lt Cdr	01-May-95	WAR	RNR MEDIA OPERATIONS
MILLS, SYDNEY D G	Lt Cdr	01-Oct-12	WAR	RNR AIR BR VL
MONK, STEPHEN R	Lt Cdr	17-Mar-10	WAR	HMS KING ALFRED
MOORE, CHRISTOPHER	Lt RN	24-Sep-05	WAR	HMS FORWARD
MOORTHY, ROHAN MICHAEL	Lt RN	02-Jul-00	WAR	HMS PRESIDENT
MORAN, SIMON	Lt Cdr	31-Mar-05	WAR	RNR AIR BR VL
MORDAUNT, PENELOPE MARY	OCdt	19-Jan-12	New Entrant	HMS KING ALFRED
MORGAN, EUGENE P.	Cdr	30-Jun-11	WAR	HMS PRESIDENT
MORGAN, GARETH W	Lt Cdr	31-Mar-01	LOGS	HMS SHERWOOD
MORGAN, PHILLIP D J	Lt RN	26-Sep-11	WAR	RNR MEDIA OPERATIONS
MORGANS, DANIEL J.	Lt Cdr	01-Oct-08	WAR	HMS FERRET - RNRIU
MORLEY, DIETMAR)	Lt Cdr	31-Mar-06	WAR	HMS SHERWOOD
MORRISON, JOSEPH	OCdt	01-Jun-13	New Entrant	HMS HIBERNIA
MOSELEY, ALLISON	Lt RN	29-Apr-04	WAR	HMS CALLIOPE
MOULTON, SIMON J	Lt RN	01-Jan-92	WAR	RNR AIR BR VL
MUNSON, EILEEN PATRICIA RD	Lt Cdr	01-Oct-08	QARNNS	HMS CAMBRIA
MURPHY, DICCON A.	Lt Cdr	01-Oct-12	WAR	RNR AIR BR VL
MURPHY, STEPHEN M	Lt Cdr	13-Jan-06	RNR Media (OF)	RNR MEDIA OPERATIONS
MURRAY, ANITA	Lt Cdr	01-Oct-09	LOGS	HMS VIVID
MURRISON, ANDREW	Surg Cdr	31-Dec-97	MED	HMS PRESIDENT
MURRISON, MARK	Cdr	06-Nov-06	WAR	HMS PRESIDENT

N

NEALE, DANIEL F.	Lt RN	01-Sep-05	WAR	HMS PRESIDENT
NEWMAN, VIRGINIA HELEN	Lt RN	01-Oct-09	WAR	RNR MEDIA OPERATIONS
NIBLOCK, GILLIAN	Lt RN	09-Nov-11	WAR	HMS WILDFIRE
NICHOLAS, BRYAN JOHN MBE	Lt Cdr	01-Oct-01	WAR	RNR AIR BR VL
NICHOLSON, JOHN K.	Lt RN	01-Apr-06	WAR	HMS FERRET - RNRIU
NICOLSON, VERNON	Lt RN	03-May-05	WAR	HMS FERRET - RNRIU
NISBET, JAMES THORNTON	Lt RN	31-Jul-04	WAR	HMS FERRET - RNRIU
NOAKES, DAVID	Lt Cdr	01-Oct-12	LOGS	HMS CALLIOPE
NOBLE, ALEXANDER	Lt RN	02-Feb-06	WAR	HMS KING ALFRED
NOBLE, ROBERT H.	Lt Cdr	31-Mar-97	WAR	HMS FORWARD

Name	Rank	Seniority	Brach/Arm/Group	Unit
NOLAN, GRAEME ALAN R	OCdt	06-Feb-12	New Entrant	HMS KING ALFRED
NORTHCOTT, JOHN	Lt Cdr	31-Mar-98	LOGS	FLEET CMR
NOTLEY, RICHARD MARK	Lt RN	04-Aug-10	WAR	HMS PRESIDENT

O

Name	Rank	Seniority	Brach/Arm/Group	Unit
OAKLEY, RICHARD	Lt RN	29-Sep-98	WAR	HMS PRESIDENT
OARTON, JAMIE C	SLt	01-Mar-10	WAR	HMS FERRET - RNRIU
OATES, EDWARD	Lt Cdr	16-Feb-93	WAR	RNR AIR BR VL
O'DOOLEY, PAUL	Lt RN	30-Jun-06	WAR	HMS SHERWOOD
ODRISCOLL, EDWARD H	Lt RN	25-Jan-03	WAR	HMS FERRET - RNRIU
OKUKENU, DELE	Lt Cdr	01-Oct-08	WAR	RNR AIR BR VL
OLVER, JEREMY	Lt RN	01-Mar-10	WAR	RNR MEDIA OPERATIONS
ORD, ELIZABETH	Lt Cdr	01-Oct-09	WAR	HMS FERRET - RNRIU
ORMSHAW, ANDREW	Cdr	15-Jul-04	WAR	RNR AIR BR VL
OVENS, JEREMY J	Lt Cdr	01-Dec-91	WAR	RNAS CULDROSE - AED HQ

P

Name	Rank	Seniority	Brach/Arm/Group	Unit
PACKHAM, CRAIG N R	Lt RN	01-Mar-96	WAR	RNR AIR BR VL
PADDOCK, LEE	Lt RN	01-Mar-94	WAR	HMS EAGLET
PARKER, KELLY	Lt RN	31-Oct-09	WAR	HMS EAGLET
PARKHOUSE, MARK JONATHAN	Lt RN	04-Oct-09	WAR	HMS FERRET - RNRIU
PARRY, CHRISTOPHER	Lt Cdr	05-Oct-10	WAR	HMS VIVID
PARSONAGE, NEIL	Lt Cdr	31-Mar-00	WAR	HMS EAGLET
PATEMAN, JASON E	Lt RN	15-Apr-11	WAR	HMS CALLIOPE
PATERSON, MATTHEW	Lt RN	09-Mar-07	WAR	HMS WILDFIRE
PATTEN, MARK	Surg Lt Cdr	29-Mar-96	MED	HMS WILDFIRE
PEACOCK, ANOUCHKA	Lt RN	01-Dec-05	WAR	HMS FERRET - RNRIU
PEARSON, CRAIG	Lt RN	02-Nov-10	WAR	HMS KING ALFRED
PEARSON, ROBERT J	Lt RN	01-Jun-05	WAR	HMS FLYING FOX
PEDLEY, MICHAEL	Lt RN	10-Dec-04	WAR	HMS PRESIDENT
PETHICK, IAN	Cdr	30-Jun-10	LOGS	HMS VIVID
PHILLIPS, JACOB L	Mid	25-Nov-08	WAR	HMS PRESIDENT
PHILLIPS, JAMES	Lt RN	20-Jun-11	WAR	HMS VIVID
PHILPOT, DAVID	Lt Cdr	18-Jul-00	WAR	HMS VIVID
PIKE, STUART	Lt Cdr	31-Mar-05	WAR	RNR AIR BR VL
PINFOLD, THOMAS DANIEL	SLt	25-Mar-13	WAR	HMS EAGLET
PIPE, DIANA Z	Lt RN	01-Jan-03	WAR	HMS PRESIDENT
PITTOCK, STEPHEN J	Lt RN	07-Jul-08	WAR	HMS KING ALFRED
POGSON, ANDREW D	Lt RN	10-Nov-08	WAR	HMS FERRET - RNRIU
POINTON, MICHAEL JAMES	OCdt	01-Jul-12	New Entrant	HMS PRESIDENT
POLLOCK, MALCOLM P	Lt Cdr	03-Aug-03	WAR	RNR AIR BR VL
POSNETT, DICKON	Lt Cdr	31-Mar-99	WAR	RNR AIR BR VL
POULTON-WATT, ANDREW	Lt Cdr	01-Oct-09	WAR	HMS SCOTIA
POWELL, WILLIAM	Lt Cdr	31-Mar-99	ENG	RNR AIR BR VL
PRATT, IAN	Lt Cdr	06-Oct-93	WAR	RNR MEDIA OPERATIONS
PUGH, NEIL	Lt Cdr	31-Mar-06	LOGS	HMS CAMBRIA
PYKE, THOMAS F P	RN Chpln	13-Jun-07	RN Chaplaincy Service	HMS PRESIDENT

Q

Name	Rank	Seniority	Brach/Arm/Group	Unit
QUINN, MARTIN	Cdr	30-Jun-10	WAR	FLEET CMR
QUINN, MICHAEL	Lt RN	01-Oct-11	WAR	RNR MEDIA OPERATIONS

R

Name	Rank	Seniority	Brach/Arm/Group	Unit
RAE, ALISTAIR L	Lt Cdr	01-Apr-05	WAR	HMS FERRET - RNRIU
RAMSAY, BRIAN	Lt Cdr	31-Mar-01	WAR	FLEET CMR
RANDLES, PHILIP	Lt RN	22-May-02	WAR	HMS CALLIOPE
RANKIN, CHRISTOPHER A	Lt RN	01-Mar-04	QARNNS	HMS PRESIDENT
RASOR, ANDREW M	Lt Cdr	01-Oct-12	WAR	RNR AIR BR VL
RAVENSCROFT, LOUISE M	Mid	22-May-08	New Entrant	HMS KING ALFRED
READ, DAVID A RD	Lt Cdr	31-Mar-97	WAR	HMS FERRET - RNRIU

Name	Rank	Seniority	Brach/Arm/Group	Unit
REDMOND, ROBERT	Lt Cdr	01-Nov-04	WAR	HMS PRESIDENT
REID, DOUGLAS R	Lt RN	01-Jul-04	WAR	RNR AIR BR VL
RENNELL, IAN	Lt Cdr	31-Mar-06	WAR	HMS EAGLET
RENOUF, ROBERT	Lt RN	24-Apr-05	WAR	HMS SCOTIA
REYNOLDSON, HOWARD B V	Lt Cdr	03-Nov-85	WAR	RNR AIR BR VL
RHODES, MARTIN J	Lt Cdr	01-Oct-04	WAR	FLEET CMR
RICHARDS, GUY	Lt Cdr	01-Apr-03	WAR	HMS CAMBRIA
ROBERTS, MARTYN	Lt Cdr	19-Jan-03	WAR	RNR AIR BR VL
ROBERTS, PHILIP E	OCdt	21-Feb-12	New Entrant	HMS EAGLET
ROBERTS, ROBERT	Lt RN	27-May-05	WAR	HMS SCOTIA
ROBERTS, STEPHEN	Lt RN	01-Feb-03	WAR	HMS VIVID
ROBERTS, STUART ALEXANDER G	Surg Lt RN	01-Feb-09	MED	HMS FORWARD
ROBERTSHAW, PAMELA	Lt Cdr	10-Sep-02	ENG	RNR AIR BR VL
ROBERTSON, LORNE THOMAS	Cdr	30-Jun-09	WAR	HMS DALRIADA
ROBERTSON, STUART	Lt Cdr	08-Nov-99	WAR	HMS SCOTIA
ROBINSON, ANDREW	Lt Cdr	01-Oct-11	WAR	FLEET CMR
ROBINSON, IAN MICHAEL OBE	Capt RN	30-Sep-01	WAR	HMS SHERWOOD
ROBINSON, JAMES	Lt RN	24-Feb-90	WAR	HMS FERRET - RNRIU
ROGERS, ALAN	Lt Cdr	25-Dec-02	WAR	RNR AIR BR VL
ROLL, SUSAN	Lt Cdr	31-Mar-01	WAR	HMS FLYING FOX
ROSINDALE, PHILIP RD	Lt Cdr	31-Mar-06	WAR	HMS VIVID
ROSS, JONATHAN ANTONY DUNCAN	Cdr	30-Sep-06	WAR	HMS DALRIADA
ROURKE, KEVIN HENRY	Surg Lt Cdr	05-Feb-08	MED	HMS EAGLET
ROWE, KEVIN CHRISTOPHER	Lt RN	04-May-01	WAR	RNR AIR BR VL
ROWLANDS, GEOFFREY A	Lt Cdr	16-Nov-85	WAR	RNR AIR BR VL
RUSS, PHILIP J	Cdr	30-Sep-05	WAR	HMS EAGLET
RUTHERFORD, KEVIN J	Lt RN	01-Oct-93	WAR	RNR AIR BR VL
RYAN, PATRICK D B	Lt RN	07-Feb-03	WAR	HMS PRESIDENT
RYAN, PETER ANTHONY	Lt RN	18-Jan-03	WAR	HMS PRESIDENT

S

Name	Rank	Seniority	Brach/Arm/Group	Unit
SAINTCLAIR-ABBOTT, SIMON	Lt Cdr	01-Jun-92	WAR	HMS FERRET - RNRIU
SAIR, MARK	Surg Lt Cdr	21-Jun-06	MED	HMS VIVID
SALT, HEDLEY	Lt Cdr	01-Oct-09	WAR	RNR AIR BR VL
SAMPSON-JONES, CHRISTOPHER J	OCdt	18-Jul-12	New Entrant	HMS EAGLET
SAN, HOWARD	Lt Cdr	31-Mar-06	WAR	HMS PRESIDENT
SANDERSON, JENNIFER P	Lt Cdr	31-Mar-05	WAR	HMS FERRET - RNRIU
SATCHELL, PETER J	Lt Cdr	31-Mar-00	WAR	HMS PRESIDENT
SAUNDERS, ALICE	Lt Cdr	01-Oct-09	WAR	RNR AIR BR VL
SCARTH, MARTIN	Lt RN	18-Jan-01	WAR	RNR MEDIA OPERATIONS
SCOTT, ANTHONY	Lt RN	15-Oct-05	WAR	HMS PRESIDENT
SCRIMGEOUR, JOHN	Mid	31-Mar-04	WAR	HMS SHERWOOD
SEARLE, GEOFFREY D	Lt Cdr	31-Mar-00	WAR	HMS KING ALFRED
SETON, JAMES	Lt RN	24-Nov-05	WAR	HMS PRESIDENT
SEVERS, ANTHONY	Lt Cdr	01-Apr-06	WAR	RNR AIR BR VL
SHAKESPEARE, MARTIN	Lt Cdr	31-Mar-97	WAR	HMS FERRET - RNRIU
SHAYLER, STEPHEN A	SLt	12-Jul-09	WAR	HMS FERRET - RNRIU
SHELLEY, JAMES	Surg Lt Cdr	05-May-08	MED	HMS PRESIDENT
SHEPHERD, PAUL R	Lt Cdr	01-Oct-02	WAR	RNR AIR BR VL
SHEPHERD, STEPHEN	Lt RN	22-Aug-02	LOGS	HMS KING ALFRED
SHEPPARD, KEVIN JAMES	Lt RN	22-Jul-94	WAR	RNR AIR BR VL
SHERRIFF, JACQUELINE MBE	Lt Cdr	31-Mar-06	WAR	RNR MEDIA OPERATIONS
SHINNER, PATRICK A	Lt Cdr	31-Mar-99	WAR	HMS PRESIDENT
SHINNER, STEPHANIE K F	Lt Cdr	31-Mar-00	WAR	HMS WILDFIRE
SHINNER, THOMAS	Lt RN	20-Feb-12	WAR	HMS WILDFIRE
SHIPLEY, JOANNE	Lt Cdr	05-Oct-10	WAR	RNR MEDIA OPERATIONS
SHORT, KEVIN	Lt RN	01-Feb-08	WAR	HMS VIVID
SHORT, MATTHEW	Lt RN	05-Dec-09	WAR	HMS FERRET - RNRIU
SHOULER, MARTIN	Lt RN	15-Nov-02	WAR	HMS PRESIDENT
SHOULER, MATTHEW F	Lt RN	30-Aug-07	WAR	HMS FERRET - RNRIU
SIGLEY, ARTHUR	Lt RN	05-Sep-02	WAR	HMS SCOTIA
SIMMONDS, TIMOTHY	Lt Cdr	31-Mar-05	WAR	HMS PRESIDENT

Name	Rank	Seniority	Brach/Arm/Group	Unit
SIMMS, DAVID M.	Lt Cdr	01-Oct-12	WAR	RNR AIR BR VL
SIMONIS, DOMINIC V	OCdt	01-Nov-12	New Entrant	HMS WILDFIRE
SIMS, DEBORAH L	Lt RN	01-Jan-94	WAR	RNR AIR BR VL
SIMS, RICHMAL	Lt Cdr	31-Mar-07	WAR	HMS PRESIDENT
SINGH, NEEL	Lt RN	16-Feb-10	WAR	RNR MEDIA OPERATIONS
SKELLY, ANDREW	Lt RN	06-Jun-08	LOGS	HMS HIBERNIA
SKELLY, ROSALIND JENNIFER	OCdt	30-Oct-08	New Entrant	HMS SCOTIA
SKELTON, MICHAEL G.	Lt RN	18-Apr-13	WAR	HMS PRESIDENT
SKINNER, NIGEL GUY	Lt RN	15-Nov-99	WAR	HMS VIVID
SLONECKI, ADAM T.	Lt RN	05-Apr-08	WAR	HMS FERRET - RNRIU
SMALL, PAULINE	Lt Cdr	31-Mar-05	QARNNS	HMS SCOTIA
SMALL, PETER	Surg Cdr	30-Sep-97	MED	HMS CALLIOPE
SMITH, DAVID T.	Lt RN	08-Sep-93	WAR	RNR AIR BR VL
SMITH, GORDON	Lt Cdr	31-Mar-01	WAR	RNR AIR BR VL
SMITH, JAMIE R	OCdt	01-Oct-12	New Entrant	HMS KING ALFRED
SMITH, PETER	Lt Cdr	01-Oct-98	WAR	RNR AIR BR VL
SMITH, STEPHEN AE	Lt Cdr	31-Mar-07	WAR	HMS WILDFIRE
SMITH, WILLIAM	Lt RN	26-Feb-02	LOGS	HMS SCOTIA
SNOSWELL, JANE L C	OCdt	01-Sep-12	New Entrant	HMS PRESIDENT
SPARKE, PHILIP R W	Lt Cdr	01-Mar-00	WAR	RNR MEDIA OPERATIONS
SPAYNE, NICHOLAS J	Lt Cdr	01-Oct-98	WAR	HMS WILDFIRE
SPEAKE, JONATHAN	Lt Cdr	01-Oct-08	WAR	RNR AIR BR VL
SPENCER, MICHAEL DAVID	Lt RN	25-Nov-03	WAR	HMS FERRET - RNRIU
SPRING, JEREMY	Lt Cdr	03-Aug-97	ENG	RNR AIR BR VL
STANLEY, NICHOLAS J	Lt RN	16-Sep-93	WAR	RNR AIR BR VL
STARR, THOMAS W	Lt RN	11-Oct-07	WAR	HMS PRESIDENT
STEPHEN, LESLEY RD.	Lt Cdr	01-Oct-08	LOGS	HMS DALRIADA
STEPHENSON, MICHAEL	Lt RN	25-Apr-04	WAR	HMS KING ALFRED
STEVENSON, PAUL M	Lt RN	01-Sep-04	WAR	HMS FLYING FOX
STICKLAND, ANTHONY	Lt Cdr	31-Mar-98	WAR	HMS KING ALFRED
STIDSTON, DAVID	Lt Cdr	01-Oct-94	WAR	HMS FORWARD
STOBO, ALEXANDER	Lt RN	02-Oct-00	WAR	RNR AIR BR VL
STOCKER, JEREMY	Capt RN	01-Mar-10	WAR	FLEET CMR
STONE, PAUL	Lt Cdr	01-Oct-98	WAR	RNR AIR BR VL
STOREY, NAOMI AVICE	Lt Cdr	01-Jan-09	WAR	HMS WILDFIRE
STRACHAN, ROBIN	Surg Cdr	30-Sep-95	MED	HMS PRESIDENT
STRINGER, KARL	Lt RN	16-Mar-97	WAR	RNR AIR BR VL
STRONG, JAMES	Mid	09-Oct-07	New Entrant	HMS HIBERNIA
STUBBS, GARY	Lt Cdr	01-Oct-08	WAR	RNR AIR BR VL
STYLES, SARAH	Lt RN	29-Oct-02	WAR	HMS PRESIDENT
SWANN, ADAM PETER D	Lt RN	01-Apr-08	LOGS	HMS WILDFIRE
SYDES, HEATHER C	Lt Cdr	01-Oct-11	QARNNS	HMS EAGLET

T

Name	Rank	Seniority	Brach/Arm/Group	Unit
TAYLOR, JAMES E H	Lt RN	01-Sep-02	WAR	HMS FLYING FOX
TAYLOR, LESLIE	Lt Cdr	01-Oct-94	WAR	RNR AIR BR VL
TAYLOR, NEIL	Lt RN	01-Jun-12	WAR	HMS VIVID
TAYLOR, RUPERT	Lt Cdr	31-Mar-99	WAR	HMS KING ALFRED
TAYLOR, TIMOTHY	Lt Cdr	01-Oct-00	WAR	RNR AIR BR VL
TEASDALE, DAVID ANDREW	Cdr	30-Jun-11	WAR	HMS EAGLET
TELFER, ALISON A.	Lt Cdr	30-Sep-91	WAR	HMS EAGLET
TEMPLE, MILES	Lt Cdr	31-Mar-06	WAR	HMS FERRET - RNRIU
TENNANT, MICHAEL I	Surg Cdr	29-Jun-09	MED	HMS CALLIOPE
THOM, MATHEW F	Lt RN	22-Jul-06	WAR	HMS FERRET - RNRIU
THOMAS, ANDREW	Lt RN	19-Jun-05	WAR	HMS PRESIDENT
THOMAS, DAVID	Lt RN	04-May-07	WAR	HMS CAMBRIA
THOMAS, DAVID	Lt Cdr	01-Oct-09	WAR	HMS KING ALFRED
THOMAS, KEVIN I	Lt Cdr	01-Oct-92	WAR	RNR AIR BR VL
THOMASON, MICHAEL	Cdr	30-Jun-12	LOGS	HMS EAGLET
THOMSON, COLIN	Lt RN	28-Oct-11	WAR	HMS DALRIADA
THOMSON, FRED D.	Lt RN	23-Jan-05	WAR	HMS DALRIADA
THOMSON, SUSIE	Lt Cdr	31-Mar-99	WAR	RNR MEDIA OPERATIONS

Name	Rank	Seniority	Brach/Arm/Group	Unit
THORNE, LEE J	Lt Cdr	31-Mar-02	WAR	HMS KING ALFRED
THORNLEY, JEREMY G C	Lt Cdr	01-Oct-11	WAR	HMS SHERWOOD
THURMOTT, ROBERT	Lt RN	01-Apr-12	WAR	RNR MEDIA OPERATIONS
TONG, STEVEN	Lt RN	12-Jun-08	WAR	HMS FERRET - RNRIU
TOOR, JEEVAN J S	Lt Cdr	01-Sep-98	WAR	HMS FERRET - RNRIU
TOOTH, MARK COLIN	SLt	07-Dec-11	WAR	HMS KING ALFRED
TOPPING, MARK	Lt Cdr	31-Mar-97	WAR	HMS CAMBRIA
TRELAWNY, CHRISTOPHER C	Lt Cdr	31-Mar-06	WAR	HMS PRESIDENT
TRIBE, JEREMY D	Lt RN	16-Oct-87	WAR	RNR AIR BR VL
TRIGG, MARK ANTHONY W	Lt RN	28-Jan-13	WAR	HMS SHERWOOD
TRIMMER, PATRICK DAVID M	Lt Cdr	31-Mar-96	WAR	HMS FERRET - RNRIU
TROMANHAUSER, KERRY	Lt RN	23-Nov-11	WAR	RNR MEDIA OPERATIONS
TROTT, CRAIG MICHAEL J	Lt Cdr	31-Mar-05	WAR	RNR AIR BR VL
TURLEY, RICHARD ANTHONY	Lt RN	04-Mar-08	WAR	HMS EAGLET
TURNER, JONATHAN S	Lt RN	02-Aug-00	WAR	RNR AIR BR VL
TURNER, SIMON	Lt Cdr	11-Mar-99	WAR	HMS VIVID
TWEEDIE, HOWARD JAMES	Lt Cdr	22-Oct-97	WAR	FLEET CMR
TYRRELL, CAROL	Lt Cdr	11-Apr-90	WAR	HMS FERRET - RNRIU

U

Name	Rank	Seniority	Brach/Arm/Group	Unit
URE, FIONA	Lt RN	03-Oct-06	WAR	HMS HIBERNIA
URQUHART, RODERICK	Lt RN	19-Sep-06	WAR	HMS PRESIDENT

V

Name	Rank	Seniority	Brach/Arm/Group	Unit
VALENTINE, ROBERT	Lt Cdr	31-Mar-99	WAR	HMS SCOTIA
VALLANCE, MICHAEL S	Lt RN	16-Jun-98	WAR	RNR AIR BR VL
VAN DEN BERGH, MARK	Lt Cdr	05-Oct-10	LOGS	HMS PRESIDENT
VENABLES, ADRIAN R	Lt Cdr	01-Dec-00	New Entrant	HMS KING ALFRED
VERSALLION, MARK ANTHONY G	Lt RN	30-Mar-05	WAR	HMS WILDFIRE
VICKERS, MARK	Lt RN	13-Jan-11	WAR	HMS PRESIDENT
VINCENT, PETER H	Lt Cdr	01-Dec-12	WAR	RNR AIR BR VL
VITALI, JULIE	Lt Cdr	31-Mar-05	WAR	HMS FERRET - RNRIU

W

Name	Rank	Seniority	Brach/Arm/Group	Unit
WAINWRIGHT, BARNABY	Lt Cdr	01-Sep-89	WAR	RNR AIR BR VL
WALES, FREDERICK	Lt Cdr	31-Mar-98	WAR	HMS KING ALFRED
WALKER, DAVID	Lt Cdr	31-Mar-97	LOGS	HMS DALRIADA
WALLER, JAMES	Lt RN	10-May-03	WAR	HMS FERRET - RNRIU
WALTERS, RICHARD	Lt Cdr	31-Mar-04	WAR	RNR MEDIA OPERATIONS
WARNOCK, GAVIN	Lt Cdr	01-Oct-95	WAR	RNR AIR BR VL
WATERWORTH, ANGELA	OCdt	07-Dec-05	New Entrant	HMS KING ALFRED
WATERWORTH, STEPHEN	Lt Cdr	31-Mar-06	WAR	HMS KING ALFRED
WATSON, CATHERINE J	Cdr	30-Jun-08	WAR	HMS EAGLET
WATSON, LLOYD JAMES	Lt Cdr	01-Oct-94	WAR	RNR AIR BR VL
WATTERS, OWEN PETERS	OCdt	08-Dec-10	New Entrant	HMS CALLIOPE
WATTS, NICHOLAS HENRY C	Lt RN	31-May-07	WAR	HMS FLYING FOX
WATTS, THOMAS	Lt RN	10-Oct-10	WAR	HMS VIVID
WAUDBY, LINDSEY	Lt RN	23-Mar-07	WAR	RNR MEDIA OPERATIONS
WAUGH, GILLIAN NONA	Lt RN	10-Sep-12	WAR	HMS FERRET - RNRIU
WEBB, CHRISTOPHER	Cdr	30-Jun-08	LOGS	FLEET CMR
WEBBER, CHRISTOPHER J	Lt Cdr	05-May-98	WAR	RNR AIR BR VL
WEBBER, STEVEN JOHN ANTHONY M	Capt RN	01-Dec-09	LOGS	FLEET CMR
WEBSTER, ANDREW	Lt Cdr	05-May-99	WAR	RNR AIR BR VL
WEBSTER, ELIZABETH	Lt RN	09-Jul-06	WAR	HMS CALLIOPE
WEDGWOOD, JONATHAN	Surg Lt Cdr	26-Nov-98	MED	HMS SCOTIA
WEIGHTMAN, NICHOLAS E	Lt Cdr	29-Feb-04	WAR	RNR AIR BR VL
WEST, JEFFREY	Lt RN	04-Sep-04	WAR	HMS FERRET - RNRIU
WEST, MICHAEL W	Lt Cdr	05-Aug-92	WAR	848 SQN
WHATLEY, MARK	Lt RN	03-Feb-13	WAR	RNR MEDIA OPERATIONS
WHEATLEY, WENDY	Lt Cdr	04-Oct-97	WAR	RNR AIR BR VL

Name	Rank	Seniority	Brach/Arm/Group	Unit
WHEELER, ROBERT	Lt RN	19-Aug-06	WAR	HMS KING ALFRED
WHEELER, SOPHIA	Lt RN	17-Oct-01	WAR	HMS KING ALFRED
WHITE, IAN	Cdr	30-Jun-08	WAR	FLEET CMR
WHITE, MICHAEL E L	Lt Cdr	31-Mar-06	WAR	FLEET CMR
WHITEHEAD, KEITH S RD	Lt Cdr	31-Mar-00	WAR	HMS FERRET - RNRIU
WHITFIELD, JOE A	Lt Cdr	01-Oct-03	WAR	RNR AIR BR VL
WHITING, MARK	Lt RN	11-Oct-07	WAR	HMS FLYING FOX
WILCOCKSON, ALASTAIR	Surg Cdr	01-Apr-05	MED	HMS KING ALFRED
WILCOCKSON, MOIRA	Lt Cdr	31-Mar-05	QARNNS	HMS KING ALFRED
WILKINSON, DOUGLAS A	Surg Lt Cdr	28-Oct-04	MED	HMS PRESIDENT
WILKINSON, MICHAEL CHARLES P	Surg Lt Cdr	01-Jul-99	New Entrant	HMS PRESIDENT
WILKINSON, RICHARD THOMAS M	OCdt	03-Aug-11	WAR	RNR MEDIA OPERATIONS
WILKINSON, ROBIN N	Lt Cdr	13-Oct-98	WAR	RNR AIR BR VL
WILLIAMS, KEVIN	Lt RN	01-Feb-06	WAR	HMS FLYING FOX
WILLIAMS, TIMOTHY	Lt Cdr	31-Mar-07	WAR	HMS WILDFIRE
WILLIAMS, TIMOTHY ROBERT	OCdt	06-Oct-09	New Entrant	HMS CAMBRIA
WILLING, NIGEL P	Lt RN	16-Aug-93	WAR	RNR AIR BR VL
WILLIS, DEBRA JAYNE	OCdt	02-Aug-11	New Entrant	HMS PRESIDENT
WILSON, PETER NEIL	Lt Cdr	07-Sep-99	WAR	RNR AIR BR VL
WILSON, ROLAND DELAMERE	Lt RN	03-Feb-13	Maritime Operations	HMS SCOTIA
WINDOW, STEPHEN	Lt Cdr	01-Sep-95	WAR	HMS KING ALFRED
WINFIELD, ADRIAN R	Lt Cdr	31-Mar-99	ENG	RNR AIR BR VL
WINKEL VON HESSE-NASSAU, FRIEDRICH	Lt Cdr	01-Oct-11	WAR	HMS KING ALFRED
WINSTANLEY, NICOLA	Lt Cdr	31-Mar-95	WAR	RNR MEDIA OPERATIONS
WOLSTENCROFT, PAUL	Lt Cdr	01-Oct-11	LOGS	HMS KING ALFRED
WOOD, JUSTIN NOEL A	Cdr	30-Sep-06	WAR	RNR AIR BR VL
WOOD, SUZANNE	Lt RN	05-Apr-93	WAR	HMS PRESIDENT
WOODARD, MATILDA JANE	Lt RN	14-Dec-04	WAR	RNR AIR BR VL
WOODMAN, CLARE F J	Lt Cdr	31-Mar-07	WAR	RNR MEDIA OPERATIONS
WOODWARD, IAN MARK H	Lt RN	03-Feb-12	WAR	HMS FLYING FOX
WORMAN, ROBIN	Lt Cdr	01-Oct-98	WAR	RNR AIR BR VL
WRAY, RONALD	Cdr	30-Jun-12	WAR	HMS KING ALFRED
WRIGGLESWORTH, PETER J	Surg Lt Cdr	02-Aug-88	MED	HMS FLYING FOX
WRIGHT, ANTONY	Lt Cdr	01-Oct-97	WAR	RNR AIR BR VL
WRIGHT, DOUGLAS	Lt Cdr	31-Mar-05	WAR	HMS FERRET - RNRIU
WRIGHT, IAIN ALASTAIR M	Lt Cdr	18-Aug-97	WAR	HMS FERRET - RNRIU
WRIGHT, SAMUAL	SLt	29-Sep-09	WAR	HMS PRESIDENT
WRIGHT, STEPHEN	Lt Cdr	01-Nov-04	WAR	HMS KING ALFRED
WRIGHT, STEPHEN	Lt Cdr	31-Mar-01	WAR	RNR AIR BR VL
WRING, MATTHEW	Lt Cdr	31-Mar-03	WAR	HMS FLYING FOX
WYATT, MARK	Capt RN	08-Mar-09	WAR	FLEET CMR
WYLIE, DAVID	Lt RN	02-Aug-02	WAR	RNR MEDIA OPERATIONS

Y

Name	Rank	Seniority	Brach/Arm/Group	Unit
YATES, STEVEN RD	Lt Cdr	31-Mar-00	WAR	HMS FLYING FOX
YEE, SOU YAN SAMUEL	OCdt	01-Jan-11	New Entrant	HMS KING ALFRED
YIBOWEI, CHRISTOPHE	Lt RN	02-Feb-09	LOGS	HMS PRESIDENT
YONG, ANDREW	Lt RN	21-Mar-09	WAR	HMS PRESIDENT
YOUNG, CARL	Lt Cdr	31-Mar-98	WAR	RNR AIR BR VL
YOUNG, COLIN STUART	Lt RN	24-Apr-12	WAR	HMS DALRIADA
YOUNG, DUNCAN	Lt Cdr	31-Mar-98	WAR	HMS CALLIOPE
YOUNG, GREGORY	Lt Cdr	01-Oct-09	WAR	RNR MEDIA OPERATIONS
YOUNG, JOSEPHINE	Lt RN	28-Apr-07	WAR	RNR MEDIA OPERATIONS
YOUNG, WILLIAM D	Lt Cdr	31-Mar-05	LOGS	HMS KING ALFRED

ROYAL MARINES RESERVE

Name	Rank	Seniority	Branch	Unit

A

| ADAMS, MARTYN | Capt | 18-Jul-08 | RN Royal Marines GS | RMR BRISTOL |

B

BOWYER, RICHARD	Maj	01-Oct-06	RN Royal Marines GS	RMR LONDON
BROWN, ROGER F RD	Maj	16-Jul-04	RN Royal Marines GS	RMR MERSEYSIDE
BRUCE, RORY M	Col	01-Mar-11	RN Royal Marines GS	FLEET CMR
BUCKLAND, CHRISTOPHER	Capt	17-Apr-12	RN Royal Marines GS	RMR MERSEYSIDE
BURNHAM, PAUL	Capt	01-Jun-10	RN Royal Marines GS	RMR MERSEYSIDE

C

| COLE, SIMON | Maj | 01-Oct-08 | RN Royal Marines GS | RMR BRISTOL |
| CRICHTON, DAYLE | Capt | 24-Oct-05 | RN Royal Marines GS | RMR SCOTLAND |

D

| DARE, CLIFFORD MBE | Maj | 16-May-06 | RN Royal Marines GS | RMR BRISTOL |
| DOWLEN, HENRY T B MBE | Capt | 02-Aug-06 | RN Royal Marines GS | RMR LONDON |

E

| EDGAR, ALASTAIR W L | Capt | 01-Jun-10 | RN Royal Marines GS | RMR MERSEYSIDE |

F

FENWICK, ROBIN J	Maj	01-Oct-04	RN Warfare FAA	RNR AIR BR VL
FIELDER, DAVID A	Maj	10-Apr-99	RN Royal Marines GS	RNR MEDIA OPS
FOREMAN, NEIL	Capt	21-Sep-05	RN Royal Marines GS	RMR SCOTLAND

G

| GOLDSMITH, ANDREW | Capt | 01-Sep-05 | RN Royal Marines GS | RMR SCOTLAND |
| GRIFFITHS, NICHOLAS | Capt | 17-Jun-08 | RN Royal Marines GS | RMR BRISTOL |

H

HALE, WILLIAM	Capt	01-Oct-09	RN Royal Marines GS	RMR LONDON
HALL, DAVID	Capt	29-Dec-00	RN Royal Marines GS	RMR SCOTLAND
HAMILTON, CORMAC	Capt	29-Mar-06	RN Royal Marines GS	RMR MERSEYSIDE
HAMILTON, STUART	Capt	02-Feb-06	RN Royal Marines GS	RMR SCOTLAND
HESTER, JAMES FRANCIS	Maj	25-Oct-03	RN Royal Marines GS	RMR SCOTLAND
HILLMAN, DAVID	Maj	29-Oct-02	RN Royal Marines GS	RMR SCOTLAND

I

| ILLINGWORTH, RICHARD | Capt | 19-Feb-07 | RN Royal Marines GS | RMR MERSEYSIDE |

K

| KEDWARD, CHRISTOPHER | Capt | 31-May-09 | RN Royal Marines GS | RMR BRISTOL |
| KENNEDY, ROBERT | Capt | 04-Dec-13 | RN Royal Marines GS | RMR SCOTLAND |

L

| LAW, DUNCAN J F | Capt | 01-Aug-07 | RN Royal Marines GS | RMR LONDON |

M

MANNION, STEPHEN	Maj	26-Mar-96	RN Royal Marines GS	RM POOLE - STS
MAROK, JANI	Col	08-Oct-13	RN Royal Marines GS	FLEET CMR
MASON, ANDREW C	Capt	17-Dec-96	RN Royal Marines GS	

Name	Rank	Seniority	Branch	Unit
MCCULLOUGH, IAN	Maj	02-Oct-97	RN Royal Marines GS	RMR SCOTLAND
MCGINLEY, CHRISTOPHER	Capt	13-Dec-06	RN Royal Marines GS	RMR SCOTLAND
MCGOVERN, JAMES	Capt	30-Jul-12	RN Royal Marines GS	HMS FERRET - RNRIU
MCLEISH, ROBIN	Capt	31-Mar-01	RN Royal Marines GS	
MOULTON, FREDERICK	Lt Col	31-Dec-95	RN Royal Marines GS	FLEET FOSNNI - NRC

O

OUSELEY, DANIEL	Capt	31-Aug-07	RN Royal Marines GS	RMR LONDON

P

PICKETT, ALEXANDER	Maj	01-Oct-13	RN Royal Marines GS	RMR SCOTLAND
PUGSLEY, ANDREW	Capt	30-Jul-09	RN Royal Marines GS	RMR LONDON

R

ROBERTS, JOHN	Lt Col	30-Jun-08	RN Royal Marines GS	FLEET CMR
ROCHESTER, ANDREW D	Maj	01-Jun-12	RN Royal Marines GS	RMR BRISTOL

S

SAWYER, TREVOR	Lt Col	30-Jun-09	RN Royal Marines GS	FLEET CMR
SHAW, ANDREW PHILIP	Capt	01-Aug-07	RN Royal Marines GS	RMR LONDON
SMITH, FRASER RD ACA	Maj	01-Nov-05	RN Royal Marines GS	RMR LONDON

T

THOMAS, JEFFREY	Capt	22-Jul-03	RN Royal Marines GS	RMR BRISTOL
TOTTENHAM, TIMOTHY	Capt	04-Jul-07	RN Royal Marines GS	RMR LONDON

W

WADDELL, IAN S RD	Maj	01-Oct-08	RN Royal Marines GS	RMR LONDON
WATKINSON, NEIL	Lt Col	27-Feb-01	RN Royal Marines GS	FLEET CAP LLM
WILLIAMS, MATTHEW	Capt	01-Sep-03	RN Royal Marines GS	RMR BRISTOL

SEA CADET CORPS

Name	Rank	Seniority

A

Name	Rank	Seniority
ABLETT Michael	SLt (SCC) RNR	14-May-07
ACKFORD Christopher	Ch RNR	28-May-09
ADEY Kay	Lt (SCC) RNR	14-May-10
AIREY Robert	Ch RNR	17-Aug-05
ALLAM John	Lt (SCC) RNR	25-May-94
ALLEN Leslie	Lt Cdr (SCC) RNR	01-Jan-99
ALLISON Neil	SLt (SCC) RNR	16-May-10
ANDERSON Alex	Lt Cdr (SCC) RNR	18-Feb-13
ANDERSON Kevin	A/Lt (SCC) RNR	20-Nov-11
ANDREWS James Edward	Ch RNR	06-Sep-13
APPLEBY Gary	A/SLt (SCC) RNR	03-Jun-13
APPLEBY Keith	Lt (SCC) RNR	21-Feb-98
AQUILINA Rene	A/Lt (SCC) RMR	20-Mar-12
ARCHBOLD Dennis	Lt Cdr (SCC) RNR	11-Aug-99
ARCHBOLD Theresa	Lt (SCC) RNR	20-Nov-97
ARCHER Barry	Lt (SCC) RNR	01-Jun-94
ARCHER Dudley Ian	Ch RNR	03-Mar-98
ARMSTRONG Leslie	Ch RNR	08-May-10
ARNOLD Bernard	Ch RNR	18-Sep-13
ASHLEY Victoria	Ch RNR	04-Dec-12
ASHWORTH John	SLt (SCC) RNR	26-Jun-11
ASTON Courtney	Mid (SCC) RNR	09-Sep-12
ATKINS Doreen	Lt (SCC) RNR	08-Apr-92
ATKINSON Terence	Ch RNR	06-Sep-06
ATLING Brian	Ch RNR	15-Nov-11
AVILL Fraser	Lt (SCC) RNR	25-Sep-10
AVILL Susan	Lt (SCC) RNR	01-Nov-89

B

Name	Rank	Seniority
BAGSHAWE Allen	Ch RNR	01-Feb-89
BAILEY Arthur	Lt (SCC) RNR	03-Oct-10
BAKER Mark	Ch RNR	31-Jan-13
BALDACCHINO Saviour	Lt (SCC) RNR	20-Apr-94
BALL Alan	Ch RNR	18-May-98
BALL Philip	Ch RNR	16-Sep-08
BARBER Anthony	Lt (SCC) RNR	12-Mar-91
BARBER Martyn	SLt (SCC) RNR	26-Jun-11
BARKER David	Lt (SCC) RNR	21-Jun-99
BARKER Paul	A/Lt (SCC) RNR	12-Jul-13
BARKER Robert	Ch RNR	07-Sep-10
BARLOW Steuart	SLt (SCC) RNR	07-Feb-11
BARR William	Lt (SCC) RNR	15-Feb-00
BARRAS Hugh	Cdr (SCC) RNR	01-Aug-09
BARTHOLOMEW Julia	Ch RNR	24-Apr-04
BARTLE Jennifer	SLt (SCC) RNR	07-Nov-10
BASSETT Gary	Lt (SCC) RNR	28-Nov-96
BASSETT Karen	Ch RNR	12-Apr-10
BASSETT Lindsay	A/SLt (SCC) RNR	24-Mar-13
BATES Cecil	Ch RNR	08-Feb-02
BATTLE Stephen	Ch RNR	02-Feb-05
BAXTER Grant	Capt (SCC) RMR	01-Nov-12
BAYLEY George	Lt Cdr (SCC) RNR	01-Jan-11
BAYLISS John	Lt Cdr (SCC) RNR	14-Feb-87
BEARNE Jeremy	Cdr (SCC) RNR	01-Aug-09
BEDDOW Jay	Lt Cdr (SCC) RNR	02-Jan-13
BEECH Nicholas	A/Lt (SCC) RMR	25-Mar-12
BELL David	Ch RNR	12-Apr-10

Name	Rank	Seniority
BELL Fred	Ch RNR	15-Sep-10
BELL Joseph	Lt (SCC) RNR	13-Sep-01
BELL Ruth	A/Lt Cdr (SCC) RNR	01-Jun-13
BELL VERONICA	Lt Cdr (SCC) RNR	01-Jan-08
BENNETT Barbara	Ch RNR	04-Aug-11
BENNETT Stephen	Lt (SCC) RNR	01-Dec-08
BENTON Anthony	Maj (SCC) RMR	01-Jan-08
BERESFORD-HARTWELL Christopher	Lt (SCC) RNR	09-May-09
BERRIDGE Grahame	Ch RNR	02-May-00
BEVAN Mark	A/SLt (SCC) RNR	07-Mar-10
BICKLE Margaret	Lt (SCC) RNR	01-Mar-13
BILES Kathleen	Ch RNR	14-Oct-09
BILVERSTONE Brian	Lt Cdr (SCC) RNR	22-Nov-05
BINGHAM Keith	Cdr (SCC) RNR	01-Aug-09
BISHOP Peter	Lt (SCC) RNR	01-Nov-95
BISSON Keith	Lt (SCC) RNR	16-Nov-06
BLACK Karen	Lt (SCC) RNR	06-Nov-12
BLACKBURN Alan	Lt (SCC) RNR	15-Jun-04
BLUMENTHAL Adrian	A/SLt (SCC) RNR	02-Jun-13
BONFIELD Christopher	Lt (SCC) RNR	06-Nov-96
BONJOUR Andre	Lt (SCC) RNR	27-May-92
BOORMAN Nicholas	Lt (SCC) RNR	01-Dec-88
BOSWELL Robert	Lt (SCC) RNR	01-Jan-07
BOURNE Jack	Lt (SCC) RNR	23-Nov-12
BOURNE Nigel	Ch RNR	13-Dec-08
BOWEN-DAVIES Alison	Lt (SCC) RNR	12-Mar-10
BOWMAN John	SLt (SCC) RNR	28-Jun-09
BOWSKILL Michael	Lt Cdr (SCC) RNR	01-Jul-02
BOYES Stephen	Lt (SCC) RNR	25-Feb-99
BRADBURY David	Lt (SCC) RNR	07-Sep-85
BRADFORD David	Lt Cdr (SCC) RNR	01-Nov-00
BRANDIE Beaumont	Ch RNR	01-Feb-84
BRATLEY Charles	Lt (SCC) RNR	25-Jul-05
BRAZIER Colin	Lt Cdr (SCC) RNR	01-Feb-03
BRENNAN-WRIGHT Alison	Lt (SCC) RNR	25-Jan-09
BRIGGS Donald	Lt Cdr (SCC) RNR	01-Sep-77
BRINDLE Dawn	Lt (SCC) RNR	13-Oct-07
BRISTER Andrew	Ch RNR	30-Nov-09
BRISTOW Roger	Ch RNR	18-Apr-06
BROADBENT Graham	Lt Cdr (SCC) RNR	01-Aug-84
BROCKWELL Graham	Lt (SCC) RNR	31-Mar-06
BROUGHTON James	Ch RNR	29-Aug-00
BROWN Damien	Lt Cdr (SCC) RNR	01-Feb-13
BROWN John	Lt Cdr (SCC) RNR	04-Jul-78
BROWN Michael	Ch RNR	12-Apr-00
BROWNING Martin	A/Capt (SCC) RMR	02-Aug-02
BROWNING Tony	Lt (SCC) RNR	19-Dec-93
BROXHAM Roy	Lt (SCC) RNR	21-Sep-90
BRYANT Charles	Lt (SCC) RNR	19-Feb-87
BUCKELS Emma	SLt (SCC) RNR	01-Apr-10
BUCKETT Vivienne	SLt (SCC) RNR	01-Nov-09
BUCKINGHAM Buck	SLt (SCC) RNR	28-Mar-10
BUCKLEY Andrew	A/SLt (SCC) RNR	22-Jun-11
BUDDEN Paul	Capt (SCC) RNR	25-Jan-09
BULLOCK Lynn	Lt (SCC) RNR	01-Dec-14
BUNDOCK Anthony	Ch RNR	08-Nov-04
BURNS Cliff	A/Lt Cdr (SCC) RNR	01-Jan-13
BURNS Desmond	Lt (SCC) RNR	18-Feb-78
BURNS Philip	Lt Cdr (SCC) RNR	14-Feb-03

Name	Rank	Seniority	Name	Rank	Seniority
BURT Christopher	Lt (SCC) RNR	20-Aug-99	COLES Jane	A/SLt (SCC) RNR	02-Jun-13
BURTON Martyn	A/Lt Cdr (SCC) RNR	01-Feb-12	COLES Thomas	Lt Cdr (SCC) RNR	19-Dec-87
BUTCHER Colin	Lt (SCC) RNR	26-Nov-02	COLLIER Billy	Lt (SCC) RMR	25-Mar-12
BUTCHER Sarah	SLt (SCC) RNR	29-Mar-09	COLLINS David	Lt Cdr (SCC) RNR	01-Feb-82
BUTTERFIELD Peter	Ch RNR	23-Jan-13	COLLINS Timothy	Lt (SCC) RNR	27-Jan-07
BUTTERWORTH John	Lt (SCC) RNR	23-Mar-87	COMER Kieran	Mid (SCC) RNR	24-Jun-12
			CONNOR Christopher	Lt (SCC) RMR	09-Aug-13
C			CONWAY Paul	Lt (SCC) RNR	27-Mar-11
			COOK Richard	Ch RNR	11-May-12
CADDICK David	A/Lt (SCC) RMR	10-Nov-13	COOKE John	Ch RNR	20-Apr-98
CADDICK Keith	A/Lt (SCC) RMR	02-Jun-13	COOMBES Peter	Ch RNR	11-Nov-10
CADDICK Natalie	SLt (SCC) RNR	11-May-10	COOPER Alan	Lt (SCC) RNR	01-Apr-06
CADMAN John	Lt Cdr (SCC) RNR	26-Nov-86	COOPER Anthony-Paul	SLt (SCC) RNR	24-Aug-10
CAINES Danny	SLt (SCC) RNR	29-Mar-09	COOPER Tristan	SLt (SCC) RNR	31-Jan-13
CALDWELL David	Ch RNR	24-Sep-07	COPELAND Derek	Ch RNR	01-Oct-00
CALVER Russell	SLt (SCC) RNR	28-Jun-09	COPELIN Maureen	Lt Cdr (SCC) RNR	01-Feb-05
CAMILLERI Carmel Lino	Lt Cdr (SCC) RNR	12-Oct-97	CORMACK Raymond	Lt (SCC) RNR	25-Apr-00
CAMPBELL Donald	Ch RNR	30-Jul-10	CORNELL Helga	Ch RNR	03-May-10
CAMPBELL Gordon	Ch RNR	20-Apr-01	CORNISH RACHEL	Ch RNR	12-Dec-13
CAMPBELL James	Ch RNR	19-Nov-08	COSTERD David	Lt (SCC) RNR	06-Dec-00
CARLILL Adam	Ch RNR	01-Mar-05	COUSINS Karen	A/SLt (SCC) RNR	24-Mar-13
CARR Barry	Lt (SCC) RNR	25-Mar-05	COX Donald	Lt (SCC) RMR	07-Aug-06
CARR Helen	Ch RNR	10-Mar-11	COX Jon	Lt (SCC) RNR	16-Jan-09
CARR Leonard	Lt Cdr (SCC) RNR	13-Oct-77	COX Simon	Ch RNR	25-Sep-95
CARROLL Kenneth	Capt (SCC) RMR	13-Oct-12	CRAIG Neil	Lt (SCC) RNR	01-Apr-86
CARTER David	Lt Cdr (SCC) RNR	06-Nov-06	CRAWLEY Stephen	Maj (SCC) RMR	01-Jan-09
CARTER Marion	Ch RNR	24-Aug-11	CREIGHTON Edward	Lt (SCC) RNR	26-Nov-92
CARTER Rebecca	SLt (SCC) RNR	24-Jun-12	CRICK Philip	Ch RNR	11-May-04
CARTWRIGHT Michael	A/Maj (SCC) RMR	01-Feb-13	CRITCHLOW Jonathan	Lt (SCC) RNR	19-Feb-89
CARVER Steven	A/SLt (SCC) RNR	24-Sep-13	CROSBY Bernard	Ch RNR	16-Dec-98
CASHMORE Matthew	Lt (SCC) RNR	09-May-09	CROWE Keith	Capt (SCC) RMR	15-Jun-09
CASLAW Paul	Lt (SCC) RNR	01-Aug-94	CROWTHER Jonathan	SLt (SCC) RNR	19-Nov-13
CAVLAN Rebecca	2nd Lt (SCC) RMR	30-Oct-11	CRUICKSHANK Jonathan	Ch RNR	24-Aug-89
CEA Franklin	Lt Cdr (SCC) RNR	01-Jan-02	CRUMP Adam	Lt (SCC) RNR	02-Nov-13
CEA Katrina	SLt (SCC) RNR	29-Mar-09	CUSH Martin	A/SLt (SCC) RNR	25-Apr-13
CHADWICK Charles	Ch RNR	03-Jul-08			
CHALLIS Stewart	Lt (SCC) RNR	09-May-09	**D**		
CHAPMAN Paul	Lt (SCC) RNR	25-Mar-12			
CHARD Michael	Lt (SCC) RNR	14-Apr-13	DALY Shane	Lt (SCC) RNR	29-Aug-12
CHEEK Ronald	Lt (SCC) RNR	23-Mar-05	DANIELS Roger	Lt Cdr (SCC) RNR	14-Jan-91
CHEETHAM Mark	SLt (SCC) RNR	07-Nov-10	DANIELS Steven	Lt (SCC) RNR	02-Nov-13
CHESWORTH Howard	Lt (SCC) RNR	03-Dec-91	DAVIES Aled	Mid (SCC) RNR	25-Jun-13
CHINN John	Lt Cdr (SCC) RNR	01-Jan-83	DAVIES Colin	Lt Cdr (SCC) RNR	04-Apr-08
CHITTOCK Michael	Lt Cdr (SCC) RNR	01-Jan-08	DAVIES Helen	Lt (SCC) RNR	02-Oct-12
CHRISTIE Randall	SLt (SCC) RNR	02-Jul-06	DAVIES John	SLt (SCC) RNR	07-Nov-10
CIOMA Antoni	Lt Cdr (SCC) RNR	01-Jul-90	DAVIES Peter	Ch RNR	01-Jul-03
CLAMMER Thomas	Ch RNR	18-Mar-09	DAVIES William	Lt Cdr (SCC) RNR	01-Jul-04
CLAPHAM Stephen	Ch RNR	27-Jun-09	DAVIS Daniel	SLt (SCC) RNR	27-Mar-11
CLARK David	Lt (SCC) RNR	18-Jun-12	DAVIS Samantha	A/Maj (SCC) RMR	17-Oct-12
CLARK Steven	Lt (SCC) RNR	13-Apr-13	DAVISON Henry	Lt Cdr (SCC) RNR	01-Jan-11
CLARKE Aaron	Lt (SCC) RNR	03-Aug-11	DAW Nicholas William	Ch RNR	12-Dec-13
CLARKE Nigel	SLt (SCC) RNR	29-Mar-09	DAWSON Craig	Lt (SCC) RNR	29-Jan-12
CLAY Paul	A/Lt Cdr (SCC) RNR	01-Aug-12	DAWSON David	Ch RNR	17-Nov-07
CLEWORTH Dean	Lt Cdr (SCC) RNR	01-Jan-11	DAY Scott	SLt (SCC) RNR	09-Sep-12
CLIFFORD Ian	Lt (SCC) RNR	19-Jun-01	DAY Trevor	Ch RNR	15-Feb-11
CLUNAS William	A/Lt (SCC) RNR	08-Dec-05	DEACON Andrew	Lt (SCC) RNR	18-Oct-12
CLYBURN Timothy	A/SLt (SCC) RNR	24-Jun-12	DEBRUYNE Jacquelyn	Lt (SCC) RNR	21-Aug-95
COAST Philip	Lt Cdr (SCC) RNR	09-Jul-90	DELACOUR Michael	A/Lt (SCC) RMR	09-Sep-12
COATES Margaret	Lt Cdr (SCC) RNR	30-Jun-08	DEMANUELE Raymond	Lt (SCC) RNR	05-Nov-11
COCKELL Lynn	SLt (SCC) RNR	07-Nov-10	DEMUTH Alice	A/Lt (SCC) RNR	14-Sep-13
COCKELL Richard	Lt Cdr (SCC) RNR	04-Dec-96	DENYER Philip	Ch RNR	25-Apr-09
COCKRELL Victoria	Lt (SCC) RNR	29-Apr-12	DERBYSHIRE David	Lt (SCC) RNR	03-Jun-92
COLEMAN Keith	Lt (SCC) RNR	26-Nov-98	DERHAM Peter	Ch RNR	14-May-96

Name	Rank	Seniority
DEVENISH Ian	Maj (SCC) RMR	01-Oct-06
DEVEREUX Edwin	Lt Cdr (SCC) RNR	01-May-87
DEVINE Anthony	SLt (SCC) RNR	07-Nov-10
DIAPER Kevin	SLt (SCC) RNR	14-Apr-11
DIBBEN Michael	Lt (SCC) RNR	03-Nov-88
DICKINSON Keith	Lt Cdr (SCC) RNR	01-Jan-10
DICKSON Mathew	A/Lt (SCC) RMR	10-Nov-13
DIXIE Colin	Lt (SCC) RNR	15-Oct-00
DIXON Michael	Lt (SCC) RNR	19-Jan-08
DODD Gary	Lt (SCC) RNR	02-Apr-11
DONNELLY James	SLt (SCC) RNR	30-Oct-05
DRYDEN Graeme	Lt (SCC) RNR	26-Mar-02
DRYDEN Stephen	Lt (SCC) RNR	01-Mar-81
DUCKETT Raphael	Ch RNR	16-Jul-12
DUXBURY MEGAN	Mid (SCC) RNR	26-Jun-11
DYER Roger	Lt (SCC) RNR	07-Jun-97

E

Name	Rank	Seniority
EALES Geoffrey	Ch RNR	11-Jul-01
EARL David	Ch RNR	01-Jun-98
EDGE Christopher	A/SLt (SCC) RNR	10-Nov-13
EDMONDS Annette	Lt (SCC) RNR	12-Jun-10
EDMUNDS Roger	SLt (SCC) RNR	07-Nov-10
EDWARDS Mark	A/Capt (SCC) RMR	02-Jun-13
EDWARDS Paul	Lt (SCC) RMR	28-Mar-10
ELGAR Carolyn	Ch RNR	15-Mar-08
ELLIOTT William	SLt (SCC) RNR	29-Mar-09
ELLIS Christopher	Ch RNR	21-Feb-12
ERB-SMITH Darren	A/Capt (SCC) RMR	05-Nov-12
ERSKINE Richard	Lt (SCC) RNR	23-Nov-03
EVANS Janet	Cdr (SCC) RNR	01-Aug-09
EVANS John	Lt (SCC) RNR	28-Sep-00
EXCELL Timothy	SLt (SCC) RNR	28-Mar-10
EYDMANN Eileen	Ch RNR	05-Jul-93
EYNON David	Ch RNR	04-Aug-03

F

Name	Rank	Seniority
FARNWORTH Tom	SLt (SCC) RNR	17-Sep-12
FARRELL Michael	Lt (SCC) RNR	05-May-07
FAULKNER Shelley-Ann	Lt Cdr (SCC) RNR	04-Apr-07
FAULKNER Shane	SLt (SCC) RNR	26-Jun-11
FENN Paul	Lt (SCC) RNR	06-Sep-07
FENTON Keith	Ch RNR	18-Oct-11
FIELD James	Ch RNR	12-Oct-10
FIELD Kevin	A/Lt (SCC) RMR	18-Nov-12
FIELDS Dawn	SLt (SCC) RNR	27-Mar-11
FINLAY David	Lt Cdr (SCC) RNR	01-Jan-08
FITCH Michael	Lt (SCC) RNR	28-Feb-03
FLEET Gordon	Maj (SCC) RMR	18-Dec-05
FLEMING Alan	Lt Cdr (SCC) RNR	01-Jan-08
FLEMING Andrea	Lt (SCC) RNR	22-Nov-02
FLEMING Margaret	Lt (SCC) RNR	01-Jan-82
FLETCHER Malcolm	Lt (SCC) RNR	20-Feb-84
FLETCHER Suzanne	Ch RNR	20-Jan-12
FLUDE Mark	A/Lt (SCC) RMR	02-Jun-13
FORD Joseph	A/SLt (SCC) RNR	02-Jun-13
FOREMAN Waleria	Lt (SCC) RNR	22-Sep-95
FORRESTER Michael	Lt (SCC) RNR	08-Apr-10
FOSTER Andrew	Lt (SCC) RNR	19-Nov-91
FOSTER James	Capt (SCC) RMR	12-Dec-12
FOWLER Alison	Lt Cdr (SCC) RNR	01-Mar-06

Name	Rank	Seniority
FOX Jane	Lt (SCC) RNR	11-Sep-11
FRANCIS Rebecca	Lt (SCC) RNR	11-Sep-07
FRANKLIN Patrick	Lt (SCC) RNR	07-Dec-02
FRASER Sean	SLt (SCC) RNR	27-Mar-11
FREESTONE Andrew	Lt (SCC) RNR	07-Nov-95
FROOM Ian	Ch RNR	27-Mar-00
FULCHER Diane	Lt Cdr (SCC) RNR	24-Jul-09
FULCHER Scott	A/Lt (SCC) RNR	22-Apr-13
FULLER Andrew	Capt (SCC) RMR	14-May-10
FULTON Karen	Lt Cdr (SCC) RNR	01-May-05

G

Name	Rank	Seniority
GAIT David	Ch RNR	20-Apr-98
GALLAGHER Eamonn	Lt (SCC) RNR	23-Jun-92
GAMBELL Mark	Lt Cdr (SCC) RNR	01-Jan-11
GAMBLE David	Ch RNR	01-May-04
GARNER JAMES	Lt Cdr (SCC) RNR	01-Jul-01
GARRINGTON Malcolm	Lt (SCC) RNR	30-Jan-13
GATHERGOOD John	Lt (SCC) RNR	17-Apr-98
GEARING Robert	Lt Cdr (SCC) RNR	01-Sep-77
GENTILELLA Barbara	Ch RNR	14-Sep-09
GILBERT Robin	Maj (SCC) RMR	01-Jun-99
GILBERT-JONES Hilary	Lt (SCC) RNR	23-Nov-08
GILBERT-JONES Robert	Lt (SCC) RMR	30-Oct-11
GILES Andrew	Cdr (SCC) RNR	28-Jun-13
GILKS Nicholas	SLt (SCC) RNR	30-Oct-11
GILL Jacqueline	Lt (SCC) RNR	28-Feb-95
GILLARD Terence	Lt Cdr (SCC) RNR	01-Jan-95
GILLERT Valerie	Lt (SCC) RNR	19-Oct-91
GILLIAM Kevin	Lt (SCC) RNR	01-Jul-93
GIRLING Craig	SLt (SCC) RNR	28-Jun-09
GITTENS Adrian	Lt (SCC) RNR	23-Jan-09
GITTINS Susan	Lt (SCC) RNR	07-Dec-02
GLANVILLE Debra	Lt Cdr (SCC) RNR	01-Jan-11
GLANVILLE Lloyd	Mid (SCC) RNR	25-Mar-12
GLEAVE Anthony	SLt (SCC) RNR	28-Mar-10
GLOVER Katie	A/SLt (SCC) RNR	09-Sep-12
GLOVER Stuart	Lt (SCC) RNR	12-Jun-10
GODFREY Simon	Ch RNR	24-Jan-11
GOODCHILD Joanne	SLt (SCC) RNR	28-Jun-09
GOODCHILD Matthew	SLt (SCC) RNR	07-Feb-12
GOODE Victoria	Lt (SCC) RNR	08-Nov-00
GOODING Peter	Lt Cdr (SCC) RNR	01-Jan-81
GOODLEFF Deborah	Lt (SCC) RNR	04-Jun-12
GORDON Andrew	Lt (SCC) RNR	19-Feb-89
GORMAN Jacqueline	A/Lt Cdr (SCC) RNR	01-Mar-12
GRAINGE Andrew	Lt Cdr (SCC) RNR	01-Jan-09
GRAINGER Steven	SLt (SCC) RNR	27-Jun-11
GRANT Malcolm	Lt Cdr (SCC) RNR	01-Jan-09
GRANT Steven	Mid (SCC) RNR	10-Nov-13
GRAY Brian	Lt (SCC) RNR	12-Dec-87
GREEN Christopher	Mid (SCC) RNR	18-Nov-12
GREEN Derek	SLt (SCC) RNR	26-Jun-11
GREEN Malcolm	Lt (SCC) RNR	16-Aug-97
GREENFIELD Stephen	Capt (SCC) RMR	09-Apr-12
GREENFIELD Diana	Ch RNR	26-Jul-12
GREENHALGH Peter	Lt Cdr (SCC) RNR	01-Apr-07
GREGORY Dominic	Lt (SCC) RNR	14-Jan-13
GRESTY Stephen	Lt (SCC) RNR	07-Oct-09
GREY Roger	Ch RNR	02-Dec-09
GRIBBLE Michael	SLt (SCC) RNR	25-Mar-12
GRIEVE Derek	Lt (SCC) RNR	01-Jan-07

Name	Rank	Seniority
GRIFFITHS Martyn	Ch RNR	03-Jul-08
GRIFFITHS Thomas	SLt (SCC) RNR	25-Jul-10
GROGAN Kenneth	Lt (SCC) RNR	16-Sep-78
GROSS Lucy	SLt (SCC) RNR	23-Jun-07
GROVES Richard	Lt Cdr (SCC) RNR	29-Aug-86
GUILE Nigel	A/Lt (SCC) RMR	06-Jun-13
GUISHARD Mark	SLt (SCC) RNR	11-May-01
GUPPY Graham	Maj (SCC) RMR	01-Jul-99
GYI Stephen	A/SLt (SCC) RNR	13-Dec-09

H

Name	Rank	Seniority
HACKETT Clive	Lt Cdr (SCC) RNR	12-Oct-90
HAGAN George	Lt (SCC) RNR	09-Apr-06
HAINES Linda	Lt (SCC) RNR	01-Nov-89
HALL Christopher	Ch RNR	10-Jan-06
HALL Derek	Lt Cdr (SCC) RNR	19-Feb-98
HALL John	Ch RNR	27-Nov-09
HALLAM Oliver	A/SLt (SCC) RNR	12-May-12
HALLAS Jeanette	Lt (SCC) RNR	17-Jun-05
HALLIDAY Angela	Lt (SCC) RNR	11-May-00
HAMILTON Francis	A/Capt (SCC) RMR	27-Aug-13
HAMILTON Gary	A/SLt (SCC) RNR	02-Jun-13
HANKEY Carolyne	Lt (SCC) RNR	29-Sep-97
HANLEY David	Lt Cdr (SCC) RNR	01-Apr-05
HANLON Scott	SLt (SCC) RNR	30-Apr-11
HANN Peter	Ch RNR	19-Dec-10
HANRAHAN Karl	Lt (SCC) RMR	27-Mar-11
HANSON Neil	Lt (SCC) RNR	11-Nov-06
HARE Laura	SLt (SCC) RNR	07-Dec-11
HARKIN Terry	Ch RNR	22-Jun-97
HARMER Robert	Lt (SCC) RNR	28-Oct-99
HARPER James	Lt Cdr (SCC) RNR	18-Sep-12
HARRIS Duncan	Ch RNR	27-Jun-09
HARRIS Geoffrey	Ch RNR	03-May-12
HARRIS Kenneth	A/SLt (SCC) RNR	05-May-01
HARRIS Rachel	A/Lt (SCC) RNR	16-Jul-13
HARRIS Trevor	Lt (SCC) RNR	05-Dec-01
HARTFIELD John	Ch RNR	25-Jan-10
HARTWELL Neil	Lt (SCC) RNR	26-Mar-02
HARVEY Brian	Lt (SCC) RNR	09-Jan-07
HARVEY Shawn	SLt (SCC) RNR	28-Mar-96
HARVEY Stephen	A/Lt (SCC) RNR	25-Oct-13
HATHERLEY David	Lt (SCC) RNR	22-Nov-06
HAWKINS Leslie	A/Lt (SCC) RNR	22-Apr-10
HAY Robert	Lt (SCC) RNR	14-Oct-10
HAZELDON Donald	SLt (SCC) RNR	28-Apr-93
HAZZARD Michael	A/Lt (SCC) RNR	13-Jun-11
HEAD Gareth	A/SLt (SCC) RNR	10-Nov-13
HEALEY Stephen	Lt (SCC) RNR	15-May-84
HEALY Christopher	A/Lt (SCC) RNR	25-Oct-13
HEARL James	Lt Cdr (SCC) RNR	01-Dec-04
HEARL James	SLt (SCC) RNR	28-Jun-09
HEEKS Theresa	Lt (SCC) RNR	02-Nov-13
HEMSWORTH John	Ch RNR	04-Jan-08
HERSANT Michael	Ch RNR	08-Jan-03
HIBBINS Neil	Ch RNR	12-Dec-05
HIDE Brenda	Lt (SCC) RNR	02-May-84
HILL Edward	A/SLt (SCC) RNR	18-Nov-12
HILLIER Barbara	Lt (SCC) RNR	04-Sep-03
HITCHINS Graham	Ch RNR	14-Jul-10
HITHERSAY John	Lt (SCC) RNR	28-Oct-78
HOBBINS Raymond	Ch RNR	23-Jul-98

Name	Rank	Seniority
HOEY David	Lt Cdr (SCC) RNR	10-Jul-12
HOEY Richard	Capt (SCC) RMR	30-Nov-13
HOFBAUER Andrea	Ch RNR	22-Feb-11
HOLDEN David	A/Lt (SCC) RNR	09-Apr-13
HOLDEN Zandra	A/Lt (SCC) RNR	17-Jan-12
HOLDER John	Ch RNR	15-Aug-02
HOLLAND Donald	Lt (SCC) RNR	15-Sep-84
HOLLIDAY Anthony	Lt Cdr (SCC) RNR	01-Jan-01
HOLLIS Arnold	Ch RNR	09-Apr-99
HOLLOWAY Pamela	SLt (SCC) RNR	25-Jul-10
HOOKINS Eric	Ch RNR	09-Jun-07
HOPKINS Henry	Ch RNR	18-Apr-07
HORNE Allan	Lt (SCC) RNR	16-Sep-89
HORNER John	Lt Cdr (SCC) RNR	16-Sep-92
HORTON Paul	Capt (SCC) RMR	13-Apr-13
HOUGHTON Antony	Lt (SCC) RNR	04-Sep-06
HOULDEN Wendy	Lt (SCC) RNR	30-Sep-01
HOWARD Jon	Ch RNR	28-Feb-08
HOWES Alan	Ch RNR	09-Sep-85
HOWIE Thomas	Lt Cdr (SCC) RNR	01-Nov-88
HUCKETT Andrew	Ch RNR	04-Apr-00
HUGHES Sheila	Ch RNR	27-Mar-07
HUGHES Sharon	Ch RNR	01-Aug-06
HULONCE Michael	Lt Cdr (SCC) RNR	01-Mar-82
HUMPHREYS Lewis	Mid (SCC) RNR	09-Sep-12
HUNT Helen	SLt (SCC) RNR	07-Nov-10
HUNT James	A/SLt (SCC) RNR	24-Mar-13
HUNT Kevin	Ch RNR	10-Dec-98
HUNTER Philip	Lt (SCC) RNR	01-Feb-02
HURST Paul	Lt Cdr (SCC) RNR	27-Aug-09
HURST Thomas	Lt Cdr (SCC) RNR	01-Jun-85
HUTCHINGS Andrew	Lt (SCC) RNR	22-Jun-04
HUTCHINSON John	SLt (SCC) RNR	02-Nov-08

I

Name	Rank	Seniority
INGHAM Anthony	SLt (SCC) RNR	24-Feb-99
INGHAM Mark	SLt (SCC) RNR	22-Nov-00
IRVING Douglas	Ch RNR	05-Feb-02
IZZARD Michael	Lt (SCC) RNR	25-Jun-98

J

Name	Rank	Seniority
JACKSON Margaret Elizabeth	Ch RNR	02-Nov-13
JAMES Richard	Ch RNR	14-Sep-09
JAMES Robert	Lt Cdr (SCC) RNR	01-Jan-95
JANNER-BURGESS Mark	Lt (SCC) RNR	21-Jan-06
JARMAN Christopher	Ch RNR	12-Mar-08
JEFFRIES Leila	Lt (SCC) RNR	25-Jun-10
JELLIS Josephine	Ch RNR	28-Jan-08
JENNINGS Pamela	Ch RNR	20-Sep-04
JENNINGS William	Lt Cdr (SCC) RNR	01-Jan-07
JEZZARD Michael	Ch RNR	02-Apr-04
JOHNS Gareth	SLt (SCC) RNR	27-Mar-11
JOHNSON Peter	Ch RNR	09-Sep-10
JOHNSON-PAUL David	Lt (SCC) RNR	23-Feb-12
JOHNSTONE Geoffrey	Capt (SCC) RMR	01-Jul-12
JONES Christopher	Lt Cdr (SCC) RNR	11-Aug-99
JONES Clive	Ch RNR	01-Oct-05
JONES Dorothy	Lt (SCC) RNR	22-Nov-94
JONES Ian	A/Capt (SCC) RMR	12-Dec-12
JONES Jonathan	A/SLt (SCC) RNR	26-Jun-13
JONES Kelvin	Lt (SCC) RNR	07-Apr-97

Name	Rank	Seniority
JONES Mark	Lt (SCC) RNR	06-Nov-96
JONES Mark	SLt (SCC) RNR	28-Jun-09
JONES Nicholas	Lt (SCC) RNR	02-Apr-10
JONES Neil	Lt (SCC) RNR	03-Jan-96
JONES Sian	Ch RNR	20-Jan-12
JORDAN Sheila	Lt (SCC) RNR	26-Jul-90
JOREY Richard	A/SLt (SCC) RNR	18-Nov-12
JUBB Elizabeth	Lt (SCC) RNR	21-Aug-09
JUNIPER James	Capt (SCC) RMR	22-Jun-07
JUNIPER Stephanie	Lt (SCC) RNR	11-Nov-06
JUPE Paul	Lt (SCC) RNR	02-Mar-88

K

Name	Rank	Seniority
KAY Anne	Lt (SCC) RNR	21-Jan-06
KAYE Timothy	Ch RNR	01-Aug-00
KEERY Neil	Lt (SCC) RNR	18-May-01
KEERY William	Lt Cdr (SCC) RNR	01-Jan-83
KELSHALL Candyce	SLt (SCC) RNR	18-Nov-12
KENDALL George	SLt (SCC) RNR	01-Jul-07
KENRICK Peter	Lt (SCC) RNR	23-Nov-94
KERRIGAN Gareth	SLt (SCC) RNR	24-Jun-12
KERSLAKE Adrian	Lt (SCC) RNR	06-Apr-11
KETTLEBOROUGH Thomas	SLt (SCC) RNR	07-Nov-10
KILLICK Peter	Lt (SCC) RNR	08-Oct-87
KING Leslie	Lt Cdr (SCC) RNR	15-Mar-98
KINGHORN Jason	Lt Cdr (SCC) RNR	01-Jan-08
KNIGHT Robert	Lt Cdr (SCC) RNR	01-Jun-08
KNOWLES-FORREST Norman	Lt (SCC) RNR	01-Oct-08
KRISTIANSEN Karen	Lt Cdr (SCC) RNR	10-Aug-07

L

Name	Rank	Seniority
LAMPERT Brian	Lt Cdr (SCC) RNR	01-Dec-84
LAMPERT Mark	Lt (SCC) RNR	25-Jan-09
LAMPERT Susan	Lt Cdr (SCC) RNR	01-Apr-06
LANCASTER Jonathan	Lt (SCC) RMR	25-Mar-12
LANE Iain	Ch RNR	27-Jul-01
LANE Roy	Ch RNR	03-Aug-92
LAWES Sonia	Lt Cdr (SCC) RNR	01-Jan-07
LAWRENCE Kevin	Lt (SCC) RNR	01-May-01
LE-BASSE Myles	A/Capt (SCC) RMR	08-Feb-12
LEAPER Richard	Ch RNR	05-Jan-99
LEAVER Carl	SLt (SCC) RNR	27-Mar-11
LECKIE ALEXANDER	A/Maj (SCC) RMR	01-Jan-13
LECKIE LESLEY	Lt (SCC) RNR	01-Oct-11
LEE Philip	A/Lt (SCC) RNR	04-Oct-13
LEEVES Luke	SLt (SCC) RNR	10-Aug-12
LEGGATE Colin	Ch RNR	20-Oct-11
LEIGH-PEARSON Michael	Ch RNR	09-Aug-12
LEVERETT Colin	SLt (SCC) RNR	01-Jul-07
LEVERETT Rosamund	SLt (SCC) RNR	07-Apr-07
LEWIS Clifford	Lt Cdr (SCC) RNR	23-Feb-09
LEWIS David	Lt Cdr (SCC) RNR	01-Jan-07
LEWIS Deirdre	SLt (SCC) RNR	02-Nov-08
LEWIS Eleanor	Lt (SCC) RNR	23-Nov-94
LEWIS John	Capt (SCC) RMR	01-Jul-99
LEWIS John	Ch RNR	10-Jul-06
LEWIS Peter	Lt Cdr (SCC) RNR	01-Jan-04
LEWIS Walter	Lt (SCC) RNR	06-May-79
LIGHTBOURNE William	Lt Cdr (SCC) RNR	22-Jan-91
LINAKER David	Ch RNR	15-Mar-10
LINCOLN David	Lt Cdr (SCC) RNR	01-Jan-06

Name	Rank	Seniority
LINDLEY James	Lt (SCC) RNR	16-May-12
LINDSEY Helen	SLt (SCC) RNR	10-Nov-12
LISTER Richard	A/Lt Cdr (SCC) RNR	01-Jan-13
LLORET-FARINA Salvador	Ch RNR	25-Sep-08
LLOYD Esther	SLt (SCC) RNR	02-Apr-13
LOCKE David	Lt Cdr (SCC) RNR	01-Jan-05
LOGIN Brenda	Lt Cdr (SCC) RNR	01-Oct-02
LOGIN Craig	SLt (SCC) RNR	28-Mar-10
LOGIN Derek	Cdr (SCC) RNR	01-Aug-09
LOGIN Susan	A/SLt (SCC) RNR	09-Sep-12
LONDON Phillip	SLt (SCC) RNR	31-Oct-05
LOUCH Stephen	Lt (SCC) RNR	21-Nov-09
LOVERIDGE Anthony	Lt Cdr (SCC) RNR	01-Dec-89
LOW Peter	Ch RNR	16-Apr-07
LOWE David	Lt (SCC) RNR	23-Jul-77
LUCAS Peter	Lt (SCC) RNR	24-Mar-99
LUCKMAN Bruce	Lt (SCC) RNR	01-Oct-92
LUCKRAFT Christopher	Ch RNR	28-May-09
LUXTON Phillip	Ch RNR	05-Nov-00
LYNCH Matthew	A/Lt (SCC) RNR	23-Sep-13
LYSTER Cody	Lt (SCC) RNR	27-Nov-09

M

Name	Rank	Seniority
MACEY Mark	Lt Cdr (SCC) RNR	01-Sep-03
MACHIN Ian	Maj (SCC) RMR	01-Jul-99
MACKAY Charles	SLt (SCC) RNR	01-Dec-97
MACKAY COLIN	Ch RNR	30-May-13
MACKAY David	Lt (SCC) RNR	01-Jul-84
MACKINLAY Colin	Lt (SCC) RNR	08-Apr-92
MACLENNAN Glenn	Lt (SCC) RMR	30-Oct-11
MACLENNAN Robert	Lt (SCC) RNR	21-Nov-09
MACLEOD Ronnie	A/Lt (SCC) RMR	24-Jun-12
MACLEOD Talisker	Ch RNR	07-Dec-11
MACNAUGHTON Diana	Ch RNR	07-Feb-12
MAIR Brian	Lt Cdr (SCC) RNR	01-Jan-02
MALM Alexander	SLt (SCC) RNR	25-Mar-13
MANNOUCH John	Lt (SCC) RNR	14-May-90
MARK Nicholas	Ch RNR	10-Aug-10
MARLBOROUGH Andrew	SLt (SCC) RNR	29-Mar-09
MARLOWE Bernard	A/Lt (SCC) RNR	08-Mar-10
MARSHALL Dean	SLt (SCC) RNR	26-Jun-11
MARSHALL Keith	SLt (SCC) RNR	25-Nov-12
MARSON Victoria	Lt Cdr (SCC) RNR	01-Feb-05
MARTIN Kevin	Lt Cdr (SCC) RNR	01-Jan-08
MASON Edward	Lt Cdr (SCC) RNR	01-Jan-78
MATTHEWS John	A/Lt Cdr (SCC) RNR	12-Jul-12
MATTHEWS Phillip	Lt Cdr (SCC) RNR	01-Feb-89
MATTHEWS Ronald	Lt (SCC) RNR	14-Jan-97
MATTHIAS Paul	Ch RNR	12-Apr-10
MAY John (Iain)	Ch RNR	26-Apr-13
MAYLAM Nicholas	A/SLt (SCC) RNR	22-Nov-13
MCAVADY Andrew	Lt (SCC) RNR	12-Jun-98
MCCUISH Ewan	Lt (SCC) RNR	05-Oct-11
MCDERMOTT Keith	SLt (SCC) RNR	28-Jun-09
MCDONALD LESLEY	Lt (SCC) RNR	05-May-98
MCDONALD PETER	Lt (SCC) RNR	29-Jun-92
MCGARRY George	Ch RNR	08-Aug-06
MCGLONE Fergus	SLt (SCC) RNR	10-Aug-10
MCKEE David	Lt Cdr (SCC) RNR	27-Sep-87
MCKENNA Paul	Lt Cdr (SCC) RNR	01-Jun-07
MCKEOWN Glenda	Lt (SCC) RNR	24-Apr-96
MCKINLAY Thomas	Ch RNR	19-Oct-06

Name	Rank	Seniority	Name	Rank	Seniority
MCNAMARA Ian	Lt (SCC) RNR	14-Jun-10	NORRIS Anthony	Lt Cdr (SCC) RNR	01-Nov-02
MCNAUGHTAN-OWEN James	Ch RNR	20-Apr-98	NORRIS Peter	Ch RNR	20-Mar-07
MCVEAGH Paul	Ch RNR	31-Aug-04	NORWOOD Paul	Ch RNR	24-Jun-11
MCVINNIE Elizabeth	Lt (SCC) RNR	06-Nov-00	NUNN Jacqui	SLt (SCC) RNR	10-Aug-13
MEADOWS Paul	Lt Cdr (SCC) RNR	01-Apr-08			
MEADOWS Sharon	SLt (SCC) RNR	01-Nov-09	**O**		
MEEK Caroline	Lt (SCC) RNR	06-May-06			
MENDRYS Adam	SLt (SCC) RNR	29-Apr-09	O'DONNELL Adrian	Lt (SCC) RNR	06-Nov-90
MENHAMS Angela	Lt Cdr (SCC) RNR	01-Jan-09	O'DONNELL David	Lt (SCC) RNR	02-Oct-12
MERRIN Roy	Ch RNR	02-Feb-12	O'DONNELL Wendy	SLt (SCC) RNR	01-Feb-05
MERRY ANDREW	Capt (SCC) RMR	29-Oct-11	O'DONOGHUE Amanda	A/Lt Cdr (SCC) RNR	01-Jul-13
MILLER Luke	Ch RNR	11-May-09	O'KEEFFE Richard	Lt Cdr (SCC) RNR	01-May-02
MILLER Martin	Ch RNR	08-Nov-06	O'SULLIVAN Michael	SLt (SCC) RNR	29-Mar-09
MILLIGAN Kevin	A/Lt Cdr (SCC) RNR	30-Mar-12	OGLESBY Simon	Lt (SCC) RNR	08-Dec-05
MILLIGAN Victoria	Lt (SCC) RNR	01-May-98	ORCHARD Richard	Ch RNR	25-Nov-11
MILLS John	Lt (SCC) RNR	04-Oct-04	ORR Jake	Lt (SCC) RNR	30-Apr-12
MILLS William	Lt (SCC) RNR	23-Jun-93	ORR Robert	Lt (SCC) RNR	26-Mar-02
MILNE Janet	Lt Cdr (SCC) RNR	18-Sep-87	ORTON Adrian	Capt (SCC) RMR	01-Jan-99
MITCHELL Alec	Ch RNR	01-Mar-00	OSBORNE Brian	Lt (SCC) RNR	01-Jan-87
MITCHELL Barry	Lt (SCC) RNR	19-Jan-08	OSBORNE Dawn	Lt (SCC) RNR	01-Feb-86
MITCHELL Craig	SLt (SCC) RNR	19-Jan-11	OUTERBRIDGE Julie	SLt (SCC) RNR	06-May-95
MITCHELL Jane	Lt (SCC) RNR	01-Jun-00	OWEN William	Lt (SCC) RNR	05-Jun-96
MITCHELL Ray	Lt Cdr (SCC) RNR	05-Jan-05	OWENS Christopher	A/Lt Cdr (SCC) RNR	11-Nov-13
MITCHISON Robert	Lt (SCC) RNR	12-Jun-10	OWENS Christopher	Ch RNR	17-Jul-09
MOIR Brian	Lt Cdr (SCC) RNR	01-Jan-09			
MOLLART Oliver	SLt (SCC) RNR	06-Dec-13	**P**		
MONKCOM Susan	Lt (SCC) RNR	01-Jan-98			
MONTGOMERY Nina	SLt (SCC) RNR	30-Oct-11	PAGETT Marie	SLt (SCC) RNR	27-Mar-11
MOODY Roger	Lt Cdr (SCC) RNR	01-Jan-85	PAINE Peter	Ch RNR	01-Aug-00
MOONEY Paul	Lt (SCC) RMR	26-Jun-11	PAINTER Lorretta	Lt (SCC) RNR	28-Jan-93
MOORE Brian	Lt (SCC) RNR	23-Nov-08	PALMER Alan	Capt (SCC) RMR	20-Nov-01
MOORE Geoffrey	Ch RNR	18-Oct-07	PARK Peter	Ch RNR	30-Jul-10
MORGAN Angus	SLt (SCC) RNR	25-Jul-10	PARRIS Stephen	Capt (SCC) RMR	01-Jul-99
MORGAN John	Lt (SCC) RNR	10-Feb-88	PARSONS Jack	SLt (SCC) RNR	04-Sep-13
MORGAN Norman John	Lt Cdr (SCC) RNR	23-Jul-04	PARTINGTON Kenneth	Ch RNR	23-May-13
MORRIS Angela	Lt (SCC) RNR	01-Jul-07	PASCOE William	Lt (SCC) RNR	26-Jul-84
MORRIS Kevin	A/Lt Cdr (SCC) RNR	01-Sep-13	PASK Thomas	Lt (SCC) RNR	25-Sep-10
MORTON Rita	Lt (SCC) RNR	13-May-98	PASSANT Keith	Ch RNR	11-Feb-98
MOSLEY E Peter	Ch RNR	10-Sep-12	PATERSON Debbie	A/Lt (SCC) RNR	29-Aug-12
MOULTON Nicholas	Lt Cdr (SCC) RNR	21-Nov-98	PATERSON Gordon	A/Lt Cdr (SCC) RNR	01-Dec-99
MOUNTFORD Robert	Lt (SCC) RNR	30-Mar-13	PATTERSON Paul	Lt (SCC) RNR	01-Jul-00
MOWATT Marleen	SLt (SCC) RNR	02-Jul-06	PATTERSON Phillip	Cdr (SCC) RNR	01-May-10
MOYSE David	Ch RNR	13-Nov-98	PAYNE Derek	Lt Cdr (SCC) RNR	01-Jan-01
MULHOLLAND Ross	Lt Cdr (SCC) RNR	08-Jan-07	PEAKE Christopher	A/SLt (SCC) RNR	10-Nov-13
MULLIN William	Lt (SCC) RNR	10-Nov-86	PEARCE Gaynor	A/SLt (SCC) RNR	24-Mar-13
MUSSELWHITE Ruth	Lt (SCC) RNR	19-Dec-02	PEEL Tracy	SLt (SCC) RNR	26-Jun-11
			PERCHARD Ronald	Lt (SCC) RNR	08-Sep-05
N			PERKIN Simon	Ch RNR	13-Dec-12
			PERKINS Douglas	Ch RNR	16-Apr-10
NAGGS Darren	A/Lt (SCC) RNR	15-Feb-10	PERKINS Jonathon	Lt (SCC) RNR	09-Mar-03
NAIRN Kenneth	Ch RNR	16-Aug-05	PERKINS Kevin	Lt (SCC) RNR	05-Nov-97
NASH Benjamin	SLt (SCC) RNR	28-Jun-09	PERRY Paul	Lt Cdr (SCC) RNR	04-Feb-94
NEEDHAM Peter	Ch RNR	26-Aug-08	PETERS Adam	A/Lt Cdr (SCC) RNR	18-Feb-13
NESLEN Tina	Lt (SCC) RNR	17-Feb-13	PETERS-JONES Lauren	SLt (SCC) RNR	28-Jun-09
NEWMAN Carl	A/SLt (SCC) RNR	09-Sep-12	PETHER Marc	Lt (SCC) RMR	13-Jun-11
NEWMAN Raymond	Lt (SCC) RNR	20-Jul-82	PETHER Phillip	Lt (SCC) RNR	02-Dec-72
NEWTON Robert	Ch RNR	24-Sep-12	PHILIP Charles	Ch RNR	20-Jul-11
NEWTON Simon	Capt (SCC) RMR	09-Dec-11	PHILLIPS Paul	Lt (SCC) RNR	12-Jan-99
NICHOL David	SLt (SCC) RNR	28-Mar-10	PHILPOT Paul	Lt (SCC) RNR	09-May-04
NICHOLLS David	Lt (SCC) RNR	25-Jul-01	PHILPOTT Matthew	2nd Lt (SCC) RMR	02-Nov-08
NICOL-GENT William	SLt (SCC) RNR	26-Jun-11	PICKERING Jean	Lt (SCC) RNR	03-Jul-90
NIMMO Emsley	Ch RNR	03-Jan-90	PIERCY Peter	Lt Cdr (SCC) RNR	25-Oct-86
NIXON Joseph	Lt (SCC) RNR	30-Jun-84	PIKE John	Lt (SCC) RNR	31-May-96

Name	Rank	Seniority
PITSIKAS Anastasios	SLt (SCC) RNR	09-Sep-12
PLUMMER Thomas	Lt (SCC) RNR	24-May-91
POKE Claire	Lt (SCC) RNR	14-Jun-97
POKE David	A/Lt Col(SCC) RMR	11-Nov-13
POLLARD Colin	SLt (SCC) RNR	10-Oct-07
POOLTON Martin	Ch RNR	01-Aug-01
POPE Darren	Lt (SCC) RNR	22-Apr-93
PORTER John	Lt Cdr (SCC) RNR	01-Jan-02
POWELL Diane	Ch RNR	06-May-98
POWELL Robert	Capt (SCC) RMR	24-Sep-01
POWELL Terry	Lt (SCC) RNR	09-Feb-13
POWNALL Edwin	Lt (SCC) RNR	25-Oct-08
PREECE Colin	Ch RNR	16-Dec-98
PRENTICE Paul	Ch RNR	20-Jun-12
PRIEST Derek	Lt (SCC) RNR	17-Jan-12
PRIOR-SANKEY Adrian	Ch RNR	08-Feb-07
PRITCHARD Carol	Lt Cdr (SCC) RNR	05-Oct-08
PRITCHARD David	Lt Cdr (SCC) RNR	01-Jan-95
PROCTER Michael	SLt (SCC) RNR	25-Jul-09
PROLLINS Mark	Lt (SCC) RMR	19-Jan-08
PUGH Heather	Lt Cdr (SCC) RNR	28-Apr-98

Q

Name	Rank	Seniority
QUINN David	Lt (SCC) RMR	17-Aug-13

R

Name	Rank	Seniority
RADCLIFFE Brian	Lt Cdr (SCC) RNR	29-Oct-95
RANKLIN Adam	Lt (SCC) RNR	01-Jan-12
RASHLEIGH Carol	A/Lt (SCC) RNR	01-Jan-14
RAWCLIFFE Michael	Lt (SCC) RNR	17-Apr-98
RAYSON Trevor	Lt Cdr (SCC) RNR	01-Jan-01
READ Christopher	Lt Cdr (SCC) RNR	01-Apr-12
READ Clare	Lt (SCC) RNR	26-Oct-07
REDHEAD Julie	Lt (SCC) RNR	13-Jun-02
REDVERS-HARRIS Jonathan	Ch RNR	23-Apr-03
REEVES Angela	Lt Cdr (SCC) RNR	01-Jan-01
REEVES Mark	Lt (SCC) RNR	11-May-01
REID Jeffery	Lt (SCC) RNR	04-Nov-03
REYNOLDS Lee	A/SLt (SCC) RNR	02-Jun-13
REYNOLDS Nicola	Ch RNR	07-Oct-04
RHODES Adrian	A/Capt (SCC) RMR	15-Apr-12
RIDGWAY Paul	Lt Cdr (SCC) RNR	21-Feb-00
RINGER Philip	Ch RNR	02-Dec-09
ROAF Alistair	SLt (SCC) RNR	07-Jun-96
ROBBINS Allan	Lt Cdr (SCC) RNR	01-Oct-01
ROBERTS Euphemia	Lt Cdr (SCC) RNR	27-Nov-03
ROBERTS Tammy	SLt (SCC) RNR	01-Nov-09
ROBERTSON Robbie	SLt (SCC) RNR	23-Mar-09
ROBINSON Charlotte	SLt (SCC) RNR	09-Oct-13
ROBINSON John	SLt (SCC) RNR	29-Apr-07
ROBINSON Paul	Lt (SCC) RNR	11-Mar-03
ROCK William	Lt (SCC) RNR	12-Nov-00
ROCKEY David	SLt (SCC) RNR	11-Mar-98
ROGERS Carol	Lt (SCC) RNR	26-Feb-10
ROGERS Neil	Lt (SCC) RNR	30-Sep-00
ROGERS Sally-Anne	Lt (SCC) RNR	22-Nov-97
ROLSTON Helen	SLt (SCC) RNR	22-May-08
ROOTS Joseph	Lt (SCC) RNR	21-Sep-01
ROSS David	Lt (SCC) RNR	13-Oct-90
ROSS Malcolm	Lt (SCC) RNR	09-May-95
ROWLAND Sebastian	SLt (SCC) RNR	25-Jul-10

Name	Rank	Seniority
ROWLES David	Lt Cdr (SCC) RNR	03-May-74
ROWLEY Julian	Ch RNR	06-Aug-07
RUSHTON Steven	Lt (SCC) RNR	15-Mar-95
RUSSELL John	Lt (SCC) RNR	01-Nov-89
RUSSELL James	A/Lt Cdr (SCC) RNR	05-Aug-13
RUSSELL Robert	Lt (SCC) RNR	14-Jan-13
RUST Darren	A/SLt (SCC) RNR	02-Jun-13
RUTHERFORD Sarah	SLt (SCC) RNR	08-Oct-10
RYCROFT Louise	Lt (SCC) RNR	25-Sep-10
RYCROFT Paul	Lt Cdr (SCC) RNR	09-Aug-89
RYDER Emma	Lt (SCC) RNR	03-Jul-12

S

Name	Rank	Seniority
SABEY-CORKINDALE Charmaine	Ch RNR	10-Dec-09
SADLER Simonetta	SLt (SCC) RNR	28-Jun-09
SALISBURY Linda	Lt (SCC) RNR	02-Apr-99
SAMIEC George	Ch RNR	15-May-05
SAMUELS Patrick	Ch RNR	19-May-11
SANDERS James	Mid (SCC) RNR	24-Jun-12
SANDERSON Lee	Lt Cdr (SCC) RNR	14-Sep-09
SANDILANDS James	A/Capt (SCC) RNR	06-Jul-13
SANDISON Michael	Ch RNR	08-Dec-08
SAUPE Peter	Lt (SCC) RNR	01-Jul-87
SCHOFIELD Hannah	SLt (SCC) RNR	09-Sep-12
SCHOLES David	Capt (SCC) RMR	01-Jul-99
SCHOLES Peter	A/SLt (SCC) RNR	08-Aug-13
SCHOLES Sian	A/Lt (SCC) RMR	18-Nov-12
SCHUMAN Andrew	Ch RNR	23-Aug-05
SCOTT Guy	Lt (SCC) RNR	10-Oct-11
SEABURY Paul	Lt (SCC) RNR	16-Aug-97
SEARLE David	Ch RNR	27-May-06
SEARLES Andrew	Lt Cdr (SCC) RNR	30-Mar-13
SEDGWICK Mark	Lt (SCC) RNR	03-Jun-00
SEEX Lucy-Anne	SLt (SCC) RNR	25-Mar-12
SEGGIE Andrew	Lt (SCC) RNR	26-Jun-09
SEKKAT Fiona	SLt (SCC) RNR	30-Aug-11
SEYCHELL Charles	Lt (SCC) RNR	01-Jan-90
SHAW David	Lt (SCC) RNR	14-May-84
SHAW Margaret	Ch RNR	30-Jul-00
SHELTON Clive	Lt Cdr (SCC) RNR	24-Apr-98
SHELTON Julie	Lt (SCC) RNR	07-Oct-89
SHEPHERD Carl	Capt (SCC) RMR	21-Nov-08
SHERWIN Peter	Lt Cdr (SCC) RNR	30-Oct-80
SHIELS Robert	Lt Cdr (SCC) RNR	08-Sep-86
SHIELS Suzanne	Lt Cdr (SCC) RNR	01-Apr-06
SHINTON Bertram	Ch RNR	11-Jan-11
SHONE Michael	Lt (SCC) RNR	15-Jun-00
SHORT Keith	Lt Cdr (SCC) RNR	06-Apr-86
SHUTTLEWORTH James	SLt (SCC) RNR	28-Mar-10
SHUTTLEWORTH Tye	Lt (SCC) RNR	27-Jan-13
SICKELMORE Barry	Lt Cdr (SCC) RNR	05-Apr-99
SIDWELL Victoria	Lt (SCC) RNR	09-Jun-10
SIGLEY June	Lt (SCC) RNR	02-May-05
SILK Ian	Ch RNR	24-Apr-08
SILVER Barry-John	Lt (SCC) RNR	30-May-08
SILVERTHORNE Robert	Lt (SCC) RNR	31-Oct-91
SIMISTER Alan	Lt (SCC) RNR	14-Sep-03
SIMM JOHN	A/SLt (SCC) RNR	16-Jan-12
SIMMONS Melvyn	Lt (SCC) RNR	10-Apr-93
SIMPSON Alfred	Lt Cdr (SCC) RNR	08-Feb-84
SIMS Bernard	Ch RNR	01-Nov-94
SIMS Martin	A/SLt (SCC) RNR	02-Jun-13

Name	Rank	Seniority
SINCLAIR Derek	Lt (SCC) RNR	30-Aug-11
SINDEN Daniel-Paul	Lt Cdr (SCC) RNR	01-Nov-10
SKINGLE Stephen	Lt (SCC) RNR	05-May-03
SKINNER Michael	Ch RNR	26-May-07
SMALL Stephen	A/Lt Cdr (SCC) RNR	28-Feb-12
SMEDLEY Monty	SLt (SCC) RNR	21-Aug-04
SMEETON Karen	Ch RNR	27-Nov-09
SMITH Adrian	Lt (SCC) RNR	21-Nov-94
SMITH Deborah	Lt (SCC) RNR	30-Jan-07
SMITH Don	Ch RNR	03-Jul-11
SMITH Frank	SLt (SCC) RNR	30-Oct-12
SMITH Graham	Lt (SCC) RNR	05-Apr-97
SMITH Janet	Lt (SCC) RMR	29-Mar-09
SMITH Lee	SLt (SCC) RNR	01-Nov-12
SMITH Nigel	Ch RNR	04-Apr-01
SMITH Noel	SLt (SCC) RNR	25-Jun-13
SMITH Sally	A/SLt (SCC) RNR	24-Mar-13
SMITH Sean	Capt (SCC) RMR	12-Jun-11
SNEDDEN David	A/Lt Cdr (SCC) RNR	23-Sep-13
SPEAR Keith	Lt (SCC) RNR	06-Jul-12
SPICER David	Lt (SCC) RNR	23-Feb-87
SPICER Janice	Lt (SCC) RNR	01-Jul-87
SPINK James	Lt Cdr (SCC) RNR	01-Apr-07
SPINKS Sally	SLt (SCC) RNR	29-Mar-08
SPREADBRIDGE Paul	Ch RNR	30-Aug-13
SQUIRES Anna	Lt (SCC) RNR	23-Feb-13
SQUIRES John	Lt Cdr (SCC) RNR	01-Jan-07
STAMP Jacqueline	Ch RNR	08-Jan-02
STANIER Tina	Capt (SCC) RMR	21-Jan-08
STEGGALL Mark	Lt Cdr (SCC) RNR	01-Jan-11
STEPHEN Kenneth	Ch RNR	04-Oct-07
STEPHENS Mark	A/Lt (SCC) RMR	24-Jun-12
STEPHENSON Claire	SLt (SCC) RNR	01-Nov-09
STEVENSON David	A/SLt (SCC) RNR	13-Feb-13
STEWART Alan	Lt Cdr (SCC) RNR	01-Jun-07
STEWART Keith	Ch RNR	11-Aug-04
STINTON Douglas	Mid (SCC) RNR	23-Sep-11
STOKER Andrew	Ch RNR	05-Sep-05
STONE Kathleen	SLt (SCC) RNR	21-Nov-04
STONE Terence	Lt (SCC) RNR	26-Feb-91
STONEMAN Allan	A/SLt (SCC) RNR	10-Nov-13
STREET Steven	Lt (SCC) RNR	14-Apr-99
STUPPLES Susan	SLt (SCC) RNR	25-Jul-10
STYLES Marc	Lt (SCC) RNR	21-Nov-09
SUMNER Robert	Lt (SCC) RNR	06-Dec-99
SUMPTER Clive	Lt (SCC) RNR	10-Jul-11
SURREY Elizabeth	SLt (SCC) RNR	03-Aug-08
SUTTON Ryan	A/Lt (SCC) RMR	03-Dec-07
SVENDSEN Peter	Lt Cdr (SCC) RNR	01-May-02
SWARBRICK David	Lt (SCC) RNR	15-Jan-99
SWATTON Jennifer	SLt (SCC) RNR	01-Feb-11
SWEETING Peter	Ch RNR	18-Jun-03

T

Name	Rank	Seniority
TAIT Graham	Lt Cdr (SCC) RNR	01-Jul-08
TANNER Roland	Lt Cdr (SCC) RNR	21-Jul-87
TAPP Maria	Lt (SCC) RNR	23-Oct-95
TAYLOR Ashleigh	A/SLt (SCC) RNR	24-Mar-13
TAYLOR Alexander	Lt (SCC) RNR	09-Aug-13
TAYLOR Fay	Lt (SCC) RNR	21-Jan-06
TAYLOR Roy	A/Lt (SCC) RNR	14-Feb-11
TAYLOR Sheila	Lt (SCC) RNR	03-May-11

Name	Rank	Seniority
TEBBY Christine	Lt (SCC) RNR	05-Sep-89
TEMPLE Edward	Lt Cdr (SCC) RNR	14-Oct-91
TEMPLETON James	Ch RNR	14-Aug-98
THACKERY Richard	Lt Cdr (SCC) RNR	01-Jan-08
THEOBALD Robert	Lt (SCC) RNR	11-Sep-90
THEOBALD Wendy	Lt Cdr (SCC) RNR	01-Jan-96
THICKETT David	Lt (SCC) RNR	11-May-08
THOMAS Alan	Lt (SCC) RNR	14-Apr-98
THOMAS Christopher	Ch RNR	12-Sep-05
THOMAS Michael	Lt (SCC) RNR	19-Jul-80
THOMAS Nancy	Ch RNR	12-Apr-00
THOMAS Stephen	SLt (SCC) RNR	02-Jul-06
THOMAS William	Lt Cdr (SCC) RNR	01-May-07
THOMPSON David	Lt (SCC) RMR	18-Jun-10
THOMPSON Mark	SLt (SCC) RNR	30-Oct-11
THOMSON Andrew	Lt (SCC) RNR	07-Apr-95
THOMSON Robert	Lt (SCC) RNR	17-Mar-71
THORN Simon	Ch RNR	18-Nov-10
THURGOOD Anthony	A/Lt (SCC) RNR	08-Feb-13
THURLAND Joseph	Lt (SCC) RMR	23-Oct-07
TILLBROOK Richard	Ch RNR	18-Mar-09
TIMOTHY Emile	Maj (SCC) RMR	01-Jul-99
TITLEY John	Lt (SCC) RNR	04-May-93
TOBIN Richard	Ch RNR	27-Feb-06
TOLLEY George	SLt (SCC) RNR	27-Sep-10
TORBETT Philippa	Lt (SCC) RNR	09-Apr-04
TOWNSEND Graham	Lt Cdr (SCC) RNR	01-Jan-11
TOWNSEND Stephen	SLt (SCC) RNR	30-Mar-03
TRAHAIR Estella	Lt (SCC) RNR	01-Apr-06
TRANTER John	Ch RNR	22-Feb-07
TRICK Matthew	Ch RNR	08-Oct-12
TROJAN Margaret	Lt (SCC) RNR	30-Nov-99
TROTT Dwayne	A/Lt (SCC) RNR	01-Jul-00
TRUELOVE Gary	Lt Cdr (SCC) RNR	01-Jul-04
TRUSCOTT Gary	Lt Cdr (SCC) RNR	01-Jan-96
TRUSCOTT Sally	SLt (SCC) RNR	28-Jun-09
TRUSWELL Jacqueline	Lt (SCC) RNR	03-Nov-07
TRUSWELL Simon	SLt (SCC) RNR	01-Nov-09
TSANG Wing	Ch RNR	15-Mar-10
TUDOR Simon	Lt (SCC) RNR	28-Sep-12
TULLY S.	SLt (SCC) RNR	16-Nov-00
TURNER Ian	Lt Cdr (SCC) RNR	01-Jan-07
TURNER Mark	SLt (SCC) RNR	28-Jun-09
TURNER Sarah-Jane	Lt (SCC) RNR	23-Nov-08
TWEED Alan	Lt (SCC) RNR	06-Jan-93
TYSON Michael	Lt (SCC) RNR	22-Mar-83

U

Name	Rank	Seniority
UMFREVILLE Robert	SLt (SCC) RNR	10-Dec-13
UNDERWOOD Andrew	A/SLt (SCC) RNR	03-Oct-13
UNSWORTH John	Lt (SCC) RNR	11-May-08
URQUHART John	Lt Cdr (SCC) RNR	01-Nov-04
UTTING Joseph	A/Lt Cdr (SCC) RNR	01-Jan-14

V

Name	Rank	Seniority
VALENTINE Andrew	SLt (SCC) RNR	26-Jun-11
VAN-HENTEN Nicola	SLt (SCC) RNR	01-Nov-09
VANDENBERGH Victor	Ch RNR	07-Nov-05
VANDERLELY Jan	Ch RNR	18-Sep-13
VANNS Jonathan	Lt Cdr (SCC) RNR	06-Nov-06
VOKES Simon	Lt (SCC) RNR	27-Jan-07

Name	Rank	Seniority

W

Name	Rank	Seniority
WADDINGTON Janet	Ch RNR	01-Nov-92
WAGSTAFF Paul	A/Maj (SCC) RMR	09-Aug-13
WAGSTAFF Voirrey	Lt (SCC) RMR	28-Mar-10
WALES Stephen Francis	Ch RNR	30-Aug-13
WALKER Keith	Lt (SCC) RNR	05-Feb-88
WALKER Pamela	Lt (SCC) RNR	01-Jun-07
WALKER Stanley	Ch RNR	01-Feb-89
WALLACE Douglas	Ch RNR	24-Aug-06
WALLACE Thomas	Lt (SCC) RNR	01-Apr-06
WALSH Joshua	Mid (SCC) RNR	10-Nov-13
WALSH Richard	SLt (SCC) RNR	28-Mar-10
WANLISS Hector	Lt (SCC) RNR	21-Jan-13
WARD Christopher	Mid (SCC) RNR	24-Mar-13
WARD John	Lt Cdr (SCC) RNR	01-Oct-03
WARD June	Ch RNR	18-Aug-11
WARE-JARRETT David	Ch RNR	17-Jun-08
WARING Peter	Lt Cdr (SCC) RNR	01-Jan-09
WARNER Derrick	Lt (SCC) RNR	01-May-13
WARWICK Stephen	Lt (SCC) RNR	12-Mar-98
WASLEY John	Ch RNR	01-Feb-01
WATERFIELD Robert	SLt (SCC) RNR	27-Mar-11
WATERS Scott	Lt (SCC) RNR	21-Apr-94
WATKINS Colin	Lt Cdr (SCC) RNR	17-Nov-03
WATSON Adrian	Lt (SCC) RNR	06-May-06
WATSON Sheila	Lt (SCC) RNR	04-Feb-00
WAYLETT Graham	Lt Cdr (SCC) RNR	01-Apr-01
WAYLETT Matthew	A/Lt Cdr (SCC) RNR	01-Aug-11
WEBB Colin	Lt (SCC) RNR	17-Nov-95
WEBB John	Lt Cdr (SCC) RNR	09-Nov-85
WEBB John	Lt Cdr (SCC) RNR	28-Aug-03
WEBSTER John	Lt Cdr (SCC) RNR	14-Dec-90
WELSH Michelle	Lt Cdr (SCC) RNR	01-Jan-09
WEOBLEY Malcolm	Maj (SCC) RMR	23-Aug-86
WEST Phil	SLt (SCC) RNR	29-Jun-08
WEST Timothy	A/Lt (SCC) RNR	01-Nov-12
WESTON Mark	Lt Cdr (SCC) RNR	01-Jan-10
WESTOVER Robert	Lt (SCC) RNR	09-Jun-78
WHATMOUGH Mark	Lt (SCC) RMR	25-Sep-10
WHEATLEY Noel	Cdr (SCC) RNR	01-Aug-09
WHITE David	Lt (SCC) RNR	29-Nov-02
WHITE Robert	Lt Cdr (SCC) RNR	01-May-08
WHITEAR Colin	A/Lt (SCC) RNR	01-Jan-12
WHITEHEAD Adam	A/SLt (SCC) RMR	02-Jun-13
WHITEHEAD Michael	A/SLt (SCC) RNR	10-Nov-13
WHITLEY Glenda	Lt (SCC) RNR	08-May-87
WHITLEY Roger	Lt (SCC) RNR	14-Apr-99
WHITTLESEA Grahame	Ch RNR	09-Oct-01
WHORWOOD Julia	Lt (SCC) RNR	07-May-97
WICKENDEN Frances	Lt (SCC) RNR	14-Oct-00
WILKES Robert	Ch RNR	28-Jun-11
WILKINSON David	Lt (SCC) RNR	01-Feb-06
WILKINSON Graeme	SLt (SCC) RNR	29-Mar-09
WILKS Stephen	Lt (SCC) RNR	27-Jul-01
WILLETT Marion	Lt (SCC) RNR	21-Dec-88
WILLIAMS Alan	Lt Cdr (SCC) RNR	01-May-84
WILLIAMS David	Lt (SCC) RNR	15-Mar-00
WILLIAMS Deborah	Lt (SCC) RNR	04-Nov-92
WILLIAMS David Neil	SLt (SCC) RNR	26-Mar-00
WILLIAMS John	Ch RNR	13-Oct-00
WILLIAMS Michael	A/Lt Cdr (SCC) RNR	01-Mar-12
WILLIAMS Susan	Lt (SCC) RNR	26-Mar-02
WILLIS David	Ch RNR	01-Dec-11
WILSON Ethel	Lt (SCC) RNR	01-Nov-98
WILSON George	Lt Cdr (SCC) RNR	01-Jan-11
WILSON Ian	Cdr (SCC) RNR	17-Nov-12
WISHART Michael	Ch RNR	18-Aug-12
WITHAM Susan	Ch RNR	22-May-13
WOOD Norman	Lt Cdr (SCC) RNR	01-Mar-90
WOODWARD Stewart	Lt Cdr (SCC) RNR	26-Oct-84
WOOLGAR Victor	Lt Cdr (SCC) RNR	01-Apr-88
WRIGHT Alan	Lt (SCC) RNR	29-Apr-12
WYLIE William	Lt Cdr (SCC) RNR	05-Dec-83
WYNNE David	Lt (SCC) RNR	21-Apr-93

Y

Name	Rank	Seniority
YATES Daniel	Lt (SCC) RNR	03-Apr-09
YORKE Barrie	Lt (SCC) RNR	01-Jul-87
YOUNG Barry	Lt (SCC) RNR	17-Feb-13
YOUNG Craig	A/SLt (SCC) RNR	29-Jul-13
YOUNG Rosalyn	Ch RNR	24-Jun-10
YUILLE Benjamin	2nd Lt (SCC) RMR	24-Mar-13

YACHT CLUBS USING A SPECIAL ENSIGN

Yachts belonging to members of the following Yacht Clubs may, subject to certain conditions, obtain a Warrant to wear a Special Ensign.

Club	Address (where applicable)

WHITE ENSIGN

Royal Yacht Squadron	Royal Yacht Squadron, The Castle, Cowes, Isle of Wight PO31 7QT

BLUE ENSIGN

Royal Naval Club & Royal Albert Yacht Club	17 Pembroke Road, Portsmouth PO1 2NT
Royal Brighton Yacht Club	253 The Esplanade, Middle Brighton, Victoria 3186, Australia
Royal Cinque Ports Yacht Club	5 Waterloo Crescent, Dover CT16 1LA
Royal Cruising Club	C/O Royal Thames Yacht Club, 60 Knightsbridge, London SW1X 7LF
Royal Dorset Yacht Club	11 Custom House Quay, Weymouth DT4 8BG
Royal Engineer Yacht Club	BATCIS DT, Yew 0 1039, MOD Abbeywood, Bristol BS36 8JH
Royal Geelong Yacht Club	P.O. Box 156, Geelong, Victoria 3220, Australia
Royal Gourock Yacht Club	Ashton, Gourock PA19 1DA
Royal Highland Yacht Club	Achavraid, Clachan, Tarbert PA29 6XN
Royal Marines Sailing Club	
Royal Melbourne Yacht Squadron	P.O. Box 2001, St Kilda West, Victoria 3182, Australia
Royal Motor Yacht Club	Panorama Road, Sandbanks, Poole BH13 7RN
Royal Naval Sailing Association	10 Haslar Marina, Haslar Road, Gosport PO12 1NU
Royal Naval Volunteer Reserve Yacht Club	The Naval Club, 38 Hill Street, Mayfair, London W1X 8DB
Royal New Zealand Yacht Squadron	P.O. Box 46 182, Herne Bay, Auckland 1147, New Zealand
Royal Northern and Clyde Yacht Club	Rhu, By Helensburgh G84 8NG
Royal Perth Yacht Club of Western Australia	P.O. Box 5, Nedlands, Western Australia 6909

Royal Port Nicholson Yacht Club......................................Clyde Quay Boat Harbour, P.O. Box 9674, Wellington, New Zealand

Royal Queensland Yacht Squadron .................................P.O. Box 5021, Manly, Queensland 4179, Australia

Royal Scottish Motor Yacht Club ....35 Brueacre Drive, Wemyss Bay PA18 6HA

Royal Solent Yacht Club ....The Square, Yarmouth, Isle of Wight PO41 0NS

Royal South Australian Yacht Squadron .........................P.O. Box 1066, North Haven, South Australia 5018

Royal Southern Yacht Club..Rope Walk, Hamble, Southampton SO31 4HB

Royal Sydney Yacht Squadron ....P.O. Box 484, Milson's Point, New South Wales 1565

Royal Temple Yacht Club...6 Westcliff Mansions, Ramsgate CT11 9HY

Royal Thames Yacht Club..60 Knightsbridge, London SW1X 7LF

Royal Victorian Motor Yacht Club ....260 Nelson Place, Williamstown, Victoria 3016, Australia

Royal Western Yacht Club of England ....Queen Anne's Battery, Plymouth PL4 0TW

Royal Western Yacht Club of Scotland............................Shandon, Helensburgh G84 8NP

Royal Yacht Club of Tasmania...Marieville Esplanade, Sandy Bay, Tasmania 7005, Australia

Royal Yacht Club of Victoria..................... ....120 Nelson Place, Williamstown, Victoria 3016, Australia

Sussex Motor Yacht Club ...'..

BLUE ENSIGN DEFACED BY BADGE OF CLUB

Aldeburgh Yacht Club...Slaughden Road, Aldeburgh IP15 5NA

Army Sailing Association ....Clayton Barracks, Thornhill Road, Aldershot GU11 2BG

Bar Yacht Club ....47 Tower Bridge Wharf, 86 St Katharines Way, London E1W 1UR

City Livery Yacht Club ....79 Palace Gardens Terrace, London W8 4EE

Conway Club Cruising Association...................................

Cruising Yacht Club of Australia......................................New Beach Road, Darling Point, New South Wales 2027, Australia

Household Division Yacht Club...RHQ Scots Guards, Wellington Barracks, Birdcage Walk, London SW1E 6HQ

Little Ship Club ....Bell Wharf Lane, Upper Thames Street, London EC4R 3TB

Little Ship Club (Queensland Squadron) .......................P.O. Box 8036, Cleveland 4183, Queensland, Australia

Medway Cruising Club..Anchorage Yard, Waterside Lane, Gillingham ME7 2SE

Old Worcesters Yacht Club...21 Brunel Quays, Lostwithiel, PL22 0JB

Parkstone Yacht Club...Pearce Avenue, Parkstone, Poole BH14 8EH

Rochester Cruising Yacht Club ....10 The Esplanade, Rochester ME1 1QN

Royal Air Force Yacht Club ....Riverside House, Rope Walk, Hamble, Southampton SO31 4HD

Royal Akarana Yacht Club...P.O. Box 42-004, Orakei, Auckland, New Zealand

Royal Anglesey Yacht Club...6-7 Green Edge, Beaumaris LL58 8BY

Royal Armoured Corps Yacht Club ....Kings Royal Hussars, Aliwall Barracks, Tidworth SP9 7BB

Royal Artillery Yacht Club..

Royal Australian Navy Sailing Association ....Edgecliffe, New South Wales 2027, Australia

Royal Bermuda Yacht Club...P.O. Box 894, Hamilton HM DX, Bermuda

Royal Bombay Yacht Club ....P.O. Box 206, Apollo Bunder, Fort Bombay, 400 001, Mumbai, India

Royal Burnham Yacht Club...The Quay, Burnham-on-Crouch, CM0 8AU

Royal Channel Islands Yacht Club...................................Le Mont du Boulevard, St Brelade, Jersey JE3 8AD

Royal Corinthian Yacht Club...The Quay, Burnham-on-Crouch, CM0 8AX

Royal Cornwall Yacht Club..Greenbank, Falmouth TR11 2SP

Royal Dee Yacht Club...Siglen, Pulford, Chester CH4 9EL

Royal Forth Yacht Club...Middle Pier, Granton Harbour, Edinburgh EH5 1HF

Royal Freshwater Bay Yacht Club of Western Australia ...Keanes Point, Peppermint Grove, 6011, Western Australia, Australia

Royal Gibraltar Yacht Club ....26 Queensway, Gibraltar

Royal Hamilton Yacht Club...Foot of McNab Street North, Hamilton, Ontario, Canada

Royal Harwich Yacht Club ....Wolverstone, Ipswich IP9 1AT

Royal Hong Kong Yacht Club ....Kellett Island, Causeway Bay, Hong King

Royal Irish Yacht Club ....Harbour Road, Dun Laoghaire,
County Dublin, Eire

Royal Jamaica Yacht Club..Norman Manly International Airport,
Palisadoes Park, Kingston, Jamaica

Royal London Yacht Club ....The Parade, Cowes, Isle of Wight PO31 7QS

Royal Malta Yacht Club..Couvre Point, Fort Manoel, Manoel Island,
Gzira, Malta

Royal Mersey Yacht Club..Bedford Road East, Rock Ferry,
Birkenhead CH42 1LS

Royal Motor Yacht Club of New South Wales.................Wunulla Road, Point Piper 2027,
New South Wales, Australia

Royal Nassau Sailing Club ....P.O. Box SS 6891, Nassau, Bahamas

Royal Natal Yacht Club...P.O. Box 2946, Durban 4000, South Africa

Royal North of Ireland Yacht Club ....7 Seafront Road, Holywood,
County Down BT18 OBB

Royal Northumberland Yacht Club ....South Harbour, Blyth NE24 3PB

Royal Ocean Racing Club ....20 St James' Place, London SW1A 1NN

Royal Plymouth Corinthian Yacht Club ....Madeira Road, The Barbican
Plymouth PL1 2NY

Royal Prince Alfred Yacht Club .....................................P.O. Box 99, Newport Beach 2106,
New South Wales, Australia

Royal Prince Edward Yacht Club...................................P.O. Box 2502 Bondi Junction,
New South Wales 1355, Australia

Royal Southampton Yacht Club....................................1 Channel Way, Ocean Village,
Southampton SO14 3QF

Royal Suva Yacht Club ....P.O. Box 335 Suva, Republic of Fiji

Royal Torbay Yacht Club...12 Beacon Terrace, Torquay TQ1 2BH

Royal Ulster Yacht Club...101 Clifton Road, Bangor,
County Down BT20 5HY

Royal Welsh Yacht Club ....Porth Yr Aur Caernarfon LL55 1SN

Royal Yorkshire Yacht Club...1-3 Windsor Crescent, Bridlington YO15 3HX

Severn Motor Yacht Club..Bath Road, Broomhall, Worcester WR5 3HR

Sussex Yacht Club..85-89 Brighton Road,
Shoreham-by-Sea BN43 6RE

Thames Motor Yacht Club...The Green, Hampton Court, Surrey KT8 9BW

The Cruising Association ....CA House, 1 Northey Street, Limehouse Basin, London E14 8BT

The House of Lords Yacht Club ....Overseas Office, House of Lords, London SW1A 0PW

The Medway Yacht Club...Lower Upnor, Rochester ME2 4XB

The Poole Harbour Yacht Club ....

The Poole Yacht Club...The Yacht Haven, New Harbour Road West, Hamworthy, Poole, BH15 4AQ

RED ENSIGN DEFACED BY BADGE OF CLUB

Brixham Yacht Club ....Overgang, Brixham TQ5 8AR

House of Commons Yacht Club ....C/O RYA, RYA House, Ensign Way, Hamble, Southampton SO31 4YA

Lloyd's Yacht Club..

Royal Dart Yacht Club ....Priory Street, Kingswear, Dartmouth TQ6 0AB

Royal Fowey Yacht Club..Whitford Yard, Fowey PL23 1BH

Royal Hamilton Amateur Dinghy Club............................P.O. Box 298 Paget PG BX, Bermuda

Royal Lymington Yacht Club..Bath Road, Lymington SO41 3SE

Royal Norfolk and Suffolk Yacht Club............................Royal Plain, Lowestoft NR33 0AQ

Royal St George Yacht Club ....Dun Laoghaire, County Dublin, Eire

Royal Victoria Yacht Club ....91 Fishbourne Lane, Ryde, Isle of Wight PO33 4EU

Royal Windermere Yacht Club.......................................Fallbarrow Road, Bowness-on-Windermere LA33 3DJ

St Helier Yacht Club ....South Pier, St Helier, Jersey JE2 3NB

West Mersea Yacht Club...116 Coast Road, West Mersea, Colchester CO5 8PB

DEFACED RAF ENSIGN

The RAF Sailing Association...HQ Air Command, RAF High Wycombe, HP14 4UE

ROYAL NAVAL RESERVE AND OTHER VESSELS AUTHORISED TO FLY THE BLUE ENSIGN IN MERCHANT VESSELS (FOREIGN OR HOME TRADE ARTICLES) AND FISHING VESSELS

1. A list of Royal Naval Reserve and other vessels authorised to fly the Blue Ensign will no longer be published in the Navy List.

2. It inclusion was intended for the information of Captains of Her Majesty's Ships with reference to provisions of Article 9153 of the Queen's Regulations for the Royal Navy under which they are authorised to ascertain whether British Merchant Ships (including Fishing Vessels) flying the Blue Ensign of Her Majesty's Fleet are legally entitled to do so.

3. However, the usefulness of this list serves only a limited purpose as the list of vessels that could fly the Blue Ensign can change frequently. British merchant ships and fishing vessels are allowed to wear the plain Blue Ensign under the authority of a special Warrant, subject to certain conditions being fulfilled, and which are outlined below.

4. Vessels registered on the British Registry of Shipping may wear a plain Blue Ensign providing the master or skipper is in possession of a warrant issued by the Commander Maritime Reserves under the authority of the Secretary of State for Defence, and the additional conditions outlined below are fulfilled. The Blue Ensign is to be struck if the officer to whom the warrant was issued relinquishes command, or if the ship or vessel passes into foreign ownership and ceases to be a British ship as defined by MSA 95.

    a. Vessels on Parts I, II and IV of the Register. The master must be an officer of the rank of lieutenant RN/RNR or Captain RM/RMR or above in the Royal Fleet Reserve or the maritime forces of a United Kingdom Overseas Territory or Commonwealth country of which Her Majesty is Head of State, or an officer on the Active or Retired Lists of any branch of the maritime reserve forces of those countries or territories.

    b. Vessels on Part II of the Register. This part of the Register is reserved for fishing vessels. The skipper must comply with the same criteria as for sub-clause 4.a. above, however the crew must contain at least four members, each of whom fulfils at least one of the following criteria:

    Royal Naval or Royal Marine reservists or pensioner Reservists or pensioners from a Commonwealth monarchy or United Kingdom Overseas Territory, Ex-ratings or Royal Marines who have completed twenty years service in the Reserves, members of the Royal Fleet Reserve.

5. Action on sighting a merchant ship wearing a Blue Ensign. The Commanding Officer of one of HM ships on meeting a vessel wearing the Blue Ensign may send on board a commissioned officer to confirm that the criteria outlined above are being met in full. If it is found that the ship is wearing a Blue Ensign, without authority of a proper warrant, the ensign is to be seized, taken away and forfeited to the Sovereign and the circumstances reported to the Royal Naval Reserves, acting on behalf of the Chief of Naval Personnel and Training/Second Sea Lord, who maintains the list of persons authorised to hold such warrants.

    However, if it is found that, despite the warrant being sighted, the ship is failing to comply with the criteria in some other particular, the ensign is not to be seized but the circumstances are to be reported to the Commander Maritime Reserves.

HM SHIPS BFPO NUMBERS

ALBION (Albion)
BFPO 204

AMBUSH (Astute)
BFPO 205

ARGYLL (Type 23)
BFPO 210

ASTUTE (Astute)
BFPO 214

BANGOR (Sandown)
BFPO 222

BLYTH (Sandown)
BFPO 221

BULWARK (Albion)
BFPO 243

CATTISTOCK (Hunt)
BFPO 251

CHIDDINGFOLD (Hunt)
BFPO 254

CLYDE (River)
BFPO 255

DARING (Type 45)
BFPO 270

DASHER (P2000)
BFPO 271

DAUNTLESS (Type 45)
BFPO 272

DIAMOND (Type 45)
BFPO 273

DRAGON
BFPO 268

ECHO (SVHO)
BFPO 275

ENTERPRISE (SVHO)
BFPO 276

GLEANER (CSV)
BFPO 288

GRIMSBY (Sandown)
BFPO 292

HURWORTH (Hunt)
BFPO 300

ILLUSTRIOUS (Invincible)
BFPO 305

IRON DUKE (Type 23)
BFPO 309

KENT (Type 23)
BFPO 318

LANCASTER (Type 23)
BFPO 323

LEDBURY (Hunt)
BFPO 324

MERSEY (River)
BFPO 334

MONMOUTH (Type 23)
BFPO 338

MONTROSE (Type 23)
BFPO 339

NORTHUMBERLAND (Type 23)
BFPO 345

OCEAN (LPH)
BFPO 350

PEMBROKE (Sandown)
BFPO 357

PENZANCE (Sandown)
BFPO 358

PORTLAND (Type 23)
BFPO 361

PROTECTOR (Antarctic Patrol Ship)
BFPO 367

PURSUER (P2000)
BFPO 363

QUEEN ELIZABETH (Carrier)
BFPO 365

QUORN (Hunt)
BFPO 366

RAMSEY (Sandown)
BFPO 368

RICHMOND (Type 23)
BFPO 375

SABRE (Fast Patrol)
BFPO 378

SCIMITAR (Fast Patrol)
BFPO 384

SCOTT (OSV)
BFPO 381

SEVERN (River)
BFPO 382

SHOREHAM (Sandown)
BFPO 386

SOMERSET (Type 23)
BFPO 395

ST ALBANS (Type 23)
BFPO 399

SUTHERLAND (Type 23)
BFPO 398

TALENT (Trafalgar)
BFPO 401

TORBAY (Trafalgar)
BFPO 403

TRENCHANT (Trafalgar)
BFPO 405

TRIUMPH (Trafalgar)
BFPO 406

TURBULENT (Trafalgar)
BFPO 408

TYNE (River)
BFPO 412

VANGUARD (Vanguard)
BFPO 418

VENGEANCE (Vanguard)
BFPO 421

VICTORIOUS (Vanguard)
BFPO 419

VIGILANT (Vanguard)
BFPO 420

WESTMINSTER (Type 23)
BFPO 426

Since the last edition of the Navy List was published, the following ships have been decommissioned:

HMS LIVERPOOL
HMS MIDDLETON
HMS EDINBURGH
HMS TIRELESS

SHIPS OF THE ROYAL FLEET AUXILIARY SERVICE

ARGUS, Aviation Training Ship
BFPO 433

BLACK ROVER, Small Fleet Tanker
BFPO 435

CARDIGAN BAY, Bay Class Landing Ship
BFPO 436

DILIGENCE, Forward Repair Ship
BFPO 438

FORT AUSTIN, Fleet Replenishment Ship
BFPO 439

FORT ROSALIE, Fleet Replenishment Ship
BFPO 441

FORT VICTORIA, Fleet Replenishment Ship
BFPO 442

GOLD ROVER, Small Fleet Tanker
BFPO 443

LYME BAY, Bay Class Landing Ship
BFPO 447

MOUNTS BAY, Bay Class Landing Ship
BFPO 448

ORANGELEAF, Support Tanker
BFPO 449

WAVE KNIGHT, Fast Fleet Tanker
BFPO 432

WAVE RULER, Fast Fleet Tanker
BFPO 431

ABBREVIATIONS OF RANKS USED BY JPA

A/ .... Acting
Adm .... Admiral
Adm of Fleet... Admiral of The Fleet
Brig..Brigadier
Capt ....Captain, Royal Marines
Capt, RN..Captain, Royal Navy
Cdr..Commander
Cdre ....Commodore
Chpln of The Fleet ....Chaplain of The Fleet
Col .... Colonel
FTRS .... Full Time Reserve Service
Gen .... General
Lt..Lieutenant, Royal Marines
Lt Cdr ....Lieutenant Commander
Lt Col... Lieutenant Colonel
Lt Gen .... Lieutenant General
Lt RN .... Lieutenant, Royal Navy
Maj.. Major
Maj Gen .... Major General
Mid.. Midshipman
OCdt ....Officer Cadet
R Adm .... Rear Admiral
RN Chpln ....Chaplain, Royal Navy
RN Prncpl Chpln ....Chaplain, Royal Navy
RNR Chaplain.. Royal Naval Reserve Chaplain
SLt..Sub-Lieutenant
Surg.. Surgeon
Surg (D) .... Surgeon (Dental)
V Adm...Vice Admiral
2Lt... Second Lieutenant, Royal Marines

LIST OF BRANCH ABBREVIATIONS

CS .... Careers Service
Ch S ....Chaplaincy Service
DENTAL .... Dental
ENG.. Engineering
LOGS... Logistics
MED .... Medical
QARNNS..Queen Alexandra's Royal Naval Nursing Service
RM ....Royal Marines
RMR .... Royal Marines Reserve
RNR ....Royal Naval Reserve
WAR...Warfare

LIST OF MAIN TRADE ABBREVIATIONS

AE	Air Engineer
AE O	Air Engineer Observer
AE P	Air Engineer Pilot
ATC	Air Traffic Controller
AV	Aviation
BAR	Barrister
BS	Royal Marines Band Service
C	Communications
CIS	Communication Information Specialist
CMA	Management Accountant
CONSULTANT	Consultant
FAA	Fleet Air Arm
FC	Fighter Controller
FS	Family Services
GDP	General Dental Practitioner
GD (RES)	General Duties (Reserves)
GMP	General Medical Practitioner
GS	General Service
GSX	General Service Warfare
L	Logistics
LC	Landing Craft
MCD	Mine Warfare Clearance Diver
ME	Marine Engineering
MESM	Marine Engineering Submariner
METOC	Meteorology & Oceanography
MLDR	Mountain Leader
MS	Medical Services
MW	Mine Warfare
O	Observer
O LYNX	Observer Lynx
O MER	Observer Merlin
O SK6	Observer Sea King 6
O SKW	Observer Sea King AEW
OTSPEC	Operating Theatre Specialist
O UT	Observer Under Training
P	Pilot
P GAZ	Pilot Gazelle
P GR7	Pilot Harrier GR7
P GR9	Pilot Harrier GR9
P HAWK	Pilot Hawk
P HELO	Pilot Helicopter
P LYN7	Pilot Lynx 7
P LYNX	Pilot Lynx
P MER	Pilot Merlin

P SHAR ....Pilot Sea Harrier
P SK4..Pilot Sea King 4
P SK6..Pilot Sea King 6
P SKW ....Sea King AEW
P UT...Pilot Under Training
PWO...Principal Warfare Officer
PWO(A)...Principal Warfare Officer (Above Water)
PWO(C) ....Principal Warfare Officer (Communications)
PWO(N) ....Principal Warfare Officer (Navigator)
PWO(U) ....Principal Warfare Officer (Underwater)
REG ....Regulator
SCC ....Senior Corps Commission
SM...Submariner
TM...Training Management
UT ....Under Training
WE ....Weapons Engineering
WESM ....Weapons Engineer Submarines

ABBREVIATIONS OF ORGANISATIONS WHERE OFFICERS SERVE
WHEN NOT AT SEA

1 ACC ....1 Air Control Centre
1 ASSLT GP RM.. 1 Assault Group Royal Marines
1 PWRR. .... .1st Battalion Princess of Wales Royal Regiment
1 REGT AAC .... 1 Regiment Army Air Corps
1 IG. ....,. .... 1st Battalion Irish Guards
1 RIFLES.., ...1st Battalion the Rifles
10 TRG SQN 1 ASSLT GP RM................. 10 Training Squadron, 1 Assault Group Royal Marines
11 (ATT) SQN................................. 11 (Amphibious Trials & Training) Squadron, Royal Marines
101 LOG BDE...101 Logistics Brigade
102 LOG BDE...102 Logistics Brigade
148 FO BTY RA............ .148 (Meiktila) Commando Forward Observation Battery Royal Artillery
1SL/CNS... . First Sea Lord & Chief of Naval Staff
202 SQN – E FLT .... E Flight, 202 Squadron Royal Air Force
26 REGT RA..26 Regiment, Royal Artillery
3 CDO BDE RM   .... 3 Commando Brigade Royal Marines
3 REGT AAC .... 3 Regiment Army Air Corps
30 CDO IX GP RM..................... 30 Commando Information Exploitation Group Royal Marines
4 REGT AAC .... 4 Regiment Army Air Corps
40 CDO RM.. .. 40 Commando Royal Marines
42 CDO RM...42 Commando Royal Marines
45 CDO RM.. .. 45 Commando Royal Marines
5 REGT AAC .... .5 Regt Army Air Corps
5 SCOTS .... 5th Battalion the Royal Regiment of Scotland
539 ASSLT SQN RM ....539 Assault Squadron Royal Marines
7 AA BN REME..........................7 Air Assault Battalion, Royal Electrical & Mechanical Engineers

AACen.. Army Aviation Centre
ACHQ... Air Command Headquarters
ACDS(Nuc & Chem, Bio)........ Assistant Chief of Defence Staff (Nuclear & Chemical, Biological)
ACNS(A&C) ....Assistant Chief of Naval Staff (Aviation & Carriers)
ACNS(Cap) .... Assistant Chief of Naval Staff (Capability)
ACNS(Pers)/NAVSEC.................... . Assistant Chief of Naval Staff (Personnel) & Naval Secretary
ACNS(Pol)...Assistant Chief of Naval Staff (Policy)
AFCC .... Armed Forces Chaplaincy Centre
AIB .... Admiralty Interview Board
ARRC ....Allied Rapid Reaction Corps
ASG RM .... Armoured Support Group, Royal Marines
AWC .... Air Warfare Centre
BDS .... British Defence Section
BF BIOT.. ..British Forces British Indian Ocean Territory
BF C .... British Forces Cyprus
BF G .... British Forces Germany
BF GIBRALTAR...British Forces Gibraltar
BFSAI... British Forces South Atlantic Islands
BFPO.. British Forces Post Office
BMATT... British Military Attache
BMM ....British Military Mission
BRNC .... .Britannia Royal Naval College
CATCS ....Central Air Traffic Control School
CATD .... .Combined Arms Tactics Division
CDI..Chief of Defence Intelligence
CDO LOG REGT RM............................. Commando Logistics Regiment Royal Marines
CFPS...Commander, Fishery Protection Squad
CGRM .... Commandant General Royal Marines
CHF HQ .... Commando Helicopter Force, Headquarters
CJO ....Chief of Joint Operations
CNP&T/2SL .... Chief of Naval Personnel & Training and Second Sea Lord
CoM(Fleet)/CFS.......................... Chief of Materiel (Fleet) and Chief of Fleet Support
COM(Ops)... Commander, Operations
COMPORFLOT... Commodore, Portsmouth Flotilla
COMUKAMPHIBFOR .... Commander UK Amphibious Forces
COMUKMARFOR ....Commander UK Maritime Forces
COMUKTG ....Commander United Kingdom Task Group
COS CC MAR FOR ..... .Chief of Staff to the Commander, Allied Naval Forces, Southern Europe
COS (Ops) PJHQ.............................. Chief of Staff (Operations) Permanent Joint Headquarters
COS SACT .... Chief of Staff to Supreme Allied Commander, Transformation
CSSE.. Chief Strategic Systems Executive
CTCRM..Commando Training Centre Royal Marines
DCAE .... Defence College of Aeronautical Engineering
DCBRNC.................Defence Chemical, Biological, Radiological & Nuclear Centre
DCCIS.............................. Defence College of Communications & Information Systems
DCEME ....Defence College of Electro-Mechanical Engineering
DCLPA .... Defence College of Logistics & Personnel Administration

DCMH ....Department of Community Mental Health
DCNS.. Deputy Chief of Naval Staff
DCOS Force Readiness .... .Deputy Chief of Staff, Force Readiness
DCPG .... Defence College of Police & Guarding
DCSU..Defence Cultural Specialist Unit
DDG EUMS .... Deputy Director General, European Union Military Staff
DDS..Defence Dental Services
DE&S .... Defence Equipment & Support
DEFENCE ACADEMY ....Defence Academy of the United Kingdom
Def Reform (Mar) ITL.........................Defence Reform (Maritime) Implementation Team Leader
DEMSS................................... Defence Explosive Ordnance Disposal Munitions & Search School
DEPCOMSTRIKFORNATO.. Deputy Commander Strike Force NATO
DHFS .... Defence Helicopter Flying School
DIO.. Defence Infrastructure Organisation
DISC .... Defence Intelligence & Security Centre
D(MarCap & Transformation) /CofN ....Director (Maritime Capability & Transformation) and
Controller of the Navy
DMLS ....Defence Maritime Logistics School
DMOC..Defence Media Operations Centre
DMRC.. Defence Medical Rehabilitation Centre
DMS ....Defence Medical Services
DMSTG ....Defence Medical Services Training Group
DPMD..Defence Post-Graduate Medical Deanery
DSAS ....Defence Security & Assurance Services
DSEA.. .Defence Safety and Environment Authority
DSL ....Defence School of Languages
DST ....Defence School of Transport
DSTL .... Defence Science & Technology Laboratory
DTOEES ....Defence Technical Officer & Engineer Entry Scheme
ETPS .... Empire Test Pilots' School
EU OHQ.. European Union Operational Headquarters
FCO.. Foreign & Commonwealth Office
FDS ....Fleet Diving Squadron
FOSNNI.........Flag Officer Scotland, Northern England & Northern Ireland, Flag Officer Regional
Forces and Flag Officer Reserves
FOSNNI NRC EE......Flag Officer Scotland, Northern England & Northern Ireland, Naval Regional
Commander, Eastern England
FOSNNI NRC NE .....Flag Officer Scotland, Northern England & Northern Ireland, Naval Regional
Commander, Northern England
FOSNNI NRC SNI ....Flag Officer Scotland, Northern England & Northern Ireland, Naval Regional
Commander, Scotland & Northern Ireland
FOSNNI NRC WWE.Flag Officer Scotland, Northern England & Northern Ireland, Naval Regional
Commander, Wales & Western England
FOST..Flag Officer Sea Training
FPGRM .... Fleet Protection Group Royal Marines
FWO ....Fleet Waterfront Organisation
HMNB ....Her Majesty's Naval Base

HQ 2 MED BDE .... HQ 2 Medical Brigade
HQ EUFOR (SAR) .... HQ European Force (Sarajevo)
HQ IADS .... HQ Integrated Area Defence System
HQ NI .... HQ Northern Ireland
HQLF .... HQ Land Forces
IBS .... Infantry Battle School
IMATT .... International Military Advisory & Training Team
INM .... Institute of Naval Medicine
JCTTAT .... Joint Counter Terrorism Training & Advisory Team
JEFTS .... Joint Elementary Flying Training School
JFC .... Joint Forces Command
JHC .... Joint Helicopter Command
JSCSC .... Joint Services Command & Staff College
JSMTC .... Joint Services Mountain Training Centre
JSSU .... Joint Services Signals Unit
JSU .... Joint Support Unit
LATCC(MIL) .... London Air Traffic Control Centre (Military)
LSP .... Loan Service Position
LWC .... Land Warfare Centre
MAA .... Military Aviation Authority
MASF .... Maritime Aviation Support Force
MCM1 .... Mine Countermeasures Squadron 1
MCM2 .... Mine Countermeasures Squadron 2
MCTC .... Military Corrective Training Centre
MDHU .... Ministry of Defence Hospital Unit
MHRF(F) .... Military High Readiness Force (France)
MOD .... Ministry of Defence
MSSG .... Military Stabilisation Support Group
MWC .... Maritime Warfare Centre
MWS .... Maritime Warfare School
NAIC .... Naval Aeronautical Information Centre
NAS .... Naval Air Squadron
NATO .... North Atlantic Treaty Organisation
NATO JFC .... NATO Joint Force Command
NATO JWC .... NATO Joint Warfare Centre
NCHQ .... Navy Command HQ
NCISS .... NATO Communication & Information Systems School
NDG .... Northern Diving Group
NETS .... Naval Educational & Training Service
NOC .... Naval Outdoor Centre
OCLC .... Officer Career Liaison & Recruiting Officer
OPTAG .... Operational Training & Advisory Group
PJHQ .... Permanent Joint HQ
RBAF .... Royal Brunei Armed Forces
RCDM .... Royal Centre for Defence Medicine
RCDS .... Royal College of Defence Studies
RM BICKLEIGH .... Royal Marines, Bickleigh, Plymouth

RM CHIVENOR .... Royal Marines, Chivenor, Barnstaple
RM CONDOR .... Royal Marines Condor, Arbroath
RM NORTON MANOR .... .Royal Marines Norton Manor Camp, Taunton
RM POOLE .... Royal Marines Hamworthy, Poole
RM STONEHOUSE .... Royal Marines Stonehouse, Plymouth
RMSM .... Royal Marines School of Music
RMAS .... Royal Military Academy Sandhurst
RMBS .... Royal Marine Band Service
RNAC .... Royal Naval Acquaint Centre
RNAESS .... Royal Naval Air Engineering & Survival School
RNAS .... Royal Naval Air Station
RNCR... Royal Naval Centre of Recruiting
RNEAWC .... Royal Naval Element Air Warfare Centre
RNIO.. Royal Naval Infrastructure Organisation
RNLA .... Royal Naval Leadership Academy
RNLO ....Royal Navy Liaison Officer
RNLT .... Royal Navy Liaison Team
RNPT ....Royal Navy Presentation Team
RNSME .... Royal Naval School of Marine Engineering
RNSMS .... Royal Navy Submarine School
SACT .... Supreme Allied Commander, Transformation
SDG ....Southern Diving Unit Group
SETT .... Submarine Escape Training Tank
SGD.. .Surgeon General's Department
SHAPE .... Supreme Headquarters Allied Powers Eúrope
SHTC .... Salmond House Training Centre
SMC .... Sea Mounting Centre
SP WPNS SCH .... Support Weapons School
SPVA .... Service Personnel & Veterans Agency
UKHO..United Kingdom Hydrographic Office
UKJSU..United Kingdom Joint Support Unit
UK MCC.. United Kingdom Maritime Component Commander
UKTI-DSO ....United Kingdom Trade & Investment Defence & Security Organisation
UN...United Nations
US CENTCOM..United States Central Command

Explanatory Notes

1. Any Officer who has the unit MCM1 or MCM2 will be assigned to one of the two Mine Countermeasure Squadrons and will be part of a rotating squad assigned to the Hunt & Sandown Class Mine Countermeasure vessels.

2. The location stated in the list of addresses may not necessarily be the Headquarters of that unit; it may simply be a location where an officer is serving.

3. Any Officer serving in a Defence Section, Exchange Post, Loan Service, Military Mission or Service Attache position, can be contacted by using the 'Yellow' book, as detailed on page 247.

ADDRESSES OF ORGANISATIONS WHERE OFFICERS SERVE WHEN NOT AT SEA

NAVAL STAFF & NAVY COMMAND HEADQUARTER FUNCTIONS

First Sea Lord & Chief of Naval Staff
1SL/CNS
Ministry of Defence
Main Building
LONDON
SW1A 2HB

Fleet Commander/
Deputy Chief of Naval Staff
Northwood HQ
Sandy Lane
NORTHWOOD
HA6 3AP

Chief of Naval Personnel & Training and
Second Sea Lord Command
CNP&T/2SL
Leach Building
Whale Island
PORTSMOUTH
PO2 8BY

Deputy Fleet Commander
Leach Building
Whale Island
PORTSMOUTH
PO2 8BY

Admiralty Interview Board
AIB
HMS Sultan
GOSPORT
PO12 3BY

Chief of Joint Operations
JHQ 205
JHQ Northwood
HA6 3HP

Commander Fishery Protection Squad
CFPS
HMNB
PORTSMOUTH
PO1 3LS

Commander Operations
COM(Ops)
Northwood HQ
Sandy Lane
NORTWOOD
HA6 3AP

Commander UK Amphibious Forces
COMUKAMPHIBFOR
Fieldhouse Building
Whale Island
PORTSMOUTH
PO2 8ER

Commander UK Maritime Forces
COMUKMARFOR
Fieldhouse Building
Whale Island
PORTSMOUTH
PO2 8ER

Commander UK Task Group
COMUKTG
Fieldhouse Building
Whale Island
PORTSMOUTH
PO2 8ER

Chaplain of the Fleet
Leach Building
Whale Island
PORTSMOUTH
PO2 8BY

Flag Officer Scotland, Northern England &
Northern Ireland, Flag Officer Regional
Forces and Flag Officer Reserves
FOSNNI
HMNB Clyde
HELENSBURGH
G84 8HL

Flag Officer Scotland, England & Northern Ireland, Naval Regional Command Eastern England
FOSNNI NRC EE
HMS President
LONDON
E1W 1UQ

Flag Officer Scotland, England & Northern Ireland, Naval Regional Command Eastern England
FOSNNI NRC EE
AFCO
Cambridge Road
PORTSMOUTH
PO1 2EN

Flag Officer Scotland, England & Northern Ireland, Naval Regional Command Eastern England
FOSNNI NRC EE
21 Hereward Centre
PETERBOROUGH
PE1 1TB

Flag Officer Scotland, Northern England & Northern Ireland, Naval Regional Command Northern England
FOSNNI NRC NE
RNHQ Northern Ireland & Isle of Man
East Brunswick Dock
LIVERPOOL
L3 4DZ

Flag Officer Scotland, Northern England & Northern Ireland, Naval Regional Command Northern England
FOSNNI NRC NE
Sobaron Barracks
LINCOLN
LN1 3PY

Flag Officer Scotland, Northern England & Northern Ireland, Naval Regional Command Northern England
FOSNNI NRC NE
AFCO
New England House
10 Ridley Place
NEWCASTLE-UPON-TYNE
NE1 8JW

Flag Officer Scotland, Northern England & Northern Ireland, Naval Regional Command Scotland & Northern Ireland
FOSNNI NRC SNI
HMNB Clyde
HELENSBURGH
G84 8HL

Flag Officer Scotland, Northern England & Northern Ireland, Naval Regional Command Scotland & Northern Ireland
FOSNNI NRC SNI
29-31 Bank Street
DUNDEE
DD1 1RW

Flag Officer Scotland, Northern England & Northern Ireland, Naval Regional Command Wales & Western England
FOSNNI NRC WWE
46 Stephenson Street
BIRMINGHAM
B2 4DY

Flag Officer Scotland, Northern England & Northern Ireland, Naval Regional Command Wales & Western England
FOSNNI NRC WWE
HMS FLYING FOX
Winterstoke Road
BRISTOL
BS3 2NS

Flag Officer Sea Training
FOST
NCHQ
Leach Building
Whale Island
PORTSMOUTH
PO2 8BY

Flag Officer Sea Training (North)
FOST (North)
HMNB Clyde
HELENSBURGH
G84 8HL

Flag Officer Sea Training (South)
FOST (South)
Grenville Block
HMS Drake
HMNB Devonport
PLYMOUTH
PL2 2BG

Fleet Diving Squadron
FDS
Horsea Island
West Bund Road
COSHAM
PO6 4TT

Headquarters Combined Cadet Force (Royal Navy)
HQ CCF (RN)
Room 21 South Terrace
PP 72
HMNB
PORTSMOUTH
PO1 3LS

Mine Warfare Centre
MWC
HMS Collingwood
Newgate Lane
FAREHAM
PO14 1AS

Naval Personnel & Family Service (Eastern)
NPFS (EASTERN)
HMS Nelson
HMNB
PORTSMOUTH
PO1 3LS

Naval Personnel & Family Service (Western)
NPFS (WESTERN)
HMS Drake
HMNB Devonport
PLYMOUTH
PL2 2BG

Naval Personnel & Family Service (Northern)
NPFS (NORTHERN)
1-5 Churchill Square
HELENSBURGH
G84 9HL

Officer Career Liaison & Recruiting Offices
OCLC
46 Stephenson Street
BIRMINGHAM
B2 4DY

Officer Career Liaison & Recruiting Offices
OCLC
HMS Flying Fox
Winterstoke Road
BRISTOL
BS3 2NS

Officer Career Liaison & Recruiting Offices
OCLC
21 Hereward Centre
PETERBOROUGH
PE1 1TB

Officer Career Liaison & Recruiting Offices
OCLC
Pilgrim House
PLYMOUTH
PL1 2SW

Officer Career Liaison & Recruiting Offices
OCLC
Petersfield House
26 St Peter's Street
MANCHESTER
M2 5QJ

UK Hydrographic Office
UKHO
Admiralty Way
TAUNTON
TA1 2DN

SHORE BASES, ESTABLISHMENTS & OTHER NAVY ORGANISATIONS

Her Majesty's Naval Base Clyde
HMNB CLYDE
Faslane
HELENSBURGH
G84 8HL

Her Majesty's Naval Base Devonport
HMNB DEVONPORT
PLYMOUTH
PL2 2BG

Her Majesty's Naval Base Portsmouth
HMNB PORTSMOUTH
PORTSMOUTH
PO1 3LS

HMS Bristol
Whale Island
PORTSMOUTH
PO2 8ER

HMS Caledonia
ROSYTH
KY11 2HX

HMS Collingwood
Newgate Lane
FAREHAM
PO14 1AS

HMS Drake
HMNB DEVONPORT
PLYMOUTH
PL2 2BG

HMS Excellent
Whale Island
PORTSMOUTH
PO2 8ER

HMS Nelson
HMNB PORTSMOUTH
PORTSMOUTH
PO1 3LS

HMS Neptune
HMNB CLYDE
Faslane
HELENSBURGH
G84 8HL

HMS President
72 St Katharine's Way
LONDON
E1W 1UQ

HMS Sultan
Military Road
GOSPORT
PO12 3BY

HMS Temeraire
Burnaby Road
PORTSMOUTH
PO1 2HB

HMS Victory
HMNB PORTSMOUTH
PORTSMOUTH
PO1 3LS

Maritime Aviation Support Force
MASF
RNAS Culdrose
HELSTON
TR12 7RK

Naval Aeronautical Information Centre
NAIC
RAF Northolt
West End Road
RUISLIP
HA4 6NR

Royal Naval Air Station Culdrose
RNAS Culdrose
HMS Seahawk
HELSTON
TR12 7RK

Home to:
750, 771, 814, 820, 824, 829, 849, 854 &
857 Naval Air Squadrons

Royal Naval Air Station Prestwick
RNAS Prestwick
HMS Gannet
PRESTWICK
KA9 2PL

Royal Naval Air Station Yeovilton
RNAS Yeovilton
HMS Heron
YEOVIL
BA22 8RT

Home to:
700W, 702, 727, 815, 845, 846, 847, 848
Naval Air Squadrons & Commando Helicopter
Force HQ.

Royal Naval Presentation Team
RNPT
RAF Northolt
West End Road
RUISLIP
HA4 6NR

ROYAL MARINES ESTABLISHMENTS AND UNITS

3 Commando Brigade Royal Marines
3 CDO RM
Royal Marines Barracks
Stonehouse
PLYMOUTH
PL1 3QS

1 Assault Group Royal Marines
1 ASSLT GP RM
Triumph Building
HMNB Devonport
PLYMOUTH
PL2 2BG

10 Training Squadron 1 Assault Group Royal Marines
10 Trg Sqn 1 Asslt Gp RM
RM Poole
Hamworthy
POOLE
BH15 4NQ

11 (Amphibious Trials & Training) Squadron
11 (ATT) SQN
1 ASSLT GP RM
Instow
BIDEFORD
EX39 4JH

131 Independent Commando Squadron Royal Engineers (Volunteers)
131 INDEP CDO SQN RE (V)
Training Centre

148 (Meiktila) Commando Forward Observation Battery Royal Artillery
148 FO BTY RA
RM Poole
Hamworthy
POOLE
BH15 4NQ

1st Battalion the Rifles
1 RIFLES
Beachley Barracks
CHEPSTOW
NP16 7YG

24 Commando Regiment Royal Engineers
24 CDO REGT RE
RMB Chivenor
BARNSTAPLE
EX31 4AZ

29 Commando Regiment Royal Artillery
29 CDO REGT RA
Royal Citadel
PLYMOUTH
PL1 2PD

30 Commando Information & Exploitation Group Royal Marines
30 CDO IX GP RM
RM Stonehouse
PLYMOUTH
PL1 3QS

40 Commando Royal Marines
40 CDO RM
Norton Manor Camp
TAUNTON
TA2 6FP

42 Commando Royal Marines
42 CDO RM
Bickleigh Barracks
PLYMOUTH
PL6 7AJ

45 Commando Royal Marines
45 CDO RM
RM Condor
ARBROATH
DD11 3SP

539 Assault Squadron Royal Marines
539 ASSLT SQN RM
RM Turnchapel
Barton Road
Turnchapel
PLYMOUTH
PL9 9XD

Armoured Support Group Royal Marines
AS GP RM
Yeovil Block,
RNAS Yeovilton
YEOVIL
BA22 8HT

Commando Helicopter Force HQ
CHF HQ
RNAS Yeovilton
YEOVIL
BA22 8HT

Commando Logistic Regiment Royal Marines
CDO LOG REGT RM
RM Chivenor
BARNSTAPLE
EX31 4AZ

Commando Training Centre Royal Marines
CTC RM
Lympstone
EXMOUTH
EX8 5AR

Fleet Protection Group Royal Marines
FPGRM
Gibraltar Building
HM Naval Base Clyde
Faslane
HELENSBURGH
G84 8HL

HASLER COMPANY
HMS Drake
PLYMOUTH
PL2 2BG

Royal Marine Band Service
RMBS
Walcheren Building
HMS Excellent
Whale Island
PORTSMOUTH
PO2 8ER

Royal Marine Band Collingwood
RM Band Collingwood
HMS NELSON
Queen Street
PORTSMOUTH
PO1 3HH

Royal Marine Band CTCRM
RM Band CTCRM
Lympstone
EXMOUTH
EX8 5AR

Royal Marine Band Plymouth
RM Band Plymouth
HMS RALEIGH
TORPOINT
PL11 2PD

Royal Marine Band Scotland
RM Band Scotland
HMS Caledonia
ROSYTH
KY11 2HX

Royal Marines Bickleigh
RM Bickleigh
Bickleigh Barracks
PLYMOUTH
PL6 7AJ

Royal Marines Chivenor
RM Chivenor
RM Chivenor
BARNSTAPLE
EX31 4AZ

Royal Marines Condor
RM Condor
RM Condor
ARBROATH
DD11 3SP

Royal Marines Norton Manor
RM Norton Manor
Norton Manor Camp
TAUNTON
TA2 6FP

Royal Marines Poole
RM Poole
Hamworthy
POOLE
BH15 4NQ

Royal Marines Stonehouse
RM Stonehouse
RM Stonehouse
PLYMOUTH
PL1 3QS

Royal Marines School of Music
RMSM
HMS NELSON
Queen Street
PORTSMOUTH
PO1 3HH

MEDICAL UNITS

Defence Dental Agency
DDA
Evelyn Woods Road
Aldershot
GU11 2LS

Defence Medical Rehabilitation Centre
DMRC
Headley Court
Headley
EPSOM
KT18 6PF

Defence Medical Services
DMS
DMS Whittington
Whittington Barracks
LICHFIELD
WS14 9PY

Defence Medical Services Training Group
DMSTG
Keogh Barracks
Ash Vale
ALDERSHOT
GU12 5RQ

Defence Medical Services Training Group
DMSTG
Selly Oak Hospital
Raddlebarn Road
Selly Oak
BIRMINGHAM
B29 6JD

Defence Post-Graduate Medical Deanery
DPMD
ICT Centre
Birmingham Research Park
Vincent Drive
Edgbaston
BIRMINGHAM
B15 2SQ

Department of Community Mental Health
DCMH
PP6, Sunny Walk
HMNB
PORTSMOUTH
PO1 3LT

HQ 2 Medical Brigade
HQ 2 MED BDE
Queen Elizabeth Barracks
Strensall
YORK
YO32 5SW

Institute of Naval Medicine
INM
Alverstoke
GOSPORT
PO12 2DL

MDHU Derriford
Derriford Hospital
Derriford Road
Crownhill
PLYMOUTH
PL6 5YE

MDHU Frimley
Frimley Park Hospital
Portsmouth Road
FRIMLEY
GU16 7UJ

MDHU Northallerton
Friarage Hospital
NORTHALLERTON
DL6 1JG

MDHU Peterborough
Peterborough District Hospital
Thorpe Road
PETERBOROUGH
PE3 6DA

MDHU Portsmouth
Queen Alexandra Hospital
Albert House
Southwick Hill Road
Cosham
PORTSMOUTH
PO6 3LY

Royal Centre for Defence Medicine
RCDM
Queen Elizabeth Hospital
Queen Elizabeth Medical Centre
Edgbaston
BIRMINGHAM
B15 2TH

Royal Centre for Defence Medicine
RCDM
Selly Oak Hospital
Raddlebarn Road
Selly Oak
BIRMINGHAM
B29 6JD

Surgeon General's Department
SGD
Coltman House
DMS Whittington
Lichfield Barracks
LICHFIELD
WS14 9PY

ROYAL NAVY & ROYAL MARINE RESERVE UNITS

ROYAL MARINE RESERVE UNITS

RMR Bristol
Dorset House
Litfield Place
Clifton Down
BRISTOL
BS8 3NA

RMR London
RMB Wandsworth
351 Merton Road
Southfields
LONDON
SW18 5JX

RMR Merseyside
East Brunswick Dock
LIVERPOOL
L3 4DZ

RMR Scotland
37-51 Birkmyre Road
Govan
GLASGOW
G51 3JH

RMR Tyne
Anzio House
Quayside
NEWCASTLE-UPON-TYNE
NE6 1BU

ROYAL NAVY RESERVE UNITS

HMS Calliope
(Including Ceres Division)
South Shore Road
GATESHEAD
NE8 2BE

HMS Cambria
Hayes Point
Hayes Lane
Sully
PENARTH
CF65 5XU

HMS Dalriada
Navy Buildings
Eldon Street
GREENOCK
PA16 7SL

HMS Eaglet
Naval Regional Headquarters
Northern Ireland & Isle of Man
East Brunswick Dock
LIVERPOOL
L3 4DZ

HMS Ferret
Building 600
DISC DHU
Chicksands
SHEFFORD
SG17 5PR

HMS Flying Fox
Winterstoke Road
BRISTOL
BS3 2NS

HMS Forward
42 Tilton Road
BIRMINGHAM
B9 4PP

HMS Hibernia
Thiepval Barracks
Magheralave Road
LISBURN
BT28 3NP

HMS King Alfred
Fraser Building
Whale Island
PORTSMOUTH
PO2 8ER

HMS President
72 St Katharine's Way
LONDON
E1W 1UQ

HMS Scotia
(Including Tay Division)
HMS Caledonia
Hilton Road
ROSYTH
KY11 2XH

HMS Sherwood
Chalfont Drive
NOTTINGHAM
NG8 3LT

HMS Vivid
Building SO40A
HM Naval Base Devonport
PLYMOUTH
PL2 2BG

HMS Wildfire
Brackenhill House
Oxhey Drive South
NORTHWOOD
HA6 3EX

ROYAL NAVAL RESERVE AIR BRANCH

RNAS Culdrose
Duke of Cornwall Building
RN Air Station
Culdrose
HELSTON
TR12 7RH

RNAS Yeovilton
Cormorant House
RN Air Station
Yeovilton
YEOVIL
BA22 8HL

UNIVERSITY ROYAL NAVAL UNITS

Aberdeen University
Royal Naval Unit (HMS Archer)
Gordon Barracks
Bridge of Don
ABERDEEN
AB23 8DB

Birmingham University
Royal Naval Unit (HMS Exploit)
HMS FORWARD
42 Tilton Road
BIRMINGHAM
B9 4PP

Bristol University
Royal Naval Unit (HMS Raider)
Lunsford House
Cantocks Close
BRISTOL
BS8 1UP

Cambridge University
Royal Naval Unit (HMS Trumpeter)
2 Chaucer Road
CAMBRIDGE
CB2 2EB

Glasgow University
Royal Naval Unit (HMS Smiter)
Officer Training Centre
95 University Place
GLASGOW
G2 8SU

Liverpool University
Royal Naval Unit (HMS Charger)
Naval Regional Headquarters
Northern Ireland & Isle of Man
East Brunswick Dock
LIVERPOOL
L3 4DZ

London University
Royal Naval Unit (HMS Puncher)
206 BROMPTON ROAD
LONDON
SW3 2BQ

Manchester University
Royal Naval Unit (HMS Biter)
Crawford House
Precinct Centre
Oxford Road
MANCHESTER
M13 9GH

Northumbria University
Royal Naval Unit (HMS Example)
South Shore Road
GATESHEAD
NE8 2BE

Oxford University
Royal Naval Unit (HMS Tracker)
Falklands House
Oxpens Road
OXFORD
OX1 1RX

Southampton University
Royal Naval Unit (HMS Blazer)
3rd Floor
Capella House
Kingsway
SOUTHAMPTON
SO14 1NJ

Sussex University
Royal Naval Unit (HMS Ranger)
Mantell Building
University of Sussex
Falmer
BRIGHTON
BN1 9RF

Wales Universities
Royal Naval Unit (HMS Express)
HMS CAMBRIA
Hayes Point
Hayes Lane
Sully
PENARTH
CF64 5XU

Yorkshire Universities
Royal Naval Unit (HMS Explorer)
Navy House
22 Pearson Park
HULL
HU5 2TD

TRAINING ESTABLISHMENTS

Air Warfare Centre
AWC
RAF Waddington
LINCOLN
LN5 9NB

Armed Forces Chaplaincy Centre
AFCC
Amport House
Amport
ANDOVER
SP11 8BG

Army Aviation Centre
AACen
Middle Wallop
STOCKBRIDGE
SO20 8DY

Britannia Royal Naval College
BRNC
DARTMOUTH
TQ6 0HJ

Central Air Traffic Control School
CATCS
RAF Shawbury
SHREWSBURY
SY4 4DZ

Commando Training Centre Royal Marines
CTCRM
Lympstone
EXMOUTH
EX8 5AR

Defence Academy of the United Kingdom
Greenhill House
SHRIVENHAM
SN6 8LA

Defence Chemical, Biological, Radiological & Nuclear Centre
DCBRNC
Winterbourne Gunner
SALISBURY
SP4 0ES

Defence College of Aeronautical Engineering
DCAE
RAF Cosford
Albrighton
WOLVERHAMPTON
WV7 3EX

Defence College of Communications & Information Systems
DCCIS
HMS Collingwood
Newgate Lane
FAREHAM
PO14 1AS

Defence College of Communications & Information Systems
DCCIS
Blandford Camp
BLANDFORD FORUM
DT11 8RH

Defence College of Electro-Mechanical Engineering
DCEME
HMS Sultan
Military Road
GOSPORT
PO12 3BY

Defence College of Logistics & Personnel Administration
DCLPA
Princess Royal Barracks
Deepcut
CAMBERLEY
GU16 6RW

Defence College of Logistics & Personnel Administration
DCLPA
Southwick Park
FAREHAM
PO17 6EJ

Defence College of Police & Guarding
DCPG
Southwick Park
FAREHAM
PO17 6EJ

Defence Cultural Specialist Unit
DCSU
RAF Henlow
HITCHIN
SG16 6DN

Defence Diving School
DDS
Horsea Island
West Bund Road
COSHAM
PO6 4TT

Defence Explosive Ordnance Disposal Munitions & Search School
DEMSS
Bldg 650
Marlborough Barracks
Southam
CV47 2UL

Defence Helicopter Flying School
DHFS
RAF Shawbury
SHREWSBURY
SY4 4DZ

Defence Intelligence & Security Centre
DISC
Chicksands
SHEFFORD
SG17 5PR

Defence Maritime Logistics School
DMLS
HMS Raleigh
TORPOINT
PL11 2PD

Defence Medical Services Training Group
DMSTG
Keogh Barracks
Ash Vale
ALDERSHOT
GU12 5RQ

Defence School of Languages
DSL
Wilton Park
BEACONSFIELD
HP9 2RP

Defence School of Personnel Administration
DSPA
Worthy Down
WINCHESTER
SO21 2RG

Defence School of Transport
DST
Normandy Barracks
Leconfield
BEVERLEY
HU17 7LX

Defence Technical Officer & Engineer Entry Scheme
DTOEES
Defence Academy of the United Kingdom
SHRIVENHAM
SN6 8LA

Defence Technical Officer & Engineer Entry Scheme
DTOEES
Loughborough University
LOUGHBOROUGH
LE11 3TU

Defence Technical Officer & Engineer Entry Scheme
DTOEES
Southampton University
Capella House
Cook Street
SOUTHAMPTON
SO14 1NJ

Defence Technical Officer & Engineer Entry Scheme
DTOEES
South Shore Road
GATESHEAD
NE8 2BE

Empire Test Pilots' School
ETPS
RAF Boscombe Down
SALISBURY
SP4 0JE

HMS Raleigh
TORPOINT
PL11 2PD

Infantry Battle School
IBS
Dering Lines
BRECON
LD3 7RA

Institute of Naval Medicine
INM
Crescent Road
Alverstoke
GOSPORT
PO12 2DL

Joint Elementary Flying School
JEFTS
RAF Cranwell
SLEAFORD
NG34 8HB

Joint Services Command & Staff College
JSCSC
Faringdon Road
Watchfield
SWINDON
SN6 8TS

Joint Services Mountain Training Centre
JSMTC
Plas Llanfair
ANGLESEY
LL61 6NT

Land Warfare Centre
LWC
Imber Road
WARMINSTER
BA12 0DJ

Maritime Warfare Centre
MWC
HMS Collingwood
Newgate Lane
FAREHAM
PO14 1AS

Maritime Warfare School
MWS
HMS Excellent
Whale Island
PORTSMOUTH
PO2 8ER

Naval Outdoor Centre
NOC
P.O. Box 2021
SONTHOFEN
BFPO 105

Operational Training & Advisory Group
OPTAG
Risborough Barracks
FOLKSTONE
CT20 3EZ

Royal College of Defence Studies
RCDS
Seaford House
37 Belgrave Square
LONDON
SW1X 8NS

Royal Marines School of Music
RMSM
HMS Nelson
HMNB
PORTSMOUTH
PO1 3HH

Royal Military Academy Sandhurst
RMAS
CAMBERLEY
GU15 4PQ

Royal Naval Air Engineering & Survival School
RNAESS
HMS Sultan
Military Road
GOSPORT
PO12 3BY

Royal Naval Element Air Warfare Centre
RNEAWC
RAF Waddington
LINCOLN
LN5 9NB

Royal Naval Leadership Academy
RNLA
HMS Collingwood
Newgate Lane
FAREHAM
PO14 1AS

Royal Naval Leadership Academy
RNLA
Britannia Royal Naval College
DARTMOUTH
TQ6 0HJ

Royal Naval School of Marine Engineering
RNSME
HMS Sultan
Military Road
GOSPORT
PO12 3BY

Royal Naval School of Physical Training
RNSPT
HMS Temeraire
Burnaby Road
PORTSMOUTH
PO1 2HB

**Royal Navy Pre Deployment Training &
Mounting Centre**
RN PDTMC
HMS Nelson
HMNB
PORTSMOUTH
PO1 3HH

Royal Naval Centre of Recruiting
RNCR
Stanley Barracks
Bovington Camp
WAREHAM
BH20 6JB

Royal Navy Submarine School
RNSMS
HMS Raleigh
TORPOINT
PL11 2PD

Salmond House Training Centre
SHTC
Rheindhalen Military Complex
BFPO 40

Submarine Escape Training Tank
SETT
Fort Blockhouse
GOSPORT
PO12 2AB

Support Weapons School
SP WPNS SCH
Land Warfare Centre
Imber Avenue
WARMINSTER
BA12 0DJ

MINISTRY OF DEFENCE DEPARTMENTS & ORGANISATIONS

Ministry of Defence
MOD
Main Building
LONDON
SW1A 2HB

Ministry of Defence
MOD
Old War Office
LONDON
SW1A 2EU

Ministry of Defence
MOD
St George's Court
2-12 Bloomsbury Way
LONDON
WC1A 2SH

Ministry of Defence
MOD
Castlewood House
77-91 New Oxford Street
LONDON
WC1A 1PX

Ministry of Defence
MOD
45-59 Kingsway
LONDON

Defence Infrastructure Organisation
DIO
Kingston Road
SUTTON COLDFIELD
B75 7RL

Defence Infrastructure Organisation
DIO
RAF Brampton
HUNTINGDON
PE28 2EA

Defence Media Operations Centre
DMOC
RAF Halton
AYLESBURY
HP22 5PG

Defence Science & Technology Laboratory
DSTL
Ively Road
FARNBOROUGH
GU14 0LX

Defence Science & Technology Laboratory
DSTL
P.O. Box 325
COSHAM
PO6 3SX

Defence Science & Technology Laboratory
DSTL
Porton Down
Salisbury
SP4 0JQ

Defence Security & Assurance Services
DSAS
Minerva House
Delta Office Park 800
Welton Road
SWINDON
SN5 7XQ

DEFENCE EQUIPMENT & SUPPORT ORGANISATIONS AND LOCATIONS

Defence Equipment & Support
DE&S
Abbey Wood
BRISTOL
BS34 8JH

Defence Equipment & Support
DE&S
Gazelle House
YEOVILTON
BA22 8HJ

Defence Equipment & Support
DE&S
MOD Ensleigh
Granville Road
BATH
BA1 9BE

**Defence Equipment & Support
DE&S**
Cormorant House
YEOVILTON
BA22 8HW

**Defence Equipment & Support
DE&S**
Unicorn House
Yeovilton
BA22 8HJ

**Defence Equipment & Support
DE&S**
Basil Hill Site
CORSHAM
SN13 9NR

**Defence Equipment & Support
DE&S**
Dounreay Site
THURSO
KW14 7TZ

**Defence Equipment & Support
DE&S**
Castle Court
Coldharbour Business Park
SHERBORNE
DT9 4JW

**Defence Equipment & Support
DE&S**
3100 Massachusetts Avenue
NW, 2008
WASHINGTON DC
USA

**Defence Equipment & Support
DE&S**
Skimmingdish Lane
Caversfield
BICESTER
OX25 8TS

**Defence Equipment & Support
DE&S**
West Moors
WIMBORNE
BH21 6QS

**Defence Equipment & Support
DE&S**
Drummond Barracks
Ludgershall
ANDOVER
SP11 9RU

Augusta Westland
P.O. Box 188
Lysander Road
YEOVIL
BA20 2YB

BAE Systems Ltd
First Floor,
Main Shipyard Offices
BARROW-IN-FURNESS
LA14 1AF

British Forces Post Office
BFPO
RAF Northolt
West End Road
RUISLIP
HA4 6NG

**UK Trade & Investment Defence &
Security Organisation**
UKTI-DSO
Kingsgate House
66-74 Victoria Street
LONDON
SW1E 6SW

Vector Aerospace
Building 165
Fleetlands
Fareham Road
GOSPORT
PO13 0AA

TRI-SERVICE UNITS

Allied Rapid Reaction Corps
ARRC
Imjin Barracks
Innsworth
Gloucester
GL3 1HW

British Forces British Indian Ocean Territory
BF BIOT
Diego Garcia
NP 1002
BFPO 485

British Forces Cyprus
BF C
BFPO 53

British Forces Germany
BF G
BFPO 40

British Forces Gibraltar
BF GIBRALTAR
BFPO 52

British Forces Post Office
BFPO
RAF Northolt
West End Road
RUISLIP
HA4 6NG

British Forces South Atlantic Islands
BFSAI
BFPO 655

Defence Intelligence & Security Centre
DISC
Chicksands
SHEFFORD
SG17 5PR

HQ EUFOR
Camp Butmir
SARAJEVO
Boznia Herzegovina

HQ Integrated Area Defence System
HQ IADS
185 Jalan Ampang
Kuala Lumpar

HQ Joint Forces Command Brunssum

Joint Counter Terrorism Training & Advisory Team
JCTTAT
Risborough Barracks
FOLKSTONE
CT20 3EZ

Joint Forces Command
JFC
Sandy Lane
NORTHWOOD
HA6 3AP

Joint Helicopter Command
JHC
HQ Land Forces
Marlborough Lines
Monxton Road
ANDOVER
SP11 8HJ

Joint Service Signal Unit
JSSU
Ayios Nikolaos
CYPRUS
BFPO 59

Joint Service Signal Unit
JSSU
Hubble Road
CHELTENHAM
GL51 0EX

Joint Support Unit
JSU
CASTEAU
Belgium
BFPO 26

Joint Support Unit
JSU
LISBON
BFPO 6

London Air Traffic Control Centre (Military)
LATCC(MIL)
Swanwick
SOUTHAMPTON
SO31 7AY

Military Aviation Authority
MAA
Abbey Wood
BRISTOL
BS34 8JH

Military Corrective Training Centre
MCTC
Berechurch Hall Camp
COLCHESTER
CO2 9NU

Military Higher Readiness Force (France)
MHRF(F)
238 Ave Auguste Batta
TOULON
France

Military Stabilisation Support Group
MSSG
Gibraltar Barracks
Blackwater
CAMBERLEY
GU17 9LP

NATO Supreme Allied Commander Transformation
NATO SACT
US Naval Base
NORFOLK
Virginia
NP 1964 via BFPO 63

NATO
MONS
Belgium
BFPO 26

NATO
BRUSSELS
BFPO 49

NATO Joint Forces Command Naples
NATO JFC
NAPLES
Italy
BFPO 8

NATO Joint Forces Command Brunssum
NATO JFC
BFPO 28

NATO Joint Forces Command Lisbon
NATO JFC
LISBON
BFPO 6

NATO Joint Warfare Centre
NATO JWC
4068 STAVANGER
Norway
BFPO 50

NATO School
OBERAMMERGAU
Box 2003
Germany
BFPO 105

Permanent Joint Headquarters
PJHQ
Sandy Lane
NORTHWOOD
HA6 3AP

Royal Brunei Armed Forces
RBAF
Bolkiah Camp
BRUNEI
BFPO 11

Sea Mounting Centre
SMC
Marchwood
SOUTHAMPTON
SO40 4ZG

Service Personnel & Veterans Agency
SPVA
Centurion Building
GOSPORT
PO13 9XA

Service Personnel & Veterans Agency
SPVA
Building 182
Imjin Barracks
Innsworth
GLOUCESTER
GL3 1HW

Service Personnel & Veterans Agency
SPVA
Kentigern House
65 Brown Street
GLASGOW
G2 8EX

Supreme HQ Allied Powers Europe
SHAPE
CASTEAU
Belgium
BFPO 26

UK Mission to the United Nations
UN
P.O. Box 5238
NEW YORK
NY 10150-5238 USA

ARMY UNITS

HQ Land Forces
HQLF
Marlborough Lines
Monxton Road
ANDOVER
SP11 8HJ

1st Battalion Irish Guards
1IG
Mons Barracks
Prince's Avenue
Aldershot
GU11 2LF

1 Regt Army Air Corps
1 REGT AAC
GUTERSLOH
BFPO 47

131 Independent Commando Squadron
Royal Engineers (Volunteers)
131 INDEP CDO SQN RE (V)
Training Centre
Honeypot Lane
Kingsbury
LONDON
NW9 9QY

148 (Meiktila) Commando Forward
Observation Battery Royal Artillery
148 FO BTY RA
RM Poole
Hamworthy
POOLE
BH15 4NQ

148 (Meiktila) Commando Forward
Observation Battery Royal Artillery
148 FO BTY RA
The Royal Citadel
PLYMOUTH
PL1 2PD

1st Battalion the Rifles
1 RIFLES
Beachley Barracks
CHEPSTOW
NP16 7YG

101 Logistics Brigade
101 LOG BDE
Buller Barracks
ALDERSHOT
GU11 2DE

102 Logistics Brigade
102 LOG BDE
GUTERSLOH
BFPO 47

24 Commando Regiment Royal Engineers
24 CDO REGT RE
RMB Chivenor
BARNSTAPLE
EX31 4AZ

26 Regiment Royal Artillery
26 REGT RA
GUTERSLOH
BFPO 47

29 Commando Regiment Royal Artillery
29 CDO REGT RA
Royal Citadel
PLYMOUTH
PL1 2PD

3 Regiment Army Air Corps
3 REGT AAC
Wattisham Airfield
IPSWICH
IP7 7RA

4 Regiment Army Air Corps
4 REGT AAC
Wattisham Airfield
IPSWICH
IP7 7RA

5 Regiment Army Air Corps
5 REGT AAC
RAF ALDERGROVE
BFPO 808

5th Battalion Royal Regiment of Scotland
5 SCOTS
Howe Barracks
CANTERBURY
CT1 1JU

7 Air Assault Battalion, REME
7 AA BN REME
Wattisham Airfield
IPSWICH
IP7 7RA

Army Aviation Centre
AACen
Middle Wallop
STOCKBRIDGE
SO20 8DY

Army Recruiting & Training Division
ARTD
Trenchard Lines
Upavon
PEWSEY
SN9 6BE

Combined Arms Tactics Division
CATD
Land Warfare Centre
WARMINSTER
BA12 0DJ

Royal Military Academy Sandhurst
RMAS
CAMBERLEY
GU15 4PQ

ROYAL AIR FORCE UNITS

Air Command Headquarters
ACHQ
RAF High Wycombe
Walters Ash
HIGH WYCOMBE
HP14 4UE

1 Air Control Centre
1 ACC
RAF Boulmer
ALNWICK
NE66 3JF

ROYAL AIR FORCE UNITS

202 Squadron, E Flight
202 SQN E Flight
RAF Leconfield
BEVERLEY
HU17 7LX

RAF Aldergrove
BFPO 808

RAF Barkston Heath
SLEAFORD
NG34 8HB

RAF Benson
Benson
WALLINGFORD
OX10 6AA

RAF Boscombe Down
SALISBURY
SP4 0JE

RAF Boulmer
ALNWICK
NE66 3JF

RAF Brampton
HUNTINGDON
PE28 4YG

RAF Brize Norton
CARTERTON
OX18 3LX

RAF Cottesmore
OAKHAM
LE15 7BL

RAF Cranwell
SLEAFORD
NG34 8HB

RAF Digby
LINCOLN
LN4 3LH

RAF Halton
AYLESBURY
HP22 5PG

RAF Henlow
HITCHIN
SG16 6DN

RAF High Wycombe
Walters Ash
HIGH WYCOMBE
HP14 4UE

RAF Kinloss
Forres
Moray
IV36 3UH

RAF Leeming
Gatenby
NORTHALLERTON
DL7 9NJ

RAF Linton-on-Ouse
YORK
YO30 2AJ

RAF Lossiemouth
LOSSIEMOUTH
IV31 6SD

RAF Northolt
West End Road
RUISLIP
HA4 6NG

RAF Odiham
Hook
BASINGSTOKE
RG29 1QT

RAF Shawbury
SHREWSBURY
SY4 4DZ

RAF St Athan
BARRY
CF62 4WA

RAF St Mawgan
NEWQUAY
TR8 4HP

RAF Valley
HOLYHEAD
LL65 3NY

RAF Waddington
LINCOLN
LN5 9NB

RAF Wattisham
IPSWICH
IP7 7RA

RAF Wittering
PETERBOROUGH
PE8 6HB

RAF Wyton
HUNTINGDON
PE28 2EA

OTHER ADDRESSES

Ministry of Defence Police & Guarding Agency
MDPGA
Wethersfield
BRAINTREE
CM7 4AZ

Royal Navy & Royal Marines Film Charity
(Regn No. 1117794)
Registered Office:
M.P. 1-3
NCHQ
Leach Building
Whale Island
PORTSMOUTH
PO2 8BY

Sea Cadet Headquarters
202 Lambeth Road
LONDON
SE1 7JF

The Cabinet Office
Whitehall
LONDON
SW1A 2AS

The Foreign & Commonwealth Office
King Charles Street
LONDON
SW1A 2AH

ATTACHES AND ADVISERS

The International Policy and Planning Overseas Directory, commonly known as The Yellow Book, lists the UK MOD Attaché corps based at Defence Sections in British Embassies and High Commissions, together with Loan Service Personnel and Special Advisors Overseas. The Directory is maintained by the International Policy and Planning Division. It is an extensive and comprehensive publication that is updated throughout the year on the Web and bi-annually in a limited run of hard copy (International Policy & Planning Overseas Directory (The IPPYellow Book)).

For access to Attaches and Advisers you should refer to these sources for accuracy.   A full and comprehensive listing of Attaches and Advisers can be accessed through the MoD intranet, the URL is:

http://defenceintranet.diif.r.mil.uk/libraries/library1/MOD/ Aug2013/20130805%20IPP%20Overseas%20Directory%20-%20The%20 Yellow%20Book.pdf

Hardcopy: Authorised users without ready access to the DefenceNet can obtain copies of the concise Directory on application to the Editor:

> Peter McCarney
> International Policy & Planning-Overseas Support-Admin
> Main Building
> Level 4, Zone L, Desk 17
> Whitehall
> LONDON, SW1A 2HB.

DIIF: IPP-OS-Admin@mod.uk Role (UNCLAS)
          peter.mccarney781@mod.uk Personal (UNCLAS)

Phone: 020 7218 9176

OBITUARY

ROYAL NAVAL SERVICE

LIEUTENANT COMMANDER

Lt Cdr Timothy BARKER RN   17 Oct 13

ROYAL MARINES

Lt Damien MORAN RM   3 Aug 13

AMENDMENTS TO NAVY LIST ENTRY

This edition of the Navy List has been produced largely from the information held within the Ministry of Defence's "Joint Personnel and Administration" system". The efficiencies and data handling of JPA affect the way in which individual entries are extracted and recorded in the Navy List.

Serving Officers who note errors or omissions in the Active or Seniority Lists should ensure that their data held within JPA is accurate and up to date. If you are unable to make these corrections within your JPA account you should seek assistance from either your JPA administrator or Career Manager.

Please note that all personnel data for the Navy List is derived through Career Managers/Data Owners and/or extracted direct from JPA; it is neither compiled nor maintained by the Editor. If you notice errors or omissions you should contact your Human Resources Manager.

All other errors or omissions should be brought to the attention of the Editor of the Navy List.

Readers who wish to comment on this edition of the Navy List are invited to write to:

Cliona Willis
The Editor of the Navy List
MP 2.2
West Battery
Whale Island
PORTSMOUTH
PO2 8DX

Service Number (mandatory)...

Surname..

Forenames...

Rank..

Comments:

Signed .... Date ....